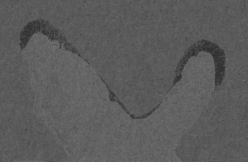

Revolution *&* Romanticism

David's *Death of Marat*

HOWARD MUMFORD JONES

Revolution *&* Romanticism

THE BELKNAP PRESS OF
HARVARD UNIVERSITY PRESS
CAMBRIDGE, MASSACHUSETTS
1974

FOR

Elex

IN ADMIRATION

Preface

This book is not for specialists, although I have shamelessly drawn upon them. In his fine study of the French revolution, which I quote later on, J. M. Thompson says that his volume hopes to be trusted. So does this one. It is written for the fun of writing it, and it can be read by anybody who is curious, as I am, about the roots and activities of revolutionary activity in the Western world and about the social results of romanticism in the arts and in general thought. I have concentrated on the American and French revolutions, and I have principally drawn my examples of revolution and romanticism from the political and cultural history of Great Britain, the United States, France, and Germany. This is to omit the Mediterranean world, the Low Countries, and Scandinavia, not to speak of the Slavs, but the book is long enough as it stands. My treatment is general. All that is necessary for an understanding of this study is some general knowledge of the American and the French revolutions, some general knowledge of the eighteenth-century world (which I find more chaotic than many historians indicate), and a willingness to think that romanticism was intelligent.

This is the third and final volume in a trio of studies devoted to the complex problem of the relationships in art and thought between the New World, more particularly the United States, and the Old. The first of these books in time of publication is *O Strange New World: American Culture — The Formative Years* (1964) and principally explores the years from 1492 to about 1830. The second in date is *The Age of Energy: Varieties of American Ex-*

perience, 1865–1915 (1971) and deals with the transformation of these relationships between the end of the Civil War and the sinking of the *Lusitania*, which ensured our entry into World War I. The present volume, which deals with the American revolution and the French revolution, fits between the earlier titles. Each book is independent, and since I have no cast-iron theory of historical writing, in each volume the method follows the materials. Necessarily there is some overlapping.

I am grateful for a grant-in-aid from the American Council of Learned Societies. Much of the material on the American revolution I gathered more years ago than I care to remember when I was a Fellow at the Huntington Library in San Marino. I have been helped in my German extracts by Henry C. Hatfield and in my French ones by W. M. Frohock, who has translated or paraphrased all the important ones, but my mistakes are all my own. I have also been aided by objurgations, help, criticism, and suggestions from so many persons I scarcely know how to list them, but I must name Herschel C. Baker, Philip Dawson, John P. Dawson, Jack Stein, David Robbins, Jane Hatfield, Sue Walcutt, Bessie Z. Jones, Maud Wilcox, Phoebe Wilson, Sheila Hart, the staff at the Widener Library, and the little group of earnest Victorians at Harvard University. I also express my gratitude to hundreds of scholars, living and dead, from whose work I have profited.

Howard Mumford Jones

Cambridge, Massachusetts
March 31, 1973

Contents

Revolution & Romanticism

I

Romanticism and Revolution

Approximately a century separates the end of the Seven Years War in 1763 from the beginning of the American Civil War in 1861. In that period the civilization of the Western world was shaken by two convulsions, one in the areas of thought and art, and one in the area of politics. The first of these is romanticism, the second, revolution. It is the purpose of this study to try to work out some of the relations between these two movements for at least a portion of this large arc of time. The study will concentrate on the American revolution of 1775 and the French revolution of 1789, though references will be made to the revolutionary movements of 1830 and 1848 where they prove illuminating. Romanticism is a term that rather defies temporal boundaries.

Theories of romanticism are numerous. Concerning the period under survey romanticism has been identified with a new interest in external nature, a new interest in the human soul, a new interest in the relation of man to God, and a new interest in certain sorts of cultures, particularly those distant in time or space from the then contemporary Western world. It was characterized by one of its practitioners as a return to the Middle Ages (the "Age of Faith"), and by another as modernity. It has been identified with philosophical idealism, including that of the transcendentalists, with a new interpretation of history, with a dynamic rather than a mechanical view of the universe, with a revaluation of the emotions and emotional life, with the virtues of children, peasants, old people in the village or the countryside, and some sorts of savages. It has been made responsible for whatever is emotionally extreme; for example, the plot of a Gothic novel or the exploitation of terror in a story by Edgar Allan Poe. It has been equated with the perverse. In the famous preface to *Cromwell* (1827) Victor Hugo seems to indicate that romanticism is a fusion of the beautiful and the grotesque. Nietzsche identified romanticism with the Dionysian rather than the Apollonian approach to life, and Goethe, who thought that classicism was per se healthy, thought that romanticism was per se sick. Others, among them Byron, Leopardi, Chateaubriand, and Schopenhauer, seem to equate romanticism with despair; yet artists of the standing of Beethoven, J. M. W. Turner, Delacroix, and Wagner insist upon romanticism as activity directed toward, and often achieving, a goal, a conquest, an affirmation, or some similar statement of hope and purpose. A leading American historian of ideas, the late Arthur Lovejoy, so despaired of finding any common denominator among these notions that he advised us to use the word only in the plural.

In the century being considered three or four allied or opposed elements complicate the puzzle. Many literary historians find in most of the literatures of the West during the eighteenth century, and sometimes earlier, something they call pre-romanticism, a term that has been debated, repudiated, and re-established. In the eighteenth century, moreover, there developed in most Western countries something called the movement of sensibility, sentimentalism, or *la sensibilité*, a movement with goals of its own that would not, in all probability, have taken the course it followed if it had not been urged as a necessity of correcting too much rationalism during the Enlightenment. Romanticism is also sometimes seen as an opponent of classicism, or at least of that sort of classicism the eighteenth century inherited from the Augustan age of Louis XIV, who died in 1715. Confusion is further compounded by the fact that classicism is one thing and neoclassicism frequently another. The great romantic artists did not, because they were romantic, turn their backs upon the antique world; on the contrary many of them revitalized that world in new, human, and occasionally revolutionary terms. Thus Shelley, a leading romantic poet, humanized the Prometheus legend, Keats, another such poet, humanized Hellenic art in his "Ode on a Grecian Urn," Schiller, who had a romantic streak in him, wrote "Die Götter Griechenlands," André Chénier in France revived the classical elegy, and the Italian Leopardi, a pessimist by temperament, mourned over the ruins of Rome in his famous poem, "All' Italia." It will therefore be necessary to indicate what is meant by neoclassicism, and to this I shall come.

In the arts realism is commonly regarded as a rebellion against romanticism, but in the decades under inspection realism proves to be almost as baffling a concept as romanticism, with which it is frequently interfused. Thus Sir Walter Scott, usually regarded as the great master of historical romance, in the Waverley novels painted earthy pictures of peasant life, life in Edinburgh, and life in the Highlands; in *Rob Roy*, for instance, he moves easily from the bourgeois values of the city to the wild life of the Highlands, and from a romantic plot about the Stuarts to a problem of bankruptcy, fraudulence, and recovery. In the end the Benjamin Franklin virtues triumph. On the other hand Balzac, who, as somebody said, made the forty-franc piece the hero of his prodigious *Comédie humaine*, also published such romantic hocus-pocus as *Séraphita* and *La Peau de chagrin*. A leading English romantic, William Wordsworth, is capable of such fine romantic writing as:

> the burthen of the mystery,
> In which the heavy and the weary weight
> Of all this unintelligible world,
> Is lightened;

and

> A voice so thrilling ne'er was heard
> In spring-time from the Cuckoo-bird,
> Breaking the silence of the seas
> Among the farthest Hebrides.

But he was also capable of giving his readers an exact topographical location for a tree:

> Not five yards from the mountain path,
> This Thorn you on your left espy:
> And to the left, three yards beyond,
> You see a little muddy pond.

He addresses one poem to a street telescope "upon its frame, and pointed to the sky," tells how a wagon was pulled up a hill, addresses one set of lines to a steamboat, a second to a railway company, a third "To the Spade of a Friend," and writes as

3

pitilessly as might Flaubert about the deaths of thousands of soldiers in Russia, as Winter

> bade the Snow their ample backs bestride,
> And to the battle ride.
> No pitying voice commands a halt,
> No courage can repel the dire assault;
> Distracted, spiritless, benumbed, and blind,
> Whole legions sink — and, in one instant, find
> Burial and death: look for them — and descry
> When morn returns, beneath the clear blue sky,
> A soundless waste, a trackless vacancy!

Beside this ruthlessness Charlet's famous picture, "Episode of the Retreat from Moscow" (1836), is compassion itself.

What is one to do amid this semantic confusion? It seems futile to lose oneself in a metaphysical maze to be called a theory of romanticism. I shall in this study not attempt to define romanticism but accept, instead, a considerable body of French commentary as central, and assume that whatever else it may be or do, romanticism implies or invokes a new formula for the individual — *le moi romantique*. The ego is of course no invention of romanticism, since without a primary concern for the self, literature would scarcely exist, nor, for that matter, would philosophy, religion, or politics. Moreover, a sense of the *moi* is quite as strong in Corneille's *Le Cid* in 1636 as it is in Byron's *Manfred* in 1817. For that matter a sense of self-importance obviously conditions the heroes of Homer just as it conditions the Freudian subjectivism of the anti-heroes in contemporary novels. But on the long road of interpretations of the self stretching from the *Iliad* to B. F. Skinner there are important way stations, and one of these is in the first quarter of the eighteenth century. In that period men, especially philosophers, artists, and theologians, began to think about themselves as individuals in a new way. Their sense of being, so far as one can judge from the arts, the memoirs, and the letters of the time, became at once more intense and more problematical than it had been in the age of Louis XIV. Of course no general proposition in the field of cultural history is infallible, and it is probable that Pascal's sense of self was quite as intense as that of Chateaubriand. But the intensity slowly came to be expressed in a new way. New modes of self-identification and self-expression

4

were invented, and this revolution in the concept of the ego is basic to any theory of romanticism.

A couple of historical comparisons may clarify what I mean. In Shakespeare's tragedy, Hamlet suffers a great wrong and lacerates himself terribly in thinking about it, but it is to be observed that his self-torture is expressed in soliloquies, and these are not public confessions after the manner of Rousseau. In the burial scene, when he leaps into Ophelia's grave, he discovers himself with the royal cry:

> This is I,
> Hamlet, the Dane!

It is the crown prince who speaks, not a romantic egotist, and he carries the play forward in that character. When Hamlet is dead, Fortinbras bids four captains bear him off the stage like a soldier,

> For he was likely, had he been put on,
> To have prov'd most royally

— a far cry, indeed, from the Werther of Goethe and the Atala of Chateaubriand.

This example concerns a man. Let us consider women. Among the heroines of Greek tragedy the Antigone of Sophocles is one of the greatest, a woman who goes proudly to her death because she knows she obeys eternal law in burying her brother despite the prohibition of her uncle, the king. There is in Sophocles no interview between Antigone and Haemon, her betrothed. But in a recent film version of the *Antigone* of Anouilh the neurotic heroine insists on quite unnecessarily mystifying her nurse, her sister, and her betrothed as Sophocles' Antigone never does, and the film version plays up an emotional and romantic interview between Haemon and Antigone, who is self-willed rather than pious. Both Antigones love life, but the truly tragic one, when she finds her sister, Ismene, too cowardly to help her, says with grave irony:

> Suffer me
> And my unwisdom to endure the weight
> Of what is threatened. I shall meet with nothing
> More grievous, at the worst, than death with honor.

What separates these two readings of the same character is romanticism. This is not to say that Anouilh's play is not good in its kind, it is merely to say that it is not tragic in the Sophoclean sense. We have greatly altered our concept of the ego. To tracing some part of this great alteration in the way man (and woman, too) thinks of himself this study is devoted. The reader must not expect, however, that the going will be easy. He will have to face inconsistencies, partly inherent in the nature of romanticism, and partly arising from the imperfect knowledge of the writer.

ii

Revolution is a term as loosely construed as is romanticism. The word is often applied to any change that is startling, drastic, or fundamental in the opinion of some writer or observer in any field of human activity. In our times the mass media consistently misuse the word as a means of gaining attention in broadcast or newspaper story — instant change, instant attention. This is unfortunately also true of books and magazines. Thus one hears of a revolution in physics, or in fiction, or in cancer research, or in theology, or in education. What is usually meant is the emergence of some new phase of a continuing process. Even in contemporary politics the word is misused. For example, a revolution in the Democratic party may mean nothing more than the replacement of older members of its national committee by younger members. If socialists or communists, operating on a program arising out of theory, were to take over the Democratic (or any other) party, that might be a genuine revolution.

In a stricter political sense the word revolution refers to an illegal seizure of governmental forms and powers by a group or allied groups alleging a grievance so great that the "people" cannot hope to secure relief or reform by any standard political process. The frustration of such a group or groups may be of long standing, and a sense of desperation or of opportunism may lead them suddenly to seize power after some event, crisis, or potential menace gives them opportunity, so that they may plausibly take over government by force. A revolution that sets up its own government in place of another, with little bloodshed, is more likely to be a *coup d'état* than a revolution, although this is not invariably true. The *coup d'état* may be the work of a few persons only, even if such

6

persons are backed up by some sort of military force or the threat of military force. A familiar example is the *coup d'état* by which Napoleon III seized power in France in 1851. Those who bring about a *coup d'état* will of course declare that they do so because the safety of the state would otherwise be endangered or because the good of the "people" requires this sudden switch in government. Leaders of any revolution tend to think they have a wider basis of popular support than do the leaders of a *coup d'état*, even if they may be mistaken. In the case of a revolution that fails, the result is usually termed a rebellion and is summarily suppressed.

In either event leaders of a revolt will almost invariably declare that they understand and carry out the will of the "people," and they will appeal to religion, national or racial tradition, ancient customs, liberty, and the like magnificent terms as sanctions. In any event revolutionaries, if they succeed, instantly assume the administrative and legislative functions of government, then the judicial one, and in modern times the educational and informational systems of the regime as well. Commonly revolutionaries promise a return to traditional procedures, once the revolution is securely in the saddle, and sometimes these promises are kept.

When the traditional names and forms of government are retained, even though their inner force is altered, the populace is apt to acquiesce peacefully in the revolution on the assumption that, the old government having proved unsatisfactory, the new government, even though revolutionary, should be given its chance. If, however, the revolution basically alters traditional forms, peaceful acceptance of this novelty by the populace is less likely, and the mere fact that the new forms are novel may become an excuse for a counterrevolution. But no rule is universal.

It is a historical truism that, despite appeals to the people, most revolutions are the work of a minority group or groups who declare that they, and they alone, represent the popular will. Thus the American revolution in the judgment of most historians was the achievement of a minority, nor did all the members of that minority intend to sever American allegiance to the British crown. The Declaration of Independence of 1776 perfectly illustrates the principle that revolutionaries act in the name of the "people" to rid the country of "despotism." The document asserts four fundamental principles: (1) it describes, though it does not define, a popular right of revolution; (2) it throws all responsibility for wrong upon the British government, and paints George III as a bloody-minded tyrant; (3) it affirms the right of the "people" to initiate a new form of government satisfactory to them, though the meaning of "people" is not made clear; and (4) it declares that there are certain unalterable principles in political theory and in so doing appeals to the enlightened part of mankind. That the most considerable part of enlightened mankind was in 1776 living contentedly enough under monarchies did not persuade these revolutionaries that a republic is not the proper form of the state.

It is probable that in the history of mankind some form of revolution is quite as common a mode of altering government as are peaceful elections or the peaceful succession to a vacated throne by the lineal heir. To pursue this general proposition would, however, lead us far astray. Let us therefore confine ourselves to glancing at revolutions before the eighteenth century and looking at the eighteenth century itself. Let us also remember that to economic historians revolutions are thought of as being physically determined, even though their outward form may be religious or dynastic, libertarian or Spartan.

In the sixteenth and seventeenth centuries in Europe, though some revolutions were dynastic in appearance, a religious coloring was often given to revolutionary activity. Thus the revolt of the Netherlands against Spain, which resulted in independence, was a rising of Protestants against Catholics, though it had its dynastic overtones. The wars of religion in France in the same century would be called revolutionary by most definitions since the aim of the Huguenots was to gain sufficient power in government to alter policy in favor of tolerating Protestantism, and the Huguenots so far succeeded that the Edict of Nantes (1598) granted them political status though it did not give them religious equality, and their leader, Henry of Navarre, became king of France, even if he abjured the Protestant religion in order to mount the throne. The Thirty Years War, which ravaged central Europe from 1618 to 1648, was launched by the irritation of Bohemian Protestants against a Catholic establishment. The rebels appointed a revolutionary government of thirty men in Prague; and if the resulting war involved dynastic quarrels, economic problems, opportunism among states and rulers, and, inevitably, because of the ruin it created, economic power sufficient for survival, the general result was to recognize the existence of Protestant states as equals to Catholic states in the Holy Roman Empire of the German People. The English civil wars of the mid-seventeenth century obviously included strong religious components, since the Stuarts were suspected of Catholicism, the Scots and the English Independents, though they quarreled, were at one in detesting the Anglican church, and the unsettled state of the realm during the revolution permitted the emergence of various odd religious and religio-political sects such as the Diggers. The civil wars eventuated in the execution of Charles I, the Protectorate of Cromwell, really a dictatorship disguised as a republic, and the restoration of monarchy through the revolution of 1660. But the restored Stuarts were again dethroned in the Glorious Revolution of 1688–89, which assured a Protestant succession to the throne and put down Catholicism in Ireland with a heavy hand.

Our interest, however, is primarily in a later period, and the point of taking this glance at seventeenth-century (and earlier) revolutions is twofold: one learns that the Western world was again and again disturbed by revolutionary fervor long before Lexington and Concord; and there develops a basic difference between the ostensible motives of the seventeenth-century revolutionaries and those of the eighteenth century. To be sure, revolutionary activities in both centuries were manifold. Europe was so disturbed that the first volume of Albert Sorel's influential *L'Europe et la Révolution française*, published in 1885, is virtually a Carlylean indictment of the *ancien régime* not only in France but elsewhere:

. . . I should consider my work not to have been useless if I had attained this result: to have shown the French Revolution, which appeared to some to be the subversion and to others the regeneration of the old European world, as the natural and necessary consequence of the history of Europe, and to have demonstrated that this Revolution brought no development with it, even the most surprising, that did not flow from this history, and is not explicable by the precedents of the ancien régime.*

* Sorel's first volume is available in an English translation entitled *Europe and the French Revolution: The Political Traditions of the Old Regime*, translated by Alfred Cobban and J. W. Hunt, New York, Doubleday Anchor Books, 1969. Cobban died before the work was through the press. My quotation is from the conclusion of Sorel's introduction, p. 32 in this edition.

But if revolutionary activity in the eighteenth-century Western world was no novelty, it acquired, at least, a novel character. It seems to be in general true that, in contrast to revolutionary movements before 1763, or many of them, those coming after 1763, or most of them, arose more particularly from political, economic, and nationalistic (or racial) discontents than from religious differences, though religious contention by no means disappeared. On the whole this later eighteenth-century activity seems to spring from a secular philosophy of the state rather than from religious or dynastic discontents.

This does not mean that a secular philosophy of the state had not appeared long before 1763. On the contrary, the literatures of Greece and Rome are rich in political observation and theory; the endless struggle between pope and emperor in the Middle Ages and after turned on a theory of the state; and the Renaissance produced a library of political treatises, of which Machiavelli's *Il Principe* is the most widely known. From Dante through Shakespeare into our own time the theory and conduct of rulers have been repeatedly examined. Toward the end of the seventeenth century that branch of theorizing which concerned the divine right of a monarch to demand and receive the obedience of his subjects reached a sort of climax in sermons and treatises by Bishop Bossuet and a kind of anticlimax in the fatuous essay by Sir Robert Filmer, *Patriarcha; or, the Natural Power of Kings* (1680). Filmer argues that monarchs derive absolute authority from the will of God expressed in His approval of Adam, Noah, and the patriarchs, a theory effectively demolished in John Locke's *Two Treatises of Civil Government* (1689–1690), which belong essentially to the eighteenth century. An Englishman, Locke has been called America's philosopher because his political philosophy was often cited in the quarrel between Great Britain and the future United States. In a general sense, therefore, although secular theories appeared long before Locke, his treatises are a turning point in political theory, since after their publication it became increasingly difficult to associate a theory of the state with supernaturalism, albeit some romantics were to return to this doctrine after the French revolution.

The four great revolutions of modern times are presumably the American revolution, which established a viable form of non-monarchical government over a vast territory; the French revolution, which seriously weakened or abolished feudal patterns of government in the Western world; the Russian revolution of 1917, which not only got rid of despotism but also created a new mode of dictatorship over a vast land mass and over millions of human beings; and the Chinese revolution (or revolutions), which is apparently destined to bring about a fateful confrontation of the Oriental world and the world of the West. Religion is involved in all four of these revolutions, of which the first two particularly concern us, since their management and outcome helped to determine the nature of the other two. One of the complaints of the Americans involved attempts of the British to establish an Anglican hierarchy in their mainland colonies, a movement interpreted by the colonials as a concealed attempt at "tyranny," albeit, despite Jefferson's famous statute of religious freedom in Virginia, some of the American states — Massachusetts is an example — maintained the ghost of an established church for some years after 1800. The French revolution not merely deprived the Catholic church of its property, confiscated in the interests of the state, but at one stage of its feverish career tried to create a queer religion of its own, the Festival of the Supreme Being. The Russian revolution repudiated any and every form of religion, theoretically establishing the state on the basis of materialism and atheism. To speak of a Chinese religion involves us in difficulties; suffice it to say that the sayings of Chairman Mao seem to usurp in China the place once occupied by Confucius.

The Russian revolution and the Chinese revolution were not the only consequences of the American and the French revolution. In Latin America revolution became, in place of orderly elections, virtually the standard mode of changing governments, and in the twentieth century revolutionary activity (witness revolutions in Turkey, Spain, Italy, Greece, Germany, the Balkan countries in general, India, parts of Africa, and Indonesia, not to speak of the intent of the Québecois to attain national identity and of the Walloons in Belgium to secure autonomy) no longer shocks us. But the leading revolutions in modern times are still that in America and that in France. They are not only the patterns of subsequent revolutions, they are of intense and continuing interest because of their immediate effects upon the arts, philosophy, and religion and upon doctrines of the state. It will also be a purpose of this study to demonstrate that in the American revolution leadership remained in the domain of the high eighteenth century, whereas in the French revolution leadership more and more took on the character of the romantic *moi*, which, by an odd paradox, though it did not immediately determine French romanticism, basically colored European romanticism outside of France and in France after the revolution. It also established a pattern for later revolutionary leadership. Personages such as Garibaldi, Jefferson Davis, and Kossuth in greater or less degree exemplify the workings of *le moi romantique* in the political sphere, as personages like Byron, Chateaubriand, Heine, Chopin, Delacroix, Victor Hugo, and Verdi continue to exemplify *le moi romantique* in the arts. This curious fact helps to explain why almost all the arts in the Western world today are *arts against*. Note the contrast with the arts during the Augustan age in Europe, and for that matter the arts during the first forty or fifty years of American independence. Artists formerly supported the state, though they criticized it; artists today denounce or find fault with the state, although they expect the state to support them by government grants, fellowships, and arts councils.

iii

We shall come in the next chapter to a more particular analysis of European society and government as they were in 1763. But since the two revolutions principally under survey occur in the eighteenth century; since the American revolution was the culmination of certain tendencies in that century, though originating earlier, and the French revolution, though an eighteenth-century affair, anticipated a good many nineteenth-century elements; and since romanticism, however defined, was nursed by, or revolted against, components of eighteenth-century culture, it will be useful to find a base from which to measure change. Such a base is found in the reign of Louis XIV of France. Whatever the military defeats of his later years, *le grand monarque* bestrode the last half of the seventeenth century like a colossus and imposed upon it a theory of the state and a theory of culture.

The legacy of Louis XIV to the eighteenth century was classicism, the classicism one has in mind when one speaks of the Augustans. The great writers of France were encouraged to bring order out of aesthetic and intellectual turmoil. Possibly the seventeenth-century classicism they helped to create and sustain sprang from a deeper philosophical theory than its successor in the eighteenth century, which one refers to as neoclassicism, though this term, too, is inexactly used. At any rate there emerged from the Europe of the Thirty Years War a unified theory of the state and a concomitant unified theory of the arts. The interest of the young king in the first of these was necessarily intimate. Despite the efforts of Cardinal Mazarin to strengthen the royal power, during the troubled period one knows as the Fronde the boy king and his family were twice compelled to flee from Paris. From this experience and from Cardinal Mazarin, whom he both disliked and admired, Louis XIV learned the necessity of centralizing power. Therefore, upon the death of that wily Italian, Louis at the age of twenty-two, in order to keep the *parlements* under control, to quiet ferment among the higher nobility, and to end intrigues among the ministers and councils of state, resolved to be his own prime minister. When during his coronation ceremony the presiding bishop placed a ring on his royal finger, pronouncing that this was "to wed him to France," Louis was deeply impressed by a marriage thus consummated, which seemed to him sacred and inviolable. Some of his first acts therefore, in building up the power of the throne, were to receive that leading Frondeur, Cardinal de Retz, affably and then arrest him, to break and imprison Fouquet, who had made millions for himself out of French finances, and to discover in Colbert an intelligent agent and adviser, who had no interest in becoming an *intrigant*. To awe the public Louis maintained even the smallest detail of the ceremonial rites of royalty, and by and by he built Versailles, that extravagant palace, partly out of vanity but also as a symbol of authority and success. All the great officials had to report to him, all the great nobles were supposed to attend the court, all the social life of the establishment centered upon the throne and, so far as possible, all the arts were, so to speak, focused on the king. It was, says Cazamian, the French literary historian, the victory of rule. In rhetoric, poetry, culture, didactic or amusing books, as Voltaire observed two hundred years ago, the French were the legislators of Europe. It was, in sum, the age of Pascal, Molière, La Fontaine, Racine, Bossuet, and Boileau.

This centralization of power and ordering of culture had great virtues and great defects. The virtues were evident to Voltaire, who begins the first chapter of his *Siècle de Louis XIV* with this paragraph: "Ce n'est pas seulement *la Vie de Louis XIV* qu'on prétend écrire; on se propose un plus grand objet. On veut essayer de peintre à la posterité non les actions d'un seul homme, mais l'esprit des hommes dans le siècle le plus éclairé qui fut jamais." Voltaire could find only four enlightened ages in all history — that in Athens from Pericles to Alexander, in Rome under Caesar and Augustus, the Renaissance, and the age of Louis XIV.

The weakness inherent in Louis's program of reform is tersely put by Alfred Cobban: "The great king had endowed France with a modern system of government while retaining a semi-medieval system of financing it." More particularly, his political program had three characteristic defects, one of them external, the other two internal. The external one was his passion for waging war too many times for *la gloire*, that besetting weakness of all French history. The internal ones were, first, that, necessary though it might be to concentrate everything in his own hands — no man worked harder at the job of being both a responsible and a stately king — he failed to allow for old age and death and he therefore left an impossible, even a dangerous, legacy to his successors. In the second place, centralization was never made complete. In the search for religious unity he drove out the Huguenots and frowned on the Jansenists; yet Pascal, one of the great thinkers of his time, was in fact a Jansenist. Except for the language of the court there was no national idiom, each district or province speaking its own patois. Nor could the king obliterate the constitutional differences between the *pays d'état*, which clung to their general assemblies, and the *pays d'élection*, which did not. He could not quite subdue the *parlements*. (From the American point of view, French *parlements* were queer bodies, half-judicial and half-legislative; they were later interpreted in the reign of Louis XVI as representing traditional French "liberties.") He could take political responsibility away from the great nobles, but he put nothing in its place. He could insist on some measure of independence for the Gallicanism of the French church but, a devout son of the church, he could not sweep aside the authority of the pope. Above all, he was more and more cut off from the peasantry, who constituted about nine-tenths of the subjects over whom he ruled.

Yet *le roi soleil* succeeded in focusing Western political ideals upon monarchy as he interpreted it, just as he centered the values of culture upon his court and *la haute bourgeoisie*. It is difficult for us, to whom kings have become an anachronism, to understand why to Europeans in the seventeenth and eighteenth centuries monarchy was a natural — indeed, *the* natural — form of the state, exceptions being only republics so small as not to count. Here it is sufficient to say that since, in the opinion of political theorists such as Hobbes, sovereignty must lie somewhere, statesmen were content to let it lie with the king. If the monarch was competent, well and good; if he was mediocre or worse, the standing order could be managed well enough through a mistress, or a favorite, or a prime minister, or a chief of state, and, excepting as intrigue increased, was a nation much worse off? Theorists could make no sense out of the history of Great Britain in the seventeenth century, though by and by Voltaire and Montesquieu were to try to, but the decapitation of one king, the banishment of a second, the bringing in from abroad of a third, the trying out of oligarchy under Cromwell, and the perpetual religious tensions in that island seemed to show there was something wrong about a mixed government. The British could neither live with their kings nor get along without them. Let all good men stick to monarchy, therefore, which has the approval of God Himself.

Doubtless in the long perspective of time any great cultural epoch takes on a semblance of unity that hides its actual restlessness, but there is persuasive evidence that high culture during the time of Louis XIV approached the victory of rule of which Cazamian speaks. By classicism is usually meant the pattern of culture supposed to be characteristic of the Periclean age in Greece (though not exclusively so) and the Augustan age in Rome. Temporal boundaries for ancient classicism cannot, of course, be strictly defined; Pericles, for example, died in 429 B.C. whereas Plutarch, whose *Parallel Lives* is one of the central books of classicism, lived in the first century after Christ. With reference to whatever is classical in painting, architecture, sculpture, music, and "modern" literature, moreover, opinion differs widely, and much depends upon the prejudices of the writer or critic who is making the survey. In addition, during the seventeenth century and to some degree in the eighteenth, what is classical is also in the opinion of competent judges sometimes what is baroque.

However one defines classicism, two matters seem to be clear: the age of Louis XIV thought it was establishing eternal systems of value in the arts and in thought; and the need for such an ordering of culture becomes evident as soon as one looks at the years before the Augustan period of Louis XIV. After Montaigne's "Que sais-je?" after Hamlet's ironical cry, "What a piece of work is a man!" after the declaration of Sir Thomas Browne, "For the world, I count it not an inn, but an hospital; and a place not to live, but to die in," it seemed essential to hit upon something less frail than skepticism, mysticism, frustration, and melancholy. Many found their model in Periclean Athens and in Augustan Rome, which had imposed peace upon the world and, profiting from the great example of Greece, had established in Horace a poetical law-giver comparable to Solon or Lycurgus in politics.

In the arts, as I have hinted, much is now denominated baroque, even though specialists do not quite know what baroque may be. But works of art commonly labeled baroque apparently threw into disorder fundamental principles latent in materials. Thus Bernini, undoubtedly a great sculptor, in carving "The Ecstasy of St. Theresa" seemed to want to reduce marble to a kind of luminous cloud that denied the real existence of stone. Where was sculpture to go from there? Bernini, says H. W. Janson, the art historian, floated the throne of St. Peter in the Vatican in mid-air; was the only possible next step in architecture that colored soap bubble, the Wieskirche in Bavaria, wherein even St. John seems to develop a wiggle and a singularly athletic cherub holds up the pulpit? El Greco is a mannerist of genius, but what about mannerists without genius? Was "space" to become more and more an ocular trick, coloring more and more "acrimonious," symbolism increasingly intricate and obscure? Johann Sebastian Bach wrote double fugues of great strength and beauty, but when one runs across a musician in Rome writing "masses, psalms, motets, and anthems" for 12, 16, 24, and even 48 voices, not to speak of a mass in 56 parts (how did he manage to get all 56 parts on a single page of music as he went along?), one might wonder whether the progress of music was to lie in further multiplicity. As for literature, what was to come of

Gongorism? Of Marinism? Of *les précieux*? Of writers of witty conceits in verse and shapers of sentences that were more like valentines than arrows? Why not a higher degree of order in music, in sculpture, in architecture, in poetry, drama, and prose?

Enfin Malherbe vint — Malherbe, that sturdy bourgeois who died in 1628 and who had no patience with finicky writing. But his generation did not seem to pay attention to Malherbe. Looking back at him over a half century, another bourgeois, Nicolas Boileau-Despréaux, known as Boileau, declared that Malherbe was the first Frenchman to bring metrical order into verse, to put words in their proper places, to control the muse, to purify language, and to manage a stanza properly. Boileau therefore proposed to reinforce the work of Malherbe. This codifier of literary classicism and so-called legislator of Parnassus produced by 1674 *L'Art poétique*, a poem in four parts, everywhere read, admired, and eventually obeyed. Boileau's statement became, so to speak, the constitution of the new classicism. Boileau was also a satirist, and his satires are today livelier than *L'Art poétique*, but the satires are directed to making men behave rationally and well, and the poem insists that reason, truth, beauty, and nature are all parts of one stupendous whole. To this Parisian, in whom prudence mingled with a profound aversion to disorder, the best of the ancients were the best of all possible models for the literature of France. They had demonstrated what lesser men must understand, namely, that the business of literature is with nature but with nature codified, regularized, made intelligible to rational and truly cultured readers. Boileau was not putting the writer into a straitjacket; he argued that if you have great, eternal patterns tested by time, you ought to study them as eternal expressions of truth, beauty, and wisdom. The doctrine was to be adapted to the English climate by Alexander Pope in his *Essay on Cricitism* in 1711, four years before Louis died:

> These RULES of old discovered, not devised,
> Are Nature still, but Nature methodised;
> Nature, like liberty, is but restrained
> By the same laws which first herself ordained.

This concept of changeless patterns in art is not acceptable to the contemporary world, but in its time (and the parallel with Horace is interesting) it was as innovative as the ideas of Freud in our time. In fact Boileau's doctrine remained for so long influential that as late as 1817, in a shapeless poem called "Sleep and Poetry," Keats rather splenetically attacked the poetasters of his era, whom he classified as

a schism

Nurtured by foppery and barbarism,

not realizing that in an odd way he was redoing the work of Boileau. Keats blamed an "ill-fated, impious race" of bad writers on the long since deceased Frenchman, saying that they

> blasphem'd the bright Lyrist [Apollo] to his face,
> And did not know it, — no, they went about,
> Holding a poor, decrepid standard out,
> Mark'd with most flimsy mottos, and in large
> The name of one Boileau!

However literary historians may now argue as to the effect of Boileau upon writing in his own time, there is no dispute about his long-run power in literature. Even if it be argued, as it can be, that geniuses of the stature of Racine, Molière, Pascal, and Bossuet were not necessarily edified by Boileau's principles or by others like them, it is still true that he clearly expressed what one is almost tempted to call a rage for order — except that the word "rage" is clearly indecorous in this context. But the lucidity and cunning of Molière, the transparent yet powerful simplicity of the tragedies of Racine, the easy manipulation of prose in, say, the *Lettres à un provincial* of 1656–57 (Pascal's style moves in one direction, his religious belief in another) — such geniuses exemplify the claim of a revived classicism to be universal, to be clear, to be orderly. And if the French language came to replace Latin as the language of diplomacy, of polite conversation, and of the international exchange of ideas, this, too, was, so to say, part of the campaign. The French Academy took the French language under its protection.

As in the case of the Royal Society in England, the origins of the French Academy were informal and, indeed, even obscure. But in 1635, a little before the birth of Louis XIV, Cardinal Richelieu, then the greatest man in the kingdom, caused letters patent to be issued creating the Academy and charged it particularly with the duty of perfecting the language of France. It was, if possible, to give French the universality, the preeminence, and the perfection alleged to be true of classical Greek and classical Latin. The *parlement* of Paris opposed the idea and momentarily retarded the progress of the Academy, but by 1667 that institution had won a permanent place in France, by 1671 it was giving its first prize for eloquence, by 1672 Louis XIV, seeing in it another force for centrality, lodged it at the Louvre "dans un appartement magnifique avec toutes les commodités qu'il lui faut pour ses assemblées," and had limited its number to the sacrosanct Forty. By 1694 it had issued the first edition of the dictionary it was supposed to sponsor, the first of many editions to come. If not all the great literary figures were members, some of them — for example, Racine — were elected. With the unwilling assent of Corneille, its author, the Academy issued its lengthy critique of *Le Cid*, which touched off a famous literary quarrel, and the Academy also furnished both the background and the arena for various stages of the dispute between the ancients and the moderns. To linguists now it seems the utmost absurdity to try to fix a language for all time; nevertheless the Academy, by its mere existence, declared that style is the morality of literary art. Style is a civic responsibility, not an individual idiosyncrasy, and the influence of the Academy upon language is in its way a cultural parallel to the influence of monarchy upon the state.

Classicism in the grand manner is, then, one of the achievements of the age of Louis XIV. The grand manner is evident in the sonorous funeral orations of Bossuet, in the concentration of the tragedies of Racine, in the sense Molière conveys that these characters of his are eternal forms of humanity, in the irony of the *Pensées* of Pascal and the *Maximes* of La Rochefoucauld, who takes a sardonic view of the eternal weaknesses of men, and in the *Caractères* of La Bruyère, who felt that types are timeless and do not change. The somber pages of the *Mémoires* of Saint-Simon are as different from the sprightly flow of the diary of Samuel Pepys as the grandeur of Louis XIV differs from the gaiety of Charles II. The same grandeur informs the great building projects of the time; for example, the vast palace and its gardens at Versailles with its Galerie des Glaces, its Salon de la Guerre, its Salon de la Paix, and its mean little cupboards of rooms under the roof. Its principal rival is possibly Blenheim Castle, which came a little later and was built to honor the conquerer of the French armies, and is so vast and uncomfortable, one passes from a sense of grandeur to a sense of pity for elegance so high it would not stoop to the common wants of man. In painting and in sculpture likewise the set pieces such as the equestrian statue of Louis XIV by Girardon, of which only a model now remains, or the frozen dignity of Lely's portrait of the Comtesse de Gramont at Hampton Court exist in a universe without change and make one long for an earthy caricature by Hogarth or a bit of Goya's disillusioned realism. But all this grandeur, this attempt at eternity, this artificial geometrizing of space by Descartes or Le Nôtre in theory or in example, generates a melancholy induced by vanity on so grand a scale. Poussin, by general consent the leading painter of the *grand siècle*, though he has his allegiance to antiquity, cannot avoid expressing this melancholy, evident, for instance, in the "Landscape with the Burial of Phocion," which subordinates the litter with the dead body and its two bearers to a landscape classically arranged, to be sure, but filled here and there with figures indifferent to the dead hero, with melancholy trees, and with temples, houses, steps, lights and shadows that have everything painterly except joy. This is the melancholy of Pascal, a sensitive soul eternally suspended between two abysses, the melancholy of Molière in Le *Misanthrope*, wherein Alceste, the supposed hero, one by one discards his friends and eventually his mistress and in the best manner of Byron informs them:

> Meanwhile, betrayed and wronged in everything,
> I'll flee this bitter world where vice is king,
> And seek some spot unpeopled and apart
> Where I'll be free to have an honest heart.*

But though the age ended in the religious austerity of Mme de Montespan, which, however harsh, had in it something stoic and heroical, it could shape, but it could not control, the age which was to follow, that of the Regency of France and that of Walpole in Great Britain. Neoclassicism was not classicism in the grand manner, though it derived from it. Yet le *grand siècle* was not as futile as this seems to sound. The Augustan age in France left to

---

* I quote from the admirable translation of Le *Misanthrope* by Richard Wilbur, New York, Harcourt, Brace, 1955, p. 140 (published in Great Britain by Faber and Faber Ltd.).

succeeding decades in Europe the invaluable gift of a sense for style. Can one imagine a Voltaire following hard upon the heels of somebody such as Cyrano de Bergerac? Or an Addison writing immediately after the *Sermons* of John Donne? Here, to make the point quite clear, is a typical extract from Sir Thomas Browne's *Religio Medici*, written in the 1630's:

At my nativity, my ascendant was the watery sign of *Scorpius*; I was born in the planetary hour of *Saturn*, and I think I have a piece of that leaden planet in me. I am in no way facetious, nor disposed for the mirth and galliardize of company; yet in one dream I can compose a whole comedy, behold the action, apprehend the jests, and laugh myself awake at the conceits thereof. Were my memory as faithful as my reason is then fruitful, I would never study but in my dreams; and this time also would I choose for my devotions . . .

And here is Goldsmith in *The Vicar of Wakefield* in 1766, more than a century later:

I was ever of opinion, that the honest man who married and brought up a large family did more service than he who continued single, and only talked of population. From this motive, I had scarce taken orders a year before I began to think seriously of matrimony, and chose my wife, as she did her wedding-gown, not for a fine glossy surface, but such qualities as would wear well.

You cannot in a direct line derive *The Vicar of Wakefield* from the *Religio Medici*; something has intervened. What has intervened is the sense for style that developed in the era of Louis XIV and radiated from Versailles to the rest of Western Europe. Sir Thomas Browne is excellent in his way, and Oliver Goldsmith is excellent in his, but they are not of the same category of artists. Why not? Neoclassicism in the eighteenth century was to weaken or alter a good many traits of Augustan classicism, but it did not refuse the demand for lucidity, whatever the language of the writer might be. It requires only a change of proper nouns and adjectives to make Dr. Johnson's famous statement about Addison's prose apply to Voltaire in France, Lessing in Germany, and Franklin in America: "Whoever wishes to attain an English style, familiar but not coarse, and elegant but not ostentatious, must give his days and nights to the volumes of Addison." * This did not satisfy the romantics, who

---

* I have not in this brief survey said anything about the emergence of rational order in music. I take it that Lully's organization of the orchestra, Monteverdi's

were to return to the idiosyncratic style of the seventeenth century, but amid a variety of other cultural changes, it applies to the entire neoclassic world of the eighteenth century.

iv

Before we plunge into a more particular discussion of our central theme, it may be clarifying to say one more general word about romanticism. In 1617 Sir William Thompson wrote about "the romantic and visionary scheme of building a bridge over the river at Putney"; in 1690 Burnet said: "We must not imagine that the pamphlets . . . feigned an idea of a romantick state, that never was nor ever will be"; in 1705 Addison remarked of an Italian landscape: "It is so Romantick a Scene, that it has always probably given occasion to such Chimerical Relations"; and as late as 1771 Smollett in *The Expedition of Humphry Clinker* described Scarborough as "romantic from its situation along a cliff." Romantic, it is clear, could be used as an appropriate term for wild, primitive, and presumably uncultivated natural landscape; and it is significant that the word was applied to paintings by Claude Lorraine (1600–1682) and Salvator Rosa (1615?–1673),* admired for their delineation of "wild" nature and, incidentally, ruins, peasantry, and banditti.

Such uses of the word indicate a link between the melancholy of high classicism and romantic emotionalism, but it is important to remember that romanticism did not overthrow the rationality of the age of Louis XIV or that of the eighteenth century. It sought, instead, to make of it a sharper and subtler instrument for the analysis of ideas, of the universe, and of man. Nor did romanticism, I repeat, turn its back upon classical grandeur. In poetry, for example, Byron, that supreme incarnation of romantic suffering,

---

remarkable *L'Incoronazione di Poppea* (1642), the slow emergence of the solo sonata for various instruments, in which the development of Corelli is representative, the work of such German musicians as Buxtehude (ca. 1637–1707), and the better parts of the music of Henry Purcell, whose *Dido and Aeneas* (1689) is still occasionally revived, are representative of a movement out of complexity for its own sake into music displaying a greater sense of structure (architectonics) than is evident in the floridity of the earlier seventeenth century.

* It is suggestive that Salvator Rosa sympathized with Masaniello, the Neapolitan revolutionary, and that his best picture is possibly "The Conspiracy of Catiline," now in the Pitti palace. I borrow my illustrations of the word "romantic" from the *OED*.

looked back wistfully upon the lost perfections of Greece, to which he desired Greece to return in a revolution in which he died, and the greatness of Rome, the wreck of which he lamented as sincerely as did Leopardi. Schiller became more and more of a classicist; and in the life of Goethe his journey to Italy is crucial, producing, among other matters, the *Roman Elegies*, his *Iphigenia*, and the *Helena* that is now the third act of the second part of *Faust*. Romantic composers did not deny the genius of Handel and Haydn, Gluck and Mozart (Bach seems to have been more or less forgotten), they learned from them and went beyond them, Beethoven beginning with Haydn and Berlioz going beyond Beethoven. Romanticism did not, furthermore, deny validity to historical painting, portraiture, or formal landscape, all topics discussed by Sir Joshua Reynolds; it enriched these genres, inventing new colors, new color combinations, new techniques to express what was then a modern version of human existence. German thinkers of the romantic and transcendental sort based themselves on Kant, but on a Kant who had corrected and refined the rationalism — and the skepticism — that goes back to the seventeenth century. The romantics could not accept the aesthetics of Boileau or of Pope (except occasionally), they did not care for the formal symmetry of Augustan gardens, they broke, or at least many of them did, with the classical hexameter and the rhymed couplet, and for the famous saying, "L'état, c'est moi," revolutionaries among them proposed to substitute the vision of Robespierre:

We wish to substitute in our country morality for egotism, probity for a mere sense of honor, principle for habit, duty for etiquette, the empire of reason for the tyranny of custom, contempt for vice for contempt for misfortune, pride for insolence, large-mindedness for vanity, the love of glory for the love of money, good men for good company, merit for intrigue, talent for conceit, truth for show, the charm of happiness for the tedium of pleasure, the grandeur of man for the triviality of grand society, a people magnanimous, powerful, and happy for a people lovable, frivolous, and wretched — that is to say, all the virtues and miracles of the Republic for all the vices and puerilities of the monarchy.*

Bearing in mind that Robespierre has in view the France of Louis XVI and not the France of *le grand monarque*, one finds much in

---

* This translation, frequently quoted in histories of the French revolution, seems to originate with F. M. Anderson, though I have not identified the actual source.

this eloquent paragraph that might have won the approval of Louis XIV. The important thing is not to deny reason to the romantics, nor a sense of history to the age of Louis XIV; the important fact is that in the Western world generally, romanticism and revolution, though they seemed at times to repudiate the whole doctrine of monarchy, sought not so much to destroy a theory of the state and of culture as to bring these great matters, from their point of view, up to date.

Let us now turn to a survey of Europe in the eighteenth century proper. After that let us have a look at the rationalism of the Enlightenment and at the strong currents of emotionalism which sought in favor of the heart to correct the dryness of too much reasoning. We shall then be better able to appreciate the elements that make the American revolution so crucial an event in the history of the West.

The Eighteenth Century

To the cultivated observer of today the eighteenth-century world seems at once remote and stable. Across two centuries of revolution, war, and change, the decades of Jefferson and Mrs. Siddons, the Adam brothers and Jean Antoine Watteau, Lessing and Frederick the Great are incredibly distant, as if these worthies existed on some other planet. Their world appears to be changeless, partly because we are familiar only with its superficial aspects — upper-class culture, the philosophy of the Enlightenment, and the arts patronized by royalty and the nobility. But not all our university courses, not all our museums, not all our adoration of Vivaldi and Gluck, colonial Williamsburg (restored) and the Wallace Collection in London really revive a period when servants knew their place, life was formal, Lady Mary Wortley Montagu wrote her charming letters, and Voltaire published *Candide*.

It is true we amuse ourselves with many eighteenth-century productions. We like Chippendale chairs, and collect snuff boxes. We produce *Don Giovanni* and (sometimes) *Orfeo ed Euridice*, we play Handel and Haydn, we admire Mrs. Siddons as portrayed by Sir Joshua Reynolds and the *Vedute di Roma* of Piranesi. By and large, however, we do not play Rameau or composers of the great Mannheim school, once the most capable musical group in Europe; and if we revive *The School for Scandal* or *She Stoops to Conquer*, we do so as if we were reanimating Madame Tussaud's waxworks. Nobody thinks of reviving Home's *Douglas*, once thought to rival Shakespeare, or Lillo's *The London Merchant*, which made the rounds of the theaters of Europe. We read *Candide* and *Tom Jones*; we do not, except under compulsion, read the essays of Joseph Addison or Voltaire's *Mahomet, ou le Fanatisme*, which he dedicated to the pope, or *Nanine*, his theatrical tribute to the tear-compelling power of Samuel Richardson. We admire Christopher Smart, who wrote *A Song to David*, which was omitted from his collected works because the author went mad; we do not read Gray's *Elegy Written in a Country Churchyard*, which is, as the old lady said of *Hamlet*, all quotations, though Gray was one of the most civilized of English writers. Philip Guedalla somewhere pictures Edward Gibbon serenely gazing across the tumultuous centuries at the age of the Antonines, the representative of one age of stability looking with admiration on another such epoch, and we tend to accept both eras in Guedalla's terms.

Gibbon's case is illuminating. The first volume of the great *The Decline and Fall of the Roman Empire* appeared in February 1776, the year the unpredictable Americans were to issue their Declaration of Independence, and Gibbon, as all the world knows, voted steadily with the king's friends in the House of Commons during the American war. The work opens with a picture of a fair, happy, and rational administration:

The frontiers of that extensive monarchy were guarded by ancient renown and disciplined valor. The gentle but powerful influence of laws and manners had gradually cemented the union of the provinces. Their peaceful inhabitants enjoyed and abused the advantages of wealth and luxury. The image of a free constitution was preserved with decent reverence: the Roman senate appeared to possess the sovereign authority, and devolved on the emperors all the executive powers of government. During a happy period . . . of more than fourscore years, the public administration was conducted by the virtue and abilities of Nerva, Trajan, Hadrian, and the two Antonines.

Under the general impression that George III and Lord North were managing a new Age of the Antonines and putting down a minor insurrection in a distant province, Gibbon sided with the king's friends, unshaken in his allegiance to the British imperial system. Some weeks after the first volume of his masterpiece appeared General Howe evacuated the British army and about a thousand Loyalists from Boston, and a few months later the Second Continental Congress ordered the final draft of the Declaration of Independence engrossed. These events mark the break-up of the peace of the empire. This was no revolt in Dacia, it was a revolution in the New World, and by and by the historian made the awful confession: "I sometimes doubt Lord North."

Where Gibbon developed dubiety, we have developed doubt or contradiction. Thus the librettist and the composer labeled *Il Dissoluto punito, ossia il Don Giovanni* a "dramma giocoso"; we assume they did not know what they intended, and turn the opera into the Tragedy of Man, since, though we can be satirical about sex, we cannot be satirical about sensuality. We think of Rousseau as a political revolutionary; in fact *Du Contrat social* is pessimistic about man, favors monarchy, and limits effective "democratic" government to a town about the size of Burlington, Vermont. The founding fathers accepted as a matter of course — read the first paragraph of the Declaration of Independence — the theory that all government is a social contract, but our young radicals do not give rational assent to a social contract, and wonder why the founding fathers were silly enough to do so. We read the eighteenth century in terms of our own lack of belief in the capacity of man to be rational, but we emotionally proclaim civil liberties. True, the eighteenth century had no atom bomb hanging over it; it merely had a succession of revolts, the American revolution, the French revolution, the bloody history of the dragonnades in Languedoc before it began and the bloody massacres in Haiti after it closed. Alexander Hamilton has been much abused by liberals for asseverating that your people, sir, is a great beast, but consider how the people often behaved in the eighteenth century. Let us list some riots at random.

In France, for example, when Law's Mississippi Bubble burst, angry crowds gathered around the office of the Company of the Indies and trampled various persons to death, Law's carriage was overturned, and he and his family were compelled to go into hiding. Girls assigned by the royal government to emigrate to Canada or Louisiana were often "rescued" by mobs. Under the Regency in that country murders were as frequent as they are in Gothic romances, and a master thief named Cartouche organized criminals into military units that terrified Paris and its environs. In 1754 thousands of peasants around Nantes and Meudon, most of them armed with cudgels and some with scythes, assembled under the direction of their parish priests to slaughter hares and partridges (the prerogative of the nobility) in order to save their crops. In London the Calves' Head Club * was mobbed and came to an inglorious end. The Haymarket Theatre was threatened by a mob in 1738 because it employed French performers, and a little later Drury Lane Theatre was demolished because Garrick hired some French dancers. The "half-price" riots of 1763 virtually destroyed both the rebuilt houses. In May 1765, in Bloomsbury, a mob tried to pull down the house of the Duke of Bedford and had to be driven off by the Horse Guards. During the agitation in London over the expulsion of John Wilkes from parliament a mob took possession of all the streets and avenues leading to the polling places, held the city in its grip for two days, smashed windows, dragged the Austrian ambassador from his stately coach, and threatened to wreck the jail where Wilkes was imprisoned. Four thousand mutinous sailors once stopped every ship trying to leave the Port of London. In 1780 the Lord George Gordon anti-Catholic riots in that city occasioned immense property damage and brought about the death of some seven hundred persons. In Bohemia in 1772 peasant rioting mounted into virtual civil war. Paoli led a revolt in Corsica. In Madrid there was a riot against the king's Neapolitan minister — "el motín de Esquilache." In Boston, that staid city, there were mobs in 1725, 1729, 1734, 1741, 1757, 1763, 1769, 1770, and annually thereafter until the siege. Not only does Hamilton's famous remark make a good deal of sense in its time, but the peace of the century was perhaps a superficial affair. Violence produces counterviolence, but violence may help one to realize that the eighteenth century was not so very different in this respect from the world of the 1970's.

ii

Yet when one speaks of the eighteenth century one does not have this violence in mind. One means rather the high culture of Western Europe and parts of the New World over a period extending from about 1715 to about 1789, when the French revolution began its tortuous and unpredictable career.

* The Calves' Head Club, which dated from sometime in the seventeenth century, met annually to burlesque Charles I and those who talked about the memory of a martyred saint. Calves' heads were used to ridicule that monarch and his courtiers. I am not certain why the club was mobbed; it was suppressed in 1735.

In France the light-hearted Regency succeeded the stately gloom of the Sun King's declining years, and in Great Britain the Age of Anne slid smoothly into the age of Robert Walpole. In various minor states — for example, Sweden, Poland, and sundry German and Italian kingdoms, duchies, principalities, and the like — rulers conceived they were not properly installed unless they imitated, though on a smaller scale, the geometric balance and baroque splendor of Versailles. In the empire of the Hapsburgs Vienna was thought to be another and more religious Paris, a capital that was, except for Mannheim, the musical center of Europe or about to become so; and in far-off Russia Peter the Great pushed a recalcitrant nobility and a stubborn church into a facsimile of modernism. He created a new capital at St. Petersburg and founded a Russian Academy of Sciences in 1725. It is true that the original membership of the Academy, sixteen in number, was made up of thirteen Germans, two Swiss, and a solitary Frenchman; true also that his illiterate widow, Catherine I (*not* the great Catherine) claimed credit for an enterprise she did not comprehend. But upper-class circles in St. Petersburg, despite Germanic rulers, became French in culture. In Massachusetts, equally far away, the Century of Enlightenment, in Samuel Eliot Morison's amusing phrase, opened somewhat belatedly when in January 1708, over the opposition of the Mather family, the more worldly John Leverett became president of Harvard College.

It is better to survey an epoch at midpoint rather than at its origin, and the best point from which to look at the Age of Enlightenment is at the end of the Seven Years War in 1763. Ranging from Niagara Falls and Cuba to the Philippines and India, this conflict was the great world war of the eighteenth century. Alliances altered during the struggle, combatants withdrew or changed sides, and there was a network of diplomatic bargaining behind the scenes; but in general Prussia and Great Britain confronted France, Austria, and Russia. Frederick the Great struggled valiantly against overwhelming military odds. At the end of 1761 it seemed as though he had come to the end of his resources. The death of the Czarina Elizabeth early in 1762 brought to the Russian throne the half-mad Peter III (he called Frederick "the king my master"). Peter changed Russia overnight from a foe to a friend of the Prussian monarch, and though Peter was quietly got out of the way by midsummer, his widow, Catherine the Great, had no desire to seem to favor Prussian aggrandizement and did not renew hostilities. During the last two years of this bloody business a tangle of considerations — secret offers of peace, more alliances, more enmities, the dilatoriness of the British in supporting Frederick's armies with gold, problems in the Baltic, problems concerning Gibraltar and Portugal, and above all the exhaustion of the treasuries of the principal Continental states — led to a series of treaties that finally ended the struggle. Frederick kept Silesia and some other territories, the Hapsburgs gained and lost possessions but came out rather unchanged, France retained her normal boundaries and her normal internal disarray, the Spanish evacuated Portugal, the British evacuated the West Indies (or most of those they had been occupying), the Germanies returned to their traditional anarchy as theoretical fiefs in a Holy Roman Empire of the German People in which virtually no German believed, France lost an empire in India and Canada, and Britain gained one. British North America was to be lost, except for Canada, twelve years later. The map of Europe remained about the same.

But the results of warfare are never what they seem at first sight to be. Frederick had won an epic struggle, but Prussia was exhausted. It is said that one of every nine of his subjects died because of the war, and he spent the rest of his life grimly restoring order and economic stability to his somewhat inchoate kingdom. He died in 1786 and left to his successors an army so lacking in leadership that twenty years later Napoleon destroyed it at Jena. France had lost prestige, and her finances never were straightened out; yet within a generation French military and naval power had so far recovered that during the American revolution the French navy at times controlled the Atlantic, and a French fleet and an army under Rochambeau were the principal factor in compelling the surrender of Cornwallis at Yorktown in 1781. Despite these occasional brilliant forays against the British, the primary result of the war was to confirm the fact that Britain, not France nor Holland nor Spain, was the mistress of the seas.

One truth that strikes the modern reader, used as he is to cries of nationalism, racial discrimination, and religious fanaticism (consider the hatred of the Arabs for the Jews), is the relative weakness of such elements in the high eighteenth century. It cannot be said that there was no feeling of nationality — the French and the British had eyed each other across the Channel for centuries — but peoples and territories were often passed from ruler to ruler during the Age of Enlightenment as if they were packaged goods exchanged by wholesale distributors. The Austrians usually controlled much of what we now know as Belgium, not to speak of a variegated empire of Hungarians, Bohemians, Slavs, and Italians. Hanover, which was German, belonged in theory to George I of England and his successors. The Finns were ruled by the Swedes. The ethnic make-up of the Russian Empire was as kaleidoscopic as that of the Ottoman Turks. The Spaniards governed a vast Indian population in the New World; and even in the North American colonies there were English, Welsh, Scotsmen, Irishmen, Germans, Jews, Frenchmen, Spaniards, Portuguese, Dutchmen, Swedes, and Africans, most of them later claiming "the rights of Englishmen."

Nothing in the century makes consistent sense. A French-speaking Swiss, by name Jean-Jacques Rousseau, converted to Catholicism and reconverted to Protestantism, lived peacefully in France, which denied toleration to Protestants, until 1762 when one of his books was condemned as seditious. In London Lord Bute, prime minister to George III, dared not appear in the streets without a bodyguard of prizefighters largely because he was a Scotsman, an unpopular breed in England. In Ireland race and religion combined to lead many of the Irish to detest Protestants and eventually attempt the overthrow of the English invaders. A French deist, Denis Diderot, was called to the court of Russia as a personal guest of Catherine the Great, who was in theory the head of the Greek Orthodox Church. One has, however, to await the American and French revolutions and the full tide of the romantic movement with its evocations of a national past to discover that nationality and race are primary forces in politics.

Probably language and religion were more divisive. A linguistic map of the Western world in the mid-eighteenth century, which took into account the innumerable dialects that were spoken, would look like a crazy quilt. In the seventeenth century Latin was still an international language, and it remained the language of much learned discourse in the eighteenth century and even lingered among the elite: Casanova, for example, in his incessant wanderings, when he could not speak a tongue native to a city, often fell back on Latin. French became the language of the polite world and of diplomacy. But the growing importance of this tongue for cosmopolitan culture should not conceal the fact that the French of Paris was not universal in France: one of the benefits of the French revolution was to extend its use into all parts of the kingdom, some of which spoke only the local vernacular. In Italy there were almost as many dialects as there were principalities and powers; and although most writers employed the standard Tuscan, Goldoni wrote some of his comedies in Venetian, a variant that had the dubious honor of sheltering the scandalous poetry of Giorgio Baffo. A Sicilian peasant could not understand a peasant from the valley of the Po.

At the other end of Europe Norway nourished a clutter of provincial dialects; the literary and political language was Danish (Riksmaal), and not until relatively late in the next century was "Norwegian" (Landsmaal) developed by philologists, writers, statesmen, and ardent nationalists. In the Germanies, though standard "literary" German was at last coming to the fore, Bayerisch and Swabian were not always mutually comprehensible. Linguistic difficulties continually plagued the polyglot empire of the Hapsburgs. In Great Britain the language of the Highlander differed importantly from that of the Lowlander, a cockney could not understand somebody from Glasgow, and one has only to read some of the novels of the age to learn how unintelligible variants of English were to Britons of another sort. "I have known a member of the House of Commons," writes Matthew Bramble in *Humphry Clinker*, "speak with great energy and precision, without being able to engage attention, because his observations were made in the Scottish dialect." Probably the necessity of giving swift and uniform orders in the army and the navy was an important force in diminishing linguistic differences among the subjects of this or that ruler.

Historians make much of the weakening power of the papacy and the growing power of toleration in this century. The papacy steadily declined in public influence, among other reasons because the period failed to produce a great pope; and the worldliness of the higher clergy, the ignorance of village curés and country priests are often cited as another reason for the waning power of religion. Certainly the eighteenth century saw nothing comparable to the bloody wars of religion of the preceding age, and it is true that philosophers and *philosophes* were freer to speak their minds in the Age of Enlightenment than they would have been during the century of the Thirty Years War. Religious zealotry cannot, however, be dismissed thus casually. In the vast domains of the Spanish and Portuguese kings and queens it seems probable that Protestants, Jews, atheists, Epicureans, materialists, conjurors, Mohammedans, witches, impostors, and mystics tended to be classed as children of the devil. The Inquisition worked away in Spain until Napoleon abolished it temporarily in 1804, and "heretics" were tortured, whipped, put in solitary confinement, or executed for the greater glory of God. The same thing was true in some degree in the Latin-American colonies of Spain, though Portugal was more tolerant, and it should be said that the Bourbon kings of Spain sought to control the worser features of this institution. In France, the bloody revolt of the Camisards, militant heirs of the Huguenots, ran from 1702 to 1711; in the Upper Cévennes 466 villages were burned and their inhabitants massacred in the name of God and the king. The bitterness dividing Catholic Irishmen from Orangemen is older than the present tension in Ulster; and John Wesley, the founder of Methodism, never knew when a meeting of his in field or village would be broken up by a mob. Socinians were expelled from Poland at one time, and at another (1766–67) used by Catherine the Great as an instrument for weakening Polish independence. In that unhappy country a Catholic countermovement from 1768 to 1772 further injured the state. Mennonites and Dunkards found it more comfortable to live in Pennsylvania than under their German overlords; nor should one forget that in writing *Hermann und Dorothea* Goethe merely transferred to a later decade the story of Protestant refugees driven out of Catholic Salzburg in 1732.

Even at higher levels religion divided rather than united many intellectuals. In France the tension between those in the Jansenist tradition and the Jesuits continued; a papal bull, *Unigenitus*, issued in 1713, condemned more than a hundred errors in a theological work by one Pasquier Quesnel; and, in the long-drawn-out controversy that followed, French bishops were now and then sent into virtual exile. The abolition of the Jesuit order by the pope followed upon the banishment of the order by several monarchs, who found that Jesuits troubled the peace and policy of their kingdoms. One may be amused by the story of miracles wrought at the grave of a holy deacon, a member of the so-called convulsionary group in France, and by the solemn sign: "Further miracles are forbidden here by order of the King"; but civil authorities were inevitably uneasy when "enthusiasts" took over some area, or "mystics," real or feigned, led the unthinking away from doctrines of orderly theology that made the church useful to the state. On the other hand Voltaire aroused most French intellectuals when he denounced the judicial murder of Jean Calas (1762), accused of strangling his younger son to prevent the young man from embracing Catholicism. The pious people of Toulouse alleged that such was common practice among inveterate Protestants.

iii

Nevertheless there existed a cultural unity in the Western world, which one may call the Enlightenment or the Age of Reason, misleading but convenient terms. Talleyrand is supposed to have remarked that no one had ever tasted the sweetness of life unless he had lived before the French revolution; and Sir Isaiah Berlin writes that the eighteenth century was the last period in which intelligent men thought that human omniscience might be attainable. Despite dynastic rivalries, some racial animosities (the Greeks did not, to put it mildly, love the Turks), linguistic blocks to easy communication, and perpetual religious quarreling, one finds a common pattern in the society of Europe and its dependencies.

Europe, to be sure, must be divided into an eastern and a western zone by a line along the Oder, then south to Vienna, and then southwest to the Venetian republic. In the Atlantic community society was organized on a status basis into ranks and classes, but the social function and responsibility of the various ranks in eastern Europe and those in western Europe often differed. In general, eastern Europe was a spread of territory in which cities counted for little, roads (and therefore communications) were bad, illiteracy was commonplace, and the nobility retained a great deal of local power. Peasants were bound to the soil in one or another pattern of serfdom. Wealth was agricultural, or wealth came, as it sometimes did in Russia, from the bulk products of a simple exploitative economy. Where there was a middle class, it was small, exerted little influence on the state or its economic life, and had virtually no political power, though it sometimes attained high rank in the church. Tradition reigned in religion, education (or lack of it), the status of women, and the fear of "modernism," even though a ruler or a court aristocracy might imitate or envy the fashions of far-off Paris. The agricultural revolution of the century, except in East Prussia and Silesia, left this part of Europe untouched, the tax systems were primitive, and though there were kindly landowners here and there who looked after their serfs, dirt, disease, and drink were commonplace on the farms and in the towns and villages, where the wretched Jews, herded into ghettos, carried on such trade and banking as was possible. During the Enlightenment eastern Europe was a debtor, not a creditor, culture.

Yet the structure of society, east and west, was much the same. Nobody had thought of any other form of government than a monarchy, despite the existence of Geneva and Venice as oligarchical republics; and society under a monarch was organized into three, sometimes four, estates.* The classic instance is France where, under the crown, the three estates were the clergy, the nobility, and the commoners. By the commoners one really meant the middle class and the richer farmers. In Prussia (and to some degree in Russia) the nobility was kept sternly at work profitable to the state, whether on their farms or in governmental service. In Poland, Hungary, and Sweden the nobles regarded themselves as in fact constituting the state: the famous *liberum veto* of the Polish diet was a chief reason for the continuing political anarchy in that nation; and in Sweden the aristocracy (with the clergy), whatever internal division they might suffer, constituted the government from about 1720 to 1772 when Gustavus III overthrew the oligarchy and set out to rule as the enlightened despot of the North. In Spain, Portugal, and Italy the nobles occupied a more ambiguous role. The traditional signature of the Spanish king,

* How difficult and tentative all generalizations about the social structure of central Europe must be is evident if one goes back to the seventeenth-century shape of these patterns. See chapter xvii, "The Hapsburg Lands, 1618–1657," by V. L. Tapic, in vol. IV of *The New Cambridge Modern History* (Cambridge, 1970).

"Yo el rey," hinted at a degree of absolutism no king of Poland ever dreamed of; and the nobles tended to flock to the court and neglect their estates. In France the noble families were either nobles of the court, who spent their lives under the eyes of their master, hoping for favors and a sinecure, or nobles too poor to live at Versailles, who, proud as Lucifer, starved with what dignity they could on their rural properties. The British situation was characteristically mixed and empirical: the lords temporal and spiritual constituted one branch of the British Parliament, and the House of Commons the other, to which the younger sons of noblemen could be elected. Most ministries were dominated by men of title. But the British aristocracy was not the Venetian oligarchy that Disraeli later called it, and the aristocrats, if they owned land, usually took pride in their estates, their farms, and their tenants, as did "Turnip" Townshend, who, deprived of office, took to modernizing farming. Nor did they, as the French aristocracy wanted to do, monopolize all the principal posts in government, the church, the army, and the navy. There was no such split between the court aristocracy and an impoverished landed gentry in Great Britain as there was in France.

If the social and economic, not to say political, function of the nobility in all countries was ambiguous, it must be remembered that what Frantz Funck-Brentano pointed out forty years ago is true: in the age of gunpowder a castle in the country was not now needed as a fortress for vassals and retainers under the captainship of a great lord. The ingathering of feudal retainers that Scott picturesquely describes in *The Lay of the Last Minstrel* and, more humorously, in *Old Mortality* was obsolete in an age when artillery had become a formidable weapon. The country nobleman, no longer under obligation to protect his followers or be protected by them, had only two choices: he could live, a parasite on their toil, by insisting on feudal dues and feudal services under regulations long out of date; or he could, by improving their lot, teaching better agricultural methods, housing them better, and looking after their health and welfare, modernize his responsibility. It is at least possible that the vogue of romantic medievalism among the gentry in many nations was owing in part to the fact that the country nobleman, having lost his real social function, imaginatively restored that function by reading stories of the past when his ancestor was a genuine warlord, justiciar, and patron of his people. Byron's thoughts were definitely turned to the feudal ages when he at last tried to live in Newstead; and it is difficult not to believe that the bitterness of Chateaubriand's father and the social alienation of his family from Breton society, pictured in the melancholy opening volume of *Mémoires d'outre-tombe*, did not have something to do with turning that writer's thoughts to a romanticized version of the wars and sufferings of Christianity and the vague chivalric atmosphere of *Les Aventures du dernier des Abencérages*.

It is today fashionable to regard monarchy as so naive a form of government that articles appear wondering whether Elizabeth II may not be the last British sovereign. The American and French revolutions and the wars of the nineteenth and twentieth centuries succeeded in sweeping away most dynasties from China and India to Germany and Spain, and the worship of throne and altar, part of the mystique of romanticism, strikes us nowadays as merely quaint. Yet in 1763 monarchy was taken as a matter of course, whether the ruler's title was that of emperor, king, prince, pope, archduke, duke, or elector. Except in a few states (Poland was such an exception), monarchy was hereditary, and despite the vicious attacks of a propagandist like Tom Paine on monarchy as an evil institution mistakenly adopted by the ancient Jews, despite the ludicrous picture of George III in the American Declaration of Independence, it does not appear that a hereditary crown was thought to be inevitably an instrument of wrong. Incompetent and licentious kings there certainly were, and one or two who were mad, but it would require an exhaustive comparison to prove decisively that the abilities of European rulers in the eighteenth century were necessarily feebler than, say, those of the presidents and president-dictators of the Latin-American republics following the wars of liberation during and after Napoleon. Some sovereigns were dull and undistinguished, but so were some princes of the church.

A system that produced such talented personages as Frederick II of Prussia, Catherine the Great of Russia, Maria Theresa, who held an empire together by force of personality and political skill, Charles III of Spain, who expelled the Jesuits and almost succeeded in modernizing the machinery of his empire, and Joseph I of Portugal, no genius, who nevertheless had the sense to keep Pombal, ruthless and efficient, as his minister from 1750 to 1777,* compares favorably with the system that produced the line of eighteenth-century popes, each theoretically elected by his cardinal peers.

Historians nowadays are beginning to think more favorably of Louis XV and George III than did their scholarly predecessors. The difficulty with eighteenth-century monarchy was that if the ruler adopted some version of Bolingbroke's famous *Idea of a Patriot King* (1749) he gradually absorbed all the principal powers of the state into himself and his successors, and if he viewed his function as that of an enlightened reformer, as did Frederick the Great and Joseph II of Austria, he either antagonized the states of the realm or failed to create an efficient civil service to carry on reform after his demise. As I have earlier remarked, Louis XIV made both mistakes. Bolingbroke had argued that the business of the king is to maintain the constitution of the realm, espouse no party (commonly called "faction," a term used by the American founding fathers), employ ministers who would serve him, and govern after the Christian, Hebraic, and Homeric pattern of being a parent to his people. This was all very well; and a ruler like Maria Theresa, without benefit of Bolingbroke, more or less succeeded in such a program. It can, incidentally, be argued that George Washington's conception of the presidency of the United States has a strong Bolingbrokian tinge.

The common concept of an absolute monarch is more or less a fiction. Burke's famous statement that the Sultan of Turkey secured only such obedience as he could get is, even if mythical, enlightening. Louis XV once sighed and remarked that if only he were the Paris superintendent of police, he could do something toward making Paris a safer city. Even the *lettres de cachet*, long supposed to be the utmost in absolute power, seem to have been rather carefully guarded by law and custom. The kings of France in this century were hemmed in by a complex pattern of custom, provincial traditions, divisions of the realm between the *pays d'état* and the *pays d'élection*, and, as I have indicated, the stubborn conservatism of the *parlements*. In his later years, out of sheer weariness, Louis XV virtually ceased to govern at all.

Even in the minor instance of Goethe's enlightened duke, Charles

* Joseph I went mad in 1774, and his wife, Maria Anna, became regent. Pombal was dismissed only when she became queen in 1777. (She married her uncle, Peter, and herself went insane in 1792.)

Augustus of Saxe-Weimar, though that ruler could call in leading writers, philosophers, and scholars, there were some things he could not do. In 1790 Goethe wrote with some bitterness that the Germans might be a decent enough people but they had no taste; and, returning from Italy to Weimar, from which he had fled in virtual secrecy, he found himself no longer the duke's chief minister but only the director of the court theater. In his *Commentaries on the Laws of England* (1765–1769) Sir William Blackstone wrote that the king was the fountain of honor, an idea generally true of Europe, but again a difficulty arose. In dealing out honors kings had also to deal out emoluments, and these, like unsavory governmental contracts in modern times, were not always without suspicion of personal or political pull. Kings were too often so cut off from their subjects that they had insufficient knowledge of men of talent in their dominions and an insufficient mode of ascertaining what talent truly might be. Besides, most monarchies were still operating the primitive machinery of the feudal system, which meant that, apart from random encounters with the peasantry, they lived wholly in the midst of courtiers both secular and ecclesiastical, and were therefore often as helpless to know what the mass of the people felt as is an American president. In the century radicals assailed monarchy because it was tyrannical, an indictment rarely justified; they could have said with greater truth that monarchy is wrong because it is inefficient. Yet neither Jeremy Bentham nor any other utilitarian seriously presses this charge, and the great French *Encyclopédie* discusses monarchy so gingerly that it may be said not to discuss it at all. From Fénelon's *Télémaque* in 1699 to Wieland's *Der goldene Spiegel* in 1772, on the other hand, eighteenth-century writers spent a good deal of intellectual energy on the education of princes.

iv

It seems to me that the most puzzling difficulty in any simple analysis of the social make-up of the West in the eighteenth century lies less in monarchy or in the aristocracy than in that vast, vague, and powerful group, the middle class. Because the eighteenth century is considered in some sense to have eventuated in the triumph of the middle class (in *Representative Men* Emerson was to attribute to Napoleon the virtues and vices of that social element), it is important not to sophisticate the term by reading back into it the pejorative connotation common today. "Middle class" now almost invariably implies stuffiness, mere domesticity, aesthetic sluggishness, and unwillingness to face "realities." In the eighteenth century, however, except among a few, and these mainly found in the romantics, middle class meant nothing of the kind. The middle class was progressive. The middle class demanded freedom of trade. The middle class, possibly out of envy, wanted to take privilege away from the aristocracy and the clergy. Moreover, although the aristocracy might be corrupt, in the eighteenth century the middle class was by definition virtuous. Everybody said so — Richardson, Diderot, Lessing, even some of the more radical leaders of the French Revolution (Danton and Robespierre are instances), men who felt they were pulling down kings, nobles, and the church to exalt the middle class and virtue.

Once past the fallacy that to be middle class is to be looking for profits rather than for progress, the inquirer faces a second problem. Throughout history the middle class has always been rising. It was rising in Periclean Athens and in republican Rome. It was rising in medieval Europe, as the English mystery plays and the mercantile success of the Hanseatic League demonstrate. It was rising in the Renaissance — for example, in Florence of the Medici and in Tudor England; and exploration, the growth of oceanic trade, the development of banking, and the invention of modern bookkeeping are among its achievements. It was rising in Cromwellian Britain. Obviously, then, the middle class did not cease to rise in the Age of Reason. But why was it necessary, after all these centuries, to continue to rise? Or was the quality of its ascendancy changing? In our epoch the middle class was all for laissez faire and freedom, yet the middle class frowned on laborers and "radicals" who were also in favor of freedom, perhaps because the "lower orders" were not altogether pleased with the results of laissez faire. The middle class was in favor of curtailing "privilege"; yet it took a series of riots amounting to virtual rebellion in England of the 1830's to carry through parliament a reform bill that mainly enfranchised the middle class. One wonders why the middle class waited so long to secure a juster parliamentary representation. In the British mainland colonies the middle class was opposed to the Stamp Act and other "repressive" measures, but the ragged Continentals who made up Washington's army were not, to put it mildly, scions of the middle class. The court and the middle class were all for domesticity; when Goethe, after some years of adultery, made an honest woman of Christiana Vulpius in Weimar by marrying her, they would have little to do with the now virtuous Frau von Goethe. It is all a little puzzling.

In the eighteenth century, in fact, two cultures developed side by side, sometimes harmoniously, sometimes in conflict — the culture of the aristocracy and the culture of the middle class. On the one side there were the elegant couplets of Mr. Pope, the rococo charm of the great Frederick's Sans Souci, the delicate sensuousness of Watteau and Fragonard, the music of Rameau, and Voltaire's *La Pucelle*, which is scarcely family reading. On the other side were the *Spectator* papers, Greuze's sentimental painting of "The Broken Pitcher," William Law's *A Serious Call to a Devout and Holy Life*, Lessing's *Minna von Barnheim*, Handel's very proper and very Protestant *Messiah*, Diderot's eulogy of Richardson ("O my friends, *Pamela, Clarissa Harlowe* and *Grandison* are three dramas of sublimity!"), and the *Poor Richard* of Benjamin Franklin, that breviary of how to get on in the world. It cannot be said that the *Messiah* was heard only by the middle class — we still rise when the "Hallelujah" chorus is sung because George II once stood up — nor can it be argued that the middle class took no pleasure in court painting, rich costumes, formal gardens, and good wine. The point is rather the simultaneous existence of two value systems, the one exemplified by Chesterfield's *Letters to His Son* (1774), the other by Rousseau's *Emile* (1762).

The middle class obtained, as it were, cultural equality but not cultural conquest. Beethoven's *Fidelio* is clearly a paean to wifely devotion (and incidentally to a wise minister of state), but Mozart's *Così fan tutte*, which preceded it by only fifteen years, is no celebration of sexual fidelity. *Die Leiden des jungen Werthers*, which came out in 1774, seems to demonstrate the folly of falling madly in love with a married woman; yet twenty-five years later Friedrich von Schlegel published *Lucinde*, a formless, passionate apology for the senses and for idleness. I extract two remarkable sentences: "Industry and utility are the angels of death with the flaming swords who stand in the way of man's return to Paradise" and "The highest, most perfect life is a life of pure vegetation." The first is a total denial of Benjamin Franklin; the second is quite incompatible with Isaac Watts's famous injunction to imitate the bee and improve each shining hour. Before we dismiss these sentences as eccentric folly let us remember that the hero of Shelley's *Alastor* in 1816 does nothing in particular because of the "selfish, blind, and torpid . . . multitudes who constitute . . . the lasting misery and loneliness of the world," and that in 1821 Richard Henry Dana, Sr., edited in the United States a magazine called *The Idle Man*, which in fact preached idleness as beneficial to the soul. Perhaps the triumph of the middle class was not as universal nor as dull as historians have alleged.

There is a third, if minor, difficulty — the problem of terms. Words that seem to have "middle class" as their referent carry different connotations in different countries. In Great Britain the state consisted of king, lords, and commons, and the commons were theoretically the people of Great Britain. But the commons in fact came from a minority group, persons of status in communities, of course — yet not all persons of status, even in boroughs that sent representatives to parliament, were entitled to vote. The British middle class, moreover, included as a characteristic element Dissenters who could not hold office except by special annual dispensations and could not be graduated from the two universities but who were nevertheless a principal source of invention, industry, and new modes of commerce as the United Kingdom slowly swung into the main stream of the industrial revolution. In France there were important distinctions between *la haute bourgeoisie* and *la petite bourgeoisie*, and these distinctions were both administrative and social. No term is more troublesome than the German *Bürger* and its derivatives. A *Bürger* might mean either a citizen of a free city entitled to vote or to representation, or it might mean any respectable subject of a sovereign, not of aristocratic lineage and not a *Bauer*. As for *bürgerlich*, it may connote the civic or the civil virtues, or a fixed social status, or being a "respectable" person, or the kind of taste that blossomed into the Biedermeier style of the early nineteenth century. *Bürgersinn* means, roughly, public spirit; a *Bürgereid* is an oath publicly taken; *bürgerliche Recht* is civil law; *bürgerliche Küche* implies a plain family meal;

Bürgerlichkeit means, on the whole, solid respectability with an eighteenth-century flavor to it. I have no doubt that linguists and historians have to confront similar puzzles in other languages and other countries.

Whatever judgment one passes on the social and cultural dynamics of the middle class in the eighteenth century, it seems clear that its members were more numerous, influential, and wealthy in the cities and towns than in the countryside, and a stronger body in western Europe than they were in eastern Europe, where they were but a thin wedge, mostly composed of governmental officials, between the mass of peasants below them and the aristocracy above them. They were also more evident in the British colonies in North America than they were in the Spanish and Portuguese dominions in the New World. In the West Indies leading families were proprietors of plantations, as was true of the Southern colonies of North America, and such persons were to be distinguished from the more humble port-merchants and factors in the islands and on the seacoasts. But whether a George Washington or a Thomas Jefferson is to be thought of as a member of an American aristocracy, not to be confused with royal governors having noble titles, is a problem of definition to be revived, in a sense, by the controversy over slavery. How did the Washingtons, the Curtises, and the Lees differ from the Adamses in Massachusetts?

The association of middle-class status with trade and banking is a very old one, reinforced in the century in countries where by custom or royal edict the nobility were forbidden to enter trade or finance and were expected to appoint an agent to collect dues and rentals from those who lived on their estates. Land was still the great source of wealth in Prussia and France. But one reason for both the economic and political power and the international influence of the middle class was the wars of the eighteenth century, since only the great banking houses could furnish loans to the state or, in many cases, collect taxes to pay the expenses of government and the armed forces. The activities of Robert Morris in financing the American revolution are familiar, and so is the rise of the Rothschilds, who became virtually a third force on the international stage during the struggles between Napoleon and the countries allied against him. A like history can be traced in the

43

growth of some of the banking houses in France and England, even when the names are "foreign." The rise of the house of Baring (the founder was originally a Lutheran minister from Bremen) is a classic example of this sort of thing in England. These great banking houses flourished alongside of "official" banks, such as the Bank of England, which dates from about 1694, and these the banking families sometimes overshadowed and controlled.

Commerce and trade, usually wholesale and sometimes retail, though small shopkeepers were not always "genteel," were of course other important activities of the middle class. So was the support of the growing factory system, albeit the immediate impact of invention upon industry before 1800 has been somewhat exaggerated. In the 1760's and the 1770's most factories were still literally manu-facturing establishments, the rationalization of industry had only begun, and though pumps, rather simple machines, and new mechanical devices were clearly making inroads, the charming plates of the *Encyclopédie* showing happy workmen operating machines are more hopeful than factual. The desperate needs of the French revolutionary armies for weapons, clothing, ammunition, and supplies in 1793 were enormous, but they had to be met by the mobilization of man- (and woman-) power rather than by the multiplication of machines. As late as 1800 the Watt-Boulton engineering partnership had turned out only some five hundred condensing steam engines for "industrial" England, and inventors like Hargreaves had sometimes been in peril of their lives from outraged hand-workers who thought with some justice that mechanical spinning and weaving would throw them out of employment. It is not here argued that there was no industrial revolution; it is argued only that the industrial revolution came more haltingly than a good many textbooks claim.

It is commonly said that a distinguishing mark of the middle class, particularly in the eighteenth century, is that it emphasized the domestic virtues, setting up family life as central to culture and society in contrast to the licentiousness of the Restoration in England and the license of the Regency in France. The middle-class housewife was expected to devote herself to home and husband, children and church as the fashionable great lady need not; the middle-class father and husband was supposed to exercise a firm, benevolent control over his spouse and his offspring. Children were brought up to reverence their parents and not only obey them in their younger years, but, if males, when they married, continue the family occupation. Appeal is made to literature during the period as proof of these ideals — an appeal epitomized in Burns's famous lines:

> To make a happy fire-side clime
>   To weans and wife,
> That's the true pathos and sublime
>   Of human life.

That Burns was no model of domestic propriety is not felt to be a fatal commentary on a century in which Squire Allworthy recognizes Tom Jones as his heir, Charlotte remains faithful to Albert despite the wild passion of young Werther, Julie in *La Nouvelle Héloïse* refuses to elope with Saint-Preux because her father wills her to stay home and marry de Wolmar, and even Lemuel Gulliver returns to his family in England, though, after living with the Houyhnhnms, the human race fills him with disgust. *The Vicar of Wakefield* conquered Europe as a poignant picture of family distress, family virtue, family forgiveness, and family reunion; and Restif de la Bretonne, few of whose publications are "virtuous," in *La Vie de mon père*, quotes his father as saying to his mother: "My dear wife, the most dangerous fault in a husband is to be a weak husband, one who does not know how to grasp the scepter of conjugal authority." In his great speeches on the American colonies Edmund Burke attributed the prosperity and increase of "this fierce people" to the thrift, industry, dissenting vigor, and philoprogenitiveness of the principal part of their inhabitants, members of the middle class.

All this is true enough, but some qualifications must be kept in mind. In the first place, during the eighteenth century parental insistence that sons should so marry as to maintain the family tradition and daughters should not marry out of it was quite as strong among the peasantry and the aristocracy as it was in the bourgeoisie — perhaps stronger among the nobility, which was on the defensive in France and elsewhere. Moreover, the whole power of government and the church was employed to enforce the pattern of family discipline. I have mentioned the *lettres de cachet*. These seem to have been used far more often to prevent undutiful behavior or to preserve domestic purity than for political purposes, and this at all social levels. The family ideal, however, was not uniform in any class. If George I complained that his son, the future George II, was totally unfilial, George III seems to have been worse as a father than he was as a king. At the other end of the social scale Jean-Jacques Rousseau, son of a Genevan watch maker, though in the second *Discours* he informed Europe that the "chaste influence" of the "amiable and virtuous daughters of Geneva" was "solely exercised within the limits of conjugal union," records in the *Confessions* the extremely free use that certain Swiss females made of his boyish body. Virtue, then, was not the monopoly of the middle class, and neither was vice. Consider the amorous career of Robert Burns among the Lowland lassies, or count the number of "betrayed" females in *The Lyrical Ballads*.

If it may be doubted whether a strong sense of the family as a continuum was peculiarly true of the middle class and whether that part of society was supposed really to possess per se a superior morality — a doubt not decreased by the irregular lives of such proponents of domesticity as Benjamin Franklin, who had two illegitimate children — one should also bear in mind that themes like family solidarity, the restoration of a long-lost or alienated child to the domestic hearth, maternal sacrifice and paternal power were no inventions of the eighteenth century. They run from the story of Cain and Abel to *The Forsyte Saga* and beyond. The *Antigone* of Sophocles turns on familial obligation as against one's duty to the state. The *cri du sang* is standard in neoclassic French and Spanish tragedy. The cry of "Absalom! My son!" the tale of Sohrab and Rustum, the plot of *King Lear*, and the resolution of *Cymbeline* involve family stories as much as do *Clarissa Harlowe*, Kotzebue's international success *Menschenhass und Reue*, known in English as *The Stranger*, and Diderot's *Le Père de famille*, written among other reasons to demonstrate that the French stage should abandon tragedy and take on either *drame* or *comédie larmoyante* — in other words, domestic pieces that would move the feeling heart to tears.

Though I think it wise to keep in mind these hazards to sweeping generalizations about the bourgeoisie of the eighteenth century, the middle class was a central element in the history of the Western world from 1715 to 1789 — and, of course, before that time and beyond it. As I have hinted, the enormous increase in trade both internal and external to any territory was mainly due to the assiduity of the middle class. On the whole this class rather than the aristocracy supported and managed the banks, oceanic commerce, voyages of exploration and discovery which, sometimes scientific in theory, created new markets, agricultural reform (in conjunction with enlightened noblemen), new tendencies in education, and such influential educational creations as the Dissenting academies in Great Britain. The bourgeoisie also supplied personnel to most of the professions, though in many countries the lower clergy sometimes verged on illiteracy. Lawyers, who were not, however, necessarily "genteel" (witness the *avocat* of French comedy); civil servants; and members of the medical profession (though physicians and surgeons were, with notable exceptions, perilously close to the barber-surgeons) — these professional types tended to originate in the middle class. In some countries the middle class could absorb the richer yeomanry, marry into the lesser aristocracy, and, *ex officiis*, acquire noble titles by purchasing certain offices of state. A lad of parts could achieve status as a scholar, a scientist, a writer, a painter, a sculptor, a musician, or an architect, though he could never be sure when he might run into the stupidities of social conventions; and one of the oddities of the social pattern is that a *grande dame* might without impropriety conduct a salon to which men of genius or talent without a title could come.

Careers in the church or in the armed forces were unpredictable: in some Catholic lands even a peasant might become a cardinal, but in others this was impossible, and it is, I think, illuminating that though army commissions could be purchased by wealth for promising sons, virtually every British command of any size in the American war was headed by someone with a title — instances include Lord Howe, Sir John Burgoyne, and Cornwallis, who had been an earl since 1762. Wives and mothers of the upper middle class could also have salons. Some of them were bluestockings, and some of them were artists or thinkers in their own right. Angelica Kauffmann, for example, was one of the first members of the Royal Academy; Suzanne Necker, the wife of Jacques Necker the banker, the mother of Madame de Staël and herself an author, was the daughter of a Protestant clergyman; Mrs. Montagu, who rebuked

Voltaire in her essay on the genius of Shakespeare in 1769, was born Elizabeth Robinson; and Elizabeth Ann Linley, the wife of Richard Brinsley Sheridan, a concert and oratorio soprano, was the daughter of Thomas Linley, himself a composer and theater director. The economic interests of the middle class are easier to discuss than their cultural achievements. Before we too hastily conclude that in the eighteenth century all middle-class women were housebound, let us remember that two years before the French Revolution Mary Wollstonecraft published *Thoughts on the Education of Daughters*, in which she argued that a woman should be entitled to the same education as that of a man — far beyond anything Rousseau claimed in *Emile*.

A summarizing statement seems necessary. The middle class after 1763 had, as it were, a special task to do, and it therefore became unusually conscious of the obstacles that stood in the way of movements of political, economic, and social change. After the peace treaties, a large part of the responsibility for restoring credit and confidence and of rebuilding states fell upon this class. Except for taxation, a matter over which it often had little control (nor is it argued that bourgeois interests in this question were unselfish), the bourgeoisie performed this necessary work with surprising speed and efficiency. This efficiency made its members an increasing power in much of western Europe and in the colonies. Even in Portugal, Naples, and Spain they exercised a considerable influence. They could not of course control "absolute" monarchs, though they often acted as royal representatives, nor did they radically alter feudal traditions on the Continent. In many lands they were unable greatly to influence the laws — consider the absurdities of the judicial system of the Holy Roman Empire. Members of the bourgeoisie often manipulated the law and the bench for their own benefit. Yet to modify public practices and to protect their own property interest, they had to know more about the theory of the law and the structure of the state than many of them did. Blackstone therefore addresses his famous lectures to the gentlemen of England. By this term he meant not only the landed gentry but also middle-class persons of status. These he found more deficient in the knowledge of law than they should be. He wrote: "Indeed, it is perfectly amazing, that there should be no other state of life . . . in which some method of instruction is not looked upon as requisite, except only the science of legislation, the noblest and most difficult of any." Rousseau's *Du Contrat social* is but one of many expositions of the theory of politics.

If England witnessed a renascence of legal studies as part of humane learning (incidentally educating ignorant justices of the peace), it is also evident that the dependence of the author upon the nobleman was slowly being replaced by the appeal of the artist to middle-class purchasers. A significant document is Dr. Johnson's famous letter to Lord Chesterfield repudiating his condescending patronage. The rebirth of German literature was possible not because of princely concern for the humanities but because the serious middle class believed in instructive reading; witness the extraordinary vogue of Klopstock's *Der Messias*. The French situation was of course complex. Jealous of the aristocracy, the middle class tended to rally around the throne, but it could do nothing to straighten out French finance, whereas the support of the arts, particularly of "radical" writing and of new musical trends represented, for example, by Gluck, was shared by the middle class and the nobility. In the Iberian and Italian peninsulas the bourgeoisie had influence here and there in modernizing the patterns of justice. Thus Beccaria's *Of Crimes and Punishments*, published in 1764, went through six editions in eighteen months and was influential, among other things, in both abolishing torture as a judicial measure and questioning capital punishment.* But it would be difficult to demonstrate that Italian, Spanish, or Portuguese support of the arts by the middle class in these domains was comparable to the support given writers, painters, musicians, and, for that matter, scientists and inventors in the British Isles. As for the British mainland colonies there was, as I have hinted, a patrician class; yet "limners," authors, musicians, and architects, to succeed, had to appeal in the main to the bourgeoisie. It is a truism that problems of finance — the right of the colonies to issue paper money, questions of taxation, the payment of colonial salaries to royal officials, and the duty to support ministers out of public funds — lay at the very heart of the American revolution.

---

* Beccaria was a *marchese*, which, however, is not quite the same as the English *marquis*. He anticipated or influenced writers such as Jeremy Bentham and Adam Smith.

49

v

At the bottom of the social pyramid was the peasantry, though whether this term can be properly applied to the small farmer in the British colonies or to the vast mass of mestizos and Indians in the Latin-American world is problematical. A great difficulty in arriving at any conclusion about the peasants is the lack of direct evidence from them as a class, and the nature of the indirect evidence available. Peasant culture did not rest on reading and writing, most peasants were illiterate, many were obstinate in their views, and even in the *cahiers*, or statements of grievances in France collected before the meeting of the States General, peasant communes submitting statements tended to adopt stereotype bills of complaint proposed to them by interested members of the bourgeoisie.

Literary evidence is subject to extreme oscillation. One pole is represented by a famous passage in *Les Caractères* of La Bruyère, published, it is true, in 1688 but often quoted or imitated by propagandists throughout the eighteenth century. La Bruyère describes

certain wild animals, male and female, scattered about the countryside, black, leaden in color, and deeply tanned by the sun, bound to the soil, which they dig and till with unconquerable persistence; they have, so to say, an articulate voice, and when they rise to their feet, they show a human face and they are in fact men. At night they withdraw into their dens . . .

(De *l'Homme*, paragraph 128)

Such creatures are barely above the brute level. Contrast this with an equally notable passage in Goldsmith's *The Deserted Village* of 1770:

> Ill fares the land, to hastening ills a prey,
> Where wealth accumulates, and men decay;
> Princes and lords may flourish, or may fade;
> A breath can make them, as a breath has made:
> But a bold peasantry, their country's pride,
> When once destroyed, can never be supplied.

Like a score of other writers, Goldsmith is denouncing "luxury," a favorite scapegoat of eighteenth-century theorizing, and believes in rural virtue, on which the strength of the state is supposed to rest. Both selections have an obvious rhetorical (or literary) bias.

Yet in Arthur Young's exemplary *Travels in France & Italy During the Years 1787, 1788, and 1789*, published in 1792, this shrewd agricultural expert also presents contrasting pictures. Near the Dordogne river he found the country maids "in reality walking dung-hills" in an *auberge*, and coming to Payrac he wrote that we

> meet many beggars, which we had not done before. All the country, girls and women, are without shoes or stockings; and the ploughmen at their work have neither sabots nor feet to their stockings. This is a poverty that strikes at the root of national prosperity . . . It reminded me of the misery of Ireland . . . Women picking weeds into their aprons for their cows, another sign of poverty I observed, during the whole way from Calais.

One cannot easily forget his vivid description of a country inn at Pezenas, not far from Montpellier:

> At supper, at the table d'hôte, we were waited on by a female without shoes or stockings, exquisitely ugly and diffusing odours not of roses: there were, however, a [gentleman wearing a] croix de St. Louis, and two or three mercantile-looking people that prated with her very familiarly: at an ordinary [inn] of farmers, at the poorest and remotest market village in England, such an animal would not be allowed by the landlord to enter his house; or by the guests their rooms.

Yet near Pau he passed

> a succession of many well built, tight, and COMFORTABLE farming cottages, built of stone and covered with tiles; each having its little garden enclosed by clipt thorn hedges, with plenty of peach and other fruit trees, some fine oaks scattered in the hedges, and the young trees nursed up with so much good care that nothing but the fostering attention of the owner could effect anything like it . . . It is all in the hands of little proprietors without the farms being so small as to occasion a vicious and miserable population.

Like contrasts could be found in other countries. Yet by and large the lot of the European peasant was coarse and miserable.

An important historical puzzle is how peasant communities communicated with each other promptly over considerable distances. It seems clear that news could be transmitted from one Russian estate to another and from one French commune through a chain reaction to a commune far distant, by some mysterious process akin to the diffusion of intelligence among the American Indian tribes or the Highland clans of Scotland. Otherwise it is difficult to account for the peasant uprisings that occurred from time to time in the various Continental countries, as, for example, the various "Jacqueries" in eighteenth-century France. How did the Great Fear spread over that nation in 1789, and who spread it? A more melodramatic instance is the greatest of Russian rebellions in the century, that under Emelyan Pugachev in 1773, a Cossack whose motley horde was gathered from Asia, the Volga river, the Ural mountains, and various other parts of Russia in sufficient force to besiege and capture cities. It required the return of General Suvarov from the Turkish frontier for the rebellion to be put down in the bloody manner customary in suppressing peasant uprisings. The peasantry were commonly not politically minded; that is, they were ignorant of international affairs and of national policies, and were aroused to action only when their religious belief seemed to be threatened or local customs were endangered by unfamiliar economic restraints, uncommon brutality, or some change that seemed to them "radical."

A peasant is commonly defined as one who lives in the country and works on the land as serf, tenant, sharecropper, or, more rarely, proprietor of a small plot of ground. In his excellent discussion of the European peasantry in volume V (1937) of the *Oxford History of European Civilization* Montague Fordham makes two important points. It is, he writes, a common mistake to think of the peasant as stupid, for this is the judgment of a verbal culture upon a non-verbal one. The peasant was oftener shrewd than stupid, ingenious in manipulating such tools and knowledges as he had, capable of judging weather and the ways of nature, and capable also of sizing up his superiors even when he could not alter their ways. This suggests that a profound resignation to things as they are was, however, basic to his view of the world. The second point made by Fordham is that the organization of the peasantry was one of kinship or of commune that was in fact an extension of the kinship pattern; yet the custom of accepting the decision of the commune was combined with the contradictory quality of an individualism so rugged and sometimes so selfish as to work for the destruction of the social unit and of the peasant himself. Such an individualism would seem to be the product of a virtually Darwinian struggle for existence in a world in which mere survival, if one considers the high mortality rate among the peasantry, was itself a triumph of shrewdness. For, whatever the philanthropists might say or do in the eighteenth century, their reforms seldom or never reached down into the peasant world.

In a general sense peasants were either free or serfs, or if not serfs, bound to the soil or the service of the lord by custom or by law. In the eighteenth century and later, poets often associated liberty with the mountains; among the peasantry it seems to be true that those who lived among the Urals, or the Alps, or the Pyrenees, or in the mountain valleys of the Scandinavian peninsula were free, whereas those who lived on the plains of Germany or the Russian steppes were unfree. This freedom presumably came about through several causes. It was more difficult for a great lord to control mountain valleys and mountain hideouts than it was to control a plains population. Moreover, mountain agriculture was seldom as productive as agriculture on the plains, so that the expense of subduing mountaineers could not necessarily be met by conquering the region. Finally, peasant families in such environments, as population grew, faced a simple dilemma: they could either starve or emigrate, legally or illegally. And leave they did. The Swiss furnished a mercenary soldiery to Europe for decades, a practice of which the Swiss Guards at the Vatican are the last surviving remnant. One should not forget the gallant and hopeless defense of the French royal family by the Swiss Guards in 1792, commemorated, as all the world knows, by the monumental dying lion at Lucerne. Similarly the Scottish Highlands, after the last Jacobite rebellion of 1745, by and by furnished excellent fighting units to serve under what was from the Highland point of view a foreign, because a Hanoverian, king. It is probably more important to observe that the free peasantry, if the term can be applied to this class in the British Isles, reach a kind of climax of respectability in the yeoman class of England. Elsewhere small farmers, however free, did not always attain a like prestige.

The miserable serfs of Russia and Poland (though in these countries, too, there were grades among the peasants) represented the extreme degradation possible under the feudal system. Their owners could do almost anything with these "souls" it pleased them to do; and on many a Slavonian estate the lord, however ignorant or malicious he might be, was the sole judge of how he might treat a population that could be traded like cows or sent like slaves to die in the mines or to establish "colonies" in Siberia. Theoretically, appeal was possible from the cruelty of a particular nobleman; in fact, however, serfs were too ignorant, too timid, too poor, or too docile to make such a legal appeal. If such protests were occasionally made, the peasants too often discovered that the judiciary was necessarily on the side of the owner. On most of the Continent the peasants were required to abandon their own fields to work on those of their overlord, or to keep up the roads, or to protect his fishing or hunting rights (though they might not themselves hunt or fish), or, in extreme cases, to furnish women for his pleasure. The taxes fell most heavily and most unfairly upon the lower orders in all of Europe. Inasmuch as the Physiocrats taught that the wealth of a nation lies in its land and agriculture, it is somewhat surprising to discover how content feudality was to let well enough alone; in other words, to continue with primitive plowing and reaping, wasteful, if traditional, methods of sowing crops, scrawny and therefore unprofitable livestock, and hovels for the peasants without light and often without fuel so that the occupants on occasion literally perished of the cold. One of the paradoxes of the century was this: that if the rise of the peasant to better status in the nation depended upon his owning his bit of land, the breaking up of larger areas into minuter parcels militated against agricultural improvement. Enclosure movements deprived the peasants of homes, but unless large estates could be created and scientifically farmed, mechanism could not be applied to agriculture and crop rotation became difficult.

It is, however, possible to paint too gloomy a picture of the peasantry in the eighteenth century. Wars took their toll since professional soldiers were expected as a matter of course to live off the land where possible; pillage and rape were so commonplace in any fought-over area as to awaken little comment. Moreover, in most countries each village or other social unit was expected to provide its quota of sturdy young men for the royal or ducal forces, a drain on manpower which meant that seedtime and harvest had to be managed in many instances by old men, women, and children. Yet even warfare had its better emotions, armies sometimes paid for what they needed, and tales of battles and sieges by a returning soldier added to village lore. Religion was a continuing solace, and in Catholic countries a colorful one. In eastern Europe mystics, saints, and holy beggars added something to community life. Saints' days and other church festivals could be celebrated by festivities traditional in character and colorful in form. A wedding was not quite the bucolic idyll of sentimental poets and painters in the century, but there were wedding feasts and jollities, even in the poorest communities. Birth and death had their rituals, christenings might be an event, and traditional holidays, religious or secular, had their customs. Nor should one forget that the treasury of ballad, folk tale, folk song, and dance music of the peasantry was later to be plundered by the romantic artists. It would be a mistake, moreover, to picture the relation of owner and serf, or tenant farmer, or renter as invariably that of master and slave, since even in France, that most aristocratic of societies, the lord of the manor could be affable to his followers.

Enclosure movements of all kinds, it is true, forced peasants off the lands into the ranks of sturdy beggars or, what was worse, into the mass of unskilled labor in the cities, the *Lumpenproletariat* of Marxian theory, an aimless migration that often increased the total of human misery. Dreadful as the cost of this displacement was, however, the future of culture in the Western world lay in the cities, not in the land, and in the long run this obscure social drift served to stir the stagnant countryside. Yet in the eighteenth century there is little reason to suppose that the general lot of the peasantry was greatly improved.

Upon examination, eighteenth-century stability proves to be far less secure than Guedalla's quip near the opening of this chapter makes it out to be. Passing over dynastic rivalries and family quarrels among monarchs, one finds beneath the smooth surface of apparent absolutism that the nobility were frequently discontented (so were the clergy). The middle class in many areas seethed with resentment against being kept below the salt, and practiced the abrasive arts of getting on in the world; yet by insisting upon the virtues of industry, frugality, and Christian love this group presented a solidity of class-interest more apparent than real. The peasantry were neither as virtuous as eighteenth-century pastorals made them out to be, nor as docile as their royal or noble masters wished they were. Jealousy among peasant groups was quite as active as it was between the lesser and the higher nobility. When one adds to these sorts of tensions the inadequate financial systems of most European nations and the queer mixture of "progress" and feudalism that most countries present, one sees that the elements of revolutionary and cultural change were present in all the Western lands long before either 1775 or 1789.

III

The Enlightenment

One reason why the century seems stable to the superficial view is that eighteenth-century intellectuals, or most of them, tended to live in the light of something called the Enlightenment, to which we now turn. But it is first necessary to understand something of the context in which the Enlightenment came into being. Although the eighteenth-century aristocracy * and the middle class developed separate, though like, value systems, these not only tended to duplicate each other, they tended to revolve around the great central puzzle of the age. This problem was how to reconcile supernaturalism and actuality, the world of tradition and the world of science, the universe of religious belief and the universe of utilitarian philosophy, monarchical government and the equality of man. On the one hand was monarchy, an ancient institution everywhere accepted. On the other hand was man, or at least man as most philosophers conceived him, a creature with certain weaknesses but a being whose good qualities, once they were released from "tyranny," would produce the almost perfect state. Kings were often stupid and were sometimes deposed. But man also exhibited a good many awkward traits, including stupidity (against which, wrote Schiller, even the gods contend in vain), cowardice, self-interest, and a stubborn refusal to follow light: witness the Tories in North America. If in the eyes of some rationalists man, despite monarchs, was inevitably headed for perfection, in the eyes of other rationalists humanity was well described by Dean Swift, who had written that though he might love John, Peter, and Thomas, he hated and detested the animal called man.

* I ignore distinctions among "aristocracy," "nobility," "noblemen," "gentlemen," and "gentry" and other categories of the elite.

57

On the one side was authority, not merely political authority celebrated by Burke and Gentz but also the authority of tradition in taste, in forms of art, in law, in education, in philosophy, in the doctrine of the superiority of the ancients over the moderns, and of course in Christian revelation. On the other side were empiricism, the excitement of scientific discoveries and voyages of exploration, the doctrine of progress, the experiment with republican government in North America, the assumption that man was so far master of his fate and captain of his soul, if he had one, that by possessing life and liberty he could pursue happiness here and now without reference to heaven or hell. Perhaps, as Paul Hazard remarks, the history of happiness is an eternal history of an eternal illusion, but the Enlightenment — despite cynics and pessimists, even despite the darker implications of the theory that human nature has never changed, a favorite assumption among most philosophers — lived in that illusion. In one way the Enlightenment was continuing the battle of the ancients and the moderns, that queer, yet profound, debate of the seventeenth century. In another way it was re-examining, even rewriting, history as a paradigm of the vices of rulers and the virtues of republics, or as proof positive of a necessary forward development in the affairs of humanity. In any event life was here and now, science and pseudo-science were as up-to-date in the eighteenth century as they are in the twentieth, and only those matters were "relevant" that could be proved to have utility, or give satisfaction, or increase the pleasure of altruism or the charm of the arts.

The succession of philosophical thinkers that begins with Bacon, runs through Spinoza and Descartes, John Locke and Newton, Bishop Berkeley and David Hume, and culminates in Immanuel Kant is one of the most distinguished in the history of thought. A second line, equally important though on occasion not formally metaphysical, descends from Descartes and Pierre Bayle to Fontenelle, Montesquieu, Voltaire, Diderot, d'Alembert, La Mettrie, Rousseau, Condillac, Cabanis, Helvétius, and Holbach, and ends in the intellectual fireworks of innumerable French revolutionary pamphlets and Condorcet's *Esquisse d'un tableau historique des progrès de l'esprit humain* (1794). This is to neglect the Physiocratic school, of which Quesnay and Turgot are representative.

The Germans contribute Leibniz, the Italians Vico, the Americans Jonathan Edwards. A thousand other, lesser lights cluster around the greater figures: epigrammatists like the German Lichtenberg with his *Aphorisms*, Vauvenargues, and Chamfort, whose *Maximes et pensées* defines the French revolution as "Be my brother or I will kill you" and describes love as the exchange of two imaginary pictures and the contact of one epidermis with another.* Probably Franklin's *The Way to Wealth* belongs in this category. Then there are second-string but able philosophic thinkers, teachers of philosophical or scientific subjects, and general essayists, of whom in the Germanies Moses Mendelssohn and Christian Wolff and in Scotland Adam Smith and Thomas Reid are examples. There are pamphleteers, statesmen full of wise saws and modern instances (for example, John Adams and Thomas Jefferson), political theorists from Frederick II to the Abbé Siéyès, and writers of philosophic or propagandistic plays and novels — Alfieri's tragedies, or some of them, novels by Klinger or Robert Bage, and in Britain a whole repertory of Godwinian and anti-Godwinian dramas, among which Wordsworth's *The Borderers* is at least readable. There were of course poems innumerable in all languages on philosophical, social, political, and theological themes.

Around and among these intellectuals, these secular campaigners for progress, for science, and for happiness, there lay an eternal smog of theological controversy, of which, so far as Britain is concerned, Sir Leslie Stephen's *History of English Thought in the Eighteenth Century* (1876) contains a classic account. On the Continent there were clashes between Catholic thinkers and Protestant thinkers, between Jansenists and Jesuits, between deists and Christians, among various types of radical or orthodox theologians, Catholic, Protestant, Jewish, and free-thinkers, between materialists who thought that physiology was the source of reason and sentimental writers who wanted to live, beautiful souls, in an atmosphere of Christian idealism. Were there miracles? How explain the Trinity to Unitarians? How defend or attack the divinity of Christ? How strike down theists, deists, atheists in the name of revealed religion? How overturn the Christian church in the name

* Here is a characteristic apothegm by Vauvenargues: "One cannot be just if one is not human," and here, while I am about it, is one by Rivarol: "There is only one morality as there is only one geometry, for these words have no plural. Morality is the daughter of justice and of conscience: it is a universal religion."

of liberty and yet police society in the name of virtue? If you tolerated Protestants in a Catholic country, should you not also tolerate Jews? And if Jews, why not Mohammedans? And if Mohammedans, why not skeptics, agnostics (a term not yet invented), materialists, the heathen in general? If the contemplation of nature led to God, why read the Bible? If the mind was only a blank piece of paper on which sensory experience was to write, where was the soul? In the pineal gland as Descartes had once suggested? Or was it a kind of spiritual replica enshrouding or accompanying the body, made occasionally visible to mystics, as the Rosicrucians and William Blake seemed to believe?

Whole libraries have been published about an individual "philosopher"; examples are Kant and Rousseau. The writings of Voltaire alone run to seventy volumes, those of Diderot to twenty fatter ones,* and the publication of his correspondence increases these indefinitely. A book such as Hettner's *Geschichte der deutschen Literatur im achtzehnten Jahrhundert* weighs as much as a large dictionary. Buffon's *Histoire naturelle*, published from 1749 to 1804, is in forty-four quarto volumes. The first part of Peter Gay's erudite *The Enlightenment: An Interpretation* (1966) runs to 555 pages, of which 130, or about a quarter of the whole, are devoted to a bibliography and an immense bibliographical essay. The Jefferson papers, if they are finished, will run to more than seventy volumes. It is evident that no single mind can comprehend this brilliance, this intellectual kaleidoscope, this glittering play of thrust and counterthrust among that minority of gifted persons who created the intellectual climate of the high eighteenth century.

Moreover, the combatants changed sides, altered alliances, retreated in terror from advanced positions they found dangerous to maintain. Thus Diderot, who was all for the family virtues, wrote *Le Neveu de Rameau*, a pitiless and cynical dialogue questioning whether virtue is either possible or profitable, and Hume, who pushed skeptical inquiry so far that the next step would have plunged him into nihilism, drew back from the abyss and took to writing profitable history and gentlemanly essays on moral and political subjects. One must add to this confusion, notably in

---

* A new edition launched in 1969 by Le Club Français du Livre promises to be far more voluminous. Some items in the standard edition are not by Diderot.

France, the operations of the censorship and of style — censorship, which led one of the editors of the *Encyclopédie* to hope that posterity would distinguish what they meant from what they said, and style, which, polished, clear, polite, also permitted a fine quality of hypocrisy evident in Bayle's *Dictionnaire* and even more evident in Voltaire's *Dictionnaire philosophique* (1764), and which invited the alert reader to read into a phrase or sentence subtleties of meaning not evident to a crass official mind. Thus under "Dog" Voltaire in the *Dictionnaire philosophique* discusses Cerberus: "But of all dogs, Cerberus has had the greatest reputation; he had three heads. We have remarked that, anciently, all went by threes — Isis, Osiris, and [H]Orus, the three first Egyptian divinities; the three brother gods of the Greek world — Jupiter, Neptune, and Pluto; the three Fates, the three Furies, the three Graces, the three judges of hell, and the three heads of this infernal dog." There is nothing here the censor can blue-pencil, but the reader will of course think of another and more powerful Trinity.

Some elements in the intellectual controversies among thinkers remain relatively constant. Thus the emerging study of economics had three heads also: the mercantilist theory that wealth lay in accumulating gold and silver within nationalist boundaries; the physiocratic theory — the adjective was invented by Du Pont de Nemours — that wealth lay in agriculture; and the Adam Smith theory that wealth lay in freedom of trade. If one reaches the sardonic conclusion that the principal product of this economic ingenuity was Napoleon's attempt by monopolizing the trade of Europe and blockading the ports to reduce the British fleet to futility, he would be unjust: the foundations of modern economics were stabilized in the eighteenth century.

Most writers tended to agree that "Nature" as revealed by science ("natural philosophy") was a way to contentment, for in the period, as Hazard remarks, to "Nature" was attributed a talismanic quality, a more efficacious virtue, since Nature was the source of intelligence, the guarantee of reason, the home of wisdom and goodness, a model for the universal society of mankind. If there was a science of Nature, why not a science of man? And most philosophers, whether they belonged to the school of rationalism or to the school of sensibility, tried to set up ethical systems apart from theology; the extreme question in this area was, as Sir Leslie

Stephen put it: can a society of atheists be maintained? Not that there were many atheists. But if you gave up the commands of Moses and the teachings of Jesus, how did you know what super-natural sanctions the dubious God of deism imposed upon man-kind? Wrote Voltaire:

The earth is but a vast field of destruction and carnage. Either the great Being was able to make it an eternal abode of delight for all sentient creation, or He was not able to do so. If He was able and did not do so, He must be thought of as malevolent; but if He was unable, do not hesitate to think of Him as a very great power, though hemmed in by Nature. Whether or not His power is infinite is nothing to you. It is a matter of indifference to a subject whether his master owns five hundred leagues of territory or five thousand; he is still a subject equally in either case.

(*Dictionnaire philosophique*, under "Omnipotence")

Obviously this merely pushed the problem back upon man. It therefore seemed to some in the eighteenth century that the world was what Matthew Arnold later called it, a darkling plain, swept with confused alarms of struggle and flight, where ignorant armies clash by night.

ii

But such a gloss is unfair. The mighty maze was not without a plan. Advanced or liberal thinkers threw off Augustinian or Calvinist theology because they could not accept an interpretation of human nature which held that by the decrees of God men were utterly depraved, or, at the best, certainly weak and usually wicked. How could such a race produce a Newton? Had living theologians really examined the nature of reason or were they, because of their vested interests, merely repeating by rote a medieval formula long outworn? Were Plato and Aristotle, were the virtuous Cornelia and Portia, Cato's virtuous daughter, were the admirable heroes of Plutarch, a biographer much read in the period — were all these to be condemned merely because they had come into the world before Christ? Were the virtuous Chinese, were the philosophic Brahmins, were the happy natives of some far Pacific island living in the light of Nature and of Nature's God — were all these to be damned for the greater glory of the Almighty?

The philosophers were struck by the absurdity of such a judgment, especially when they studied the uniformity of Nature and the resulting uniformity of reason in man. The axiomatic truth that man was a rational animal implied as axiomatic also a principle of individualism, not a mass condemnation under an arbitrary divine decree, nor, for that matter, a mass stagnation under "tyranny." Nothing in Nature argued, for example, that a nobleman was per se more sensitive or more intelligent than a yokel. "What have you done," asks Figaro apropos of Count Almaviva in Beaumarchais's *Le Mariage de Figaro* of 1784, "to deserve so many privileges except to take the trouble of being born?" When Hamlet tells Claudius a king may go a progress through the guts of a beggar, he is commenting upon the democracy of death; Figaro, or Beaumarchais for him, is announcing the democracy of life.

Whether man is born possessed of innate ideas or whether he acquires their equivalents through the operation of the wonderful machinery of the mind operating on sensations was disputed; nevertheless the main tenet of the new interpretation of man was the identical quality of sensory experience and of rationality among all human beings. This identity made for atomism and for egalitarianism. Men were separated by the truth that every person's sensory experience was unique and private; men were united by their common power of rational thought. Born into a universe immensely filled with useful, pleasant, or awe-inspiring objects, men fitted neatly into their environment, received their primary impressions from the physical world, and from these impressions formed congruent notions about things, men, the universe, and deity. Men of course differed in customs and opinions, but this was not because rationality was untrustworthy but because of climate, or a backward education, or bad government, or a perverse theology. Each man was an island of self-rule, independent of all other souls, a self-sufficing physiological and nervous mechanism (man, said one French thinker, is his nervous system), functioning in an environment admirably suited to him. The universe was itself an immense machine, timeless, perfect, glorious, put together by a divine engineer who watched over it, a machine that furnished energy to myriads of little machines who lived within its immensities. La Mettrie got out a book entitled *L'Homme machine* in 1748; David Hartley demonstrated in *Observations on Man, His Frame, His Duty, and His Expectations* in 1749, as he thought on Newtonian lines, that man is, so to speak, the product of vibrations in his nerves and associations of ideas in his mind.

On the affirmative side Addison's "Ode" put the matter admirably:

> The spacious firmament on high,
> With all the blue ethereal sky,
> And spangled Heavens, a shining frame,
> Their great Original proclaim.
> Th' unwearied Sun from day to day
> Does his Creator's pow'r display;
> And publishes, to every land,
> The work of an Almighty hand.

On the negative side it was observed that this Creator seemed not to live up to his philanthropic character. For example, a great earthquake destroyed most of Catholic Lisbon in 1755 and combined with a tidal wave to kill between ten and twenty thousand believers. How explain such a catastrophe? Voltaire produced a poem, *Le Désastre de Lisbonne*, the next year, in which, insisting upon the uncertainty of life, he noted sardonically that while men had been dancing in Paris, men had been dying in Portugal. Three years later he sent Candide through the world, and also the virtuous Mademoiselle Cunégonde and the optimistic Dr. Pangloss, each of whom undergoes incredible misfortunes, most of them uncalled for. Candide concludes, or Voltaire concludes for him, not that the world is tragic but that quiet and comfort may be obtained if one will but stay home and attend to his own affairs. This conclusion had already been reached in *Zadig* (1747) and was echoed by Johnson's *Rasselas* in 1759. Stoicism was, indeed, no uncommon gloss upon the theories of the philosophers, in whom a strain of pessimism appears as frequently as does an expression of future hope. But all this did not mean that one should not strive to overthrow theology and undermine tyranny.

For the Enlightenment the universe was made up of physical atoms attracting each other according to a uniform principle that could be mathematically expressed. As the universe was constructed out of physical atoms held together by general law, so the human psyche was a myriad of psychological atoms (impressions and ideas) held together by the principle of association. On the same line the state was thought of by advanced thinkers as an aggregate of human beings kept in harmony by a mysterious contract which paralleled, as it were, the law of association in psychology and the law of gravitation in physics. The Dark Ages were displeasing because rationalism had been overlaid by theology, and empirical science had waned because Aristotle (or at least a medieval version of him) and theology (or at least a medieval form of that "science") had forbidden inquiry. Philosophers, however, were not therefore interested in a revolution of a political sort. They wanted to instruct kings in the principles of the Enlightenment and turn them into philosophical rulers. Eighteenth-century theorists, while they seemed to repudiate history, in fact revalidated an ancient concept of primordial agreement as the origins of government and society. Even Rousseau in *Du Contrat social* (1762), supposed by many to be a radical attack on society, merely refurbished a theory of the state much older than the century of Locke and Hobbes. He held that the state results from an a priori agreement separately assented to by individuals who, living originally in a state of nature and eventually finding that life intolerable, consent to pool their individual wills in something called the general will, the quintessence of civil society, and so exchange natural freedom for civil liberty. Perhaps even liberty is not the right word, since in England, supposed to be a liberal monarchy, men talked of the liberties of Englishmen, that is, a set of separate and traditional formulae descended from the Anglo-Saxons or the Goths or the Germans.* Monarchy was usually tolerable unless taxes on property or restrictions on individual freedom of movement or expression became utterly unbearable, and in that case, the contract having been broken by a ruler whose duty it is to rule justly and, if he could, wisely, his subjects might set up a new government as the British had done in 1688–89 and as the Americans were to do in 1775–76.

Being finite, the world was imperfect. It was not the best of worlds but only the best of possible worlds, given the materials out of which it was made. If philosophers differed as to the degree of

---

* In his invaluable handbook, *The French Revolution: Ten Years That Shook the World*, Leo Gershoy notes that among the *cahiers* presented to the States-General in 1789 those from the middle class emphasized "liberty" but those from the nobility emphasized "liberties," which meant in fact privileges.

imperfection to be found in life, most theorists felt that men were rational and that happiness, or at least satisfaction, or in the utmost case philosophical resignation, was our being's end and aim. Some, however, were persuaded that things were necessarily improving, and that, given the light of the new rational philosophy, in a relatively short time humanity could simultaneously return to the primitive virtues of the noble savage and advance to some higher form of life based on the benefits of science and industry. In that not-too-distant future wealth would be better distributed and, a result of self-love to rule and reason to restrain, there would be no more wars. Such, for example, was the dream of the German Herder (theologically trained), who published between 1784 and 1791 a four-volume work entitled *Ideen zur Philosophie der Geschichte der Menschheit*, less an examination of historiography than a rosy account of the gradual evolution of humanity. Even Immanuel Kant, who did not care for Herder's book, set forth in 1759 a project for perpetual peace. The most striking of such prophetic works is Condorcet's *Esquisse d'un tableau historique des progrès de l'esprit humain*, written while he was hiding from the agents of the French Republic One and Indivisible and published after he had died from exhaustion or poison in 1794. In that famous essay mankind progresses through ten stages, the ninth beginning in 1789, the tenth to come about through popular education, the perfecting of human nature, the withering of Christianity in favor of the God of Nature, and the disappearance of present governments. This was to be the theory of William Godwin and the dream of Percy Bysshe Shelley.

But Shelley was of the next generation, and meanwhile the rule of the philosophers was somewhat limited. Putting aside Christian theologians who attacked him, and putting aside also the mystics, the pietists, the quietists and other religious groups, including the English Methodists, who regarded the world as a vale of tears and temptations from which the Christian soul ought to withdraw, one notes that sensualists and cynics sometimes translated the right to pursue happiness into an epicurean enjoyment of the pleasures of the senses, thus turning the philosophers' arguments, or at least their value systems, inside out or upside down. If the universe was made for men, why not enjoy it? Enjoyment frequently took the form of sensuality in fact and voluptuousness in fiction. No period was more prolific in pornography and in works of art erotic in their appeal. The books are sometimes delicately written and sometimes not, sometimes veiled social satires and sometimes frank celebrations of sexuality. They include Montesquieu's *Lettres persanes* (1721), John Cleland's *Fanny Hill; or, Memoirs of a Woman of Pleasure* (1748-1749), the tales of Crébillon *fils* (for example, *Le Nuit et le moment*), Morlière's *Angola* (supposedly printed at Agra in 1748!), Boufflers's *Aline, Reine de Golconda* (1761), Nerciat's *Felicia, ou mes fredaines* (1778), the scandalous writings of Mirabeau and of John Wilkes, Casanova, Restif de la Bretonne's *Monsieur Nicolas* (1794-1797), an enormous work, longer than Rousseau's *Confessions*, a narrative, says Havelock Ellis, of Gilles de Rais in Arcadia. There were anthologies of erotic verse, and seven editions of Nicholas Chorier's *Satyra Sotadica de Arcanis Amoris et Veneris*, one of them, a translation, purporting to be printed "à Cythere, dans l'imprimerie de la Volupté." The light but titillating sensuality of Fragonard and Boucher, the pornographic drawings of Fuseli, the scabrous cartoons of Rowlandson, their date a little uncertain, all celebrate the pleasures of the flesh. It was in vain for Hogarth to depict "Gin Lane," "The Harlot's Progress," or the sad history of male rakishness. The century of George Washington was also that of the Marquis de Sade, and the same period in which the priggish Sir Charles Grandison in the most unreadable of Richardson's novels saves Harriet Byron from a fate worse than death presents Tom Jones, a healthy son of nature, sleeping with various females, some of whom pursue him and some of whom he pursues, before he weds the lovely Sophia Western, who seems to think this the usual conduct of the male animal. The century of the *Encyclopédie* saw that famous brothel, the Parc aux Cerfs, maintained for the pleasure of the king of France. Every petty ruler had his mistress, sometimes two or three at a time, some of whom had conscientiously trained for sensual joys. The bastard children of Augustus the Strong, elector of Saxony, are said to have numbered three hundred, including the famous Marshal Saxe; if they were not that numerous, they were numerous enough. "Nature," says one of the speakers in Diderot's *Supplément au voyage de Bougainville* (1772; published 1796), "though you may call her immodest for it, impels both sexes toward each other indiscriminately." One

recalls the epitaph, perhaps legendary, of the Marquise de Boufflers:

> Ce gît dans une paix profonde
> Cette Dame de volupté,
> Qui pour plus grande sûreté
> Fit son paradis de ce monde.*

No age is dominated by a single pattern of thought, but since
the Enlightenment came closer to uniformity than most periods,
it is disconcerting to find that one and the same intellectual climate
produced the epicurean and the stoic, an altruist of the type of
John Howard, the prison reformer, and a charlatan of the type
of Cagliostro, who got himself involved in the infamous affair of
the diamond necklace. How explain this ethical diversity? The
difficulty seems to lie in the nature of philosophical empiricism.
It was possible, or at least plausible, by introspection and the observation of others to conclude that all men possess the faculty of
reason, that through the application of this faculty to nature they
could arrive at general scientific principles, that mathematical
truths were as valid in London as they were in Lapland, whither
Maupertuis went to measure a degree of latitude. One could also
infer a God of universal Nature everywhere ruling under what
one may call a cosmic constitution.

When, however, one passed from the truths of science to the
field of morals, generalizations broke down. A transcendental ethics
seemed impossible. Men might agree in logical matters, but ages,
races, and individuals differed widely about what right conduct
might be. In the moral sphere the Enlightenment found itself
confronting the paradox of Pascal: what was truth on one side of
the Pyrenees was error on the other. The Great Engineer sufficed
for the planets and perhaps for the universe of minds, but the
Great Engineer was a mechanic, not a moralist. After empirical
philosophy had subtracted all theological sanctions from the sum
of things, it left a world in which it was quite possible for everybody to do what was right in his own eyes. Men preached virtue,
and virtue remained ambiguous. It is perhaps significant that
Rousseau has been claimed as a spiritual godfather by anarchists,
socialists, communists, democrats, individualists, and fascists — but

---

* Here lies in deep peace / That Lady of pleasure, / Who to be surer of having
one / Made her paradise in this world.

what moral system did Rousseau maintain? Was there a universal moral sense? A moral faculty? If there was, why did it not operate uniformly? Why did it sanction acts that were wildly in conflict, motives that could not be reconciled, customs that could never be universalized? Perhaps the final comment on this problem was the spectacle of agents of the Committee of Public Safety under the Terror drowning men and women, two by two, in the Loire river, in the name of a virtuous republic.

iii

Although it owed much to English thought, especially the empiricism of Bacon, the psychology of Locke, and the cosmogony of Newton, the French Enlightenment is thought to be central to the Age of Reason, and as a result there is a tendency to regard its advocates as members of a unified movement, an intellectual bloc, a school of reformers conducting a common campaign. There is enough agreement among the *philosophes* to give coloring to this point of view. But literary groups seldom stay together very long, and the philosophers quarreled among themselves, grew jealous of each other, parted company, came together again, and found fault with each other's conduct or theories in a manner normal among literary "schools." Some, such as Buffon, Fontenelle, d'Alembert, Condillac, and Quesnay, led relatively quiet and stable lives. But a considerable fraction of their number were nomads, partly as a result of temperament, partly as a result of governmental or ecclesiastical persecution, albeit both government and church on occasion showed a leniency inconsistent with the general doctrine that heretical books should be burned and radical writers silenced.

Two of the ancestors of the movement lived much of their lives in exile: Descartes began his journeys with a military adventure in Holland, wandered through Denmark, Poland, Hungary, and Bohemia, entered Italy, returned to Holland, where the Dutch intellectuals furiously assailed him, and died in Sweden in 1650. Pierre Bayle, because of his religious tergiversation, was forced to flee to Geneva, then returned to the Protestant university at Sedan, lost his professorship when the university was suppressed, joined the faculty of the university in Rotterdam, was deprived of that post, and died there, an exile, in 1706.

The outcry against La Mettrie's *Histoire naturelle de l'âme* drove its author out of France to Leyden; he was forced to leave Holland for Berlin, and died in Germany; his works had to be published in London, Berlin, and Amsterdam. Montesquieu was no vagabond, but he found it safer to live on his country estate. His *L'Esprit des lois* was published not in France but in Geneva. The *De l'esprit* of Helvétius was condemned to be burned. He went to England in 1764, to Berlin in 1765. Though he seems to have been unmolested by the authorities, Maupertuis visited Prussia in 1740, was taken prisoner by the Austrians at Mollwitz, returned to Berlin in 1744, became president of the Royal Academy of Sciences there, and died at Basle in Switzerland. Diderot, at once a genius and a booksellers' hack, was imprisoned, led a precarious bohemian life, was hounded by the authorities, got out most of the volumes of the *Encyclopédie* surreptitiously, and later, in a remarkable reversal of fortune, spent half a year at the court of Catherine the Great. Raynal's *Histoire philosophique et politique . . . des . . . deux Indes* dates from 1770 and was published in Amsterdam; in February 1779, in France, it was condemned to be burned, and in order to escape arrest Raynal fled to Spa, then to Berlin, and thence to St. Petersburg. He returned to France but not to Paris in 1787. Turgot was made controller-general in 1774; having incurred the enmity of every powerful group associated with the regime, he was forced out of office in less than two years, retired to the country, and devoted the rest of his life to noncontroversial scientific and literary pursuits. The wanderings of Rousseau are incredible: they cover Europe from Venice to London, involve exile from France, exile from Berne, interminable quarrels, abnormal suspicions of conspiracy against him, and a life more unsettled than even that of Diderot.

As for Voltaire, he was several times sent to the Bastille, was beaten by ruffians in the employ of the Chevalier de Rohan, traveled to Brussels, to Holland, to England, to Lorraine, to Berlin, to Frankfurt (where he was ignominiously arrested), to Geneva, and to Ferney, four miles from Geneva, the city that had expelled him. Voltaire alternated between fear of arrest and imprisonment and the sunshine of being appointed the historiographer royal.

He returned to Paris in 1778, after twenty-eight years of forced or voluntary exile, for a famous apotheosis. D'Alembert quit the *Encyclopédie* from motives of prudence and retired to the safer business of writing eulogies on deceased members of the Academy. Others flattered rulers (read the correspondence of Voltaire and Frederick II), sometimes because they hoped to educate a truly philosophical monarch but more often because they needed outside protection. Holbach brazened it out as a Very Important Personage in Paris, for the reason that he had money. Cabanis prudently hung on to a series of administrative medical posts from 1789 to the time of Napoleon. A good many published their books in Amsterdam or in some imaginary place, usually Oriental, or pretended they had not written them.

In sum, however they might agree in a general point of view, it was impossible in these circumstances for the liberals to have either devised or carried through a consistent campaign of propaganda; and though some writers speak of them in military terms of organization, strategy, and tactics, it is, I think, virtually impossible to picture the *philosophes* as a coherent group advocating step by step a program of change or revolution after the fashion of, say, the Bolsheviks in Russia or, for that matter, the American abolitionists. Hounded by the police, quarreling among themselves, now exiled, now flattered, their books at one time the intellectual fashion, at another time despised and rejected by the elite, the *philosophes* are a movement but not a party, a truth that invalidates a good many rash generalizations about the connection between the printed word and a revolution supposed to have been incited or supported by it.

Nevertheless, rationalism, often of a radical nature, was a fact in eighteenth-century France and therefore in eighteenth-century Europe, and amidst this clash of personalities and opinions, if one looks for some central document to serve as a paradigm of the movement, one turns to the great *Encyclopédie, ou Dictionnaire raisonné des arts et des métiers*, which, originally edited by Diderot and d'Alembert, and carried through by Diderot, that giant of industry, began publication in 1751 and was not really completed until 1780. Most of the material has only curiosity value nowadays, but the famous *Discours préliminaire* of d'Alembert not only is a prime example of eighteenth-century French prose at its clearest and best, it also tells us why the *Encyclopédie* is central in the total Enlightenment. D'Alembert did not seek to be oracular, but his essay illustrates the ideal of an intellectual elite. The encyclopedists sought to divorce science from any transcendental presuppositions; they argued that utilitarianism rather than beatitude was the desire of man; in that sense they assumed that the business of philosophy was to deal not with supernatural order but with the world here and now. They would have agreed with Schleiermacher that the essence of philosophy is that there is no philosophy and no enlightenment.

Diderot carried the *Encyclopédie* to its conclusion, but if one looks for a norm among the *philosophes* one can do worse than select Jean le Rond d'Alembert (1717–1783), who, born illegitimate, raised himself by perseverance, prudence, and talent to an honorable place in French society, lived modestly, became a distinguished mathematician, physicist, and astronomer, and was honored by the friendship of kings, of his foster-mother, a glazier's wife (with whom he lived for thirty years), and of Mademoiselle de Lespinasse, Voltaire, David Hume, Rameau, and a chosen circle of intellectuals, young and old, from all classes of society. Concerning d'Alembert, Condorcet in his famous *Eloge* wrote that there assembled around him "all the men who, zealous for the interests of humanity but differing in their occupations, their tastes, and their opinions, were called together only by an equal desire to hasten the progress of intelligence, an equal love for the good, and a common respect for the illustrious man whom genius and glory had naturally placed at their head." D'Alembert was neither flamboyant nor piquant; a man of caution and good sense, in personality and career he is much nearer to Franklin than is almost any other French philosopher. Most of d'Alembert's writing was scientific and mathematical, but as secretary to the Academy he produced a number of *éloges* in a clear, energetic, and elegant style, and the *Discours préliminaire de l'Encyclopédie* is a model. He did not, it is true, go in for martyrdom, and he has been blamed for withdrawing from the superintendency of that great work precisely when a more heroic soul might have defied church and state. But good sense is as important a quality of the eighteenth century as rebelliousness, and it is possible that d'Alembert accomplished as much cultural reform by modesty as Voltaire accomplished by bravura. Men have, says Leatherstocking solemnly, a variety of gifts.

Nature, wrote Buffon in an essay on the theory of the earth, is the system of laws established by the Creator for the existence of things and for the succession of what the early nineteenth century was to call animated beings. This is the postulate which the *Encyclopédie* assumes and d'Alembert endorses in his great preliminary essay. The idea of the *Encyclopédie* originated in a translation, begun in 1743, into French of Ephraim Chambers' *Cyclopaedia; or, a Universal Dictionary of Arts and Sciences, containing an Explication of the Terms and an Account of the Things Signified thereby in the several Arts, Liberal and Mechanical, and the several Sciences, Human and Divine*, printed in two volumes in 1728. I give the full title since, except for "divine science," Chambers' sonorous title is in effect the program of the French compilation. It is unnecessary to rehearse here the story of the petty intrigues that prevented the appearance of the translation of Chambers and ended by placing such manuscripts as had been assembled by one Jean Paul de Gua de Malves, professor of philosophy in the Collège de France, in the hands of Diderot, nor the story of the delay in producing a totally new work, outlined in a prospectus by Diderot of November 1750.

Publication began in 1751 and almost immediately ran afoul of the royal council and of the church, bodies which declared that the first volumes were injurious to the authority of the king and to religious faith. Nor is it necessary to rehearse the devious ways, often amusing, by which friendly officialdom, warning Diderot in advance, gave that extraordinary genius time to remove papers in danger of being seized, connived at illicit printing, and secretly favored the enterprise because it was inimical to the Jesuits. At night the frightened printer removed whole sections of articles he thought dangerous. Because of these untoward circumstances the work was uneven. Enemies described the *Encyclopédie* sometimes as a work of disorder and sometimes as the gospel of Satan. D'Alembert, who did not care for controversy, ceased to contribute in 1758 (volume VII, through the letter G, appeared in 1757). But by 1765 seventeen volumes had been printed, together with four volumes of plates; a supplementary five volumes and two volumes of indexes, not to speak of other volumes of plates, were later published in Amsterdam, and by 1780 the great *Encyclopédie* in thirty-five volumes was done.

D'Alembert quit after volume VII, but the *Encyclopédie* never departed from the lines laid down by his famous *Discours*. An encyclopedia (*dictionnaire raisonné*) of the sciences, the fine arts, and the mechanical arts, d'Alembert begins, should present for each science and each art, liberal or mechanical, the general principles on which any branch of knowledge is based, together with the essential details of the substance and working of the art, science, or trade under consideration. We ought therefore to begin by asking how we know anything, and how, from our primitive notions, we rise to general principles and concepts of beauty and morality. There follows an exposition of the psychology of Locke, including the origin of the sensations we have of pleasure and pain. By and by we discover in the world not merely objects that make impressions upon our senses but also a number of beings who seem to behave as we do and whom we find it is to our interest to join. This commerce with others augments our ideas and increases our curiosity, and after a while we, and they, tend to infer the existence of some all-powerful being who called us into existence, sustains that existence, and deserves in turn our reverence. We profit from our own experiences and from the researches of others, and so agriculture, medicine, and other crafts are born.

Our experience with objects in nature leads us to observe qualities, such as impenetrability, that they have in common, and by and by we come to the concept of real space, penetrable and immobile, in which these objects (and we) exist. Geometry results from our curiosity about extension and space; the combination of objects produces arithmetic, our interest in relationships brings algebra into being. In the same way we arrive at mechanics and at the most sublime field of thought, a combination of geometry and mechanics, the glorious notions of astronomy. Sciences can, of course, be abused: for example, in medicine, where doctors seem to treat the body as a mere machine, an attitude that awakens d'Alembert's skepticism. But we are finite beings, nature is at bottom a mystery, though illuminated here and there by the light of reason, and nothing is more necessary to contentment than revealed religion, which instructs us, or should instruct us, to be content with the limits of mortality.

74

Logic extends the sphere of general thought by teaching us to arrange our ideas in the most natural order, analyze complex ideas into simple ones, look at them from every point of view, and present them to others in forms that can be easily understood. Grammar is a branch of logic; and d'Alembert next discusses style, finding fault with eccentricities and trying to distinguish true rhetoric from rhetorical falsities. The sciences of time and place (chronology and geology) are the daughters of history and astronomy, and if this idea now seems a little peculiar, his discussion of government and political science and the relation of public morality to private morality is also a touch confused, though he insists that all such matters lead us back to the principles of natural law. He then goes (following Aristotle) to the arts as imitations of nature, and distinguishes between the sciences and the arts, and between the liberal arts and the mechanical arts, a little regretting the conventional inferiority of the latter, though he admits that the mechanical arts, depending as they do on routine, are necessarily lower in the scale. Yet the names of the great benefactors of mankind who invented or discovered the rudiments of the mechanical arts are unfortunately unknown. The mechanical arts can be reduced to principles, but so can the fine arts, although the principles differ in subtlety and clearness.

There are, also, he thinks, some general rules governing the theory of truth in any branch of organized knowledge: evidence, certitude, probability, sentiment, and taste. Evidence is a function of those ideas of which the mind instantly perceives the connection. Certainty results from ideas the connection among which can be known only by a chain of intermediary ideas. Probability has its principal home in history: we attribute events to chance when we cannot uncover their true causes. Sentiment he divides into two categories; one is the acceptance of moral truths (conscience), which results from natural law and from our ideas of good and evil — this he calls the evidence of the heart as distinguished from the evidence of the mind. The other sort of sentiment has to do with our pleasure in the imitation of the beauties of nature or in beauty of expression, and to this we owe taste and perhaps genius, genius being the sentiment which creates, taste the sentiment which judges. One is conscious that the French *sentiment* has nuances lacking in its English equivalent.

D'Alembert now discusses what he calls "the tree of knowledge," explaining that he means by this the ordering of knowledge, not its origin in sensory experience, and this classification ("the tree") he refers to memory, reason, and imagination. History comes under memory, philosophy under reason, and the fine arts under imagination. Then comes a historical excursus which will convince those who do not care for eighteenth-century thinking that it dismissed the Gothic past as lacking in intelligence. But we next reach a significant survey of the progress of thought from Bacon to d'Alembert's time. Of Bacon he writes: "To consider the sane and extensive views of this great man, the multitude of objects on which his mind expatiated, the boldness of a style which everywhere united the most sublime images with the most rigorous precision, one is tempted to regard him as the greatest, the most universal, and the most eloquent of all philosophers."

D'Alembert touches also upon the importance of the seventeenth-century quarrel between the ancients and the moderns, insisting, however, that the ancients amply deserve study, since present-day literature is inferior to that of the preceding century, which was more firmly based on classical precedent, and declaring with a touch of humor that possibly our inferiority to the age of Louis XIV or that of the ancients comes from our anxiety to surpass them: we have, he says, a greater number of good judges and a lesser number of good books. D'Alembert's generosity of spirit is nowhere better shown than in his discussion of a problem that seems remote from the professional interest of a mathematician and a physicist:

The philosophy which forms the dominant taste of our century, by the progress it has made among us, seems to want to make up for the time it has lost in the past and to avenge itself for the sort of contempt which our fathers accorded it. This contempt has today been transferred to erudition, and is no more justified for having changed its object. People imagine we have taken from the works of the ancients everything it is important for us to know, and on that basis they willingly dispense with the trouble created by those who still wish to consult them. It seems that people regard antiquity as an oracle which has already said everything and which is now useless for us to interrogate . . . But it would be ridiculous to believe that there is nothing more to discover in anatomy because anatomists sometimes seem to give themselves over to researches apparently futile, yet often useful in their results; it would be no less absurd to wish to interdict erudition under the pretext that the researches are unimportant to which our savants give themselves over. It is ignorant or presumptuous to believe that everything is now known in any existing area and that we can find no advantage to be got from the study and reading of the ancients.

And he concludes the main part of the *Discours* with this very sensible observation on the relation between government and science, that problem of our day:

Let us finish this history of the sciences by remarking that the different forms of government which so much influence both men's minds and literary culture also determine the kinds of knowledge that can flourish under them . . . It is in general true that there are more orators, historians, and philosophers under a republic, and under a monarchy more poets, theologians, and geometers. This rule, however, is not so absolute that it cannot be modified by an indefinite number of causes.

When the *Encyclopédie* resumed publication in 1765 Diderot wrote an "Avertissement" to volume VIII, in which he paid heartfelt tribute to the Chevalier de Jaucourt, that incredible gnome who labored fourteen or sixteen hours a day on the work, asking for no glory, satisfied with very little, and selling his house to pay for the work of others. Diderot wrote with genuine, if somewhat self-conscious, pathos of all he had himself endured. Throughout time, he said, those who have tried to benefit the human race have suffered persecution and injury, and history transmits to us the baseness, the deceits, the ignorance, the fanaticism directed against philanthropists. He has, he says, experienced all these woes. For twenty years of unremitting labor he has never known a moment of real repose, spending his days in toil and awaiting each night whatever malice might bring upon him. How often, he exclaims, has he got up in the morning, not knowing whether he would not be torn from his family, his friends, his fellow-citizens, to avoid imprisonment — fleeing to some strange sky for the tranquillity necessary to his work and the protection he needed to continue it. Only his attachment to his country has kept him in France. But, he unctuously adds, a good man is susceptible to enthusiasm the wicked can never know; he comes to despise the perils which menace him. Let readers who find faults in the *Encyclopédie* consider the odious calumnies and the evils with which it has been menaced. If enlightenment continues to grow, in twenty years or so the *Encyclopédie* will be outmoded, but he and his colleagues will have done something for mankind.

Few have studied the *Encyclopédie* as a whole. The work is inconsistent, its arrangement is faulty, its purpose as often propagandistic as informative. Charges of plagiarism were constantly brought against it and many of these are justified, albeit the notion of literary property in the eighteenth century was not what it is today. Subjects were assigned to hack writers. Even in certain major fields such as mathematics the contributor is not always aware of current research in particular areas. Moreover, to avoid conflict, major information was sometimes hidden away in articles of apparently innocuous or minor significance. It can be taken as a matter of course that the church and theology fare badly in a compilation that had to pretend to be both objective and orthodox and was frequently neither. Writers came and went — the connection of Voltaire with the enterprise, for example, was intermittent. Nor was the *Encyclopédie* as novel as it is sometimes made out to be: in a compact work of astonishing erudition entitled *L'Encyclopédie* (1965), Jacques Proust has written a history of encyclopedias in Europe and indicates that the French compilation was great but not unique. The intellectual drive behind it, the social work it had in mind to do, and, with all its contradictions on its head, the general acceptance of a particular notion of ethics and of the state by its managers — these are qualities that make the *Encyclopédie* a central document in the intellectual history of the Western world.

The encyclopedists were concerned for modernity and the middle class. They sought to undermine and, if possible, destroy the hold that traditional scholasticism had upon French education, and they desired to modernize the state. As Proust points out, they were against the court, against the great nobles, against the military leaders, against the merely fashionable men of letters. They did not speak for the peasants, or even for the rich farmers. Articles on agriculture in the compilation were not by practicing agriculturists. Their use of the words "arts" and "artists" more often implied the "mechanical arts" and "artisans" than it did the paintings of Boucher, the music of Rameau, or the architecture of Jacques-Ange Gabriel, who built Le Petit Trianon. They wanted reform, they wanted progress, but they did not want rebellion or revolution. If by and large they tended to sustain the French *parlements* in their contests with the crown, they did not think of dethroning the monarch — who but a king, preferably enlightened, could impartially study the interests of all the classes that made up a nation? They spoke, in short, for the bourgeois enlightenment in language that was clear, precise, definite, for the most part un-poetical, and for the most part unambiguous except for purposes of concealing what they meant under what they wrote. They believed not alone in science but in science as an aid to life in a clear and coherent scheme of things which made religion possible but which was not dependent upon revelation for its comprehension. And the influence of the *Encyclopédie*, difficult to define, spread over the boundaries of France, spread even to England and North America, though its impact upon the empirical British mind was less revolutionary, less dazzling than it was in other countries. Of course, tracing the influence of a work of this character is much like tracing the influence of a rainstorm.

Wrote Locke in the *Essay Concerning Human Understanding*: ". . . many cardinal errors are due to the mistaking of words for things. . . . the findings of philosophers must not depart too widely from the beliefs of balanced common sense." This was, I think, axiomatic with the encyclopedists; and though from the Catholic point of view the work was an unfortunate performance by free-thinkers and rationalists, from the point of view of progressive thought in the eighteenth century the *Encyclopédie* seemed to show that belief in God was possible without theology, that ethics were practicable without revelation, that the natural order was intelligible without the church, and that stable forms of the state and of social life could be worked out on rational lines to the benefit of all men without the intervention of the clergy. God, wrote Diderot in an article on political authority, permits men to establish a hierarchical order among themselves and to obey the commands of one of their own number; but he wishes this subordination to be reasonable and moderate. A prince holds his authority from his subjects, an authority limited by the laws of nature and of the state. The state does not belong to the prince; the prince belongs to the state.

Here is no argument to overthrow monarchy; but here is the critique the Third Estate was to apply to the crown when it took the famous Oath of the Tennis Court in 1789. The *Encyclopédie*

79

was in no sense a "cause" or even one of the "causes" of the French revolution. But it strengthened the views of an influential minority, it insisted that rational change was possible, it appealed to enlightened self-interest, and it assisted the middle class in achieving what the Scots call a good conceit of themselves. It must not be forgotten that the French revolution began, at least, as a middle-class drive for moderate and sensible reform.

On the other hand it was quite possible from premises very like those of the encyclopedists to arrive at dark and gloomy conclusions about the degeneration of mankind and the hopeless future of the human race. A startling commentary on the general optimism of the "progressives" in France is Henry Vyverberg's remarkable study, *Historical Pessimism in the French Enlightenment*, which, after carefully examining the principal writers of the time, concludes:

The Enlightenment was characterized by a heightened sense of earthly destiny, and if it was conscious of progress so too was it conscious of decadence and historical flux. In force and attraction these pessimistic doctrines could not compete on even terms with the greater lure of historical optimism, but the notions of decadence and flux stubbornly resisted destruction by progressionist imperatives. The strength of this resistance, moreover, was not an accident. Historical pessimism was by no means an obscure and irrelevant reaction against the ideals of the Enlightenment; it was firmly rooted in the thought of the age.*

We shall hear the dark trumpets of doom sounding loudly in the romantic movement that is to come.

* Cambridge, Mass., Harvard University Press, 1958, p. 231.

IV

Sensibility

The Enlightenment was not ignorant of the role of emotion in human life. It could not be. The one sentence by Pascal that is universally known occurs in the fourth section of the *Pensées* (1670) and runs: "The heart has its reasons reason does not know." In 1697 Dryden, in "Alexander's Feast; or, the Power of Music: An Ode in Honor of St. Cecilia's Day," pictures Timotheus swaying the emotions of Alexander the Great and his court by the power of music:

> Thus, long ago,
>
> . . . .
> Timotheus, to his breathing flute,
> And sounding lyre,
> Could swell the soul to rage, or kindle soft desire.

"Half the misery of human life," wrote Addison in *The Spectator* September 13, 1711, "might be extinguished, would men alleviate the general curse they lie under, by mutual offices of compassion, benevolence, and humanity." "Great thoughts," declared Vauvenargues in 1747, "come from the heart." Poetry, asseverated Hamann, the Magus of the North, about 1767, is the mother-tongue of the human race. Even that admired poet of the genteel, Thomas Gray, sorrowed in his "Ode on a Distant Prospect of Eton College" that the "sprightly race" of urchins disporting themselves on the green would soon experience assaults from a regiment of capitalized emotions — black Misfortune, disdainful Anger, pallid Fear, Shame, pining Love, Jealousy, Envy wan, faded Care, comfortless Despair, Sorrow, bitter Scorn, hard Unkindness, keen Remorse, and moody Madness. He naturally concluded that

> where ignorance is bliss,
> 'Tis folly to be wise.

Gray also wrote the "Elegy Written in a Country Churchyard" (1751), which, said Dr. Johnson, "abounds in images which find a mirror in every mind and with sentiments to which every bosom returns an echo." The odd figure of bosoms returning an echo has its attractiveness; but the point is the universality in the literature of the age of what was commonly known as the passions. The whole man included the passions no less than reason, and one of the then current philosophical and poetical problems was how to bring both sides of human nature into a manageable whole. If God had dowered man with reason in order to understand the universe, what good were the emotions? If God had given man emotions, what relation did they have to the cosmic scheme of things, particularly to beauty and morality?

It cannot, then, be argued that neoclassicism even at its highest and dryest was ignorant of emotion. A standard subject in neoclassicism was the conflict of love and honor, a theme essential to Spanish drama, to the tragedies of Corneille and Dryden, and central to the interminable love-romances of the seventeenth century in France. Nor did Locke and his followers deny that the passions exist; they saw that the problem was the intricate one of demonstrating the reliability of the reasoning faculty and simultaneously proving that the passions, which everybody possesses, should never be allowed to control the reason. Or, what was easier, they demonstrated that self-regard was a primary motive and that there was a symbiotic relation between the force of self-regard and the force of rationality. This doctrine of selfishness has an ancient history but it is a doctrine then supposed to enlist the passions on the side of a reasonable regard for other human beings. That confused and elegant writer, Anthony Ashley Cooper, third Earl of Shaftesbury, in a series of essays known as *Characteristics of Men, Manners, Opinions, Times*, in two volumes (1711),* though he opposed "enthusiasm," which for his generation meant religious fanaticism, took a gentler view of human nature than did Locke. He denied that man is essentially vicious and essentially selfish. Why, he asked, should self-interest be the only "natural"

---

* A third volume, *Miscellaneous Reflections on the preceding Treatises, and other Critical Subjects*, really an introductory essay to the whole, was added later.

passion? Were this true, society could not exist. But society does exist, and there is a harmony in social relationships as well as a harmony between society and the universe as a whole, because men have affection for their fellow beings:

When, in general, all the affections or passions are suited to the public good, or good of the species . . . then is the natural temper entirely good. If, on the contrary, any requisite passion be wanting, or if there be any one supernumerary, or weak, or any wise disserviceable, or contrary to that main end; then is the natural temper, and consequently the creature himself, in some measure corrupt and ill.

. . . to explain, "How much the natural affections are in themselves the highest pleasures and enjoyments," there should, methinks, be little need of proving this to any one of human kind who has ever known the condition of the mind under a lively affection of love, gratitude, bounty, generosity, pity, succour, or whatever else is of a social or friendly sort. He who has ever so little knowledge of human nature is sensible what pleasure the mind perceives when it is touched in this generous way.

Thus it [appears] how much natural affection is predominant; how it is inwardly joined to us, and implanted in our natures; how interwoven with our other passions; and how essential to that regular motion and course of our affections, on which our happiness and self-enjoyment so immediately depend.

This affirmation of the excellence of pity, gratitude, and the like springs in part from the moral sense, a term Shaftesbury seems to have invented, though he made less of it than did his successors. Whether all this be logical or not, Shaftesbury stands near the head of a movement in Great Britain that countered too much trust in "reason" by emphasizing the relationship between morality and emotion, an assumption that was to eventuate in the celebration of emotional situations for their own sake. Shaftesbury also enjoyed considerable vogue in Europe, notably in Germany, and it is not surprising that before the celebration of rationality reached its absurd anticlimax in the French "Worship of Reason" of 1793, the practice of "sensibility" in literature, drama, painting, and actual life produced absurd excesses of its own. The difficulty with rationalism was twofold: it emphasized the reason and tended to blur over the appeal of the heart; and its cultural doctrine was directed in the main only to those groups who represented high culture in the Western world. The laborers and the peasants it did not touch.

ii

An inevitable countermovement developed, first in religion, second in a new philosophy of the tomb, third out of a renewed interest in racial traditions, and fourth from a doctrine of sensibility and art implicit in Shaftesbury and ripening in the second half of the eighteenth century.

Let me begin with the religious problem. In one sense this was simply another phase of the eternal conflict between theology and emotion. In a more specific sense it has its roots in various quietist developments of the seventeenth century. Quietism is a form of mysticism. It includes the doctrines of the Moravians, of the Society of Friends (or Quakers), and Quietism proper. To theologians, particularly to Catholic theologians, Quietism is a specific heresy condemned by the Inquisition and by Pope Innocent XI in 1687 but continuing nevertheless. For present purposes it will suffice to define quietism in general as a search in the Christian world for spiritual exaltation arising from self-abnegation that withdraws the soul from all outward actions and inclines it to deny not merely reason but also any outward form or ceremony, theological or secular, regarded by ecclesiastical or civil authorities as necessary to the well-being of church and state. It looks backward to Christian mystics of the early centuries; it prophesies the transcendental philosophies of the centuries to come.

So far as Quietism proper has any immediate literary ancestry this lies in *The Spiritual Guide, which disentangles the Soul, and brings it by the inward way to the getting of perfect contemplation and the rich treasure of internal peace*, published at Rome in Italian in 1675 by Miguel de Molinos (1640–1697), a Spanish priest. Molinos was protected for a while by the pope and at one time or another was approved by various church dignitaries and by the Holy Office itself. But the Jesuits were outraged by a treatise that went through twenty editions in various European languages within six years, which attained great popularity among Catholic readers, and which seemed to threaten not only their own power but the whole pattern of the existing church. Bringing pressure to bear upon the Vatican through Louis XIV, they caused Molinos to be imprisoned and his teachings condemned by the Inquisition in 1687. The Inquisition forced him to a formal recantation and imprisoned him for the rest of his life.

To the modern reader *The Spiritual Guide* scarcely seems alarming. Human life, Molinos argues, seeks perfection; and perfection is attainable by meditation, in which reason fixes its attention upon the capital truths of Christian theology, and then by contemplation, in which the soul neither reasons nor reflects but passively receives the impressions of divinity, desiring nothing, not even salvation, and fearing nothing, not even hell. Here is a typical passage:

The truly spiritual men . . . are those whom the Lord, in His infinite mercy, has called from that outward way in which they had been wont to exercise themselves; who had retired into the interior part of their souls; who had resigned themselves into the hand of God, totally putting off and forgetting themselves, and always going with an elevated spirit to the presence of the Lord, by means of pure faith, without image, form, or figure, but with great assurance found in tranquillity and internal rest. . . . These blessed and sublimated souls take no pleasure in anything of the world, but in contempt of it, in being alone, forsaken and forgotten by everybody; keeping always in their hearts a great lowliness and contempt of themselves; always humbled in the depths of their own unworthiness and vileness. . . . No news makes them afraid. No success makes them glad. Tribulations never disturb them, nor [do] the interior, continual Divine communications make them vain and conceited; they always remain full of holy and filial fear, in a wonderful peace, constancy, and serenity.*

* In *Dialogues sur le Quiétisme* La Bruyère writes a dialogue between a priest and a penitent, which hints at the basis for charges of heresy brought against the Quietists. The penitent has rewritten the Lord's Prayer as follows: "O God, who art no more in Heaven than on Earth or in Hell, who art everywhere, I neither wish nor desire your name to be sanctified. You know what is suitable for us, and if You wish it to be, it will be without my wishing or desiring it; whether Your Kingdom comes or not is to me indifferent. Neither do I ask that Your will be done on Earth as it is done in Heaven. It will be done in spite of my wishes, and it is for me to be resigned. Give us all our daily bread which is Your grace, or do not give it; I neither desire to have it or to be deprived of it. So if You pardon my crimes as I have pardoned those who have wronged me, so much the better. If, on the other hand, You punish me by damnation, still so much the better, since such is Your will. Finally, my God, I am too entirely abandoned to Your will to ask You to deliver me from temptations and from evil." I find this in John Bigelow's lively little study, *Molinos the Quietist* (New York, 1882), pp. 9–10. The original is in Dialogue V of the "Dialogues sur le Quiétisme," in La Bruyère, *Oeuvres* (Paris, 1865), II, 267. Bigelow's translation is not wholly accurate.

85

Thousands, especially in the Mediterranean countries but also including Catholic Germany, found in Quietism a guide to living.

The general mystical doctrine of Molinos was supported by Madame Guyon (1648–1717), whose troubled life vaguely anticipates that of some of the women advocating emancipation of the female sex a century later. Her father and mother neglected or spoiled her; as a child she was pushed in and out of convents, often for no good reason; and she was married by her parents to an uncongenial husband, by whom she had three surviving children. Madame Guyon had her first mystical experience at eighteen. Thereafter she went about seeking to do good and also seeking to avoid popular distrust, one reason for hostility being that she traveled a good deal with Father François La Combe,* who, however, was a good man filled with charity. Madame Guyon was "detained" in France, released in 1688, shut up at Vincennes in 1695–96, kept in another convent from 1696 to 1698, and imprisoned in the Bastille from 1698 to 1702. Nevertheless, the great Fénelon took up cudgels in her behalf, and for two years European orthodoxy wavered between his interpretation of religion and that of Bossuet and the Jesuit party. The Jesuits won.

A characteristic work of Madame Guyon is *La Moyen court et très-facile de faire oraison. Que tous peuvent pratiquer très-aisément et arriver par là dans peu de tems à une haute perfection*, published at Grenoble in 1685. According to this doctrine prayer comes from the heart, not from the head, and the mystic is to go beyond meditation into the contemplation of the Eternal God. One must will (or desire) only what God wills in eternity and be indifferent to everything else, whether it concerns the body or the soul, temporal goods or eternal ones. Leave the past and the future to Providence and live in the present — in fact, give the present wholly to God, since to content oneself with whatever happens now is to content oneself with the eternal order that is timeless and present in God, who is love. All things are of Him and come infallibly from His hand. In Madame Guyon's view such contemplation educes love and love educes contemplation. But since in a state of extreme beatitude the soul knows not any distinct

---

* La Combe was arrested and imprisoned for life in 1687. I omit for the sake of clarity the complicated story of Fénelon's relationship to Madame Guyon's mysticism.

ideas, not even, for example, the idea of the Son of God and His mission, it is clear why her pronouncements were from the point of view of Catholic orthodoxy both destructive of religion and heretical in point of doctrine.

While Quietism was thus disturbing the Catholic world, a similar movement known as Pietism gathered force in the Lutheran parts of Germany — Lutheran, because Luther's theology was more malleable than that of the rigid Calvin. To a degree that Quietism never knew, German Pietism was propounded by university men — Philipp Jakob Spener (1635–1705), preacher and professor of theology, whose *Pia Desiderata* appeared at Frankfort in 1675; August Hermann Francke (1663–1727), a formidable professor of Hebrew and Greek at the University of Halle, a philanthropist and a founder of various eleemosynary institutions and movements; and Gottfried Arnold (1666–1714), also an academician, associated with Dresden, Quedlinburg, and Giessen, minister, wanderer, hymn-writer, and author of various books of mysticism and church history, such as his *Unpartheiische Kirchen- und Ketzerhistorie von Anfang des neuen Testaments bis auf das Jahr Christi 1688.* This formidable study argues that the true march of Christianity is to be detected among the persecuted and heretical minorities rather than in synods and church councils. Of course it created an immense theological controversy.

One of the last phases of German Pietism was that dominated by Count Nikolaus Ludwig von Zinzendorf (1700–1760), whose wishes from his youth were all "directed toward the Bridegroom of my soul," who wrote little notes and letters to Christ, and who on his estate at Berthelsdorf sheltered the Moravian Brethren driven out of Catholic Bohemia. Very shortly he helped create a "religious" village at Herrnhut, which in 1727 was constituted an Erneuerte Brüderkirche (Renovated Church of the Brotherhood), an attempt to carry out an idea of Spener's, who had proposed private assemblies of Christians to replace, or be added to, the existing church system. It would be tedious to summarize the contents of even the leading books of these Pietists, since in their emphasis on simplicity and subjectivism they do not greatly differ from books by Molinos and Madame Guyon, albeit the goal of a mystical communion seems to be less evident among the Germans then among the Quietists proper. The Pietists deprecated quarreling; nevertheless, they occasioned a good many ecclesiastical arguments, got into difficulties with various political and church authorities, and sometimes differed sharply among themselves. Their emphasis was, however, upon love rather than logic, theirs was an advocacy of the priesthood of all believers, and, as is usual in such movements, they developed a belief not merely in love as an individual Christian experience but also in some sort of Christian commune (Spener called such gatherings *ecclesiolae* or little churches), a return, they thought, to the purity of the primitive faith. German Pietism was a more complicated affair than the mystical movements in France and elsewhere, and it was also a more lasting and important movement because the Thirty Years War had profoundly disturbed German belief in the providence of God. The Germans needed faith, not theology, and faith was somehow to bring the world together again. Moravian communities in contemporary Pennsylvania testify to the lasting quality of the German "renewal"; moreover, it has been argued that German Pietism helped create German nationalism. Pietism also spread to the Netherlands and the Scandinavias.

The English equivalent of these movements is more difficult to define, but we may content ourselves with a single book, William Law's *A Serious Call to a Devout and Holy Life* (1728), with the Society of Friends, or Quakers, and with certain phases of the Wesleyan movement. The tenets of the Society of Friends are too widely known to require presentation here, since, like the Quietists and Pietists, they emphasized peacefulness, love of man and of God, and the artificial quality of all church establishments. The Wesleyans, the future Methodists, are a more complicated matter, because John Wesley tried to remain within the framework of the Anglican Church, distrusted seclusion as a means of salvation ("the Bible knows nothing of solitary religion"), and set up an organization with himself as the head of it that reminds the modern reader of the military pattern of the Salvation Army. Moreover, a sect of Calvinist Methodists broke off from the main Wesleyan body because they preferred the elaborate intellectualized theology of Geneva to the looser forms of Wesleyan "conversion." Although Wesley came to distrust any doctrine that was based on a merely emotional state, there is no doubt that the meetings he and others addressed were sometimes characterized by the physical convulsions of a few (like the Holy Rollers), even if Wesley took care to follow up "conversions" of this sort by a system of checking on the later conduct of the converted. On the other hand he deplored the insensibility of all high and dry theologians.

But the great impact of Wesleyanism upon the emotional life of the British Isles came from field preaching, which Wesley adopted only after the astonishing success of George Whitefield, one of the great natural orators of the century. Field preaching began in 1739 at Kingswood, about four miles from Bristol, where in a barren tract that had once been a royal game preserve, and was now a colliery area, crowds of lawless, illiterate miners learned from Whitefield for the first time of Christianity, of the possibility of hell-fire, and of the means of attaining grace. Wesley's religious views were shaped in part by a Moravian named August Gottlieb Spangenberg, whom he met on shipboard and later talked with during Spangenberg's brief residence in the fire-new colony of Georgia; by personal experience (dare one speak of a certain spiritual egotism in this regard?); and by such writers as Thomas à Kempis, Jeremy Taylor, and William Law. The Wesleyan societies as organized curiously anticipated the pattern of the Jacobin clubs in revolutionary France and like them may owe something to Freemasonry. That Wesleyanism frightened the establishment is evident in a letter from the Duchess of Buckingham to Lady Huntingdon, a famous convert, quoted in Arnold Lunn's *John Wesley* (Dial Press, 1929, p. 200):

I thank your ladyship for the information concerning the Methodist preachers. Their doctrines are most repulsive, and strongly tinctured with impertinence and disrespect towards their superiors, in perpetually endeavoring to level all ranks, and to do away with all distinctions. It is monstrous to be told that you have a heart as sinful as the common wretches that crawl on the earth. This is highly offensive and insulting; and I cannot but wonder that your ladyship should relish any sentiments so much at variance with high rank and good breeding.

Since the Wesleyan movement then appealed chiefly to the laboring classes and the poor, the societies were compelled to meet at night — another suspicious circumstance.

William Law's *Serious Call* has some pretension to be a literary classic, its substance being a fusion of the edifying literature common in the seventeenth century with a succession of literary

"characters" descending from the same period. The "characters"
— Flavia, Miranda, Julius, Susurrus, Claudius, and the rest, all
from the upper social ranks — incarnate this or that dominant trait
inimical or favorable to true religion, and the appeal of the whole
book is to the thoughtful literate public. Law's principles are very
like those of Molinos, Madame Guyon, Spangenberg, and the rest,
except that he underplays mysticism:

If we are to be wise and holy as the new-born sons of God, we can no
otherwise be so, but by renouncing every thing that is foolish and vain
in every part of our common life.

Having . . . stated the general nature of devotion, and shown that it
implies not any form of prayer, but a certain form of life, that is offered
to God, not at any particular times or places, but everywhere and in
every thing; I shall now descend to some particulars, and show how
we are to devote our labour and employment, our time and fortunes,
unto God.

. . . we must eat and drink, and dress and discourse, according to the
sobriety of the Christian spirit, engage in no employments but such
as we can truly devote unto God, nor pursue them any further than
so far as conduces to the reasonable ends of a holy, devout life.

Nothing, therefore, can be more false than to imagine, that because
we are private persons, that have taken upon us no charge or employment of life, therefore we may live more at large, indulge our appetites,
and be less careful of the duties of piety and holiness; for it is as good
an excuse for cheating and dishonesty. Because he that abuses his
reason, that indulges himself in lust and sensuality, and neglects to act
the wise and reasonable part of a true Christian, has everything in
his life to render him hateful to God, that is to be found in cheating
and dishonesty.

A devout man makes a true use of his reason: he sees through the
vanity of the world, discovers the corruption of his nature, and the
blindness of his passion. He lives by a law which is not visible to vulgar
eyes; he enters the world of spirits; he compares the greatest things,
sets eternity against time; and chooses rather to be for ever great in
the presence of God, when he dies, than to have the greatest share of
worldly pleasure whilst he lives.

In considering the probable relation of these movements, their
leaders, and their books to revolution, it will of course be remembered that the "literature" of a heart religion (so the phrase sometimes went) necessarily was available only to that minority of the
Western world that could read and, indeed, only to a minority

of that smaller fraction. Moreover, it does not follow that the impact of such religious revivals was inevitably on the side of radicalism; Wesley, for example, published an abridged edition of Samuel Johnson's anti-American tract *Taxation No Tyranny* as *A Calm Address to Our American Colonies*, and historians of the American revolution can find no enthusiasm among American Methodists for rebelling against the crown. Molinos may by implication have assaulted the church; there is no substantial evidence that he wanted to overturn the state, and neither the Herrnhuters nor any other branch of the German Pietists attacked prince or state with fire and sword. Though we have statistics for some things — the number of Quakers, the number of persons imprisoned by the Inquisition, and so on — there are no reliable figures for the percentage of the vast, silent, illiterate populace of Western Europe who embraced doctrines that tended to substitute private emotion for social and intellectual order.

Nevertheless, these movements as a whole worked against the Enlightenment. They viewed reason as an enemy rather than a friend. They insisted that all souls, from that of the monarch to that of the slave, were equal in the sight of God and in the possibility of eternal salvation. A "heart religion" was quintessentially a democratic religion because it had no place for ecclesiastical expertise, the church as a policeman for the state, or, at least consciously, the doctrine that religion is the opiate of the masses. On the contrary, this international ground swell of egalitarian emotionalism sapped, without intending to do so, the foundation of a society structured in rank and class; and it is characteristic that such great creations of the Enlightenment as the *Encyclopédie* were thought of by these followers of Christ as irreligious documents. Had it been otherwise, Robespierre would not have encountered some of the difficulties he met when, after some years of revolution, he tried to establish in France a religion of the state. The masses remained obstinately of Wesley's opinion rather than Robespierre's, and as a result one of the striking paradoxes of a revolutionary century is that a religious revival prepared the way for an overturn of the Christian commonwealth as intelligence then conceived such a commonwealth.

The ethical system of Benjamin Franklin is anticipated in Law's *Serious Call* as when, for example, Law writes: "It is as much your duty to rise to pray, as to pray when you are risen. And if you are late at your prayers, you offer to God the prayers of an idle, slothful worshipper, that rises to prayers as idle servants rise to their labour." More striking, however, is Law's reduction of the aristocracy and the servant class to a plane of humble equality: "The fine lady must teach her eyes to weep, and be clothed in humility. The polite gentleman must exchange the gay thoughts of wit and fancy, for a broken and a contrite heart. The man of quality must so far renounce the dignity of his birth, as to think himself miserable till he is born again. Servants must consider their service as done unto God, masters must consider their servants as their brethren in Christ, that they are to be treated as their fellow-members of the mystical body of Christ." This is from chapter ten, significantly entitled "Showing how all orders and ranks of men and women, of all ages, are obliged to devote themselves unto God."

iii

A second phase of this countermovement has to do with death. The Thirty Years War had acquainted all Europe afresh with death, and the wars of the eighteenth century did nothing to lessen its propinquity. Infant mortality was high, too many diseases were treated by blood-letting, epidemics were common, and starvation, even in the fertile land of France, was not unknown. The century often surrounded death with pomp and circumstance, but sometimes it did not; for example, the body of Louis XV was hurried off to interment with unparalleled indecency. Death came immediately home to the farmer, the villager, and the peasant: Courbet's fine "Burial at Ornans" in the Louvre undoubtedly pictures family burial rites traditional among the peasantry. "Undertaker" in the American sense of funeral director does not get into the language until 1698; and as in many small American towns today, the eighteenth-century undertaker was also a carpenter or had some other employment. His services could be had only by families of means.

Death is an ancient theme in art. For a variety of reasons there developed in English literature, spreading thence to the Continent, a fashion in poetry known as the Graveyard School. Writers in this category had their relation to Quietism and the Pietists in that they, too, concentrated on the vanity of human life; and they expressed the melancholy, deepening into pessimism, basic to much rationalistic thought in the century. Minor poets such as Anne, Countess of Winchelsea, and Thomas Parnell touched lightly on the dark side of mortality: the Countess's "A Nocturnal Reverie" of 1713 doesn't even get to the cemetery, and although Parnell's "A Night-Piece on Death" of 1721 describes a lakeside "place of graves," decaying tombs with "arms, angels, epitaphs, and bones," and pictures Death as the "King of Fears," the poet rises from a funeral procession to consider "pious souls" who "clap the glad wing and tow'r away." The grisly masterpiece of the school is Robert Blair's "The Grave" (1743), which among other gloomy topics pictures the yew tree, that "cheerless unsocial plant," growing

> Midst skulls and coffins, epitaphs and worms;
> Where light-heeled ghosts and visionary shades,
> Beneath the wan cold moon . . .
>   . . . perform their mystic rounds.
> No other merriment, dull tree, is thine.

But Blair had less vogue outside the British Isles than did Edward Young's solemn *The Complaint, or Night Thoughts on Life, Death and Immortality*, which dragged along from 1742 to "Night the Ninth and Last," printed in 1745. The European vogue of Gray's "Elegy Written in a Country Churchyard" of 1751 was also notable.

Taken in small doses, Young's *Night Thoughts* is not unreadable, and he is capable of occasionally striking off so memorable a line as

> The undevout Astronomer is mad.

But Europe did not take him in small doses; his poem, as long as the *Aeneid*, was translated into all the major languages, Ebert being his principal German purveyor and Le Tourneur his French one. Young saw the world, says Van Tieghem, the French scholar, across the pages of the Book of Job, and another Frenchman thinks that Young invented the *mal du siècle* before the French romantics had got around to this literary disease. In Germany the vogue of Young began in the sixties, and Klopstock, the author of *Der Messias*, Hamann, and Herder read him with enthusiasm, despite the ridicule of classicists such as Lessing and Wieland. Even the aristocratic Chateaubriand found something in *The Complaint*. Young's greatest European vogue was apparently in the Germanies, partly because he was not French and frivolous, partly because these exercises in solemn piety from the land of the Anglo-Saxons emphasized the superior moral worth of the Teutonic peoples.

The nights grew longer and longer as the poem progressed from "Life, Death, and Immortality" to "The Consolation, Containing, among other Things, i. A Moral Survey of the Nocturnal Heavens. ii. A Night-Address to the Deity." The folly of man, says the poet, lies in his failure to reform, and the deaths of friends, nighttime, and the gloom of the cemetery ought to teach even the infidel that "if man's immortal, there's a God in Heaven." How much of the poem is vaguely autobiographical, and how much of it grew from the writer's sense that he had a popular theme and might as well exploit it, is anybody's guess. There is a vague, antiskeptical progression of thought in the work, but one section is so much like another in tone that this passage from Night One is representative:

> O ye blest scenes of permanent delight!
> Full above measure! lasting, beyond bound!
> A *perpetuity* of bliss is bliss.
> Could you, so rich in rapture, fear an end,
> That ghastly thought would drink up all your joy,
> And quite unparadise the realms of light.
> Safe are you lodg'd above these rolling spheres;
> The baleful influence of whose giddy dance
> Sheds sad vicissitude on all beneath.
> *Here* teems with revolutions every hour,
> And rarely for the better; or the *best*,
> More mortal than the *common* births of fate.
> Each *Moment* has its sickle, emulous,
> Of *Time's* enormous scythe, whose ample sweep
> Strikes *empires* from the root; each *moment* plays
> His little weapon in the narrower sphere
> Of sweet *domestic* comfort, and cuts down
> The fairest bloom of sublunary bliss.

One can of course remark, as Byron said of another platitude, that all this is extremely true. During the Seven Years War and its aftermath, however, Europe was looking for precisely the consolation Young's polysyllabic lines seemed to offer. Like other works of literary mediocrity, the *Night Thoughts* translates extremely well.

The somber blank verse of Young had a prose rival, even more unreadable nowadays, the Rev. James Hervey's *Meditations among the Tombs* (1746), the first of two volumes of lugubrious "meditations" and "contemplations" completed in 1747. *Meditations among the Tombs* was many times reprinted and often translated. The reverend author wanders alone in "deep silence" in "a large *burial-ground*: remote from all the noise and hurry of tumultuous life" somewhere in Cornwall, and contemplates in succession the monument of an infant, the monument of a youth, the monument of a young man cut off in his prime, the monument of a middle-aged person, the graves of the aged, and various other tombs with their "awful aspect." Any page is as lugubrious as any other, but this visit to a vault will serve as a specimen of Hervey's prose:

Yonder entrance leads, I suppose, to the *Vault*. Let me turn aside, and take one View of the Habitation, and it's tenants. — The sullen *Door* grates upon it's Hinges: Not used to receive many Visitants, it admits me with Reluctance and Murmurs. — What meaneth this *sudden Trepidation*, while I descend the Steps, and am visiting the pale Nations of the Dead? — Be composed, my Spirits; there is nothing to fear, in these quiet Chambers. "Here, even the Wicked cease from troubling."

Good Heavens! what a solemn Scene! — how dismal the *Gloom*! Here is perpetual Darkness, and Night, even at Noon-day. — How doleful the *Solitude*! Not one Trace of chearful Society; but Sorrow and Terror seem to have made This, their dreaded Abode. — Hark! how the hollow Dome resounds at every Tread.

The darkness is pierced by a beam or two of light that "reflects a feeble Glimmer, from the Nails of the *Coffins*," and two or three pages later, "solemn and slow" the clock strikes, reminding author and reader: "May it teach me that *Heavenly Arithmetic*, of 'numbering my Days, and applying my Heart unto Wisdom.' " Wisdom seems chiefly to consist in the thought that man is doomed to die. This masterpiece was shaped as "a Letter to a Lady," and neither flower gardens, nor a walk at evening, during which Hervey contemplates the night, nor the starry heavens, nor winter snows, the topics of the five later funereal essays, cheer the author or break what Dr. Johnson might call his inspissated gloom. As he was incapable of an original idea, Hervey was read by pious readers everywhere.

It would be tedious to trace the whole history of the school of melancholy in the British Isles and on the Continent, even if it could be done. Night and the terrors of the tomb became necessary elements in Gothic novels and horror fiction generally. On the Continent the Germans seemed prone to religious meditation, and with them solemn poetry reached two climaxes in *Der Messias* and in the famous *Hymnen an die Nacht* of Friedrich von Hardenberg (known as Novalis), written about 1798 and published in 1800. Better than any other bit of German romanticism, these express a Freudian death-wish, and probably have something to do with the fascination death exercises in Wagner's music. In style Novalis' *Hymns* are incomparably above Young or his kind. They are the expression of Novalis' sorrow at the demise of Sophie von Kühn, a very young girl whom he loved and who died in 1797: Novalis himself died of tuberculosis, that standard romantic complaint, the year after the *Hymnen*, six in all, were printed. The work is sometimes in unrhymed verse, sometimes in prose, and sometimes in stanzaic form, and as literary art it represents a fusion of classical restraint (even classical borrowings) with romantic emotions arising from night, hopelessness, Christian faith, and a longing for death. Here are extracts from the sixth hymn, "Sehnsucht nach dem Tode" (Longing for Death), which will serve to hint at Novalis' achievement:

> Hinunter in der Erde Schoss,
> Weg aus des Lichtes Reichen,
> Der Schmerzen Wut und wilder Stoss
> Ist froher Abfahrt Zeichen.
> Wir kommen in dem engen Kahn
> Geschwind am Himmelsufer an.
>
> .   .   .   .   .   .
>
> Die Vorzeit, wo noch blütenreich
> Uralte Stämme prangten,
> Und Kinder für das Himmelsreich
> Nach Qual und Tod verlangten;
> Und wenn auch Lust und Leben sprach,
> Doch manches Herz für Liebe brach.

Die Vorzeit, wo in Jugendglut
Gott selbst sich kundgegeben
Und frühem Tod in Liebesmut
Geweiht sein süsses Leben,
Und Angst und Schmerz nicht von sich trieb,
Damit er uns nur teuer blieb.

Mit banger Sehnsucht sehn wir sie
In dunkle Nacht gehüllet,
In dieser Zeitlichkeit wird nie
Der heisse Durst gestillet.
Wir mussen nach der Heimat gehn,
Um diese heil'ge Zeit zu sehn.*

The terrors of death and a longing to die overran Europe years before the death-wish became a standard theme in romantic art. What could the Enlightenment do with this universal, this ambiguous, emotion? Thoughts about death with all their overtones were commonplace and horrid long before the guillotine had become the symbol of the Reign of Terror.

iv

The dark emotional currents underlying the fair surface of the Enlightenment had still other springs: the ballad revival with its emphasis on primary emotions, the vogue of Ossian and the accompanying concept of primitive poetry (the bards), an increasing interest in the Volkslied and popular song in general, and the development of the hymn. Ballads were of course originally sung or chanted, or so the theory ran; in the eighteenth century they might or might not have a tune associated with them. What Addison stressed in his notable discussion of "Chevy Chase" in *The Spectator* was not the music of the ballad but the healthy epic simplicity of subject and style. The culmination in mid-century

---

* Deep down in the womb of earth, far from the realms of light, the anguish of our pain and its wild impact are signs of a happier departure; we shall come in our narrow boat [the coffin] quickly to the shore of heaven. . . . In the foretime when aged trunks were yet rich with blossoms, and children for the sake of the kingdom of heaven longed for suffering and death, and even if life and pleasure spoke, many a heart was broken for love. The foretime when God [i.e. Christ] revealed himself glowing with youth and dedicated His sweet existence to an early death, out of his love and courage, nor spared Himself pain and anguish; wherefore He remained dearer to us. With melancholy longing we see them wrapped in dark night, and we shall never quench our burning thirst in this world. We must go on to heaven if we are to see that sacred hour.

97

English literature of ballad interest was Thomas Percy's famous three-volume *Reliques of Ancient English Poetry: Consisting of Old Heroic Ballads, Songs, and other Pieces of our Earlier Poets (Chiefly of the Lyric kind), Together with some few of later Date.* This came out in 1765, and went into new editions in 1767, 1776, and 1794. The confusion in the title is symptomatic of the confusion at mid-century about what was "ancient," what primitive, and what "popular" in any sense of the word. The only music in Percy's first edition is a single page in volume two, purporting to be a specimen of a ballad tune; the vignette on the title pages, however, has a harp for its central ornament, and the frontispiece of volume three shows a minstrel playing this harp before an assorted set of "medieval" types, including a knight in armor lying on the ground.

The introduction of the collection gets the good bishop involved with theories about ancient bards (minstrels), who are supposed to have chanted most of these poems to "the people" or at court in some vague era in the past. Percy's historical importance is great. One of his virtues is that his example encouraged Scott to translate, from the German, Bürger's powerful pseudo-ballads "Lenore" and "Der wilde Jaeger" and to collect *The Minstrelsy of the Scottish Border,* also in three volumes, in 1802–1803. Moreover, Percy's example led Herder to bring out a two-volume collection of *Volkslieder* in 1778–1779 (without music), later rearranged and republished as *Stimmen der Völker in Liedern,* by which title it is more commonly known. Herder's is an international collection, everything, however, being translated into German. He justifies his labors by passages from Montaigne, Milton, Sidney, Addison, Luther, Agricola, Lessing, Gerstenberg, Percy, and Dr. Burney, who furnishes the only hint that ballads might have something to do with popular music.

Whoever opens a copy of *Stimmen der Völker* comes at once upon a German rendering of "Darthula's Grave Song." This is a version in irregular verse of a paragraph of *Dar-Thula: a Poem* (in prose!), one of the pieces included in Macpherson's *Fingal, an Ancient Epic Poem . . . and Several Other Poems,* 1762. We are at once confronted with the vast puzzle of Ossian, Macpherson, the bards, the druids,* the Celtic revival, and the "Gothick North."

---

* A characteristic effusion on the druids is Thomas Warton's "Sonnet Written

98

Even before Macpherson's first publication, Europe had seen a considerable stimulating and contentious literature about bards, minstrels, the Celts in Gaul, Ireland, and the Highlands of Scotland, and the habits of the ancient Germans. The bards were supposed to sit by the primitive springs of language and of poetry; they were usually pictured as gray-haired men plucking a harp, and the themes on which they improvised concerned heroism, love, warfare, and death. Partly out of a desire to vindicate the importance to history of the Highlanders and the Irish (he is a little vague on this racial distinction), James Macpherson (1736–1796), two-fifths of him talent and three-fifths sheer fraud, published in 1760 in Edinburgh a small book entitled *Fragments of Ancient Poetry, Collected in the Highlands of Scotland, and Translated from the Galic [sic] or Erse Language*. A mere seventy pages of print have seldom set off so continuing a controversy. A second edition with an additional "fragment" appeared that same year. Admiring friends paid for two trips into the Highlands by Macpherson to collect more fragments, and he presently printed two "epics," purportedly also composed in Gaelic by Ossian, *Fingal* in 1762 and *Temora* in 1763, each accompanied by shorter "poems." By 1765 the *Works of Ossian* in two stout volumes, which included an admiring dissertation by the Rev. Hugh Blair, was on the market (they were still translated from the "Galic"); by the end of the century there were at least ten reputable editions, some forgeries, and a great many imitations and selections on the British market, and innumerable versions in German, Italian, Spanish,

---

at Stonehenge" (1777):

> Thou noblest monument of Albion's isle!
> Whether by Merlin's aid from Scythia's shore
> To Amber's fatal plain Pendragon bore,
> Huge frame of giant-hands, the mighty pile,
> T'entomb his Britons slain by Hengist's guile:
> Or Druid priests, sprinkled with human gore,
> Taught 'mid thy massy maze their mystic lore:
> Or Danish chiefs, enriched with savage spoil,
> To Victory's idol vast, an unhewn shrine
> Reared the rude heap; or, in thy hallowed round,
> Repose the kings of Brutus' genuine line;
> Or here those kings in solemn state were crowned:
> Studious to trace thy wondrous origin,
> We muse on many an ancient tale renowned.

One notes the confusion of Arthurian, Anglo-Saxon, Danish, Celtic, and even Roman antiquity in this odd performance.

French, Dutch, Danish, Swedish, Polish, and Russian appeared in the half-century.

A long quotation (in German) in *The Sorrows of Werther* (1774) increased the vogue of Ossian, and Goethe contributed a design to the title page of a German translation of 1773–1777. Napoleon at one time kept a copy of "Ocean," as he called it, under his pillow. Infants were christened Oscar, Malvina, or Selma. A great painter took opportunity to gratify royalty by using Macpherson's cloudy hills and cloudier heavens to depict the souls of departed generals in the skies. A vast musical literature, most of it now forgotten, developed,* and tragedies were of course produced on Ossianic themes. Was not Ossian the equivalent of Homer, an epic poet who revealed the mystic "North" (Ireland, Scotland, Scandinavia, Germany, the Low Countries) as filled in "ancient times" with poetry, music, heroes, lovely women, death, and racial tradition? "Das Volk dichtet," ran the German, gleaned from the theories of Herder and the linguistic researches of the Brothers Grimm, and a new race of philologists was persuaded that modern speech was fossil poetry, that the business of art was to go back to the wellsprings of life, music, poetry, heroism, and simplicity, and so bring about a new instauration of virtue and

---

* Since all one has to go on in most cases is the title, my list is undoubtedly full of errors, but I have assembled the following: F. H. Barthelemon, *Cithona: A Dramatic Poem Set to Music* (?1778); John Abraham Fisher, *The Masque of the Druids* (spectacle with songs, 1774); William Reeves, *Oscar and Malvina* (ballet pantomime, 1791); Harriet Wainright, *Comala: A Dramatic Poem from Ossian* (incidental music, 1792); J. M. Zumsteeg, *Colma* (ballads, 1793); C. Kalkbrenner, *Scène tirée des poésies d'Ossian* (choral work, 1800 or 1809); Jean Franc Leseur, *Ossian* (also known as *Les Bardes*, 1804), which opened the Académie Impériale de Musique in Paris and occasioned three musical parodies in the same year; Méhul, *Uthel* (opera, 1806); Winter, *Colmal* (opera, 1809); Schubert, "Lodas Gespenst" (1815), "Kolmars Klage" (1815), "Das Mädchen von Inistore" (1815), "Ossians Lied nach dem Falle Nathos" (1815), "Shilrik und Vinvala" (1815), "Cronnan" (1816), "Lorma" (a fragment, 1815), "Der Tod Ossians" (1816), "Die Nacht" (1817); J. G. Kastner, *Ossians Tod* (opera, 1833); Niels Gade, *Echoes from Ossian* (overture, 1840), *Comala* (cantata, 1846); Louis M. Gottschalk, "Danse Ossianique" (1846), "Ballades d'Ossian" (1847), "Marche de Nuit" (1885); S. Millinghem, *Darthula* (cantata? 1849); E. Sobolewski, *Komala* (opera? 1858); Brahms, "Gesang aus Fingal" (1860), "Darthula: Ein Grabgesang" (1861); Bantock, *Caldmor* (opera, 1893); Goossens, *Symphonic Prelude to a Poem by Ossian* (1915). I am unable to find out anything much about *Fingal* by P. A. Coppola, apparently produced before 1835, F. L. A. Kunzen, *Ossian's Harp* (Kunzen died in 1817), a *Moina* by Sylvain Dupuis, who died in 1931, and a *Moina* (1897) by de Lara. And what is one to do with the large number of Hebridean and "Celtic" compositions by Bantock, Mendelssohn's *Fingal's Cave* of 1829, and Bellini's *Norma* of 1831?

happiness. This doctrine even colors the chapter on "Language" in Emerson's *Nature*.

The innovations ran in two parallel streams. Not only did amateurs collect ballads and folk songs (often tampering with them in the process), but poets began to imitate them — Gray, Cowper, Burns, Wordsworth, Coleridge, Scott, Keats, Blake, Byron, Bürger, Schiller, Goethe, Uhland, Tieck, Brentano, various Danes and Swedes, and French and Italian writers. The Spanish had less need to catch up, since, despite the enthusiasm of their upper classes for "taste" and neoclassicism, their popular narrative and lyrical poetry was rich and lively — so much so that Spanish ballads attracted the attention of such Germans as Herder, Jakob Grimm, Diez, and the Schlegels. Some German romantics got out anthologies of Spanish ballads and romances, which in turn interested a rising literary generation in Spain. English and French enthusiasm came a little later; an example is John Gibson Lockhart's *Spanish Ballads* of 1823.

But one ought to look at a sample of the Ossianic "poems," which are in prose, the sentences being short or, more rarely, simple compound sentences, the vocabulary monotonous, and the general mood one of melancholy, since the fiction is that the aged Ossian commemorates the deeds and virtues of the dead. It should be added that the scenery is vague and primitive, cloudiness or moonlight prevails, and a sorrowful wind forever sighs through the mournful trees. Ghosts abound. Here is a characteristic passage from "Carthon: A Poem, " "complete," says Macpherson's introductory argument, "and the subject of it, as of most of Ossian's compositions, tragical." Moina has been married to Reuda, killed in a quarrel by Clessámmor, who also loves her, but the wind prevents Clessámmor from carrying off the widow. Moina gives birth to a son, Carthon, and then dies:

RAISE, ye bards, said the mighty Fingal,* the praise of unhappy Moina. Call her ghost, with your songs, to our hills; that she may rest with the fair of Morven, the sun-beams of other days, the delight of heroes of old. I have seen the walls of Balclutha, but they were desolate. The fire had resounded in the halls: and the voice of the people is heard no more. The stream of Clutha was removed from its place by the fall of the walls. The thistle shook, there, its lonely head: the moss whistled

* A footnote informs us that Fingal is celebrated by the Irish historians for his wisdom in making laws, his poetical genius, and his foreknowledge of events.

101

to the wind. The fox looked out, from the windows, the rank grass of the wall waved round its head. Desolate is the dwelling of Moina, silence is in the house of her fathers. Raise the song of mourning, O bards, over the land of strangers. They have but fallen before us: for, one day, we must fall. Why dost thou build the hall, son of the winged days? Thou lookest from thy towers to-day; yet a few years, and the blast of the desert comes; it howls in thy empty court, and whistles round thy half-worn shield.

And so on and so on, parts of it cribbed from the Old Testament. This has a certain charm, but nine hundred pages seems a touch excessive. The eighteenth century, however, and the romantics did not think so. Macpherson's recurrent phrase: "A tale of the times of old! the deeds of days of other years!" possessed for them a kind of enchantment.

If folk poetry, why not folk music? The English had been singing catches, glees, and madrigals for years, and the so-called ballad opera, of which Gay's (and Pepusch's) *The Beggar's Opera* (1728) is the most notable, existed as a kind of protest against too much musical formalism. If one believes that high-school classic, Theodor Storm's *Immensee*, folk songs develop spontaneously; Reinhard thus defends them against Eric:

They are not made; they grow, they drop from the clouds, they float over the land like gossamer, hither and thither, and are sung in a thousand places at the same time. We discover in these songs our very inmost activities and sufferings; it is as if we all helped to write them. . . . These melodies are as old as the world; they slumber in the depth of the forest; God knows who discovered them.

The German word *Lied* has come to denote a special sort of musical composition, secular or sacred, lyrical in content, usually of more than one stanza, the stanzas being identical in form. These verbal elements in turn affect the musical setting, which must possess, to use another German expression, *Liedhaftigkeit*; that is, the musical setting, whatever demands it may make on an accomplished singer, must convey an impression of directness, must avoid the ornamentation of operatic aria and the vocal showiness of the oratorio. Early collections of *Lieder* appeared in connection with the Pietistic movement. By the 1730's a considerable interest in *Lieder* had developed. In 1767–68 the *Lieder der Teutschen* (four parts) was published in Berlin. In 1769 J. A. Hiller put together his *Lieder für Kinder*, an important collection because it insisted on directness and simplicity; and in 1785 J. A. P. Schulz brought out *Lieder in Volkston*, which contains the celebrated passage: "Zu dem Ende habe ich nur solche Texte aus unsern besten Liederdichtern gewählt, die mir zu diesem Volksgesange gemacht zu sein schienen, und mich in den Melodien selbst der höchsten Simplicität und Fasslichkeit beflissen, ja auf alle Weise der Schein des Bekannten derzubringen versuch . . . In diesem Schein des Bekannten liegt das ganze Geheimnis des Volkston." * Schulz (1747–1800), together with J. F. Reichardt (1732–1814), is one of the founders of that musical interest in German *Lieder* which had its greatest exponent in Franz Schubert.

German songs became an instrument in arousing German nationalism; and comparable attempts to make music express the "soul" of a nation developed elsewhere. In Scotland, for example, *The Scots Musical Museum*, edited by James Johnson, to which Burns contributed actual folk songs or compositions of his own, began publishing in 1771. It is merely one in a long line of such collections, the first of which is *Orpheus Caledonius* (1725); and as early as 1701 there appeared *A Collection of Original Scotch Tunes (full of the Highland Humours) for the Violin*. George Thomson's *A Select Collection of Original Scottish Airs for the Voice* began publication in 1793, with more, though mutilated, poems by Burns. Tom Moore's *Irish Melodies*, which appeared at intervals during the first quarter of the nineteenth century, would not have been possible if Edward Bunting (1773–1843), fired by a meeting of Irish harpers at Belfast in 1792, had not launched in 1796 his *A General Collection of the Ancient Irish Music*. One of Moore's *Irish Melodies* begins: "Dear harp of my country: In darkness I found thee," and the assumption of a living connection between folk music and nationalism is implicit in the line. It is to be noted that song played an important part in sustaining nationalism and revolution throughout a century which gave the world

* With this aim in mind I have chosen only such texts from our best song-writers as seem to me made for folk song, and I have tried to take pains that the melodies themselves should be of the purest simplicity and comprehensibility, in every way giving them the appearance of familiarity. The whole secret of a popular strain lies in this appearance of familiarity.

For acute comment on modern settings of modern *Lieder* see Jack M. Stein, *Poem and Music in the German Lied from Gluck to Hugo Wolf*, Cambridge, Mass., 1971.

"Rule Britannia," "Yankee Doodle," "La Marseillaise," the former Austrian national hymn, "Ça ira," and others. What "popular" music did for revolution and nationalism, the hymn did for religion: to stick to English examples only, such notable hymn writers as Isaac Watts (*Psalms and Hymns*, 1719), and John and Charles Wesley (*Collection of Psalms and Hymns*, 1738, and *Hymns for the Lord's Supper*, 1748) appealed to simple Protestant piety and blurred theological distinctions.*

The ballad, Ossianism, folk song, and hymn express a universe of discourses filled with primary emotions. Heroism, love, death, childhood, domesticity, simple religious faith, racial or national fervor are more important than arguments about the Newtonian universe, Lockian psychology, or theories of the commonwealth. If character is presented in these art forms, it is, so to speak, one-dimensional — the lover is untrue, the faithful sweetheart dies, the knight is brave, mother-love is the totality of maternity (there are also hateful parents, simply defined), the faithful foot soldier follows his captain into battle, the sailor loves both his ship and his Nancy, the true believer maintains an unquestioning piety or receives comfort in the misfortunes of life from the love of Jesus or of God. Emotional discourse in such a world, be it narrative or lyrical, knows nothing of theories of knowledge or of the state and is not concerned about relations between the passions and rationalism. The agencies of this emotionalism — simple words and singable melodies — could, however, be turned to useful ends by propagandists, politicians, and revolutionaries. One thinks in this connection of the political success of such tunes as "Malbrouk s'en va-t-en guerre," which turns up in Beaumarchais's *Le Mariage de Figaro*, and of "Lilliburlero," a song that accompanied the successful revolt against James II. Revolutions are emotional explosions. Primary passions retained their hold upon the people throughout the eighteenth century, so that the epoch may be said to have exploited the programmatic value of emotion associated through music and words, with race, death, honor, and spiritual salvation. This does not mean that revolutionary leaders were all idealists or that they lacked cynicism.

* It is interesting to remember that the Germans Tieck and Novalis once planned to collaborate on a collection of sermons and hymns.

v

Each of the movements I have sketched can conceivably be brought under the rubric of the cult of sensibility, which, during the eighteenth century, clashed with the movement of rationalism. The term sensibility (*sensibilité*) and the term sentimentalism, often equated with it, together with their cognate adjectives, are as vague, broad, and disputable as romanticism itself, and the movement (dare one call it the program?) of sensibility touched philosophy, theology, poetry, nonfictional prose, the drama, and the novel in various ways, nor does painting escape (for example, Greuze's domestic scenes, which were intended to touch the feeling heart). Harder to isolate but nonetheless an influential cultural element in the age was musical sentimentality, notably evident in airs composed to be played or sung in the salon or the drawing room. The harp became a "romantic" instrument, and writers not versed in musical history were likely to equip suffering heroines with harps which they could not possibly carry into the wild, wild woods wherein this sad sisterhood produced effusions of their own or songs alleged to be traditional "ballads."

The philosophical origins of sensibility are always in dispute: Plato, Plotinus, Christian theology, Shaftesbury, Rousseau, and scores of others have by one or another writer been singled out as the central genius in the movement. There are, moreover, scholars who minimize the international nature of this value system; F. C. Green, for example, in his admirable study, *Minuet: A Critical Survey of French and English Literary Ideas in the Eighteenth Century,** stoutly defends the cultural autonomy of France, and thinks (p. 301) that in France there was a general resistance to outside influences, though he admits the vogue among a minority in Paris of such a play as Lillo's *George Barnwell; or, The London Merchant* and of the divine *Pamela*.

The appeal of sensibility in Western culture everywhere was to the feeling heart, and standard approaches involved undeserved poverty, divine benevolence, or virtue in distress. Evil or wicked-

---

* This was first published in London in 1935. A New York reprint (1966) bears the title *Literary Ideas in Eighteenth Century France and England*.

ness was caused, so to speak, by misunderstanding of purpose in a benevolent universe. Wrote Leibniz:

The order of things, which to our confused senses appears as that of space, of time, and of cause and effect, vanishes in the clear light of thought, and gives way to an intellectual order in the mind of the Creator or God. . . . the things of the world, which are created in complete harmony with one another, continue to manifest this harmony or mutual agreement.

The failure of a right education of the moral sense and of a belief that virtue and beauty are interchangeable, or, in sum, the substitution of egotism for benevolence, creates or permits evil to develop in the soul. But such is the eventual appeal of goodness even to the hardened heart that in the long run the reprobate — for example, Lovelace in *Clarissa Harlowe* or the hypocritical Joseph Surface in Sheridan's *The School for Scandal* — will either repent or be driven by exposure from society.

A like faith in the power of the domestic virtues is evidenced in Diderot's two bad plays, *Le Fils naturel, ou les Epreuves de la vertu* and *Le Père de famille*. Here is part of the "conversion" scene (Act V) of *Le Père de famille*; it is not necessary to know the story to get the point:

Saint-Albin (à son père). Mon père, écoutez-moi . . . Germeuil, demeurez . . . C'est lui qui vous a conservé votre fils . . . Sans lui vous n'en auriez plus. Qu'allais-je devenir? . . . C'est lui qui m'a conservé Sophie . . . Menacée par moi, menacée par mon oncle, c'est Germeuil, c'est ma soeur, qui l'ont sauvée . . . Ils n'avaient qu'un instant . . . Elle n'avait qu'un asile . . . Ils l'ont dérobée à ma violence . . . Les punirez-vous de ma faute? . . . Cécile, venez. Il faut fléchir le meilleur des pères. (*Il amène sa soeur aux pieds de son père, et s'y jette avec elle.*)

Le père de famille. Ma fille, je vous ai pardonnée; que me demandez-vous?

Saint-Albin. D'assurer pour jamais son bonheur, le mien et le vôtre. Cécile . . . Germeuil . . . Ils s'aiment, ils s'adorent . . . Mon père, livrez-vous à toute votre bonté. Que ce jour soit le plus beau jour de notre vie. (*Il court à Germeuil, il appelle Sophie.*) Germeuil, Sophie . . . Venez, venez . . . Allons tous nous jeter aux pieds de mon père.

Sophie (se jetant aux pieds du père de famille dont elle ne quitte guère les mains, le reste de la scène). Monsieur.

Le père de famille (se penchant sur eux, et les relevant). Mes enfants . . . mes enfants . . . Cécile, vous aimez Germeuil?

Cécile. Mon père, pardonnez-moi.

Le père de famille. Pourquoi me l'avoir celé? Mes enfants, vous ne connaissez pas votre père . . . Germeuil, approchez . . . Je vous avais destiné ma fille. Qu'elle soit avec vous la plus heureuse des femmes.*

I repeat, the plot is of no importance; the point is that all parties in this touching scene act from the highest sentimental motives.

Poets of all the nations overflowed with sensibility — for example, James Thomson, whose *The Seasons*, published at intervals from 1726 to 1730, had an enormous vogue. Thomson's universe is not without its horrors: in "Winter" a "swain disastered" perishes in the snow close to his wife, his children, his friends, and "the fire fair-blazing and the vestment warm"; in "Summer" "all-conquering Heat" causes "all the world without, unsatisfied and sick" to "toss" at noon, and "the Thunder holds his black tremendous throne"; in "Autumn," wherein

> The meteor sits, and shows the narrow path
> That winding leads through pits of death,

"a proud city, populous and rich" is seized by an earthquake and

> convulsive hurl'd
> Sheer from the black foundation, stench-involved,
> Into a gulf of blue sulphureous flame.

* *Saint-Albin (to his father).* Father, listen. Germeuil, don't go away. You owe it to him that you still have a son. Without him you would no longer have one. What was going to happen to me? I have Sophie because of him. It is Germeuil and my sister who saved her when she was in danger from me and my uncle. They had just one moment. She had just one place of safety. They snatched her away from my violence. Are you going to punish them because I was wrong? Come, Cecile. We must soften the best of fathers. (*He brings his sister to kneel with him at his father's feet.*)

The Father. Daughter, I pardon you; what do you want from me?

Saint-Albin. To assure her happiness forever, and yours, and mine. Cecile . . . Germeuil. They love and adore each other. Father, give way to your own kindness. Let this day be the most beautiful day of our lives. (*He hurries to Germeuil, and calls Sophie.*) Germeuil, Sophie . . . Let us all kneel at my father's feet.

Sophie (kneeling before the father, whose hands she holds through most of the rest of the scene). Sir.

The Father (leaning over and lifting them up). My children . . . my children. Cecile, you love Germeuil?

Cécile. Father, pardon me.

The Father. Why did you hide it from me? Children, you do not know your father. Come, Germeuil . . . I had intended you to have my daughter. May you make her the happiest one of women.

[I have omitted one speech and a few phrases; the omissions do not affect the point of the excerpt.]

But since it would be dissonant to sing "the cruel raptures of the savage kind," Thomson turns to a shepherd on the grassy turf in the midst of his many-bleating flock, "of various cadence"; passes on to a tribute to Wealth, Commerce, Liberty, Law, and God —

> Inspiring God! who, boundless Spirit all,
> And unremitting Energy pervades,
> Adjusts, sustains, and agitates the whole.

God is especially tender of the feeling heart. When Musidora, in "Summer," goes bathing in a woodland stream, she is spied upon by Damon, who, however, behaves in the most exemplary manner:

> What shall he do? In sweet confusion lost,
> And dubious flutterings, he a while remain'd:
> A pure ingenuous elegance of soul,
> A delicate refinement, known to few,
> Perplex'd his breast, and urg'd him to retire:
> But love forbade.

Having satisfied his voyeurism to the full, Damon writes this note to Musidora, which he throws on the river bank:

> "Bathe on, my fair,
> Yet unbeheld save by the sacred eye
> Of faithful love: I go to guard thy haunt,
> To keep from thy recess each vagrant foot,
> And each licentious eye."

Not unnaturally the naked Musidora reads this document "with wild surprise" and flies

> to find those robes
> Which blissful Eden knew not.

After she gets dressed, she pens a note which she hangs on a beech tree. Her epistle coyly concludes:

> ". . . the time may come you need not fly."

Comment on this mixture of sex and sensibility would be super-fluous. The age thought it all very fine, and if there are green serpents, rattlesnakes, "the lively-shining leopard," keen hyenas, and man-eating lions in the tropics (as there are in "Summer"), this is all part of God's mysterious yet benevolent plan. A con-cluding "Hymn" leads us into the right way where "Universal Love" smiles all around,

From seeming evil still educing good.

As Thomson remarks at the very end: "I lose Myself in Him . . . Come then, expressive Silence, muse his Praise." Public "Liberty" somehow also gets involved.

So far as the general reading public is concerned, the most influential branch of this kind of writing was probably the novel of sensibility.* Such works were innumerable, but there is only room to list some leading titles and to discuss one or two of them. Here again the problem of categorization is virtually insoluble. It does not seem to me, for example, that Prévost's *Manon Lescaut* (1732), sentimental enough to have occasioned at least three major operas, comes under our classification, since "virtue" is absent from the lives of a young man without moral principle and a heroine whose main notion of success is to have a good time with males. At the other end of the temporal spectrum I assume that Jane Austen's *Sense and Sensibility*, begun in 1797 and published in 1811, marks an important turn in the vogue of the fiction of sensibility. The sentimental of course we have always with us.

Some of the devices of this eighteenth-century fictional genre — the orphan of mysterious but noble parentage, attempts at seduction or rape, imprisonment in jail or convent, enforced exile of the "Don't-darken-my-doors-again" variety, deserving poverty, the restoration of the rightful (and virtuous) heir to estates hitherto possessed by the villain — such topics were transferred to (sometimes from) the Gothic tale of terror. Novels of sensibility flooded Europe. Leading titles include Marivaux's unfinished *La Vie de Marianne* (1736–1742), known in English as *The Virtuous Orphan*; Richardson's widely disseminated *Pamela; or, Virtue Rewarded* (1740–1741), and his *Clarissa Harlowe* (1747–1748),

---

* I say this hesitantly since the theatrical vogue of certain leading plays, whether of the *comédie larmoyante*, *le drame*, the *bürgerliches Trauerspiel*, or middle-class drama type, was sometimes European and often prolonged. One runs into the problem of definition, but among representative samples of this sort of play (it commonly repudiated the heroic and stuck to the genteel) are such titles as Lillo, *The London Merchant* (1731); Nivelle de la Chaussée, *La Fausse Antipathie* (1733) and his *L'Ecole des mères* (1744); Marivaux, *La Mère confidente* (1736); Lessing, *Miss Sara Sampson* (1755; *Emilia Galotti* of 1772 is a more doubtful case); George Colman and David Garrick, *The Clandestine Marriage* (1766); Hugh Kelly, *False Delicacy* (1768); Mrs. Inchbald, *Every One Has His Fault* (1793); and A. F. F. von Kotzebue, *Menschenhass und Reue*, Englished by Benjamin Thompson as *The Stranger* (1793). This last, by the by, in some of its details curiously anticipates Oscar Wilde's *Lady Windermere's Fan*. Sentimentalism affected even Voltaire, whose *Nanine*, based on *Pamela*, was produced in 1749.

one of the great English novels; Rousseau's *Julie, ou La Nouvelle Héloïse* (1761), the subtitle of which is usually overlooked: *Lettres de deux amants, habitants d'une petite ville au pied des Alpes* (inaccurate in fact but pointing to the relation between sensibility and "Nature"); Henry Brooke's *The Fool of Quality* (1760–1762); Goldsmith's *The Vicar of Wakefield* (1766); Sterne's *A Sentimental Journey through France and Italy* (1768), which, like Rousseau, transforms erotic emotion into sensibility; Henry Mackenzie's *The Man of Feeling* (1771), which *begins* with chapter xi; and Goethe's *Die Leiden des jungen Werthers* (1774), which according to legend led sensitive young men to commit suicide and certainly increased the vogue of Ossian. A special niche should be kept for Bernardin de Saint-Pierre's *Paul et Virginie* (1786), the heroine of which drowns rather than take off her heavy clothing in order to be rescued from the sea by a naked sailor. I omit, perhaps wrongly, Marmontel's three volumes of *Contes moraux* (1765); I omit the first American novel, William Hill Brown's *The Power of Sympathy* (1789), aimed, like *Clarissa*, "to expose the dangerous Consequences of Seduction"; I omit Mrs. Inchbald and Mrs. Opie and other virtuous members of a mob of scribbling women; and I omit many shapeless German fictions that belong to this general category.

In their monumental *Samuel Richardson: A Biography* (Clarendon Press, 1971) T. C. Duncan Eaves and Ben D. Kimpel quote a letter dated December 8, 1741, from Aaron Hill to Richardson, written to smoke out the true author of *Pamela*. Part of the epistle runs:

Who could have dreamt, he should find, under the modest Disguise of a *Novel*, all the *Soul* of Religion, Good-breeding, Discretion, Good-nature, Wit, Fancy, Fine Thought, and Morality? — I have done nothing but read it to others, and hear others again read it, to me, ever since it came into my Hands; and I find I am likely to do nothing else, for I know not how long yet to come: because, if I lay the Book down, it comes after me. — When it has dwelt all Day long upon the Ear, It takes Possession, all Night, of the Fancy. . . . Yet, I confess, there is *One*, in the World, of whom I think with still greater Respect, than of PAMELA: and That is, of the wonderful AUTHOR of PAMELA.

The letter is illuminating. It exhibits the fascination this novel had for its readers, it hints at the connection between God and nature ("the *Soul* of Religion," in Hill's phrase) and virtuous feeling, and above all it assumes as a matter of course that the aim of sensibility is to reinforce the value patterns of the genteel. Indeed, one of the curious elements in this genre of fiction is the emotional attachment to social status displayed by the leading personages. The vicar of Wakefield, having been jailed, rejoices that on his release his parishioners still respect him as a minister. Pamela wants to rise from a serving maid to a lady of assured social position. Marianne in the Marivaux novel is forever fearful that somebody in good society will discover that she lives or has lived in a linen-draper's establishment. Harley in *The Man of Feeling* rescues a girl from a brothel but the girl proves to be the daughter of a genteel officer. The vast majority of the characters in *Clarissa* are "respectable," and so are those in *La Nouvelle Héloïse* — even Saint-Preux, though of "humble origin," is, like Werther, an educated young man, capable of becoming the friend of Lord Edward Bomston.*

It is a nice question in emotional arithmetic whether, in proportion to the lengths of the books that contain them, Marivaux's Marianne or Mackenzie's Harley weeps more often; both novels are among the wettest in Europe. It is a more important question to ponder whether weeping, which expressed everything from rapture to indignation, was common in eighteenth-century literature only, or found also in actual life. And it is an even more important problem, though an insoluble one, whether this excess of lachrymosity may not have produced by an understandable reaction the brutal indifference of a great many "virtuous" French revolutionaries to the terrors and the massacres they thought necessary to support the revolution.

The plots of most of these sentimental masterpieces can be reduced to three or four sentences and have little interest in themselves. Treatment is everything, and one may select *La Vie de Marianne*, translated by Mrs. Mary Collyer as *The Virtuous*

---

* In a curious monograph by Alexis François, *Le Premier Baiser de l'amour, ou Jean-Jacques Rousseau inspirateur d'estampes* (Geneva, 1920), the author reproduces a series of eighteenth-century engravings of a famous episode in *La Nouvelle Héloïse* and reprints Rousseau's instructions and comments on some of them. Neither the pictures nor the comments hint that Saint-Preux is, in the famous phrase from Daisy Ashford's *The Young Visiters* (*sic*), not quite a gentleman.

Orphan in 1743 (Mrs. Collyer "improved" the original French, omitted parts of the text, and invented an ending).* Marianne, daughter of a noble family, loses her parents, who are robbed and murdered in an attack on a stagecoach. As a child she is brought up by some virtuous villagers, but has to leave them, and under the care of a naive priest is confided to the protection of a rich hypocrite named de Climal, who lodges her with a linen-draper and, a combination of Tartuffe and Pecksniff, tries to seduce her. She attracts the attention of a handsome hero, de Valville, nephew of de Climal, moves in and out of convents, is once kidnapped through the influence of the de Valville family, and almost loses her lover to her bosom friend, Mlle Varthon. But Marianne has during her numerous mishaps won the admiration of Mme de Valville, the mother of her lover. In Mrs. Collyer's version all ends happily. But as Dr. Johnson said of Richardson's fiction, only a fool would read these volumes for the story: it is the climate of sensibility that matters.

Mrs. Collyer was obviously of this opinion. In her introduction she writes:

The reflections [mostly by Marianne] have nothing in them studied and forced, but are the language of the heart, the fruits of experience, dictated immediately by the circumstances of the person who makes them. The sentiments throughout have an uncommon delicacy and beauty in them; they do honor to morality, and ought to be cherished by everyone who would be truly polite [note the emphasis on status], and throw a luster and an attractive quality on his virtues . . .

Marianne tells her own story for the benefit of a single correspondent, and she writes, "The remembrance of these things brings tears into my eyes; and I am obliged, dear Madame, to break off, in order to dissipate the too painful ideas which crowd into my mind." When she discovers she has been put into a linen-draper's establishment she says: "Had I fallen from some superior region, I could not have been more chagrined than I was at my present situation. Persons whose sentiments are delicate are sooner cast down than others; their hearts are more sensible, their souls more tender than the rest of the world, and those humane dispositions, that make them more sensible of the superior, the God-like pleasure

---

* I have used the fine edition edited by William Harlin McBurney and Michael Francis Shugrue and printed by the Southern Illinois University Press (Carbondale and Edwardsville), 1965.

of doing good, here add an emphasis to every misery." Marianne learns to call Mme de Valville "Maman" and thus describes her:

She had a greater attachment to the moral virtues than to the peculiar duties of Christianity, regarded more the punctilious exercises of instrumental religion than she complied with them, honored more the very devout than she thought of being so herself, loved God more than she feared Him, and conceived of His justice and goodness in a manner almost peculiar to herself and, from the benevolent dispositions of her own tender heart, justly inferred what must be those in the tender Parent of mankind who had fixed them there.

On his deathbed the repentant de Climal asks Marianne's forgiveness and adjures here: "Be virtuous in spite of all opposition, and you will find that 'to be good is to be happy.' It will raise you above many of the miseries of life, give you charms that time will not be able to efface, and render you forever lovely, forever blessed."

And so on and so on. When Marianne takes from Mlle Varthon a love letter which the fickle de Valville has written to Mlle Varthon, who has become Marianne's friend and knows nothing of de Valville's expressed affection for Marianne, "I took it up with a trembling hand and durst not at first look upon those characters which had before often filled me with delight. At last, however, I cast a look upon it, and wet it with my tears." And when Marianne is at last recognized by an uncle through the agency of the inexpressibly benevolent M. de Rosand, the scene runs as follows:

Advancing hastily to me, "Oh, my dear niece," cried he, taking me in his arms and embracing me, "thou dear remains of my lost brother!" This tender exclamation at first softened me to such a degree that I was unable to speak to him. At last recovering myself, "Dear Sir," cried I, looking upon him with a tender kind of pleasure, "you are the first, the only person I know of my kindred. How happy do I think myself in being related to you!" While I was speaking M. Dorsin and another person were coming in; but how great, how inexpressible was my surprise when, lifting my eyes and looking over my uncle's shoulder, I saw a person whom I had long before thought dead — my dear friend, my indulgent [foster-] parent, M. de Rosand! I started, gave a shriek, stood motionless, while a flood of tender ideas flowed into my mind. My uncle meanwhile retired a few steps, and M. de Rosand held me in his arms while joy tied both our tongues.

At last he cried out, "Oh, my child!" Here the tears trickled down his aged cheeks, and he was too full to say more.

"Oh, my father!" then cried I and stopped too and clasped my arms about him. The tears gushed from my eyes, which, while he kissed me, mingled with his. Sure there never was a more tender interview! What a pleasing painful transport! Our minds, Madame, are capable of receiving only a certain degree of pleasure, and all beyond that is pain. Our passions are confused sensations which, when violent, swell the heart. Its emotions become turbulent, and the excess of our delight we find nearly allied to pain.

In the next pages "my uncle and M. Dorsin" are "bathed in tears," Marianne, finding herself very weak and "almost ready to faint," sits down, everybody sits down, the repentant de Valville turns up, having thoughtfully brought along a coach, and various hostile relatives appear. But the uncle invites everybody to dinner, and Marianne, assured of her social status, informs an inimical old lady, "The honor of a virtuous mind is derived from itself and can receive no addition from the accidental advantages of birth or fortune, nor can the want of them render a person truly valuable worthy of reproach." Some days after her wedding ("the porter's whistle informed us that company was at the gate, which proved to be several persons of quality"), Marianne is commanded to tell her life story to the Queen of France. Cinderella cannot ask for more.

The rest of the vast library of fictional sensibility is much like *La Vie de Marianne.* Clarissa, to be sure, is made of sterner stuff, but like Charles II she is an unconscionable time dying, and her emotional state seems to be due less to the physiological shock of having been raped than to the feeling that, in refusing to marry the detestable Mr. Solmes, she has been an undutiful daughter. The letters of Saint-Preux and Julie are bathed in rapture, desolation, melancholy, and longing; Julie, dying, desires Saint-Preux to bring up her children. *The Man of Feeling* produces sentences of this type: "There was a tear in her eye, — the sick man kissed it off in its bud, smiling through the dimness of his own," and Harley dies when he discovers that Miss Walton, whom he adores, returns his affection. The narrator then tells us: "I sometimes visit his grave, I sit in the hollow of the tree. It is worth a thousand homilies: every noble feeling rises within me! every beat of my heart awakens a virtue!"

We shall come to the stormy passions of Werther in another connection. Saint-Preux may have been a new type in European literature, the weak hero loved by woman, and he anticipates the Byronism that is to come, just as Werther's indignation at being patronized by persons of higher rank anticipates Robespierre's egalitarianism. Talleyrand once said that the French Revolution was born out of vanity. But it was nourished by this immense sea of passion — religious, erotic, nostalgic, self-pitying — emotionalism as fundamental to the age of the Enlightenment as the Enlightenment itself.

V

Neoclassicism and Its Variants

We earlier remarked on the amusing image painted by Philip Guedalla of Edward Gibbon, author of the stately *The Decline and Fall of the Roman Empire*, gazing from the security of the age of Johnson across centuries of turbulence to the security of the age of the Antonines. The Guedalla figure has at least two circumstances in its favor, one contemporary and the other traditional. To many intelligent readers the eighteenth century is all of a piece until the American revolution or that in France. It exhibits a surface tranquillity so changeless that it is easy to think of Joseph Addison and *The Spectator Papers* as contemporary with Boswell's *Life of Samuel Johnson*, issued two years after the beginning of the French revolution. The traditional support arises from a vague idea not uncommon in the eighteenth century that the states of Europe, however they might quarrel, were all, or almost all, provinces in a great Christian community, an over-arching *res publica*, the general structure of which was, so to speak, dictated by heaven. Various elements contributed to the force of this illusion. One was the continuing existence of a universal church, the Protestants being younger, and the Russians older, deviants from the one true faith, to which they would eventually return. Moreover, there was still a Holy Roman Empire, and some kings bore titles such as "Defender of the Faith," "Most Catholic King," "Most Christian King," and the like. Indeed, as late as the fall of Napoleon, the Emperor of Russia, the Emperor of Austria, and the King of Prussia solemnly bound themselves by a public announcement to conduct the affairs of the nations in the spirit of Jesus Christ — the so-called Holy

Alliance. Only the British, that nation of shopkeepers, refrained. But what could you expect from a nation of shopkeepers?

This unity, this apparent harmony in the life of Europe was enriched by the centralizing tendencies in thought and art associated, as we have seen, with the policy of Louis XIV. The Augustan age in France was founded on the historical premise that all of Europe is based upon the history of Greece and Rome. The life of this great French cultural idea, even though French replaced Latin as an international language and became the language of the polite world, proved to be both transient and in some sense specious. An earlier chapter traced the precarious balance of social and political forces in eighteenth-century Europe. Even in that "tranquil" age hereditary princes were not always sure whether they could peacefully ascend their thrones upon the deaths of their sires. It is illuminating to remember that some of the great armed conflicts of the age are called the War of the Spanish Succession, the War of the Austrian Succession, and the War of the Polish Succession; illuminating also that chapter xxvi of Voltaire's *Candide* (1759) shows that unfortunate young man taking supper at an inn with six strangers, each of whom is a monarch in exile. If monarchy was thus unstable, so in most countries was the hereditary nobility, nervously defending its privileges against the king above and against the commoners below. In all nations with an important middle class, that class was dissatisfied, now allying itself with the throne against the aristocrats and now with the aristocrats against the throne. And, as we have noted, the century is also scarred with uprisings of a greater or less degree of violence by the peasants, the yeomanry (a somewhat stabler group), and mobs in the cities.

At once idealistic and utilitarian, the Enlightenment, its roots in the seventeenth century, reached a climax in that most subtle of anti-Christian documents, the *Encyclopédie*, and seemed to impose uniformity on the intellectual world. Philosophers, however, seldom agree very long; and deists, skeptics, materialists, atheists, and "liberal" theologians broke into or broke up the intellectual order of the Enlightenment. Moreover, this insistence upon reason as the governing factor in life immediately created opposition, and a second tendency referred the great issues of existence not to the head but to the heart. As we have seen, the value patterns of

Europe grew more complicated with the vogue of the graveyard school, of emotionalized and mystical religion, of Ossian, the ballad revival, and a renewed interest in "ancient" music, an emotional drive resulting from a fresh examination of racial or national origins, the thrill from reading "horrid" novels or witnessing bloody plays, and the growing belief that the commoner joys and sorrows of ordinary persons rather than of princes were the proper stuff for fiction and the stage. The cry of the heart disturbed the empire of reason and the harmony of the eighteenth century. So much we have already seen.

Classicism itself underwent a series of developments and "modernizations," which are, to be sure, rather oddly bounded by a late return upon the classicism of the time of Louis XIV. Interest in the ancient world moved from the stateliness of such a painting as Van Dyck's "Portrait of Charles I Hunting" to the severe formalism of David's "Oath of the Horatii," but on this long journey it developed a variety of new interpretations of the past, to which we shall come. Two things, however, should be postulated. There is the puzzle of nomenclature, complicated by the term baroque; and the Augustan classicism of the age of Louis XIV did not totally disappear in the eighteenth century. To avoid confusion I shall hereafter mean by "classicism" the monumental classicism of the court at Versailles in the time of the Grand Monarque, and I shall mean by "neoclassicism" the interest of the eighteenth century in the ancient world, even when that interest includes the survival here and there of monumentality.

Classicism in the age of Louis XIV, associated with a principle of authority in the state and in the arts,* simultaneously worshiped at the shrines of such authors as Homer and Vergil and sought to draw from the works of other writers eternal principles that would raise the art of the moderns to an equality with the monumentality

---

* A succinct but illuminating discussion of the relations of classicism in the age of Louis XIV to contemporary movements in science and philosophy in that period, not to speak of a noble style as a support to the class structure of the time, is by W. H. Barber, part of chapter iii, "Cultural Change in Western Europe," of vol. VI of the *New Cambridge Modern History: The Rise of Great Britain and Russia*, Cambridge, 1970. Whatever one thinks of the "rules" nowadays, or of the apparent suppression of the emotions by a classical superstructure, harm in this contradiction, he says, "was mitigated in fact by the creative energies of the major writers, and by the general acceptance of the view that the essential function of imaginative literature was to please, to move the reader." Augustan classicism both agreed with and helped to create culture among the elite.

of the past. Architecture had this grandeur; that is, it sought to impress rather than to charm. In literature and drama the intent was to cut away all the superfluous ornamentation of the baroque and reveal basic concepts about humanity, God, and the universe. Thus, comedy, when it was successful, dwelt upon the eternal follies of mankind, and tragedy delineated man's inevitable sorrows, most striking in the lives of kings.

But edification can become monotonous, the solemn turns into the pompous, and the fable about bending the bow of Odysseus has special applicability to the lesser writers of Europe. With the passing of the great king, a new age set in. The Regency followed in France. Not only in France but elsewhere humanity rediscovered that it could dance and laugh, sing and make light-hearted love, that though stoicism was part of the classical inheritance, so was epicureanism, and that if Horace gave the law to poets, Horace also advised his contemporaries to eat, drink, and be merry, for tomorrow we die — the *carpe diem* of the *Odes*. Augustan grandeur yielded to rococo art, the solemn "correctness" of Poussin's "The Rape of the Sabine Women," in which everybody turns into statuary, is replaced by the fairy-tale landscape of Watteau's "Pilgrimage to Cythera," in which everybody is informal, and Fénelon's *Traité de l'existence de Dieu* is forgotten in Voltaire's "Les prêtres ne sont pas ce qu'un vain peuple pense" (*Oedipe*, 1718) and the *Lettres persanes* of Montesquieu of 1721. In England likewise one passes from the baroque splendors of *Paradise Lost* and *Paradise Regained* to the homely prose of *Robinson Crusoe* (1719), and the solemnity of Milton's *The Doctrine and Discipline of Divorce* is forgotten in the frivolity of Matthew Prior (1664–1721):

> The merchant, to secure his treasure,
>   Conveys it in a borrow'd name:
> Euphelia serves to grace my measure;
>   But Chloe is my real flame.
>
>   .   .   .   .   .
>
> My lyre I tune, my voice I raise;
>   But with my numbers mix my sighs:
> And while I sing Euphelia's praise,
>   I fix my soul on Chloe's eyes.

This is not classicism but neoclassicism, although, I repeat, classicism in the seventeenth-century sense did not wholly die away.

ii

To eighteenth-century culture the classical past presented three, possibly four, great phases: the Platonic phase, a tradition of ideal and changeless truth and beauty; the Plutarchian phase, a tradition of civic virtue and stoic calm; and the Anacreontic phase, a tradition of light loves and sensuous pleasures. The fourth phase would be Juvenalian, represented by the scathing satire of Swift and the bitter cartoons of Goya, but the moral indignation of such artists is essentially a variant of "republican" indignation at luxury and vice, and may for convenience be put in the Plutarchian category. The Platonic tradition, or at least the Platonic tradition as leaders of eighteenth-century aesthetic philosophy conceived it, is represented by the work of Winckelmann and Reynolds. The Plutarchian (and stoic) tradition runs all the way from the tragedies of Corneille through the austerity of John Adams. The Anacreontic strain produces the pastorals of the age, its amatory tales and poems, the light Horatian satire, the elegant compliments, and the epicurean delight in life of the period. Typical are Montesquieu's *Le Temple de Gnide*, Anacreontic poets in Germany such as Hagedorn, Gellert, Gleim and Ewald von Kleist,* Tom Moore's version of Anacreon, canvases by Watteau, Fragonard, and others, and the minor decorative arts. The hold of neoclassicism in the period varied from country to country and from decade to decade, but it was continually strengthened by the enthusiasm of archaeologists and dilettantes, by new editions, interpretations, translations, and imitations of classical authors, and by an increasing sense that useful parallels could be drawn between ancient history and the modern state.

It is difficult for the twentieth century to understand why a knowledge of the ancient world should be fundamental to almost any conceivable pattern of education, but so it was. In the eighteenth century an educable youth, once past his ABC's, was exposed as soon as possible to Lily's Latin grammar † and the

---

* Even Gottsched, commonly dismissed as a stuffy reactionary, translated some of the odes of Anacreon. See also, for an anthology, vol. 45 of the *Deutsche National-Litteratur* series, Stuttgart, 1894.

† An American equivalent was *The American Latin Grammar; or, A Complete Introduction to the Latin Tongue: Formed from a Careful Perusal of the Classic*

Colloquies of Corderius, two common school texts in English schools, and their equivalents in other countries. He was expected to learn the elements of Latin and, if possible, Greek, to read the standard Latin authors, and to know something of ancient history. Otherwise he could not advance, though in Great Britain some of the Dissenting academies showed as little enthusiasm for Latin and Greek as did Benjamin Franklin. But a promising pupil could not, for example, enter Harvard College unless he understood Vergil, Cicero, or "any such classical author," spoke or wrote "good Latin," and displayed some skill, however dim, in the making of Latin verse. The Harvard requirements merely echoed academic requirements in Europe and Latin America. The Jesuits, before their order was dissolved, were the schoolmasters of Catholic Europe, teachers who gave their students a thorough grounding in theology, philosophy (with Christian rebuttal), Latin, usually Greek, and always ancient history — Herodotus, Xenophon, Plutarch, Livy, Sallust, Quintus Curtius, Cornelius Nepos are representative names. The Jansenists, rivals of the Jesuits, offered a similar program. At Port Royal, Racine, despite Jansenist distrust of the theater, learned the stories he later turned into such great dramas as *Bérénice*, *Iphigénie*, and *Phèdre*. In his case, as Lanson puts it, a Jansenist education was imposed upon a sensibility essentially Greek. His elder rival, Corneille, a product of Jesuit training at Rouen, strayed afield into Spanish themes, but works such as his *Horace*, *Cinna*, *Polyeucte*, and *Sertorius* spring from the antique world, as did many of the "heroick" plays of the Restoration in England, groups of tragedies by Voltaire and Alfieri, and opera librettos by Metastasio. In Germany every schoolmaster was something of a classicist, though it is said that Greek was virtually unknown there until the 1690's; and in the Protestant states theologians, scholars, and schoolmasters of a right Protestant sort played the roles taken by the Jesuits in Catholic Europe. (In Protestant Prussia, indeed, Frederick the Great protected the order and let the Jesuit "colleges" continue.) The English situation was

Authors, and the Writings of the Best Grammarians, both English and Latin. By Robert Ross, A.M. Published principally for the Use of the Grammar School at Nassau-Hall, in Princeton, and particularly recommended to all those who design to send their Children to New-Jersey College. The Fifth Edition, carefully revised, corrected, and enlarged. . . . New-York, James Parker, for Garrat Noel . . . 1770.

like that in Germany, though Scotsmen had on the whole a higher reputation for learning, and sometimes for pedantry.

It seemed to no cultivated person extraordinary that a tract intended for the moral training of a future king of France should be called *Télémaque*, or that the Abbé Barthélemy should spend thirty years writing *Le Voyage du jeune Anacharsis en Grèce*, in which a young Scythian, like a young European, makes the grand tour of the Alexandrian world. If Latin was no longer a universal tongue, it was a tongue universally studied. If Greek came limping after, this was partly because of its difficulty and partly because the vast shadow of the Roman Empire hid ancient Attica from modern Europe.

Since nothing crumbles more surely than the fame of a leading scholar, it would be idle to try to trace the progress of classical studies in the decades here under survey. Some names and institutions still escape the ruin of oblivion. In France the Academy of Inscriptions and Belles-Lettres took up the heritage of the Benedictines and became a center for research in classical antiquities. From Italy Scipione Maffei (1675–1755), scholar, historian, and poet, visited Provence, was struck by its history and its ruins, and produced *Galliae Antiquitates Selectae*, which, published in Paris in 1733, heartened French antiquarianism. In England the famous Richard Bentley (1662–1742), now mainly remembered for remarking: "A very pretty poem, Mr. Pope, but you must not call it Homer," in his famous *Dissertation on the Epistles of Phalaris* demonstrated how a skilled philologian distinguishes between an honest text and a spurious one. In Italy Lodovico Antonio Muratori (1672–1750), called the father of Italian history and by no means confined to the classical world only, devoted fifteen years to the twenty-seven volumes of *Rerum Italicarum Scriptores* (1723–1751). His *Novus Thesaurus Veterum Inscriptorum* is said to be of primary importance in the science of epigraphy. In Italy also Egidio Forcellini (1688–1768) amidst immense difficulties put together his *Totius Latinitatis Lexicon* in 1753, the base from which all later Latin dictionaries take off. The Visconti family was responsible for the *Museum Pio-Clementinum* (1782–1787), which made available to Europe descriptions and illustrations of the treasures of the Vatican, and Ennio Quirino Visconti (1751–1818), who later headed the staff of the Louvre and published much on Greek antiquities, was one of the first to recognize the significance of the Elgin marbles. In Germany Johann August Ernesti (1707–1781), orator and theologian, produced a famous edition of Cicero (1739), the most commonly read of Latin prose writers. Johann Jakob Reiske (1716–1774) edited Plutarch, Dionysius of Halicarnassus, and others, and wrote an influential autobiography, published in 1783. The famous Christian Gottlob Heyne (1729–1812) brought out the first "scientific" study of Greek mythology, edited classical texts, and at his seminar in Göttingen trained, it is said, some 150 professors of the classics. Friedrich August Wolf (1759–1824), who did not like Heyne, published among other matter his *Prolegomena ad Homerum* (1795), which, though anticipated by an odd *Essay on the Original Genius of Homer* (1769) from the British traveler and antiquarian Robert Wood (ca. 1717–1771), raised the vast question of the origins of the *Iliad* and the *Odyssey*. And Joseph Eckhel (1737–1798), bringing out his *Doctrina Numorum Veterum* (1787–1789), put a flooring under numismatics. He was a Jesuit and became director of the mint at Vienna.

These shards and fragments of a lost world of learning cannot convey the excitement of scholarship in the eighteenth century. Yet even such leading minds as these probably had smaller immediate general effect upon the politics, art, and thought of the age than did two other sorts of classicists: translators, and the authors of more humble textbooks, who derived from advanced scholarship what they put into the schoolbooks. The purpose of such volumes can be gleaned from this characteristic passage in Anthony Blackwell's *Introduction to the Classics* (1718). By the writers of antiquity, he says,

the Precepts of a virtuous and happy life are set off in the Light and Gracefulness of clear and moving Expression; and *Eloquence* is meritoriously employ'd in indicating and adorning *Religion*. This makes deep *Impressions* on the minds of young Gentlemen, and charms them with the love of Goodness so engagingly dress'd out and so beautifully commended.*

* I find this in M. L. Clarke, *Greek Studies in England, 1700–1830*, Cambridge, 1943, but I have not been able to lay hands on the original. Most classical instruction had this moral aim. In a note to the first canto of *Don Juan* Byron wryly illustrates the naiveté of such pedagogy. He tells of a school text of Martial he was given to study, the grosser epigrams all excised from the text and then collected in the appendix. Thus both scholarship and morality were served.

In all the Western world, even in North America, an area in which Sandys, the historian of classical scholarship, could find nobody worth mentioning before 1800, elementary textbooks having to do with the ancients insisted that morality was the great lesson to be learned. The implanting of virtue was more important than historical curiosity. Persons as varied as Madame Dacier, Thomas Jefferson, and Lord Chesterfield in *Letters to His Son* (1774) insisted that this was true. The phrase ran: "Reason the guide; classicism the adviser."

As for translations, the text of every principal author of antiquity and most of the minor ones was turned into one or more modern languages in the period under survey, often two, three, four, or more times. In the single instance of Homer, Madame Dacier brought out her controversial French versions of the *Iliad* in 1699, the *Odyssey* in 1708; and a new edition of these, corrected and augmented, published at Paris in 1766, included in the prefatory matter a discussion of Pope's preface to his *Iliad*, which had appeared at intervals between 1715 and 1720. An *Odyssey* only partly by Pope was printed in 1725–26. In the German of Johann Heinrich Voss the *Odyssey* (in 1781) and the *Iliad* (in 1793) appeared in versions so influential as to have colored Homeric scholarship in Germany ever since. The Italian poet Monti translated the *Iliad* in 1810 and revised his poem in 1812.

What strikes a modern reader of these and other translations of Homer during the later seventeenth and the eighteenth centuries (and the same is true of other translation of other classics) is a paradox. On the one hand they are as up-to-date in tone and treatment as our own "modern" versions of Sophocles or Catullus. On the other hand they seem to us oddly artificial. Possibly every age gets the translations it deserves. Homer, said Pope in his preface, is universally allowed to have had the greatest invention of any writer whatever. His work is "a wild paradise, where, if we cannot see all the beauties as distinctly as in an ordered garden, it is only because the number of them is infinitely greater." He is "a copious nursery," wherein "if some things are too luxuriant it is owing to the richness of the soil," and if other things are weak, it is because "they are overrun and oppressed by those of a stronger nature." Homer, he avers, is filled with sublimity, the first poet to teach the language of the gods to men.

After such flourishes the modern reader expects something wild and disorderly, perhaps a poem such as John Donne or Christopher Smart might produce. He gets nothing of the sort. The eighteenth century takes over. Waiving all question of Pope's knowledge of Greek and of the appropriateness of the rhymed couplet for a translation of the Homeric hexameter, one finds, with a certain wry amusement, that the wrath of Achilles has here been transmuted into a political problem in a status society. The gods have demanded that Agamemnon give up Chryseïs, and when he balks at doing so, a divine plague breaks out in the besieging army, as such plagues had done during the Thirty Years War. A leading general, by name Achilles, in character much like Wallenstein in Schiller, demands a meeting of the privy council. The council meets and in turn consults the church in the person of Calchas, whose function lies somewhere between that of a royal astrologer and that of an archbishop of Canterbury. When, though advised to do so by the priest, Agamemnon still refuses to dismiss his mistress unless he is compensated by getting another woman, Achilles taunts him, the king then announces he is going to take over Achilles' doxy, by name Briseïs, Achilles grows more and more vituperative, and Agamemnon opposes his insolent subordinate by the doctrine of the divine right of kings.

> Jove himself shall guard a monarch's right,

he says, and also

> kings are subject to the gods alone.

The privy council supports the king, and the embittered general removes himself and his forces from the allied army. Although Achilles asserts in very rough terms the right of the individual to keep what he has — a philosophy of individualism prophetic of romantic individuality — at heart he remains an eighteenth-century nobleman, who, when the two timid heralds approach him to take his Briseïs to the king's tent, declares he has nothing against them as ambassadors but that, a gentleman in his own right, he will not be put upon by tyranny. All this has some remote likeness to Homer, but, as Bentley said, it is not Homer; and eighteenth-century cynicism must have been further increased, despite the assumption that the classics were supposed to teach virtue, by the fact that divinity enlists simultaneously on the sides of both the Trojans and the Greeks. The gods not only lie to each other, but, invited to an imperial feast, they set off to eat, drink, and be merry, forgetting all about the little wretched race of men. At the end of the tale, Hector, the only thoroughly decent character in Pope's story, is killed and his body treated with a ferocity suggesting the future judicial torture of Damiens, who attempted to assassinate Louis XV. As Arnold Hauser observes in *The Social History of Art*, an aristocratic society threatened by change and longing for permanence clung to neoclassicism in all fields as a philosophical insurance against revolt. He notes also that aristocratic society encouraged two great enemies of neoclassicism, sensibility and the Gothic revival. It is equally important to notice that eighteenth-century versions of antiquity are often little more than eighteenth-century problems transferred backward in time.

It is of course difficult to estimate the effect of any educational pattern or the reading of any book or set of books upon those who study them. Only a few outstanding personalities in any generation show the direct influence of classical learning. It is also clear that many young gentlemen did not always improve either their religion or their morals by reading Vergil, Cicero, Ovid, Horace, and the rest. So far as one can guess, two great leaders of political upset, Washington, who established a republic, and Napoleon, who tried to revive a Roman empire, though one was called the Cincinnatus of the West and the other denounced as a tyrannical Caesar, owed little to their classical reading. Obviously also two arch-conservatives, Montesquieu with his *Considérations sur les causes de la grandeur des Romains et de leur décadence* (1734) and Gibbon with his *History of the Decline and Fall of the Roman Empire* (1776–1788), each of whom knew far more ancient history than did either Washington or Napoleon, drew gloomy conclusions about virtue in the ancient world. They left sprightly influences to a popular writer, Charles Rollin, who wrote a *Histoire ancienne des Egyptiens, des Carthaginois, des Assyriens, des Mèdes et des Perses, des Macédoniens, des Grècs* (in fourteen volumes!) in 1730–1738 and followed it in 1738 with a *Histoire romaine*. Rollin was often reprinted, widely translated, and enormously read, partly because he was thought to be a martyr (he defended Jansenism, came out against the bull *Unigenitus*, and was persecuted by the Jesuits), partly because he united the Bible with classical history, but mainly because he was heavily on the side of virtue. Among other leading revolutionary figures the results of classical studies seem very contradictory. The few classical allusions in Tom Paine and Marat are little more than easy journalism. But Rousseau's egalitarianism and his celebration of virtue owe much to Plutarch, Thomas Jefferson was forever recommending classical authors to young men and importing classical texts and translations from abroad, Benjamin Rush praised the Greek commonwealths, John Adams read soberly in ancient literature, and a study by Harold T. Parker, entitled *The Cult of Antiquity and the French Revolutionaries* (1937), not only demonstrates the central place of classical teaching in the *collèges* (secondary schools) but documents the study of Vergil, Horace, Livy, Cicero, Phaedrus, Sallust, Cornelius Nepos, Quintus Curtius, Ovid, and Tacitus in all or some of the schools he examined.

After analyzing representative revolutionary newspapers in France, Parker turns up numerous quotations and allusions to Latin writers (none, apparently, to the Greeks), most of which have to do with the glory and decline of the Roman republic. Charlotte Corday, the great-granddaughter of Corneille, read Plutarch, Tacitus, and Cicero, and in assassinating Marat thought she had acted like a Roman. Madame Roland, the Egeria of the Girondins, often spoke of herself as Cato's wife (Roland as Cato is an interesting idea), said she ought to have been a Roman or a Spartan woman, and thought the French theater should devote itself to plays like *Catiline* or *The Death of Caesar*. Stanley Loomis gives us this picture of the Girondins as orators in the Constituent Assembly:

Toga-like coats and large flowing bows of muslin worn as cravats became the uniform of their 'party'. Their long hair, hanging loose and cut in a Brutus fringe, set them apart from the common run of Deputies. In addressing the Assembly they made frequent use of their profiles, lifting and slightly turning their heads away from the audience. Barbaroux, whose nose was much admired as being 'Roman', made frequent use of this conceit. Their passion for the Rome of Plutarch, the Rome of Charlotte Corday's dreams, carried them beyond reasonable limits. One of their number, Gaudet, never referred to 'God' in his oaths; he always spoke of 'the gods'. Vergniaud preferred to have it said that he and his groups were deputies from the Peloponnesus rather than from the homely Gironde. Louis XVI was generally either 'Tarquin' or 'Caligula'; their references to Cato, the Gracchi, to Brutus and Caesar became as tiresome as they were cryptic.*

Abigail Adams, the wife of John Adams, though she had no formal classical tutoring and lamented that women were not better educated, consciously modeled herself upon a Roman matron, and referred in the 1780's and 1790's to Cicero, Catiline, the Myrmidons of Achilles, Aurelian, the Amphictyonic League, Solon, Seneca, Jugurtha, and others. She wrote Mrs. Warren from London in 1787:

Had Pericles lived in the present day, he could not have made the boast which he does in his funeral oration over the Athenians, saying, that they were the *only people* who thought those who did not lend their assistance in State affairs, not indolent but good for nothing. It is indeed a pleasing presage of future good when the most promising youth shrink not from danger through a fondness for those delights which a peaceful affluent life bestows . . . esteeming it a dishonor that their country should stand in need of any thing which their valor can achieve.†

Not all neoclassicists were conservative. Not all revolutionaries were neoclassicists. It is therefore difficult to identify closely among the eighteenth-century elite a cause-and-effect relation between what they were taught and what they later thought and did. Nevertheless, the eighteenth-century world was as steeped in neoclassicism as the twentieth-century world is steeped in technology.

iii

Let us turn to the three great phases of antiquity interesting to the eighteenth century. Every man, says Emerson, is either a Platonist or an Aristotelian; and it is probable that at no time in the history of the West has Platonism (or Neoplatonism), however distorted, totally disappeared from the stream of thought. In

* Stanley Loomis, *Paris in the Terror*, Penguin Books, 1970, p. 47. I owe much to this study and to Harold T. Parker's monograph, mentioned in the text.
† This is from Charles Francis Adams, ed., *Letters of Mrs. Adams*, 4th ed., Boston, 1848, pp. 324–325. But see also Stewart Mitchell, ed., *New Letters of Abigail Adams, 1789–1801*, Boston, 1947, and Lyman H. Butterfield and others, eds., *Adams Family Correspondence*, vols. I and II (1761–1778), Cambridge, Mass., 1963, vols. III and IV (1778–1782), Cambridge, Mass., 1973.

seventeenth-century England the Cambridge Platonists were important, and on the Continent seventeenth-century mystics, combining Christian theology with some form of Platonism or its offshoots, were likewise significant. Among writers influential on eighteenth-century thinking Lord Shaftesbury, who thought the mind of man is attuned to the cosmic order, was notably influential in Germany, particularly in German thinking about art. The Germans developed no great political ardor, though they admired the American revolution and the creation of the American republic, and some of them were enthusiastic, at least for a time, about the French revolution. The great alteration in German culture was to be philosophic, not political, and the revolution in aesthetic theory was important in two ways: under the urging of Lessing German writers were encouraged to throw off the hegemony of the French and return to a national tradition; and under the influence of Winckelmann the Germans were encouraged to believe that perfect models in art were not Gothic but Hellenistic. The reconciliation of these two tendencies was not easy, and perhaps it was never achieved.*

Winckelmann, who was one of the strangest geniuses of the century, created a never-never land that he called Greece, a timeless Arcadia filled with beautiful people, a utopia that attracted the interest of such leading German writers as Wieland, Schiller, Hölderlin, Goethe, Heinse, and eventually Heinrich Heine. The son of a poor shoemaker, Johann Joachim Winckelmann (1717–1768) was born in a small Brandenburg village. After some preliminary schooling, he went to Berlin at seventeen to study under Christian Tobias Damm, one of the few Grecians then in Germany. At nineteen he managed to visit Hamburg with just enough money to buy a few classical texts from the library of Fabricius. In order to keep alive he taught a village school at Seehausen, where, wrapped in an old coat and curled up in a chair on winter nights,

---

* An immediate instance of the difficulty of reconciling neoclassical theory and nationalizing tendencies is Lessing himself. He was so far a classicist as to accept Winckelmann's theories with reservations, but in his influential set of theatrical essays and reviews, *Hamburgische Dramaturgie* (1767–1769), written with the intent of fostering a truly national German theater, he argued against the three neoclassical unities, saying that the only unity prescribed by Aristotle is unity of action, and even this Lessing construes loosely. Lessing's doctrine made room not only for Shakespeare but, in the event, for German Storm-and-Stress dramas. The best known of these are Goethe's *Götz von Berlichingen* (1773) and Schiller's *Die Räuber* (1781).

he read Greek (including Plato) till midnight, then awoke at four in the morning to read Greek for two more hours. In Dresden he saw marble statuary in the baroque style, paintings by Veronese, Titian, and Raphael, and in packing-cases he was not allowed to open, a collection of statues known as the Vestal Virgins (in reality funerary urns) dug up at Herculaneum and later brought to Dresden by Augustus III. His homosexual tendencies were expressed by passionate friendships for young men, usually of superior social station, and by his celebration of male friendship among the ancients. He attracted the notice of Heinrich von Bünau, who had retired to his estate at Nöthnitz, near Dresden, who had a library of 42,000 books, and who hired Winckelmann as a secretary.

At Dresden, as elsewhere, the study of coins and intaglios was an important basis of instruction in the arts of antiquity, and there the Academy of Art was directed by Christian Ludwig von Hagedorn, the brother of the poet. Despite his poverty, Winckelmann seems to have moved with some degree of ease in the artistic and academic circles of Saxony. But Saxony was not classic ground. A passionate desire to go to Rome obsessed the shoemaker's son. With a cynicism anticipating Heine's "conversion" to Christianity, Winckelmann allowed himself to be "converted" to the Roman Catholic religion. He sufficiently impressed the Elector of Saxony to receive from that ruler a stipend of two hundred thalers for his journey to Italy. In Rome he took on various library or custodial jobs, commonly under prelates, and also became a friend of Raphael Mengs, the painter. Though Winckelmann's first impressions of the Eternal City had been lukewarm, he grew more and more enamored of what was for him, as it was for Europe, the capital of antiquity. To chronicle his friendships, his quarrels, his enthusiasms, and his various posts is here unnecessary. Yearning to visit Greece but feeling he must first revisit Germany, he traveled to Vienna, where the Empress Maria Theresa praised him and gave him some medals; then, abruptly deciding to return to Italy, he stopped at an inn in Trieste, where he was murdered in 1768 by a chance acquaintance, to whom he had incautiously shown his coins and medals.

Of the six principal titles associated with Winckelmann the most influential were the first and the last — his *Gedanken über die Nachahmung der griechischen Werke in Malerei und Bildhauer-*

kunst (1755) and his *Geschichte der Kunst des Alterthums* (1764), which he was revising when he was murdered.* The *Gedanken*, written before he had seen Italy, announced, and the *Geschichte der Kunst* amplified, the doctrine that Greek art, notably in its architecture and its statuary, especially if the statue were that of a beautiful youth such as the Apollo Belvedere,† was not only the most perfect in the world but also incarnated an ideal humanity to which modern man can aspire even though he cannot return to it. The perfection of the Greeks followed upon the imperfections of the Egyptians, the Phoenicians, the Persians, and the Etrurians, and was the result of a variety of causes. In the first place, argued Winckelmann, physical perfection is commoner in temperate climes than it is elsewhere. In the second place there was a harmonious relationship among the forms of government, the teaching of the philosophers, and the love of beauty in ancient Greece. In the third place the Greeks, especially the Spartans (but did Sparta produce great art?) encouraged nakedness and loved beautiful male forms. In the fourth place the relation between art and religion was then such that the sublime expression of humanity in sculpture among the Greeks was also the expression of a noble simplicity, a calm grandeur, and an ethical harmony.

How did Winckelmann know all this? By intuition: as Walter Pater says, "he catches the thread of a whole sequence of laws [principles?] in some hollowing of the hand, or dividing of the hair." Winckelmann, however, remained persistently hazy about "Greece." Attica and Sparta, Arcadia and Boeotia are all left in a beautiful dream (the Ionians first developed a musical-sounding language under a smiling sky); and all the Greeks honored their artists as other nations honored statesmen and soldiers. This was because they enjoyed "liberty," an indefinite term that ignores the existence of slavery in the ancient world. Winckelmann in some degree endorses the Platonic doctrine that a beautiful soul in a beautiful body is what makes that body beautiful. His identification

* The others are *Description des pierres gravées du feu Baron de Stosch* (1760), *Anmerkungen über die Baukunst der Alten* (1762), *Sendschreiben von den herculanischen Entdeckungen* (1762), and *Nachricht von den neuesten herculanischen Entdeckungen* (1764). The essay on Winckelmann in Walter Pater's *Studies in the Renaissance* (1873), though incorrect in some details and marked by typical Paterian flourishes, is still the most sympathetic English interpretation.
† I exalted myself beforehand, says Winckelmann, in order to be worthy to see it.

of the idealism of art with an ideal form of culture associated his theory with the eighteenth-century search for an ideal form of the state.

It is clear that Winckelmann omitted much from his Grecian utopia. In his Greece there were no economic struggles, no wars of conquest, no treachery, no old age, no diseases, but only perfect friendship, ideal love, and perpetual summer. He admits the existence of politics, since he divides the story of Greek art into periods. The "beautiful style," for example, developed just before Alexander the Great, and the "imitative style" in the post-Alexandrian world. It is useless to argue that his history is shaky, his dating and identification of the Hellenic or Roman statues imitative of the Greeks frequently wrong, that he never saw a Greek painting and never examined really Greek art. Winckelmann's importance is not archaeological but cultural. The Germans considered that he had substantiated the doctrine of a calm and noble Ideal as the goal of humanity, of art, and of life. For the narrowly neoclassical "imitation" of the ancients he substituted emulation, a striving upward, the autonomy of art and the autonomy of humanity. He substituted Hellenism for Christianity as a goal of mankind. In the long run the revolutionary cult of humanity owes much to Winckelmann.

In his famous essay, *Laokoön, oder über die Grenzen der Malerei und Poesie* (1766) Lessing endeavored simultaneously to correct Winckelmann's notion concerning that famous statue (Laocoon and his sons express anguish only in a noble way) and to define the difference between the treatment of a subject in the plastic arts (."Painting" in the title is very loosely employed in the text) and in literature — in this case the comparison is with the episode in the *Aeneid* wherein Vergil describes the death agonies of a father and two sons, strangled by huge serpents divinely sent. Lessing's argument is that the faces do not express physical anguish (Vergil makes the victims shriek) but, as it were, a refined or idealized form of anguish, an interpretation not now accepted. The difference must be true, says Lessing, because "painting" (that is, the representative arts) can express but a single moment, in spatial terms, whereas literature must move from point to point in time. This interpretation was followed by another influential essay, *Wie die Alten den Tod gebildet* (1769), its point being that to represent death the ancients did not employ skeletons as in the late medieval "Dance of Death" but used instead the symbol of a youth with crossed feet and an inverted torch. Both essays are important contributions to the development of a doctrine of the Ideal, albeit the *Laocoon* is a large fragment, and the second essay is marred by spiteful references to Professor Christian Adolf Klotz of the University of Halle, with whom Lessing had been feuding in his *Antiquarische Briefe* (1768).

In England the *Discourses: Delivered to the Students of the Royal Academy* (1797), which Sir Joshua Reynolds had been delivering almost annually, though they show little direct influence from Winckelmann, encouraged young artists (Reynolds talks mainly about painting) to proceed in the spirit of Winckelmann's idealistic theory: Look to the Ancients, Reynolds says in the Third Discourse, for "nobleness of conception." Learn the art of

animating and dignifying the figures with intellectual grandeur, of impressing the appearance of philosophic wisdom, or heroic virtue. This can only be acquired by him that enlarges the sphere of his understanding by a variety of knowledge, and warms his imagination with the best productions of ancient and modern poetry. . . . [The painter must] exhibit distinctly, and with precision, the general form of things.

The Thirteenth Discourse contains the observation:

Upon the whole, it seems to me that the object and intention of all the arts is to supply the natural imperfection of things, and often to gratify the mind by realizing and embodying what never existed but in the imagination.

For Sir Joshua imagination is not what it would be for Blake, or Poe, or E. T. A. Hoffmann, but rather an idealizing faculty through which the artist moves from the locally imperfect to the Ideal. The great, but by no means the only, example of such an artist was to be Goethe.

Outgrowing the stormy passions of his youth and longing for inner peace, Goethe stole off to Italy in 1786 — an experience he recorded in two volumes, the *Italienische Reise* (1816–1817), a nostalgic memory of what Rome, Sicily, and Venice had meant to him. His experience in Italy confirmed him in the belief that proper style is not capricious but, as Karl Vietor says, "law-abiding and normative." It can attain perfection only in the reconciliation of nature and intellect, in a cultivated humanity, of which Faust, ever struggling forward through errors, becomes the supreme type. More immediately, in Goethe's central period, it brought him into serenity, clarity, harmony, and measure, the influence of Winckelmann enriching Goethe's acceptance of Spinoza. The great poet's attempts to embody his ideal in his own works were not invariably successful, many of them remaining fragmentary, but we owe to the Italian experience of antiquity his *Iphigenie auf Tauris* in its final form (1787) and the third act of *Faust* II, issued independently as *Helena* in 1827. At a lower level is *Hermann und Dorothea* (1797), technically an epyllion or small epic. An analogue to this in American letters is Longfellow's *Evangeline*, which, however, is scarcely neoclassical. Latin rather than Greek, the *Römische Elegien* (1790) and some of the *Venetianische Epigramme* (1796) express the paganism, erotic and joyous, of the ancient world. In *Winckelmann und sein Jahrhundert* (1805) he paid tribute to the better parts of that genius. Goethe found in Rome — but especially in Sicily, that great fragment of Magna Graecia — "the key to all." The Greeks, he thought, followed the laws that nature observes, and like other German writers and painters he contrasted the blue skies of the Mediterranean world with the somber heavens of Germany. For him his Italian experience was a revolution, not of politics, but of the soul; yet since an idealized form of humanity was the goal of political revolutions, Goethe's Olympian attitude toward art and man was not without an influence upon the thought of even radicals in the Western world.

iv

To couple the terms "Plutarchian hero" and "stoic philosophy" in that order violates history, inasmuch as Zeno, the founder of stoicism, died about 262 B.C. and Plutarch died in A.D. 120, almost four centuries later. Except among specialists, however, the chronology of the ancient world was as blurred in the eighteenth century as it is to us, and if Plutarch was, as some have argued, a Platonist at heart, Platonism has little to do with his masterpiece, *The Parallel Lives of Eminent Greeks and Romans*, read in the eighteenth century by all thoughtful men. There are fifty biographies, thirty-eight of them arranged in nineteen pairs. The

Plutarchian hero may be the founder of a state, such as Romulus, a lawgiver, as in the case of Solon, an outstanding general, an example being Titus Flaminius, an orator discussing large public issues as Demosthenes did, or a public figure of extraordinary merit, instances being Cato the Censor, the Gracchi, and Marcus Brutus. They live in various periods of political and social peril and change. They are capable of extraordinary grandeur of soul, heroism, and magnanimity, and of that extreme form of self-effacement, suicide. If a Plutarchian figure fails as Mark Antony and Alcibiades fail, it is because he has violated one or more of the cardinal tenets of stoic morality: wisdom, justice, benevolence, and propriety (or decorum). Whatever inconsistencies appear in stoic thought with respect to cosmology, religion, and epistemology, its ethical teaching is relatively simple and clear. The aim of a good life is not pleasure but control, conformity to cosmic law, resignation to the will of the gods, duty, and a self-abnegation that scorns riches and sinks itself into some larger civic good. Such is the lesson of Plutarch.

We probably do not have the work as Plutarch designed it, and some scholars believe that the famous comparisons were written by another author. But for purposes of discussing the Plutarchian (and stoic) tradition in eighteenth-century thought, Plutarch's *Lives* is a whole and may be taken as a single influential work. Plutarch's moral judgments can be extracted from almost any one of the biographies, but one finds them easily in the famous comparisons, as in these extracts from the Dryden-Clough translation:

[From "The Comparison of Numa with Lycurgus"] It was glorious to acquire a throne by justice, yet more glorious to prefer justice before a throne; the same virtue which made [Numa] worthy of regal power exalted [Lycurgus] to the disregard of it.

[From "The Comparison of Alcibiades with Coriolanus"] After harshly repelling public supplication, the entreaties of ambassadors, and the prayers of priests, [for Coriolanus] to concede all as a private favour to his mother was less an honour to her than a dishonour to the city which thus escaped, in spite, it would seem, of its own demerits, through the intercession of a single woman.

[From "The Comparison of Aristides and Marcus Cato"] Questionless, there is no perfecter endowment in man than political virtue. . . . Lycurgus, by prohibiting gold and silver in Sparta, and making iron, spoiled by the fire, the only currency, did not by these measures discharge them from minding their household affairs, but cutting off luxury, the corruption and tumour of riches, he provided there should be an abundant supply of all necessary and useful things for all persons, as much as any other lawmaker ever did; being more apprehensive of a poor, needy, and indigent member of a community, than of the rich and haughty. And in his management of domestic concerns, Cato was as great as in the government of public affairs; for he increased his estate, and became a master to others in economy and husbandry. . . .

[From "The Comparison of Philopoemon and Flaminius"]   The equity, clemency, and humanity of [Flaminius] towards the Greeks display a great and generous nature, but the actions of Philopoemon, full of courage and forward to assert his country's liberty against the Romans, had something yet greater and nobler in them.

[From "The Comparison of Dion and Brutus"] . . . the chief glory of both was their hatred of tyranny and abhorrence of wickedness. This was unmixed and sincere in Brutus; for he had no private quarrel with Caesar, but went into the risk singly for the liberty of his country.

These are snatches from what, to use Bernard Shaw's phrase, became a revolutionist's handbook. It requires no great acumen to infer from the explicit denunciation of wealth, the fear of the mob and of the rich, the praise of courage exercised to preserve the state, the scorn of egotism, and the emphasis upon civic virtue in Plutarch that he had his appeal to the whole eighteenth century.

Plutarch wrote in Greek, as did Marcus Aurelius Antoninus, who died in 180, and whose *Meditations* is the latest and in some regards the greatest of the classics of stoicism. Among his important readers was Montesquieu. Marcus Aurelius thought this of death: "Thou hast taken ship, thou hast sailed, thou art come to land, go out to another life, there also are gods, who are everywhere" (III:iii). And he said of life:

Whatsoever is expedient unto thee, O World, is expedient unto me; nothing can be either unseasonable to me, or out of date, which unto thee is seasonable. Whatsoever thy seasons bear, shall ever by me be esteemed as happy fruit, and increase. O Nature! from thee are all things, in thee all things subsist, and to thee all tend. Could he say of Athens, Thou lovely city of Cecrops, and shalt thou not say of the world, Thou lovely city of God?
(IV:xix. The Casaubon translation, 1634)

But though these masterpieces are in Greek, for the eighteenth century stoicism was, by and large, Roman. Cicero and Seneca, Horace and Vergil, Livy and Lucan were familiar names, whereas Zeno, Cleanthes, and Chrysippus, founders and shapers of stoic philosophy, were more remote. Cicero, in a work like *De officiis*, is derivative, but he is elegant. Seneca may remind the cynical modern of a do-gooder columnist, but he is clear. Horace flattered both Maecenas and Augustus and had a roving eye, but he was a sagacious man of the world. Vergil, however stupid we find the pious Aeneas, extols a man who founded an empire and who reverenced the gods. In Aeneas, as E. V. Arnold points out, the sovereignty of mind is never upset:

mens immota manet; lacrimae volvuntur inanes.*

Stoic morality appealed to some republican Americans and to many republican Frenchmen. They admired the Spartan virtues preached by the stoics, they admired their doctrine that to live in harmony with the laws of the universe as determined by the gods is wisdom, they applauded the dictum that a good citizen should sacrifice his private desires to the public good, and since both the American and the French revolutionaries asserted the rights of man as a general proposition that could be exported to, and even imposed upon, foreign countries, they applauded the theory that the aim of political action is the creation of a cosmopolis, or universal state, in which all local, municipal, racial, dynastic, and national differences are to be dissolved into that universal whole Cicero called *humanitas*.

Moreover, the principal exemplars of Roman stoicism lived in eras of special meaning to eighteenth-century revolutionaries. They lived and wrote in an arc of time that ran through the heroic struggle of the Roman republic to preserve itself from external enemies as in the case of Carthage, and from internal enemies as in the case of Catiline, or through the great days of the Roman empire. The principate, to be sure, had its good and its bad phases. Augustus was followed by a succession of wicked rulers, except for Vespasian,† until the gods sent from 96 to 180 a succession of good

---

* *Aeneid*, IV:449. His mind (i.e., conscience, spirit, soul) remains unmoved, and his tears roll down but in vain (i.e., his emotions will not deter him from his destined aim).

† Modern historians do not altogether accept Gibbon's judgment, but his phrasing is memorable: "the dark, unrelenting Tiberius, the ferocious Caligula,

emperors: Nerva, Trajan, Hadrian, and the two Antonines. In Roman stoicism Seneca, the tutor of Nero, who committed suicide at the command of that tyrant, represents the good man struggling in the storms of fate, and Marcus Aurelius, though he persecuted the Christians (but why should that trouble a skeptic or an atheist?) represented that ideal of eighteenth-century liberalism, a philosopher on a throne.

Since stoicism flourished for many centuries and in its later years absorbed elements essentially hostile to its purpose, one must not expect perfect congruity among its representatives. But over the decades its ethical system proved both central and relatively stable. The aim of philosophy is virtue, since philosophy is right thinking, right thinking leads to right action, and right action is by definition virtuous; that is, virtuous action is in harmony with the pattern of things as they are. Unlike the animals, man has both freedom of choice and something like Shaftesbury's moral sense, though the stoics would not say so and though they had some difficulty in disentangling freedom from fate. An important point is the difference between pleasure and virtue. Pleasure may be immoral, whereas virtue may require the philosopher to face — indeed, to create — extraordinary difficulties and to endure pain. But those who look upon pleasure as the highest good are simply the slaves of pleasure, whereas those who are truly virtuous hold pleasure (by which the stoics commonly meant sensuality) in check. The wise man achieves inward composure in contrast to the emotional man who is hurried into pleasure by impulse. The wise man will not regard pain as an evil to be avoided per se, since pain is a part of the scheme of things. He therefore enjoys — indeed, commands — an area of moral freedom which he who seeks only pleasure can never know. Since domesticity and the state are essential parts of the scheme of things, the virtuous man will be a good husband and a responsible father, he will be a faithful friend to those deserving of friendship, and, because stoicism stresses individual responsibility, the wise man will be drawn into the society of other wise men. Therefore he lives not for himself or his family alone, but also for the state, being bound to subordinate individual desire to

---

the feeble Claudius, the profligate and cruel Nero, the beastly Vitellius, and the timid, inhuman Domitian." The years of tyranny ran from the death of Augustus in A.D. 14 to the accession of Marcus in 96. Vespasian ruled from 69 to 79.

the good of the whole society precisely as the individual is bound to accept universal law. Austerity, the result of "decorum," was inevitably the "note" of stoicism, even though benevolence was one of the four cardinal virtues. Self-restraint, self-discipline, a capacity to renounce and to endure, a submission to the course of things are all admirable attributes; nevertheless stoic rigidity in morals sometimes passed into self-righteousness, and the stoic, though an admirable (for example Cato the Censor), was not always a lovable man.

Virtue was to play an important role in the value systems of the revolutionaries. In general the stoics meant by virtue both right thinking and right conduct in an orderly universe. But virtue and virtuous, in any language that uses these terms or their derivatives, are unfortunately ambiguous words. Virtue may mean merely chastity, as when Pamela in the novel battles to preserve her "virtue." It may connote righteousness, but righteousness can become a little overpowering. It may mean an occult efficiency. But the real problem goes back to the root of the word, the Latin *vir*, meaning literally *man* but connoting virility, maleness, masculinity, force, and power. Virtue in the sense of power can be illustrated by the use of it in *Paradise Lost*, wherein Milton, heir of Jewish, cabbalistic, and Christian speculation, makes God address the angelic host as "Thrones, Dominations, Princedoms, Virtues, Powers" (V:602), thus ranking the status society of heaven by the degree of authority or power the angels are allowed to have. Virtue as power, virtue as efficacy, especially when that power is exercised in the name of righteousness, may turn into ruthlessness as in the instance of Robespierre, who talked much of virtue and sought by judicial murders to purge the state of those who seemed to him actual or potential traitors. On the other hand, Montesquieu had argued that virtue, by which he meant the love of country, is the one quality necessary for the life and safety of a republic. He thought that Rome fell, among other reasons, because its elite went over to an Epicurean philosophy * of happiness, whereas in earlier

---

* Again one has to deal with an ambiguous word. "Epicurean" may mean mere sensuality, as in Milton's coarse phrase about the "Epicurean sty." Or it may mean setting pleasure as the goal of life. True Epicureanism is exemplified in Lucretius' poem about the universe, *De rerum natura*, which had considerable vogue among French *philosophes*. Lucretius teaches that the gods are remote, that matter is the basic constituent element in things, and that religion derives

decades its great men had practiced republican virtue, avoiding the excesses of wealth and demanding that Roman citizens live up to ideals of duty and responsibilities.

If Plutarch furnished the revolutionaries with antique heroes whom they could admire, Cicero and Seneca, writers whom we do not now regard as profound, furnished them with a philosophy they could adapt to their purposes. One example — a treatise on Seneca — will illustrate the point. In his *Essai sur les règnes de Claude et de Néron et sur la vie et les écrits de Sénèque pour servir d'introduction à la lecture de sa philosophie*, Diderot combines a history of two tyrants with an exegesis of Seneca's thought. He published this in 1778 and revised it, somewhat for the worse, in 1782, seven years before the meeting of the States-General. His work is in two books, the second including a sort of epilogue. Book one is a fusion of Diderot's version of Roman history with the career of Seneca, in whom he could find little to blame:

O Sénèque! tu es et tu seras à jamais, avec Socrate, avec tous les illustres malheureux, avec tous les grands hommes de l'antiquité, un des plus doux liens entre mes amis et moi, entre les hommes instruits de tous les âges, et leurs amis. Tu es resté le sujet de nos fréquents entretiens; et tu resteras le sujet des leurs. Tu aurais été l'organe de la justice des siècles, si j'avais été à ta place et toi à la mienne. Combien de fois, pour parler de toi dignement, n'ai-je pas envié la précision et le nerf, la grandeur et le véhémence de ton discours, lorsque tu parles de la vertu? Si ton honneur te fut plus cher que la vie, dis-moi, les lâches qui ont flétri ta mémoire n'ont-ils pas été plus cruels que celui qui te fit couper les veines? Je me soulagerai en te vengeant de l'un et des autres.*

Among the detractors of Seneca against whom Diderot lashes out are Rousseau, La Mettrie, and La Harpe. Seneca, he says, is more honored by a single page of his own writing than by all the

---

from fear. Much of his doctrine was attractive to those who wanted to undermine supernatural religion.

* O Seneca! You are and always shall be, with Socrates, with all the illustrious unfortunate, with all the great men of ancient times, one of the sweetest ties between my friends and me, between educated men and their friends through all the ages. You have been the subject of our frequent talks, and you will remain the subject of theirs. You would have been the voice of justice through the centuries if I had been in your place and you in mine. How many times, wanting to speak worthily of you, have I not envied the precision and sinew, the grandeur and vehemence of your speech, when you talked of righteousness? If honor was dearer to you than life, tell me, haven't the cowards who smirched your memory been more cruel than the one who made you open your veins? I shall take comfort in avenging you upon him and upon them.

dignities he won under the empire; and Diderot clears Seneca of sycophancy by saying that he and Burrus were posted as sentinels in the palace of Nero, and like sentinels they watched over virtue to the end of their lives. The gods had placed Seneca at his post and despite Poppaea, despite the intrigues of the base freedmen of the court, despite the increasing hostility of Nero, he stayed on — if they want to cut my throat, he said, they will at least have to cut it in a palace. Book two is a running commentary on the letters and essays of Seneca, applausive and enthusiastic. Throughout the work there are frequent direct or indirect allusions to European monarchies, including France. It seems possible that Seneca's defense of suicide (Diderot ignores the Christian argument against it), and his essays on the tranquillity of the soul, the brevity of life, and the constancy of the wise man, not to speak of his attempt to console Marcia, the daughter of Cremutius Cordus, put to death under Sejanus for praising Brutus and Cassius, contributed something to the quiet heroism with which many victims of the guillotine went to their doom.

If the courage never to submit or yield to injustice is central to the Plutarchian-stoic tradition, the ideal was not new in eighteenth-century Europe. Not to speak of Shakespeare, the *pundonor* plays in Spain, and perhaps even Milton's Satan, the emphasis of the theater of Corneille was upon the autonomy of the will and the submission of the heroic soul, when necessary, to reasons of state. Everyone knows that *Le Cid* (1636) turns upon the duty of Rodrigue to avenge a stain on the honor of his aged father by challenging the insulter, Don Gomez, father of Chimène, the fiancée of Don Rodrigue, to a duel. Don Gomez is killed, Chimène demands the head of her father's slayer, and things are put right only when Don Rodrigue wins so glittering a victory over the Moors that the king orders Chimène to forgive the lover who has killed her parent. The play is a clash of wills throughout, and the celebrated line (the very heart of Cornellian heroism), "Je le ferais encore, si j'avais à le faire," is repeated in *Polyeucte*. A Cornellian tragedy has a love story imposed upon it, but the titles of these dramas — *Médée, Oedipe, Rodogune, Suréna, Horace, Sophonisbe, Nicomède, Cinna* — not only demonstrate their sources in history or supposed history, they demonstrate also that the problem of civic duty versus individual desire is paramount.

The most perfectly organized of these plays is probably *Horace* (1640), in the better sense of the word a problem of casuistry — the clash of domestic affections and public duty. Despite its complexities, the plot is worked out with an almost geometrical logic. The cities of Alba and Rome are at war, when it occurs to their leaders that if the conflict becomes general, both cities will be weakened for any possible war waged on them by other hostile states. It is therefore agreed that three champions shall be chosen from either army and that the undefeated three (or a survivor) shall *ipso facto* win for their city the suzerainty of the other. The three Romans are the sons of old Horatius, the three defenders of Alba are the Curatii. The assignment has been made in each case because the trio designated are the bravest and most skillful warriors in the army. But one of the Horatii is married to Sabina, a sister of the Curatii, and Camilla, the sister of the Horatii, is the fiancée of one of the Curatii. Complications ensue. The young Horace, who is the only survivor of the conflict, early on meets his proposed brother-in-law among the Curatii (Act II), both proclaim eternal friendship, and each declares that his primary duty is to the state. Also before the duel Horace talks to his sister, Camilla, saying that if he returns from the fray he does not wish to be received as the murderer of her lover. His speech includes this key line:

> Mais en homme d'honneur qui fait ce qu'il doit faire.

Horace survives, the others are killed, and when, in spite of the passage just noted, Camilla curses Rome —

> Rome enfin que je hais parce qu'elle t'honore

— Horace slays her. At the end of the play, although justice demands the death of young Horace, Tullius, king of Rome, appears in the character of a Euripidean *deus ex machina*, and in a long *tirade* bids Horace live:

> Vis donc, Horace, vis, guerrier trop magnanime:
> Ta vertu met ta gloire au-dessus de ton crime.
>
> . . . .
>
> Vis pour servir l'état . . .
> Qu'il ne reste entre vous ni haine ni colère;

> Et soit qu'il ait suivi l'amour ou le devoir
> Sans aucun sentiment resous-toi de le voir.*

To the modern this may seem to mean: murder your sister and be forgiven because you have increased the power of the state, but this is not quite a fair gloss on a drama in which civic virtue is shown to be superior to private grief.

A like theme with deeper emotional coloring is presented by Racine. If Corneille put the will first and the emotions second, Racine in one sense reverses this order. Nevertheless, in *Bérénice*, in *Andromaque*, in *Iphigénie*, in *Phèdre* the plots turn on the *res publica*, the welfare of the state as against private emotions. A subtler psychologist than his predecessor, Racine will not sacrifice the public good to private passions. In *Bérénice* Titus puts Bérénice away because Rome will not suffer a foreign queen, and in *Iphigénie*, which, following Euripides, ends with a divine intervention, the welfare of the allies is more important than paternal love, maternal jealousy, or any other domestic motive. *Phèdre* is not merely a tragedy of incestuous passion, it also illustrates the wickedness of despotism, since Hippolytus is put to death through the false accusation of the queen. Racine may have, as someone said, substituted the tragedy of passion for the tragedy of character, but for him civic virtue is outraged in either event.

These plays and others like them permeated the whole theater of Europe in the eighteenth century, and in so doing helped to shape conventional notions of tyrants and kings. The eighteenth century also produced innumerable operas of heroism, many of them of the "rescue" type, in which tyranny is either exposed or overthrown and, whatever the love story, virtue is honored — *Muzio Scevola* (1721), *Catone in Utica* (1727), *Orazio* (1737), *Serse* (Xerxes, 1738), *Attilio regolo* (1740), *Alessandro* (1767), *Antigone* (1772), *Iphigénie en Tauride* (1779), *Euphrosine ou le tyran corrigé* (1790), *Médée* (1797) are typical titles. Beethoven's *Fidelio* (1805/1806) is perhaps the climax of this tradition, with

---

* But as a man of honor who knows what he must do.
  In fact I hate Rome because it honors you.
  Live then, Horace, live, O too magnanimous warrior: your virtue puts your reputation above your crime. . . . Live to serve the state . . . Let there be neither hatred nor anger between us; and whether he was led by love or duty, resolve yourself to see him without emotion.

143

its unforgettable chorus of prisoners released to light and air and then reconfined, the sufferings of the imprisoned Florestan, and the heroic defiance of death and tyranny by Leonora.

Nothing more clearly indicates the continuity of the Plutarchian and stoic tradition than the masterpiece of Jacques Louis David, "The Oath of the Horatii" (1785), in which the older Horatius of Corneille's drama swears his three sons to do their civic duty while the weeping women cower in the background of a chamber austerely classical. For that matter, as late as 1842 Samuel J. Ainsley, traveler and amateur artist, sketched "The Tomb of the Horatii and the Curatii at Albano." The tomb dates from the first century B.C., the ascription is legendary only, and the picture is mediocre, but the important fact is the long time the legend continued to grip the imagination. If the Platonic strain in neoclassicism furnished revolutionaries and romantics with ideal patterns in art, public life, philosophy, and general life, the Plutarchian and stoic tradition helped men to identify tyranny, to oppose it, and to will the means by which it was to be overthrown.

v

The Anacreontic strain in neoclassicism seems at first glance to have no connection with either revolution or romanticism. The supreme values in the world of the Anacreontic poets are youth, health, joy, love, and wine, and the inescapable misfortune which one tries to forget is time — time that brings old age and death. When in the "Ode on a Grecian Urn" Keats tells the fair lad on the urn, though he can never catch his beloved,

> do not grieve;
> She cannot fade, though thou hast not thy bliss,
> For ever wilt thou love, and she be fair!

he gives one side of the Anacreontic view of life. When, some two centuries earlier, Nicolas Poussin in his canvas "Shepherds in Arcadia" pictured a tomb inscribed with the legend "Et in Arcadia ego," he presented the other side, for the "ego" is death, which even life in Arcadia cannot avoid. But age and death are to be shunned as long as possible; love, youth, and light sensual joys are to be cherished, and no one in Arcadia has any civic responsibility, since in the Anacreontic universe politics do not exist.

Anacreon lived in the sixth century B.C., and little of his work survives. But the Anacreontic tradition in Greek literature continued deep into the Byzantine empire, and in general Anacreontism never disappears. In writers as recent as Edna St. Vincent Millay and Dorothy Parker one finds examples of Anacreontic values. Ode vii in Thomas Moore's version of what he thought were the odes of Anacreon ends with these lines:

> But this I know, and this I feel,
> That still as death approaches nearer,
> The joys of life are sweeter, dearer;
> And had I but an hour to live,
> That little hour to bliss I'd give.

This is a far cry from the loftiness of Plato and the austerity of Plutarch.

But it is a human cry. During and after any considerable war the expectation of death, the fear of dying, or a well-nigh hysterical obsession with the five senses as an affirmation of vitality is greater than in normal times. In such periods important elements in society find that patriotism and religion lose their appeal. A philosophy of "Eat, drink, and be merry, for tomorrow we may be shot" has an immediate allure to the young and to those who fear they are likely to be the next victims of the conqueror or the headsman. The Seven Years War developed an increase in luxury and gaiety all over the Western world. During the American revolution austerer patriots complained that in cities such as New York and Philadelphia (even Boston!) pleasure reigned when austerity should have prevailed. (One thinks of the Mischianza in Philadelphia in May 1778.) The hectic gaiety of imprisoned aristocrats during the French revolution, hourly expecting the tumbril that would carry them to the guillotine, has passed into legend. Sensuality and corruption characterized Parisian life during the Terror and the Directorate. English society was never giddier than during the wars against the French Republic and Napoleon. Revolutionaries could of course be austere, but they could also be drunkards and sensualists, thinking that any woman would yield to them and taking no thought for the morrow, partly to veil their sense of guilt for violence already done, partly to veil their dread of violence to come. The uncertainty of life in a revolution invites hedonism, and in this sense the Anacreontic tradition has its understandable relation to revolutionaries.

But there is another aspect to this relationship. The Anacreontic tradition, relaxed and anti-intellectual — youths passing the drinking bowl from hand to hand, maidens dancing in a fair meadow, shepherds and villagers who never pay taxes, the gods reduced to cupids and nymphs or satyrs, old men longing to be young, who put off the majesty of age in favor of Bacchic revelry — types such as these reduced classical man to human proportions. The Plutarchian hero was larger than life. Platonic idealism required thinking on an exalted level. But one could not live forever on the high plateau of Platonic idealism or imitate Cato's dyspeptic denunciations of the follies of mankind. The perfection of humanity is not necessarily sublimity. The idealized Greece (or Sicily) of Winckelmann had to be peopled, but peopled by beings who were not demigods; and while it was admirable to elevate mankind, how high, so to speak, was the elevation to rise? Let us be nymphs and shepherds before we play the part of Prometheus.

It is an odd but understandable conjunction that the Anacreontic dream of Greece (or Magna Graecia) was strengthened by the increasing interest in archaeology, notably the rediscovery of Herculaneum and Pompeii. One significant organization was the Society of the Dilettanti, apparently founded in 1734 though the official records go back only to 1736. The original members, some of them associated with the notorious Medmenham Abbey group, were scarcely Hellenists. They included Sir Francis Dashwood of dubious memory, the Earl of Sandwich, who appears as Jemmy Twitcher in Charles Churchill's bitter satire, *The Candidate* (1764), the Earl of Middleton, and other worldly-minded hedonists. Later members were soberer men, such as Sir Joshua Reynolds, but the history of the Society quotes these minutes of an early meeting:

The Committee met. Resolved, That it is the opinion of this Committee that Mr. Brand will be Damned. Resolved, That it is the opinion of this Committee that all Publick pious Charities are private impious alms.

The Dilettanti were nevertheless often men of considerable education, many of whom had made the Grand Tour, seen ruins,* and

---

* The attractiveness of the Anacreontic tradition was in all probability set off by the craze for engravings and paintings of Roman (and other) ruins and the taste for artificial ruins set up in "English" gardens in the eighteenth century.

were fascinated by archaeology. In 1751 James Stuart and Nicholas Revett, painters and architects, were elected to the Society, which financed a journey by these two into Greece and the Levant. In 1762 the two men published under the auspices of the Society *The Antiquities of Athens*, an illustrated volume widely influential in forming taste, a second volume appearing in 1787, a third and a fourth even later. Meanwhile Robert Chandler got up his *Ionian Antiquities* for the Society, and books were also published on the ruins of Palmyra and those at Baalbek. On the Continent similar volumes appeared.

Peasants digging wells in the area of Pompeii and Herculaneum came upon inexplicable statues and stones bearing inscriptions. In the sixteenth and seventeenth centuries other persons of a higher degree of education uncovered an aqueduct and other evidences of civilization. In 1709 Prince d'Elboeuf of the Austrian army bought a plot of ground near Portici, a modern village lying over Herculaneum, and was told by a peasant he could by digging get marble for making plaster and find statues as well. In 1713 Elboeuf sunk a shaft and made underground tunnels from which workers clumsily extracted statues, columns, cornices, and the like. Not until 1738 did the king of Naples realize the importance of these findings, when he ordered a military engineer (without archaeological training) to supervise the "digs." In 1750 Carl Weber, a far more intelligent engineer, was set to work under the first one. After 1750 and particularly during the 1760's the work was carried forward with some intelligence, but not until the early nineteenth century were the poorer quarters of Herculaneum uncovered. The record of blunders, thievery, and thoughtless destruction makes the modern archaeologist wince; nevertheless the domestic life of the Romans was now made tangible; statuary of human size,

---

Such ruins emphasized the transience of men and empires. Painters, engravers, and etchers flocked to Rome and its vicinity, and books containing pictures of classical buildings and aqueducts in decay were popular among the elite during most of the century. Of scores of such artists the best known is the Venetian, Giovanni Battista Piranesi (1720–1778), whose *Le Antichità romane* in four volumes (1756), *Della Magnificenza ed architettura de' Romani* (1761), and *Vedute di Roma* (1748–1778), are among the masterpieces of engraving, so much so that forged Piranesis still flood the market. On the taste for "English" gardens and the significance of that taste see B. Sprague Allen's magnificent study, *Tides in English Taste, 1619–1800: A Background for the Study of Literature*, 2 vols., Cambridge, Mass., 1937. The English garden in Munich was laid out by Benjamin Thompson, Count Rumford, a refugee from the American revolution.

domestic ornaments, tripods, vases, kitchen utensils, hair ornaments, buckles, and furniture came to light. Various worthies, English, French, Italian, German, published accounts of these discoveries — for example, Thomas Gray, Horace Walpole, the Comte de Caylus (who wanted to "restore antiquity to life"), the Duc de Choiseul, and of course the great Goethe — as well as accounts of archaeological discoveries elsewhere in the Mediterranean world. Collections were put together, for instance, that of Sir William Hamilton, whose vases, bronzes, gold ornaments, and the like were sold to England in 1772. Other enthusiasts, such as D'Hancarville, who compiled a vast *Récherches sur l'origine et le progrès des arts de la Grèce* in 1785, tinged their work with mysticism; and Payne Knight daringly brought out a book on Priapic worship among the ancients, an idea not unassociated with the eroticism of the Anacreontic tradition. An anonymous *Mémoire sur la ville souterraine découverte au pied du mont Vésuve*, printed in Paris as early as 1748, talks about wall paintings removed to the Naples Museum as fresh as when they were painted and representing cupids, a Hercules of natural size, Theseus receiving the thanks of the children of Athens, and so on, and speaks also about lamps, household objects, furniture, and the like. The heroic interpretation of antiquity slowly turned into a human one.

Two elements in this confusion seem important. In the first place the sensuality evident in many decorative motifs seemed to endorse the view that all was life and love in parts of the ancient world. In the second place the fact that a happy culture had been buried by a convulsion of nature strengthened the kind of paganism revived in Goethe's *Roman Elegies*, Wieland's *Geschichte des Agathon* (1766–1767), Heinse's *Ardinghello* (1787), and Hölderlin's *Hyperion*, which took final shape in 1799, books which, novels or not, picture an ideal Greece (or Sicily) as the backdrop, the locale, or the climax of the narrative. Novels are of human size. A Corneille portrayed epic heroes sublime in will; the German *Bildungsroman* of this type pictured more ordinary mortals seeking happiness in a simpler culture. Had not Winckelmann pronounced that nakedness was a virtue? If nakedness, why not amorousness? One result was that fashionable ladies at the end of the century were dressed *à la mode antique* in clothing virtually diaphanous, their bosoms exposed, as may be seen in Proudhon's portrait of the Empress Josephine, David's picture of Mme Vigée-Lebrun, and Gérard's famous painting of Mme Récamier, not to speak of fashion plates of the time such as may be found in the *Berlinischer Damen-Kalendar*. Younger women adopted the "Grecian bend" or curvilinear pose. All this sort of thing was supposed to represent "freedom."

The chairs and couches of the classical past in these pictures were perhaps studio properties, but they shortly made their appearance in real life. In 1769 in a place named Hanley, significantly christened Etruria, Josiah Wedgwood, an enthusiast for the discoveries at Pompeii and for the results at other archaeological diggings, began the manufacture of his famous blue-and-white Wedgwood ware, its designs, often by John Flaxman, originating in imitations of Greek vase designs. Since it is a touch difficult to produce household pottery of epic proportions, Flaxman's designs and those of others reduced the ancients again to human proportions and, what is more, portrayed the figures on the pottery as forever unconscious of disease or death.

If pottery, why not other household furnishings? In the last third of the century, chairs, tables, bookcases, couches, beds, candelabra, "ebony work," and footstools all over Europe among the circles of the elite showed a taste for classicism that preceded the coarser Empire style. The acanthus leaf, the egg-and-dart motif, the cross-framed curule chair, lion masks with rings in their mouths, table-legs terminating in classical forms were "in." The famous furniture designer, Sheraton, actually called some of his chairs Herculaneums. Sir William Gell, whom Byron once fell foul of, brought out in 1817 his *Pompeiana*, which included plates of "restored" Pompeiian houses. In England and on the Continent Pompeiian and Greek motifs mingled with designs even more exotic from China and Egypt. But classicism meant "Freedom" and also melancholy at the passing of time. Pictures from Italy and Greece now came to lack the grandiosity of Piranesi; painters put modern figures (a trick used by Poussin) among the ruins, a device hinting that life and death go on. An inevitable gloss was the Anacreontic comment: "Gather ye rosebuds while ye may."

"Freedom" takes many forms. It is not inappropriate to quote in connection with the Anacreontic mode of interpreting antiquity another seventeenth-century poet, Richard Lovelace:

> If I have freedom in my love,
>   And in my soul am free,
> Angels alone, that soar above,
>   Enjoy such liberty.

This is not "classical," though it is hedonistic. Is it a far cry from Byron's dream that Greece might yet be free? The lyric poet in Canto III of *Don Juan* sings on an Aegean isle of the possibility of a Greek revolution, but his poem includes this stanza:

> Fill high the bowl with Samian wine!
>   Our virgins dance beneath the shade —
> I see their glorious black eyes shine;
>   But gazing on each glowing maid,
> My own the burning tear-drop laves,
> To think such breasts must suckle slaves.

The hedonistic and the heroic strains in the classical revival here fuse in the words of the greatest romantic rebel of the European nineteenth century.* The paintings of David, whether they deal with the ancient world or such dramatic modern events as "The Oath of the Tennis Court," return us to the austerity of Corneille and Addison's *Cato*.†

---

* Herculaneum and Pompeii continued to be of importance after the close of the eighteenth century. See in this connection the remarkable article by Jean Seznec, "Herculaneum and Pompeii in French Literature of the Eighteenth Century," *Archaeology*, II (3/7), 150–158 (September 1949). Bulwer-Lytton's *The Last Days of Pompeii* appeared in 1834.

† One of the most illuminating ways to trace the movement from the austerities of the age of Louis XIV through the frivolities of Pompadour and Marie Antoinette neoclassicism back to the austerity of the time of David is to study the series of exquisite miniature rooms devised by Mrs. James Ward Thorne or an illustrated catalog of them. I add that throughout this chapter I have been greatly helped by two studies by Henry C. Hatfield, *Winckelmann and His German Critics, 1756–1781: A Prelude of the Classical Age*, New York, 1943, and his *Aesthetic Paganism in German Literature from Winckelmann to the Death of Goethe*, Cambridge, Mass., 1964. For an interesting interpretation of pagan mythology by the seventeenth and eighteenth centuries in Europe see Frank E. Manuel, *The Eighteenth Century Confronts the Gods*, Cambridge, Mass., 1959. Professor Manuel's interest is in the religious history of the period; mine more particularly in the political.

VI

The American Revolution

In the American revolution some of the major tensions of the eighteenth-century world broke through the cake of custom and produced for the first time in the century a new and radical state on a pattern theorists had dreamed of but had thought impossible to carry out in fact. The new nation was a state without a king, without a hereditary aristocracy, and without a national established church. Except in the lamentable matter of slavery, the new republic was established on a theory of man eighteenth-century philosophers had talked about and eighteenth-century rulers had smiled at as chimerical. The governing idea was not merely that men are born free — that was an old concept — but also that they are entitled not merely to individual liberty but to equality and happiness. Happiness was supposed to spring not alone from freedom and equality but also from three other important theories of the century: the physiocratic theory, which, among other matters, held that an agrarian nation was likely to be contented; the laissez-faire theory, which held that the mercantilist theory was wrong and that contentment would be increased if government interfered as little as possible with trade and manufacture; and the utilitarian theory, which held that happiness was possible here and now and need not be postponed to heaven. It argued that individual fulfillment arose from a surplus of pleasure over pain, a doctrine which in turn required men to live amicably together.

None of these ideas was new in 1775. But their fusion into a political philosophy that set up a popular republic in a large, extended territory was startling. The immediate inciting forces of the American revolution are generally known, but in their search for doctrine the promoters of American "liberty" went back to ancient Rome, to British tradition as the Americans interpreted that tradition, and to a considerable body of philosophic thought more or less recent, such as the political doctrine of Locke and the theory of the state set forth in Montesquieu's *L'Esprit des lois*. Some phases of American discontents coincide with some phases of romanticism, but it cannot be argued that the Americans operated on a doctrine of romanticism. It is, however, true that the American revolution gave a powerful push toward validating romanticism, or at least some parts of it. The appeal of the New World led Chateaubriand to visit Indians in central New York and make Louisiana the locale of his celebrated romantic tale, *Atala*; the supposed happiness of the Americans caused young Coleridge, Southey, and their partners to dream of founding an ideal commonwealth in Pennsylvania; and Goethe could write: "Amerika, du hast es besser." It becomes necessary therefore to inquire with some particularity into the history of this great event.

Possibly the sources of all revolutions lie in the nature of man himself — in that disharmony between freedom and necessity which most philosophies struggle, often vainly, to reconcile. Eighteenth-century society did not succeed in reconciling these two elements. A state ordered in ranks and classes, the king on top and the peasants down below, could not by its very nature easily adjust to new pressures of population, new economic developments, and disturbing ideas about the relation of the nation to its population. Western culture had accepted the picture of an orderly universe and an orderly population, but it also had to face a new concept of progress, a new emphasis upon individualism, and, oddly enough, a doctrine of historical pessimism (found also among the Americans) which worked to destroy the very uniformity then thought to be the last word in human wisdom. The Enlightenment produced the countermovement of sensibility, a movement which insisted that man faces death as well as life, that he is more than the sum of his ideas, that a beneficent God has given him passions as well as reason, and that there are purer and more lasting emotions than those of a frivolous sensuousness. Even the tradition of classicism, on which the eighteenth-century world heavily relied, though it presented its stately image of beauty, courage, harmony, calm, and virtue, proved but a frail reed. Antiquity had too many tyrants, too many regicides, too many skeptics, too many epicureans for thoughtful persons to believe that Great Britain or France or any other European nation had only to model itself on Periclean Athens, the Roman republic, or the world of Augustus Caesar to be both stable and virtuous.

The American revolution was an unpredictable event, so unpredictable that even when it was well along, many acute observers thought it was only a local rebellion that the British forces would put down. No previous revolution had been quite like it. Perhaps the Corsican revolution, though on a small scale, was the nearest immediate analogue. Corsica had been a possession of Genoa, its inhabitants felt oppressed, and under the leadership of Pasquale Paoli they tried to establish a "democratic republic." But the inhabitants were not united in their aims, in 1768 Genoa sold Corsica to France, and in 1770 this sale was accepted by a "general assembly" of Corsicans. Paoli fled to England. He had, said Dr. Johnson, the loftiest port of any man he had ever seen and he therefore became a modern Plutarchian hero. The Americans, however, when they sought precedents for their rising, preferred Plutarch to Paoli and did not read Rousseau's proposals for a Corsican constitution, which the embattled island revolutionaries had asked that philosopher to draw up.

In one sense the creation of the American republic was the last great triumph of the Enlightenment. The motto of the young republic was — and is — *e pluribus unum*, a phrase so enigmatic as to have received varying interpretations, but a phrase symbolizing a unity among men the Enlightenment desired to achieve. This unity is also expressed in two central papers: the Declaration of Independence and the federal Constitution, each of which repudiates kings in favor of the people. As there is a rich sheaf of documents illustrating the appeal of the Enlightenment to American leaders — Jefferson's *Summary View of the Rights of British America*, the "Suffolk Resolves" penned by Dr. Joseph Warren, John Adams' constitution for the Commonwealth of Massachusetts, and, for that matter, most of the writers discussed in Moses Coit Tyler's old-fashioned but powerful *The Literary History of the American Revolution* (1897) — the truth that the American revolution grew out of the Enlightenment no less than out of the troubles of its century need not surprise us. At the beginning of our inquiry, however, it will be helpful to look at the two fundamental documents creating the new republic. They should be more familiar to Americans than they generally are.

Here is the relevant part of the Declaration:

When in the Course of human Events, it becomes necessary for one People to dissolve the Political Bands which have connected them with another, and to assume among the Powers of the Earth, the separate and equal Station to which the Laws of Nature and of Nature's God entitle them, a decent Respect to the Opinions of Mankind requires that they should declare the causes which impel them to the Separation. — We hold these Truths to be self-evident, that all Men are created equal, that they are endowed by their Creator with certain unalienable Rights, that among these are Life, Liberty and the Pursuit of Happiness. —— That to secure these Rights, Governments are instituted among Men, deriving their just Powers from the Consent of the Governed, — that whenever any Form of Government becomes destructive of these Ends, it is the Right of the People to alter or to abolish it, and to institute new Government, laying its Foundation on such Principles, and organizing its Powers in such form, as to them shall seem most likely to effect their Safety and Happiness. Prudence, indeed, will dictate that Governments long established should not be changed for light and transient Causes; and accordingly all Experience hath shewn, that Mankind are more disposed to suffer, while Evils are sufferable, than to right themselves by abolishing the Forms to which they are accustomed. But when a long Train of Abuses and Usurpations, pursuing invariably the same Object, evinces a Design to reduce them under absolute Despotism, it is their Right, it is their Duty, to throw off such Government, and to provide new Guards for their future Security.

That, said Jefferson, was the common sense of the matter. The opening passage is followed by a series of accusations and denunciations of George III, also written by Jefferson. It charges that the "direct object" of that monarch and his government is "the establishment of an absolute Tyranny over these States" (one would scarcely guess from this flaming rhetoric that there was such a thing as a British parliament)* and it specifies a series of horrendous acts.

The Constitution begins:

We the People of the United States, in Order to form a more perfect Union, establish Justice, insure domestic Tranquility, provide for the

---

* The single reference is to "their Acts of pretended Legislation."

common defence, promote the general Welfare, and secure the Blessings of Liberty to ourselves and our Posterity, do ordain and establish this Constitution for the United States of America.

The Constitution follows the theory of the separation of powers the founding fathers read about in various representatives of the Enlightenment, particularly in Montesquieu. It creates a nation not only without a monarchy, an established church, a hereditary nobility, or any other privileged order, but also without bills of attainder, without internal tariffs, and without authorization for spending public money except as this is appropriated for specific purposes by bills originating in the popular branch of a bicameral legislature. The first ten amendments, adopted in 1791 as a result of popular protest against their absence from the original document, embody an American version of the rights of man: freedom of religious worship, freedom of speech and of the press, freedom of peaceable assembly, freedom to bear arms, freedom from billeting soldiers in private houses, freedom from unreasonable search and seizure, freedom from unwarranted trial (spelled out at length), and freedom from excessive fines and cruel and unusual punishments. There are also two amendments (IX and X) of a somewhat ambiguous nature, one to the effect that the enumeration of certain rights in the Constitution shall not deny others retained by the people, and one saying that powers not delegated to the United States nor prohibited to the states are reserved to the states respectively or to the people.

These documents are the products of the Enlightenment and they are something more. Those who then argued for them appealed to customary law among the Saxons and to theorizing by authors writing before the Enlightenment; for example, Hooker's *Laws of Ecclesiastical Polity*, which dates from the late sixteenth century. They appealed to the ancient Greeks and Romans. Those who opposed the Declaration of Independence and those who opposed the federal Constitution sometimes cited authors customarily categorized as representing one or another phase of the Enlightenment — for example, Hobbes, Hume, and Blackstone — but they also appealed to antiquity. As Bernard Bailyn demonstrates, there was also an appeal by both sides to seventeenth-century political theorists and theologians and to ecclesiastical history — had not the Puritans revolted against "tyranny"? Nevertheless the Declaration and the federal Constitution may be fairly thought of as powerful statements of eighteenth-century civic theory and of the rational nature of man.

Upon closer inspection certain other elements emerge. Except for the dating of the Constitution "in the year of our Lord," the deity appealed to (and the same is evident in Adams' constitution for Massachusetts) is not the Christian deity, but "Nature's God," the "Supreme Judge of the world," a deity who has instituted and upholds the "Laws of Nature." Both documents rest upon a social contract. In the Declaration it is alleged that governments derive their just powers from the consent of the governed, and that when governments exceed their powers, they break the compact and the people have a right to institute new governments on such principles as may appeal to them. The Constitution is ordained and established by "the People of the United States," a phrase that greatly troubled Patrick Henry, populist though he was, and was to trouble the nation in the nullification controversy and in the Civil War (and, for that matter, since). It is true that the contract theory was not confined to the Enlightenment, since its history goes back to antiquity, but it was a theory so favored by exponents of the Enlightenment, it may be regarded as a hallmark of their thinking. The Declaration enumerates three great rights — "life, liberty, and the pursuit of happiness" — and the Constitution and its amendments are specific about certain other enumerated rights, among other reasons, to serve as bulwarks against royal or aristocratic government.

The theory of the pursuit of happiness adopted in the Declaration is, as various provisions of the federal Constitution and as provisions of many of the new state constitutions make clear, essentially Lockian. For Locke happiness could not be possible without property, and in the second *Essay Concerning the True Original Extent and End of Civil Government* property becomes a kind of extension of the human personality. The preamble to the federal Constitution does not mention property, but since it was difficult for the founding fathers to think of domestic tranquillity or the general welfare unless property values were secure, they said a good deal about property directly or indirectly in the total document. For example, congressmen are to be chosen in each state by electors having the qualifications necessary for the electors of the most numerous branch of the state legislature; and it takes very little reading in the early state constitutions to discover that some sort of property qualification for voters was required in virtually every one of them. Moreover, the enumeration of the powers of Congress in section viii of Article I has much to do with the currency, taxes, debts, credit, bankruptcy, weights and measures, patent rights, and the like essentials to property. Article IV guarantees to Congress the right of regulating both the property and the territory of the United States, and Article VI assures the payments of debts contracted under the Articles of Confederation.

Such are some of the positive aspects of the Enlightenment in these documents. But there are some queer lapses. The Declaration asserts that "one people" have the right to dissolve the political bonds which have connected them with another; but inasmuch as late in 1775 most leaders of the revolutionary movement declared they were Englishmen desiring only the rights of Englishmen, when and how did they suddenly discover that they were not Englishmen but a peculiar people? The word "people" is in fact defined in neither document; and inasmuch as the federal Constitution was ratified in some states by the narrowest of margins, sometimes by a special convention and sometimes by a legislature, the members of either body being usually chosen on a property basis, the phrase "We the People of the United States" is a little mysterious.

The founding fathers agreed with Montesquieu that virtue (that is, love of country) is essential to any successful republic. But Montesquieu says:

C'est dans le gouvernement républicain que l'on a besoin de toute la puissance de l'éducation. . . . On peut définir cette vertu, l'amour des lois et de la patrie. Cet amour, demandant une préférence continuelle de l'intérêt public au sien propre, donne toutes les vertus particulières; elles ne sont que cette préférence. . . . Tout dépend donc d'établir dans la république cet amour; et c'est à l'inspirer que l'éducation doit être attentive.*

Jefferson thought so too, and his famous bill for the general diffusion

* It is under a republican government that all the strength of education is needed. . . . One can define this virtue as love of the law and of the fatherland. This love, requiring a continual preference for the public interest over private ones, is the source of all the individual virtues: they are only this preference. . . . Everything turns on establishing this love in the republic, and education must be always intent on inspiring it. (Book IV, chap. v.)

of knowledge was presented to the Virginia House of Burgesses in 1778. "What a plan was here," exclaimed William Wirt in *The Letters of the British Spy* (1803), "to give stability and solid glory to the republic!" Quite as illuminating is a letter from Samuel Adams to John Adams in 1790:

We agree upon the Utility of universal Education, but 'will nations agree in it as fully and extensively as we do'? . . . The feelings of humanity have softned the heart: . . . Tyranny in all its shapes, is more detested, and Bigotry, if not still blind, must be mortified to see that she is despised. Such an age may afford at least a flattering Expectation that Nations, as well as individuals, will view the utility of universal Education in so strong a light as to induce sufficient national Patronage and Support.

Nothing can be clearer than these instances. Yet the word "education" does not appear in either the Declaration of Independence or the Constitution.

Finally, though both documents are classical statements of republican theory, and though the first asserts everybody's right to life, liberty, and the pursuit of happiness, despite the efforts of a minority to abolish slavery, all that the federal Constitution has to say on slavery is: first, that the "migration or importation of such persons as any of the States now existing shall think proper to admit" shall not be prohibited by Congress prior to 1808, though a head tax may be imposed on each of these persons; second, that any person held to service or labor in one state shall, if he escapes to another state, be delivered up on claim of the party to whom such service or labor may be due; and third, that in taking the decennial census a slave shall count but as three-fifths of a human being (Article I, section ii). This denial of life, liberty, and the pursuit of happiness to a considerable section (400,000) of the American population was a compromise between the northern and the southern interests. But it is also a peculiar sort of protection for a peculiar sort of property.

That events in North America should have eventuated in two documents that, whatever their defects, unify a philosophy of the state and of the individual and emphasize the freedom of the self rather than the subordination of individualism to status is amazing for two reasons. The first is that the incitement to revolution seems on the whole to have been weaker in America than it was in the mother country or on the continent of Europe. The second is that the formal intellectual and political unity which shapes these documents was born out of a series of conflicts, jealousies, and disorders. Let us examine these striking facts.

ii

The British mainland colonies were not particularly oppressed, despite the cries of tyranny uttered by a radical minority. They exhibited, say, in 1770 no such melodramatic contrasts of splendor and squalor, no such gulf between opulence and poverty as travelers report of eighteenth-century France. Even though slavery and the slave trade were still legal, American slave-owners seem as a class not to have been as brutal as were many masters of serfs in eastern Europe. North America as a whole did not exhibit such ravishment of land and livestock, resources and people as the Seven Years War left behind it in Prussia and adjacent lands. Unlike the peasants in Hungary, the American colonists suffered under no feudatory overlords. They were in fact working in 1763 toward the abolition of such remains of proprietary government as persisted. They supported no class of hereditary nobles on landed estates who skillfully avoided taxation, nor were they called upon to pay for an opulent and worldly church. There were in the colonies no dungeons, no *lettres de cachet*, no secret police (in fact virtually no police), no midnight arrests followed by imprisonment or execution at dawn, no forced labor by peasants, no real monopoly of land, no despotic emperor as in Russia or Turkey, no personal rule as in Naples or Portugal; and despite the outcries of Whigs and radicals, the royal governors, who might sometimes be inept and occasionally venal, were not despots appointed by an unfeeling and distant tyrant to wring treasure out of an enslaved people. The idea of a gubernatorial Parc aux Cerfs in, say, Williamsburg or Boston is as unthinkable as the idea of a colonial Marquis de Sade in Philadelphia.

In truth, a disinterested observer skilled in reading political omens might have prophesied that revolution was more likely to break out in the British Isles than in the British colonies after the Seven Years War. Enclosure acts, Irish landlordism, rack-rents in that unhappy country, the arrogance of some of the great nobles in Britain, poverty in the three kingdoms, the economic depression which followed on the heels of victory, bad harvests, insufficient food for the very poor, disease, loose morals, and technological unemployment created by the nascent industrial revolution — social and economic factors such as these increased pauperism, discontent, and radicalism, as the government of the younger Pitt was to discover at the opening of the next long war with France. Indeed, as late as 1812, Byron, in one of his few speeches in the House of Lords, was to protest on humanitarian grounds against a bill to put down frame-breaking by unemployed weavers. "I have traversed," he said, "the seat of war in the [Iberian] peninsula. I have been in some of the most oppressed provinces of Turkey, but never, under the most despotic of infidel governments, did I behold such squalid wretchedness as I have seen since my return, in the very heart of a Christian country."

The Stamp Act may have been unwise and was badly managed by the imperial government, but it was not oppressive, and would not in all probability have seriously injured colonial economy. It was, moreover, quickly repealed, not so much because of colonial opposition as because British merchants found its results deplorable — a truth that diminishes the charge of tyrannical rule by George III. A good many parliamentary statutes were unwise or unwisely administered, but they were passed, whatever radicals might say, by a legislature that, however awkwardly, represented the commons of Great Britain. Even the Quartering Act of 1765, later revived, was not unusual. Colonial legislatures or governors were directed to billet troops in inns or private houses when barracks were unavailable, a practice against which the British occasionally objected, but a practice so standard that towns in England occasionally complained when troops were not quartered in or near them. It is remarkable that in 1764 a stout American, Benjamin Franklin, rather welcomed the thought of stationing British soldiers in America both as a measure of imperial defense and as security against popular disorders.* In sum, the actual

---

* In *Cool Thoughts on the Present Situation of our Public Affairs. In a Letter to a Friend in the Country*, Philadelphia, 1764. The passage runs: "That *we shall have a standing army to maintain* is another Bugbear rais'd to terrify us from endeavouring to obtain a King's Government [in place of the proprietary one in Pennsylvania]. It is very possible that the Crown may think it necessary to keep Troops in America henceforward, to maintain its Conquests, and defend the Colonies; and that the Parliament may establish some Revenue arising out of

amount of "tyranny" in North America scarcely justified a revolution. Perhaps uneasily conscious of his labors as a propagandist, Jefferson late in life wrote to Madison concerning a Fourth of July oration by Timothy Pickering:

Timothy thinks . . . that the Declaration, as being a libel on the government of England . . . should now be buried in utter oblivion, to spare the feelings of our English friends and Angloman fellow citizens. But it is not to wound them that we wish to keep it in mind; but to cherish the principles of the instrument in the bosoms of our own citizens: and it is a heavenly comfort to see these principles are yet so strongly felt . . .

In short, it was the philosophy of the revolution that mattered, not the wrongs of the aggrieved colonials.

iii

The American revolution was born not so much out of unsupportable tyranny as out of dissensions, and the dissensions were many, contradictory, and in some instances irrational. The first anomaly arose out of the odd variety of ways by which the colonies had come into being from 1607 to 1733. Some were chartered commercial enterprises, some were crown grants, some were refuges, some had been conquered, and some were in theory feudal domains. Some were set up to maintain a church establishment, and others were created precisely to avoid so grievous a burden. Those secured by conquest — New Amsterdam and New Sweden * — had to have English laws, customs, and language imposed upon them. In others — for example, Pennsylvania — the coming of too many "foreigners" became a grievance. Proprietary governments had to yield to governments more or less representative. But no colonial government in 1763 was representative in our sense, since a royal governor was in most cases imposed from without, even though he might be, like Thomas Hutchinson, a native of the

---

the American Trade to be apply'd towards supporting those Troops. It is possible too, that we may, after a very few Years Experience, be generally very well satisfy'd with that Measure, from the steady Protection it will afford us against Foreign Enemies, and the Security of internal Peace among ourselves without the Expence or Trouble of a Militia." Leonard W. Labaree, ed., *The Papers of Benjamin Franklin*, vol. XI, New Haven, 1967, p. 169. So far as I can discover there were no barracks maintained by the colony on the Pennsylvania frontier.
* Canada was of course a special case.

161

colony.* Historians note that from 1763 to 1775 forms of government in the colonies more and more approximated each other. Nevertheless the chief magistrate, commonly appointed by a distant ministry, and the governor's council, mostly chosen from the rich and conservative gentry, were not "democratic"; and the lower house in any colonial legislature was also not "democratic," revisionist historians to the contrary notwithstanding. In every colony there were property qualifications for the suffrage, and in almost all the colonies the new, more sparsely settled western areas were not equitably represented. If the legislature quarreled with the royal governor, western men wondered why they had to pay any tax whatever to colonial governments that did little for them.

The very notion of being colonial was with many a source of irritation. The British had no comprehension of the colonies or of colonial life. Thus in his *History of the Province of New-York* (1757) William Smith, Jr., complained that the main body of the English people

conceive of these plantations, under the idea of wild, boundless, inhospitable, uncultivated deserts, and hence the punishment of transportation hither, in the judgment of most, is thought not much less severe, than an infamous death. . . . we may safely assert that even the publick boards, to whose care these extensive dominions have been more especially committed, attained, but lately, any tolerable acquaintance with their condition.

On the other hand John Dickinson in *The Late Regulations respecting the British Colonies on the Continent of America considered* (1765) complained of a precisely opposite British misunderstanding:

We are informed, that an opinion has been industriously propagated in *Great-Britain*, that the colonies are wallowing in wealth and luxury,

---

* In a careful study, *Royal Government in America*, New Haven, 1930, Leonard Woods Labaree found that between 1624 and the close of the revolution about three hundred governors were appointed to colonial posts, and says the average level was rather high, even though, or because, one in every four was a peer, the son of a peer, or held some sort of title. These officials, whatever their individual merits, were constantly beset by pressures from the colonial assemblies, demands from the English mercantile class, and instructions from the king in council, the board of trade, or some other administrative authority in Great Britain. It is to be remarked that, aside from the undependable colonial militia and the sheriffs and constables (who were often sympathetic with the crowd or mob and therefore lax or disobedient), no governor had an unpartisan permanent police force upon which he could depend to put down disorder.

while she is labouring under an enormous load of debt . . . This opinion has arisen from slight observations made in our cities during the late war, when large sums of money were spent here in support of fleets and armies. Our productions were then in great demand, and trade flourished. . . . But the cause of this gaiety has ceased, and all the effect remaining is, that we are to be treated as a rich people, when we are really poor.

A postwar depression in Great Britain in 1765 and another in 1774 affected the health of colonial economy. Add that, as a result of colonial resistance to the Townshend acts, English imports into New England and the middle colonies, which had been £1,363,000 in 1768, sank to £504,000 in 1769, and one can see that colonialism per se became a continuing irritation, not cured by the haughty attitude of British military officers toward colonial troops in the French and Indian War. This attitude, rather justified by the uncertain behavior of the colonial militia and intercolonial jealousies, necessitated that William Johnson receive five separate commissions as major-general from five separate colonies in 1755 before he could lead a "provincial army" against Crown Point. "Never," writes Parkman, "did general take the field with authority so heterogeneous." In London colonial representatives were summoned before parliamentary bodies as though they were high-class clerks rather than as representatives of autonomous political bodies possessing dignity and status.

Theorists, whether Tory or Whig, went back to the ancient world to "explain" the nature of a colony. They argued that the Greek colonies had carried with them the political characteristics of the mother city-state, yet retained local autonomy; but precisely what allegiance a colony then or now owed to its parent was never quite clear. Others pointed to the tyranny of Rome over her colonies, an assertion which also created dispute, since Roman colonies were more often conquests than separated hives of the Roman people, and, moreover, Rome finally extended citizenship first to all Italy and afterwards to the entire empire. Still other theorists held that the first settlers had fled from the Old World and its "tyranny" and then, by virtue of the law of nature, had entered into social compacts of their own (for example, the Mayflower compact); or they argued they were subject only to those parliamentary statutes in effect when the founders left England; or that their original charters, even if annulled, gave them a special relation to the crown or to the king in council or to parliament.* But this, too, got its proponents into difficulties, inasmuch as the colonies had quietly accepted the authority of many British statutes passed since their founding. Indeed, the question of internal versus external taxation, the last being within the "right" of parliament, was debated up to the time of the revolution.

The Albany Convention of 1754, intended to unify Americans, had been wrecked by, among other causes, colonial jealousy. Fear of the French and the Indians did something toward unifying the mainland colonies, so much, indeed, that when victory was won, the Rev. Thomas Barnard, preaching before Governor Bernard in Massachusetts, reflected a common feeling by saying: "Here shall our indulgent Mother [England], who has most generously rescued us and protected us, be served and honoured by growing Numbers, with all Duty, Love, and Gratitude, till Time shall be no more. Here shall be a perennial Source of her Strength and Riches." Against this, however, may be set many discordant expressions. Thus Charles Chauncy in *Two Letters to a Friend*, Boston, 1755, hoped that Braddock's defeat would arouse the "soporific south," scarcely a flattering expression if one lived in Virginia. That same year William Clarke said that only Massachusetts had acted with vigor against the French, but an unflattering sermon by the Rev. William Vinal, preached at Newport in 1755, declared that New England was a den of "thieves and robbers." In Philadelphia in 1756 William Smith blamed the Quakers for Braddock's defeat, and Ames's *Almanac* announced that convicts transported to Maryland from Tyburn plagued that colony more than its native rattlesnakes. In 1755 the Rev. Samuel Davies harangued the militia of Hanover County, Virginia, on "The Sin of Cowardice." The reader of Parkman's *Montcalm and Wolfe* learns a good deal about the scorn of the British for the colonials, the resentment of the colonials, interprovincial rivalry, and the unpredictability of colonial troops who sometimes fought bravely, sometimes ran away, sometimes deserted, and at no time showed

* The classical theory is set forth in Richard B. Gummere, *The American Colonial Mind and the Classical Tradition*, Cambridge, Mass., 1963; the colonial version of sixteenth- and seventeenth-century origins may be glimpsed in Michael Kammen, "The Meaning of Colonization in American Revolutionary Thought," *Journal of the History of Ideas*, 31 (1970), 337-358.

much sense of discipline. Such pronouncements, such judgments, did not make for unity.

Nor did an increasing uniformity of pattern among colonial governments end particularism. Thus control of Vermont real estate was long disputed among New Hampshire, Connecticut, and New York. Vermont later existed for a short time as a shadowy independent republic. In 1778 Ethan Allen, "major-general" of its militia, conducted a minor war against New York, and in 1780 he and his brother flirted with the idea of an agreement with military authorities in Canada, by which Vermont would become or continue a province of Great Britain. Westward expansion in New York was hindered by the existence of vast estates, holdovers in many cases from the Dutch regime, and also by the need for not overrunning the lands of the Six Nations, allies of the British in the French and Indian war. The early history of New Jersey is a queer compound of claims and counterclaims among various British noblemen and among the Swedes, the Dutch, and the English, not to speak of an emotional division between the Quakers and everybody else. Once split into East Jersey and West Jersey, that colony was united in 1702 under the administration of the governor of New York; in midcentury there were riots over land claims, and in the seventies Jersey farmers sold produce to both the American forces and the British forces, rather preferring the British, who paid cash. Pennsylvania, indeed, was the keystone colony, and is traditionally associated with the peace-loving Quakers, Benjamin Franklin, and the Pennsylvania Dutch. The Quakers, however, angered other inhabitants by refusing to protect the western frontier; boundary disputes with five other colonies sometimes led to blood-letting; the Penn family was stubborn; tensions among the Quakers, who were wealthy, the Germans, who were thrifty, and the Scotch-Irish, who were pugnacious, continued through the eighteenth century; and late in 1763 a "Presbyterian" mob known as the Paxton boys massacred a group of peaceful Indians at Lancaster living under the protection of the colonial governor.*

* The passions of the age are well represented in two accounts. The first, *The Conduct of the Paxton-Men, Impartially Represented: With Some Remarks on the Narrative*, possibly by Thomas Barton, Philadelphia, 1764, assails the Quakers and indicts the Indians. The Quakers "neglected and despised the Complaints of an injured and oppressed People; refused to redress their Grievances; they promoted *a military Apparatus; fortify'd the Barracks; planted Cannon*, and strutted about in all the Parade of War, as if they chose rather to have the Province

Although Philadelphia was to be the seat of the First and Second Continental Congresses, when the British army occupied it in 1777–78 resident Loyalists apparently had no qualms about including British officers in their jolly social life while Washington's fragment of an army froze at Valley Forge.

Besides internal dissensions over religion, land titles, and proprietary government, Maryland quarreled with Virginia concerning fishing in Chesapeake Bay. In Virginia the bloodshed of Bacon's rebellion in the seventeenth century, when frontiersmen burned Jamestown, was succeeded by the violent rhetoric of Patrick Henry, elected a burgess from Louisa County, then near the frontier, who in 1763 denounced George III, threw the House of Burgesses into an uproar, piloted a set of resolutions through that body in a somewhat illegal manner, and, says the staid *Dictionary of American Biography*, became "as complete a master of the public life of Virginia as Samuel Adams was of that of Massachusetts." In the Carolinas opposition between the Low Country and the back counties was notorious, climaxing at the Battle of Alamance, North Carolina, in 1771, when Governor Tryon and 1,200 militia defeated an estimated 2,000 "Regulators," executed some of their leaders, and required about 6,000 settlers in the Piedmont to take the oath of loyalty. Carolina frontiersmen, rightly or

involv'd in a Civil War, and see the Blood of perhaps 5 or 600 of his Majesty's Subjects shed, than give up, or banish to their native Caves and Woods, a Parcel of treacherous, faithless, rascally Indians, some of which can be proved to be Murderers . . . a *drunken, debauch'd, insolent, quarrelsome Crew*." The second item, *Copy of a Letter from Charles Read, Esq; to the Hon. John Ladd*; . . . *Gloucester*, also printed at Philadelphia in 1764, takes the opposite point of view: "The late outrage committed in *Lancaster*, is such a notorious Violation of the Rights of Government, and a Crime of so black a Dye, that I have not the least Doubt but that the Perpetrators of it will, in good time, suffer the Punishment the Law inflicts upon Murderers. . . . such an inhuman Murder as that at *Lancaster* can only serve to convince the World, that there are among us Persons more savage than *Indians*." An anonymous poem, *A Dialogue, Between Andrew Trueman and Thomas Zealot; About the killing the Indians at Cannestogoe and Lancaster*, Philadelphia [Ephesus], 1764, attempts to reproduce the Scotch dialect because the Paxton men were supposed to be Scotch-Irish. Another attack on the Presbyterians as whisky guzzlers and murderers, also anonymous, is *The Paxtoniade: A Poem by Christopher Gymnast*, Philadelphia, 1764. The legislature ordered the arrest of the Paxton men, who thereupon marched east to attack the legislature, but were persuaded by the governor to go home. The remnant of Indians had fled to Philadelphia; the frontier mob apparently intended to destroy them. See also *A Touch on the Times: A New Song to the Tune of Nancy Dawson*, apparently published in Philadelphia, in which the marauders are "Beasts of Prey and Murd'ring Fellows." The Paxton incident is representative of tension between the frontier and the seacoast.

wrongly, were not happy about their share of representation in the colonial legislatures, which laid taxes on them they often refused to pay, partly because they had no money with which to pay them. The gentry in South Carolina seem to have had little concern for either Georgia or North Carolina and not much for their own back country. Though it has been argued that inequalities in suffrage and in representation have been exaggerated, statistical research does not explain away emotional biases. It was, moreover, easier to go to a town meeting in, for example, eastern Massachusetts than to attend one in the western part of that province; and, besides, revision of any system of political apportionment is a slow, laborious process. Finally, if seaboard gentry could not pay their debts to London factors and resented new imperial taxes, westerners in the several colonies, once hard money was drained out of America by British mercantile economics, could not pay their rents or their debts to the seaboard gentry. Intercolonial jealousies and interclass suspicions were not easily subdued. Washington's army was to suffer from this particularism, as was the Continental Congress of the Confederation.

iv

Religion contributed importantly to tensions. The Anglican church was supported by taxation in some colonies, for example, New York, Virginia, and South Carolina; in other colonies — for instance, Massachusetts and Connecticut — the established church was Congregational or Congregational/Presbyterian. Still other colonies — Rhode Island and Georgia — prided themselves on being cities of refuge for religious underdogs. The history of Maryland is itself a curious story. Founded as a place to which Roman Catholics might safely go, Maryland saw the rise of a Puritan group to power in the seventeenth century; after the Glorious Revolution there was rumor of a popish plot to slaughter Protestants; and in 1715, proprietary government being once more in the saddle, Roman Catholics were nevertheless disfranchised. Yet Maryland counted Charles Carroll of Carrollton, educated by the Jesuits, among the signers of the Declaration of Independence and made him a member of the first United States Senate. At one time the Maryland delegates to the Second Continental Congress were instructed not to vote for independence; and a Maryland constitution of 1776 contained a property qualification for voting, retained until 1802. In Pennsylvania the Quakers, the Mennonites, and the Presbyterians seldom saw eye to eye. In Connecticut and Massachusetts conservative Congregationalists exhibited a siege psychology as rents appeared in the seamless robe of Calvinism; Baptists, Methodists, and other sects won toleration; the Anglican church slowly made headway; nascent Unitarianism appeared; and the sailing of three Congregationalists associated with Yale to England as early as 1722, to be ordained as Anglican clergymen, created an ecclesiastical furor. Rhode Island was a law unto itself.

In 1700 there were about 28 Presbyterian congregations in the future United States, in 1740 about 160. In the same years the Baptists virtually tripled the number of their churches, the Lutherans grew from 7 to 93, the Dutch Reformed from 28 to 68, and the Anglicans from 111 to 246. By the end of the colonial era it is estimated there were more than three thousand religious organizations in the future United States. From the standpoint of our secular age these figures are mere statistics. In a century when religion was central to thought, this multiplication of sects implies heated disputes among the several creeds.

Thus, preaching at Stanford on April 10, 1763, the Rev. Noah Welles lamented the efforts of the Anglican churches to lure believers away from the Presbyterian faith:

The restless endeavours of some among them, to draw away persons from our communion, and their unwearied attempts to increase their party, by constantly insinuating to you, the danger of continuing in fellowship with churches, in which (as they would bear you in hand) there is no authorized ministry, no regular gospel administrations; at last convinced me, that it was high time something should be publickly offered for your satisfaction, in this important point.

The reverend Mr. Welles then vigorously went on to do just that. He was courteous compared to some of the others. Jonathan Mayhew, for example, himself a vigorous controversialist, wrote against the Anglican Society for the Propagation of the Gospel in Foreign Parts (SPGFP); whereupon one John Aplin, a Rhode Islander, attacked him in bitter satiric verse:

> By Nature vain, by Art made worse,
> And greedy of false Fame;

> Thro' Truth disguis'd, and Mobs deceiv'd,
>   Thou fain would'st get a Name,

and in a footnote referred to "this blind Bigot [who] is for setting up an Inquisition against the Religion of the Nation, within his Majesty's own Dominions," a fine return, he added sarcastically, for "a fanatic Preacher" to give for the "blood and treasure poured out by England" to preserve the colonies from French conquest. Mayhew could give as good as he got. In a quarrel with John Cleaveland of Ipswich, who did not care for Mayhew's views of God, Mayhew retorted:

Can you then possibly think it became you, an obscure person from another province, and one so unletter'd as you are; an outcast from the college [Yale] to which you was a disgrace; for some time a rambling itinerant, and prompter of disorders and confusion among us; so raw and unstudied in divinity; one hardly ever heard of among us, but in the frequent reports of your follies and extravagances, and at length set up as a minister to an assembly of separatists . . . to turn author upon this occasion?

The Rev. Henry Caner, an Anglican clergyman in Boston, who profoundly distrusted Mayhew and all his works, in *A Candid Examination* (1763), was capable of this sort of writing: "Every gentleman who has had a liberal and polite education, thinks it beneath his character to enter the lists with one who observes no measures of decency or good manners, nay who does not scruple to sacrifice the meek and gentle spirit of the Gospel to the gratification of a licentious and ungovern'd temper." Clerical disputants hit hard at each other in the second half of the eighteenth century. They also profoundly disturbed the minds of their parishioners and of the reading public. The rhetorical extravagance of the American revolution has a lengthy forehistory.

While the branches of Protestantism disputed among themselves, Daniel Coxe in 1730 became Grand Master of the Masons in America — and many of the founding fathers were Masons. In 1733 Jews were formally admitted to Georgia, and in 1755 Joseph Salvador bought 100,000 acres in South Carolina for a Jewish colony. As early as 1725 Benjamin Franklin published, though he later tried to suppress it, *A Dissertation on Liberty and Necessity*, and in 1728 he wrote his *Articles of Belief and Acts of Religion*, documents virtually deistic and forerunners of such books as Ethan

Allen's *Reason the Only Oracle of Man* (1784),* a characteristic effusion of the "republican religion" that went along with the revolution and prospered on the frontier. There it was contested by Presbyterians and Methodists, and there at the very end of the century a new wave of revivalism developed, of the camp-meeting order with all its wild emotional upheavals.

Old Side and Old Light churches in New England fought a determined rear-guard action against liberal theology, but they lost ground. From the Seven Years War to the Declaration of Independence American religious life more and more emphasized the autonomy of the individual and the privacy of his emotions.† Probably the middle term between old-line theology and republican religion was this same Jonathan Mayhew, who carried Christianity to the borders of Unitarianism and who, as Herbert Schneider said, transformed a Calvinist Jehovah into a benevolent ruler who "governs his great family, his universal Kingdom, according to those general rules and maxims which are in themselves most wise and good[, having only] good and gracious purposes respecting his creatures." Minister of the new and liberal West Church in Boston, Mayhew was shunned by the orthodox, came to distrust the emotional populism in the Great Awakening and its aftermath, questioned some of the principal theological tenets of the standing order, said that Christianity was rational, upheld free will, and in his sermons tended to equate theology virtually with deism, or at least Unitarianism,‡ took an ambiguous view of the Trinity, and

---

* *Reason the Only Oracle of Man* is something of a bibliographical and historical puzzle. It was apparently the joint product of Ethan Allen and Thomas Young, the agreement being that the book should be published by the survivor. It was published, but a fire in the printer's garret destroyed all but thirty copies of the original edition. An abridged edition was, however, published in New York in 1836 and another in Boston in 1854. On the whole curious story see chapter i ("Ethan Allen, Freethinking Revolutionist") of G. Adolf Koch, *Republican Religion*, New York, 1933, and its references to various biographies and studies of Allen.

† For a differing interpretation and a well-documented one see Alan Heimert, *Religion and the American Mind: From the Great Awakening to the Revolution*, Cambridge, Mass., 1966.

‡ Mayhew accepted the philosophy of Newton. In a sermon "Occasioned by the Earthquakes in November 1755" he denied that the earthquake was a "special providence," though he admired God as a great supervisory power: "A little reflection upon the operations of our own minds, will indeed make it evident, that all wonder, surprise, astonishment, at bottom proceed from, and connote ignorance; for nothing which we fully understand, ever excites our wonder or admiration." The earthquake was, indeed, the work of God, and in view of the unprosperous war against the French might be construed as a "warning of the

in his most celebrated performance, *A Discourse Concerning Unlimited Submission and Non-Resistance to the Higher Powers*, preached at Boston in 1750, outlined what a late biographer has called a catechism of revolution. Here Mayhew substantiated the right of the people to throw off tyranny and argued vehemently against the Anglican church:

The people know for what end they set up, and maintain, their governors, and they are the proper judges when they execute their *trust* as they ought to do it.

For a nation . . . abused to rise unanimously, and to resist their prince, even to the dethroning of him, is not criminal; but a reasonable way of vindicating their liberties and just rights; it is making use of the . . . only means, which God has put into their power, for mutual self-defence.

People have no security against being unmercifully *priest-ridden*, but by keeping all imperious BISHOPS, and other CLERGYMEN who love to "lord it over God's heritage," from getting their foot into the stirrup at all.

Tyranny brings *ignorance* and *brutality* along with it. It degrades men from their just rank, into the class of brutes. . . . There can be nothing great and good, where its influence reaches. For which reason it becomes every friend to truth and human kind; every lover of God and the christian religion, to bear a part in opposing this hateful monster.

Here again is an example of the theological lineage of revolutionary rhetoric.

Mayhew exemplifies the spread of Arminianism among the colonials, a doctrine that not only stressed freedom of the will but also tended more and more to stress the practical aspects of Chris-

---

need of reformation in morals." But it must be remembered that the "general laws" in nature "are themselves mysterious and inexplicable." In *Two Sermons On the Nature, Extent and Perfection of the Divine Goodness* (1763) he virtually fuses the God of the deists with the God of Christianity. Thus: "For, please to consider, that when God makes creatures capable of happiness and misery, in whatever degree; if he does not also make provision for their comfortable subsistence, and take kind care of them, he of consequence dooms them to inevitable pain and misery, even without any fault of theirs; since if a creature is actually made, and preserved in a state of sensibility, it must be either in a degree of pleasure or pain. . . . let some very acute distinguisher shew the difference betwixt this and positive cruelty." Tom Paine could have subscribed to this doctrine. The latest life of Mayhew is by Charles W. Akers, *Called unto Liberty: A Life of Jonathan Mayhew, 1720–1766*, Cambridge, Mass., 1964.

tianity, not its theological subtleties, and argued that to make God the author of sin was false theology. The secularity of the seaport towns and some of the unruly elements along the frontier found this view of religion more acceptable than hell-fire and damnation, and again one notes the renewed belief in individualism. Indians and Frenchmen might be born wicked, but not white Protestant American colonials.

One must next consider the effects of the Great Awakening, that vast religious revival which swept over the colonies from the middle thirties through the Seven Years War. In 1726 the Rev. Gilbert Tennent founded the Log Cabin College (the date is in dispute) in Delaware for the training of evangelists who, if they were not illiterate, were not learned in the New England sense; in 1734 the Rev. Jonathan Edwards began preaching a series of powerful sermons that, somewhat to his distress, produced the hysteria associated with revivalism; in 1738 George Whitefield, a powerful exhorter, arrived in Georgia on the first of several visits to the British colonies; and in Virginia the Rev. Samuel Davies proved to be a great mover and shaker. Some of the revivalists preached Calvinism in the sense of stressing the depravity of man; the same men, and others, encouraged the individual sinner to repent; and though sinners might repent in crowds, by an understandable psychological contagion, the religious experience was emotional and individualized. A central principle of many revivalists (Whitefield and John Wesley are famous in this regard) was that if the people would not go to the church, the church should go to the people. A doctrine of individual salvation, Calvinist or not, created in a few years a vast movement of dissent from the establishment that weakened ecclesiastical authority by underlining, in Burke's phrase, the dissidence of dissent and the protestantism of the Protestant religion. Evangelists more than hinted that churches of the establishment were spiritually dead. Salvation, they felt, was an individual and private matter, an emotional awakening, not a problem in logic and theology. The paradox of the movement is that although the Great Awakening was directed at individual souls, it rested upon a crowd psychology, evident, for example, in a letter of 1764 from the Rev. Samuel Buell of East-Hampton, Long Island, to the Rev. Mr. Barber of Groton:

Never did I see such an Assembly before! God's Glory filled the

House. Our Pews, Alleys, Stairs, Seats, above and below, contained therein wounded and distressed Souls; and from Time to Time, Day after Day, the Holy Ghost evidently came down as a mighty rushing Wind; sometimes almost as sudden as a Flash of Lightning; bowing our Assembly, and producing the most amazing Agonies of Soul, & Cries that ever you heard.

Without meaning to, the Great Revival taught the power of mob action, and, together with Arminianism, smoothed the road for revolution. If everybody was to find his private way to God, what difference did it make whether the deity was Anglican or Congregationalist, Calvinist or Arminian, Baptist or Edwardsian? The "experience" of salvation could do without logic and author-ity; and though colonials, notably in the northern states, continued to be fascinated by fine points of theology, the Great Awakening appealed to the common man. The Declaration of Independence and the federal Constitution assumed as a matter of course what the Great Awakening assumed as a matter of conscience, namely, the autonomy of the adult.

In addition to intercolonial jealousy and emotional differences among the dissenting sects, a third great source of ecclesiastical and political conflict was fear of an Anglican establishment, a fear that strikes us nowadays as absurd but was nonetheless a real anxiety undoubtedly played up by propagandists. Separatists had of course got out from under episcopal rule, for which they could not find scriptural warrant. Scotsmen and the Scotch-Irish looked back to their own Church of Scotland, which rejected the idea of epis-copacy. The Quakers, the Mennonites, the Baptists, and other denominations could not accept the English prayer-book and the Thirty-Nine Articles. Puritans who had once thought of themselves as misunderstood members of the Anglican flock had ceased to belong to that sheepfold, and Methodists, who had once regarded themselves as within the Church of England, held their first in-dependent American "conference" in 1773. Francis Asbury, called the "Wesley of America," had come here in 1771 and organized American Methodism. Some Methodists, it is true, remained Tories and returned to England after the revolution broke out.

During the colonial period the American Anglican church was under the supervision of a deputy of the Bishop of London. That high official was also at times the head of the Society for the

Propagation of the Gospel in Foreign Parts. The king was the head of the church, and colonies in which the Anglican church was established necessarily supported it by taxation. The SPGFP had as its theoretical aim the conversion of the heathen — that is to say, the Indians — but sturdy colonials protested it was more interested in establishing Anglicanism among the whites than in carrying the gospel among the savages. Americans remembered the traditions of Stuart autocracy and the tyranny of Archbishop Laud. Colonials who had come hither to get out from under the rule of bishops saw in this cautious campaign of the Church of England to create one or more American bishoprics a plot, under cover of which the imperial government might gain some control of the colonies and of colonial taxation.

In Virginia the Anglican clergy, poorly supported, were paid not in tax money but in tobacco. In the 1750's the price of tobacco fluctuated, the clergy, in need of a decent wage, complained to London, and the practice of paying them in tobacco at a fixed price was found unconstitutional. In Louisa County a colonial court reached the same conclusion. But Patrick Henry there made a fiery speech opposing an encroachment upon the rights of Virginians and denounced the clergy for not observing the laws of the colony. Technically he lost his case, but the fame of his address spread beyond the borders of that colony. Clearly the Anglicans were infiltrating the colonies, for what dark purpose nobody really knew. Had they not created King's College in New York City as their own? This support was spiritedly attacked by William Livingston, who published an influential paper, *The Independent Reflector*. In vain the Rev. East Apthorp in Boston in 1763 appealed for tolerance and moderation; in vain the Rev. John Beach in New York declared the Church of England stood in need of support; in vain the Rev. Henry Caner in 1763 in a pamphlet, on the whole well-mannered, declared that, though an Anglican, he was "unwilling to renew the memory of those severities, that were too commonly practiced by all parties in the last century"; in vain did the Rev. Thomas Bradbury Chandler of Elizabeth-Town, New Jersey, plead in 1767 that if bishops came to America, they "shall have no Authority, but purely of a Spiritual and Ecclesiastical Nature, such as is derived altogether from the Church and not from the State."

The fat was in the fire. The Rev. Charles Chauncy, by no means a bigot, denied the doctrine of the apostolic succession, denounced episcopal power, said there was absolutely no need for an American episcopate, more than hinted that the papists were upon us, and roundly concluded:

We are, in principle, against all civil establishments in religion and as we do not desire any such establishments in support of our own religious establishments, or practice, we cannot reasonably be blamed, if we are not disposed to encourage them in favor of the Episcopal-Colonists.

A footnote adds that "bishops being once fixed in America, pretexts might easily be found, both for encreasing their number, and enlarging their powers." The *Pennsylvania Journal* on December 22, 1769, quoted *The Centinel* to the effect that true-blue Americans, "far from allowing the *Church of England* the rank of ADMIRAL in the *protestant fleet*, will not give her so much as the privilege of a cock-boat, but [are] for turning her adrift without any commanding officer she can acknowledge; and that too in a *rotten and leaky* condition; her whole works being 'corrupted,' &c." The paper would not "even take her in tow" but would allow her to sink. *The American Whig* said that the Rev. Thomas Bradbury Chandler ought to confine himself to his pastoral duties and not meddle with secular affairs, since

the Christian clergy seem to have surpassed the Pagan priesthood, as much in their cruelties, as in the refined morality they were sent out to inculcate. Power in the hands of ecclesiastics raised antichrist to the very bosom of the Christian church; and if we may judge from what is past, civil authority can never be intrusted to the clergy with safety to the people. Secluded from the world, and ignorant of mankind . . . they grow sour and vindictive, over-rate their order, are impatient of opposition, and are enemies to freedom of thought.

They are also "intriguing, speculative, systematical and enterprising," "an overmatch for the vulgar,"

and by the advantage of their numbers, and the devotion of their weak and biggoted adherents, naturally acquire a dominion the more to be feared, as their operations proceeding upon the flattering principles of advancing the glory of God, and the good of souls, rarely cease until an implicit submission to their opinions is extorted.

As for the SPGFP, the vocabulary of ecclesiastical abuse was poured upon it.

In a general sense respectability — the gentry, the royal governors and their retinues, many southern planters, and many well-placed merchants, though of course not all — favored Anglicanism, whereas dissenters, intellectual liberals, farmers, and the plain people, again in a loose sense, were against it. As Carl Bridenbaugh phrases the situation, the Great Fear of the Episcopacy reached its highest intensity during the years 1767 to 1770, the period of the Townshend acts. Episcopal tyranny, parliamentary tyranny, and royal tyranny, patriots thought, were three phases of some mysterious system of oppression. This is amusingly evident in a passage from John Trumbull's *M'Fingal*, written in the early 1770's:

> The power display'd in Gage's banners,
> Shall cut their fertile lands to manors;
> And o'er our happy conquer'd ground
> Dispense estates and titles round.
> Behold the world will stare at new setts
> Of home-made Earls in Massachusetts;
> Admire, array'd in ducal tassels,
> Your Ol'vers, Hutchinsons and Vassals;
> See joined in ministerial work
> His Grace of Albany and York.
> What lordships from each carved estate,
> On our New-York Assembly wait!
>
> .   .   .   .   .   .
>
> In wide-sleeved pomp of godly guise,
> What solemn rows of Bishops rise!
> Aloft a Card'nal's hat is spread
> O'er punster Cooper's rev'rend head.
> In Vardell, that poetic zealot,
> In view a lawn-bedizen'd prelate;
> What mitres fall, as 't is their duty,
> On heads of Chandler and Auchmuty!
> Knights, Viscounts, Barons shall ye meet,
> As thick as pebbles in the street;
> Even I, perhaps (heaven speed my claim!)
> Shall fix a *Sir* before my name.*

* The persons named were all Loyalists. The clergy among them were ardent Church of England men. Thus Myles Cooper, the second president of King's College, guided a meeting of Episcopalian clergymen in 1765 in New York, and John Vardill (Vardell) wrote Tory articles for the New York papers; the "Poplicola" essays were apparently their joint production.

v

Although historians are agreed that there were economic tensions between Great Britain and her colonies before 1775, disagreement among interpreters arises about the strength of these tensions, their effects upon publics often ill-defined, and about the puzzle as to whether the revolution was rebellion against Great Britain or some sort of social struggle in the colonies between the haves and the have-nots. One school of thought contends that the suffrage was more widely held and the ownership of land less of a problem than earlier writers had assumed. It is, however, one thing to possess the right to vote and another thing to exercise it. It also seems to be true, first, that many land titles were suspect and, second, that under the disastrous methods of farming then common, small farmers (the yeomanry of some writers) frequently quit one farm to move to some other area nearer the frontier, usually without warning the tax-collector. The point is not that class distinctions may have been overemphasized; the point is that save for the coastal towns and their environs, population was more scattered, more disorganized, and less able to balance both sides of a disputed policy than mere written evidence from the eighteenth century leads one to assume. Hence, once the "radicals" got control of a colonial legislature or a popular assembly as well as the printers in a colony, the propaganda they were able to spread, high-keyed as such propaganda is, had nothing to counteract it in emotional or intellectual appeal. Loyalists like Daniel Leonard and Joseph Galloway might write on economic or political issues with clarity and skill, but the voice of reason was often drowned in the shriller prose of such revolutionaries as James Otis, Patrick Henry, and Thomas Paine.

It is useful to look briefly at some economic discontents. These arose out of the mercantilist doctrine, common in the Western world since the days of Colbert, the financial genius of Louis XIV. Under this doctrine national prosperity consisted in the physical possession of as much gold and silver as possible, a surplus of exports over imports (hard money therefore stayed in a country, or at least a surplus of it did), control over shipping (no foreign bottoms), and such a monopoly of goods produced in the nation as prevented its colonies, if it had them, from competing with the mother country. Colonies existed to supply the mother country with materials and goods it could not produce itself and to consume such goods as the mother country produced, without setting up rival manufactures or other productive units. In such a system colonies were neither masters of their own economic lives nor equal partners in an imperial order.

The so-called Navigation Acts regulating and restricting colonial commerce either by forbidding the colonials to export materials they produced to any other country than Great Britain or by enumerating the articles they must send to that nation dated from the seventeenth century, but until the period of the Seven Years War they had been laxly enforced. Even at that, however, Virginia planters in particular found themselves perpetually in debt to London, and merchant-shippers in the middle and northern colonies, to keep alive and make a profit, had to exercise considerable ingenuity in smuggling. Because hard money drained out of the colonies to Britain, colonial legislatures turned to paper currency in the eighteenth century, but paper money was in any circumstances an uncertain medium and, moreover, its issue was soon forbidden by the imperial government. When, after the Seven Years War, British political leaders rightly turned to modernizing the imperial government, they could not understand why their own laws drew hard money to London or why the colonists were helpless to replace it except with French, Spanish, or other foreign coinage acquired by illegal trading with the West Indies, the continent of Europe, or Africa. It has been estimated that hard money seldom stayed in the colonies more than six months. It was also true that the various colonies could not agree on the value to be given foreign coins, and that clipping and "sweating" — that is, wearing away hard metal and saving the gold and silver dust — further rendered the value of any foreign coin uncertain.

If economic conditions in the mother country and in the colonies had remained relatively stable, possibly something could have been worked out. But the Seven Years War was costly to many of the colonies and more costly to Great Britain. International wars upset shipping: privateering was a favorite eighteenth-century device, under which hundreds of vessels were seized — it increased both public and private debts and swelled some sorts of private profits. The Seven Years War, like other world wars, induced an economic slump in Europe, which had its repercussions in the American colonies, suffering smaller depressions of their own. The uncertainties of commerce filled a port town like Boston with restless unemployed seamen. There were at least two bad harvest years in Britain during the period 1763–1775, and in America, notably in the southern colonies, plantations ceased to give their earlier yields because bad farming exhausted the soils, and, as we have noted, the small farmer, having allowed one farm to deteriorate, moved on to another piece of ground usually more distant from a market. If he sold anything at all, he had to face an increase in the cost of getting his wares to market.

British cabinets during the fifteen years from 1760 to 1775 were not either as stupid or as "tyrannical" as American propaganda sometimes pictured them. Parliamentary leaders had to devise means of paying for the most expensive war of the eighteenth century, one which involved the very existence of the colonies and which ended by assuring that existence. From the point of view of the colonies, they had paid a goodly share of that expense, but the ministry seemed resolved to prevent them from enjoying any of the profits. In London minister succeeded minister, but as the system of genuine party responsibility had not yet been invented, the result was a succession of uncertainties. The Stamp Act became law in 1765, a law laying a moderate tax on all sorts of legal forms, newspapers, and other items. As we have remarked, it cannot be said that from the point of view of taxation the Stamp Act was anything very terrible. But colonial "radicals," who had not liked the Sugar Act of 1764, a complicated measure that laid taxes on the import-export trade with Britain and restricted colonial commerce with other countries, found the Stamp Act the very thing for their purpose — it was "tyranny." In most of the colonial port towns there were violent anti–Stamp Act riots that endangered lives, destroyed property, and showed a general disrespect for law and authority. Parliament repealed the act in 1766, but insisted at the same time on voting the so-called Declaratory Act, which asserted that parliament had authority to pass legislation binding on the colonies in all cases whatsoever. The colonists, who had in October 1765 set up a Stamp Act Congress, issued a "Declaration of Rights and Grievances," principally the work of John Dickinson. This asserted that there could be no taxation without representation, and asked colonial merchants to do no business with Great Britain. Merchants now assumed that victory was theirs and overlooked the significance of the Declaratory Act.

In 1766 a ship carrying two companies of British artillerymen was storm-driven into Boston harbor. When the governor and his council ordered supplies to be sent to the unfortunate soldiers and sailors, temporarily housed in Castle William in Boston harbor, the Massachusetts lower house, swayed by the oratory of James Otis, refused to vote money for supplying them. The governor was helpless and could only report to London his inability to enforce the laws. About the same time the New York assembly refused to obey the Mutiny Act — that is, to supply British forces stationed in New York; and other colonies tried to get out from under the obligation of housing, supplying, or paying for the armed forces of the king. Colonial politicians, ministers, economists, and other intellectuals argued endlessly in sermon and pamphlet, newspaper article and speech about two central issues essentially economic: trade and taxation. By the later sixties there was, except among "radicals," a vague feeling that parliament had the right to lay external taxes but no right to impose internal taxes. But what was an internal tax? What was an external tax? What, for that matter, was representation?

The parliamentary history of Great Britain in the sixties and seventies is a complicated and separate problem. But in 1767 the Townshend administration, conforming, as it thought, to the American distinction between external and internal taxation, imposed duties on various imported articles, including tea, and established or reinvigorated various boards and courts charged with the duty of enforcing the revenue laws. The response of colonials was once again to enter into nonimportation agreements, which, more and more generally adhered to by the colonies from 1767 to 1769, proved extraordinarily successful, British imports into the colonies being cut about in half from 1768 to 1769. (Unfortunately for the colonies British trade with the continent increased during the same years.) The Sons of Liberty were more and more active. In 1768 John Hancock's sloop, *Liberty*, obviously engaged in smuggling, was seized by customs officials and towed to lie under the guns of the British frigate *Romney* in Boston harbor. This occasioned an assault upon the customs officials by a mob, and this riot in turn compelled the governor to call in troops to maintain order. Two British regiments came to Boston in October 1768.

vi

In January 1770, at New York, where troops were also stationed, rioters led by Alexander McDougall brought about the Battle of Golden Hill, in which many were wounded. In March occurred the famous Boston Massacre, in which three persons were killed outright and two mortally wounded. Samuel Adams, the leading Boston radical, demanded that the troops be withdrawn to Castle William, and the governor was forced to comply. The Boston Massacre became a *cause célèbre*, which fired the flames of radical propaganda. Here, for instance, is a sample of the language used by Dr. Joseph Warren in an oration commemorating the Boston Massacre, delivered in 1772:

[The creators of the Massachusetts Bay colony had found it] so hard . . . to resolve to embrue their hands in the *blood* of their brethren, that they chose rather to quit their fair possessions and seek another habitation in a distant clime. — When they came to this new world, which they fairly purchased of the Indian natives, the only rightful proprietors, they cultivated the then barren soil by their incessant labor, and defended their dear-bought possessions with the fortitude of the christian, and the bravery of the hero.

But now behold

the ruinous consequences of standing armies to free communities [which] may be seen in the histories of SYRACUSE, ROME, and many other once flourishing STATES, some of which have now scarce a name.

Boston threatens to be among these unhappy cities:

When our alarmed imagination presented to our view our houses wrapt in flames — our children subject to the barbarous caprice of the raging soldiery — our beauteous virgins exposed to all the insolence of unbridled passion, — our virtuous wives endeared to us by every tender tie, falling a sacrifice to worse than brutal violence, and perhaps like the famed LUCRETIA, distracted with anguish and despair, ending their wretched lives by their own fair hands,

let all good citizens remember that the villains wore "the royal GEORGE's livery." That the few bewildered British privates who, fearing their lives were endangered, unluckily fired into a group of men and boys, were actually the "Bloody butchers," the "villains high and low," the "wretches . . . who executed the inhuman deed" (John Hancock's language in 1774) may at this distance in time be doubted by the thoughtful historian. The regiments exiled to Boston harbor were not the profligate soldiery who pillaged Rome in 1527; they were, on the contrary, the same sort of men whose victory at Quebec under Wolfe had been hailed with delight by colonial preachers.

The next event to transform economic problems into the politics of emotion was even more dramatic. This was the burning of the *Gaspee*, a schooner of the royal navy, by an organized mob in 1772, and the shooting of its commander in circumstances of coarse brutality. The *Gaspee* was engaged in putting down smuggling operations in Narragansett Bay, then a notorious haven for illegal traffickers; and its commander, Lieutenant William Dudington, brave but rash, had been seizing vessels bearing contraband. Tempers rose among the Rhode Islanders, who proposed to arm a vessel of their own to rescue by force ships captured by the *Gaspee*. Thereupon the British admiral on that station declared he would hang as pirates any persons engaged in so unlawful an enterprise. Unfortunately Lieutenant Dudington ran the *Gaspee* aground. Bands of "patriots" set out in small boats to capture and destroy the vessel, shot and wounded the commander, set him adrift in an open boat on the waters of the bay, destroyed his schooner, and dispersed to their homes. No other single act hitherto so directly challenged the British government not only because of the open defiance of law by the rioters but also because imperial officials were unable to get any witness to testify to the facts.

We have passed beyond economic differences into the politics of revolution. The Sons of Liberty were gradually overshadowed by the organization of Committees of Correspondence, first proposed in Massachusetts in 1772, then in Virginia in 1773, and eventually appearing in most of the colonies. Their leaders sought concerted action. In 1773, all the Townshend duties having been repealed except a tax on tea, the British government passed a complicated measure designed to rescue the East India Company from bankruptcy, which retained and enforced the tax on tea but which, had it gone into effect, would probably have resulted in making tea cheaper in America than it had been. Alert colonial agitators viewed this measure, however, as a cunning device to get money out of the colonies indirectly. The tea was never sold to the Americans. The most famous episode resulting from the Tea Act was the Boston Tea Party, involving the destruction of imported tea through actions obviously planned ahead of time and paralleled by similar, if less violent, actions in other seaports. This celebrated event occurred on December 16, 1773. In March there was more violence in Boston; on April 22, 1774, New York radicals repeated the formula of the Boston Tea Party; and cargoes of tea were burned in Annapolis and at Greenwich, New Jersey, the Annapolis rioters burning not only the tea but also the ship that brought it.

From the point of view of Great Britain the colonies had now put themselves beyond the possibility of reasonable negotiation, Edmund Burke to the contrary notwithstanding. Parliament therefore in the spring of 1774 passed the so-called Coercive Acts and the Quebec Act.* The colonials responded by the "Suffolk Resolves" drawn up by Dr. Joseph Warren, which declared with a good deal of defiance that taxes should be withheld from the British until the government of Massachusetts was restored, that Boston was in danger of attack from British forces, and that Americans were justified in jailing any officer of the crown. The First Continental Congress assembled at Philadelphia in September 1774 and, voting down such conservatives as Joseph Galloway of Pennsylvania and George Read of Delaware, endorsed the Suffolk Resolves, desired all colonists not to obey the Coercive Acts, urged

* The Coercive Acts were three in number (four, with the Quartering Act of June 1774) and were intended (1) to close the port of Boston as a punishment; (2) to transfer to Great Britain from Massachusetts all indictments and trials for capital offenses arising out of riots, inciting riots, or interfering with the collection of the revenue; and (3) to annul the existing government of Massachusetts, substituting for it one virtually dependent upon the king's pleasure. The Quartering Act of June 2 applied to all colonies and legalized the housing of troops in taverns, deserted buildings, and, when necessary, occupied houses. The Quebec Act (May 20) not only gave Canada a permanent civil government but extended the boundaries of Quebec to the Ohio River. This, with the Proclamation Line, if enforced, annulled the claims of various colonies to lands north of that river and also (a result of the conspiracy of Pontiac in part) confined the colonies to the land between the top of the Appalachian mountain chains and the seacoast. The Quebec Act further offended Protestants by giving a preferred place to the Roman Catholic Church and annoyed political liberals by reserving local taxation in that province to the British parliament and vesting legislative authority in the governor and his council. Colonials saw in these provisions the wave of the future and dreaded it.

Massachusetts to form its own government, exhorted the several colonies to organize and arm a militia, and recommended the revival or continuance of the nonimportation agreements. This took form as the Continental Association, created in October, eventually spreading to all thirteen colonies, and enforced by the "people" or committees of the people. To a Loyalist such as Samuel Seabury, anarchy had settled in:

The American Colonies are unhappily involved in a scene of confusion and discord. The bands of civil society are broken; the authority of government weakened, and in some instances taken away: Individuals are deprived of their liberty; their property is frequently invaded by violence, and not a single Magistrate has had courage or virtue enough to interpose.

What harm had the manufacturers of Great Britain or the people of Ireland done the Americans?

Shall we then revenge ourselves upon them . . . ? Shall we attempt to unsettle the whole British Government — to throw all into confusion, because our self-will is not complied with? Because the ill-projected, ill-conducted, abominable scheme of some of the colonists, to form a republican government, independent of Great-Britain, cannot otherwise succeed? — Good God! can we look forward to the ruin, destruction, and desolation of the whole British Empire, without one relenting thought? *

Samuel Seabury argued in vain. The New England colonies were especially forward in creating new governments, arming the militia, sending them out on raids against the British, and collecting stores of arms and ammunition. In 1775, on instructions from Lord Dartmouth, Secretary of State for the Colonies, General Gage sent his troops from Boston through Lexington to Concord to capture or destroy colonial military supplies. Who fired the first shot heard round the world has never been settled, but the battles of Lexington and Concord and the retreat of the British to Boston

---

* Samuel Seabury, *Free Thoughts on the Proceedings of the Continental Congress, Held at Philadelphia Sept. 5, 1774: Wherein Their Errors are exhibited, their Reasonings Confuted, and The fatal Tendency of their Non-Importation, Non-Exportation, and Non-Consumption Measures, are laid open to the plainest Understandings; and The Only means pointed out For Preserving and Securing Our present Happy Constitution: in A Letter to The Farmers and other Inhabitants of North America In General, And to those of the Province of New York In Particular. By a Farmer. Hear me, for I Will Speak!* New York, November 16, 1774.

under fire from militia skirmishers rendered futile the conciliation plan of Lord North, formed in February. The British army was now shut up in Boston by the motley intercolonial force that became the Continental Army under George Washington. It was so designated by the Second Continental Congress that met in May 1775. In June the Americans fought the British at Bunker Hill. During the ensuing winter the Americans vainly, if gallantly, tried to invade and subdue Canada. In December Governor Dunmore of Virginia placed that province under martial law, tried to raise a regiment of slaves, lost a battle at Great Bridge, retreated to a British naval force, and on January 1, 1776, burned most of Norfolk. (Americans burned the rest of it in February.)

In January 1776 Thomas Paine printed *Common Sense*, a pamphlet that electrified patriot opinion and disheartened the Loyalists, calling George III a royal brute and demanding American independence. In June 1776 Richard Henry Lee of Virginia moved in the Second Continental Congress that "these United Colonies are and of right ought to be free and independent States." On July 4 the Declaration of Independence was voted, a document that threw all the blame on the British king. The war was to last until 1783, a period of time about as long as the Seven Years War. Out of such confusions was born a new nation conceived in liberty and dedicated to the proposition that all men are created equal. The problem was how to unify thirteen suspicious states. Not until 1789 was unity really achieved.

Economic and political (or constitutional) disputes had passed into passion. Two examples may be given to illustrate revolutionary emotionalism. When the Boston Port Bill went into effect, a day of "fasting, humiliation and prayer" was declared in most of the colonies. That stout Anglican, the Rev. Jonathan Boucher, refused to recognize this or any other appeal in aid of Boston because, he thought, contributions in the name of charity were intended to buy arms and ammunition. On the appointed fast day, a Thursday, he went to his church, found his curate, "a strong republican," in the pulpit, and the building filled with about two hundred armed men under the command of one Osborne Sprigg. Sprigg forbade Boucher to preach. According to Boucher's autobiography,

at the proper time, with my sermon in one hand and a loaded pistol in the other, like Nehemiah I prepared to ascend my pulpit, when one of my friends, Mr. David Cranford, having got behind me, threw his arms round me and held me fast. He assured me that he had heard the most positive orders given to twenty men picked out for the purpose, to fire on me the moment I got into the pulpit, which therefore he would never permit me to do. . . . I maintained that, once to flinch was forever to invite danger; but my well-wishers prevailed, and, when I was down, it is horrid to recollect what a scene of confusion ensued. Sprigg and his company contrived to surround me and to exclude every moderate man. Seeing myself thus circumstanced, it occurred to me that there was but one way to save my life, — this was by seizing Sprigg, as I immediately did, by the collar, and with my cocked pistol in the other hand, assuring him that if any violence were offered to me, I would instantly blow his brains out. I then told him he might conduct me to my house, and I would leave them. This he did, and we marched together upwards of a hundred yards, guarded by his whole company — whom he had the meanness to order to play the rogues' march all the way we went.

The second instance is (or was) more familiar. Note the emotional appeal of the famous speech of Patrick Henry as put together by William Wirt in *Sketches of the Life and Character of Patrick Henry* (1817), an oration once declaimed by thousands of American schoolboys. The occasion was a meeting of county delegates in Richmond, Virginia, in March 1775, seemingly resolved to approve of conciliatory measures and a renewed pledge of allegiance to the crown. Patrick Henry stopped this action by uttering one of the most famous (and inflammatory) speeches in American history. Parts of it apparently ran something like this:

I know no way of judging the future save by the past. And judging by the past, I wish to know what there has been in the conduct of the British ministry for the last ten years, to justify those hopes with which gentlemen have been pleased to solace themselves and the house. Is it that insidious smile with which our petition has been lately received? Trust it not, sir; it will prove a snare to your feet. Suffer not yourself to be betrayed with a kiss. . . . Ask yourselves how this gracious reception of our petition comports with those warlike preparations which cover our waters and darken our land. Are fleets and armies necessary to a work of love and reconciliation? . . . These are the implements of war and subjugation — the last arguments to which kings resort. . . . Our petitions have been slighted; our remonstrances have produced additional violence and insult; our supplications have been disregarded; and we have been spurned with contempt, from the foot of the throne. . . . Gentlemen may cry peace, peace — but there is no peace. . . . The next gale that sweeps from the north will bring to our ears the clash of resounding arms! Our brethren are already in the field! . . . Is life so dear, or peace so sweet, as to be purchased at the price of chains and slavery! Forbid it, Almighty God! — I know not what course others may take, but as for me, give me liberty or give me death!

Wirt reports that when Henry ceased, the auditors sat silent because "the supernatural voice still sounded in their ears, and shivered along their arteries." Wirt was a second-rate writer and a rhetorician, and his account was published years after Henry had died. Nevertheless he is probably telling the approximate truth about the speech and its startling effect. It is thus that revolutions are energized.

VII

Effects of the
American Revolution

The great controversy running from 1763 through 1789, which eventuated in the American revolution and the creation of the United States, was waged, military contests aside, on three levels. The highest of these, one on which ministers, statesmen, political theorists, and other intellectuals joined battle, dealt in the main with constitutional theory and proved to be one of the basic discussions of the age. The exchange of views between such writers as John Adams, Stephen Hopkins, John Dickinson, James Wilson, and Thomas Jefferson on the "Whig" side and opponents of the caliber of Martin Howard, Samuel Seabury, Joseph Galloway, and Jonathan Boucher among the Loyalists, like the arguments over framing the federal constitution (unfortunately preserved in fragments only), is among the high reaches of eighteenth-century thought. In Britain, moreover, colonial dissatisfaction brought out some of the best prose of Edmund Burke, although it must be said that careful reading of his renowned speech on conciliation with the American colonies reveals that, whatever Burke's present prestige as a political thinker, he was there more deeply concerned with trade than with constitutional theorizing.

The colonial issue had raised three great political problems. (1) Did the British parliament represent all the subjects of the British crown? (2) Did colonial charters and other grants give the colonies in North America a special, if disputable, status within the empire; and if they did, since sovereignty was supposed to be indivisible, where did sovereignty lie? (3) If taxation without representation was a valid phrase, did colonial grievances spring from the fact that the colonies were not represented in the House of Commons; or, if their basic allegiance was to the crown, did this mean that the king in council could permit the colonies to tax themselves, paying what they thought right into the imperial treasury while simultaneously demanding that the royal army and navy protect them from their enemies? If so, where was equity as between the colonials with their own system of taxation, and the British people with theirs? These problems were of intense interest to other countries possessing colonies — for example, France — and the solution of them was of considerable interest to liberals in the Western world.

It is interesting and curious that the West Indian colonies were not involved in this controversy. It is even more interesting and curious to realize that the famous phrase, "no taxation without representation," was never clearly defined. Nobody had as yet seriously proposed a graduated income tax for the British empire, and nobody had thought that a poll tax was feasible. The only possible direct tax was therefore a tax on property — real estate or merchandise, imports or exports, manufactured goods or raw materials, shipping or inherited wealth. Confusion was inevitable. If the protestors were saying that owners of property should not be taxed without their consent, this implied that only property owners should vote, or at least that suffrage should be confined to persons who had acquired status in society, as in Great Britain and in most of the states in the new republic. A few English "Jacobins" held otherwise. If the phrase meant that nobody should be taxed without his consent, populist-minded radicals here and abroad were justified in railing against the "tyranny" of the British government and afterwards, as in the case of Shays's rebellion, against the oppression of a state legislature. What did the Americans really want?

From the American point of view the answer was the publication of *The Federalist* in 1787–1788, eighty-five papers in all, most of them written by Alexander Hamilton, the rest by James Madison and John Jay. *The Federalist* is an American literary classic. It is also a classic statement of a political theory, and its essays are perhaps the last great achievement of Enlightenment prose in the New World. If Jefferson said of the Declaration of Independence that he had merely put down the common sense of the matter, Hamilton and his associates could have said of *The Federalist* that they had only set forth common sense about the new federal constitution. *The Federalist* favors a strong central government, and its interpretations of the powers and responsibilities of the various branches of that government have influenced interpretation ever since. Written in the generalized prose of its century, *The Federalist* nevertheless had a practical purpose: it sought to show how the new government would work. It therefore shunned brilliant rhetorical flights and never presented its readers with metaphysical ideas about liberty, humanity, and the philosophy of the state.*

Perhaps the wisest words ever written on the great constitutional issue were penned half a century ago by Charles H. McIlwain in his *The American Revolution: A Constitutional Interpretation* (1923):

The American Revolution began and ended with the political act or acts by which British sovereignty over the thirteen English colonies in North America was definitely repudiated. All else was nothing but cause or effect of this act. Of the causes, some were economic, some social, others constitutional. But the Revolution was none of these; not social, nor economic, nor even constitutional; it was a political act, and such an act cannot be both constitutional and revolutionary. . . . So long as American opposition to alleged grievances was constitutional, it was in no sense revolution. The moment it became revolutionary it ceased to be constitutional.

So his book begins, and toward the end he observes:

If the opposition to Parliament of some of the leading American statesmen just before the American Revolution is not to be called in large part a constitutional opposition, one of three other explanations of their actions would seem the only reasonable alternative: they were either trying to throw off an actual economic burden . . . or the rights which they professed to be asserting were only the creation of heated imaginations or uninstructed minds; or, if neither of these views be tenable, they were from the beginning merely cloaking under a specious claim of constitutional right in which they did not really believe, a settled determination to be absolutely independent of Great Britain.

The middle level of discussion is represented by large groups in

---

* Attacks on the new Constitution had continually alleged that it violated the principles for which the American revolution had been fought. It is illuminating to read an article by Frederick R. Black, "The American Revolution as 'Yardstick' in the Debates on the Constitution, 1787–1788," *Proceedings of the American Philosophical Society*, 117 (June 1973), 162–185.

all the colonies, men who, though they would not have put it this way, were ill at ease under the mercantilist doctrine of trade and economics. These groups are difficult to define, just as their opinions are troublesome to isolate. In a sense most of them were timorous liberals. They could not see why American enterprise should be circumscribed by the selfishness of British merchants, as, for example, seemed to be true in the iron industry. But with few exceptions they never dreamed of demanding political independence. What they seemed to desire was that the British government should accept the ideas in Adam Smith's *Inquiry into . . . the Wealth of Nations*, which, however, did not appear until 1776. Smith did not wholly free himself from the presuppositions of mercantilism, nor was he the first to propound the doctrine of laissez faire, but his great classic, from which many historians date the rise of modern economic theory, substantiated the feeling of colonial merchants, manufacturers, planters, and farmers, that if they were let alone to make what they wanted to make and to trade where they wanted to trade, the wealth of the colonies would grow and the prosperity of the empire would increase. I do not know that there is any single great statement of this doctrine on the American side, but this idea informs the prose of Edmund Burke, who both feared and admired American commercial enterprise. Here is a part of his speech on conciliation:

As to the wealth which the colonies have drawn from the sea by their fisheries . . . you surely thought those acquisitions of value, for they seemed even to excite your envy; and yet the spirit by which that enterprising employment has been exercised ought rather, in my opinion, to have raised your esteem and admiration. . . . Pass by the other parts, and look at the manner in which the people of New England have of late carried on the whale-fishery. Whilst we follow them among the tumbling mountains of ice, and behold them penetrating into the deepest frozen recesses of Hudson's Bay and Davis's Straits, whilst we are looking for them beneath the arctic circle, we hear that they have pierced into the opposite region of polar cold, that they are at the antipodes, and engaged under the frozen serpent of the South. Falkland Island, which seemed too remote and too romantic an object for the grasp of national ambition, is but a stage and resting-place in the progress of their victorious industry. Nor is the equinoctial heat more discouraging to them than the accumulated winter of both the poles. . . . No sea but what is vexed by their fisheries. No climate that is not witness to their toils. . . . When I know that the colonies in general owe little or nothing to any care of ours, and that they are not squeezed into this happy form by the constraint of watchful and suspicious government, but that . . . a generous nature has been suffered to take her own way to perfection . . . I feel all the pride of power sink, and all presumption in the wisdom of human contrivance melt and die away with me. . . . I pardon something to the spirit of liberty.

If one strips the splendid rhetoric from this passage, one sees that by "liberty" Burke means little more than commercial laissez faire.

There is, as I say, small indication that colonial merchants dreamed of national independence. Commenting in later life on what he had written during the Stamp Act agitation of 1765, John Adams wrote:

I thought [in later years] a man ought to be very cautious what kinds of fuel he throws into a fire, when it is thus glowing in the community. Although it is a certain expedient to acquire a momentary celebrity, yet it may produce future evils which may excite serious repentance. I have seen so many firebrands thrown into the flame, not only in the worthless and unprincipled writings of the profligate and impious Thomas Paine, and in the French Revolution, but in many others, that I think every man ought to take warning! *

Even the unstable James Otis in *A Vindication of the British Colonies* declared in 1765: "God forbid these colonies should ever prove undutiful to their mother country! Whenever such a day shall come, it will be the beginning of a terrible scene. Were these colonies left to themselves to-morrow, America would be a meer shambles of blood and confusion." Commonly regarded as the incarnation of commercial prudence, Benjamin Franklin long sought reconciliation, thought to bind the British empire together, and accepted independence late. A classic study by Arthur Meier Schlesinger, *The Colonial Merchants and the American Revolution, 1763–1776* (1917), notes that merchants and their natural allies, the established lawyers, tended to hold aloof from their radical followers, even when the merchants had originally egged them on, and that, having urged purchasers to assist in enforcing nonimportation agreements, they saw with growing uneasiness that they had sown the popular wind and reaped the populist whirlwind.

* For this entry in John Adams's diary see Charles Francis Adams, ed., *The Life and Works of John Adams*, vol. II, Boston, 1856, p. 153.

The Articles of Association adopted by "his majesty's loyal subjects" of twelve colonies in congress assembled in 1774 laid down explicit rules concerning nonimportation of goods and against inflation of prices; they also urged the necessity of improving the breed of American sheep and of killing them "as seldom as may be," in order to "encourage frugality, economy, and industry, and promote agriculture, arts, and the manufactures of this country." They also discountenanced many popular pleasures, especially "all horse-racing, and all kinds of gaming, cock-fighting, exhibitions of shews, plays, and other expensive diversions and entertainment," and forbade the use of mourning-dress at funerals. All this might have been borne with equanimity, but incentives to disorder appeared in articles 11 and 12 of this agreement:

11. That a committee be chosen in every county, city, and town, by those who are qualified to vote for representatives in the legislature, whose business it shall be attentively to observe the conduct of all persons touching this association; and when it shall be made to appear, to the satisfaction of a majority of any such committee, that any person within the limits of their appointment has violated this association, that such majority do forthwith cause the truth of the case to be published in the gazette; to the end, that all such foes to the rights of British-America may be publicly known, and universally contemned as the enemies of American liberty; and thenceforth we respectively will break off all dealings with him or her.

12. That the committees of correspondence . . . do frequently inspect the entries of their custom-houses, and inform each other, from time to time, of the true state thereof, and of every other material circumstance that may occur relative to this association.

These resolutions were adopted by the First Continental Congress October 24, 1774, and were undoubtedly well meant. But the method of spying out opponents ("foes to the rights of British-America"), of reporting their supposed lack of loyalty, and of informing not only the colonial committees at large of misdeeds discovered by any one of them but also of publishing their findings "in the gazette" was an open invitation to mob violence. The Association unconsciously anticipated the methods of the Committee of Public Safety and the Committee of General Security in the French Revolution (1793) and the work of their agents. Moreover, if merchants could thus set up a wholly extralegal system of espionage and pressure, and if their customers were necessarily to be involved in supporting these measures, why should the populace at large be ruled out?

The unruly crowd is a characteristic element in American colonial history, particularly in New England. The mob got out of hand. After the Boston Massacre, the Boston Tea Party, and the Boston Port Bill, it was impossible to control the radicals, whose ideas in fact triumphed in the actions of the First Continental Congress. A movement for commercial reform eventuated in armed rebellion. An attempt to cooperate with liberal British merchants ended in revolution. Schlesinger's massive study concludes:

They [the merchants] had the mournful satisfaction, when the war closed, of finding their worst fears confirmed in the inefficient government which the radicals established and in the enfeebled state of American commerce and business at home and abroad. In the troubled years that followed, the merchants of the country regardless of their antecedents drew together in an effort to found a government which would safeguard the interests of their class.

Revisionist historians suspect a study that seems to substantiate the economic determinism of an older historical school, but they overlook the character of eighteenth-century mobs, who, wrote Jonathan Boucher in 1774, "find the Movement of the Passions a more easy and agreeable Exercise than the Drudgery of sober and dispassionate Enquiry. Hand Bills, News Papers, party Pamphlets, are the shallow and turbid Sources from whence they derive their Notions of Government." Boucher, of course, was a Tory, but he had had some experience of mob rule. Gouverneur Morris, however, was a patriot. He wrote in that same year of "daring coxcombs" who worked

to rouse the mob into an attack upon the bounds of order and decency. These fellows become the Jack Cades of the day, leaders in all the riots, the belwethers of the flock. . . . The belwethers jingled merrily, and roared out liberty, and property, and religion, and a multitude of cant terms, which every one thought he understood, and was egregiously mistaken. . . . In short, there is no ruling them; and now, to change the metaphor, the heads of the mobility grow dangerous to the gentry, and how to keep them down is the question.

I quote James Otis again, apropos of the historical precedent presented by the abdication of James II and the problem of "liberty": "If upon the abdication all were reduced to a state of nature, had not apple women and orange girls as good a right to give their respectable suffrage for a new king as the philosopher, courtier, petit maitre and politician?" Why not, if kings were to be chosen at all? Said Tom Paine, "our plan is commerce," and "I challenge the warmest advocate for reconciliation to show a single advantage that this Continent can reap by being connected with Great Britain." "The King's negative *here* is ten times more dangerous and fatal than it can be in England," he declared.

O! ye that love mankind! Ye that dare oppose not only the tyranny but the tyrant, stand forth! Every spot of the Old World is overrun with oppression. Freedom has been hunted round the globe. Asia and Africa have long expelled her. Europe regards her like a stranger, and England hath given her warning to depart.

Only — what did Tom Paine mean by freedom? Even French supporters of the Americans were not quite clear, and cautious French statesmen were troubled by this attitude.

Lower social levels, often stirred to action by those above them, were necessarily the areas of violence. One must of course distinguish. Not all farmers, not all artisans, not all small shopkeepers wanted to plunder and destroy, ride Tories on a rail, or tar and feather them. Responsible men in town and country were sometimes faithful members of regiments of the Continental Line or of the militia, or local legislators, local officials, deacons, and the like. But there were also the rioters, the *mobile vulgus* as Dr. Johnson called them. Instigators of opposition to the Stamp Act had employed or aroused the passions of the crowd and proved unable or unwilling to control the rioting in Boston and other seaports during the Stamp Act agitation. When things quieted down for a time, the passage of the Townshend Acts (1767), the Tea Act (1773), and the Coercive Acts (1774), as we have seen, released popular passions. Merchants who refused to abide by the nonimportation agreements and who stood, they said, for freedom of thought, speech, and action, faced not merely the ruin of their business but also physical danger to themselves and their families. A prime instance is rioting in Boston, where a "secret" group known as the Loyal Nine, feeling that intimidation was the remedy for redressing grievances, initiated the organizing of unemployed seamen, local toughs, rowdies, young men out of work, and the unthinking generally into formidable mobs, and thus revealed the inability of government to enforce the laws without a police force. Was this a prelude to the mob pressure of the Paris Commune after 1789?

In Charleston, South Carolina, an organization of artisans known as the Sons of Liberty — the name spread widely — at first favored by the commercial interests, expanded into a populist movement that shook the city and the province. In New York City there were popular uprisings that took over the control of the port, destroyed printing presses, seized powder from government forts, threatened Tories with physical violence, and compelled some Loyalists to flee with their families into Connecticut in fear of their lives, nor were these mobs controlled until the British military occupation of New York. The dilemma of a quiet man who wished to be ruled by neither mobs nor monarchs is set forth in Crève-coeur's *Letters of an American Farmer* (I quote a London edition of 1783): "I am conscious that I was happy before this unfortunate Revolution. I find I am no longer so; therefore I regret the change. . . . If I attach myself to the mother-country, which is three thousand miles from me, I become what is called an enemy to my own regime; if I follow the rest of my countrymen, I become opposed to our ancient masters. Both extremes appear equally dangerous to a person of so little weight and consequence as I am.*

The lowest level on which the debate was waged was that of sheer propaganda. Mass propaganda must be repetitive, simple, and emotional. The "people" were repeatedly told that they were about to become the slaves of a distant and bloody tyrant, that British troops were there to burn their houses, ravish their wives and daughters, and carry off their property, that all Loyalists were traitors and all patriots valorous citizens, worthy of the ancient traditions of the Roman people. The language of a broadside of 1770, having a color reproduction of Paul Revere's rather unhis-torical engraving of the Boston Massacre, concentrates but does not misrepresent the idiom of populist propaganda:

> Unhappy Boston! see thy Sons deplore,
> Thy hallow'd Walks besmear'd with guiltless Gore:
> While faithless P-----n and his savage Bands,
> With murd'rous Rancour stretch their bloody Hands;

* On the general problem of propaganda and crowd psychology see Philip Davidson, *Propaganda and the American Revolution, 1763–1776*, Chapel Hill, 1941.

Like fierce Barbarians grinning o'er their Prey,
Approve the Carnage, and enjoy the Day.
If scalding drops from Rage, from Anguish Wrung
If speechless Sorrows lab'ring for a Tongue,
Or if a weeping World can ought appease
The plaintive Ghosts of Victims such as these;
The Patriot's copious Tears for each are shed,
A glorious Tribute which embalms the Dead.
But know, FATE summons to that awful Goal,
Where JUSTICE strips the Murd'rer of his Soul,
Should venal C---ts the scandal of the Land,
Snatch the relentless Villain from her Band,
Keen Execrations on this Plate inscrib'd,
Shall reach a JUDGE who never can be brib'd.*

Terms like "Murderers," "Tyranny," "Royal Despot," "Nero," "Caligula," "Rebel," "Foul Traitor," "Bloodybacks" and the like inflamed the populace. When Samuel Adams wrote in 1780 to the governor of Rhode Island that Massachusetts had sustained injuries from the "Arts of too many internal Enemies," and that "it is indeed much to be regretted, that the greatest Vigilance is insufficient to detect the most virulent Enemies of Publick Liberty in every instance, and bring them to condign Punishment," he was anticipating the language of the French revolutionaries.

Yet underneath this emotional violence the current of change flowed irresistibly on. The concept that all men are created free and equal, though freedom was denied in the case of slaves, and equality in any social sense was not attained, fortified and enriched a new value placed upon individualism. True, even in the United States, though all men were equal, social divisions still obtained — between the rich and the poor, between the master and the servant, between men, that superior race, and women, that delicate sex, between the landed gentry and the roving frontiersmen, between the squire in the village and the topers in the tavern, between the white man and the Indian, between the Protestant and the Catholic, between the Christian and the Jew, between those who acquired some sort of status and those who had none or who had lost what had been attained. But the language of revolutionary argument, of the Declaration of Independence, the federal Constitution, and

* "P-----n" is Captain Preston, the unhappy officer called in when the main guard was summoned during the so-called massacre; and "C---ts" is courts. The Massachusetts court gave the accused soldiers a fair trial.

republican propaganda had gained something. In the New World the individual was now made the primary foundation of a philosophic state.

Individuals could be taken separately or they could be added together, in which case they became the people. In this view the people were to be differentiated from mobs destroying property and endangering lives. As a unit in political theory the individual, divested of all his idiosyncratic qualities — something the romantic movement would not do — was a rather faceless unit in a vast political game of chess. The people, however, became sacrosanct. Their voice, it appeared, was the voice of God. Men of liberal feelings, weary of priesthood, turned from theology to the Religion of Humanity, and the Religion of Humanity became credible to them because it was working, or about to work, in the United States. What happened to individualism here and elsewhere is a complicated matter to which we shall later turn.

ii

In 1827 the aging Goethe wrote a poem more remarkable for its content than for its artistic worth:

> Amerika, du hast es besser
> Als unser Kontinent, das alte,
> Hast keine verfallene Schlösser
> Und keine Basalte.
>
> Dich stört sich nicht im Innern,
> Zu lebendiger Zeit,
> Unnützes Errinern
> Und vergeblicher Streit.
>
> Benutzt die Gegenwart mit Glück!
> Und wenn nun eure Kinder dichten,
> Bewahre sie ein gut Geschick
> Vor Ritter-, Räuber- und Gespenstergeschichten.*

From China to Peru the history of man has been haunted by

---

* America, you have things better than does our aged continent; you have no ruined castles and no basalt rocks; you are not inwardly troubled in the present age by useless memories and futile conflict. Employ the present time and its happy state! And if your offspring write anything, shield them from any move toward tales of knights, brigands, and ghosts.

either or both of two visions: a paradise lost in the past or a golden age to come. The Enlightenment, for example, thought it had found a model of political perfection in Periclean Athens, republican Rome, or the Age of Augustus or of the Antonines. Others looked to the South Seas or some other remote portion of the globe — for example, the virtuous Chinese — for proof that mankind, if only certain restraints, certain corruptions were removed, could be virtuous and happy. The term, "The New World," implied a place where man could begin again, especially after voyagers and discoverers, sometimes from interested motives, dwelt upon the innocence of its natives, the inexhaustible fertility of its soil, and the abundance of its metals. The image, it is true, had been clouded by human greed, the terrors of unknown continents, and the strife of European imperialisms, not to speak of a struggle between white man and Indian. Now, with the creation of a New World nation on the philosophic principles of life, liberty, the pursuit of happiness, the dream was again made vivid. Accounts of this new hope for man run through the colonial period, through Crèvecoeur's famous essay "What Is an American?" (the answer was that he *is* a new man), through the period of the melting pot, into the anti-racist and integration movements of our own time.

Eighteenth-century Americans were pleased to applaud their own virtues, and their unexampled opportunities. Especially after 1783 the potential goodness of society in the mainland colonies, where food was cheap, land was plentiful, and population could expand indefinitely, was repeatedly celebrated. The new republic was supposed to lead mankind to happiness. It is illuminating to examine some of this propaganda. Commonly it rests upon the assumption that an agrarian society is the best society, but it does not dodge the problem of cities.

For example, as early as 1755 one finds in Ames's *Almanac* this hortatory paragraph:

Breathe not the Air of Ceties [Cities], where breathless Winds imbibe Effluvia from the Sick and Dying, from the Dead, from Docks and Dung-hills; where Thousands of Lungs with Exhalations foul, sate the Air with strange Corruption. . . . You who would breathe in pure balsamic Air, see yon Blue-Hill invites you, where western Gales from *Dedham* Plains with sweet ambrosial Breezes fan the undulating Skies and chase those Mists which cloud his lofty Summit.

This, obviously, is excessively local, but in 1757 Benjamin Church in *The Choice* widened the range of felicity. He wanted a "handsome Seat not far from Town,"

> Where safe from Damps I'd snuff the wholesome Gale,
> And Life and Vigour thro' the Lungs inhale,

a "plantation"

> Where gamesome Flocks and rampant Herds might play,
> To the warm Sun-Shine of the Vernal Day,

and where he might adore his Creator and "let no future . . . my Peace destroy, / Or cloud the Aspect of a present Joy."

In the *Almanac* for 1759, declaring that if the colonies would only awaken to their opportunities, the French could not keep the Ohio country, Ames wrote:

> HAD we wak'd early from an idle Dream
> On yonder smooth OHIO's winding Stream,
> Our Cities might have stood, and Structures shone,
> Magnificently built with curious Stone,
> With all the Stores of Nature there possest,
> And vast Conveniences for Man and Beast.

By 1762 his publication was even firmer in its prophecy:

> AMERICA kind Heav'ns peculiar Care,
> Vast Heaps of Nature's Stores are treasur'd here:
> Here the kind Earth produces yearly Grain,
> Soften'd by Waters and descending Rain:
> In Time thy Towers will vie with *Europe's* Pride,
> And scepter'd Heads will gladly here reside.

I pass over an election sermon of the Rev. Thomas Barnard in 1763 to the effect that "Here shall be a perennial Source of . . . Strength and Riches. Here shall Arts and Sciences, the Companions of Tranquility, flourish," to note that *Poor Richard Improved* (1764) foretold the glories of the Middle West:

> Her Eye, far piercing, round extends its Beams
> To *Erie's* banks, or smooth *Ohio's* Streams,
> It fixes where kind Rays till then have smil'd
> (Vain Smile) on some luxuriant houseless Wild;
> How many Sons of Want might here enjoy
> What Nature gives for Age but to destroy?

. . . . . .

Fair Order here shall from Confusion rise,
Rapt I a future Colony survey . . .
Where prowls the Wolf, where roll'd the Serpent lies,
Shall solemn Fanes, and Halls of Justice rise.

By 1769 *The Farmer's and Monitor's Letters to the Inhabitants of the British Colonies*, printed in Williamsburg, for which Arthur and Richard Henry Lee were responsible, declaring that "the great Author of nature has created nothing in vain" and had joined the life of man to "liberty, the virtuous enjoyment and free possession of property honestly gained," offered humanity a wonderful new life in North America: "The nature of the climate, the soil, and its various produce, point out the ease and extent with which manufactures may be conducted here . . . the bountiful Author of nature has furnished his creatures with the means of securing their proper rights —" hence, presumably, the revolution. The year before Lexington and Concord, the *Royal American Magazine* printed an address of "AMERICA'S GENIUS" to the people:

AMERICA blossoms as the expanding rose, and rises like the towering cedar; every morning sun views her encreased fame, and each new day extends her domain and adds new glories to her crown. — Here the streams of wealth, the beams of science, the stars of wisdom, the light of virtue, and the sun of liberty, will all unite their rays, and form the sublime circle of human splendor and felicity.

That same year Richard Wells's *A Few Political Reflections Submitted to the Consideration of the British Colonies, by a Citizen of Philadelphia* had this to say:

The genius of America is agriculture, and for ages to come must continue so. An extensive wilderness to the westward will long receive the gradual overflowings of population; and the Manufacturer of Great-Britain will never meet with a formidable rival in the shape of an American Farmer, so long as he can purchase the cloathing of his family with the produce of his fields . . . OUR fields, through the wonted providence of the great Lord of the soil, produce their usual crops — our barns expand with the pressing load of unnumbered sheaves; and a joy 'like unto the joy of harvest' spreads a serenity of countenance through thousands.

Unfortunately, when the laboring wains of "ten thousand families" reached the sea to sell their grain as export, they found that the wretched British had shut up the ports.

At the end of the revolution the thirteenth number of *The American Crisis* by the ebullient Tom Paine exulted in the whole history and unshakable idealism of the United States:

Never, I say, had a country so many openings to happiness as this. Her setting out in life, like the rising of a fair morning, was unclouded and promising. Her cause was good. Her principles just and liberal. Her temper serene and firm. Her conduct regulated by the nicest steps, and everything about her wore the mark of honor. It is not every country (perhaps there is not another in the world) that can boast so fair an origin. Even the first settlement of America corresponds with the character of the revolution. Rome, once the proud mistress of the universe, was originally a band of ruffians. Plunder and rapine made her rich and her oppression of millions made her great. But America need never be ashamed to tell her birth, nor relate the stages by which she rose to empire.

Whether Indian leaders such as Powhatan or Pontiac would have applauded America's rise to empire may be doubted, but Paine's interpretation was exhilarating alike in the Old World and in the New.

The Rev. William Smith, preaching at Christ-Church, Philadelphia, in 1790 before the local chapter of the Society of the Cincinnati was, if possible, even more rhetorical than the radical Paine:

Be wise, then, be instructed, ye rising *American States!* Let it be your glorious contention which of you shall stand foremost in making liberal provisions for the advancement and support of *Freedom* and *Virtue*; without which, neither the Ordinances of *Religion* nor the *Laws* can be duly administered. . . . by wise establishments for the Instruction of Youth, the Advancement of the Arts and Sciences, the encouragement of Industry, and the maintenance of *Religion* and *Morality* — this shall become a great and happy land!

The minister looked forward to "new *States* and *Empires*, new Seats of *Wisdom* and *Knowledge*, new *Religious* domes, spreading around."

The second volume of *The Monthly Register, Magazine and Review of the United States* (apparently printed simultaneously in Charleston, S.C., and New York in 1806/7) declared that in free states "the efforts of arts to correct the faults, and to surpass the beauties of former models, are unwearied, incessant, and often successful. . . . Hence, will men, gradually, and progressively advance towards the *perfection of taste*, that is, *the general opinion*

of excellence, entertained by sensible and enlightened minds,"
whereas in despotic countries the opposite is true: "The unbending
loftiness of genius is not likely to be found in the porticoes of
princes and of lords, proffering the servile strains of interested
adulation; neither will it be seen offering up the incense of prosti-
tuted praise to the lap dogs and the parrots of *ladylings and queens.*"
This may be a touch unhistorical, to be sure, but the writer says:
look at the "voluptuous and immoral literature" of the court of
Charles II and the "licentious profligacy" of the court of Louis
XIV. Free governments "exalt the people into the dignity of thinking beings."

Perhaps the climax of this rapturous differentiation between the
corrupt life of Europe and the fair promise of America is a poem
by the gifted and eccentric Joel Barlow, who was elected a member of the French Assembly. He toiled for years at the *Columbiad*
(1807), originally *The Vision of Columbus.* In this poem "Hesper"
obligingly furnishes the discoverer with a vision of things past,
present, and to come. Here is a part of Book VIII; it concerns "the
West":

> Then shall your works of art superior rise,
> Your fruits perfume a larger length of skies,
> Canals careering climb your sunbright hills,
> Vein the green slopes and strow their nurturing rills,
> Thro' tunnel'd heights and sundering ridges glide,
> Rob the rich west of half Kenahawa's tide,
> Mix your wide climates, all their stores confound,
> And plant new ports on every midland mound.
> Your lawless Mississippi, now who slimes
> And drowns and desolates his waste of climes,
> Ribb'd with your dikes, his torrent shall restrain
> And ask your leave to travel to the main;
> Won from his wave while rising cantons smile,
> Rear their glad nations and reward their toil.

Once the Mississippi had been "ribb'd" with dykes, there was to be
a general federal parliament and perpetual peace among the nations
of the world.

iii

The American propagandist might assume one of two or three
general philosophical positions. He might believe that the history

of nations runs in a cycle and that the United States was now in the bloom of youth and that centuries must elapse before its inevitable decline. Or, following the assumptions of some proponents of the Enlightenment, he might hold that, progress being the law of life, the new republic was the latest birth of time and therefore the best, prepared for by ancient history, Anglo-Saxon tradition, the English Civil Wars, and British — that is to say "Whiggish" — liberal thought. Or he might believe that the revolution was something, though secular, like Creation or the Incarnation, an event unpredictable by time though occurring in time. In this view something called liberty triumphed over something called tyranny, to benefit, by enforcing natural rights, something called the people. Just as in much Christian theology salvation was available to all men, so the revolution demonstrated that any virtuous nation could be saved for (or by) freedom. If to the deist this interpretation called for a little juggling with strict logic, if to the devout the theological parallel savored slightly of blasphemy, the ardent patriot simply followed Tertullian: *certum est quia impossibile est* — it is true because it is impossible. Probably no writer stuck consistently to any of these positions. But victory had been won. The easiest explanation of victory was twofold but not self-contradictory: triumph was due to virtue in itself or to God's providence working through human agency. Virtue or providence or both created a George Washington, a devoted people, and a citizenry rushing to arms. True, Washington lost as many battles as he won, the virtue of the people then as now was moot, and the militia was usually unreliable. Still, there were the Declaration of Independence and Yorktown, the swarming of minutemen after Lexington and at Bennington, the stubborn defense of Bunker Hill, the crossing of the Delaware, and the inability of Lord Cornwallis or any of his predecessors to conquer and hold the southern states.

American propaganda faced various difficulties. These included the treatment of Loyalists during the dispute, the failure to compensate Tories as stipulated by the treaty of peace, the truth that victory was made possible mainly by the aid of the French, mutinies in the Continental armies, and the refusal of self-seeking states to pay attention either to financial requisitions or to rules about trade and tariff set up by the congress under the Articles of Confederation. Moreover, the development of national feeling, though genuine, was impeded by the emotional claims of localism. Many Americans, however, and most foreigners were not especially conscious of these matters. The republic existed. American annals should therefore be recorded, American history made known, American leaders, those modern equivalents of Plutarch's men, written up for foreigners and for posterity.

It cannot be contended that any central agent controlled the line of this patriotic propaganda. But in his illuminating study, *Republican Religion* (1933), G. A. Koch exhumes a Fourth of July oration of 1797 by Elihu Palmer, Dartmouth graduate and leading deist, that is virtually a program for mankind in the light of American experience:

Among all the events recorded in history the most important is that of the American Revolution. . . . we already behold some of the effects which have flowed from this political contest. We behold them in the operations of the human mind — in the energy which has been displayed by the intellectual powers of man, and the consequent general decay of superstition and fanaticism — in progressive and extensive improvements exhibited in the American country — in the cultivation of science, the discovery and application of principles, the more general diffusion of knowledge, and the melioration of that unfortunate condition to which man by the tyrants of the earth has been devoted — in the French Revolution, an event of the most astonishing nature, and extremely dissimilar to any thing recorded on the page of ancient history, but which presents to afflicted humanity the consoling hope of suffering alleviated or wholly destroyed.*

The Americans had reshaped government and society into a nation embodying the best ideas of the Enlightenment about public order and the state. Difficulties arose under the Articles of Confederation and, in the minds of many, greater difficulties were created by the federal Constitution. Nevertheless Rousseau was clearly wrong.

---

* Palmer also avers that "it is not to be presumed, that men will long remain ignorant of their moral condition in nature, after being instructed in the principles of civil science. The moral condition of man will be as essentially renovated by the American Revolution as his civil condition. . . . awakened by the energy of thought, inspired by the American Revolution, man will find it consistent with his inclination and his interest to examine all the moral relations of his nature, to calculate with accuracy the effects of his own moral energies; and to relinquish with elevated satisfaction, those supernatural schemes of superstition which have circumscribed the sphere of beneficial activity, for which Nature designed him." "Moral" in this context has both ethical and psychological overtones, as in Wordsworth's "all my moral being." Palmer was of course rowing against the strong current of revived religion in the United States in the 1790's.

The arts and sciences do not decline as civilization advances. Under freedom they blossom. In free societies men were responsible human beings, whereas under *"military* despotism" and "other *despotic* principalities," as the *Monthly Register* had said, the people are "sunk in mental darkness," "the sleep of ignorance and death."

It is important to remember that in this period "democratic" and "democratical" were pejorative terms. To the Enlightenment a proper state might be a republic. In this country the Jeffersonians, the "Jacobin" clubs, and most foreign radicals were tagged as "democratical," democracy being thought of as an "odious conclave of tumult." Despite the ambiguity of these and other terms Jefferson, replying to an address of welcome at Alexandria, Virginia, in 1790, said: "Convinced that the republican is the only form of government which is not eternally at open or secret war with the rights of mankind, my prayers and efforts shall be cordially contributed to the support of that we have so happily established." In Jefferson's time, to avoid the pejorative adjective and to distinguish it from the "monarchical Federalists," the present Democratic party was known as the Republican party. In France "Federalism" was to be, from the point of view of true republicanism, an evil term.

In the revolutionary and postrevolutionary years local history (commonly that of a state) was a more usual publishing product than it has since become, and in such books, of which Jeremy Belknap's *History of New Hampshire* (1784–1792) is an excellent example, the notes of patriotism and progress were sounded. Four or five histories on a national scale apparently exerted considerable influence on opinion, on education, and on foreign interpretations, even though so excellent a historical scholar as John Adams informed a French friend that no competent history of the American revolution could be written until the great bulk of archival material, foreign and domestic, was made available.* Here, however, one is not so much concerned with either depth or accuracy as with point of view. Of these books William Gordon's *History of the Rise, Progress, and Establishment of the Independence of the United*

---

* A beginning was made by Ebenezer Hazard, who as surveyor-general of the United States Post Office from 1776 to 1782 traveled extensively. He published two volumes of *Historical Collections* in 1792 and 1794, but these do not get beyond the records of the New England Confederation.

States of America (4 vols., 1788) seems earliest in point of time, and Mrs. Mercy Otis Warren's *History of the Rise, Progress and Termination of the American Revolution: Interspersed with Biographical, Political and Moral Observations* (3 vols., 1805) was possibly the most influential. In between one finds David Ramsay's *The History of the American Revolution* (2 vols., 1789) and Jedidiah Morse's *The History of America: In Two Books* (1790). Morse accepted the cyclical interpretation of history, and Ramsay thought that the revolution was inspired by providence, a unique event in the history of man. These historians and others felt entitled to draw freely upon the *Annual Register*, founded in 1758 and edited for over thirty years by Edmund Burke and members of his circle. It was published in London by the great Robert Dodsley, admired by Horace Walpole for the quaint reason that "Doddy" was "little apt to forget or disguise his having been a footman." But let us examine one or two of these titles at length.

William Gordon (1728–1807) as a historian has more claim to realism than most commentators realize. Born in England, coming to America in 1770, and returning to England in 1786, he was at one time chaplain to the provincial congress of Massachusetts, a post he lost because of his outspoken opinions. He early determined to write a history of the American revolution, a work that eventually included a sketch of Britain's struggle with hostile Continental powers. He alleged that an impartial history could not be printed in the United States, but he found prejudice quite as strong in England, where his manuscript had to pass through several hands before being printed in London. A New York edition appeared one year after the original. Gordon's history takes the odd form of a series of imaginary letters, some of them dated from European cities, most of them supposed to be from America. His preface acknowledges his indebtedness to the *Annual Register*, and he seems to have had access to documentary material in this country. He is tough-minded about looting, rape, cruelty, insubordination, filth, disease, cowardice, and the cynicism of some American patriots and some loyalists. Of the German mercenaries he observes that they had been led to believe the Americans were savages, and that when a private soldier had been captured his body would be stuck full of pieces of pine and burned. Of more importance is his comment on the German mercenaries: "Officers and men are together ignorant of the nature of the quarrel between Britain and the United States; and have high notions of subjection to princely authority. They detest the thought of rebellion, and the Americans being stiled rebels, they are hearty in desiring and attempting their reduction."

Gordon describes small episodes vividly, details at length pro-American speeches in the British parliament, and says that on the Continent public opinion favored the revolutionaries. His vignettes of Benedict Arnold are lively, his praise of the humanity of Sir Guy Carleton is manly, and in the fourth volume he eulogizes Washington with intelligence: "It would be absurd to expect, that he should equal in military skill the first European generals, when he has enjoyed neither their opportunities nor experience for perfecting himself; but it may be justly asserted concerning him, that he was the best general the Americans could have had to command them . . . whose natural temper possesses more of the *Marcellus* and less of the *Fabius* than has been generally imagined." Unexpected but deserved is a tribute to General Nathanael Greene, even if Gordon misspells his name. Greene was a man "of a humane disposition; but resolutely severe when the same was necessary . . . of a firm, intrepid and independent mind." Gordon admires the Declaration of Independence and says, somewhat coldly, that its abuse of George III was allowable since the rebels were no longer his subjects.

Gordon is important also because he both quotes and deplores the rhetoric of revolution. Thus in volume two he writes:

Many of your [British] papers, it is observed, are very liberal in bestowing upon the colonists the appellation of rebels, traitors, cowards, &c., while those printed on this side of the Atlantic are calling the parties employed against the Americans by sea and land, pirates, banditti, ministerial butchers, butchering assassins, cut-throats, thieves, &c. These abusive names take with the unthinking multitude, whether in high or low life, and set a keener edge upon the spirit of party; but are productive of much cruelty, and tend to beget a rooted antipathy.

Unfortunately leaders of the French revolution did not characteristically read Gordon or took no warning from such a paragraph.

No book more vividly illustrates the innumerable small, forgotten, and sometimes brutal episodes in the war. In his final volume Gordon quotes from the address of the president of congress on receiving Washington's resignation as commander-in-chief. The president (Thomas Mifflin), he writes, spoke "but not without such a sensibility as changed and spread a degree of paleness over, his countenance":

Called upon by your country to defend its invaded rights, you accepted the sacred charge, before it had formed alliances, and whilst it was without funds or a government to support you. You have conducted the great military contest with wisdom and fortitude, invariably regarding the rights of the civil power through all disasters and changes. You have, by the love and confidence of your fellow-citizens, enabled them to display their martial genius, and transmit their fame to posterity . . . the glory of your virtues will not terminate with your military command, it will continue to animate remotest ages.

Many spectators shed tears. With this address the deification of Washington may be said to have become fixed in American theology.

Mrs. Mercy Otis Warren could not write with equal specificity on military matters, and she is so far from being impartial that, as Moses Coit Tyler long ago observed, she referred to American Loyalists as "the malignant party." But she wrote with spirit if with too much rhetoric. Her sketches of figures like Governor Thomas Hutchinson are etched in acid, she despised General Charles Lee, and she adopted a New England interpretation of the revolution. She did not care for the Order of the Cincinnati when it was founded, and she felt that the American "connexion" with European powers "tainted the purity and simplicity of American manners," these countries lending "their co-operating influence to undermine the beautiful fabric of *republicanism*, which Americans had erected with enthusiastic fondness, and for which they had risked ease, property, and life." She was likewise dubious about immigrants who had "fled from the slavery of despotic courts" and become "respectable" in the United States, since among such persons "the darling system of the inhabitants of the United States, might be lost or forgotten in a growing rabiosity for monarchy."

Mrs. Warren is readable partly because, like Macaulay's, her prejudices are open and hearty. She virtually ignores the sad account of desertions and mutinies to declare:

We have seen through the narration of events during the war, the armies of the American states suffering hunger and cold, nakedness, fatigue and danger with unparalleled patience and valor. A due sense of the importance of the contest in which they were engaged, and the certain ruin and disgrace in which themselves and their children would be involved on the defeat of their object, was a strong stimulus for patient suffering. An attachment to their commanding officers, a confidence in the faith of congress, and the sober principles of independence, equity, and equality . . . all united to quiet any temporary murmurs that might arise . . .

Although, she avers, the war cost America thousands of soldiers and citizens, immense property damage, its simplicity of manners, and "those ideas of mediocrity which are generally the parent of content," the Americans retained "their veneration for religion," so that in the end it all comes right. Mrs. Warren then really lets lets herself go:

. . . the young republic of America exhibits the happiest prospects. Her extensive population, commerce, and wealth, the progress of agriculture, arts, sciences, and manufactures, have increased with a rapidity beyond example. Colleges and academies have been reared, multiplied and endowed . . . on the broad scale of liberality and truth . . . The wisdom and justice of the American governments, and the virtue of the inhabitants may, if they are not deficient in the improvement of their own advantages, render the United States of America an enviable example to all the world, of peace, liberty, righteousness, and truth. . . . this last civilized quarter of the globe may exhibit those striking traits of grandeur and magnificence, which the Divine Oeconomist may have reserved to crown the closing scene, when the angel of his presence will stand upon the sea and upon the earth . . . and there shall be time no longer.

It is fair to this fervid rhetoric to remember that her work was published in 1805, the year of Trafalgar and Austerlitz.

If the angels of the Apocalypse were to stand upon the shores of North America, it was proper that an American hagiography should be prepared against their coming. Pietistic biographies could not, however, be written until the deaths of the patriots, though there were important exceptions to the rule. That what one may call the marble-bust concept was shaped early is evident in William S. Baker's collection, *Early Sketches of George Washington* (1894), in which Jedidiah Morse's essay (1789) is characteristic:

The virtuous simplicity which distinguishes the private life of General Washington, though less known than the dazzling splendor of his military atchievements, is not less edifying in example, or worthy the attention of his countrymen. The conspicuous character he has acted on the theatre of human affairs, the uniform dignity with which he sustained his part amidst difficulties of the most discouraging nature, and the glory of having arrived through them at the hour of triumph, have made many official and literary persons, on both sides of the ocean, ambitious of a correspondence with him . . . [He is] the *focus of political intelligence for the new world.**

Collections of filio-pietistic biographies began with Jeremy Belknap's *American Biography* (2 volumes, Boston, 1794, 1798), and by the end of the first quarter of the nineteenth century a considerable library of these collections had appeared:

> James Hardie, *The New Universal Biographical Dictionary and American Remembrancer of Departed Merit*, 4 vols., New York, 1801–1802.
>
> *Public Characters; or, Contemporary Biography*, Baltimore, 1803.
>
> John Eliot, *A Biographical Dictionary*, Boston, 1809.
>
> Joseph Delaplaine, *Delaplaine's Repository of Distinguished American Characters*, Philadelphia, 1815–1818.
>
> Benjamin Franklin French, *Biographia Americana*, New York, 1825.
>
> *Biography of the American Military and Naval Heroes of the Revolutionary and Late Wars*, 2 vols., New York, 1826.

Eulogy of course extended backward to explorers and settlers, unconscious prophets of the republican glory to come; and commemorative addresses, sermons, and Fourth of July orations fed the sacred flame. It is a commentary upon this enthusiasm that the full text of Lorenzo Sabine's *Biographical Sketches of Loyalists of the American Revolution* had to wait until 1864 to get into print

---

* This paragraph was first printed as a sort of extended note in the first edition (1789) of Morse's *American Geography*. The text proper is quite as awe-stricken: "while true merit is esteemed, or virtue honored, mankind will never cease to revere the memory of this Hero; and while gratitude remains in the human breast, the praises of Washington shall dwell on every American tongue." The first lengthy biographical sketch of the hero during his lifetime is apparently that by Thomas Condie, editor of the short-lived *Philadelphia Monthly Magazine* (1798). This is entitled "Memoirs of George Washington," ran through several numbers, and compares Washington to Moses, Leonidas, and various other immortals. In his *George Washington in American Literature 1775–1865* (New York, 1952) William Alfred Bryan amusingly records Thackeray's impatient query: "No, no, Kennedy, that's not what I want. Tell me, was he a fussy old gentleman in a wig? Did he take snuff and spill it down his shirt front?"

(there was a first version published in Boston in 1847), for your true American during the romantic decades could see small difference between the traitorous Benedict Arnold and an American "Tory." It was impossible in these years to compete with an emotional attitude like that expressed by William Tudor in his *The Life of James Otis of Massachusetts* (Boston, 1823, p. 4):

The characters of the great leaders in the American revolution, are gradually emerging from the jealous level of their own times. As this sinks away, they will become daily more conspicuous, and when their contemporary age shall be enrolled among the past; these founders of a nation will remain the lofty land-marks of history, sublime as the mountains of the globe appeared in all their majestic elevation, after the waters of the deluge had subsided.

The iconographic equivalent of this attitude is perhaps the frontispiece to the third volume of *The Columbian Magazine, or Monthly Miscellany, Containing a View of the History, Literature, Manners & Characters of the Year*, reproduced in the first volume of Frank Luther Mott's great *History of American Magazines*, opposite page 94. The editor obligingly explained the symbolism of this crowded plate:

The Genius of Federate America is represented sitting under a palm-tree, the emblem of Peace. The tree is adorned with a wreath of laurel entwining the badges of liberty — the pole and cap. Around the Genius of America, are the symbols of Commerce, Science, Agriculture and Plenty. — The American Eagle affords support to her arm; and, in this situation, she is supposed to be unconscious of her proximity to the temple of Fame, a view of which is represented in the background. Apollo, having heard the trumpet of the goddess [the winged figure of Fame is perched precariously on the dome of the temple], celebrating her [Federate America's] praise, appears, — and announces the honors to be conferred on her — At the same time, he points to the temple; and casts a splendour on the path leading to its portal.

The most widely influential, as it is the most ludicrous, patriotic biography of the period was of course Weems's *The Life, and Death, Virtues and Exploits, of General George Washington* (?1800), which by its second printing purported to be "faithfully taken from authentic documents." This immortal work began as an eighty-page pamphlet; by the "fifth edition" it had become a book of 250 pages by the "former rector of Mt. Vernon Parish," which Weems never was. The cherry tree suddenly bloomed and was cut down in this edition. John Marshall's stately *Washington* in five large volumes appeared from 1804 to 1807, Aaron Bancroft's *Washington* and David Ramsay's *Washington* were published in 1807, but they got nowhere. What scholar could compete with a writer who not only gave you a stainless revolutionary leader, but sent the hero's soul to meet both God and "the brother band of thy martyred saints," pouring forth "from heaven's wide-opening gates" to greet their beloved chief.

At sight of him, even these *blessed spirits* seem to feel new raptures, and to look more dazzling bright. In joyous throngs they pour around him — they devour him with their eyes of love — they embrace him in transports of tenderness unutterable; while from their roseate cheeks, tears of joy, such as angels weep, roll down.

As Senator Albert Beveridge once gravely remarked, Weems "profoundly influenced the American conception of Washington." Weems's only rival in creating folklore of this sort was William Wirt in his *Sketches of the Life and Character of Patrick Henry* (1817).

iv

The birth of an independent republic in the New World thus created a new mythology, part of it local to the United States, part of it appealing generally to the world. A renewal of vitality of interest in the classical past here and in Europe engendered or kept alive an odd symbiotic relationship between antiquity and romanticism. The new American mythology enriched this symbiosis and fed the hopes of a younger generation of liberals and radicals in Europe.* The first fabulous figure in the American pantheon was Benjamin Franklin, the rival of Voltaire, a Quaker, a philosopher, a lover of mankind, a benevolent sage from a simple and honest society wherein all men strove for the good and the practical. He became a European legend in his lifetime. The bland, shrewd face, the "primitive" costume (he refused to wear a wig

---

* For a more detailed account of the classical element in American culture of the period and of the cultural relation between the United States and France, see the relevant portions of my *O Strange New World*, New York, 1964, and *America and French Culture*, Chapel Hill, 1927, together with the references listed in these volumes. One may also consult with pleasure and profit Robert Rosenblum, *Transformations in Late Eighteenth Century Art*, Princeton, 1967.

and frequently appeared in a fur cap), the homely wisdom of *le bon homme Richard* — were not these outer attributes proof of republican virtue? Only a few, among them the French foreign minister Vergennes, realized that beneath this mask of simplicity there was a wily and subtle diplomatic mind.

In addition, there was Jefferson, an American *philosophe*, a cosmopolitan who developed in France and Italy a passion for classical architecture and in Virginia built a classical home. Falling in love with the Maison Carrée at Nîmes, he insisted that the state capitol in his beloved Virginia should be a copy of it. Jefferson was also a Francophile, in Paris he helped to frame proposals for the constitution of a limited monarchy, he was perpetually recommending the study of the classics to young men in order to make virtuous citizens of them, and like Quesnay he believed that an agrarian culture must ipso facto produce a moral society. Then there was John Adams, more Roman than Greek, the "celebrated Adams" visited at Braintree, Massachusetts, by Brissot de Warville, the future revolutionary, in 1788. The Frenchman applauded the rise of honest John from the lowly status of schoolmaster to the first dignities of his country. Adams had returned to his Sabine farm near the Blue Hills at Quincy. Such, exclaimed the delighted Brissot, were the generals and ambassadors of Rome and Greece; such were Epaminondas, Fabius, and Cincinnatus.

Houdon, the greatest French sculptor of the age, modeled busts of Franklin, Jefferson, and John Paul Jones, as he did of Lafayette, Mirabeau, and Buffon, and, moreover, came to America in 1785 to make sketches for his statue of Washington, which is now in the capitol at Richmond. Washington is more than six feet high. His face, according to Houdon, rejects with scorn some dishonorable proposal. He is clad in modern dress but he strikes a noble Roman pose, his cloak is carelessly flung over a bundle of thirteen fasces (the rods of the Roman lictors), his sword, now that peace has come, hangs on one side of the bundle, there is a plowshare behind his feet, and he carries a staff after the manner of the aediles. Washington incarnated the republican qualities developing in the new nation. He was the Father of his Country, the Cincinnatus of the New World, returning home after heading the armies of his country, then abandoning retirement again to be the first president of the United States. Had he not scorned an opportunity to become king or dictator? Survived plots against him? Led citizen soldiers to victory and yet met with Continental noblemen — De Kalb, Lafayette, Rochambeau, the Vicomte de Noailles, Lafayette's brother-in-law, de Broglie, a future marshal of France — on terms of lofty social equality? As Michael Kraus remarks, it was also true that European representations of American Indians suggest the world of the Greeks, so that behind Washington, Jefferson, and the rest, a sort of Greek-Roman-Indian-American image developed, which fascinated European liberals and fascinated many of the romantics.

As for the more local elements in this iconography, they were more classical than indigenous, despite the substitution of corncobs for acanthus leaves on columns in the national capitol. Probably the romanticized classicism of the new republic would not have been congenial to the age of Louis XIV. By 1774 the word *campus* was used to designate the grounds of a college. In 1789 basic elements in the new federal government included such classical derivatives as a president and a senate, and, for that matter, the building supposed to house the new government was a capitol, not a house of parliament or a *hôtel de ville*. Political life soon divided into the federalists and the republicans, terms springing from the Latin. Washington, who journeyed from Mount Vernon to the Hudson through an endless succession of classical arches and endless rows of maidens clad in white, took the oath of office on the balcony of a classical building in New York City. The government shortly authorized a great seal of the United States, thoroughly republican and thoroughly Roman: it includes an eagle of the legions clasping in one talon an olive branch and in the other thirteen sharpened arrows; three Latin phrases — *e pluribus unum*, *annuit coeptis*, and *novus ordo seculorum*; and the eye of a deistic God looking out from a triangle set in a glory over a truncated pyramid, though there were no pyramids in the United States. A decimal coinage (note the Latin adjective) included coins on which eagles were embossed, or a deified Liberty (or Columbia) in classical garments, commonly wearing a Phrygian liberty cap. (Shades of Robespierre!) The motto of North Carolina is *esse quam videri*, that of Virginia the famous *sic semper tyrannis*, and that of Massachusetts the more complicated *ense petit placidam sub libertate quietem*. The young republic rejuvenated classical symbolism, and the feeling spread that a great romantic revival of the best ages of Greece and Rome was possible. This rejuvenescence of antiquity affected or paralleled a revived romantic Hellenism in Europe, participated in by such artists as David, Canova, André Chénier, Hölderlin, Alfieri, and innumerable novels by Germans who wrote about ancient Greece as an erotic utopia. It was not that a new Rome was to rise on the banks of the Potomac, even though the name of Goose Creek was altered to Tibur; it was that a nation principally composed of independent farmers was to demonstrate in modern times that Vergil, Horace, and Columella were right in attributing political morality to independent agriculturists. *Hoc erat in votis* runs the famous passage in Horace's *Satires* — "this used to be among my prayers: a bit of land not too large, which should contain a garden and near the house an ever-flowing spring, and beyond that a wood lot." Had not the Americans fulfilled this ideal — farmers who had left their fields, seized their muskets, defeated the armies of a tyrannical monarch, founded a republic, and gone home again to cultivate their land? *

v

How did Europe, particularly European liberals and a dissatisfied younger generation, learn the particulars of this attractive renewal of the hopes of humanity? A current of information about the revolution and the young republic ran steadily from North America to the Old World during the decades under survey, but it cannot be described as a clear stream from a pure source. Like other great political, economic, or cultural upheavals, the revolution aroused prejudice and bias, admiration and envy, and these characteristics colored the reports. The sources of information varied widely, and of what must have been one of the most powerful kinds of reporting — conversation — we have virtually no records. Loyalists driven from their homes to Canada, the West Indies, or the British Isles were necessarily unsympathetic to what they considered an

---

* In the matter of a revival of antiquity in the young United States historians have hitherto been compelled to neglect one of the most important sorts of evidence — the coins and medals struck by a republican government. On this consult the invaluable study by Cornelius Vermeule, *Numismatic Art in America: Aesthetics of the United States Coinage*, Cambridge, Mass., 1971.

enormous act of treason, nor was their bitterness assuaged by the continuing failure of the Americans to fulfill that part of the peace treaty in which the Americans promised to pay off legitimate claims by Loyalists and British merchants covering property losses and debts. In some cases the revolution divided families; one can see in some of the historical novels of James Fenimore Cooper and William Gilmore Simms the bitter nature of these feuds. Returning soldiers might or might not like what they saw in the New World. They had been beaten, some of them had had frightful experiences with frontier Indians and white frontiersmen, and the prisoners of war, notably those constituting Burgoyne's army, might complain with reason that the Americans had not met the stipulations under which they had surrendered. Others, however, were impressed by the rich promise of the American land. Some German mercenaries remained in the United States to become citizens; those who returned had varying stories to tell, some of them highly colored because they knew no English and because they were bewildered by the American modes of waging war. Young French liberals, chiefly of the officer class, of whom Lafayette is the type, seemed to feel what a celebrated American journalist felt when he visited Russia shortly after the Russian revolution: "I have seen the future, and it works." It must also be remembered that the uncertainties of crossing the Atlantic in the days of sail meant that many reports, whether oral or printed, were months or years behind the facts.

Another generalization should be made. Although it may be true, as one scholar remarks, that in the last quarter of the eighteenth century the United States promised to be the almost perfect state, by 1825 the image had turned into that of a pushing bourgeois nation anticipating Guizot's famous mandate: "Enrichessez-vous." Nor was this unflattering interpretation long delayed. Moreover, a major difficulty in estimating the American impact on Europe lies in the ambiguity of such terms as "liberty," "freedom," "the people," "tyranny," "happiness," and the like. Investigation, exemplified by Carl B. Cone's *The English Jacobins: Reformers in Late Eighteenth Century England* (1968), makes it clear that although radicals like Richard Price consistently supported the Americans, the body of English Whigs, Dissenters, and reformers talked of liberties rather than of liberty and the rights of Englishmen rather than the rights of man. They looked back to a rather mythical Anglo-Saxon past for justification; and the Italians, the Spaniards, the Germans, and the French, when they talked about reform, also turned to history — to ancient Rome, to the Visigothic *cortes*, to an idealized feudal order, and, in the case of France, to a seventeenth-century precedent, the States General. Talk about equality seldom resulted in universal male suffrage. Our doctrine of "one man, one vote" would have made no sense in 1789. "Tyranny," "liberty," and "freedom" were fine words to throw about, but happiness was one thing to Bentham the utilitarian, another to Mirabeau the reformed rake, a third to Thomas Jefferson, and a fourth to Goethe's Faust ("Verweile doch, du bist so schön"). These meanings were incommensurable. I have earlier touched on the indefiniteness of "taxation without representation." Confusion was increased by differences in the political structures and cultural traditions of various nations and among the several reformist movements, not to speak of the shifting policies of any liberal or radical group in any nation over a space of years.

Let us look at Great Britain. It used to be said that British liberals, which usually meant the Whigs, supported colonials demanding the rights of Englishmen, a theory that received powerful support from the implications of Trevelyan's massive *The American Revolution*, in six volumes, completed in 1914. Nor is that theory now defunct.* But English reformers mainly based themselves upon the Glorious Revolution; that is, the shape given their political structure at the accession of William and Mary. After 1689, therefore, their conflict was not between king and people but between the crown ("the prerogative") and parliament. Parliament was only in part an elected council, and George III was not the tyrant of the Declaration of Independence but a political boss in the sense that the speaker of our House of Representatives has been the boss of the actions of that body. British radicalism has therefore to be thought of as pragmatic and historical rather than as universal and

---

* As late as 1930 in her *British Opinion and the American Revolution* Dora Mae Clark affirmed that "the history of British radicalism in the period of the American Revolution shows that the reformers in the two countries were a source of inspiration to each other. They corresponded with one another and exchanged philosophical ideas" (p. 176). "Inspiration" is a slippery word, and correspondence across three thousand miles of ocean was difficult in times of peace and much more difficult during seven years of war, since there were hundreds of privateers prowling the seas.

philosophic. Eighteenth-century radicalism begins indeed with the end of the Seven Years War, since in 1763 the forty-fifth issue of John Wilkes's *North Briton* was found actionable, Wilkes fled to France, and the interminable problem of the Middlesex election followed. Had parliament the right to refuse a seat to a person elected by a majority? By and by the House of Commons tired of the whole puzzle. There were strikes, riots, murders, and enforced boycotts during the economic depression of the 1760's. In 1769 a Society of Supporters of the Bill of Rights was formed, a date from which many British historians trace eighteenth-century British radicalism. It will be remembered that the Stamp Act crisis occurred in 1765–1766. Radicals looked abroad when it was useful to do so and cheered on the Americans, but British radicalism was, by and large, a home product, not a universal philosophy. Moreover, the colonies were distant and their troubles not always understood. The consequence was an alternation between intermittent support of the Americans and intermittent support of the ministry trying to bring them to heel. One has an amusing glimpse into the vagaries of radicalism when one learns that, without government objection, the Society for the Support of the Bill of Rights unanimously elected John Adams, that leading revolutionary, a member in 1773, whereas the government of the younger Pitt exiled Paine in 1792 for his treasonable writings, though Paine claimed to have been a friend of Burke!

It is therefore not surprising that British opinion about troubles in America was inconsistent and contradictory. British information was usually belated or untrustworthy even in government circles. Information for the general public ran the gamut from news in a recent letter from an American worthy, to a total blackout. It commonly took three months for an official report to reach the Secretary of State for the Colonies when that office was created, and about the same length of time for an instruction to be returned. What the ministry made public in parliament was often distorted, nor were random letters from America to merchants in Bristol or London necessarily objective. British officials in the New World were too often placemen, unworthy of a post at home, who sent back the kind of information they thought their patrons or superiors wanted to hear. British officials were not characteristically curious travelers who rode over bad roads and crossed "savage rivers" to collect popular opinions. And as Trevelyan says, royal governors, even when they were compassionate men, were not necessarily skilled in dealing with the Americans. Finally, bias and ignorance were increased whenever British army or naval units were stationed in America, inasmuch as military drinking, wenching, gambling, and contempt for civilians failed to ingratiate British officers with the colonial gentry. Some officers sent home reports that the colonials were meek and priggish or wild and uncivil. Colonial agents in Great Britain were put off by flaunting luxury, upper-class debauchery, and general excess in Britain after the Seven Years War. Finally, among the friends of the Americans John Wilkes was a woman-chaser, Charles Fox a gambler, the elder Pitt eccentric, and Burke suspected of being a secret Papist. Was America a purer country? Did it owe allegiance to an empire as corrupt as the Roman empire in its decadence? The question was often raised.

What did the unpredictable Americans really want? After the repeal of the Stamp Act, things seemed to settle down, and loyal addresses poured in from the colonials. Then came the Boston Massacre (less bloody than many a fight between smugglers and revenue officers in some obscure Scottish port), the Boston Tea Party, the assault by minutemen upon his majesty's troops at Lexington and Concord, and, finally, Bunker Hill. As a consequence, even the disaffected in Britain tended to lower their voices or rally to the crown. If the surrender of Burgoyne increased opposition to the ministry, the Franco-American alliance of 1778 rallied British opinion to the king. Eventually, as the number of Britain's enemies increased and the American war dragged on, many honest Britons concluded that the proper business of the armed forces was to defend the British Isles and such British possessions as were profitable or militarily advantageous. Yorktown and the final recognition of American independence were received with something like a sigh of relief. In addition, the infamous Lord George Gordon riots of 1780 frightened peaceful citizens. In 1785, says Cone, the reform movement was so quiescent, it seemed to be dead. It was reactivated, notably by the first news of the French revolution, but the younger Pitt's repressive measures after the French declaration of war in 1793 again smothered it.

The colonies had not enjoyed an altogether favorable image in

Britain. Andrew Burnaby, whose *Travels* was published in 1775, said of the colonies that "nothing can exceed the jealousy and emulation, which they possess in regard to each other." William Russell of Gray's Inn published a *History of America* in 1778; in this it appears that "neither moderation nor submission were to be expected from the wild fanatics of Massachusetts Bay." An anonymous *Account of the Rise and Progress of the American War*, which came out in 1780, attributed the rebellion to a "few violent and unprincipled scoundrels" deceiving peaceable Americans opposed to "violence and sedition." In that year George Chalmers published his *Political Annals of the Present United Colonies*, saying that "at all times" the New Englanders "found delight amid scenes of turmoil." So closely was the idea of citizenship bound in with that of status that in his famous *Taxation No Tyranny* of 1775 Dr. Johnson had written:

He who goes voluntarily to America, cannot complain of losing what he leaves in England. . . . By his own choice he has left a country, where he had a vote and little property, for another where he has great property, but no vote. But . . . this preference was deliberate and unconstrained . . . he has reduced himself from a voter to one of the innumerable multitude that have no vote.

British colonists "have the happiness of being protected by law, and the duty of obeying it." In his *Reflections on the Rise and Progress of the American War*, published five years later, John Wesley, who had been in the New World, said the Americans talked the "uniform language of malcontents" but that only "republicans" wanted independence. Liberals in England, wrote the author of an anonymous *Short but Comprehensive Account of the Rise and Progress of the Commotions in America* (1780), deceive themselves: the colonists are not prosperous — they are dying, they are "on the brink of ruin," prices there are exorbitant, manufactured goods scarce, and labor unavailable. Let us, he implied, push on to victory. But Yorktown was to be surrendered the next year.

It is true that in 1775 Burke had prophesied that if the British denied the Americans their proper "participation in freedom," they would break the sole bond that held the empire together; true also that, ten years later, in his *Observations on the Importance of the American Revolution, and the Means of Making it a Benefit to the World* Richard Price declared: "Perhaps, I do not go too far when

I say that, next to the introduction of Christianity among mankind, the American Revolution may prove the most important step in the progressive course of human improvement"; true that George III received John Adams, the first American minister to his court, with complete courtesy; true also that excitable young men named Coleridge and Southey dreamed of establishing a pantisocratic commune on the banks of the Susquehannah (the philosophic anarchism of Godwin, however, had only a remote connection with the American war). But the *Annual Register* under the control of Burke or his friends, though it reported the political recriminations consequent upon the American Declaration of Independence, spoke in 1777 of the "general indifference among the English people about the American war," and later calmly chronicled the surrender of Cornwallis in 1781, but it also said that the "news of the taking of Charleston" seemed to "revive all the sanguine hopes of the speedy subjugation of the colonies," and defended the treaty of peace in 1783. In 1787 it wondered how far the calling of the Assembly of Notables in France resulted from the American example and how far it resulted from the vogue of British writers on government and philosophy. Thereafter it concentrated on Europe, though in 1795 it hinted that the Whiskey rebellion in Pennsylvania may have been incited by British agents. But some commentators thought American minutemen displayed Indian savagery in picking off British officers, and by 1794 in his two-volume *History of the Origin, Progress, and Termination of the American War* Charles Stedman, dedicating his work to the Earl of Moira, comforted British pride by saying that "the military spirit of Britain shone forth with undiminished lustre; and the noblest families exhibited bright examples of true courage, exalted genius, and consummate vision." To most Britons in the troubled 1790's the United States was not a land of freedom. Isaac Weld, Jr., who traveled in North America in 1795–1797, expressed a common view in his *Travels* (1799):

there is no country on the face of the globe, perhaps, where party spirit runs higher, where political subjects are more frequently the topic of conversation amongst all classes, and where such subjects are more frequently the cause of rancorous disputations . . . I have repeatedly been in towns where one half of the inhabitants would scarcely deign to speak to the other half, on account of the difference of their political opinions.

On the other hand, British radicals dreamed of emigrating to America, and some did so; for example, Joseph Priestley. British radicalism, it is clear, drew only partial nourishment from the example of the United States.

The Irish response to the American revolution was, if possible, more confused than that of Great Britain. The first years of George III had seen the rise and fall of violent movements of discontent — the Whiteboys in the south and the Oakboys in the north, both groups protesting against enclosure movements, the rental system, inequitable taxation, and the iniquities of an Irish parliament that did not represent the Irish people. Many fled from Ulster to America, settling in the western parts of Pennsylvania, the Shenandoah valley, and the western Carolinas, and this group was an important element in the American story. The American theory that though the British parliament might legislate for the empire and for "external" taxation, it could not legislate for the internal affairs of the colonies struck a responsive chord.

But Ireland had a parliament, however inadequate, and by 1782–83 this parliament had won a considerable degree of legislative independence. The Irish gentry, Catholic or Protestant, seem to have taken a dim view of American rebels. Unemployment in Ireland made the army attractive to many Irishmen, the Irish gentry offered bounties to those who would enlist, and the Irish parliament, however unrepresentative, expressed indignation against the American rebels and consented to the reduction of the British armed forces in Ireland, for service abroad. This reduction became the more interesting after the Franco-American alliance, when an Irish volunteer movement, at first only military, spread over the island to protect it against a possible French invasion. The surrender of Cornwallis was felt to be a blow to the prestige of the empire. But though trade with America was cut off after 1775 and Irish coastal waters so swarmed with hostile privateers that trade with British ports was hazardous, and though there were serious riots in Dublin in the late 1770's, the principal result of the American revolution was not political independence but a greater degree of legislative independence won in 1782–83. Doubtless this legislative independence was in part illusory; if, for example, Great Britain declared war on a foreign country, Ireland was forced to go along with it. The mirage of a happy republic across the Atlantic drew some Irishmen thither and teased others — for example, Napper Tandy — into the thought of going, yet rebellion in Ireland had to await the French revolution and the second war against France to become formidable. It does not appear that during the years of the American struggle Irish Catholics exhibited any notable discontent, nor did they seize this opportunity to rise in rebellion, partly because the British government relaxed some of the harsher laws restricting their freedom of movement and of trade.

If one turns to other European countries, one begins by putting France aside as a special case. Possibly Germany (or "the Germanies") is characteristic. There were three special elements in the German relation to the American revolution: German mercenaries had been hired by the British; George III was also king of Hanover; and there were many German immigrants in the colonies and some German officers in the American forces, many of whom kept up correspondence with German relatives and friends. Of what notable interest was the American revolution to the Germanies?

The second half of the eighteenth century saw an increase of correspondence between German immigrants in the New World and their relatives at home. Moreover, there was some attempt to encourage emigration. Thus an anonymous pamphlet published at Sorau in 1771, *Das britische Reich in America*, said the climate of New England was healthy, liked the schools, praised the absence of beggars, admired the commerce of New York and Philadelphia, and remarked on the availability of good farming land. Franklin's personality impressed the Germans, as did the fame of Washington, admired by Frederick the Great, who was miffed at the British and rather wanted the Americans to win, though he distrusted republics. Various lesser German poets, among them Klinger, Voss, von Stolberg, Schubart, and Gleim, praised the revolution in occasional pieces, as did Wieland and Klopstock. There have been attempts to demonstrate that Schiller and Goethe were on the side of the Americans. At a celebration of the centenary of Schiller's death William Herbert Carruth made a case for Schiller as the bard of freedom but said that during the poet's lifetime

Germany was . . . more provincial than England or France. The American Revolution does not appear to have touched her deeply at any point excepting that of her deported soldiers. Steuben and Kalb came into the service of the colonies by way of French introduction. The Sturm und Drang writers do not keep an eye on America. Seume, who was himself among the Hessian soldiery sent to this country, treated the subject perforce in his diary. Klinger, indeed, locates his drama *Sturm und Drang* in America, but betrays no intimate acquaintance with the colonies nor much concern for their cause.

There is, he adds, little evidence to show an appreciation of the real significance of the struggle.*

Nevertheless opinions were sometimes vigorously expressed. Thus one Schlötzer edited a rather anti-American paper in Göttingen (in Hanover!), in which he wavers between admiration and prophesying that if the revolt succeeded, the result would be a new form of tyranny. More interesting is Wilhelm Ludwig Wekherlin, who, born near Stuttgart in 1739 to a tempestuous career, retired at forty to the village of Balden (Baldingen) near Nördlingen and published his *Chronologen*, an influential magazine with, for those days, a wide circulation. He denounced the American rebels, prophesied mob rule, said that freedom was a ghost, and expressed the political ideas of a Bonald or a de Maistre in language anticipating the diatribes of H. L. Mencken:

* William Herbert Carruth, "Schiller and America," *German-American Annals*, 4 (May 1906), 131–146. Attempts to show from Schiller's works that he had a genuine concern for things American amount to little. He was at one time (1781) vaguely associated with a Stuttgart periodical, *Nachrichten zum Nüzen und Vergnügen*, but those who have examined a file of this rare item cannot determine whether it had any policy. Carruth points out that in the plays and poems most of the "American" allusions have to do with the gold of Peru. Goethe, as we have seen, wrote an indifferent poem on America, but his central statement is in *Wilhelm Meisters Lehrjahre*: "Hier oder nirgend ist Amerika!" (in other words, don't emigrate). If Kant "supported" the dissident Americans against the despotic English, this seems to have been as late as 1784.
Let me express my indebtedness not only to Carruth but to three or four pioneering articles, from which I take excerpts in the next page or two of my text. The earliest is Karl Biedermann, "Die Nordamerikanische und die Französische Revolution in ihren Rückwirkungen auf Deutschland," which appeared in four installments in vol. III of the *Zeitschrift für deutsche Kulturgeschichte* (1858). Biedermann reprints a lengthy ode. The other contributions are by John A. Walz: a series entitled "The American Revolution and German Literature" running through vol. XVI of *Modern Language Notes* (1901); and another series, "Three Swabian Journalists and the American Revolution," scattered through various issues of *Americana Germanica*, which became *German-American Annals*, the pagination of the one and the volume numbering of the other being confusing. See also J. G. Rosengarten, "American History from German Archives with reference to the German soldiers and Franklin's visit to Germany" in the thirteenth volume of the *Proceedings* of the Pennsylvania-German Society (1904); and for some later phases of the subject Paul C. Weber, *America in Imaginative German Literature in the First Half of the Nineteenth Century*, New York, 1926.

Was ist Freiheit? Ein Ding, das niemals in der Welt war, das niemals in der Welt seyn kan, ein Phantom. . . . Keine Gesellschaft kan ohne oberschwimmende Macht bestehen. Ohne Macht ist der Begriff Gesezz leer. . . . Der Pöbel in Amerika hascht also einen Schatten nach.

Die Amerikaner sind Rasende, welche bey heller Sonne mit der Fackel in der Hand umrennen dem Tag zu suchen.

Als ein Kampf zwischen Freiheit und Tiraney, wär er diss gewesen, müsste er ein grosses ein interessantes Specktakel gewesen seyn. Aber als der Kampf der Ungebundenheit miet der gerechten Gewalt, also ein Streit zwischen der beneidsten Aemsigkeit und der drückenden Habsucht verliert er sein Schimmer. Gepriesener Sieg! *

Such were some representative antirevolutionary comments. The puzzle of liberals is evident in the case of C. F. D. Schubart, poet and journalist, who began printing his *Deutsche Chronik* in Augsburg, whence he was forced to remove to Ulm. This periodical ran from 1774 to 1777, when Schubart was imprisoned, and if it began by praising the English, it ended by applauding the Americans. Then in 1787 Schubart started a continuation, the *Vaterländische Chronik*; perhaps imprisonment had altered his views, since in this periodical the United States has become the country where his ideals are being realized, and his interest in England has been superseded by his interest in the French attempts to modernize their government. One of his remarkable statements runs: "Auch die Weiber in Amerika wandelt der Heroismus der alten Amazonen an" (heroism transforms American women into the ancient Amazons). Other "articles" are dated "Aus dem Lande der Freyheit" — the land of freedom is of course the United States. But perhaps the most remarkable pro-American piece is an endless ode printed in the *Berlinische Monatschrift* sometime in 1787, which congratulates the United States on achieving liberty, calls Washington a Hercules, says the new nation is a land of plenty and of promise, opposes tyranny, and exclaims: "O Land, dem Sänger theurer ist

---

* What is freedom? Something that never was in the world and that will never be, a phantom. Unless it have an overriding power, no society can exist. Lacking power, the idea of law is empty. The mob in America has been trying to lay hands on a shadow.

The Americans are maniacs who with torches in their hands run around looking for daylight in the bright sunshine.

As a struggle between freedom and tyranny, supposing it were that, the spectacle might have been vastly impressive. But as a battle between license and proper power, as warfare between active envy and driving greed, it loses its luster. A praiseworthy victory!

als Vaterland!" (O nation dearer to the poet than his fatherland!).
Thus the pendulum of opinion swung back and forth.

But Germany had its internal troubles, America was far away,
and the French revolution and Napoleon warring against German
states altered Germany's status as well as German opinion. The
problem of a mercenary soldiery was replaced by the necessity of
defending — indeed, of creating — a fatherland, the theme of
Fichte's famous *Reden an die deutsche Nation* delivered in Berlin
in 1807–8, the year after the Prussians had been totally defeated at
Jena, Auerstädt, and Halle. The American example was no longer
emotionally remote. It is true that Dietrich von Bülow had brought
out his *Der Freistaat von Nordamerika in seinem neuesten Zustand*
(that is, the latest report on the American republic), in which he
accused the United States of bringing up its youth in stupidity
and declared that country could never be powerful, but two years
earlier, in an examination of the American constitutional system
(*Die Staatverfassung der Vereignigten Staaten von Nord-
Amerika*), Franz Seidel had proclaimed that the American revolution surpassed anything in the history of the Roman republic.
Other books — histories, travels, books on emigration, political
accounts — multiplied, one of the most important being Johann
David Schöpf's *Reise durch den mittleren und südlichen vereinigten
nordamerikanischen Staaten nach Ost-Florida und den Bahamainseln
. . . 1783–1784* (Erlangen, 1788), one of the best and fullest reports on life in America under the Articles of Confederation. Paul
C. Weber, who analyzes this library, tells us that in 1808 the great
von Humboldt, talking to the Prussian king, Frederick William
III, said: "Your Majesty, it is a government which nobody sees
and nobody feels, and yet it is by far mightier than the government
of Your Majesty." This was a pleasant tribute to the results of the
American revolution, but one may wonder whether the king, when
he thought it over, felt that Humboldt's sentence might not cut two
ways.

So much for Great Britain, Ireland, and the Germanies. For the
French response to the American revolution let us wait until that
great movement is discussed. In the meantime it is important to
study a profound change in the concept of individualism.

VIII

Romantic Individualism

It now becomes necessary to solve a confusing chronological and thematic puzzle. Revolutionary political movements in the Western world can be taken in chronological order from 1763 through 1848, a task made simpler (if anything historical is ever simple) by the truth that the ending of the Seven Years War closed one great chapter in European history and opened another — the century of revolutionary change. The need of improving the fiscal system in Great Britain and of modernizing the empire awakened American distrust of the imperial intentions of the crown and led to independence; and the success of the American revolution, though scarcely a "cause" of the French revolution, encouraged liberals in France to think that they, too, could throw off a vicious tax system and install some form of government more aware of reality than was Versailles under Louis XVI. When, however, we try to discover what one may call a linear approach to romanticism, we discover the thing cannot be done. Romanticism is not linear but elusive. Aspects of romantic art can be identified in masterpieces created long before the Seven Years War, and elements of romanticism are evident in movements of sensibility, in the neoclassical revival, and in the antiquarian and anthropological interests of the eighteenth century years before Goethe published *Götz von Berlichingen* in 1773 and Wordsworth and Coleridge brought out *The Lyrical Ballads* in 1798. There was a continual interplay between the political forces making for individualism and the Dionysiac forces making for romantic individualism. Romantic individualism produced its most characteristic personalities *after* both revolutions had ended. Yet to understand the French revolutionaries one must first understand romantic individualism.

The shift in the nature of individualism about to be studied is one of the basic changes in European culture and one of the most difficult to analyze. In the world of politics considered simply as politics the initial phase of this alteration offers no great problem: the American revolution found man as subject and left him as citizen. The French revolution, again considered simply as politics, is only slightly more complicated because the movement there is triadic: the French revolution found man as subject, turned him into citizen, and then turned him back into subject. But the simple succession of monarchy-republic-empire-monarchy is not now the point. A more important difference develops in the few short years between the beginning of the American revolution and the beginning of the French revolution.

American leaders such as Washington, Franklin, John Adams, Jefferson, and Alexander Hamilton seem to be in one category of human beings, and French leaders such as Mirabeau, Marat, Danton, Robespierre, and Saint-Just seem to be in another. Washington, Adams, and their kind are thoroughly eighteenth-century personalities, content with eighteenth-century postulates and seeking a limited, eighteenth-century, utilitarian goal. French leaders seem to want to suppress and to surpass the eighteenth century. The great men of that revolution make totally incalculable appearances on the stage of the world. Indeed, their biographers, whether the leader whose life is examined be genius or devil, seem to wonder how his quiet earlier years produced such flaming energy. The great names of the French revolution are the names of men who are at once passionate egotists and devoted doctrinaires, men who have passed beyond rationalism into ideology, who have no genius for compromise, and who proclaim: "He who is not for me is against me." The American revolution and the early years of the republic found the Americans content with eighteenth-century canons of thought and behavior. But the French, of course with exceptions, seem driven to destroy the century of reason and to move into a stormy universe of emotion, thought, and behavior. They are not so much democratic as demoniac. They differ substantially from the Americans. One can by an effort of the imagination think of Patrick Henry delivering an oration by Mirabeau, but it is impossible to think of Washington in the role of Danton or Robespierre. An American court-martial regretfully sentenced

Major André to be hanged as a spy, but no committee of the Continental Congress ruthlessly butchered Tories as the committees and subcommittees of the Legislative Assembly allowed hundred of "suspects" to be butchered. This is not to argue that the Americans are a just people and the French an unjust one; it points only to the frenetic personal drive behind ruthlessness as something that must be understood. Hamilton extruded Jefferson from Washington's cabinet; he did not send him to death at the hands of an executioner as Robespierre sent Danton to death. Obviously, then, we are dealing with disparate types of leadership, and what makes the difference between the time of the beginning of the French revolution and the time of the beginning of the American revolution is the intrusion of a novel theory of individualism. That theory seems to me a theory of romantic individualism. It has two great aspects: romantic individualism proper and the romantic theory of genius. To these I turn.

To get from Lexington and Concord to the Committee of Public Safety and the Terror in France requires that we take a roundabout way. We must look at the images of individualism shaped by the romantics and then look at the French revolution. Unfortunately for chronology, because these romantic images were often perfected after the revolutions and not before or during their time, we must temporarily invert the chronological order. This inversion may be clarifying. Perhaps an illustration or two may help. Sam Adams was so thoroughly an eighteenth-century American, it would be difficult to picture him writing, say, Byron's *Childe Harold's Pilgrimage*, which began appearing during the war against Napoleon's armies in Spain. But Marat is chronologically also an eighteenth-century figure. Temperamentally he is so different from Samuel Adams, it is quite possible to imagine him, supposing he had the gift, sitting down in a white heat of anger and writing, say, Shelley's *The Mask of Anarchy*, that great attack upon political reactionaries. Yet Shelley's poem was written in 1819, a quarter of a century after Marat's assassination. To put the matter another way, if Byron had been born in an earlier time, we might say that it would be plausible to think of the succession Jefferson-Byron-Marat. Byron is chronologically out of order, but from the point of view of interpreting personalities, Jefferson's neoclassicism passes into Byron's passion for Greece and Rome, and Marat's perfervid insistence that he is a Friend of Man frustrated by tyrants parallels Byron's passionate belief that he is a friend of mankind frustrated by reactionaries.

Let us begin, even at the risk of repetition, by briefly examining the notion of individualism which the American revolution helped to bring into being, and then analyze at greater length romantic individualism and some of its expressions. Before the American revolution, unless he happened to be born into the purple, man was almost everywhere a subject and frequently a serf. If he was a citizen, the term usually meant that he was a member of some oligarchical minority as in Genoa or Venice, the rest of his compatriots being thought of merely as Genoese or Venetians, who might in their way be useful denizens of a state, but who were not to be entrusted with choosing those who conducted the affairs of the state. Even in Great Britain, thought by Voltaire and Montesquieu to be the most enlightened monarchy on earth, men were subjects, and suffrage was so ludicrously distributed and restricted that the system could not be rationally defended. Apologists had to fall back upon tradition. Moreover, although a Dissenter might be a highly respectable person, and Hodge the farmer a very worthy man, often neither Hodge nor the Dissenter could either vote or hold office, albeit in the case of Dissenters a special act of parliament sometimes cleared them of the obloquy of not being Anglicans. In the Western world in general women were subordinated to men, and by law and custom tended to assume meekly the social or political status or nullity of their male relatives. There were of course exceptional women everywhere. Thus the United States produced Abigail Adams and Mercy Otis Warren. But it is interesting to note that the United States, in its day the most radical nation on earth, produced nobody like Madame du Pompadour, Mary Wollstonecraft, or Charlotte Corday.

The American revolution, as I have said, transformed subjects into citizens. If they were male, most of them could vote and hold office. They were equal, so to speak, in their public capacity. But romantic individualism was not satisfied with the merely civic interpretation of man. It was a good thing that man as citizen was freed of such restrictions on his liberty as had been imposed by a fading feudal order and a status society in which everyone kept his place in an absolute order of rank and class. To strike the chains of "slavery" from the citizen, even though he could not vote, and to abolish compulsion on his labor and restriction on his industry were all excellent things, in themselves a step forward. But in another point of view political equality, though it ended servility, merely substituted for it uniformity.

Political equality released the public individual from bondage, but this principle, mainly operative in elections, reduced the citizenry to a sort of general facelessness. At elections everyone who could vote counted for one and only as one; from an electoral point of view A, B, and C could be replaced by X, Y, and Z and no change would be wrought in the result. Arithmetical summation was fine, but arithmetical summation had nothing to do with individual differences. Even in France, after the adoption of the first written constitution, which divided the populace into active citizens and passive ones, it did not matter who the active citizens were, taken individually, provided they voted, just as it makes no difference in American opinion polls what are the names of persons polled, provided the fraction of the populace they represent be a fair sampling. Idiosyncratic traits are thus subordinated to representational status. It would be too much to say that idiosyncratic traits disappeared from politics, since clearly they did not, but in the voting process, that triumph of the revolutionary program, one counted bodies, not personalities.

Against this anonymity the romantic doctrine of individualism set its face. For romantics it was less important that a human being be a citizen than that he be a soul. In the romantic point of view uniqueness, not generalization, is the key to humanity. In the romantic version of Christianity, for example, God created each individual as an isolated being, and in deism or pantheism, the same argument still held, since supernatural intelligence manifested itself not by creating masses but by creating men. Even the materialist, romantic or not, did not desire a robot political world. If the materialist dispensed with deity, he commonly held that the fecundity of nature is endless, that this fecundity delights in variations, and that education, by varying the physical environment of children taken individually, can vary the natures of the adults into which they develop. In this point of view, unless men were created different and, in some sense, unequal, how explain the appearance of genius in the most unlikely places?

ii

Although this theory of individualism did not originate with Rousseau, as in the case of other leading ideas phrased by that extraordinary character the theory of romantic individualism seemed to be his. To Rousseau man was more than the sum of his public appearances. Human life is, he thought, subjective; it lies within, it is of the soul; and it cannot be generalized except in the case of slavery, and even in that case real existence is merely subdued, it is neither eliminated nor transformed. In the Cartesian tradition man was an inhabitant of a geometrical universe; Rousseau denied the validity of such an analysis and approached the point of saying that man lives in a musical universe. The natural state of man, he thought, was not regular order but a sort of genial anarchy, which, when it became unbearable, was reluctantly transformed into some sort of social order, in which, nevertheless, the expression of the self was still paramount.

Rousseau begins his *Confessions*:

I am commencing an undertaking without precedent . . . which will never find an imitator. I desire to set before my fellows the likeness of a man in all the truth of nature, and that man myself. Myself alone! I know the feelings of my heart, and I know men. I am not made like any of those I have seen. I venture to believe that I am not made like any of those who are in existence. If I am not better, at least I am different.

At least I am different! Here is the central issue, new and powerful. This emphasis upon the uniqueness of personality and experience is to be discovered later in a thousand places — in the eternal "Ich" of the Germans, in Chateaubriand, de Vigny, Lamartine, Shelley, Byron, in Poe and Emerson, in painters of the stature of J. M. W. Turner, in artists such as Fuseli and Blake, in musical geniuses — Beethoven, Paganini, Berlioz, in dandies transforming clothing into aesthetic form (for example, Beau Brummell), in women who, insisting that their sex had been wronged, avenged themselves upon the world by being extravagantly and insistently themselves, among them Mary Wollstonecraft, Madame de Staël, Caroline Schlegel, Lady Hester Stanhope, Charlotte Corday, who proposed to purify society by assassination, and Harriet Wilson, who hoped to become important by sleeping with as many men of rank as she could.

European literature in the last decades of the eighteenth century and the opening ones of the nineteenth sometimes seemed to transform itself into an enormous autobiography in many languages. Chapters might take the form of dramatic poetry as in *Manfred* and *Faust*, or philosophic discourse as in the instances of Kant, Fichte, Hegel, Schopenhauer, and Coleridge, or fiction as in the *Hyperion* of Hölderlin, the *Werther* of Goethe, the *Adolphe* of Benjamin Constant, and (incredible!) the *Waverley* of Walter Scott and *The Pioneers* of Cooper. The collected poems of Wordsworth are a gigantic confession, the fantastic tales of E. T. A. Hoffmann are what they are because Hoffmann was himself a fantast. The *Génie du Christianisme* and *Les Martyrs* of Chateaubriand are as personalized as his *Mémoires d'outre-tombe* and no more reliable.

> Fratelli, a un tempo stesso, Amore e Morte
> Ingenerò la sorte,

begins a celebrated poem by Leopardi, that most classical of melancholy romantics, but it is not universal love, universal death that fate engenders, it is love and death as experienced by Leopardi. As for other poems by other poets, often private visions of a world gone mad, portraits, including pictures of the insane, eccentric conduct (one British swell dressed in nothing but green), subjective music, writing supposed to spring from dreams, odd architecture (gazing at the Prince Regent's Pavilion in Brighton, the Rev. Sydney Smith commented that the dome of St. Paul's had had pups) — these expressions of idiosyncrasy were acceptable, though not central, to the doctrine.

This is not to say that Western civilization produced no striking or eccentric individuals before 1763. Neoclassicism had its quota of introverts, its cases of melancholia — one thinks of those standard complaints, the vapors and the spleen — and its portion of eccentrics. Most of these would presumably have been introverts or victims of melancholia in any period. But the biographical and autobiographical information concerning eighteenth-century worthies is in the main public information rather than confessional or introspective. The individual then existed at a crossroad where his private impulses met his publicly avowed relations — a place at court, a profession, political eminence, a career in the church, in the army, in law, in commerce, in marriage, and so on. While the

Autobiography of Benjamin Franklin is personal in the sense that only Benjamin Franklin could have written it, the *Autobiography*, elaborate mystification though it is, tells us little or nothing about the inner life of its author. Johnson suffered from melancholia but Johnson did not wear his heart upon his sleeve for Boswell to peck at. In the high eighteenth-century world character was usually measured by public acts, not by introspection, except perhaps in the world of religion.

Rousseau opposed all this. He lived in the eighteenth century but he was not altogether of it. His principal works were printed from 1750 to 1782, the first part of the *Confessions* appearing four years before his death, the second part some time after it.* But it is useless to separate the *Confessions* from the rest of his work. Individual books by Jean-Jacques are not so much separate works as chapters in a universal book that is both an unending apology for Rousseau and a continued attack upon modern society. The theme of the enterprise is double: an examination, enormous, passionate, and hostile, of the origins and misfortunes of the human race, and an examination of the origins and misfortunes of Jean-Jacques. Rousseau is the single but not necessarily the representative case; history, or rather history as Rousseau conceived it to be, is the general story of humanity. Because Rousseau was a European and a deracinated figure, long an outcast, profoundly suspicious of contemporary life, and eventually persuaded that the state, his friends, and his benefactors were engaged in a conspiracy against him, he mounted this perpetual assault. He speaks for the natural man, who is imperfect, and for social man, who is enchained. The exposition begins with the human race as it should have been in a state of nature, for which Rousseau blandly says he has no evidence, and flows across recorded time into such practical issues as an improved government for Poland and a proper constitution for Corsica.

Matters of personal import may, however, turn up anywhere in this library. The discussions, the narratives, the descriptions, the

---

* Bibliographers mildly dispute the date of the publication of part one of the *Confessions*. The other principal titles are: *Discours sur les arts et les sciences*, 1750; *Discours sur l'origine et les fondements de l'inegalité*, 1755; *Lettre à d'Alembert sur les spectacles*, 1756; *Julie, ou la nouvelle Héloïse*, 1761; *Du Contrat social*, 1761; *Emile, ou de l'éducation* (includes *La Profession de foi du vicaire Savoyard*), 1762; *Lettres de la montagne*, 1763; *Reveries du promeneur solitaire*, 1776. The list omits various more or less *ad hoc* political and economic treatises and also his musical works.

invectives, and the invocations, any or all of them, are likely to be elegant, illogical, brilliant, or contradictory; they touch upon economics, the education of youth, the sentiments of love, the world as a temple of deity, the conduct of princes, the nature of the state, and the goodness of God. God is neither Christian nor Judaic, but an elementary being, a primal entity evident in the dew of the morning, the multitudinousness of society, the lonely charm of mountain and meadow, and the susceptibilities of the heart. Such a Creator, at once ineffable and intimate, reveals Himself through neither theology nor philosophy nor history. He is a taciturn yet omnipresent deity, immanent in the kiss of lovers, a mother nursing a child, personal sorrow, and the glow of artistic fulfillment, as also in such inexplicable disasters as the Lisbon earthquake and the tyranny of kings. God does not favor kings, he merely permits man to err. As for autobiography, my real purpose, says Rousseau at the opening of part two of the *Confessions*, is to contribute to an accurate knowledge of my inner being. I have promised, he writes, to relate the history of my soul. For this I need no *aides-mémoires* for I cannot be deceived in the memory of what I have felt.

In this way both his campaign against society and his treatise on the cosmos became personalized. It is I, Jean-Jacques, who have educated Emile, listened to a Savoyard vicar, and in the character of Saint-Preux gazed across the severing waters of the lake at Julie, the new Eloise; I, who was born free and am now in chains: I, Jean-Jacques, who write these books and treatises, my *Confessions* making evident to all the world my goodness, my folly, my weakness, my friendships, which are eternally misunderstood, my determination to remain poor while longing for the flattery of the rich. It is I, who put my children in a foundling home; I, who preach the duty of mothers to suckle their young; I, who respond to river and lake, mountain and garden, women who wish to seduce me and philosophers who wish to betray me to the police. Never before had the literary productions of a single man been so vehement, so subjective, so egotistical.

Rousseau is the complete manifestation not so much of romantic philosophy as of the romantic outlook. There were of course egotists before him. But never previously had a single genius turned everything — pedagogy, love, political theorizing, religious exhortation, economics, a new system of musical annotation, anthropology however naive, and psychology however unsystematic, into an attack upon the ordinary and the traditional. The assault is confused. But here is no Diogenes bidding the Bourbons stand out of his sunlight. Rousseau is a cosmic poet who writes prose, a genius who realizes that polished epigrams will not save mankind, that if one is to capture the allegiance of men, one must clothe one's ideas in melody, in long, cadenced paragraphs that haunt the mind, with here and there the shock of a terse opening sentence. This writer reinvigorates French style, transforms the rationality of prose into rhapsody, and preludes the roll of drums at the guillotine by creating a revolutionary symphony in words, a composition that anticipates the urgency and sorrow of a Beethoven or a Berlioz. Romanticism was not born with Rousseau's *First* or *Second Discourse*; yet, with the *Discours sur les arts et les sciences*, produced precisely at midcentury amid the clink of Voltaire's alexandrines and the persiflage of Piron, romantic individualism enters upon the stage of Europe and seduces the imagination of men. Rousseau transformed sensibility into rapture and despair. Des Grieux, Werther, the Agathon of Wieland, the Karl Moor of Schiller, the Childe Harold of Byron, and the René of Chateaubriand — personages such as these are his contemporaries or his imaginative offspring.

Although Rousseau perpetually attacks, he is not a political activist in the sense that Mirabeau, Danton, or Robespierre is a political activist. For Rousseau contemplation is a mode of action. To his tortured genius meditation is so important that competent critics declare that the *Confession of Faith of a Savoyard Vicar* and the *Reveries of a Solitary Walker* are the high-water marks of his prose. When one adds that little Emile is expected not merely to act but also to meditate, and that page after page of *La Nouvelle Héloïse* is devoted to the charm of landscape and the pleasures of the eye, the ear, and the soul, one realizes that *Du Contrat social* is not, as was formerly thought, one of the "causes" of the French revolution, but that *Emile* and *La Nouvelle Héloïse* cleared the way for emotional commitments to the revolution that differentiate the political convulsions in France from the political convulsion in America. The revolutionaries justified themselves by quoting from *Du Contrat social* but only after the revolution had occurred.

Consider, for example, this passage from the *Reveries*:

As evening drew on, I used to come down from the higher ground and sit on the beach at the water's edge in some hidden, sheltered place. There the murmur of the waves and their agitation, charming all my senses and driving every other movement from my soul, plunged it into delicious dreams, in which night often surprised me. The flux and reflux of the water, the ceaseless stir, swelling and falling at intervals, striking on ear and sight, compensated for the subjective movements which my musings extinguished, and were enough to give me delight in mere existence without my taking any trouble to think. From time to time some passing thought arose about the instability of the things of this world, of which the face of the waters offered me an image; but such light impressions were swiftly effaced in the uniformity of the ceaseless motion which rocked me as in a cradle, and held me with such fascination that even when I was called at the right hour and by the appointed signal, I could not tear myself away without summoning up all my energy.

Nothing is said about the rights of man. Yet a social system which would deny men the right to withdraw, to muse, to contemplate cannot be good. Hence the radicalism of Rousseau is as much emotional as intellectual. His subjectivism, because it isolates the individual, increases the value of life and is as revolutionary as the ideas of Paine. It produces a new concept of the purposes of humanity. It does not teach anybody how to launch or control a political revolution (Rousseau was at heart a conservative), but it asks what happiness is to be, once the revolution has triumphed. Happiness conceived by political theorists as the greatest good of the greatest number will not, for Rousseau, be happiness as judged by the heart.

The concept of man in a state of nature, the concept of a social contract, and the concept that a democracy, or, more accurately, a republic is possible only in a small territory did not originate with Rousseau. These are among the commonplaces of eighteenth-century theorizing, inheritances from a venerable past. The one relatively original notion in Rousseau's political philosophy is that of the general will, which means that before any society can be governed, the group must agree to be a society. But this idea is essentially mystical, since the general will cannot arise logically either from a state of nature or from any discoverable impulse in natural man. As for two other notions associated with Rousseau —

the idea that social man degenerates because of the arts and sciences he has invented and the idea of a working and disastrous relation between property and social status (inequality), these, too, do not originate with him. A dream of some simpler time when men were not burdened by anxiety haunts the history of humanity. The true originality of Rousseau lies therefore less in his theories and his simplistic ideas of human development than in his insistence upon the autonomy of the person. Here is a doctrine that did as much to overthrow the ancient regime, which defined men by custom and wealth, as did the National Assembly when it voted for the Rights of Man and of the Citizen. What good is a declaration of rights unless one first ascertains what one means by "man"? This is the terrible question Rousseau puts to eighteenth-century society. Toward a proper answer the discovery of personality (his own, to be sure, but was he not a man?) is the first step, a basic impulse which furthers both the revolutionary impulse and the romantic impulse. *At least I am different!* Who does not believe himself unique? Such a valuation of the self requires the creation of a new world in which every individual is autonomous. If the terms "society" and "unique" contradict each other — very well, let them contradict each other.

iii

I am not made like any of those I have seen. At first glance the egotism of Rousseau seems so absolute that some cultural historians (for example, the late Irving Babbitt) date all the evils of contemporary society from its expression. Egotism, however, has long been something for traditional morality and religion to correct. The Bible is full of commentaries upon egotism, its temptations, its loneliness, its strength, and its potentiality:

Naked came I out of my mother's womb, and naked shall I return thither.

I said in my haste, All men are liars.

We brought nothing into this world, and it is certain we can carry nothing out.

Blessed is the man that endureth temptation, for when he is tried, he shall receive the crown of life.

But in the eighteenth century among the elite and fashionable groups romantic individualism, a fusion of values partly from the Enlightenment, partly from the movement of sensibility, partly from neoclassicism and, oddly enough, partly from religion, could no longer be what individualism had been in the Renaissance or the Middle Ages. When the patterns of a status society slowly altered or crumbled away, the individual found himself at once less and more than he would have been if he had lived a century before; he was both more isolated and more exaggerated, so to speak. Until the Catholic revival in Germany and France, and except for evangelical or fideistic groups such as the Methodists, the Pietists, the Quakers and, of course, thousands of the illiterate, Christian faith with all its panoply of atonement, redeeming grace, salvation, and eternal life strangely weakened. In the eyes of most philosophers the great drama of the universe, despite the vogue of Milton and Klopstock, was played out. As spectators of world tragedy, human beings could at one time identify themselves with the principal actors in this play — Adam, Moses, Jesus, Judas Iscariot, and St. Paul — just as they could stare in fascination at the tremendous Wagnerian conclusion when heaven and earth should pass away, and the fearful, the unbelieving, the abominable, the murderers, the whoremongers, and all liars be cast forever into the lake which burns with fire and brimstone. Few eighteenth-century rationalists, however, would have agreed even with Edgar Allan Poe's version of the cosmic plot and its denoument:

> . . . the angels, all pallid and wan,
> Uprising, unveiling, affirm
> That the play is the tragedy, "Man,"
> And its hero, the Conqueror Worm.

How could one accept a church Voltaire had called infamous? How believe in an institution that tolerated Cardinal Rohan of diamond-necklace notoriety, and made Talleyrand bishop of Autun? For that matter, was the Church of England any better? The arts had been the handmaids of religion, but when one thinks of leading painters of the eighteenth century, although religious subjects never disappear, one thinks of Watteau, Fragonard, Boucher, Chardin, Hogarth, Reynolds, Gainsborough, Copley, West, David — men who are for the most part painters of this world, not of the next. We expect from them portraits, genre pictures, anecdotes, erotic mythology, actual landscapes, naval battles or those on land — in short the life of the world as it goes, not parables of a world to come. True, there are sentimentalists among them, for example, Greuze, whose characters seem to enjoy a pleasant Sunday-school virtue, but we are far from Michelangelo or Raphael. Only in Spain do religious themes retain their old importance; yet the greatest painter in Spain is Goya, pitiless and sardonic.* In the musical world masses are composed, oratorios on religious themes are sung, hymns are written, and sacred concerts held; but by the middle of the century composers of the Mannheim school, or Haydn, or Gluck, or Mozart write music less for the glory of God than for the glory of a royal or aristocratic patron. If they produce operas, these are on heroic legends or classical stories — Gluck's beautiful *Orfeo ed Euridice* is an example; or they dramatize with charming deftness amorous plots and counterplots or the story of a rakish life as in Paisiello's *Il Barbiere di Siviglia* or Mozart's *Così fan tutte*. *Don Giovanni* concludes in a good deal of hell-fire but it is merely magic, and at the end of the opera the surviving pairs of lovers complacently congratulate themselves on the disappearance of Don Giovanni and their own happy survival. It is true that Mozart wrote more than twenty-five masses long and short, but it is characteristic that the great "Requiem Mass," ordered by a "mysterious stranger" and left incomplete at the composer's death, is shrouded in a legend that might be part of Offenbach's *The Tales of Hoffmann*. The Saviour now took refuge among the Wesleyans or in the fields or among revivalists on the distant American frontiers; he was driven out of the national churches, the fine arts, and the current philosophies. God was banished from the American Constitution of 1789, to be replaced by that geometrical construct, a Supreme Being, whom

---

* Paintings by Caspar David Friedrich (1774–1840), the leading German romantic artist, when they picture religious edifices, show them either as ruins or buried in lonely silence, as in "The Graveyard in Snow" (1810). His famous canvas of a sailing vessel crushed by huge slabs of Arctic ice was originally "The Wreck of the *Hoffnung*" and "Hoffnung" (Hope) was painted on the bows of the vessel. Friedrich anticipates the Norwegian genius, Edvard Munch, in presenting an isolated figure or small group of figures against a melancholy empty landscape. His "Mountaineer in a Misty Landscape" (1815?) curiously recalls Wordsworth's apocalyptic vision on a mountaintop in *The Prelude*, Book XIV, ll. 35ff; and Wordsworth's "three chance wanderers" in that passage recur in Friedrich's misty seascape, "Moon Rising over the Sea" (1823)

Robespierre led the Parisians in honoring during the year 1794. When Napoleon asked Laplace, on receiving his *Mécanique céleste*, why the author of the universe was omitted from the book, the scientist replied: "Sire, I have no need for that hypothesis."

Rationalism had perhaps done its work too well. The philosophical movement that had begun with Descartes and Malebranche in France and with Locke in England ground to a halt in the skepticism of Hume and the materialism of Holbach. Not only did God, Christ, and Satan disappear except as stage properties or myths, but under the relentless pressure of skeptical analysis the world vanished also, leaving man, in the opinion of Hume, a bundle of imaginative impressions and ideas with no possible knowledge of the actual world and no possible proof for the existence of God. In the endeavor to destroy such nihilism, Kant started all over again, but though he managed to equip every mind with something he called the transcendental unity of apperception, he was unable to discover any sure way of knowing things as they really are in themselves. The transcendental unity of apperception is a mystical principle, since through its pure existence — that is, the assumption that it has qualities and powers preceding any possible sensory experience — if we cannot know the world as it truly is, we know only that existence is divided between the I and the Not-I, and that our ego so orders perception that in matters of ordinary life we get along very well. But poets and philosophers, radicals and revolutionaries are not always content with ordinary life. German metaphysicians therefore asked the inevitable next question: if the ego begins where the non-ego leaves off, must it not be equally true that the non-ego exists for the sake of the ego? Why not, therefore, assume they are simply two sides of the same thing, or, in other words, that the world as I know it must be in some sense something I generate? Fichte boldly faced the dilemma and seemed to say that the ego and the non-ego were the expressions of some sort of super-ego existing outside space and time. In connection with these early phases of German transcendentalism it is instructive to learn that Kant attended the Collegium Fredericanum at Königsberg, then under the direction of Albert Schultz, a Pietist follower of Spener, and went from there to the University of Königsberg where he worked under Martin Knutzen, who was also a Pietist. Thus does the wheel come full circle. The *Kritik der reinen Vernunft* first appeared in 1781, the year Cornwallis surrendered at Yorktown.

It cannot be argued that leaders of the French revolution read Kant, Fichte, or any other leaders of German thought. But the leaders of any great movement live in a climate of opinion, and the climate of opinion in Europe in 1789 differed radically from the climate of opinion in North America in 1763. God was remote, the universe was malleable, the future of mankind depended upon humanity itself, the world was what the ego made of it, and French revolutionary egotists were entirely prepared to assert that they and they alone, taken collectively or individually, were capable of interpreting the present wishes and probable future of mankind in terms they themselves laid down with a personal passion not evident in American patriots or the American founding fathers. The disappearance of the Christian order from French revolutionary thought turned Man into an enlarged surrogate for deity. Victory and remorse were here and now; the development of advanced thought, if it isolated the individual revolutionary leader, also permitted him to picture a perfected society and a rational future as an enlarged image of himself. This is not, of course, the whole story of the French revolution, but it is an image sufficiently cogent to illuminate the profound psychological difference between a Jefferson and a Marat, a George Washington and a Robespierre.*

iv

From about 1775 forward romantic individualism developed, it seems to me, at least three cardinal types other than the revolutionary one, each of which was influenced by revolution and in turn influenced the revolutionaries. Allowing for national variations and philosophic differences, the types seem to me to be (1) the sufferer; (2) the rebel; and (3) the liberated woman. The first of these is represented by Goethe's *Werther*, the second by poems on the Prometheus theme, and the third by such works as Schlegel's

---

* I touch only the edges of a vast philosophical problem. For a rich and profound study of the dreams of artists and thinkers principally in England and Germany, who propose revolutionary modes of constructing some sort of heavenly city on earth through an onerous self-examination, see M. H. Abrams' remarkable book, *Natural Supernaturalism: Tradition and Revolution in Romantic Literature*, New York, 1971.

Lucinde, Madame de Staël's *Corinne,* and Shelley's *Epipsychidion.* Let us examine these types.

The sufferer descends from Rousseau and from the general pool of eighteenth-century sensibility. There is, however, an important difference between the man of feeling and the romantic sufferer. Both feel intensely, but the man of sensibility — an example is Harley, the hero of Henry Mackenzie's *The Man of Feeling* (1771), more or less travestied in Robert Bage's amusing *Hermsprong; or, Man As He Is Not* (1796) — the man of sensibility feels intensely but he assumes that what he feels anyone else would feel whose emotions have not been blunted by custom or self-regard. The romantic sufferer, like Rousseau, insists that he is unique and solitary, a being born out of his due time and place, a soul who comes too late into a world too old. By the world the romantic sufferer means the world of men as they are, since the world of nature, though partially obscured to him by human stupidity, is still a world in which, like Childe Harold, the sufferer can find spots in which to breathe freely:

> There is a pleasure in the pathless woods,
> There is a rapture on the lonely shore,
> There is society where none intrudes,
> By the deep Sea, and Music in its roar:
> I love not Man the less, but Nature more,
> From these our interviews, in which I steal
> From all I may be, or have been before,
> To mingle with the Universe, and feel
> What I can ne'er express — yet cannot all conceal.

To the romantic sufferer the world is at opposite poles from the world agreeable to Alexander Pope, who in *Windsor Forest* wrote about it as "harmoniously confus'd / Where order in variety we see, / And where, though all things differ, all agree." Pope's universe is the Newtonian universe, the universe of God the great geometer, a world in which there is a chain of being with an allotted place in it for man. The universe of the romantic sufferer is the product both of abstract thought (as in the case of Fichte) and of speculative thought about such concretions as chemistry, electricity, and other branches of natural philosophy which put a new aspect on things. These changes were interpreted by many romantics as lying in the direction of vitalism, mesmerism, actual phenomena as symbols, arcane wisdom, or occult forces known to ancient man but hidden by the course of history from the vulgar mind. This universe is not mechanical but dynamic, a universe of light and power, love and terror. Its central principle is vitality. Nature is curative, but veiled from all but the melancholy sufferer by the course of civilization, "tyranny," the waxing and waning of empires, priestcraft, logical analysis, and human folly. Hence only a sensitive minority rises to an apprehension of the life-giving quintessence in nature itself. Such men, though they suffer, are by their very suffering throwbacks to a healthier life on earth and prophets of a radiant age to come. Most bards, wrote Shelley, are "cradled into poetry by wrong; / They learn in suffering what they teach in song."

Experience and longing lead the lonely sufferer to believe that the crust of falsehood can be broken, and that he can be strengthened for revolutionary idealism by the experience of love. Love, however, especially if it involves forbidden relationships, is soon crushed by convention, by society, by the tyranny of family life, or by the tyranny of the state. The romantic sufferer, divorced from his beloved, may find life intolerable and commit suicide as Werther does,* or he may live on, alone, a silent stoic, clasping to

---

* *Die Leiden des jungen Werthers* is in all probability more widely read nowadays in Europe than it is in the United States, and therefore a summary may be useful. The novel, first published in 1774, was reissued in a revised edition of 1787 but never lost its autobiographical tinge. It concerns a hyperbolically sensitive young man named Werther, who has escaped from one unlucky love situation only to fall desperately in love with Charlotte, the betrothed and later the wife of the respectable Albert, a husband for a time indulgent to the passion Werther develops for Albert's wife. This love becomes an obsession with Werther, who vainly tries to cure, or at least diminish, his frenzy by leaving the vicinity where Charlotte resides and taking service with an ambassador. But he runs into humiliating social rebuffs ("everything conspires against me"), resigns his post, and returns to Charlotte and Albert, where his unrequited passion drives him almost insane. Through a transparent trick he acquires a pair of Albert's pistols and shoots himself, but not before he has recounted the tale of another unhappy young man in love with a woman his social superior. Three-fourths of the novel is written rather naively in epistolary form; Goethe awkwardly reverts to the third person ("the editor to the reader") for the concluding section, since Werther cannot very well narrate the circumstances of his own suicide. In the early portion Werther is a happy lover of nature and of Homer; in the latter parts he gives up Homer for Ossian, which on one fatal occasion he reads aloud to Charlotte. "A tremor ran through him . . . and his eyes filled with tears." At the conclusion of the reading "a torrent of tears streamed from Charlotte's eyes and gave relief to her oppressed heart," and Werther "seized her hand, and wept bitterly." A moment later he "threw himself at Charlotte's feet, seized her hands, and pressed them to his eyes and his forehead. . . . They lost sight of

his heart the secret of his existence, the memory of the immortal beloved, some gleams of arcane knowledge, and a hatred of mankind as it is. If he dies a natural death, he dies as the wolf dies. A late poem by Alfred de Vigny, "La Mort du loup" (1843), admirably expresses this melancholy conclusion:

> Comment on doit quitter la vie et tous ses maux,
> C'est vous qui le savez, sublimes animaux!
> A voir ce que l'on fut sur terre et ce qu'on laisse,
> Seul le silence est grand; tout le reste est faiblesse.*

The romantic sufferer appears not only in the literature of the age but in actuality. Werther, René, Roderick Usher, and Ernani expire, although a few such as the Wandering Jew, Melmoth the Wanderer, the monster in *Frankenstein*, and Bulwer-Lytton's Zanoni must live indefinitely on. Biographers reveal a like typology in actual existence. Herder (1744–1803), for example, with his unhappy temperament, worsened, it is true, by a lingering ocular ailment, yearned for intuitive truth, rebelled against the *Aufklärung*, and was confident that only in intuitive truths did God reveal Himself. One commentator quotes him as saying: "My life is a progress through Gothic vaults, or at least an avenue of green shades: the prospect is always . . . sublime; I set foot in it with a sort of awe." He alternated between melancholy and exaltation, unable most of his life to govern the discontent that haunted him. He once characterized his existence as lightning flashes by night. J. G. Hamann, to whom we shall come in the next chapter, denied the validity of any intellectual order and, a hypochondriac, once announced he would have nothing to do with responsibility. The greatest Hellenist of his generation, Hölderlin felt two natures struggling within him. Born in 1770 into a lower-middle-class family, he held and abandoned one tutoring post after another in a period when the tutor was classed with the house servants. He

---

everything." Charlotte, however, does not succumb. For the vogue of Werther see Stuart Pratt Atkins, *The Testament of Werther: In Poetry and Drama* (Cambridge, Mass., 1949).
* The right way to leave life and all its suffering
  You sublime animals are the ones who know.
  Judging by what one was in life and what one leaves behind,
  Silence alone is great; the rest is weakness.

fell in love with Frau Gontard, the wife of one of these employers, called her his Diotima, and was discharged. Unable to withstand the slings and arrows of outrageous fortune, he went partially insane in 1802 and wholly so in 1807. Yet there was within him a totally different personality, that of a pagan fascinated by the culture of ancient Greece as interpreted by Winckelmann. Along with his rebellious existence in the world, Hölderlin therefore simultaneously lived a dream life of total antique beauty. This self wrote the most admirable poems about antiquity, but the self in this world complained:

> Ich verstand die Stille des Aethers,
> Des Menschen Wort verstand ich nie.*

Wilhelm Heinrich Wackenroder (1773–1798), nervous, dreamy, a fantast by temperament, despising his duties as a referendary in Berlin — that is, a man with legal training who examines legal papers, petitions, and the like — victim of a passionate friendship for Ludwig Tieck, produced his *Die Herzensergiessungen eines kunstliebenden Klosterbruders*, heart-outpourings of an art-loving friar, in 1797 and thus retreated into the Middle Ages. He died at twenty-five. One of eleven children born to a Moravian family, Novalis (Friedrich Leopold, Freiherr von Hardenberg, 1772–1801), after telling a professor at the University of Jena that "a thousand images glide before my soul vivified by imagination and memory," the magical light of which softly "summons up an infinite set of emotions, feelings, and ideas," fell in love with a girl of thirteen, who died two years later. Novalis attempted to will his own death beside her grave, wrote his six *Hymnen an die Nacht* to say that night is the night of the soul, then fell in love all over again, and died of tuberculosis. These examples are all from Germany, but leaders of the French revolution, such as Couthon, Robespierre, Marat, and even Mirabeau are also, as the Germans would say, *problematische Naturen*; they strive to impose their vision of the world as it should be on the world as it is not, and eventually develop a sort of boredom with revolution, that weariness of the soul which overcame Danton, for example, who refused to resist a death sentence imposed upon him.

* I understood the silence of the ether; the word of man I could never comprehend.

v

The Prometheus theme represents the defiant romantic rebel. In antiquity it had many variants, but the central idea is that either as the creator or the benefactor of mankind Prometheus defies Zeus, who binds him to a distant mountaintop and sends an eagle, or vultures, to prey on his liver (which is nightly restored) in the hope that, unable to endure the pain any longer, Prometheus will reveal his secret knowledge concerning the fated overthrow of Zeus, the tyrant of gods and men. Romantics translated Prometheus into a secular savior, the incarnation of a will to resist, a believer in the overthrow of despotism, and a proponent of the idea that mankind under sunnier circumstances is capable of indefinite progress without the need of Christian revelation. Prometheus replaces Christ. This faith in secular progress was the faith, for example, of Condorcet. Three leading expressions of the theme are Goethe's unfinished *Prometheus* (1773), a lofty poetical address by Byron entitled "Prometheus" (1816), and Shelley's great *Prometheus Unbound* (1820), a passionate affirmation of the revolutionary faith that man can be freed from "tyranny." In an extensive preface Shelley wrote:

The only imaginary being resembling in any degree Prometheus is [Milton's] Satan; and Prometheus is, in my judgement, a more poetical character than Satan, because, in addition to courage, and majesty, and firm and patient opposition to omnipotent force, he is susceptible of being described as exempt from the taints of ambition, envy, revenge, and a desire for personal aggrandisement, which, in the Hero of *Paradise Lost*, interfere with the interest. . . . Prometheus is, as it were, the type of the highest perfection of moral and intellectual nature, impelled by the purest and truest motives to the best and noblest ends

— in sum, the perfect revolutionary. Shelley acknowledges his own republicanism and his "passion for reforming the world." His poem appeared one year after the Carlsbad decrees imposed on the German press and on German universities a universal police censorship.

More usual versions of the Prometheus story are those of Goethe and Byron. The first two acts of the proposed play by Goethe exist only as sketchy dialogues between Prometheus and one or another god or goddess, and what remains of the third act is a single monologue by Prometheus, a poem frequently detached from the rest of the drama and printed separately. This poem Georg Brandes, the Danish critic, in his book on Goethe called unsurpassed as a revolutionary document. In Brandes' opinion the Prometheus monologue fuses into a single whole what Goethe had absorbed from Spinoza and from Lessing and his repudiation of all theological systems. God and the world are as soul is to body, man is the expression of natural force, and man creates the gods in his own image. In Goethe Prometheus calls to Zeus to cover his heaven with clouds, says that Zeus has nothing to do with earth, and declares that the gods live a really miserable existence subsisting as they do upon prayers and sacrifices. No god has aided him, Prometheus — why, then, should Prometheus honor any god? His indignation mounts:

> Ich dich ehren? Wofür?
> Hast du die Schmerzen gelindert
> Je des Beladenen?
> Hast du die Thränen gestillet
> Je des Geängsteten?
> Hat nicht mich zum Manne geschmiedet
> Die allmächtige Zeit
> Und das ewige Schicksal
> Meine Herrn und deine?
>
> Wähntest du etwa,
> Ich sollte das Leben hassen,
> In Wüsten fliehen,
> Weil nicht alle
> Blütenträume reiften?
>
> Hier sitz' ich, forme Menschen
> Nach meinem Bilde,
> Ein Geschlecht, das mir gleich sei,
> Zu leiden, zu weinen,
> Zu geniessen und zu freuen sich
> Und dein nicht zu achten,
> Wie ich! *

* I am to honor thee — why? Hast thou ever relieved the sorrow of the heavy laden? Hast thou ever dried the tears of those stricken by anguish? Was I not fashioned to be a man by Time the omnipotent and Fate the eternal, masters of thee and me? Didst ever suppose that I would learn to hate life and fly to waste-lands because not all my dream-flowers ripened? Here I sit forming mortals after

Goethe's poem appeared before the revolutions; Byron's was written when two revolutions had ended. Its fifty-nine lines fall into three sections. In the first Prometheus is addressed as an immortal Titan, who feels

> All that the proud can feel of pain,
> The agony they do not show,
> The suffocating sense of woe.

The second section, though syntactically somewhat confused, sympathizes with the sufferer because he must bear "the wretched gift Eternity," which he has done so well that

> All that the Thunderer wrung from thee
> Was but the Menace which flung back
> On him the torments of thy wrack;
> .   .   .   .   .   .
> And in thy Silence was his Sentence,
> And in his Soul a vain repentance.

The last section deserves to be quoted entire:

> Thy Godlike crime was to be kind
>   To render with thy precepts less
>   The sum of human wretchedness,
> And strengthen Man with his own mind;
> But baffled as thou wert from high,
> Still in thy patient energy,
> In the endurance, and repulse
>   Of thine impenetrable Spirit,
> Which Earth and Heaven could not convulse,
>   A mighty lesson we inherit:
> Thou art a symbol and a sign
>   To Mortals of their fate and force;
> Like thee, Man is in part divine,
>   A troubled stream from a pure source;
> And Man in portions can foresee
> His own funereal destiny;
> His wretchedness, and his resistance,
> And his sad unallied existence:
> To which his Spirit may oppose
> Itself — an equal to all woes —
>   And a firm will, and a deep sense,

---

my image, a race like me, to suffer, to weep, to enjoy, to be glad, and not to honor thee, as I do not!

The negation of Christianity could not be more sweeping.

> Which even in torture can descry
>   Its own concenter'd recompense,
> Triumphant where it dares defy,
>   And making Death a Victory.

To the romantics it is clear that Prometheus symbolized a will power that included a capacity for infinite endurance, a defiance of deity and therefore of "priestcraft," a mystical self-justification that might mount into sublime egotism, a hatred of tyranny, and a belief in the brotherhood of man and therefore in equality. But it is equally clear that the theoretical equality of man in this myth is contradicted in a sense by the superiority of the Titan. Man may be, indeed, half divine, and therefore also be half capable of shaping his future. But Prometheus is the incarnation of the aristocratic spirit, a being above those he protects, a leader and savior from outside. He has a foresight not found in the common herd.

No romantic in actuality approaches the quality of Prometheus, but it seems fair to suggest that Beethoven, Napoleon, and Byron exhibit something of Prometheus' gigantic defiance and also his sublime egotism. In the instance of Napoleon the imperial legend developed an image of the benefactor of mankind, a lonely eagle, imprisoned on St. Helena as Prometheus was chained to the mountaintop. But it should also be remembered that as First Consul Napoleon by creating the Napoleonic code and by extending many of the benefits of the French revolution to allied or subjugated peoples aided and comforted humanity. This was what Beethoven recognized in originally dedicating the *Eroica* to Bonaparte, and if, when Napoleon became emperor, Beethoven in a fury changed this to read: "To the memory of a great man," this, too, is within the Promethean story. It is scarcely necessary to point to the titanism in Beethoven's mature music, which not merely throws off the tyrannical conventions of musical tradition but also seeks to express the godlike ecstasy and anguish of life; for example, in the last piano sonata (op. 111) and the final string quartets. Indeed, the sequence Beethoven-Berlioz-Brahms expresses an ideal of titanism if ever music did.

vi

In *Prometheus Unbound* the triumph of the hero and the coming in of heaven on earth is signalized by the union of Prometheus with

Asia, the female symbol of regenerative and mystical love, so that after their union (they have been separated for endless ages), not only do the chains fall from humanity, but the earth, the moon, the stars, and the entire universe are regenerated. The important place given to women in revolutionary circles is thus signalized. Probably revolutionary salons such as that presided over by Madame Roland, who was guillotined, did not differ from those under the Bourbons; probably a revolutionary bluestocking like Mary Wollstonecraft did not differ from earlier bluestockings; probably an austere theory of the union of the sexes, such as that preached by William Godwin, who later married Mary Wollstonecraft, did not differ from the moral demands of marriage evident in *The Vicar of Wakefield*, just as there is no reason to suppose that the mistresses taken on by the leaders in the French revolution, the Directory, and the Consulate differ from mistresses taken on at the court of Louis XV or George III. But as the eighteenth century drew to its stormy close it produced a small library of books and pamphlets advocating something called the emancipation of women, and it produced a relatively new and revolutionary doctrine of sexual union.

Sexual ecstasy plays no role in Mary Wollstonecraft's *Vindication of the Rights of Woman* (1792), which is virtually a document in political revolution:

In short, in whatever light I view the subject, reason and experience convince me, that the only method of leading women to fulfil their peculiar duties, is to free them from all restraint by allowing them to participate [in] the inherent rights of mankind . . . Make them free, and they will quickly become wise and virtuous . . . make women rational creatures and free citizens and they will quickly become good wives, and mothers; that is, — if men do not neglect the duties of husbands and fathers.

Asserting the rights which women in common with men ought to contend for, I have not attempted to extenuate their faults; but to prove them to be the natural consequence of their education and station in society. If so, it is reasonable to suppose that they will change their character, and correct their vices and follies, when they are allowed to be free in a physical, moral, and civil sense.

This is purely eighteenth-century, if revolutionary, thinking, and has in common with romantic individualism only its emphasis upon "freedom." It might be noted in passing that Mary exercised her right to freedom by becoming the mistress of Gilbert Imlay, who deserted her. She gave birth to an illegitimate daughter, journeyed to the Scandinavias, became a friend of the radical-minded Helen Maria Williams,* tried to commit suicide, and finally married William Godwin in order to protect a coming child, the future Mary Shelley, though the couple maintained separate establishments. Mary Wollstonecraft is no romantic; she rather resembles Voltaire's *amie*, who knew so much about Newton and chemistry, but she does not represent the feminine mystique of the romantics. For that we must look elsewhere.

Friedrich Wilhelm von Schlegel (1772–1829), younger brother of August Wilhelm, was twenty-seven when *Lucinde* startled German readers. He had been a student at the "radical" University of Göttingen, he had traveled to Leipzig, Jena, Dresden, and Berlin, sowing wild oats as he went. In Berlin, he had joined his brother in publishing a short-lived but influential periodical, *Das Athenäum* (1798–1800), and he had fallen passionately in love with Dorothea Mendelssohn Veit, whom he persuaded to leave her husband to become his Egeria, his Phryne, his Eve. His own temperament alternated between laziness and feverish activity. He thirsted after a sense of personal fulfillment and hoped to reconcile his romantic yearning after the infinite with a revived Hellenism. To this end he had written various essays on Grecian themes, among them *Ueber die weiblichen Characteren in den griechischen Dichtern* and *Ueber die Diotima*, the last a meditation on the Mantinean seeress supposed to guide Socrates in the *Symposium* of Plato. According to Winckelmann the art and life of the Greeks were supposed to have expressed a noble simplicity. Schlegel was impressed by the fact that in Sparta nubile girls exercised naked in public, and he assumed that under the blue skies of Hellas sexual relations were open and candid as they were not in modern Europe. Indeed, a "Fragment" published in *Das Athenäum* said that prudishness will govern the female sex in

---

* Helen Maria Williams (1762–1827), a minor poet, dramatist, and writer of travels, would nowadays have in all probability been the foreign correspondent of some newspaper. She went to France in 1788, became a member of the Girondin circle, was arrested by Robespierre in 1793, and narrowly escaped the guillotine. Upon her release she apparently became the mistress of John Hurford Stone, who had deserted his wife, and there is some suspicion that she supplanted Mary Wollstonecraft in the affections of Gilbert Imlay. She should not be confused with Jane Williams, the friend of Shelley.

Europe so long as men were sentimental. What is demanded of the female is a free, beautiful, and unconditioned womanliness, and this *Lucinde* is supposed to further.

Like other books produced by the German romantics, *Lucinde* defies classification. It begins as an epistolary novel, a pretense but feebly sustained. Parts of it are written in the first person, part of it in the third. Some of it is in dialogue, some in rhapsodic prose, some of it is ironical. The work is divided haphazardly into sections, the sections having such odd titles as "Dithyrambic Fantasy over the Most Beautiful of Situations," "Metamorphosis," "An Idyll of Idleness," and "The Confessions of an Awkward Man." The last is a chronicle of the sexual education of Julius, the titular hero as Lucinde is the titular heroine. A baby suddenly appears about one-third of the way through the book, little Wilhelmina, who has a divine light on her small face and a habit of kicking off the covers and displaying her little legs and bottom, a natural act Lucinde is encouraged to imitate. Sexual intercourse is described in hyperbolical terms, and so is Lucinde's pregnancy. Everything is "intense," including Julius' fear for Lucinde's health. A major theme gradually develops: through the conjugation of the sexes Lucinde brings to herself and to Julius a sense of spiritual fulfillment. Sexual rapture blends with the ecstatic holiness of religion, and the glory of womanhood is that it is an instrument for establishing a mystical union of sense and soul. The morality of this view was defended by the theologian Schleiermacher, who declared that *Lucinde* was a new gospel, a bringing of humanity into the presence of the Eternal. Woman's individuality was to flower in an ecstatic union with the male.

Sex as sensual ecstasy does not govern *Corinne* (1807), a novel in which Madame de Staël compensated for the frustrations of her actual life by projecting an image of herself as a poetess of divine inspiration. She had preceded *Corinne* with an earlier novel, *Delphine* (1802), also autobiographical, and both a domestic melodrama and a condemnation of modern marriage. Delphine, a widow, is loved by Léonce, but Léonce is maneuvered into an engagement with Delphine's cousin, Mathilde, whom he weds largely because of the machinations of the worldly Madame de Vernon, a character based on Talleyrand. Although Delphine believes that marriage is valid only when it expresses an ideal morality, once Léonce is lost to her she takes the veil, and after Mathilde dies Delphine is too virtuous to unite herself with Léonce. The thesis of the book seems to be such an utterance as this by its heroine:

A proud and high-minded man should obey only the dictates of universal morality. Of what significance are duties which are merely the outcome of accidental circumstances and which depend upon the caprices of law or the will of a priest? duties that subject a man's conscience to the judgment of other men? . . . The Supreme Being knows our nature too well ever to accept irrevocable vows from us.

This looks like a statement of a philosophy of free love, and perhaps it is, but Delphine does not practice what she seems to preach.

Pitched on a loftier plane of idealism, *Corinne* is a tale of female genius, a guidebook to Italy, a document in nationalism, and a melodrama involving a cold-hearted stepmother, concealed identities, a wrong marriage, and a suffering heroine who dies of unrequited love. The book falls into two unequal parts. In the first and more important section Corinne (she has no last name), a mysterious female rhapsode or *improvisatrice*, is first seen as she is borne in a chariot drawn by four white horses to be crowned in the Roman capitol at a public ceremony witnessed by all the distinguished citizens of the city. Roman poets recite odes in her honor, a Roman prince delivers an oration on her genius, and after she has delivered a passionate extempore poem on the glories of Italy, she is crowned with a chaplet of bayleaf and laurel. She returns home amid the plaudits of the multitude. The ceremony is witnessed by Lord Oswald Nevil, a British nobleman (Madame de Staël is not quite clear whether he is Scottish or English), who, melancholy, solitary, and withdrawn, falls in love with her as she with him. Oswald's melancholy springs from his feeling that he has disobeyed his father, who has died.

Corinne serves as a guide to Oswald both in Rome and Italy. He discovers she speaks not only beautiful Italian but flawless English. How can this be? They exchange vows of love. But military duty requires Oswald to return to Great Britain, much to Corinne's agitation, without marrying her. Corinne is the daughter of a Lord Edgermond by an Italian wife, who has died. A thoroughly British and thoroughly disagreeable stepmother had driven Corinne out of England to Italy, where her genius flowered.

Oswald was supposed to have married into the Edgermond family. Time passes. In England Oswald gradually forgets Corinne and weds Lucille (or Lucy), her stepsister, in accordance, as he thinks, with his father's desires. He has a daughter. Corinne has secretly gone to England to remind Nevil of his promise to return to her, but she nobly conceals her presence in order not to disrupt the happiness of her stepsister and her beloved lover. Oswald, his wife, and his daughter visit Italy. Through a chance acquaintance between Corinne and Oswald's little girl, Oswald discovers all. Corinne, dying, says to Oswald: "I could exact nothing that could afflict you, only one tear and sometimes a fond look towards the heaven where I shall await you." Obviously the second part of the plot rises no higher than *Lady Audley's Secret*.

Corinne is important for its exaltation of female genius. If *Lucinde* raises the female ego to transcendent fulfillment, *Corinne* represents supernal feminine intuition. Indeed, the intrusion of Oswald into the life of the poet weakens Corinne's creative powers. Asked by Oswald where her inspiration truly lies, the poetess responds:

Sometimes . . . my impassioned excitement carries me beyond myself; teaches me to find in nature and my own heart such daring truths and forcible expressions as solitary meditation could never have engendered. My enthusiasm then seems supernatural: a spirit speaks within me far greater than my own; it often happens that I abandon the measure of verse to explain my thoughts in prose. . . . Sometimes my lyre, by a simple national air, may complete the effect which flies from the control of words. In truth, I feel myself a poet, less when a happy choice of rhymes, of syllables, of figures, may dazzle my auditors, than when my spirit soars disdainful of all selfish baseness; when godlike deeds appear easy to me, 'tis then my verse is at its best. I am . . . a poet while I admire or hate, not by my personal feelings nor in my own cause, but for the sake of human dignity and the glory of the world. . . . I cannot touch on any of the themes that affect me, without that kind of thrill which is the source of ideal beauty in the arts, of religion in the recluse, generosity in heroes and disinterestedness among men.

Corinne is a sort of political maenad, a figure like Rude's energetic "La Marseillaise" on the Arc de Triomphe or the goddess in Delacroix's painting of 1831, "Liberty Guiding the People."

Epipsychidion is more involved, a poem of 604 lines in rhymed couplets, on the meaning of which no two Shelley experts ever agree. The occasion of the piece was Shelley's rush of passionate interest in a handsome Italian girl living in a convent — a not unusual mode of life for young women in Italian society — until she should be married. Shelley was persuaded she had been immured by the jealousy of her stepmother. Nothing in Emilia's youth or her subsequent life shows her to have possessed genius. But Shelley translated her into a female embodiment of the Ideal, an emblem or figure of permanence in a world of misunderstanding and change. After the first twenty lines, his poem soars into the empyrean, where Emilia becomes not his mistress but an embodiment of that intellectual beauty to which Shelley had addressed an earlier poem. This flight occupies him for about two hundred lines. Then we have a complex section of poetical autobiography, confused in syntax and involving a series of astronomical images — the sun, the moon, and a comet — which seem darkly to hint at the poet's dissatisfaction with a number of women in his life, including Mary Shelley. In the last third of the poem (ll. 388–604) the bard invites the now transfigured Emilia to voyage with him to an island paradise in the Aegean where

> we will talk, until thought's melody
> Become too sweet for utterance,

and

> Our breath shall intermix, our bosoms bound
> And our veins beat together; and our lips
> With other eloquence than words, eclipse
> The soul that burns between them, and the wells
> Which boil under our being's inmost cells,
> The fountains of our deepest life, shall be
> Confused in Passion's golden purity,
> As mountain-springs under the morning sun.
> We shall become the same, we shall be one
> Spirit within two frames.

The poet exclaims: "Oh, wherefore two!" We are assured by experts that what is wanted is not bodily union but a transcendental fusion of souls. If one puts carnal considerations aside, one may fairly gloss *Epipsychidion* as a seraphic interpretation of the nature of womanhood, paralleled in other romantic effusions, such as de Vigny's Eloa, the Cynthia of Keats's *Endymion*, the Peri of Thomas Moore's "Paradise and the Peri" in *Lallah Rookh*, and in some sense the Undine of de la Motte Fouqué. In any case one thinks of the concluding lines of *Faust*: "Das Ewig-Weibliche / Zieht uns hinan" (the eternal-womanly leads us on).

The exaltation of feminine spirituality reached even higher levels. German and English romantics took to celebrating the earthly woes and heavenly triumphs of various female saints: Schiller's *Die Jungfrau von Orleans*, Southey's *Joan of Arc*, and Tieck's *Leben und Tod der heiligen Genoveva*. Doubtless angels have no sex, though the archangels are commonly represented as masculine. But the romantics began and the nineteenth century continued the doctrine that one's guardian angel is feminine. Possibly, the romantics simply reinforced a tradition they learned from their interest in the graphic arts.

The discrepancy between the character of many leaders of the American revolution and many leaders of the French revolution is obviously not a problem of literary "influences" but a problem of that indefinite yet powerful force one calls the *Zeitgeist* or the spirit of the age. True it is that many French revolutionaries read Rousseau's *Emile* and *La Nouvelle Héloïse* and that, once the revolution was well along, they found it politically profitable to quote from *Du Contrat social*. It is also true that Madame de Staël fancied herself as an intellectual sybil comparable at least to the more political Madame Roland. If one is looking for a direct connection between revolutionary minds and literature, one had better look, however, at Montesquieu's *L'Esprit des lois*, Raynal's *Histoire des Indes*, and such a book as the Abbé de Mably's *Entretiens de Phocion, sur le rapport de la morale avec les politiques* (1763). Nevertheless, there is such a thing as general change of opinion, and young men and women coming to maturity in society or in certain segments of society in 1789 looked on the world from premises subtly different from those of their elders. Outwardly, perhaps, the family formula had not greatly altered, and the author-of-my-being attitude which wrecked the life of Clarissa Harlowe had not everywhere disappeared. It dominates many middle-class plays and novels from 1775 to 1832. For example, it seems perfectly right to Francis Osbaldistone, the titular hero of Scott's *Rob Roy* in 1818, for his father, a merchant, to cast him out because he writes poetry and perfectly right for his father to take him back again when Francis recovers some missing papers and so restores the commercial standing of the firm. *Rob Roy* is a historical novel, but Walter Scott assumed as a matter of course that his readers would understand and accept this paternal authority.

Nevertheless, the younger generation was conscious of being "different." Their relations with God, with their families, with their peers and their elders, and with the state were changed from what had been true of 1750. They felt not so much that the world owed them a living, as that the state owed them opportunity for a full and variegated life. They were not prepared to cry with Housman's young man:

> I, a stranger and afraid
> In a world I never made,

because they were not afraid and because too many writers had told them that the world could be refashioned. They refused to be retainers, apprentices, catechumens, novices, merely obedient children. Lafayette, when he set off for America, having decided to defy his family, was only twenty years old. At the outbreak of the French revolution Danton was thirty, Saint-Just twenty-two, Barère was thirty-four, Georges Couthon thirty-three, Robespierre thirty-one, Charlotte Corday twenty-one, Madame Roland thirty-five, Talleyrand thirty-five, Napoleon nineteen, Burns, who had small patience for family obligations, whatever the domesticity of "The Cotter's Saturday Night," was thirty, Blake, now in literary opinion the most radical of English poets but ignored in his lifetime, was thirty-two, Coleridge seventeen, Southey fifteen, and William Hazlitt, a steadfast liberal throughout his life, only eleven. A famous painting by the revolutionary David depicts Brutus receiving the bodies of his dead sons in whose execution he had acquiesced. It won great acclaim. But the younger generation at eighteen, nineteen, twenty, or twenty-one in 1789 was less likely to agree to having their lives snuffed out by father than to accept the imprisonment or death of suspected relatives who wanted to return to the good old ways of the monarchy. Every tub, they seemed to think, should stand on its own bottom except as its stability might be affected by emanations from another — shall we say female? — tub. The inconsistent actions of the Assembly, too often terrified as one faction or another seized control, seemed to be actuated mainly by a *sauve-qui-peut* doctrine as the monarchy yielded to the republic, the republic to the Committee of Public Safety, the committee to the Thermidoreans and the Directory, and the Directory to the Consulate. This was less out of devotion to church, state, family, or abstract principle than out of devotion to oneself, which may have been cowardice but which also valued self above society. I do not mean to imply that individualism is the "key" to some of the uglier aspects of the French revolution.

But the last quarter of the eighteenth century, as traditional forms of state, church, and society weakened or vanished, and as more and more voices were raised to say that a new and better sort of social existence was possible to men, inevitably raised the question: who are the individuals that are to benefit from change? The human being became at once more lonely and more independent, more unpredictable and more filled with emotion, more likely to look for the satisfactions of life here and now and less likely to be put off either by promises or by assurances that class and status were more blessed than self-fulfillment. It is, I think, not without meaning that Rousseau's "I am not made like any of those I have seen" was followed by Napoleon's "Every French soldier carries a marshal's baton in his knapsack." The individual might be damned but he was to be damned on his own terms, just as, if he succeeded, his success was due to himself alone. And in the world of women were there not Angelica Kauffmann and Madame Vigée-Lebrun, Mrs. Radcliffe, Madame de Genlis, and Jane Austen, Dorothea Mendelssohn Veit Schlegel, Madame de Krüdener, and Elizabeth Fry? Progress meant that the individual was no longer merely an integer but a total human being.

IX

The Doctrine of Romantic Genius

It requires no great knowledge of either the American or the French revolution to know that the French revolution was characterized by excesses far beyond anything the Americans dreamed of. I have suggested in the preceding chapter that the difference between two kinds of eighteenth-century personalities, developing as that century drew to its close, springs from a new sense of the meaning of individualism. But a mere belief in individualism is insufficient to "explain" the charismatic qualities of many leaders of the French revolution, which, though it began only fourteen years after its American progenitor, seems to belong to a different era. There were, it is frequently said, no parties in the various revolutionary assemblies but only followers of this man or that, or at the best factions — the friends of Brissot, the friends of Danton, the friends of Robespierre, and so on. The surviving members of such a faction, when one leader had vanished (commonly by execution), often found little difficulty in transferring their allegiance to some other dominant personality; and the dominance of personalities rather than the dominance of programs strikes us in reading accounts of the revolt in France. Even when a faction rallied around an idea, the idea was sometimes incarnated in a man. Personality is therefore a more powerful force in the French revolution than was true in the American one, a fact which suggests that if all the leaders of factions in the French revolution were not geniuses, they regarded themselves as geniuses ("leaders") in theory. They expressed themselves, if they were in power or aspiring to arrive at power, in an excess of words and an excess of deeds, springing from an inward assurance of their own right-eousness and of the wrongheadedness of their opponents.

I have remarked that leaders in the American revolution remain within the moral patterns of the eighteenth century and submit as a matter of course to the sanction of "Nothing in excess." Loyalists were mistreated, but they were not systematically put to death because they were Loyalists. Indians were a nuisance, but no American leader urged a solution of the Indian problem by genocide. New World suspects were not drowned as suspects were drowned in the *noyades* (also known as republican marriages) at Nantes in 1793–1794. Except by accident, church property was not destroyed or confiscated wholesale; and in America only a few towns and villages were deliberately destroyed. Nobody threatened to wipe a city off the map as French revolutionary leaders proposed to wipe Lyons or Marseilles off the map. In truth a cynic might re-mark that the American revolution, in comparison with the French revolution, was rather an amateur affair.

The cynic would be wrong. Yet even Tom Paine, among the more violent revolutionary propagandists in America, would scarcely have demanded a wholesale execution of "Tories," as Pierre Gaspard Chaumette demanded wholesale executions when he spoke before the National Convention in September 1793:

We must destroy our enemies or they will destroy us! No quarter, no mercy to traitors! Throw between them and us the barrier of eternity! . . . we were instructed to ask from you the formation of the revolutionary army which you have already decreed. . . . Let this army be formed immediately. . . . Let it be followed by a terrible and incorruptible tribunal and by the fatal instrument which cuts off at one blow both the plots and the days of their authors.*

This is the utterance of a man (and there were others like him) convinced that he is supremely right and his opponents are su-premely evil. A minor figure in the annals of the revolution, Chau-mette is for that reason the more representative. He is a revolution-ary egotist, one who displays or demands a kind of action or speech that passes beyond the confines of convention. Such men may not

---

* This excerpt and others like it may be found in Wilfred B. Kerr, *The Reign of Terror, 1793-94*, Toronto, 1923. See especially his chapter on "The Sansculotte Committee."

be geniuses, but at least they regard themselves as unique, and they form their life styles on those of other men who are by general consent geniuses, diabolical or messianic as one prefers. It may be illuminating therefore, having in mind not only leaders in the French revolution but also other extraordinary personalities who march across the stage of the world in these decades, to say something about the development of a concept of genius that flowered in the later decades of the century. Genius or its simulacrum then carried with it an imperative of activity over and beyond what was expected of any normal theory of individualism.

Discussions of genius commonly begin with Socrates and his *daimon* or tutelary spirit, the latter an overpowering concept in the era of romanticism, the era of the French revolution and the era of Napoleon. In classical Greece it appears that there had been a doctrine of good demons and bad demons, a notion that attracted an increasing number of adherents while Greece was being infiltrated by cult religions from the East. When Christianity triumphed, it was natural that all demons should become agents of that old deluder, Satan; yet the original division between affirmation and denial survived in the Christian concepts of good angel and evil angel, good genius and wicked genius. In the earlier ages of Attica a *daimon* might be the soul of somebody who had lived in the Golden Age (Hesiod) or a guardian spirit who accompanies a human being through life (Plato). Socrates, however, particularizes. He had a *daimon* who, he said, guided him at critical moments. Thus in the *Apology* Socrates is made to speak of an oracle, or sign, which has come to him at intervals since childhood, and "the sign is a voice which comes to me and always forbids me to do something which I am going to do, but never commands me to do anything, and this is what stands in the way of my being a politician." Later in the same dialogue he is represented as saying:

O my judges . . . I should like to tell you of a wonderful circumstance. Hitherto the familiar oracle within me has constantly been in the habit of opposing me even about trifles, if I was going to make a slip or error about anything; and now as you see there has come upon me that which may be thought, and is generally believed to be, the last and worst evil [i.e., a sentence of death]. But the oracle made no sign of opposition. . . . What do I take to be the explanation of this? I will tell you. I regard this as a proof that what has happened to me is good. . . . This is a great proof to me of what I am saying, for the customary sign would surely have opposed me had I been going to evil and not to good.

In Plato's dialogue on the death of Socrates, the *Phaedo*, one finds Socrates telling his followers:

. . . the soul when on her progress to the world below takes nothing with her but nurture and education; which are indeed said greatly to benefit or greatly to injure the departed, at the very beginning of his pilgrimage to the other world.

For after death . . . the genius of each individual, to whom he belonged in life, leads him to a certain place in which the dead are gathered together for judgment, whence they go into the world below, following the guide, who is appointed to conduct them from this world to the other; and when they have there received their due and remained their time, another guide brings them back again after many revolutions of ages. . . . The wise and orderly soul is conscious of her situation, and follows in the [right] path, but the soul which desires the body . . . is after many struggles and many sufferings hardly and with violence carried away by her attendant genius . . . [whereas] every pure and just soul which has passed through life in the company and under the guidance of the gods has also her own proper home.*

These passages are complicated by various extraneous doctrines (for example, that of the transmigration of souls), but the *daimon* or tutelary genius, mainly represented as negative ("the habit of opposing me"), is a supernal guide telling Socrates what is right and contradicting his own purposes on certain occasions.

Although demons became devils in the Christian system, a guardian angel was still a good spirit. Sometimes its divine promptings were internalized, as in the Gospel of St. John or the stirrings of the spirit among Quakers, and sometimes they were externalized, as in paintings or plays: for example, Marlowe's *Dr. Faustus*. The Renaissance could not deny genius to the ancients and therefore returned to a variant of the Socratic *daimon*, allowing the tutelary genius to be more than a negative spirit, and assuming that the tutelary genius of one great figure might be superior to the tute-

* I quote Jowett's translation: from the *Apology*, sections 31D and 40A, and from the *Phaedo*, 107d in part. The confusion between *daimon* as a supernal being external to the individual and an internalized spirit gave romanticism its opportunity to set up a theory of genius. See the fine essay on demons and demonology in the Hastings *Encyclopedia of Religions and Ethics*, IV (1912), and for Greek uses of *daimon* the appropriate entry in the Pauly-Wissowa *Real-Encyclopädie der klassischen Altertumswissenschaft*, new ed., VIII (Stuttgart, 1901). There are later and more speculative studies.

lary genius of another. Thus, following Plutarch, Macbeth is made to say:

> under him
> My genius is rebuked, as it is said
> Mark Antony's was by Caesar,

an observation echoed in *Antony and Cleopatra* (again following Plutarch), when a soothsayer warns Antony not to contend with Octavius. Meanwhile immortality, another supernal notion, became attached to works of art and to records of heroic enterprise, the eccentricities of the goddess Fame now being contradicted by a sure and certain belief that great deeds and great actions, prompted by genius, must per se be immortal. The immortality due the artist is evident in two familiar passages in Shakespeare's *Sonnets*. The eighteenth begins, "Shall I compare thee to a summer's day?" and concludes:

> But thy eternal summer shall not fade
> Nor lose possession of that fair thou ow'st,
> Nor shall death brag thou wand'rest in his shade,
> When in eternal lines to time thou grow'st;
> So long as men can breathe, or eyes can see,
> So long lives this [the work of the poet], and this gives life to thee.

The nineteenth ("Devouring Time, blunt thou the lion's paws") also has transience as its theme, but assures the reader of the immortality of genius in art:

> Yet do thy worst, old Time; despite thy wrong,
> My love shall in my verse ever live young.

It should be remembered that in the so-called Dark Ages, in the Middle Ages, in the Renaissance, and even later, Christian theology allowed both secular geniuses and saints to be possessed by the Holy Spirit, the third member of the Trinity.*

In post-Renaissance Europe, though the doctrine of Christian in-

---

* Concerning both Christian doctrine and the long space of time between the Christianization of western Europe and the generation of Boileau, see the illuminating article by Courtland D. Baker, "Certain Religious Elements in the English Doctrine of the Inspired Poet during the Renaissance," *ELH*, 6 (1939), 300–323. The climax of this doctrine, at least in English poetry, is the invocation to the "Spirit" (apparently the Holy Spirit or in Protestant terminology the Holy Ghost) in Book I of *Paradise Lost*, ll. 17–26: "And chiefly Thou, O Spirit, that dost prefer / Before all Temples th' upright heart and pure, . . ."

spiration and Christian guidance by no means disappeared, the general theory of genius faced two difficulties. Almost all theorizing about genius had hitherto concerned nonscientific persons ranging from statesmen to saints. But a new philosophy put a good many things in doubt, and in the seventeenth century the influence of Bacon, the influence of Descartes, and the sudden efflorescence and modernization of science involved an awkward question about theorizers, notably Christian theorizers: the inspiration of an ancient Hebrew prophet or a medieval church father was no doubt divine, but was it divine in any geometrical, any "scientific" sense? Did the possession of genius in an exact science imply the same qualities as were evident in nonmensurative fields? The problem was not solved, it was merely postponed, a postponement possible because "science" was natural philosophy, a natural philosopher was still a philosopher, and philosophers remained within the acceptable doctrine. It was thus quite proper for Pope to write as an epitaph for Newton:

> Nature and Nature's laws lay hid in night:
> God said, *Let Newton be!* and all was light.

Such an asseveration of a new day of creation was an assertion of the theory of the divinity in, or of, genius.

Though it was perhaps possible to distinguish genius from madness, how was one — and this was the second problem — to distinguish genius from enthusiasm? In the seventeenth century and for a good many years thereafter, an enthusiast was a person suffering from pseudo-inspiration; that is, from emotional extravagance. He claimed to be filled with the god (*in* plus *theos*), whereas in fact he was really full of self-conceit, notably in matters of religion and philosophy. He lacked judgment. He might turn into an Adamite and strip off all his clothing in a fit of religious zeal, or he might become a Quaker and interrupt the decorum of a court of law with his irresponsible shoutings. If God be Supreme Reason, if the universe is rationally constructed by a Supreme Engineer, enthusiasm, whatever its origin, was simply out of line. So my Lord Shaftesbury argued in *A Letter Concerning Enthusiasm* (1708):

For Inspiration is *a real* feeling of the Divine Presence, and Enthusiasm *a false one*. But the passion they raise is much alike . . . Something there will be of Extravagance and Fury, when the Ideas or Images received are too big for the narrow human Vessel to contain. So that *Inspiration* may be justly called *Divine* ENTHUSIASM . . . This was the Spirit [Plato] allotted to *Heroes, Statesmen, Poets, Orators, Musicians* and even *Philosophers* themselves. Nor can we, of our own accord, forbear ascribing to a noble ENTHUSIASM whatever is greatly performed by any of *These.*

But what about "false" enthusiasm?

. . . to judg the Spirits whether they are of God, we must antecedently *judg our own Spirit*; whether it be of *Reason* and *sound Sense*; whether it be fit to *judg* at all, by being sedate, cool, and impartial; free of every byassing Passion, every giddy Vapor, or melancholy Fume. . . . By this means we may prepare ourselves with some *Antidote* against Enthusiasm. And this is what I have dar'd affirm is best perform'd by keeping in GOOD-HUMOUR.

Good humor is doubtless an excellent thing, but since one man's reason is another man's "byassing passion," the noble lord's argument left the situation precisely where it had been. Poets might address a fictitious muse, but was a fictitious muse the same thing as the Socratic *daimon?* And on Shaftesbury's rather dim distinction, were "reason and sound sense," was "being sedate, cool and impartial" a true criterion? Perhaps genius, true or false, enthusiastic or merely ebullient, could best be contained, notably in the arts, if it were channeled into that general experience of expression commonly known as "the rules."

Alexander Pope spoke for a whole culture, English and Continental, when in the *Essay on Criticism*, though he admitted the ancients had been born in happier days, that the meanest among them possessed some spark of celestial fire, and that even now the poet might be expected to snatch a grace beyond the reach of art, he stated:

> Nature to all things fixed the limits fit,
> And wisely curbed proud man's pretending wit.

He added:

> One science only will one genius fit;
> So vast is art, so narrow human wit;

and, a more familiar passage, already cited:

> First follow Nature, and your judgment frame
> By her just standard, which is still the same:

Unerring NATURE, still divinely bright,
One clear, unchanged, and universal light,
Life, force, and beauty, must to all impart,
At once the source, and end, and test of Art.

The artist might occasionally seek "nameless graces which no methods teach," but "let it be seldom, and compelled by need." In fact, to snatch a grace beyond the reach of art plainly implies that you had studied the art beyond which the grace was to be found. In sum, Socrates' *daimon*, if he was active at all, had better be restrained. In one sense the romantic doctrine of genius can be briefly asserted to be the exact opposite of all that Pope implied or said, but that would be to oversimplify. In fact, a new concept of genius involving the discovery or rediscovery of the *daimon* slowly shaped itself in the mid-eighteenth century amidst a vast confusion about taste, art, the classical world, the Gothic revival, uneducated poets, and the springs of national culture.* It was eventually translated to the political sphere.

ii

From the varied library of theories about taste, genius, aesthetic discrimination, psychology, the battle of the ancients and the moderns, and originality in art, produced in the Enlightenment, one may select a few English and German examples to illumine the rise of the romantic concept of genius. The most famous of these treatises is that of the Rev. Edward Young, whose *Conjectures on Original Composition* (1759), a prosy essay, won an international acclaim the modern student finds difficult to understand. Composition, the author says, is an elegant amusement for gentlemen, but it is also a consolation for the endless evils of life. Genius he compares to a fertile and pleasant field blessed with perpetual

---

* Although many romanticists turned the *daimon* into the demoniac, it is not argued that the Platonic doctrine of inspiration was superseded in the period under survey. Thus André Chénier (1762–1794), guillotined three days before the death of Robespierre, wrote in "L'Invention":

Celui qu'un vrai démon presse, enflamme, domine,
Ignore un tel supplice: il pense, il imagine;
Un langage imprévu, dans son âme produit,
Naît avec sa pensée, et l'embrasse et la suit.

As, however, some of Chénier's poetry had to be smuggled out of jail (he was imprisoned for 141 days), the first collection of his work (and that imperfect) did not appear until 1819.

spring. Genius produces both originals and imitations, but the originals are necessarily better than the imitations because imitation simply builds on the originality of somebody else. (The contemporary reader must remember that an "imitation" was a standard literary genre in the eighteenth century, one in which a living author, taking some classical work as his model, wrote a new work in the style and form of the original as if the classic poet were alive at this later date.) But if we are to be original, argues Young, let us compose in the spirit of the ancients and let us use our own materials and not theirs. The ancients are useful only as a sort of noble contagion. Winckelmann is obviously just around the corner.

But what is genius? Genius is not the immediate topic of the essay, and Young is more rhetorical than penetrating in discussing this idea. Genius is the power of accomplishing great things without the means generally reputed to be necessary for a given end. Genius resembles virtue (*virtus*); learning is like riches merely. Geniuses, says Young, are of two sorts, "infantine" and adult, and he illustrates these categories by citing, for the one, Swift, for the other, Shakespeare. The difference seems to be that the adult genius comes fresh from the hands of nature, whereas the "infantine" genius must learn its art and consciously develop its potential. Modernity, however, is not per se inferior to the ancient world; if it falls short, it is because modernity is satisfied to imitate the ancients when it ought rather to rival them. But where is genius to be found?

Dive deep into thy bosom; learn the depth, extent, bias, and full fort [*sic*] of thy mind; contract full intimacy with the stranger within thee; excite and cherish every spark of intellectual light and heat, however smothered under former negligence, or scattered through the dull, dark mass of common thoughts; and, collecting them into a body, let thy genius rise . . . as the sun from chaos . . . Let not great examples or authorities browbeat thy reason into too great a diffidence of thyself: thyself so reverence as to prefer the native growth of thy own mind to the richest import from abroad . . . The man who thus reverences himself will soon find the world's reverence to follow his own. His works will stand distinguished; his the sole property of them.

Young argues that Christianity helps this process of self-discovery and self-evaluation, and he says that the inspired enthusiast is to the well-accomplished scholar as the rising sun is to the morning star. He goes on to assay the relative merits of a line of geniuses, ancient and modern, but the essay breaks off rather than concludes. His theory is virtually solipsistic.

The modern inquirer is likely to wonder why a piece thus flat in style and confused in analysis was influential. Does Young do more than elaborate Sir Philip Sidney's line, "Fool, said my Muse to me, look in thy heart, and write"? One has therefore to explain the wide vogue of the *Conjectures*, the many translations, and the innumerable references to it by a rising generation of Europeans. The explanation seems to be twofold. In the first place Young's style translates easily, as a more idiosyncratic style does not. In the second place Young sets forth with all the vigor of repetition a doctrine the young generation longed for — one, moreover, originating in an admired literature and authenticated by a poet who was an Englishman, a Christian, and a clergyman. The doctrine was simple and clear. Unerring nature, as in Pope, was still divinely bright, but to interpret nature philosophically or aesthetically it was no longer necessary to study Homer — in other words, to continue the long and increasingly arid patterns of neoclassicism.

"Know thyself" was an axiom as old as the Delphic oracle, but it was now restated with Christian implications. The self was no longer a mere congeries of psychological atoms drawn together as a magnet attracts filings, it was something creative, primal, even godlike, something buried beneath the dull, dark mass of common thoughts, a self set apart from other men, wholly individual, wholly unique, a sun rising out of chaos, a native growth preferable to psychological borrowings from, or imitations of, others. In short, here was in the Christian soul a foretaste of the doctrine of original genius. Here was romantic individualism, though not known by that phrase, raised to an alluring, if indefinite, higher power. Moreover, the *Conjectures* contained a good many sentences that, detached from context, seemed to express oracular wisdom.

Young was not an acute reasoner, and his awkward distinction between infantine genius and genius proper was unsatisfactory. He failed to clarify a more important distinction — that between something innate and something consciously trained. Other writers took up the question, among them William Sharpe, who published *A Dissertation upon Genius* in 1755, now a relatively rare book, and William Duff, whose *An Essay on Original Genius* in

1767 propounded the theory that the two essential elements of genius were imagination and taste. The clearest writer after Young was probably Professor Alexander Gerard of King's College, Aberdeen, who, before the small, high-minded Philosophical Society of Aberdeen, had talked about genius or aspects of genius many times and had conducted discussions from which he later profited. As early as 1759, the year of the *Conjectures*, Gerard brought out *An Essay on Taste*, which ran through three editions and was translated into French and German, the Germans calling it admirable, "ein vortreffliches Buch." His claim to remembrance, however, mainly rests on his *Essay on Genius* (1774), the product of twenty years of study and reflection. Immanuel Kant admired it for its orderly presentation, evident in its division into three parts: (i) the nature of genius; (ii) the general sources of the varieties of genius; and (iii) the kinds of genius. Possibly Gerard appealed less to the romantics than did Young, since he argued that genius in the sciences appeals to the understanding and is therefore superior to other kinds of genius, whereas genius in the arts cannot exist where "the passions have not great power over the imagination in affecting the train and association of perception." *
Yet was it not the passions, precisely, that most interested the romantics? If, however, one again resorts to pointing out that science was then natural philosophy, that natural philosophy was still philosophy, and that philosophers, many theologians, and all sorts of geniuses in the arts and literature could when necessary be categorized, if they were superior, as geniuses in general, the difficulty disappears.

It is perhaps less important to worry about the differences between scientific genius and geniuses of other sorts than it is to note that Gerard, like Young, thinks that genius is vegetative, not mechanical, something that blossoms from a vital root like a plant, not something like a Newtonian machine. Genius is a power innate or "given," inexplicable but not therefore incomprehensible. To Gerard the human mind possesses four principal divisions: the sense, memory, imagination, and judgment, categories that also

---

* My attention was first called to Gerard when I read the admirable edition got out by Bernhard Fabian for a German series, *Theorie und Geschichte der Literatur und der schönen Kunst*, in which the book is vol. III (Munich, 1966). Fabian says about all that needs to be said concerning Gerard and his place in thought; I have therefore followed his excellent analysis.

seemed important to Diderot. For Gerard genius originates in the imagination, but imagination alone will not do, for genius must be guided by judgment to produce "that regularity of imagination, that capacity of avoiding foreign, useless, and superfluous connections, at the same time that none necessary or proper are passed by, which is always most perfect in the greatest geniuses." Shakespeare's judgment, for example, was not sufficiently "improved" to avoid improper subjects, improbable incidents, and quibbling expressions, yet in depicting character and the "passions" Shakespeare is supreme. Genius, or "comprehensiveness of imagination," for Gerard involved a special associational psychology:

When the associating principles are vigorous, imagination, conscious as it were of its own strength, sallies forth, without needing support or asking assistance, into regions hitherto unexplored, and penetrates into their remotest corners, unfatigued with the length of the way.

An extensive imagination, impressed with a strong association of the design, and regulated by it, will draw out from the whole compass of nature, the suitable ideas, without attending to any others.

When an ingenious track of thinking presents itself, though but casually, to true genius, occupied it may be with something else, imagination darts along it with great rapidity; and by the rapidity its ardor is more inflamed. The velocity of its motion sets it on fire, like a chariot wheel which is kindled by the quickness of its revolution.

Whatever the origins or difficulties of Gerard's ideas, a writer who likened genius to a plant was not quite of the school of Boileau or Pope, since he said that if a man shows invention, no intellectual defects in his performance can deny him genius. Such a man's "invention" may be wild and undisciplined, but he is nonetheless a natural genius. Hence it was not difficult to reconcile this analysis of genius with the idea of being possessed by one's *daimon*. This fusion was made, though it was not exclusively made, by German theorists.*

* A characteristic effort in the direction of such a fusion is that odd pre-Byronic poem by the Scottish writer James Beattie, *The Minstrel; or, The Progress of Genius*, revised in 1774. Beattie chose the Spenserian stanza because of its "Gothic" structure, and the preface says that his theme is "to trace the progress of a Poetical Genius, born in a rude age, from the first dawning of fancy and reason [note the distinction], till that period at which he may be supposed capable of appearing in the world as a minstrel . . . a character . . . not only respectable, but sacred." The poem is filled with the self-pity characteristic of many romantics. The lad who is the "hero" prefers as a boy to steal from village sports to listen

To Stendhal romanticism was the art of presenting the people with literary works that, in the actual state of popular habits and beliefs, would give them the greatest possible pleasure, whereas classicism, on the contrary, produced literature that gave the greatest possible pleasure to their great-grandfathers. This amusing statement may be wrongheaded, but it indicates why, notably in Germany, a fresh concept of genius had to be set forth if a true national literature was to be reborn. The German situation was complicated. The Seven Years War was to the renewal of German culture what the Persian wars had been to the efflorescence of culture in ancient Greece, but unlike the predecessors of Pericles, the Germans had to throw off two confining prepossessions. One of these was the authority of French neoclassicism in all the German courts and universities, and the other, notably in the Protestant states, was the equally powerful authority of religious orthodoxy. Frederick the Great was heroic, but his tastes were French; and though Lutheranism had sought to free the mind from the shackles of a foreign church, it now failed to free thought from theological control, so that there were a number of unhappy instances of freethinkers in eighteenth-century Protestant Germany dismissed from their posts because they had heretical views about God. As the Germans lived in the most apolitical culture in central Europe, the road of escape into a less narrow system of values had to be discovered not by party strife as in England, nor by an amalgam of rationalistic inquiry, anticlericalism, and speculation about forms of government as in France, but by looking within; that is, by exploring the "German soul." To such an inquiry, vague but essential, a new doctrine of individualism, notably of individualism raised to the heightened power which is genius, became basic.

Several theories were advanced. One, for example, led to the remarkable balance of intellectual energy, emotional power, and public responsibility which produced the best poems and dramas of Schiller and the total personality of Goethe. Another, far more wild and wayward, expressed itself in the ill-considered literature

---

to the voices of nature. On one such occasion he overhears a hermit pessimistically soliloquizing on the miseries of life. The lad seeks out the hermit, who gives him a great deal of advice about urban evil, philosophic history, the pleasure that is in the lonely hills, and the necessity of celebrating some patriotic prince. The reader never learns, however, what act, thought, or sequence of events matures the youthful bard.

of the Sturm-und-Drang writers and, after that, in the subjective writings, too often fragmentary, of German romanticism.

Up to the middle of the eighteenth century the German notion of genius had been bound by the "rules" and by ideas imported from England and France. Thus for Moses Mendelssohn genius represented the essential obligation of an artist to reduce multiplicity to unity and so reveal the central harmony that is the universe. Religious orthodoxy restrained speculations that might disturb or deny such a doctrine. Even Lessing never quite got over being "rational"; even Klopstock, by many considered the leading preromantic in German literature, felt that genius must submit to two limitations: that imposed by God and that imposed by nature. To compare genius to God in the matter of creativity might be blasphemous; to copy nature and idealize it was a fine accomplishment, but it expressed nothing "original" — that is, genius did not, as in the instance of Novalis, create a new universe of its own.

Romantic genius seems to spring from the doctrine that one best expresses one's self and best serves the group to which one belongs by realizing one's self completely. Realizing one's self completely is, obviously, an open invitation to any sort of whim (Emerson was to hope it would not be whim at last). To avoid solipsism one method was to find another soul or other souls full of sensibility, in whom one might confide; hence the intense friendships among romantics and revolutionaries, notably among German romantics, and hence also the intensity of erotic experience as an enlargement of the self and as a guard against too much subjectivity. The parallel with Rousseau is obvious. But subjectivity was basic to the German concept of romantic genius, and this subjective self-realization, enriched by a mistress, a friend, or external nature, had little or nothing to do with church or state, the public, or the common reader. If the common reader could not comprehend the outpouring of romantic genius, so much the worse for the reader, who was probably a philistine. On the other hand the fusion of genius, freedom, and civic responsibility in Schiller and Goethe was made possible by, among other causes, an emotional return upon Italy and ancient Greece. An emotional Hellenism proved decisive, and in the case of the two great German dioscuri it led them to repudiate romanticism and to discover a sense for the state not found in, say, Tieck or Wackenroder. It must be remembered that among the Germans generally the primary duty of the good citizen was obedience to the prince and to the pastor.

The first of the two leading theorists of a fresh doctrine of genius was that strange person, Johann Georg Hamann (1730–1788), who spent most of his life (except for two mysterious years in London) in the northern parts of Germany, and who came to be known as the Magus of the North. He had read everything, he disputed everything, he wrote a large amount of dithyrambic prose, he was a devout Christian of the Pietist sort, and he was a spiritual ancestor of Kierkegaard and Sartre. He was also a child of the Enlightenment and simultaneously one of its principal foes. His life was as complicated as his style. He read (and repudiated), for example, all the fifty-four volumes of a set of Voltaire, he turned German commercial documents into French for the benefit of the tax-collectors of Frederick the Great, he fell in love with a woman he called his hamadryad, whom he refused to marry on the ground that to do so would decrease her happiness and that of any possible children. He is remembered, among more important things, for a sentence that lies at the root of the whole romantic movement: "System is itself a hindrance to truth." His own prose has sometimes a piercing and epigrammatic force, and at other times is so encrusted with allusions that it is like a ship covered with barnacles. His pioneering work on genius is dedicated to "Nobody and to Two," the "Two" being a veiled allusion to his friend Behrens and to Immanuel Kant, whose philosophy he came to hold in contempt. No Talmudic scholar could twist the Bible into more contorted examples of wire-drawn typology.

Hamann's central document on genius was printed in 1759, the year of Young's *Conjectures*, and has a characteristically ironic title, "Socratic Memorabilia Put Together for the Boredom of the Public by an Amateur of Boredom." This curious little book bears a Latin motto from that most baroque of Latin poets, Persius, which ironically inquires: Who will read this stuff? Nobody, or at least only one or two. The *Sokratische Denkwuerdigkeiten* has a sequel assailing its critics, *Wolken: Ein Nachspiel sokratischer Denkwuerdigkeiten*, and the doctrine is enriched by another

rhapsodic afterpiece with the Latin title *Aesthetica in Nuce* —
aesthetics in a nutshell — brought out in 1762 and subtitled "A
Rhapsody in Cabbalistic Prose." The rhapsodic nature of this prose
may be sampled from the opening of the *Aesthetica in Nuce*:

Nor lyre nor paintbrush but a winnower's shovel for my Muse in
sweeping the threshing floor of holy literature! Hail to the archangel
over the relics of the language of Canaan! On fair she-asses he is victorious in the race; but the wise fool of Greece borrows Euthyphron's
proud stallions for the philological exchange of words.

Meaning can be made out of this, but only after a study of the
fifth chapter of the book of Judges and of Plato's dialogue *Cratylus*.
Hamann, like Herder who was influenced by him, argues that
poetry was the mother tongue of the human race as the garden is
older than the farmer's field, painting than writing, song than
oratory (declamation), analogies than inferences, and barter than
commerce — all favorite romantic presuppositions. A concern
about the origin of language was a continuing problem among the
romantics everywhere, but to explore this in depth would take us
from Lowth's *Praelectiones de Sacra Poesi Hebraeorum*, Lord Mon-
boddo's *Of the Origin and Progress of Language*, and Horne
Tooke's *The Diversions of Purley*, to Herder's *Ueber den Ursprung
der Sprache*, the *Geschichte der deutschen Sprache* of Jakob
Grimm, and the researches into Sanskrit, Persian, and other tongues
by Franz Bopp. Let us go back to Hamann.

The *Socratic Memorabilia* is introduced by two riddling pref-
aces, "To the Public, or Nobody Well Known" and "To the
Two," and then by an "Introduction," which readers find difficult
to grasp. The truth is that the *Memorabilia* does not concern
Socrates so much as it concerns divine ignorance and a typological
reading of Biblical history. Whoever does not believe Moses and
the prophets is like Buffon writing on the history of creation
(Buffon did not accept the account in Genesis) or Montesquieu
on the history of the Roman empire — Montesquieu, that is, did
not really know much about the Roman empire. It is true that the
records of creation and, for that matter, the Scriptures themselves
are fragmentary, but perhaps all history is mythology and like
nature itself a sealed book, a concealed or secret witness, a riddle
that does not allow itself to be read. (This passage refers obliquely
to Judges 14:18, "If ye had not ploughed with my heifer, ye had

not found out my riddle.") God, in sum, makes riddling revelations. Socrates was a great name among followers of the Enlightenment; Hamann wishes to clear him of the sin of homosexuality and simultaneously turn him into an early "type" of Christ. Socrates professed "ignorance," yet he was a wise man. His "ignorance" is, however, that of St. Paul: "If any man think that he knoweth any thing, he knoweth nothing yet as he ought to know. But if any man love God, the same is known of him" (I Corinthians 8:2–3). Did Socrates love God? Socrates shunned system-makers, he sat day and night meditating, he went among young people, he found his classrooms in the marketplace, the fields, dinner parties, and prisons, the quodlibet (medley) of human life. He refused to write formal or systematic discourse, but through his questionings he spoke from himself. Like Christ he led a heroic life and suffered a martyr's death.

Why did Socrates thus behave? His "ignorance" sprang from his sensibility (*Empfindung*), that is, his grasp of the world in sensuous terms. He accepted things as they are and tried to understand them as objects having a deeper significance, but he did not mechanize or systematize thought as did Newton and the French *philosophes*. Therefore Apollo approved his "ignorance." Why? Because in place of trying to construct physical laws, Socrates obeyed his tutelary genius, on whose wisdom he could rely, whose voice he believed in, whom he loved and feared as a god, whose peace (peace of mind) was more important a gift than "wisdom," and whose "wind" (spirit) made Socrates' ignorance fruitful as a "wind" (spirit) makes the womb of a virgin fruitful (the Virgin Mary). Whatever this tutelary genius might be, it in no wise resembled a thermometer, a microscope, or a telescope, says Hamann, and its fructifying power must not be misinterpreted by charlatans.

If this somewhat astonishing interpretation of Socrates and his *daimon* seems unhistorical, it must be remembered that for Hamann, after his "conversion," the Bible became both ahistorical and typological ("I recognized my own crimes in the history of the Jewish people") and that, repudiating the rationalism of the Enlightenment, he had in mind totally to destroy the interpretation of Socrates the rationalists favored. For Hamann self-knowledge includes the ability to rise above or ignore "wisdom" (rational knowledge), and Hamann's interpretation of the Socratic *daimon* turns that concept into a variety of divine revelation suitable to his peculiar version of Christianity.

The German romantic return upon a mystical Christianity, whether Protestant or Catholic, though it had its roots in the pietistic movements of the seventeenth century, owes a great deal to Hamann's curious Christianization of Socrates. Logic and "science" were as nothing compared with the utterances of God. Therefore to him the Encyclopedists were blind leaders of the blind, though, unexpectedly, Hume was somebody Hamann honored because Hume also professed "ignorance." To Hamann great and powerful geniuses in any age were in some measure like "that strange people of whom Moses and the prophets foretold" that they were to be as an eagle that flies, their language at once profound and laughable and not now understood among men. Hamann fused together texts from the Bible, Scriptural allusions, quotations from classical literature, references, often obscure, to works in Latin, Greek, and, more rarely, Hebrew, attacks, sometimes veiled and sometimes direct, upon rationalists and theories of rationalism, and his own idiosyncratic use of typological language. The result is a composition difficult to understand. Indeed, an afterword (*Apostille*) is an indirect apology to posterity, but the apology is itself so cryptic as to require explanation. Creativity, it appears, is so much a part of the universal work of God that paraphrases of Plato's *Ion* and an injunction to fear God and keep Him in honor follow upon this opening, with its echo of Ecclesiastes:

As the oldest reader of this rhapsody in cabbalistic prose I find myself bound by the right of the first-born to leave behind me an example of merciful judgment to younger brothers who will come after me. Everything in this aesthetic nutshell smacks of vanity — vanity.

Is there any "merciful" interpretation that we moderns can understand?

Genius is creativity, notably creativity in words. But words are not abstractions, and modern rationalism, so the discussion seems to run, leads us astray by striving for generalization, whereas men should move in an opposite direction. God created the universe and all living things. He then permitted Adam to give names to these creations (for example, the animals), and the names Adam gave them, such they became, because Adam was the only created being on earth with the gift of speech. The animals were specific entities, not abstractions, and speech was poetry in that it simultaneously created and mirrored actual things. On the basis of their success in mathematics and other logical knowledge, theorists and critics in Hamann's time had set up various false doctrines about art as the imitation of nature, but in fact such thinkers and such doctrines pushed nature out of the picture. Therefore an understanding of creativity (and creation) and an understanding of God have virtually disappeared, and so has the divine purpose of speech. How shall we recover it? How shall we reawaken the lost speech of the dead?

It is well to become true Christians once more, but neither Christianity nor creation is properly understood among the intellectuals. God is a great poet. He works in types and symbols, and through these types and symbols He revealed himself to man in the past. Thus Adam is a "hieroglyph" (that is, a secret typological figure) of all mankind. Adam dealt directly with sensuous, visible nature, and was the first creative genius working with words. God will work through genius today if civilized men will but let Him. Genius, to be original, must throw away the stale platitudes of contemporary aesthetic theory and, realizing that human speech is at best but a translation of divine speech, return not merely to Adam but also to cultures that have remained nearer the springs of language than have the Europeans; for example, the "happy" Arabians and the Orient generally. Nor are the classical languages useless, since the best of the heathens recognized the "invisible" nature that man, the creation, shares with the Creator, a relation that takes shape as poetry. To make this point even clearer Hamann casually throws in a line from the Latin poet Manilius, a favorite of A. E. Housman:

Exemplumque dei quisque in imagine parvo

— each of us is an illustration of God in a small image.

There is more to Hamann's aesthetics (and to his bibliolatry) than this. For example, he throws a divine aura around language by alluding to such Biblical passages as "Day unto day uttereth speech, and night unto night showeth knowledge" (Psalms 19:2); and he regards the Pentateuch as a sort of secret agreement between God and man, put into writing by men and therefore an example of divine revelation through men to mankind. The channels of such creative revelation are, or could be, the geniuses of our time if only geniuses would go about their business in the right way — the way of revelation or the *daimon*. Such, or something like it, seems to be the theory that one extracts from Hamann's tortuous prose.

iii

Hamann's baffling typology, his feeling, vaguely suggestive of Kant, that time and space (and therefore history) have no external significance, his passionate opposition to all theological and philosophical theorems favorable to the Enlightenment presumably confined his immediate public to a small minority. Yet his doctrine of original genius was compatible with varying systems of thought. Its influence in Germany and in Europe generally is perhaps explained by the international vogue of that curious poem *Der Messias* by Klopstock in twenty cantos, each of them nearly a thousand lines long. The successive *Gesänge* appeared at intervals between 1748 and 1773, each addition, as in the case of the *Cantos* of Ezra Pound, being received as a fresh manifestation of creative genius. The subject is the last days of the life of Christ from the bitter night on Gethsemane (there are throwbacks to Palm Sunday and other events) to his betrayal, his trials, his crucifixion, his burial, and his resurrection. An English reader ignorant of German can approximate the flavor of Klopstock if he will imagine Longfellow rewriting *Paradise Lost* in the meter of *Evangeline* and adding copious borrowings from the four gospels and the machinery of Southey's "Oriental" epics. Nowadays the reading of Klopstock is a wearying task.

Not only does the simplicity of the gospels disappear but also, to fill out his twenty ponderous cantos, Klopstock involves heaven, earth, and hell, the present, the past, and time to come. Virtually any important character in Luther's Bible from Lazarus back to Adam and Eve is likely to appear as spectator or participant in the story. Old Testament figures are invisibly or, as Blake would say, spiritually present. The dramatis personae also include God, the archangels, the seraphim, the tutelary spirits of the various apostles, including one for Judas Iscariot, and a diplomatic mission from hell (Satan and others) puzzled or delighted by the apparent contradictions in, or failure of, what had been announced as the divine plan for humanity. Among other unexpected persons is Portia, the wife of Pontius Pilate, who seems to be a proto-Christian. There is also Eloa, a kind of angelical public relations official for the Almighty. Discussing the course of events with Gabriel, Eloa finds himself as baffled as is that archangel about God's purpose in condemning the Son to die. This is all well enough, but it is difficult to suppress a smile when in Canto VIII one finds the souls of Abraham and Isaac near the hill of Calvary, invisibly present because Abraham had also been in the position of sacrificing a son for the benefit of man (Abraham implores the Lord to be easy on the Jews). An important episode in Canto IX is the presentation of Judas Iscariot, who is shown the immortal glory he has lost by his treachery and who has the terrors of eternal death vividly described to him by an angel. This raises two casuistical questions: how can an angel, by definition immortal, know anything about death? and how can Judas Iscariot be held responsible for doing something he was unable to refuse to do, if the betrayal and the crucifixion were parts of a divine plan? Like Hamann, Klopstock had Pietist leanings, and his theology is never acute.

The wide appeal of *Der Messias* either in the original or in translation is understandable. Many readers, the younger generation in particular, had grown weary of the frigidity of neoclassical doctrines of art and thirsted for something more emotionally satisfying. *Der Messias* was a gallant effort to make vivid the most dramatic event in Christian history, and Christian history, unlike deism, dramatized human beings. Here was a gigantic Christian epic ostensibly in the meter of Homer, in which angels and archangels replaced gods and goddesses. God took the place of Zeus, and, as in the case of Milton, the whole population of heaven and earth was present in a drama far more earth-shaking than the Trojan war. The fatal defect in modern hexameters is diffuseness; Klopstock not only expands the laconicism of the Bible to inordinate dimensions, he also yields to the temptation to put formal addresses of a parliamentary sort into the mouth of every leading personage, including Jesus. Yet this very laxity makes for easy reading. The "mysticism" of Klopstock was not the mysticism of Hamann or William Blake, it was good *bürgerlich* mysticism, and the characters were, most of them, familiar names in any godly household and not unknown to disciples of the Enlightenment. Moreover, the style added to the rhetorical extravagance of the age.

What has *Der Messias* to do with spreading the doctrine of original genius? Its importance was twofold. In the first place, by theatricalizing the drama of the death and resurrection of Jesus, Klopstock brought heaven nearer to earth. He insisted that divinity was neighborly and available. In the second place, Klopstock himself implores the aid of the higher powers. The poem opens with an invocation to the Holy Spirit (like Milton's opening invocation) and utters a plea to God for aid in writing this tremendous story. Throughout the poem similar appeals for divine assistance appear; in other words the Hamann doctrine of the proto-Christian significance of the Socratic *daimon* is translated into full Christian terms. Here, for example, is an excerpt from the opening of Canto VIII that illustrates both the quality of Klopstock's versification and his appeal to divinity:

> Die du am Sion den heiligsten unter den Sängern Jehovah
> Sahst, von ihm lerntest, als er von dem ewigen Geiste gelehrt sang,
> Den der Richter im Tode verliesst, den grössten der Todten,
> Lehr, Sionitin, mich wieder; du lerntest himmlische Dinge!
> Komm' und leite den Schritt des Wankenden, deines Geweihten,
> Führe mich in des Gekreuzigten Nacht. Des Heiligthums Schauer
> Fasst mich, ich will den Sterbenden sehn, ich will die gebrochnen
> Starren Augen, den Tod auf der Wange, den Tod in den schönsten
> Unter des Wunden, dich sehn, du Blut der Versöhnung! . . .*

---

*An anonymous translation of the first fifteen cantos of *Der Messias* appeared in London in 1826. The translator, really a Miss Head, gets Klopstock's name wrong, says in the preface that an accurate list of the abridgments she has made appears at the end of each volume, and paraphrases rather than translates this passage:

> Come, heavenly Muse! Thou who on Sion's mount / Didst hear of old Judah's rapt minstrel strike / His harp of inspiration, while he sung / The Holy One forsaken by his God, / The Mighty One in death! Oh teach my lips / To chaunt those sacred strains! Through the deep gloom / Of crucifixion's darkness lend thine aid / To guide my feeble steps! Though o'er my soul / Mysterious horror creeps, yet would I view / The Holy Suff'rer, see his glazing eye / Close stiffly, mark death's hue upon his cheek, / Death in his open wounds! I would behold / The blood of reconcilement!

I choose this rather than make a literal translation because it illustrates the Gothic strain in Klopstock that appealed to foreign readers.

If in the days of Frederick the Great cultivated readers could gravely accept the Homeric epics either in the original or in somebody's translation, why not Klopstock with his tutelary spirits and his archangels in place of Zeus and Aphrodite? The God of *Der Messias* is at least consistent, despite the doubts of the heavenly host, and does not, like Zeus, change his immortal mind whenever this or that god or goddess embraces his knees. If Hamann could Christianize Socrates, Klopstock's appeal for heavenly inspiration approached the problem of genius in a way that neatly got around the difficulty of potential blasphemy. The romantics sometimes ignored and sometimes embraced Christianity with fervor, but they commonly retained some theory of the supernal guidance of the muse.*

It was the general opinion that Shakespeare was an untaught genius, nature's child, one who was supposed to have had small Latin and less Greek. The wide vogue of Rousseau, notably of *La Nouvelle Héloïse*, obviously the product of an "untaught" genius, paved the way for *Die Leiden des jungen Werthers*, in which intensity of emotion is more important than common sense. A new school of poets and dramatists arose to anticipate Byronic passion, egotism, and *Weltschmerz*. A younger generation of German thinkers, among them Herder, agreed with Hamann that poetry was the original language of man and studied the origins of language from that point of view.

What may be called a translation of the theory of original genius out of the theological atmosphere Klopstock had given it into the general assumption that an undefined divinity makes a free gift of genius to particular men was the work of Johann Kaspar Lavater (1741–1801), a Swiss mystic, poet, and letter-writer, one of the founders of the alleged "science" of physiognomy, whose "fragment" on genius seems to have been written about 1774 and appeared in the fourth volume of his *Physiognomische Fragmente*.

---

* It is difficult nowadays to be fair to *Der Messias*. The poem as a whole is more grandiose than grand, but this does not mean it is all dreary. In Canto IV an oration by Gamaliel before the Sanhedrim strikes me as excellent and is an interesting contrast to the Last Supper, with which the canto ends. Klopstock manages to convey some feeling of awe and terror in Canto VIII, and has considerable success in humanizing his angels and his demons. I ought likewise to add that the tiresome beat of his hexameters is for the most part abandoned in Canto XX, which, like the Prologue to Boito's *Mefistofele*, is principally composed of angelical choruses singing in varying meters. They celebrate the triumph of Christ.

Lavater was himself an original genius, whose religious poems have been compared to those of Novalis. He had interesting views on inspiration in preaching, and his style partakes of the verbal hysteria of the later eighteenth century.

Lavater never defines genius because, according to him, he who has genius knows it not and he who has not genius cannot know what genius is. His subject gives him opportunity, however, for one of the most remarkable explosions of verbal fireworks in all romantic literature. Genius is the light of the world, the salt of the earth, the substantive of the grammar of humanity, the image of divinity, the entrance of God into man, the creator, the destroyer, the revealer of the secrets of God, the interpreter of nature, the prophet, the priest, the ruler of the world. Call it, he commands the reader, the fructifying power of the spirit, the uncreate, the source or spring of everything, the elasticity of the soul. It will always remain something unlearned, unborrowable, inimitable, and divine. Genius flashes, genius creates, genius does not contrive anything, because it *is*. It is something not manageable. Its character is revelation, not reason, it is what is surmised but not wished for, what one has in the moment of demand but what cannot be demanded. It is not of man though it may be of God or of Satan. Genius is super-nature, super-art, super-learning, super-talent. Its way is the way of the lightning or of the storm wind or of the eagle. One can only stand and be amazed at its great flights and admire its brilliance, but whence it comes or why, no man can discover.

There are pages on pages of this heady rhetoric, which, whether it be intelligible or not, clearly separates genius from the rules. Enthusiasm, the faculty Shaftesbury had found exceptionable, now becomes central to romantic genius, and since in the light of this theory genius unpredictably comes and goes, the romantics felt that structure had less to do with art than did inspiration. Hence their penchant for the fragment, the unfinished masterpiece, in painting the sketch, in music the étude, and so on. Along with this, rhetorical intensity turned into a surrogate for reason and persuasiveness. Logic and sermons, wrote Whitman, never convince. If the Storm and Stress movement has been called the French revolution of German culture, the parallel between the perfervid rhetoric of a Lavater and the perfervid rhetoric of many a revolutionary is illuminating.

iv

Our inquiry is thematic, not chronological. I therefore pass over the intense subjectivism and the frequently frenetic verbal ouput of members of the German Storm and Stress school and some of the German romantics to draw some illustrations from England, postulating that a theory of original genius or, if one prefers, of a sublime individualism slowly spread over all the Western world. Perfervid utterance came to characterize much public speech and many doctrines of "liberty." Thus in the British Isles Robert Burns was encouraged to declare:

> Gie me ae spark o' Nature's fire,
> That's a' the learning I desire,

something Milton would never have understood. His *Poems, Chiefly in the Scottish Dialect* were printed at Kilmarnock in 1786, republished in Edinburgh and London, and followed by an edition of the great Scotsman in two volumes. Blake was known only to a few, and Burns is therefore perhaps the first genuinely British revolutionary bard:

> A prince can mak a belted knight,
>   A marquis, duke an' a' that;
> But an honest man's aboon his might,
>   Gude faith, he mauna fa' that!
> For a' that, an' a' that,
>   Their dignities an' a' that,
> The pith o' sense an' pride o' worth,
>   Are higher rank than a' that.

Revolutionary rhetoric was not, however, the only mode of Burns's intensity. He advertised the supremacy of passion in such a passage as:

> The wan moon is setting beyond the white wave,
>   And time is setting wi' me, O,

lines that, as somebody has remarked, contain the essence of a thousand love songs. In an even more famous poem he wrote:

> Ae fond kiss, and then we sever;
> Ae farewell, and then forever!
> Deep in heart-wrung tears I'll pledge thee,
> Warring sighs and groans I'll wage thee,
> Who shall say that Fortune grieves him,
> While the star of hope she leaves him?
> Me, nae cheerfu' twinkle lights me;
> Dark despair around benights me.
>
> I'll ne'er blame my partial fancy,
> Naething could resist my Nancy:
> But to see her was to love her,
> Love but her, and love for ever.
> Had we never lov'd sae kindly,
> Had we never lov'd sae blindly,
> Never met — or never parted,
> We had ne'er been broken-hearted.

William Hazlitt, another great name in English romanticism and a lifelong "radical," sought repose in strength, his romantic *Sehnsucht* finding its goal in the expression of power, says Herschel Baker, his best biographer. Hazlitt conceived the imagination to be a faculty by which one rises to a level of "disinterested benevolence," a trait essential to political reform, by which "the boundary of our sympathy" becomes "a circle which enlarges itself according to its propulsion from the centre — the heart." Hazlitt identifies art with power, and power with genius: hence, in all probability, his famous praise of the prose of Edmund Burke, with whom he radically differed in politics.* But Hazlitt, though he managed to stay out of jail as some of the English Jacobins did not, is perhaps less characteristic of romantic genius than are Coleridge, Wordsworth, Shelley, and Byron.

The lack of formal structure in Coleridge's prose works † — for

---

* Herschel Baker, *William Hazlitt*, Cambridge, Mass., 1962, pp. 146–147, 271, and elsewhere. At the start of his career Hazlitt laid down the proposition that genius is the power to do what no one else has done. A man of genius is, he thinks, *sui generis* — to be known, he need only to be seen: "you can have no more dispute whether he is one, than you can dispute whether it is a panther that is shown you in a cage" (p. 276). Note the ferile nature of the figure of speech.

† Familiarity with famous passages in the *Biographia Literaria* (1817) probably leads readers to overlook its hodge-podge make-up. Besides the sections on the imagination and on Wordsworth as a poet, the book includes some letters written from Germany, an imaginary dialogue, a good deal about Coleridge's school years, "remarks on the present mode of conducting critical journals," a set of Italian

that matter in a great many of his poems, which break off or represent only the instant moment — his inability to complete the great philosophical system he dreamed of putting together, which was to reconcile Christianity, politics, and Neoplatonism, and a sense that he was losing his primal energy as a genius are all parts of a troubled story. A reading of Coleridge's "Dejection: An Ode" (1802) in its negative sadness throws as much light on the romantic theory of genius as do more positive statements:

> My genial spirits fail,
>   And what can these avail
> To lift the smothering weight from off my breast?
>   It were a vain endeavour,
>   Though I should gaze for ever
> On that green light that lingers in the west:
> I may not hope from outward forms to win
> The passion and the life, whose fountains are within.
>
> O Lady! we receive but what we give,
> And in our life alone does Nature live:
> Ours is her wedding-garment, ours her shroud!

The fact that Coleridge, like Southey and Wordsworth, turned Tory after his revolutionary youth cannot alter the truth that he accepted the doctrine of romantic genius and lamented what he felt to be its passing from him.

We shall have to postpone for later discussion the case of Wordsworth, who is, so to speak, a supreme egoist as Rousseau was a supreme egotist. In him we have a genius whose major artistic effort was a Proustian attempt to recapture the steps of his own development in order to learn how a genius comes to be. Here it is sufficient to quote a paragraph from the "Postscript" to *Yarrow Revisited and Other Poems* (1835), which characteristically ends in the key of "I":

It was with reference to thoughts and feelings expressed in verse, that I entered upon the above notices, and with verse I will conclude. The

---

madrigals in that language, ten theses on a proposed "Dynamic Philosophy," a lengthy footnote concerning somebody whose venom Coleridge discusses on only "hearsay evidence," an anonymous letter advising him to revise the *Biographia Literaria*, a defense of the church establishment, a discussion of landscape painting, an argument intended to show "why the hand of providence has disciplined all Europe into sobriety," and much else. Of course the subtitle is "My Literary Life and Opinions," but *Tristram Shandy* is not more capricious and a story by Jean Paul Richter, Hoffmann, or Tieck can scarcely be more anarchical in structure.

passage is extracted from my MSS. written above thirty years ago; it turns upon the individual dignity which humbleness of social condition does not preclude, but frequently promotes. . . . if a single workman . . . should read these lines, and be touched by them, I should indeed rejoice, and little would I care for losing credit as a poet with intemperate critics, who think differently from me upon political philosophy . . . if the sober-minded admit that, in general views, my affections have been moved, and my imagination exercised, under and *for* the guidance of reason.

In other words the rationalist had better follow *me*. The egotism of Byron was externalized for all Europe to see; the egoism of Wordsworth was internalized and turned into the most painstaking examination of the development of original genius written in the nineteenth century. "Freedom in himself," says Wordsworth in *The Prelude*, is man's "genuine liberty." Probably "freedom in himself" was one thing to Wordsworth and another thing to Burns, but in either case an intense awareness of the inner being is what the writer has in mind. So do the revolutionary leaders.

Wordsworth was, however, so completely an English poet that he scarcely counts in the development of revolutionary ideology on the continent of Europe. The two great cosmopolitan revolutionaries in Britain are Byron and Shelley. Shelley was more consistently a radical than was Byron, but his impact upon Europe in his own lifetime and later was so slight as to be negligible, whereas Byron became the thunder-voice of the revolutionary reaction against conservatism. In him power and rhetoric are fused to a degree unsurpassed in other poets of his time — he died in 1824. Except for some trifles and except for some of his satires (but not all of them), the poems and dramas of Byron are, for revolutionaries, the incomparable expression of the romantic *moi*. Most of his works fall into two categories not mutually exclusive — melodrama and ringing public address. Poems such as the "Ode on Venice" and *The Prophecy of Dante*, however inferior as art, are metrical political orations, *Childe Harold* has virtually a similar function, and *Don Juan*, the great comic epic of modernity, is an indictment of oppression and elitism. As Arnold wrote, when the Europeans read Byron, they

> *felt* him like the thunder's roll.
> With shivering heart the strife we saw
> Of Passion with Eternal Law.

And yet with reverential awe
We watch'd the fount of fiery life
Which serv'd for that Titanic strife.

It seems clear that the doctrine of genius propounded by romantic philosophy basically altered the approach to truth. The commonality of doctrine acceptable to the eighteenth century began to dissolve under the fierce assault of personalities, each of which was supposed to represent a new, a solitary, and a proper grasp on essential principles in the arts and in politics. The geometrical world of Descartes in the seventeenth century was finally to turn into the non-Euclidean world of the nineteenth century; the fixed order of creation changed during the so-called "heroic age" of geology into a principle of continuing process endlessly debated by scientific genius; philosophy grew more and more idiosyncratic in comparison with the norms of eighteenth-century thought; and the future of political man and the nation-state became problematical. Somewhere along the line of these curves romantic genius was again and again an irresistible force for basic change, not so much because it was either genius or romantic as because the very concept of genius or, if one prefers, leadership implied the inevitability of radicalism.

Our illustrations of the romantic doctrine of genius have hitherto been drawn from philosophy and the arts. But an altered attitude toward charismatic leadership is evident in the French revolution. That complex and bitter period from 1789 to 1799 (to 1815 if one includes Napoleon's empire) virtually defies analysis after almost two centuries of historical scholarship. Nevertheless, there is one relatively stable dividing line, indicated by Madame Roland, who, when the Legislative Assembly met in 1791, said that in the two years since 1789 France had grown older by two centuries. The principal names one associates with the Third Estate of 1789 (which became the National Assembly) are, with the possible exception of Mirabeau, names that one associates with the eighteenth-century world. Necker is the prudent bourgeois, Siéyès a constitution-maker after the manner of the *philosophes*; Lafayette dreams of being a new George Washington; his brother-in-law, the Vicomte de Noailles, helps to open the floodgate of sentiment on the night of August 4 when "privileges" are enthusiastically abolished but no secure financial system is instituted to replace them; Du Pont de Nemours after the manner of Voltaire proposes that the state take over the ecclesiastical revenues; Jean Sylvain Bailly, astronomer and natural philosopher, administers the famous Oath of the Tennis Court and, elected mayer of Paris, cannot understand why "citizens" do not act rationally. The minds of such leaders were shaped by the *Encyclopédie*, by the movement of sensibility, by the optimism of the century, by its faith in property, in rationalism, in an enlightened and limited monarchy. They thought they were making a revolution partially after the American model and partially after the English model of 1688–89. They wanted to be kind to peasants, whom they did not know; they confused the middle class with the whole of the kingdom; they voted a Declaration of the Rights of Man and of the Citizen not for Frenchmen only but for all mankind. They had maturity, courtesy, tolerance, faith in the future — so much so that J. M. Thompson, the English historian, quotes the volatile Camille Desmoulins as writing (after the march of the women on Versailles and the forced coming of the royal family to Paris in 1792):

Consummatum est: it is finished. The king is in the Louvre, the National Assembly is at the Tuileries, the channels of circulation are being cleared, the market is crammed with sacks of grain, the Treasury is filling up, the corn-mills are turning, the traitors are in full flight, the priests are under foot, the aristocrats are at their last gasp, the patriots have triumphed!

Beautiful illusions! The difficulty with the men of 1789 is that nothing prepared them to deal with brute human nature. Desmoulins succumbed to the irresistible genius of Danton, voted for the death of the king, was sentenced to death, announced that he was the same age as Jesus, another victim of tyranny (as a matter of fact he was thirty-four, not thirty-three), and died a coward's death on the guillotine.

When Madame Roland made her remarkable statement in 1791, the political atmosphere was changing and the great and terrible triumvirate of a new despotism — Marat, Danton, Robespierre — were about to come into power and one by one be destroyed. Such men exhibited the self-assurance of many a romantic genius. They combine egotism with grandiose phraseology. "I voice," wrote Marat, "the rage of the people," as if he alone understood the populace. Danton, a greater man, whom somebody called the

Mirabeau of the lower classes, when Théodore de Lameth came secretly to beg him to spare the life of the king, answered in effect: what is a constitution among men who want to do something and have the power to do it? Just before he was sentenced to death, Robespierre defended himself by a speech of which this is the keynote: "They say I am a tyrant. Rather I am a slave. I am a slave of liberty, a living martyr to the republic . . . I confess . . . that I am sometimes afraid that my name will be blackened in the eyes of posterity by the impure tongues of perverted men." He also implied that his opponents in the Assembly were secret traitors and that he, and he alone, had the proofs of their villainy. If this suggests the paranoia of Rousseau, the inference is right; Robespierre was nourished on that writer. One can add to this fetid rhetoric that of Hébert, who after the execution of Marie Antoinette wrote in his paper, *Le Père Duchesne*, that the greatest of all his pleasures was to have seen the head of "Madame Veto" roll into the basket. He also called Jesus a sans-culotte.

This is not to say that romantics were evil men; it merely points to the truth that, as powerful personalities, good or evil, were more and more convinced that they and they only had access to vital truth, rationalism inevitably gave way to rhetoric. Two characteristics of the revolutionary spirit are its explosive speech, especially evidenced in the use of slogans intended for crowd hypnosis ("Liberty, Equality, Fraternity" in one epoch, "All Power to the People" in another), and its assumption (one that Burke deplored) that destruction of what is wrong must inevitably be followed by the appearance of what is right. Thus, once the French had got rid of the Bourbons, it seemed a simple matter to reconstitute a stable nation on the sublime basis of the Rights of Man and of the Citizen, but in fact the nation changed its form of government nine times from 1789 to 1848.

The words of national songs lose their cutting edge by incessant iteration, and it is not argued that "La Marseillaise" is per se more bombastic than others. Nevertheless the language of terror is evident in its style. I quote some of the verses, italicizing the more strident words and phrases:

> Allons, enfants de la patrie,
> Le jour de gloire est arrivé;
> Contre nous *de la tyrannie*

291

L'étendard sanglant est levé.
Entendez-vous dans ces campagnes
Mugir ces féroces soldats?
Ils viennent jusque dans nos bras
Égorger nos fils, nos compagnes!
Aux armes, citoyens! formez vos bataillons!
Marchons, marchons!
Qu'un sang impur abreuve nos sillons!

.   .   .   .   .

Tremblez, tyrans, et vous *perfides,*
L'opprobre de tous les partis;
Tremblez! vos projets parricides
Vont enfin recevoir leur prix!

.   .   .   .   .

Mais *ces despots sanguinaires,*
Mais les complices de Bouillé,
Tous les tigres qui sans pitié
Déchirent le sein de leure mère! *

This is a far cry from the language of reason.

Of all the forms of art, except the art of acting, oratory is the most perishable. Many great speeches leave no record behind them; and even when orations are printed in full or in abbreviated form, we wonder why this turgid prose once held its hearers spellbound. A white-hot flow of words ran over Paris during at least the first half of the revolutionary decade, and men such as Mirabeau, Vergniaud, Danton, and Robespierre captivated great audiences. These wonderful outbursts of personal energy must have been as impressive as the poetry of Byron or the music of Beethoven, for they proceeded from men who were the political equivalents of the geniuses in philosophy and the arts studied by romantic theorists. It is instructive to observe that after the Thermidorean reaction of July 27–28, 1794, orators lowered their voices, a sort of hush fell over France as if under the Constitution of the Year III all Europe was waiting for the famous whiff of

* Forward, children of our country, / The day of glory is here; / The *bloody flag of tyranny* / Is raised against us. / Do you hear across our countryside / *The roar of savage soldiers?* / They are coming to *slit the throats* / *Of our children and wives* in our very arms! / To arms, citizens! Form your batallions! / Forward, forward! / *Let their impure blood soak our furrows.* / . . . *Tremble, tyrants* and *traitors,* / The shame of every party; / *Tremble! Your parricidal plots* / At last shall get their due! / . . . But these *bloody despots,* / These henchmen of Bouillé, / *All the tigers who pitilessly* / *Tear their mother's breasts!*

grapeshot that mowed down rebels on the steps of the church of Saint-Roch, prepared for the *coup d'état* of 18–19 Brumaire, and permitted Bonaparte to become the dictator of France and of Europe. True, there is a sordid side to Napoleon, the side that led Emerson to quote with approval the statement that Napoleon was a *Jupiter Scapin*, but, the greatest embodiment of the romantic theory of genius that Europe was ever to see, the little man from Corsica imposed himself upon the West. He still lives in the memory of mankind as, say, Siéyès does not, and his war bulletins still vibrate with life: "Soldiers, from yonder pyramids forty centuries look down upon you!"

It helps one to grasp the nature of Napoleon if one contrasts it with that of his most famous antagonist, the Duke of Wellington. The duke was in his way a sardonic political descendant of Frederick the Great and had no patience with idealism. His quality is endurance, he inspires his armies with fortitude — in India, in Spain, in Belgium, where he heads brigades mainly made up, he said, of riffraff. He expects prodigies of resistance from his regiments, which in fact perform these prodigies; then, having permitted the enemy to exhaust himself, Wellington moves slowly forward to take possession of a battlefield or a country with the surety of a glacier. In politics he is a conservative, in religion a conformist. In the art of war he invents little, but he employs with unrivaled simplicity the tactics of others. A believer in society permanently ordered in ranks and classes, he evinces a steady attachment to his officers, whom nevertheless he will cashier the moment they fail to live up to his concept of military duty. He has an old-fashioned courtesy and an old-fashioned morality, especially where women are concerned; he is fond of children and grandchildren; he reverences not the man but the sovereign; his taste in art, music, and literature is negligible; he accepts with chilly indifference the worship of the nation he has preserved. His aristocratic disdain nevertheless charms the man on the street. He was so firm a pillar of the state that, when he was prime minister, he could force Catholic Emancipation through the parliament because he was afraid of civil war; yet, once out of office, he resisted the Reform Bill of 1832. On one anniversary of the Battle of Waterloo he was booed by the mob; at his death he was apotheosized by the nation.

In contrast to Wellington, Napoleon is perhaps the prime instance in modern times of original genius. One says "perhaps" only because it is impossible to weigh the claims of a Beethoven, a J. M. W. Turner, or a Goethe beside his claim. On the whole, however, the statement seems justified, because Napoleon touched life on a thousand sides.

This scion of an obscure "good" family in Corsica, scarcely a Frenchman, was at once the child of the revolution and the man of destiny. As the child of the revolution he was able by force of military and administrative genius to carry French principles into more parts of the world than his predecessors had done; as the man of destiny he believed, or made others believe that he believed, in his star, as Socrates believed in his *daimon*. There was in him something superhuman and something diabolical. No man ever rose to international power more quickly from such humble beginnings; no man was slyer, falser, more *intrigant*, and on occasion crueler than he, who sacrificed whole armies to his egotism. In some sense the British were right in identifying him as an agent of Satan; but the French were also right in believing that no one since Louis XIV had raised France and *la gloire* to such eminence. At the acme of his powers his mind moved with incomparable rapidity; it was at once analytical, comprehensive, lucid, and prophetical, seeing as if in a magic glass what his opponents would do and entrapping them in consequence. He was the idol of his soldiers because, unlike Wellington, he went among them, pulled their ears, and talked the argot of the bivouac. His charm could be irresistible, his anger terrifying. He had a devouring taste for women, for aristocratic distinction, for efficiency, glamor, and flattery, but he was at the same time cold-blooded, given to pride and melancholy, distrustful, and tyrannical. He read Plutarch and Ossian, he admired David the painter and Cherubini the musician, Monge the geometer and Berthollet the chemist. He was capable of conquering Egypt in three weeks and incapable of understanding that he who rules the empire of the sea defeats him who has the empire of the land. His great campaigns he planned with the precision of a chess game, but he could not understand the psychology of the Spaniards, the Russians, or the Germans, and because of this error his gigantic visions of an empire comparable to that of Augustus or Charlemagne faded away. He completed the modernization of France, he forwarded the unification of Italy, Germany, and Spain, he abolished the Holy Roman Empire, he codified the laws, the administrations, and the police systems of France and of all the countries his genius touched and occupied. The style of his famous proclamations was Caesarian in its ring and simplicity, but he falsified military bulletins at will. Though he rode from Moscow to Madrid, he never learned the truth of his own statement: "A form of government that is not the result of a long sequence of shared experiences, efforts, and endeavors can never take root." Being a Corsican, he tried to put his mediocre brothers and sisters on gimcrack thrones in the countries he invaded.

Nevertheless, in Napoleon revolution, romanticism, and reaction fused into a single gigantic whole. He is the greatest charismatic figure in the nineteenth century; he impressed his personality upon the world as no other modern man has done, and, dying, he dramatized himself as that favorite mythological figure among the romantics, a Prometheus chained to a rock and forgotten. In Napoleon one finds the utmost height and the consequent tragedy of original genius.

X

Reflections on the
French Revolution

After learning of the fall of the Bastille, Charles James Fox, British liberal and champion of the Americans, wrote on July 30, 1789, to his friend Robert Fitzpatrick: "How much the greatest event is it that ever appeared in the world! and how much the best!" In 1818 Byron published the fourth canto of *Childe Harold's Pilgrimage*, written in 1817. Byron was a radical among aristocrats and an aristocrat among radicals. The ninety-seventh stanza opens with this memorable line:

> But France got drunk with blood to vomit crime.

Twenty-eight years separate these judgments. When Fox wrote, Louis XVI was in theory an absolute monarch. When Byron wrote, Napoleon, a dying man on St. Helena, had about three years to live. Between the two statements, one radiant with hope, the other thick with disgust, lie the idealism and the savagery of the French revolution, the glory and the tyranny of the Napoleonic empire.

A different judgment can be gleaned from Arthur Young's *Travels in France & Italy during the Years 1787, 1788, and 1789*. Young was a shrewd observer. Having spent most of the month in Paris, and convinced by June 27, 1789, that "the whole business now seems over, and the revolution complete," he set out in "a light French cabriolet" and stopped at Nangis, a town south of Meaux, to spend a day or two with his friend, the Marquis de Guerchy, who had some concern for agriculture and whose chateau was filled with "a circle of politicians." Young talked with the local hairdresser on June 30 as follows:

. . . the perruquier that dressed me this morning tells me that everybody is determined to pay no taxes, should the National Assembly so ordain. But the soldiers will have something to say. No, Sir, never: — be assured as we are, that the French soldiers will never fire on the people; but, if they should, it is better to be shot than starve. He gave me a frightful account of the misery of the people; whole families in the utmost distress; those that find work have a pay insufficient to feed them — and many . . . find it difficult to get work at all. I inquired of Monsieur de Guerchy concerning this, and found it to be true.

Local magistrates ordered that no person be allowed to purchase more than two bushels of wheat. Young comments that this regulation had a tendency to increase the evil of monopoly. He went to the market and "saw the wheat sold out under this regulation, with a party of dragoons drawn up before the market-cross to prevent violence." He adds that the people quarrel with the bakers, riot, and run away with bread and wheat for nothing, the consequence being that neither farmers nor bakers supply the market until the people are in danger of starving, and that prices "under such circumstances must necessarily rise." The marquis's chateau required for its ordinary upkeep six men-servants, five maids, eight horses, a garden, and supplying a "regular table" for invited guests. Guerchy seems to have been amiable, even progressive; Young nowhere indicates that he had much contact with the peasantry.

Three leading British judgments interpret the French revolution in terms of idealism, disillusion, and economic maladjustment. Another interpretation is expressed in Tocqueville's classic *The Old Régime and the French Revolution* (1856) and avers that in spite of its violence the revolution did not fundamentally alter a tendency evident throughout French history:

No nation had ever before embarked on so resolute an attempt as that of the French in 1789 to break with the past, to make, as it were, a scission in their life line and to create an unbridgeable gulf between all they had hitherto been and all they now aspired to be. . . . they were far less successful in this curious attempt than is generally supposed . . . they took over from the old regime not only most of its customs, conventions, and modes of thought, but even those very ideas which prompted our revolutionaries to destroy it.

The more he studied the relevant documents,

the more I was struck by the innumerable resemblances between the France of that period and nineteenth-century France. . . . the peculiarities of our modern social systems are deeply rooted in the ancient soil of France.

This may be called the traditionary or developmental interpretation of the revolution. Everything changes, yet everything is the same. Perhaps the best commentary on Tocqueville's doctrine is Balzac's vast *Comédie humaine*, in which people in the city and people in the provinces, Bonapartists and adherents of the Bourbons, ex-revolutionaries and mystics are alike actuated by undying motives of greed and self-sacrifice, cynicism and sympathy. Such, Balzac seems to say, is your French society as it is, as it has been, and as it will always be.

There have been a thousand interpreters of the French revolution. Writers close to that catastrophe could not be impartial; they saw it either as the last, best hope of man or as a vile conspiracy of philosophers, cynics, and radicals. A later school of thought is represented by Michelet, who dramatizes the revolution as the uprising of the people in their sacred might to rid themselves of centuries of wrong. There is another group, of whom Carlyle is a sample, that sees the revolution sweeping away the sham world of the eighteenth century to make room for modernity, which, though plagued in Carlyle's opinion by erroneous doctrines of democracy, will not bow down before an idle aristocracy and a futile church. Another school is that of Taine, who "explained" the revolution as a conflict between the scientific spirit and the classical spirit, the latter being the mother of misfortunes because it rested too comfortably in unproved and unprovable generalizations. Because Taine had a devouring eye for detail, some of his passages read like pages from a horror story. There is likewise the school of Aulard, which interprets the revolution mainly in political terms: one formula of government is finally vanquished by another. Historians of a socialist or Marxist inclination include Jaurès, Mathiez, and Soboul; they see the revolution as a succession of crises in a class struggle. One of their contributions is the downgrading of the Terror: ruthlessness was necessitated by the hypocrisy of the bourgeoisie. Then there is a "patriotic" school, more or less conservative, exemplified by such authors as Gaxotte and Funck-Brentano, which tends to blame "foreigners," among them Rousseau, Necker, and Marat, all of whom were Swiss, for what went wrong, and praise "Frenchmen," such as Napoleon, who was born in Corsica, for what came out right or nearly right. Among more recent scholars Georges Lefebvre has been the most influential. Sympathetic with historians of the left, Lefebvre is more aware than they of the danger latent in generalizations and more sensitive to individual differences. His American followers include such excellent writers as Leo Gershoy and R. R. Palmer, who translated Lefebvre and whose *Twelve Who Ruled* (1941) is a brilliant study of the work of the great Committee of Public Safety, which, he thinks, saved France from anarchy. The British scholar Alfred Cobban takes a moderate view of the class struggle, though the idea seems to him central, and possibly pays more attention to the relation of the French republic with foreign powers than do some of his predecessors. Still another group lays great emphasis upon the international quality of the revolutionary movement; characteristic are Albert Sorel's monumental *L'Europe et la Révolution française* (1885–1904) and Crane Brinton's brief but illuminating *A Decade of Revolution, 1789–1799* (1934).

Two other important shifts have occurred in the twentieth century. One is a movement from Paris to the provinces; that is, where most nineteenth-century writers and some in the twentieth century took their stand in the capital and cast only necessary glances at provincial France, the newer school assumes there was much more to the revolution than the Palais Royal, the Paris sections, and the revolutionary Commune, and inquires with particularity into the states of mind, the economics, and the political and religious trends in France outside of Paris. A recent American example of this view is Philip Dawson's *Provincial Magistrates and Revolutionary Politics in France, 1789–1795* (1972), an assessment of the powers, social status, and points of view in the *bailliages* and *sénéchausées* into which the ancient regime had divided France for legal purposes. Inasmuch as many *bailliage* magistrates became deputies to the Third Estate and therefore to the National Assembly, their predilections are important. Other scholars have concentrated on a province or a provincial city; an example is *The Vendée* (1964) by Charles Tilly.

The second big change has been in biography. Whatever one

may think of modern psychological analysis when it is applied to a dead man who cannot respond to questions, recent biographies, using new documents and reinterpreting old ones, have replaced the black-or-white, either-or personages of the revolution with defter analyses, often exploring the home life or lack of it of revolutionary leaders. Thus Max Gallo in *Robespierre: Histoire d'une solitude* (1968) subjects the Incorruptible to a Freudian dissection; and if one is not altogether persuaded that Robespierre's career is "to be marked by this feeling of his father's guilt, his own guilt towards his father, a deep distress born of this guilt, and his mother's death, which was also the death of his childhood," the Robespierre who emerges from this book is at least of human dimensions when compared with the cold-devil image or the mis-understood-saint formula that sufficed many earlier historians. A like analysis appears in Jacques Guilaine's *Billaud-Varenne: L'Ultra de la révolution* (1969). Billaud, says this biographer, has never been indulgently judged but has had to bear the whole weight of the inhumanity of the revolution. Guilaine traces the history of this intellectual tramp from his unhappy childhood to his mem-bership in the Committee of Public Safety, all motivated by his thirst for absolute power. Even when psychiatric analysis is not involved, twentieth-century historians can view the men of the revolution in better perspective and produce juster lives. An in-stance is Leo Gershoy's *Bertrand Barère: A Reluctant Terrorist* (1962), which it is interesting to compare with Macaulay's sinister picture in 1844 of a Barère who "approached nearer than any [other] person mentioned in history or fiction, whether man or devil, to the idea of a consummate and universal depravity." One generalization can be made: it is illuminating to discover how many of the revolutionaries suffered from loss of parents in childhood, broken homes, neglect, and lack of a permanent domicile.

The library of books on the French revolution is, then, enor-mous. In addition to historical and biographical studies, there are thousands of bound periodicals, collections of pamphlets, official reports, memoirs, exculpatory essays, orations, autobiographies, and volumes of printed correspondence. Whole societies are devoted to the French revolution or aspects of it, to contemporary diplo-macy, to warfare, and to everything else from applied science to women's clothing. When one adds an equally tremendous library about the Napoleonic period, it is clear that no single mind can compass the French revolution and its aftermath, and I do not pretend to do more than scratch the surface in this chapter. A general reader who wants a balanced view of part of the revolution should consult J. M. Thompson's *The French Revolution* (1943), which surveys the crucial period from May 1789 to July 29, 1794, the date of the Thermidorean reaction. To someone who wants to look at Europe as a whole Jacques Godechot's remarkable *Les Révolutions (1770–1799)* (1963) is a lucid bibliographical and historical guide. Possibly the clearest presentation of current French views is found in three volumes in the Editions de Seuil series (1972): Michel Vovelle's *La Chute de la monarchie, 1787–1792*; Marc Bouloiseau's *La République jacobine, 10 août 1792—9 Thermidor an II*; and Denis Woronoff's *La République bourgeoise de Thermidor à Brumaire, 1793–1799*. I suspect I have been influenced by their interpretations to a greater extent than I realize. What will concern us in this chapter is three or four aspects of a gigantic convulsion.

ii

It is said that the American revolution offered French liberals a distant paradigm of what a revolution should be. The statement must be received with reserve. In the first place North America, including Canada, was more remote to Frenchmen than it was to Englishmen (consider the operatic New World setting of the last part of Prévost's *Manon Lescaut*), and French attention was more fixed upon the sugar islands of the West Indies than upon the frozen north. Moreover, until the French alliance of 1778 most Americans viewed the French as traditional enemies. Were they not Catholic? Had they not been for centuries hostile to the British crown and hospitable to the dethroned Stuarts? Why should they suddenly turn into friends of the former British colonies? Our representatives in Paris blandly ignored Vergennes in signing the preliminaries of peace in September 1792, and from 1798 to 1800 we fought an undeclared naval war with France. Vague generalizations about the influence of the American revolution on French thought fail to define what scholars mean by public opinion. If in French literary circles the United States was regarded as a star of

301

liberty, we do not know what reports the French private soldier returning home spread abroad concerning the heretic Americans. Nor is it true that all French officers came back zealous for liberty. For example, the Marquis de la Rouërie served in America as "Colonel Armand"; and if he participated in a plot against the king upon his return to France, one finds him in 1790 a thorough royalist, organizing an antirevolutionary movement in Brittany, his plot betrayed by, of all persons, his dead wife's doctor. In America attractive young French officers in Rochambeau's army got along very well with the village belles of Newport, but whether noncommissioned officers and privates found Eden in America is more problematic.

There is, however, respectable testimony that in some circles the United States of America seemed a sort of Rousseauistic, early Roman, or Hellenic republic. After the execution of Louis XVI, Saint-Just addressed the Convention, recommending to that body the adoption of a short constitution he had drawn up; he said he imagined that if one gives men laws according to their natures and their hearts, men will cease to be corrupt and evil, since corruption is not natural to the people but is found only in the hearts of kings. Saint-Just had not been to America, but it is a safe surmise that his thesis on the moral purity of republics owes something to reports from across the Atlantic. Even so suspect a liberal as Hérault de Séchelles, who announced to the Legislative Assembly in December 1791 that he had discovered a great conspiracy against France and liberty, thought Benjamin Franklin was an American Solomon:

Franklin est l'homme du siècle dont la destinée a été la plus extraordinaire. Également grand, également créateur dans les deux genres, la nature et la société; témoin l'électricité et la liberté de l'Amérique; il a fait avec la finesse et l'étendue de sa raison ce que les autres font avec leur enthousiasme. Il observait tout, il découvrait sans cesse. J'ai ouï dire que son foyer était même entouré de ses découvertes. Homme calme, tranquille, humain, simple, être indépendant. Il se promit de bonne heure de n'accorder son assentiment qu'aux objets qu'il verrait, après les avoir bien regardés. Il pensait que l'homme peut faire lui seul sa santé. Il citait avec complaisance cette pensée de Salomon: "L'homme sage porte ses longues années dans sa main." Il entre dans tout moins de fortune qu'on se croit.*

* Franklin had the most extraordinary fate of any man of our time. Equally great, equally creative in the two orders, the social and the natural; witness elec-

This was written some time after Franklin had made his great impression on the court at Versailles as a noble primitive, a wise child of nature wearing his own hair without a wig.

What there was of an American legend may be more richly illustrated from *The Letters from an American Farmer* by "J. Hector St. John," which came out in English in 1782 and in an expanded French version in 1783. J. Hector St. John was really Michel-Guillaume Jean de Crèvecoeur (1735–1813), a Norman of good family, who is supposed to have fought against the Indians in Canada under Montcalm and who in 1759 landed in New York, whence he traveled extensively in the British mainland colonies. In 1765 he became a naturalized "American" citizen, in 1769 he married Mehetable Tippet of Yonkers and settled on a farm in Orange County, New York, in 1780 he went back to France, and in 1783 he returned to New York to learn that his wife had died, his children had disappeared, and his farmhouse had burned, all the unhappy results of an Indian raid. He recovered his children, was for a time French consul in New York City, and left the United States permanently in 1790. In addition to the *Letters*, he published in French three volumes entitled *Voyage dans la Haute Pennsylvanie et dans l'Etat de New-York.** Essentially a Loyalist, he was nevertheless also a physiocrat and something of a liberal.

---

tricity and American liberty; by finesse and breadth of reason he did what others did with their enthusiasm. He observed everything and constantly made discoveries. I have heard that his home was full of things he had invented. A calm, tranquil, humane, simple man, and an independent soul, he made up his mind early to believe only what he saw, and only after having had a good look at it. He thought that without outside help a man could control his own health, and he was pleased to quote Solomon's saying: "A wise man carries his longevity in his own hands." Nothing is so much a matter of chance as we take it to be.

I find this in a section of "thoughts and anecdotes" in the *Oeuvres littéraires et politiques* of Hérault, edited by Herbert Juin, Paris (?), 1970, pp. 219–220. No date is annexed to the entry. Like some other "liberal" aristocrats, Hérault, a *flâneur*, a lady-killer, and a wit, went over to the revolution and was for a time a member of the Committee of Public Safety. Along with Danton, he was guillotined, probably on manufactured evidence, April 16, 1794. He was thoroughly a child of the eighteenth century.

* In 1925 a hitherto unpublished manuscript of Crèvecoeur's, *Sketches of Eighteenth-Century America*, was edited by H. L. Bourdin, Ralph H. Gabriel, and Stanley T. Williams; and various other essays by him have been recovered and published in scholarly magazines. For a complete bibliography consult the appropriate entries in vol. II of Jacob Nathaniel Blanck, *Bibliography of American Literature*. My discussion in the text is confined to the *Letters from an American Farmer*, since, both in English and in French, this book was immediately influential.

The Letters from an American Farmer is an unsystematic survey of the mainland colonies and the American wilderness and includes the brutalities of Indian warfare and the famous statement about "this American, this new man." The American, declares Crève-coeur, is more than a transplanted European, he is a product of a melting pot. I knew an American family, he remarks, where a grandfather was English, the wife Dutch, one daughter-in-law French, and four other sons married women of differing nationalities. The American leaves behind him all the prejudices of the Old World (!) and brings the arts and sciences of Europe into a new and more promising environment. He works from enlightened self-interest, pays no taxes to a despotic prince, supports no state church, and is free from penury:

Wives and children, who before in vain demanded of him a morsel of bread, now, fat and frolicsome, gladly help the father to clear those fields whence exuberant crops are to arise, to feed and clothe them all, without any part being claimed either by a despotic prince, a rich abbot, or a mighty lord.

We are [he says] a people of cultivators scattered over an immense territory, communicating with each other by means of good roads [!] and navigable rivers, united by the silken bands of a mild government, all respecting the laws, without dreading their power, because they are equitable.

Yet what he writes about South Carolina includes a searing picture of a Negro shut in a cage suspended from a tree, his eyes picked out by birds and his flesh lacerated, who begged Crèvecoeur for water and who longed to die. The final letter, which concerns the frontier, gives a somber account of strife between Indians and white men and of civil wars among the colonists. He also makes the pessimistic observation: "Of all animals that live on the surface of this planet, what is man when no longer connected with society, or when he finds himself surrounded by a convulsed and a half-dissolved one?" What, indeed?

More sustained idealism is found in descriptions by other Frenchmen. One reads, for example, in *Travels in North-America in the Years 1780, 1781, and 1782* (in French, 1786; in English, 1787) by the Marquis de Chastellux, an aide-de-camp of Rochambeau, that "one is tempted to apply to the Americans what Pyrrhus said of the Romans: Truly these people have nothing barbarous in their discipline." Their armies consist of the people themselves. Samuel Adams is made to describe the Massachusetts constitution as something "proposed and agreed to in the most legitimate manner, of which there is [no other] example since the days of Lycurgus." Jefferson, though a slave-owner, "perfectly resembles the bulk of the individuals who formed what were called *the people* in the ancient republics," * and in Virginia "the philosophers and the young men, who are almost all educated in the principles of a sound philosophy [the Enlightenment], regard nothing but justice, and the rights of humanity." Though Chastellux is mildly apprehensive about the future of the United States, he describes America as a contented democracy:

such is the present happiness of America that she has no poor, that every man in it enjoys a certain ease and independence, and that if some have been able to obtain [only] a smaller portion . . . than others, they are so surrounded by resources, that the future is more looked to, than their present situation. Such is the general tendency to a state of equality, that the same enjoyments which would be deemed superfluous in every other part of the world are here considered as necessaries.

What Chastellux propounded as true of the United States was echoed by Brissot de Warville, who, though he said in 1790, "I hate royalty," strove for a constitutional monarchy in France, gave his name to a moderate faction (the Brissotins), and was guillotined in 1793. A reformer, a journalist, a liberal, a one-time prisoner in the Bastille, Brissot traveled in the United States in 1788 and published an account of his observations in 1791. I quote from a second London edition of 1794, *New Travels in the United States of America Performed in M. DDC. LXXXVIII*. He thinks the French must study men who have just acquired their liberty and the secret of preserving liberty, which, the Americans know,

consists in the morals of the people; the Americans have it; and I see with grief, not only that we do not yet possess it, but that we are not even thoroughly persuaded of its absolute necessity in the preservation of liberty.

What is liberty? It is that perfect state of human felicity, in which each man confidently depends upon those laws which he contributes

* "People" here seems to mean the *populus Romanus*, not the *plebs*, and its use by Chastellux, like its use throughout both revolutions, illustrates the ambiguity of a central term in revolutionary theory.

to make; — in which, to make them good, he ought to perfect the powers of his mind; in which, to execute them well, he must employ all his reason; for all coercive measures are disgraceful to freemen — they are useless in a free State; and when the magistrate calls them to his aid, liberty is on the decline.

Brissot is something of a Rousseauist and something of a physiocrat:

I assure you that the Americans are and will be for a long time free; it is because nine tenths of them live by agriculture; and when there shall be five hundred millions of men in America, all may be proprietors.

We are not in that happy situation in France.

Small wonder that Lafayette could speak of an "American era" or that Condorcet, who never came here, not only declared that the American revolution was the dawn of a new day but also denied the general idea that republican institutions were workable only in a small area. Lafayette, forgetting that American officers had been as much sticklers for rank and precedence as either the British or the French, pontificated that it takes citizen-soldiers to support hunger, nakedness, toil, and want of pay; and Condorcet seemed to think that, after the fashion of the Greek and Roman republics, a citizen army only was capable of defending a virtuous republic. Even under the Consulate, Jean Chas et Lebrun in *Histoire politique et philosophique de la révolution de l'Amérique septentrionale* (1801) could praise the "sublime élan" of a virtuous people who created a constitution founded on true principles and established liberty on the basis of a love of justice, of law, and of religious morality. In this book Washington appears before the American congress like a liberating god comparable to Aristides, Cincinnatus, and Fabius; Franklin deserves the glory of Solon and Lycurgus, Kepler and Newton; and the American constitution is a work of genius and wisdom attesting to all the universe the virtues of the people.

There were of course dissenting voices. Thus the Abbé de Mably, a brother of Condillac, an economist of advanced views, and a writer who never visited America, published his *Observations sur le gouvernement des Etats-Unis d'Amérique* in 1784. He admits that the new republic was founded on an enlightened philosophy and the dignity of man, but he feels sure that liberty must lead to license and idleness, is horrified by religious toleration, and prophesies that discord among the American states is inevitable. The United States, he augurs, must go to pieces as the republic of Florence had done and as the Dutch states are presently falling apart.* The abbé is also against freedom of the press because of the fallen nature of man. If one considers the tone of much French revolutionary journalism — for example, that of Hébert — he was shrewder than he knew.

Doubtless, then, some French readers saw in the United States a glimmer of hope. That the course of the French revolution was greatly influenced by New World example seems, however, to be negated by two truths: readers in the kingdom were a minority, and of that minority only a minority was prepared in 1789 to admit that a "primitive" people could teach much to the French; and the concept of a republic was in 1789 shrouded in ambiguity. It is a historical irony that the fatal effect of the American alliance on France was to bankrupt the French treasury. In his *L'Esprit révolutionnaire en France et aux Etats-Unis à la fin du xviiie siècle* (1925) Bernard Faÿ says about all there is to say concerning the parallels between the American and the French revolutions, but analogues are not cause and effect. Gouverneur Morris, in Paris from 1789 to 1794, courageously sticking to his ministerial post during the Terror, was no friend of radicalism, yet his acid observations help the historian's judgment; and the counterpoint to Faÿ is Morris' shrewd observation that the French could not immediately imitate the Americans since, having had no experience as citizens, they could not overnight cease being subjects. Under the Empire, indeed, Félix de Beaujour in a *Sketch of the United States* published in French in 1810 and in English in 1814 saw nothing but weakness in the government of that country since its inception, declared the Americans have no more stability in their character than in their opinions, and, though he found nobody in rags, affirmed that American "virtue," supposed to be the chief

* De Mably at least insisted that the American government did not treat its inhabitants as animals. It is interesting to note that de Mably's book consists of four letters addressed to John Adams, then American minister to Holland, and that an English translation (*Remarks concerning the Government and the Laws of the United States of America*) was published at Dublin in 1785, three years after Ireland had been granted the so-called "Constitution of '82," which, if it recognized the right of Ireland to be governed by laws of her own making, retained for the Crown the appointment of all the leading administrative officers.

quality of a republic, turned out to be an unbounded love of money. He thought that the republic would be balkanized because of the tensions among its various states and territories or, if not that, become a dictatorship.*

iii

There are nowadays two major modes of interpreting the French revolution. One is to see that great tragic event only as the most vivid chapter in a general revolutionary wave extending from 1775 through 1917 (and after); the other concentrates on France. The first is exemplified in E. J. Hobsbawm's *The Age of Revolution, 1789–1848* (1962). In an earlier chapter I touched briefly on a succession of popular tumults in the Western world before 1775. For Hobsbawm and historians resembling him there is a working connection among popular uprisings, the commercial and industrial revolutions, and full-fledged political revolutions in the eighteenth century and later. This connection is twofold. On the one hand, manufacturing, even in its rudimentary phase, lured simple people into the cities, leaving them to starve whenever there was an industrial slump. The unemployed melted into the *Lumpenproletariat* and frightened the middle class. On the other hand, enclosure movements dislocated the normal pattern of peasant tradition. Since in most of Europe a steady increase of population pressed hard upon the means of subsistence, as Malthus noted in 1798,† the resulting misery often took shape as political discontent, an increase in begging, and a growth in pillage and robbery which explains why, in the final cantos of *Don Juan*, Byron could plausibly

---

* What the French later thought of Americans may be gleaned from an extraordinary monograph by Simon Jeune, *De F. T. Graindorge à A. O. Barnabooth: Les types américaines dans le roman et le théâtre français (1861–1917)*, Paris, 1963. The rich American uncle, commonly beneficent, takes care of everything at the end of the many comedies analyzed.

† As had, more naively, the radical Babeuf in his *Cadastre perpétuel* (the full title is too long to transcribe) of 1789: "Mais ce n'est point là où s'est borné le mal; ces travaux sont devenus une ressource absolument insuffisante pour chaque individu. Tout ayant concouru à ce que les petites fortunes s'engouffrent dans les grandes, le nombre des Ouvriers s'est excessivement accru. Non seulement il en est résulté que les mêmes salaires ont pu être diminués de plus belle, mais qu'une très grande quantité de Citoyens s'est vue dans l'impossibilité de trouver à s'occuper même moyennant la faible rétribution fixée par la tyrannique et impitoyable opulence, et que le malheur avoit impérieusement forcé l'industrieux Artisan d'accepter." (*Cadastre perpétuel*, p. xxvi.)

308

picture his hero and his entourage held up by highwaymen at Shooter's Hill only eight miles out of London.

If one passes to a more specific listing of rebellious or revolutionary episodes in the Western world, one notes, first of all, four great revolutionary movements, successful, half-successful, or abortive, in 1775–1789, 1820, 1830, and 1848. The span of Irish discontent sometimes seems to run from the "gift" of Ireland to Henry II by Pope Adrian IV in 1154 to the present day; more particularly, Irish rebelliousness was evident from about 1779 to the corrupt Act of Union in 1801, and there were smothered movements of discontent during the wars against France and throughout the nineteenth century. In Britain a potential revolution appeared in the rise of British radicalism (the "English" Jacobins, though many were Scots), the mutiny at Spithead, the notorious Peterloo massacre (1819), the Cato Street conspiracy (1820), repressive measures by various ministries, and sporadic riotings, pillagings, and burnings, which, however, quieted with the passage of the Reform Bill of 1832, though rebelliousness flared up again during the Chartist agitation from 1839 to 1848. During 1791–1794 in what was left of Poland Kosciusko led a futile revolt against the destruction of his country. There was a succession of internecine struggles in the Low Countries, not settling down until after the revolutionary year 1830, when Belgium and Holland became separate kingdoms. Civil tensions continued in Switzerland, were deepened by French invasion and by the ending of Napoleon's Continental system, and were partially a function of religious conflict between Catholic and Protestant cantons. These tensions culminated in the Sonderbund war of 1845–1847, which produced the Swiss constitution of 1848. There were violent changes, or attempts at change, in Spain, Portugal, and Latin America, outbursts in areas as diverse as Malta, Turkey, Corsica, Sweden, India, Southeast Asia, and northern Africa, and movements toward unification, sometimes conspiratorial, sometimes public, in Italy and Germany. The Franco-Prussian war occasioned civil strife in France in 1871. The rise and fall of liberal or radical movements in Russia until 1917 are important elements in European political and intellectual history. Tensions continued between the Austro-Hungarian crown and the polyglot nations, territories, or races over which the Viennese emperor presided or hoped to preside. Greece won its independence. Various Latin-American republics took various shapes; and two of them, Mexico and Brazil, were, temporarily, empires. The concept, however rudimentary, of dominion status for Canada was worked out in Lord Durham's *Report on the Affairs of British North America in 1839*, a report necessitated by rebellion in Upper and Lower Canada (Ontario and Quebec) in 1837–1839. There were rebellions or attempts at rebellions in China and Japan. In the point of view represented by this list the French revolution was simply the most dramatic of the violent changes attempted in the period.

Of these changes taken *en bloc* it can be argued that forces of nationalism originating in romantic invention and replacing the cosmopolitan ideal of the Enlightenment, the determination of the bourgeoisie to rise in the world and dominate the state, techniques of terrorism, and the manipulation of propaganda by a relatively small, unified, and skillful minority intending to incite and control a revolution are, if not inventions by the French, modes of turmoil perfected by them. In the nineteenth century generally the struggle for controlling a revolution, once launched, lay between the middle class, which had wealth, and the laboring and peasant classes, which had numbers. These elements appear of course in the history of the French revolution; and it is a nice question of interpretation whether they were invented by the French or whether, looking backwards, we impute to the French inventions they did not intend. Most commentators agree, for example, that in the long run the French bourgeoisie* prevailed over the monarchy, the nobles, and the lower classes, but did the struggle necessitate the Consulate, the Empire, the Restoration, the Revolution of July, the Second Republic, the Second Empire, and the Third Republic? Or was the French revolution a unique experience?

If one confines himself solely to the French revolution, it should be noted that the principal phases of that movement have been

---

* "Bourgeoisie" is a term as baffling as "people." It may mean the very rich, and also those who are, as we say, well off; it usually includes many professional men but less commonly practitioners of the arts; it sometimes includes peasants with incomes in the upper bracket and their equivalents in the towns — what eighteenth-century England or Ireland would call respectable persons. Whether a small local contractor is among the petite bourgeoisie, however, is a disputable matter, and at what point a distinction is to be drawn among the trades is anybody's guess. Was — or is — a wine-seller respectable? In most cases, probably yes, but what about a plumber, even if he be a master plumber? The reader can tease his mind endlessly with these nuances. How about gardeners?

worked out by various historians. The decade 1789–1799 is the revolutionary decade par excellence, but in view of the contrast between the first five years and the last five years of that period, there are writers who virtually conclude the revolution proper in 1794. Those who wish to call the entire ten years revolutionary are compelled to label as revolutionary the constitution of the year VIII (1799), which established the Consulate. In general the French revolution may be compared to a triptych. Its prelude runs from the first meeting of the Notables in February 1787 to the first meeting of the States General in May 1789. Then comes the revolution proper; then a postlude, from the Consulate, established at the end of the century, to the Empire, established in 1804. In general the years from 1789 to 1792 form a period of general bourgeois ascendancy, the years from 1792 to 1795 are marked by attempts to create a durable democratic republic, and the bourgeoisie triumphs or seems to triumph again from 1795 to 1799. Aulard adds a fourth phase, the "plebescite republic" from 1799 to 1804. It is, however, difficult to see anything genuinely republican in our sense of the term in the military dictatorship established by Bonaparte in 1799, and it must also be noted that France became a formidable military power as early as 1793, a fact that increasingly diminished both democratic and republican "virtue." The problem, it is clear, passes beyond semantics into riddles of political and social interpretation.

When one takes the point of view that, though there were other revolutions, the French revolution was a unique and unpredictable event, it may be argued that this great convulsion created or matured forces that were copied by later movements of rebellion or revolution. If one may speak of professional revolutionaries — political radicalism exemplified by Che Guevara and by various twentieth-century revolutionary groups, commonly secretive,* seems to be of this order — the revolution of 1789 was the first training-ground for the development of revolutionary temperaments; that is, it encouraged gifted individuals to create, lead, and alter popular discontent. Marat, Danton, Hébert, Robespierre,

---

* Before, during, and after the French revolution it was often argued that this great event was a result of a mysterious conspiracy among equally mysterious secret societies, among these the Masons, the Illuminati, and the Rosicrucians, an assumption much exploited in romantic fiction. The latest study of these seems to be J. M. Roberts, *The Mythology of the Secret Societies*, London, 1972.

Saint-Just, Babeuf, Billaud-Varennes are examples and the leaders of the Constituent Assembly were, in the words of Marc Bouloiseau, "farouchement individualistes." Partly to retain their power, partly from sincere, even fanatical, conviction, some leaders took to exporting the revolution or imposing it by force on other nations in the belief that revolutionary principles as they interpreted them were of universal significance.* In the next place, French revolutionaries, apologists to the contrary notwithstanding, instituted the blood bath as an instrument of political control, either tacitly permitting massacre (as in the infamous September massacres of 1792) or deliberately executing hundreds of real or putative opponents. Thus a revolutionary tribunal at Nantes under the direction of Carrier put some 15,000 persons to death, and when in 1795 General Hoche defeated the émigrés, the British, and the Chouans in Brittany, he caused about 700 émigrés to be executed. In reprisal the royalists executed about a thousand republicans. Wholesale slaughter or individual guillotining was justified in the name of revolutionary dogma — "Was the blood shed, then, so pure?" went one justificatory phrase. Though orthodoxy shifted from group to group and from leader to leader, the system (or no-system) remained constant: seize power and liquidate the leaders of the opposite faction. Orthodoxy, it is true, became a function of leading personalities and of shifting creeds. Thus in one year Lafayette, at another time the Brissotins, at a third Danton, at a fourth Robespierre determined or seemed to determine the one true revolutionary faith. The French revolution did not, of course, invent the personality cult which has troubled later revolutions, since the Americans virtually deified Washington, but it matured this use of crowd psychology. The clash of cults is evident in the bitter internecine struggles within the revolution, struggles which, in conjunction with foreign hostility or opportunism, offered plenty of chances for espionage, counterrevolution, propaganda of all sorts, and even open revolt against the dominant faction of the day.

* The Americans tried to convert the Canadians to revolutionary principles by force (they failed) and dreamed of revolutionizing Bermuda and the British West Indies. Later American exponents of manifest destiny thought of extending the "American system" over Latin America and still hoped that British North America would join the United States. Indeed, the "expansionists of 1898," of whom Mr. Dooley was scornful, wanted to carry the flag and democratic institutions to Cuba, Porto Rico, Guam, the Hawaiian Islands, and the Philippines.

The French revolution was also forced to take over from ancient history and modernize the concept of total war, not merely the *levée en masse* (the first great national draft) but also the philosophy that warfare was not between army and army but between nation and nation. Notably in 1793 and to varying degrees later, the economic and social life of France as a whole was directed toward military success. As a necessary corollary, and to reduce the popular economic burden, French revolutionary armies, including those of the young Bonaparte, were expected not merely to live off the land — no new concept — but also to destroy a hostile government, take over the treasury and the tax system of the enemy country, "modernize" government, and possess themselves of almost anything that was movable, including works of art. Later on, French imperial forces in Spain tried to devastate the total countryside, as Sherman was to do in his famous march to the sea. But the ancient truth, *fas est ab hoste doceri* — one should learn from the enemy — soon came into play. Thus the Russians burned Moscow in order to force Napoleon's Grand Army to retreat and so destroy itself with the aid of the Cossacks and cold weather. This is not to say that murder, rape, pillage, conflagration, and laying waste the land were inventions of the French. But injuries done by professional armies fighting against professional armies in the eighteenth century were, so to speak, conventional, whereas the aim of the revolutionary armies was to break the will of a whole people to resist. This strategy succeeded for a time, but Napoleon discovered too late in Prussia, in Spain, and in Russia that laying waste a nation in order to compel it to surrender induces a counterstrategy of nationalism. The finest hour of nations determined to drive out the French was therefore that of recovering national independence. The revolution thus simultaneously proclaimed nationalism and universal truth, but in the long run nationalism overcame universality. For a time the concept of a balance of power kept the peace in Europe after 1815, but who was to define balance of power? Or the concert of Europe? It is again a historical irony that, although the "rights of the people" was a universal idea, the French revolution proposed to substitute for the status society of the old regime, which the Enlightenment defended as both rational and cosmopolitan, a new, or at any rate, a novel, concept of nationhood. Once the "rights of the people" were imposed upon by the "rights" (ambitions, desires, race, political system) of some other people, nationalism turned into an irresistible emotional force. Our modern version of this social energy turns upon "ethnic" rights.

iv

The chief events of the revolution from 1787 through the trial and execution of Louis XVI in 1793 can be briefly recounted, and follow a regular order interrupted by certain explosive events. An Assembly of Notables, called together by the king, and composed principally of members of the clergy and the nobility, sat from February 22, 1787, to May 25 of that year and, because of jealousy of the parlements and suspicion among the royal counselors, accomplished little, though it was later briefly reconvened. The one positive recommendation that came out of these sessions was the advice to summon the States General, which had not met since 1614. The aristocracy, in Leo Gershoy's phrase, overplaying its hand, insisted on the preservation of ancient forms. This meant that the States General was to meet in three separate chambers, the clergy, the nobility, and the commons, but, as a concession, the number of the commons was determined to be equal to that of the clergy and the nobility taken together. This, however, did no good unless the three chambers were fused into one. Elections of the clergy were, for the most part, direct, as were those of the nobility, but the commons were chosen through an elaborate system of indirect elections that, however, seems to have been fairly administered. As the peasantry naturally chose persons of some eminence (and were encouraged to do so in many districts), the result was that the peasantry as a class had virtually no representation in the Third Estate. The parlements meanwhile lost all hold on popular opinion and shortly ceased to be a force in French political life. Deputies to the States General numbered 1,201: 300 for the clergy, 291 aristocrats, and 610 in the Third Estate. For good or ill, membership in the latter body was strongly colored by lawyers.

It has been said the French revolution originated in vanity — the desire of the bourgeoisie to shine in the world, envy among the country nobility against the court aristocracy, and jealousy of the provinces and the provincial cities against Paris and Versailles. It can be said with equal truth that the revolution was fed by ineptitude. When the three bodies finally assembled to be presented to the king, members of the Third Estate were made to feel their social inferiority. Neither the king nor any representative of the court, including Necker, whose reputation for financial insight posterity wonders at, showed any genuine comprehension of the troubles of the kingdom. The Third Estate invited the other two orders to join them, and the other two estates stood stiffly on their dignity for something like five weeks. The Paris delegates did not join the Third Estate until more than a month after the formal opening of the sessions; after that date things began to move. On June 17, 1789, the Third Estate, after issuing a final invitation to the other two orders to join them and make a single body in which votes should be individually cast, declared that they were no longer the Third Estate, but the National Assembly, or a representative congress for all France. Members of the clergy and the nobility began drifting in to join them. The king was advised to suggest some sort of compromise measure as between voting by estates and voting by "head," and ordered that the hall in which the Third Estate had been meeting be closed for alterations so that he might address the combined bodies. Unfortunately but characteristically, nobody informed the commons. Again, ineptitude; the Third Estate (the National Assembly) put the worst construction on thus being locked out, met in a nearby indoor tennis court, and took an oath, with but one dissentient, not to separate until a constitution for the kingdom had been established. The royal government again displayed its magnificent stupidity; and when Louis XVI commanded the estates to meet separately, and when one Dreux-Brézé, the Grand Master of Ceremonies, reminded the commons that they were but one of the three estates and should leave their hall, Mirabeau told him they could be dispersed only by troops:

Les communes de France ont résolu de délibérer. Nous avons entendu les intentions qu'on a suggérées au roi; et vous, qui sauriez être son organe auprès de l'Assemblée nationale; vous, qui n'avez parmi nous ni place, ni voix, ni droit de parler, allez dire à votre maître que nous sommes ici par la volonté du peuple, et qu'on ne nous en arrachera que par la puissance des baïonnettes.*

* The commoners of France have resolved to take counsel. We have heard the intentions that have been suggested to the king; and you, who could be his voice in the National Assembly, you, who have no right to a place, or to vote, or to speak among us — go tell your master that we are here by the will of the people and that it will take bayonets to drive us out.

This is forceful language, but there is in it no hint of violence as a weapon. As bodies the clergy and the nobility virtually disappeared; many had joined the National Assembly and many of the nobility had become émigrés, a category of discontented persons that was long to trouble the French revolutionary government.

The National Assembly, a body too large for discussion and too small for true representationalism, was to produce a written constitution for France, which, all things considered, is a remarkable document, reorganizing the administrative system of the kingdom, reorganizing the legal system, reorganizing (in a somewhat less satisfactory manner) the fiscal system, and, above all, reorganizing the concept of French nationalism by instituting a limited monarchy in place of a theoretically absolute king. This constitution had a great many defects, but, given the circumstances of its creation, it is as remarkable an innovation as the American Constitution, and one that had more obstacles to sweep out of the way. Unfortunately the National Assembly voted that none of its members could be elected to the National Convention of September 20, 1792.

Unfortunately also this simple narrative conceals the hidden passions and the political storms that swept through France during these months, and were to increase. Some of these events in any other context would have been dismissed as *émeutes* — popular uprisings to be put down by the constabulary or its equivalent — and some were of great political and philosophical significance. Among the first is the storming of the Bastille on July 14, 1789, an event that has become symbolical in the history of French liberty. Parisians, principally from the lower classes, persuaded that the king had wicked designs on them, sought everywhere for weapons to defend themselves against the "tyranny" of the royal regiments. It was rumored that the Bastille, which contained almost no prisoners, had an armory that could be taken over, and the populace, together with members of the National Guard whose sympathies were popular rather than monarchical, managed to storm the fortress, a success due, again, as much to the ineptitude of those in command as it was to the patriotism of the attacking multitude. Popular victory was stained by murders prophetic of the bloody months to come; and the unpleasant sight of the severed head of the quondam governor of the Bastille paraded through the streets on a pike did nothing for conciliation. Other murders of unpopular administrative officers were to follow. On the other hand, from August 20 to August 27 the National Assembly debated and finally adopted the influential "Declaration of the Rights of Man and of the Citizen," which is to the Old World what the first ten amendments of the Constitution are to the United States. The text of the Declaration will be found in the appendix to this volume. Here it is sufficient to make three important points. First, following the night of August 4, when members of the privileged classes in the National Assembly rapidly surrendered their feudal privileges, the Declaration insists upon the "natural, inalienable, and sacred rights of man." Second, the Declaration protects the rights of property: property is "a sacred and inviolable right." Third, then and since, the Declaration has never wholly satisfied radicals. Apparently nothing in it prevented the Assembly from classifying citizens into "active" and "passive" categories, only the first having a right to vote.

Neither the king, the queen, nor the immediate royal counselors, official or unofficial, seem to have had any real acquaintance with the actualities of the general life of France, and in June 1791 the royal family tried to flee the country and were discovered, captured, and returned. Louis was now no longer the "father of his people." Meanwhile the Assembly had decreed on July 12, 1790, the so-called civil constitution of the clergy, possibly the most divisive measure emanating from that body. By this and a subsequent law clergymen were not to be instituted until and unless they had sworn an oath to abide by the constitution. They became civil officials. The law coordinated episcopal seats with the eighty-three new French "departments," insisted that all religious offices were to be filled by popular election, and required each priest, whatever his rank, to support the French constitution. No single measure of the Assembly created greater emotional resistance: the king sanctioned it with extreme reluctance and himself preferred non-juring clergymen to those who took the oath; thousands upon thousands of simple Frenchmen looked upon the "civil clergy" as heretical; and the pope, deeply offended, denounced this legislation. The civil constitution of the clergy fed the flames of old-line allegiance to church and king in those parts of France that had considerably less enthusiasm for revolution than had the radicals of the various Paris "sections."

For, in truth, France was a deeply divided country. A series of weak ministries, characteristically Brissotin in quality, tried to manage the government even after the king's flight, but the death of Mirabeau in April 1791, the so-called "massacre" on the Champ de Mars of July 17, 1791, for which Lafayette could not altogether disclaim responsibility, the "march of the fishwives" on Versailles in June 1792, and the creation of an insurrectional Parisian "Commune" on August 9, 1792, which rudely ousted the legal municipal government, were signals of widespread popular bewilderment and discontent. Most of France, notably in the summer of 1789, had been swept by a vague but portentous Great Fear. It was rumored that regiments of brigands, whom nobody had ever seen, were about to plunder the countryside, and, taking advantage of the panic, peasants in many communities seized chateaux, sometimes murdering the occupants and almost invariably burning documents on the theory that the old feudal taxes could not then be collected. There were areas in France that were heartily revolutionary, but there were also districts that were quite as heartily royalist. In general the provinces distrusted Paris, and in general Paris distrusted the provinces. People who had grain refused to sell it, and some of them were peremptorily murdered; tax collectors scarcely knew what taxes to collect, if, indeed, they could collect any; municipalities that had depended upon the local *octrois* for income now had no income; foreign trade declined; industry faltered; hostile armies threatened France from the north and west; hostile fleets, particularly the British fleet, threatened France from the west and south; and, basic to economic life, nobody knew what money might be, since the paper *assignats*, the value of which depended upon the sale of confiscated church property, grew more and more uncertain as the months crawled by. Regiments mutinied, cities rebelled, kings and émigrés uttered vague but imposing threats; and when on April 20, 1792, the Legislative Assembly, in office since October 1, 1791, declared war on Austria, it was clear that sober-minded persons such as Lafayette, Brissot, Pétion, Vergniaud, and other moderates (now known as the Girondins) were losing control. Despite Robespierre, the Girondins hoped to save themselves and France by turning bellicose.

On July 11, 1792, it was decreed that the country was in danger. On August 10 occurred the notorious massacre of the Swiss guards at the Tuileries, the result in part of royal ineptitude, and a day or two later the royal family was in fact imprisoned in the Temple never to emerge as royalty again. In August 1792 Lafayette deserted to the enemy; and in September there were the infamous prison massacres, which must forever stain the history of the French revolution. On September 25, 1792, it was declared that France was a republic one and indivisible, an important phrase, since the provinces, which had by no means lost their sense of identity, had in many instances hoped for a federal republic — that is, a nation of associated districts loosely held together by a central government. The hope was vain. On September 20, 1792, a date identical with the end of the Legislative Assembly and the inauguration of the Constituent Assembly, the Prussian (and the Austrian) forces were turned back at Valmy, and France soon was launched on that career of conquest which was to end only with the defeat of Napoleon at Waterloo June 18, 1815. After 1792 France was (temporarily) a republic. But where was the center of government? Who were the masters of France?

The monotonous rise and fall of one or another faction determined to govern France, failure commonly leading to the guillotine, cannot conceal the truth that until the grasp of power by the "great" Committee of Public Safety, France was steadily tending toward anarchy, an anarchy that permitted foreign nations to seize French ports, royalists and outraged Roman Catholics to organize antigovernmental revolts, enemy forces to destroy or menace the French armies, which, justified or not, had marched into alien territories (Avignon, for example, was made a part of France in response to a "popular" demand, not without violence), the unemployed and the poverty-stricken to rise in Paris, in provincial cities, and in the countryside, and the economic life of France to grind, haltingly, almost to a stop. It is of course possible to exaggerate the danger to the republic one and indivisible of these hostile elements, but France gained a reputation for violence, bloodshed, and anarchy in the years 1790–1794 that lent special force to the denunciations of Burke in 1790 and those of the Prussian Friedrich von Gentz in 1800. In the first half of the 1790's France offered to the impartial observer an extraordinary mélange of murders and virtuous civic celebrations.

Order was to come with the creation of a novel political body, the "great" Committee of Public Safety, theoretically one of the committees erected by the Constituent Assembly but in fact, with the aid of the Paris Commune, the master for a good many months of that convention and of all its other committees. From the execution of the king in January 1793 to the guillotining of Robespierre, Couthon, Saint-Just, and others in July 1794 (the beginning of the conservative or Thermidorean reaction), twelve men, working without a chairman, without any formal agenda, with a pragmatical rather than a specific assignment of particular duties, not only held France together but also repulsed its enemies and increased the territory of France. It cannot be said of the "great" Committee that it followed the Declaration of the Rights of Man. It cannot be said of them that they were at all points just. They toiled, however, eight, ten, twelve, fourteen, and even sixteen hours a day. No American efficiency expert could possibly approve their expertise, or if one prefers, their lack of business management, but they learned on the job. Pragmatism, not theory, was their lodestar. They saved France. They suppressed, however bloodily, local revolts, they reanimated, supplied, and applauded the armies, they executed their opponents by batches, they created and maintained the revolutionary tribunals, and one of them, Robespierre, attempted to replace God by a Supreme Being. When at length their terrified enemies reached the conclusion: "It is they or us," they went, or many of them went, to the guillotine during one of the more execrable nights and mornings of the French revolution. Nobody has ever pretended that members of the Committee of Public Safety were a lovable lot. But they created during a terrible year a terrible government, and if, after their fall from power, their successors also put down royalist revolts, instituted the "White Terror," and gave France still another constitution — that of the year III (1795), which created the Directorate, permitted Bonaparte to rise to eminence, and reached a more or less inglorious end in the constitution of the year VIII (1799) — these changes followed the lines laid down by the terrible Committee.

The world has seldom seen a greater discrepancy between the philosophy of a republic and the facts of political life than that developed in France from 1793 to 1794. The names of the chief members of this extraordinary body deserved to be remembered: Barère, wily and supple, known for some odd reason as the

Anacreon of the guillotine; Billaud-Varenne, logical, cruel, essentially inhuman; Carnot, the great "organizer of victory," who saw to it that the revolutionary armies got what they needed when they needed it; Collot d'Herbois, whom it is impossible to admire; the paralytic Georges Couthon; Hérault de Séchelles; Robert Lindet, essentially a bourgeois; Claude-Antoine Prieur-Duvernois, known as Prieur de la Côte-d'Or; Pierre-Louis Pierre, known as Prieur de la Marne; André Jeanbon Saint-André, the only Protestant in the group; Louis-Antoine Saint-Just, the inexorable "Angel of Death"; and, best known of all, Maximilien Robespierre, the most enigmatic character in the whole history of the French revolution. These men were inexorable with a clear, geometrical French logic; they were pragmatic after the fashion of the British; they were, so to speak, both idealistic and "practical" after the manner of the Americans. They were frugal, devoted, tyrannical. But whatever they might be, the long shadow of what they accomplished extended as far as the Congress of Vienna, and, after the debacle of the Napoleonic adventure, preserved France as one of the great powers in Europe.

Four principal measures by which the Committee of Public Safety ruled France were these. In the first place, they induced the Assembly to declare in October 1793 that the emergency was so great that the constitution of that year, overwhelmingly ratified by such Frenchmen as could vote, was suspended pro tempore and that the government of France was to be revolutionary until the peace. In the second place, profiting from the errors of an earlier committee and determined to wipe out "parliamentary" opposition, they secured the assent of the Assembly or its "judicial" representatives to the political murder of leaders of the opposition — for example, members of the Gironde and, after that, the principals of the Hébertist faction of the left, and Danton, Camille Desmoulins, and other leaders of the center. The aim of the Committee was in fact the creation of a one-party state. In the third place, they strengthened a mode of control they had not invented but used, that of the deputies on mission. Theoretically these representatives reported to the Assembly; in fact they were agents of the Committee of Public Safety until the death of Robespierre. Sometimes these agents were granted wide, dictatorial powers; sometimes their assignments were specific and limited. They were sent to rebellious cities, where they often put down dissent by legal massacre; they were sent to the armies, where they got rid of weak officers and of officers suspected of treason to the state, but they also saw to it that the armies were properly armed and provisioned. Some of these representatives on mission were crooks, but most of them displayed an almost fanatical zeal for the republic and made themselves both feared and respected. The contemporary equivalent would seem to be the Russian commissar sent to "advise" the commander of a Russian army. The fourth mode of control was the Terror: what Robespierre called "the despotism of liberty." The Terror included, of course, intimidation and the swift judicial murder of anybody opposed to the revolutionary government or even suspected to be so opposed. Of 1793–1794 it is estimated that about 40,000 men, women, and occasionally children were guillotined and about 300,000 jailed. The Terror also included seizing goods for the army; compelling workers to produce, and executing generals who had failed to win a battle. Intimidation and cruelty, however, grow by what they feed on; the Terror aroused the anger of property owners, failed to provide properly for the peasantry, offered convenient opportunity for bribery and corruption, and horrified both the rest of Europe and many Frenchmen, even if it produced the most formidable armies on the Continent. Moderates in the Assembly, fearful of their own lives, therefore combined to overthrow Robespierre and his chief associates. The moderates returned the revolution to its original course, carrying out their own Terror for a while but also closing the Jacobin clubs, readmitting what was left of the Girondins to the Assembly, reintroducing, though without total success, economic liberalism, and drawing up a new constitution, which created the Directory, to replace the constitution the Committee of Public Safety had caused to be suspended.

Robespierre, the virtuous, the incorruptible, by one of these swift transformations of public opinion that characterize the French revolution, now became a tyrant whom only the immortal spirit of liberty could defeat, a usurper worse, far worse as a despot than Louis XVI, a bloodthirsty monster made up of suspicion, cruelty, tyranny, and egotism. The day before his arrest, a member of the Committee of General Security, according to Barère, shouted at Robespierre: "You are a triumvirate of scoundrels — Robespierre, Couthon, and Saint-Just — conspiring against the country." On the day of his arrest Billaud-Varenne (of all people!) accused Robespierre of plotting against his country, cries of "Down with the tyrant!" were heard from all parts of the Assembly, Robespierre was accused of playing God, and somebody shouted, "He is being choked by the blood of Danton!" That evening Robespierre apparently tried to kill himself (or was he shot by an outraged guardsman?), and when, unconscious from his wound, he was borne on a stretcher to the hall of the Convention, that congress refused to receive him on the ground that the body of a tyrant would infect the whole meeting with pestilence. On July 27, 1794, Robespierre, Saint-Just, Couthon the cripple, and some twenty others were guillotined for the safety of the republic they had saved.

Life in France from 1794 to 1799 offers on the whole fewer melodramatic incidents than does life from 1789 to 1794. In an unfavorable point of view the Directory depended more and more upon military prowess and less and less on popular suffrage in its struggle to retain power. Moreover, it seems to have been more riddled by corruption than any previous revolutionary government. It winked at individual street brawls when the victims were its own opponents (these were the years of the *jeunesse dorée*, fashionably dressed young men who went about armed with cudgels to keep down "radicals" and the proletariat), and it subdued popular insurrections by armed force. The frenzied financial history of France in the decade created a class of *nouveaux riches* in place of the old nobility, and a hysterical reaction against the years of the Committee of Public Safety permitted the development of a new paganism in which costume and spending became important. Men wore the incredible costumes of the *incroyables*, women attired themselves in clothing they fondly believed to be Greek — the so-called *style Directoire*. The *style Directoire* also modified furniture, wall decoration, restaurants, the theaters, and music: ancient republican Roman virtue yielded to the softer seductions of Hellenism. Wealth and gaiety were everything, morality a more doubtful quality. In these years Madame de Staël, Madame Tallien, Josephine de Beauharnais, later the wife of Napoleon, and others of more doubtful virtue held salons, and a fashionable mode of entertainment was to attend a "bal des victimes." In order to be eligible one must count a victim of the guillotine among one's family. Gambling returned as a fashionable amusement, and visible wealth, palpable luxury, blatant sexuality smothered all denunciation. Far from these corruptions, however, ragged French armies under young Napoleon were conquering Italy and Egypt.

In a more favorable view the period of the Directory consolidated many of the gains of the revolution. The economy, the finances, and, oddly enough, the central government of France grew more and more acceptable, even to the very poor. The arts, particularly the art of music, were, if not revived, then at least revivified in the decade following the revolution. Cherubini, whom Beethoven regarded as the greatest of his musical contemporaries, settled in Paris in 1788; his *Lodoïska* (1791) and his *Médée* (1797), both of which are still in the repertory of opera, have their revolutionary overtones. Revolutionary and republican fêtes required music, and one finds d'Alayrac composing (or adapting) the *Carmagnole* and *Ça ira* from old tunes to new purposes. The "citoyen Gossec," supposed in his day to be a remarkable composer, wrote revolutionary songs and was a professor at the Conservatoire after 1795. Grétry produced a *Guillaume Tell* in 1791, Boïeldieu his *Le Calife de Bagdad* in 1800, Méhul, sometimes regarded as the artistic heir of Gluck, his *Euphrosine et Coradin* in 1790. "Civic" music was in demand; more important, the French revolution gave an impetus to the composition of "rescue" operas, of which Beethoven's *Fidelio* (1805) is now the best known, a composition which, in the words of one historian is "perfectly suited to the expression of Beethoven's passionate belief in the ideals of liberty and the universal power of human love." The libretto goes back to an inferior work performed in Paris in 1798.* There is, possibly, no such thing as revolutionary music in the 1790's, but there is small doubt that the general ideals of the French revolution radically affected

---

* It is of course notable that Beethoven's *Eroica* expresses his enthusiasm for liberty; and the last movement of the Ninth Symphony takes over Schiller's "An die Freude," that celebration of universal brotherhood:

> Seid umschlungen, Millionen!
> Diesen Kuss der ganzen Welt!
> Brüder — überm Sternenzelt
> Muss ein lieber Vater wohnen.

(Be embraced, ye many millions! / Take this universal kiss! / Brothers, o'er the starry heavens / There a loving father dwells.)

the development of music later in the nineteenth century. Bellini's *Norma*, for example, is a tale of subject people under Roman tyranny, his *I Puritani* is a story of the English civil wars, and most of Verdi's operas from his early and middle periods celebrate a virtuous hero wronged by the aristocracy.*

If the history of France produces few colorful personalities, Bonaparte aside, from 1794 to 1799, the period is nonetheless one of profound importance in European history. It was an era of intrigue, of corruption, of cynicism, but it was also a period of consolidation. Ideas theoretically justified by revolutionary philosophies were at a discount; for example, Babeuf and his equally radical colleague, Darthé, were guillotined May 27, 1797, two deaths that ended utopianism (the "conjuration des égaux"), and, whatever the intrigues and the conspiracies in upper political circles, the threat of another populist upheaval was ended. There were, it is true, the royalists; there was, it is also true, the financial crisis of 1795–1796; there were, as we have seen, various *coups d'état*. Nevertheless both industrial and commercial life slowly improved (there was even an industrial exposition in 1798 at Paris); scientific discoveries, often based on industrial needs (for example, in chemistry), were being made; there was a religious revival, so that in 1796 General Clarke could declare, "Our revolution once lacked a religion; now Roman Catholicism has returned to France," as the severe regulations of the civil constitution of the clergy were insensibly relaxed; and, bit by bit, the concept of national sovereignty rather than of departmental (or provincial) autonomy gained ground. In their study of the period from 1789 to 1848, MM. A. J. Tudesq and J. Rudel quote from an oration of Edouard Herriot delivered in May 1939 in which he described the spirit of the 1790's as follows:

La nouvelle organisation du pays fait surgir un véritable esprit national en créant les départements. . . . Du même coup apparaît, substituée à la notion antérieure de loyalisme et de fidélité, cette passion qui anime toute la masse immense. Le patriotisme, sous sa forme nouvelle, est

* Not only do many of Verdi's musical heroes (for example, Manfred in *Il Trovatore* and Ernani in the opera of that name) represent humanity outlawed or outraged by tyrants, but the letters V.E.R.D.I., scratched or painted on a wall in an Italian city under the Austrian yoke or that of some other "tyrant," were understood to mean "Vittorio Emanuele, Re d'Italia" and therefore became a piece of effective propaganda for Italian unity. See also *Don Carlo* (1867).

né; il sera le plus beau, le plus pur, le plus constant des sentiments révolutionnaires.*

France was getting ready for Napoleon, but despite the atrocities, the duplicities, the bloodshed, the cruelty, the treasons, the egotisms of the revolution, France had not forgotten and was not to forget the basic principles of the Declaration of the Rights of Man and of the Citizen.

* The new organization of the country creates a genuinely national spirit by establishing the Departments. . . . At the same time, in place of the older notion of obedient loyalty, there emerges this passion that moves the entire people: patriotism, in its new form, is born. It will be the most beautiful, purest, and most lasting of revolutionary emotions.

XI

Revolution, Classicism, Reaction

Of necessity the narrative of the French revolution just given is superficial. It makes no attempt to analyze either the profound psychological puzzle of the revolution as a whole or the scarcely less profound puzzles of some of the principal participants, who range from dedicated idealists to cynics of all kinds. One obvious problem, for example, is the need to understand the emotional drives, however sluggish, and the emotional blockages, however inconsistent, of a king whose intentions were usually good and whose conduct was almost invariably indecisive. What is one to make of a personality such as that of Talleyrand, who, like the Abbé Siéyès, managed to survive both the revolution and its aftermath, who was frequently shrewd and far-sighted, but with whom the first question seemed ever to be: what is there in this for me? Who comprehends the labyrinthine mind and soul of Robespierre, at once self-centered and idealistic, cautious and fanatical, an egotist of virtually Machiavellian deviousness and a dreamer who tried to substitute the cult of a Supreme Being (a projection of Robespierre?) for the Roman Catholic religion?

Little has been said, or can be said here, of the complex economic life of France, a problem summed up in a pithy statement by the great historian Mathiez, when he declared that the revolution was not so much a break in the history of an exhausted nation as one in the history of a nation moving forward on the tide of progress. Unfortunately progress was not uniform: the economic life of

France in 1787 was a queer compound of modernity and medievalism. Clever persons, the *nouveaux riches*, notably after 1795, were to replace or overshadow the old aristocracy as a political force in a period when unemployment in the cities was a problem and famine still threatened parts of the countryside. One must also face the curious paradox of the image of a king who was, or was supposed to be, the father of his people, faced as early as 1788 with movements of rebellion in Béarn and Dauphiné to make these provinces virtually independent of the royal government. The nobility were never a single-minded class. The bourgeoisie, however defined, wanted change but were never quite sure what change they wanted or where change should be stopped; yet, just as they wanted peace and safety in the streets, so they wanted a sound currency and freedom of commerce. The urban proletariat in Paris and lesser cities were, in the early phases of the revolution, simultaneously devoted to a king they scarcely knew, antagonistic to a court that scarcely knew them, and torn between outbursts of violence and celebrations of peace and progress.

Equally neglected has been the irregular, even anarchical, situation of internal administration. After the dethronement and execution of the king, what we would now call the civil service, both provincial (departmental) and urban, did not automatically turn to the Assembly as its director. Older administrators of the lesser sort were bewildered by the change and kept to their customary ways, nor was it possible to replace these thousands by revolutionaries untrained and unfamiliar with local situations. Moreover, the people were in many instances used to the "regular" officialdom and kept to their wonted habits. The petty court, the local constabulary, the supervisor in this or that area of roads and bridges — these were familiar figures, and the *petite bourgeoisie*, the conservative peasantry went to them rather than to new men from force of habit. What power did raw officials just sent down from Paris really have? What did they know? For a good many weeks after Louis XVI was dethroned, it may be said there were two conflicting administrative systems in most of France, neither one working fully and neither quite sure either of its own responsibility or of the response it was going to get from newly made *citoyens*.

The revolution may be said to have adopted the party system without any knowledge of the operation of a party, and tried out parliamentary government without parliamentary responsibility. After 1794, of course, parliamentary government and republican theory were more honored in the breach than in the observance. Nor did France during the revolutionary decade ever solve a central political issue brought into existence by the execution of the king: where does sovereignty lie? With the people, cried the radicals, but who were the people? All French males, or only those French males who satisfied the categories set up for "active" citizens? Voting became more and more lackadaisical; and the history of the Directory is a series of violent jerks from one *coup d'état* to another until Bonaparte ended uncertainty by a military dictatorship which turned into an ephemeral empire.

Equally difficult was the international problem. France lay at the center of Europe and, except on the sea, was the most powerful nation in the Western world. Among other European powers there was satisfaction in seeing France broken by inward turmoil, but by 1793 it appeared that inward turmoil had ended by vastly increasing the military power of France. The Bourbons had played the game of family alliances, open alliances, and secret treaties according to the rules of eighteenth-century diplomatic chess, but the revolutionaries seemed wholly unpredictable. Could you trust men who in their foreign policy usually contradicted themselves? And how far could one believe the fine phrases of groups of émigrés clustering here and there on the borders of the French kingdom? What statesman could prophesy the future of France, or of a Europe with an unpredictable republic at its center?

Whatever one's opinions or prophecies, whether they were those of Thomas Jefferson, or the younger Pitt, or Anacharsis Clootz, or the king of Prussia, or Thomas Paine, or Friedrich von Gentz, one thing seems clear: the French revolution was the most audible revolution in history. Nothing could be done without a fine flow of words — a proclamation, a decree, an oration, a new constitution, a denunciation, an emotional appeal to glittering terms such as "the rights of man." Pamphlets and journals sprang up like weeds. It is true that France did not invent political propaganda and that the American revolution produced its quota of patriotic songs, rhymed satires, declarations, and great speeches. But the French multiplied and enriched these political devices to a degree beyond anything that had yet appeared in European history. In an illuminating study, *The Spirit of Revolution in 1789* (1949), Cornell B. Rogers has brought together and analyzed popular songs in Paris and the provinces for this crucial year, finding in their lines, usually uninspired as style but revealing as document, not merely the alleged ideals of the first phase of the revolution but expressions of its emotional drive.

Such songs did not disappear in 1790, not even when a "paternal" king was adjudged to be a traitor and a tyrant and Frenchmen came to regard themselves not as royal subjects but as champions of the entire human race. Pamphlets multiplied, cartoons increased, periodicals were born and died, poems were written, spoken, and read, and the theaters were required to celebrate republican virtue and dramatize tyranny and its overthrow. In addition to political plays, domestic dramas of sentiment and satiric or patriotic vaudeville filled the stage. The monotony of a few recurring themes makes difficult the task of any literary historian of France, who, once he is past André Chénier, the early work of Chateaubriand, *Paul et Virginie*, Madame de Staël, and a few others, finds that the really compelling "literature" in the revolutionary decade is oratorical. By and by, of course, censorship was to subdue all writing to such a degree that in his classic six-volume *Main Currents of Nineteenth Century Literature* Georg Brandes, greatest of Danish critics, had to devote a whole volume to French authors in exile.

A new vocabulary, or at least the reinvigoration of an old one, carried immense emotional overtones.* The political club was not an invention of the French, but revolutionary France turned political clubs into endless debating societies, unending contests alike of ideas and of emotions. The various assemblies — National, Constituent, Legislative — were too large for genuine discussion, but they could be swayed by oratory, and orators accordingly appeared — and, it should be added, disappeared — under the Direc-

---

* "Vue 'd'en haut,' à travers les débats de l'Assemblée et des clubs, les décrets, la correspondance officielle, elle [the period of 1792–1793] paraît suivre une route droite, protégée des déviations et du hasard. L'histoire convenue nous entretient des rivalités politiques, des factions, des journées. Elle leur accorde trop de gros titres; aux ténors, aux leaders, trop de gros plans; aux idées trop d'espace, comme si l'écrit suffisait à engendrer l'action, comme s'il convenait d'ignorer l'ignorant. Par elle, les légendes conservent encore leur pouvoir sentimental; notamment celles des 'buveurs de sang' et des 'héros en guenilles.' " Marc Bouloiseau, *La République jacobine: 10 août 1792 — 9 Thermidor an II*, Paris, 1972, p. 7.

tory, the Consulate, and the Empire. Orators in large assemblies engaged in factional disputes commonly employ words not so much to conceal thought as to energize emotion, and at the clubs, in the assemblies, at the Palais Royal, or on the streets orators attempted to sway the masses; an example is Camille Desmoulins in the court of the Palais Royal in July 1789, after the dismissal of Necker and the rumor that the king was concentrating "foreign" regiments on Paris, calling the people to arms so efficiently that the mob stormed Les Invalides and then the Bastille in search of muskets and powder.* Certain words and phrases took on new, rich emotional overtones: "la patrie," "citoyens," "tyrannie," "la république," "sécurité," "liberté, égalité, fraternité," "la patrie en danger," and so on. The list is endless. Editors of journals and writers of pamphlets manipulated this new vocabulary, whether on the relatively low level of Hébert's *Le Père Duchesne*, which exploited the language of the people, as in

Il est arrivé . . . C'est maintenant, foutre, que vous allez recevoir le prix de votre salaire, foutus grédins de '89, faux patriotes qui n'êtes ni chair ni poisson. Gare la lanterne, vous tous Jean-foutres des Comités qui avez trafiqué de votre conscience et de la liberté de la nation avec le pouvoir exécutif. Votre jour approche. C'est contre vous que des milliers des voix s'élèvent et vous crient: 'Foutez-nous le camp' †

or in the elegant, if ineffectual, diction of a Roland declaring that he presented himself to his contemporaries as to posterity with his works, which "speak for me." Perhaps a median is represented by Robespierre, who like Hébert addressed himself to the people and to "l'amour de la patrie" but whose language seems to descend from the *philosophes*, as in "C'est dans la vertu et dans la souveraineté du peuple qu'il faut chercher un préservatif contre les vices et le despotisme du gouvernement." ‡

The extraordinary volubility, the extraordinary verbal dynamism of the revolution anticipates the verbal fecundity of writers to

---

* "Les mercenaires allemands sont rassemblés au Champ de Mars pour tomber ce soir sur les citoyens de Paris! Armez-vous!" Note the term *citoyens*.

† The time has come . . . It's now, by cock, that you are going to get paid off, you lousy scum of '89, false patriots, neither fish nor fowl. Watch out for your necks, all you bloody slobs of the Committees who sold out your conscience and the liberty of the country to the Executive. Your day is about here. It's you that thousands of voices are raised against, shouting at you: "Fuck off!"

‡ It is in the strength and the sovereignty of the people that we must find protection against the vices and despotism of the government.

come, such as Balzac and Hugo. The standard phrases of the Enlightenment were now being multiplied and poured forth by men who lacked the delicate irony of the eighteenth century and who sought to impose upon their auditors or their readers or the nation as a whole not merely the new emotional coloring but also the personalized force of the writer, the editor, or the orator.* The vocabulary of "humanity" was indeed noble; those who used it for political purposes in the later phases of the revolution were nevertheless romantic egotists as often as they were idealists — not that the two traits are incompatible. They resemble those great romantic egotists in music, in the fine arts, in poetry, and on the stage who assert themselves to be sublime leaders or sublime sufferers. Their power was increased by the remarkable fusion of currents of sensibility with currents of revolution. If in 1789 the king was still a father image, once he was dethroned and executed, remnants of a thirst for paternalism survived: the Marseillaise begins, "Enfants de la patrie," but the children are children not of a father but of a fatherland, unless, indeed, one wants to consider Hébert's *Le Père Duchesne* a substitute for the king. The cult of Rousseau *romancier*, the Rousseau of sensibility rather than the man of politics, enriched emotional drives in favor of love, of the family, and of the common man. Note the title of Marat's influential journal, *L'Ami du peuple*. Minor writers during the revolution sometimes exhibit sensibility to a marked degree; for example, the novels of Madame Cottin and of that exigent, if progressive, educator, Madame de Genlis, who introduced magic lanterns into the classrooms, whose "théâtre d'éducation" for young people included *Les Annales de la vertu* (1781), and who fled to Switzerland after the fall of the Girondins.†

* The habit of speaking in generalizations, often necessary in the eighteenth century to avoid censorship, was one of the most fateful legacies of the Enlightenment to revolutions. This is what Burke saw when in the famous *Reflections* he pointed out how great was the gap between these noble and even incontrovertible terms and the realities of the life of France. Consider as a lone example the flagrant misuse of "traitors."

† For one reason or another not merely the wilds of America but also the wilds of Siberia became acceptable settings for sentiment and adventure; witness Madame Cottin's *Elisabeth, ou les exilés de Sibérie* (1806) and Xavier de Maistre's *La Jeune Sibérienne* (1825). Xavier de Maistre was the brother of Joseph de Maistre and like him spent most of his life out of France. Imprisoned at Turin, he wrote his *Voyage autour de ma chambre* (1794), something of a sentimental tour de force, the title of which, at least, lingers in the history books. He combined authorship, painting, adventure, and military service in Italy and in Russia. In the Russian service he rose to the rank of major-general.

Leaders in the revolution come along in three waves. The third of the waves, that of the Directory, need not here concern us, since, profiting by the fate of many of their predecessors, they grew more cautious and, in the opinion of some historians, corrupt. In the first period (1787–1792), from the first meeting of the Notables to the fall of royalty, leaders are for the most part still men of the eighteenth century, personages in whom rationalism on the whole really governs the passions, leaders who move with caution, who announce general propositions but make practical compromises, and who, in the main, keep their voices down. The symbol of this phase is the transfer of the ashes of Voltaire to the Panthéon on June 11, 1791. But the king's flight and capture, the massacre of the Champ de Mars, and the Declaration of Pillnitz, crucial events in French history from June into August 1792, put an end not merely to monarchy but also to the fine art of political compromise. Another type of man appears, anticipated by Mirabeau, the revolutionary leader, to whom the world is either black or white, men are either patriots or traitors, and opponents must either submit or die. The center of this phase is the Committee of Public Safety. The names one associates with this stage are such as Marat, Hébert, Danton, Robespierre, Billaud-Varenne, Collot d'Herbois, and Saint-Just, the latter characterized by R. R. Palmer as "an idea energized by a passion." Such men possess not so much the rational ego as the romantic *moi*, not that all romantics were necessarily revolutionary leaders. Their language expresses not what is possible but what is terrible, passionate, and overwhelming.

Let us examine some of these rhetoricians. Their declamatory style is sometimes no more than rodomontade, but the rodomontade is frequently keyed to the first-person pronoun and announces highly personalized views of men and events or of despotism and freedom, comparable to the passionate rhetoric of some of Posa's speeches in Schiller's *Don Carlos*, to the unconditional abuse or praise one finds in Shelley, or to the tirades in Victor Hugo. Hébert was a professional vulgarian and a demagogue, and we have already looked at a characteristic passage from *Le Père Duchesne*. Marat is, however, another matter. Whether one regards him as a charlatan and a demagogue or whether one takes the view that he was a man of considerable talent who unfortunately combined chicanery with a sound scientific spirit — and both interpretations have been strongly advocated — he is, says Loomis, the incarnation of demonic energy, a spirit of elemental fury, despising rational theorists and obsessed with the idea of rooting out "traitors," whom he and he alone is capable of identifying without recourse to evidence or legal procedure. He cried out for a popular dictatorship, for the equivalent of an inspired leader of the type the visionary Shelley pictured in *Laon and Cythna* (*The Revolt of Islam*), *Prometheus Unbound*, and for that matter, *Hellas*, wherein

> The world's great age begins anew,
>   The golden years return,
> The earth doth like a snake renew
>   Her winter weeds outworn:
> Heaven smiles, and faiths and empires gleam,
> Like wrecks of a dissolving dream.

But let us hear Marat himself. He thought the deputies of the National Assembly were base servitors of the court, who deserved to be stoned, hanged, burned, impaled, and buried under the ruins of the hall they met in. He described Lafayette as a hypocritical fiend, Louis XVI as a treacherous dissembler, whereas I, he said, am the most humane of men (*le plus humain des hommes*). This is, however, paraphrase; let us listen to Marat directly — for example, in *La Constitution, ou projet de Déclaration des droits de l'homme et du citoyen, suivi d'un plan de constitution juste, sage, et libre*:

J'abhorre la license, les violences, le dérèglement; mais quand je pense qu'il est actuellement dans le royaume quinze millions d'hommes qui languissent de misère, qui sont prêts à périr de faim; quand je pense qu'après les avoir réduites à ce sort affreux, le gouvernement les abandonne sans pitié, traite en scélérats ceux qui s'attroupent, et les poursuit comme des bêtes fêroces; quand je pense que les municipalités ne leur présentent un morceau de pain que dans la crainte d'en être dévorées; quand je pense qu'aucune voix ne s'est élevée en leur faveur, ni dans les cercles, ni dans les districts ni dans les communes, ni dans l'Assemblée nationale, mon coeur se serre de douleur et se révolte d'indignation. Je connais tous les dangers auxquels je m'expose en plaidant avec feu la cause de ces infortunés, mais . . . j'ai renoncé plus d'une fois au soin de mes jours; pour venger l'humanité, je verserai s'il le faut jusqu'à la dernière goutte de mon sang.*

Or again:

O Français! peuple libre et frivole, ne pressentirez-vous donc jamais les

* I abhor license, violence, disorder; but when I think that right now fifteen million men are suffering from poverty in this kingdom and about to die of

malheurs qui vous menacent, vous endormirez-vous donc toujours sur le bord de l'abîme? . . . Peuple inconsideré, livrez-vous à la joie, courez dans les temples, faites retentir les airs de vos chants de triomphe et fatiguez le Ciel de vos actions de grâces pour un bien dont vous ne jouissez pas . . . Vos ateliers sont déserts, vos manufactures abandonnées, votre commerce est dans la stagnation, vos finances sont ruinées, vos troupes sont débandées; vous vivez dans l'anarchie et, pour surcroît de calamité, c'est en vain que le Ciel vous a ouvert les trésors de fécondité. Vous n'avez échappé aux horreurs de la famine que pour éprouver la disette, au sein même de l'abondance. . . . une Nation sans lumières, sans moeurs, sans vertus, n'est pas faite pour la liberté. . . . Insensés que nous sommes . . . ah! sortons, sortons de notre fatale sécurité. *Jamais la machine politique ne se remonte que par des secousses violentes, comme les airs ne se purifient que par des orages.* Rassemblons-nous donc sur les places publiques, et avisons aux moyens de sauver l'Etat.*

This language ranges between that of an Old Testament prophet and that of a French Patrick Henry; the important characteristic is that if one were to judge by these passages alone (there are many like them), only Marat was awake to the misery and the peril of

hunger; when I think that having reduced them to this dreadful state the government is abandoning them without mercy, treating as criminals those who come in bands, and chasing them down like wild beasts; when I think that the cities give them a crust only out of fear of being devoured by them; when I think that no voice speaks out for them in the clubs, the districts, the communes, or the National Assembly, my heart is wrung by sorrow and rises in indignation. I know all the risks I run by pleading the cause of these wretches so hotly, but . . . more than once I have left my life unprotected; to avenge humanity I will give every drop of my blood if that is what it takes.

* O free, frivolous French people! Won't you ever foresee the troubles that hang over you? Will you always go to sleep on the edge of the abyss? . . . Thoughtless people, give way to joy, rush to the temples, let the air resound with your songs of triumph and deafen heaven with your thanksgiving for a blessing you do not have . . . Your shops are empty, your factories are abandoned, your business has stagnated, your treasury is bankrupt, your troops are dispersed; you live in anarchy, and to make calamity complete you have wasted the gift heaven gave you, the fertility of the earth. You have escaped the horrors of famine only to go through shortages in the very bosom of plenty. . . . a nation without enlightenment, ill-behaved, devoid of virtue, is not made to be free. . . . Madmen that we are . . . Let us, I say, let us break out of our false security. *The machinery of state can be set in motion again only by violent shocks, just as the air is purified only by storms.* Let us gather in the open streets and take counsel on a means to save the state.

The second paragraph is from *L'Ami du peuple*, September 18, 1789, and I find this, together with the other extract, in Jean Massin's admirable *Marat*, Paris, 1970, pp. 89–90 and 99. I think this work was first published in 1960. Almost any book on Marat will yield similar passages. *L'Elite de la Révolution*, published in Paris, 1908–1914, is a collection of writings by Saint-Just, Robespierre, Marat, Mirabeau, and others.

his countrymen. He, and he only, is touched by their poverty, famine, lack of work under a selfish government in a nation without virtue; he, and he only, has seen the deserted factories, commerce stagnating, an army in disorder, disaster at hand, anarchy around the corner. But to save mankind he will surpass Prometheus and shed the last drop of his blood. Note also the exaggerations ("les municipalités ne leur présentent un morceau de pain que dans la crainte d'en être dévorées") and the loose assertion of generalities of violence; for example, the statement that the political machine cannot be made to work except by violent shocks (*secousses violentes*), just as the air can be purified only by a storm. Here is the vision of a seer in the phraseology of a demagogue. There is a kind of perfection of ferocity in this style.

Marat was the most melodramatic of journalists, but if one turns to the leading orator of the Girondins, Vergniaud, one finds the same self-righteousness, the same gloomy splendor, the same emotionalized vocabulary. Thus on July 3, 1792, in the Assembly, Vergniaud attacked the king almost as if he were exposing Iago:

Le roi a refusé sa sanction à votre décret sur les troubles religieux. Je ne sais si le sombre génie de Médicis et du cardinal de Lorraine erre encore sous les voûtes du palais des Tuileries; si l'hypocrisie sanguinaire des jésuits Lachaise et Letellier revit dans l'âme de quelques scélérats, brûlant de voir se renouveler la Saint-Barthélemy et les Dragonnades; * je ne sais si le coeur du roi est troublé par les idées fantastiques qu'on lui suggère, et sa conscience égarée par les terreurs religieuses dont on l'environne. Mais il n'est pas permis de croire, sans lui faire injure et l'accuser d'être l'ennemi le plus dangereux de la Révolution, qu'il veuille encourager par l'impunité les tentatives criminelles de l'ambition pontificale, et rendre aux orgueilleux suppôts de la tiare la puissance désastreuse dont ils ont également opprimé les peuples et les rois: il n'est pas permis de croire, sans lui faire injure et l'accuser d'être l'ennemi du peuple, qu'il approuve ou même qu'il voit avec indifférence les manoeuvres sourdes employées pour diviser les citoyens, jeter les ferments dans la sein des familles, et étouffer au nom de la divinité les sentiments les plus doux dont elle a composé la félicité des hommes †

* The massacre of St. Bartholomew is familiar. François de la Chaise (1624–1709), father confessor to Louis XIV, is thought to have been influential in inducing that monarch to revoke the Edict of Nantes and thus terminate religious toleration in France for the Huguenots. Michel Le Tellier (1603–1685), chancellor of France, likewise influenced the king in this particular. The "Dragonnades" refers to this same religious persecution. Bodies of dragoons were quartered on Protestants in France and allowed to commit all sorts of brutalities and indignities.

† The King has refused to approve your decree on religious disturbances. I don't know whether the somber shade of Medicis and of the Cardinal de Lorraine still

— with a long string of other matters one is not "permitted to believe," including the possibility of a civil war. Vergniaud ends by declaring that he respects the constitution and the king, but "je déchire le bandeau que l'intrigue et l'adulation ont mis sur ses yeux et . . . je lui montre le terme où ses perfides amis s'afforcent de la conduire." * Here is the technique of Antony's oration over the body of Caesar, and, like Antony, Vergniaud is the only man who sees the truth and has courage to expose hypocrisy and save the state. The passage is filled with appeal and grandeur. It is also the expression of a powerful personal emotion, and its vocabulary of menace is self-evident.

In March 1793, demanding that the Assembly create the famous (or infamous) revolutionary tribunal, Danton spoke with fewer historical allusions but with like ardor and equal egotism:

Je demande donc que le tribunal révolutionnaire soit organisé séance tenante; que le pouvoir exécutif, dans la nouvelle organisation, reçoive les moyens d'action et d'énergie qui lui sont nécessaires. Je ne demande pas que rien ne soit desorganisé, je ne propose que des moyens d'amélioration. Je demande que la Convention juge mes raisonnements et méprise les qualifications injurieuses et flétrissantes qu'on ose me donner. Je demande qu'aussitôt que les mesures de sûreté générale seront prises, vos commissaires partent à l'instant; qu'on ne reproduise plus l'objection qu'ils siègent dans tel ou tel côté de cette salle. Qu'ils se répandent dans les départements, qu'ils y échauffent les citoyens, qu'ils y raniment l'amour de la liberté, et que, s'ils ont regret de ne pas participer à des

---

haunts the vaults of the Tuileries, whether the bloody hypocrisy of the Jesuits Lachaise and Letellier is alive again in the souls of a few rascals who are afire to see a renewal of Saint Bartholomew's Day and the Dragonnades; I don't know whether the heart of the king is disturbed by the fantastic ideas people suggest to him, or his conscience led astray by the religious terrors they surround him with. But it is unbelievable, short of insulting him and accusing him of being the revolution's most dangerous enemy, that he should want to encourage the criminal maneuvers of papal ambition by letting them go unpunished, and hand back to the arrogant flunkies of the papal crown the disastrous power they have used to oppress kings and countries alike; one cannot believe, without insulting him and accusing him of being an enemy of the people, that he approves, or even that he is indifferent to, the underhanded tricks used to divide citizens, stir ferment in the bosom of families, and stifle in the name of God the sweetest of the emotions that make up the happiness of men.

I find this in Albert Chabrier's anthology, *Les Orateurs politiques de la France des origines à 1830*, Paris, 1898, pp. 289–294, 297. Applauded on another occasion, Vergniaud demanded silence: "Respectez mon enthousiasme: c'est celui de la liberté!" The selection from Danton in the text, which shortly follows, is also in Chabrier, p. 333.

* I tear off the blindfold that plotting and adulation have put over his eyes and . . . I show him the end to which his treacherous friends are doing their best to lead him.

décrets utiles, ou de ne pouvoir s'opposer à des décrets mauvais, ils se souviennent que leur absence a été le salut de la patrie.*

This is the same Danton who is famous for his "Il nous faut de l'audace, encore de l'audace, toujours de l'audace," and who, just before being guillotined, advised the executioner to show his head to the people — it will be worth seeing. Beyond this egotism can scarcely go.

Or can it? One comes back to the eternal riddle of Robespierre. Cold and cautious, a lonely thinker, at one time a modest lawyer, a man who sometimes smiled but seldom laughed, puritanical, absent-minded, he pursued an interior vision all his own of a perfect democracy. By prudence he slowly became a prominent figure in the Jacobin Club and in the Assembly, never advocating war, apparently favoring religious toleration (what else was the worship of the Supreme Being but a rite in which believers in any sort of God could join?); he was elected a member of the Committee of Public Safety in July 1793 and was guillotined in July 1794 as a tyrant, though all his years he protested he had followed only virtue. The Committee of which he was a member had taken to quarreling among themselves, and Robespierre was absent from its meetings in February because of illness, and inexplicably absent just before he was accused in the Assembly and condemned to be executed. Did he stay away from pride or bewilderment? Or did he picture himself as a superior being, above all factional disputes, who wanted merely to annihilate the "enemies of virtue" so that a pure republic could finally come into being? Certain it is that he was importantly involved in purge after purge of members of the Assembly — the Girondists, the Hébertists, the Dantonists — and it seems probable that he was planning another "last" purge just before his death, when from the tribune he denounced six traitorous

* So I ask that the revolutionary tribunal be set up here and now, and that the executive power, in the new organization, be given the means it requires to take energetic action. I do not ask that everything be completely reorganized; I merely propose some ways toward improvement. I ask that the Convention judge my arguments, and reject the insulting, wounding names people have dared call me. I ask that as soon as measures have been taken for the general safety your commissioners depart at once; let us not hear again the objection that they sit on one side or the other of this chamber. Let them spread out through the Departments, let them stir up the citizens, let them rekindle the love of liberty among them, and if they dislike losing the chance to write some useful decrees or to oppose some bad ones, let them remember that their absence has meant the salvation of the country.

deputies but refused to name them. Though the decree of 22 Prairial (June 10, 1794), which authorized revolutionary tribunals to put suspected persons to death without hearing evidence for the defense, was proposed by Couthon, it was widely felt to be the work of Robespierre, under which nobody, not even members of the Convention, could feel secure. When he last rose to speak to the Assembly he was shouted down by cries of "A bas le tyran!" and came to a miserable end as the chief victim of the Thermidorean reaction, which began July 26–27, 1794.

The enigma of Robespierre's personality is partially explained by what seems to be true; namely, that he was the only principal leader of France in the days of the Jacobin republic (August 10, 1792 — July 27, 1794) who belonged simultaneously to the world of the eighteenth century proper and to the emotionally lurid world of the Committee of Public Safety. His great report of 5 Nivôse An II (December 25, 1793) sets forth with clarity and logic the theory of despotic democracy, the state of Rousseau's *Du Contrat social* expanded and rationalized, a speech which, though it inevitably denounces Great Britain, Austria, Prussia, and "cinq années de trahisons et de tyrannie," also declares that "la fondation de la République française n'est point un jeu d'enfant," but that "la sagesse, autant que la puissance, présida à la création de l'univers," and a like wisdom must watch "sans cesse sur les destinées de la patrie." What is revolutionary France?

La fonction du gouvernement est de diriger les forces morales et physiques de la nation vers le but de son institution.

Le but du gouvernement constitutionnel est de conserver la République; celui du gouvernement révolutionnaire est de la fonder.

La Révolution est la guerre de la liberté contre ses ennemis: la Constitution est le régime de la liberté victorieuse et paisible.

Le gouvernement constitutionnel s'occupe principalement de la liberté civile: et le gouvernement révolutionnaire, de la liberté publique. Sous le régime constitutionnel, il suffit presque de protéger les individus contre l'abus de la puissance publique: sous le régime révolutionnaire, la puissance publique elle-même est obligée de se défendre contre toutes les factions qui l'attaquent.*

* The function of the government is to direct the moral and physical forces of the nation toward the goal it was created to serve. . . . The goal of constitutional government is to preserve the Republic; that of the revolutionary government

Voltaire could have admired these clear generalizations, this balanced and antithetical prose.

But there is another aspect to Robespierre, an aspect that links him to Hébert and Danton, whom he destroyed. This is evident in such passages as these:

C'est à l'impunité de Dumouriez, de Lafayette, de Custine, et de leurs complices, que les tyrans doivent leurs triomphes, et nous nos alarmes. . . . Je demande qu'on poursuive avec la plus grande activité l'exécution des mesures pour s'assurer des conspirations fomentées et des trames ourdies par le gouvernement anglais; . . . je demande que la France, les administrations, le gouvernement, les armées soient purgés des traîtres; que l'on s'occupe de punir les administrateurs rebelles, que le Tribunal révolutionnaire soit chargé de juger Custine sous 24 heures; qu'ensuite il poursuive sans relâche le procès des conspirateurs qui ont été mis en état d'accusation par un décret. [August 12, 1793]

Le Comité de salut public voit des trahisons au milieu d'une victoire. Il destitue un général encore investi de la confiance, et revêtu de l'éclat d'un triomphe apparent; et on lui fait un crime de son courage même! Il expulse les traîtres, et jette les yeux sur les officiers qui ont montré le plus de civisme; il les choisit après avoir consulté les représentants du peuple qui avaient des connaissances particulières sur le caractère de chacun d'eux. Cette opération demandait le secret pour avoir son plein succès: le salut de la patrie l'exigeait. [September 25, 1793]

Cependant leur délire atteste à-la-fois leurs espérances et leur désespoir. Ils espéroient jadis de réussir à affamer le peuple français: le peuple français vit encore, et il survivra à tous ses ennemis: sa subsistance a été assurée; et la nature, fidèle à la liberté, lui présente déja l'abondance. Quelle ressource leur reste-t-il donc? l'assassinat.

Ils espéroient d'exterminer la représentation nationale par la révolte soudoyée; et ils comptoient tellement sur le succès de cet attentat, qu'ils ne rougirent pas de l'annoncer d'avance à la face de l'Europe, et de l'avouer dans le parlement d'Angleterre. Ce projet a échoué. Que leur reste-t-il? l'assassinat.

There are four more paragraphs which reach their climax in

---

is to establish it. . . . Revolution is liberty at war against its enemies: the Constitution is the regime of liberty victorious and at peace. . . . The principal business of constitutional government is civil liberty; that of revolutionary government is public liberty. Under the constitutional regime it is almost enough to protect individuals against the abuse of public power; under the revolutionary regime, the public power, itself, must defend itself against all the factions that attack it.

"l'assassinat." The orator, like the others I have quoted, is a superior being, sorrowing for his own fate as Prometheus:

Quel homme sur la terre a jamais défendu impunément les droits de l'humanité? [May 26, 1794] *

Once more we are back in the mysterious, Gothic-novel world of veiled conspiracy, avowed traitors, assassins, and tyrants, in which a mysterious Titan, larger than life size, asserts his superior understanding of France and of the world. The atmosphere is compounded, so to speak, out of Volney's *Les Ruines, ou méditations sur les révolutions des empires* (1791) — Volney was thrown into jail by the Jacobins but was not guillotined — and Condorcet's *Esquisse d'un tableau historique des progrès de l'esprit humain*, to which I have several times referred. The personality is, again, alternately that of a martyr and a conqueror.

* The tyrants owe their triumphs, and we our woes, to the impunity of Dumouriez, Lafayette, Custine, and their allies. . . . I ask that measures of protection against the conspiracies and plots that the English government fomented and contrived be carried out with the greatest energy . . . I ask that France, the administrations, the government, the armies, be purged of traitors, that we get on with punishing rebellious administrators, that the Revolutionary Tribunal be directed to judge Custine within twenty-four hours; and that afterwards it prosecute without delay the cases of conspirators who have been accused under a decree. . . .
The Committee of Public Safety finds treason in the midst of victory. It breaks a general who enjoys our confidence and is in all the glory of a real triumph; and is blamed for having the courage to do it. It drives out the traitors and then starts looking at the officers who have showed the greatest civic virtue; it chose them after consulting the representatives of the people who had individual knowledge of the character of each. This operation required secrecy to be fully successful; the safety of the country demanded it. . . .
Yet their delirium reveals at once their hope and their despair. They hoped at one time to succeed in starving the French people: the French people is still alive, and will survive its enemies; its continuance has been made certain; and nature, faithful friend of liberty, has given it the gift of plenty. What have they left to try now? Assassination.
They tried to break our national effort by subvention of revolt, and they were so sure of success that they did not blush to announce it ahead of time to all Europe, and to admit it in the British Parliament. The plan failed. What do they have left? Assassination. . . .
What man on earth has ever defended the rights of humanity without paying for it?
These passages under the appropriate dates may be found (with many like them) in vol. X of *Oeuvres de Maximilien Robespierre*, edited by Marc Bouloiseau and Albert Soboul, Paris, 1967. The same volume also contains the report of 5 Nivôse II (December 25, 1793) and its great parallel, the "Report on the principles of political morality which ought to guide the National Convention in the internal administration of the Republic" of 17 Pluviôse II (February 5, 1794), perhaps a greater rationalization of the democratic state.

ii

These figures and others like them seem the more imposing, and the wild drama of the French revolution the more turbid, because both play and players take on a greater degree of movement and energy by producing their tragedy in front of a changeless backdrop. The background is a background of history, but not the history of the ancient Gauls, or the Merovingian kings, or the Normans, or, for that matter, at least until Napoleon's time, the empire of Charlemagne; it is the background of antique Rome. It is true that some French thinkers, notably the parliamentarians, conceived of the *parlements* as representing broken but authentic fragments of ancient gatherings of the people from before Caesar's Gallic wars. It is also true that in his younger years Louis XVI was sometimes compared to Henry IV, who, to be sure, threw away Protestantism because Paris was worth a mass, whereas Louis XVI was deeply impressed by the ancient religious significance of the coronation ceremony at Rheims. But an emotional return upon the glories of a medieval and a feudal past was more characteristic of German romanticism or of the historicism of Walter Scott than it was of the French revolution; it is significant that no woman in the French revolution remotely suggests Joan of Arc. There were plenty of leaders, big and small, who cast themselves in the role of Cicero denouncing the conspiracy of Catiline. It would be a mistake, however, to say that intelligent Frenchmen were totally ignorant of the history of France — indeed, the discussion about calling the States General and its proper procedures created a sort of political antiquarianism.

In a sense the revolutionary interpretation of classicism began with Montesquieu's *Considérations sur les causes de la grandeur des Romains et de leur décadence* of 1734 and reached its classical climax in "The Death of Marat" by David in 1793, or, if not that, the installation of the Consulate at the very end of 1799. Montesquieu was not writing history but what may be called a moral analysis of the Roman republic and the Roman empire. For him Rome was a successful state so long as its male citizens were also soldiers of a martial nation; once its conquests extended beyond Italy and required professional armies, Rome produced military heroes, luxury, civil war, and despotism. Rome, he observed, began with fratricide; four kings out of seven were murdered; even in the palmy days of the virtuous republic the magistrates executed not only criminals but political opponents; and all in all he found Roman history bathed in blood. Why, then, did Rome astonish the world? Montesquieu is less clear on the causes of Roman greatness than he is on the cause of Roman decline, but he seems to say that so long as Romans were actuated by *virtue*, so long as the legions were composed of citizen soldiers, and so long as Rome refused citizenship to conquered peoples, vice, luxury, and absolutism were held at arm's length. The lesson for France was obvious: the wars of Louis XIV were wrong, and — a point urged more firmly in the *L'Esprit des lois* — virtue is the quintessence of a healthy and vigorous republic. And is not "The Death of Marat" an emblem of the end of civic virtue?

As we have hinted, the pattern of French education in the eighteenth century rested upon classical learning; the chief teachers of the revolutionary leaders had been Jesuits, Oratorians, or in some cases crypto-Jansenists. In such pedagogy the classical past was a glorious epoch in time. But it was in time, not of it, a perpetual model for modernity. Most of the *philosophes* seemed to know more about ancient Greece and Rome than they did about St. Louis or the Hundred Years War; even Voltaire, who knew everything, said plainly in his *Age of Louis XIV* that everything between Augustus and the Sun King except the Renaissance was more or less dark and barbarous.

The revolution soon became a bloody Senecan tragedy played in an ageless classical theater. History repeated itself (except for those who believed in progress): the plebs rose, the nobles (*equites*) fled, the tribune — note the noun — was occupied by orators who dreamed of emulating Demosthenes. The assassination of Caesar, the suicide of Brutus, and the elder Brutus causing his sons to be executed — such things were, from this point of view, re-enacted during the French revolution. "Le peuple" were in political terms the *populus Romanus*, though the Assembly, always in a tumult, did not even vaguely suggest the Roman *senatus*. Orator after orator denounced, as it were, some new conspiracy of Catiline. The term "citizen soldier" recalled Roman farmers springing to arms and then returning to the plow; in Napoleon's time the armies were given eagles to carry; and the term "Legion of Honor" has its antique significance. The seal of the Republic One and Indivisible was patterned, not after a Gothic model, though France was full of Gothic architecture, but as a classical design; and it is curious to note that Napoleon was first proclaimed emperor of the French republic just as Augustus, though emperor, had been simply the First Citizen (*princeps civitatis*) of Rome. In the two dictatorships the forms of republican government were hypocritically preserved until the naked seizure of power could no longer be usefully concealed.

In an earlier chapter I tried to break down the classical tradition in France into two chronological and three categorical divisions, all of which interlock with each other. The classicism of Louis XIV implied the heroics of Corneille, the noble intensities of Racine, and the timeless comedies of Molière. The tradition of tragedy was carried on, though weakly, by Voltaire and lesser dramatists,* just as the tradition of Molière, notably in the comic types among his plays (like those of Plautus and Terence) was also kept up, despite the fad of *comédie larmoyante* and *drame*. But we noted that the solemn taste of the old age of Louis XIV was reversed in the Regency, when classicism took on a lighter, more erotic, and more cynical tone, and that in the eighteenth century, classicism, or rather what I have called neoclassicism, seems to run in three separate channels: the Platonic and neo-Platonic tradition, the Plutarchian-stoic strain, and the lighter and more sensuous (and also more human) outlook of Anacreon, Horace, Catullus, and others, which I ventured to christen the Anacreontic component. Of these the Platonic tradition virtually disappeared in the revolution except when it was vaguely fused with Christian belief in the writings of such counterrevolutionary figures as Bonald, de Maistre, and Chateaubriand. During the revolutionary decade, the Plutarchian and stoic strain was of greater political significance and the Anacreontic influence most potent in the lesser arts, clothing, love, and poetry, especially the poetry of André Chénier, who, though he is sometimes as vituperative as Juvenal, writes

---

* Possibly *Caius Gracchus* by Marie-Joseph Blaise de Chénier, produced in 1792 and forbidden in 1793 (because it was antimonarchical!), has some claim to remembrance, though his *Charles IX* (1789) effectively anticipated the emotional impact of *Hernani* (1830) by Victor Hugo. One contemporary said that the audience at *Charles IX* came away drunken with vengeance and thirsty for blood. Contemporary or nearly contemporary personages were recognizable under thin historical disguises.

pastorals and elegies, is as melancholy as the romantics, and seems to sigh for a lost Arcadia where he can sport with Amaryllis in the shade.

It is difficult for us, to whom Latin and Greek are dead languages, to comprehend the impact of this classical typology. The seal of the president and the secretary of the National Convention, circular in form, bears, inscribed round its frame, the words: "La République ou la mort. Liberté, Egalité, Fraternité." In its center is a classical column surmounted by a liberty cap, that Phrygian emblem of freedom from slavery, and on either side of the column are two tablets intended to represent the Rights of Man and of the Citizen. The National Guard flag of the Carmelites district bears, among other emblems, a caduceus, with clasped hands under it signifying fraternity, and a liberty cap above it. A big poster of the Declaration of the Rights of Man and of the Citizen has the text printed in two opposing tablets separated by a bundle of fasces, a liberty cap, and, over all, the eye of God in a triangle (a symbol satisfactory to the Masons), and on either side at the top of the fasces what look like laurel leaves. There are also two winged figures which may be meant for Victory and the Republic. The official letterhead of Bonaparte as First Consul was topped by Liberty in the inevitable liberty cap, her left arm leaning on a stele on which is engraved "Au Nom du Peuple Français." Proud'hon designed an allegorical engraving celebrating the victories of the First Consul in thoroughly classical style. A large oblong, it presents, beginning at the viewer's left, three or four cupids running before four horses that draw a Roman chariot. In the chariot stands Bonaparte flanked by two women, classically gowned, one of whom drives the chariot and the other of whom may represent Victory. Bonaparte is crowned with a wreath of laurel. Accompanying the chariot, to the viewer's right and slightly behind the horses, though they do not obscure Bonaparte and his companions, are three other classical females, barefoot, clothed in Greek costumes, one apparently playing on a lyre, and another bearing some sort of tray or board apparently holding more laurel leaves. An engraving by P.-L. Debucourt, supposed to represent a gathering in Madame de Staël's garden, pictures a group of a dozen or so men and women, this time fashionably clad in modern costume, who meet at the base of a pedestal which upholds Eros leaning on his bow.* In truth, since the revolution desired to rid itself of all the trappings of royalty, there was no other iconography possible but the universality of the classical past.

The central personage in the arts of design during the revolutionary decade, the Consulate, and the Empire was Jacques Louis David (1748–1825), one of the great geniuses in painting but of a somewhat pliable political nature. What he admired was energy. We have seen that his "The Oath of the Horatii" (1784) perfectly expresses the revival of classicism of the serious sort. This canvas, by reason of its fidelity to nature in musculature and its treatment of lighting, reminiscent of Caravaggio or perhaps Poussin, is sometimes thought of as the first milestone in the development of modern painting. David arranged all the revolutionary fêtes until the fall of Robespierre, after which he was briefly imprisoned, and if the classical allegories of these processions and ceremonies strike us nowadays as somewhat childlike, it must be remembered once more that classical typology was the only possible universal typology. For a time a radical, when Bonaparte came into power David became the great painter of the Empire, and the vast spread of his "Napoleon Crowning Josephine" with all its brilliant detail at first glance scarcely seems to be by the same master. The connecting link is the expression of heroism and of heroic energy; the coronation painting is, in fact, no more crowded with persons than his obviously classical "Les Sabines," in which three figures, frozen into immobility — a woman in the middle imploring peace, two warriors, one on either side of her, who fight naked except for helmet, shield, and sword or spear — stand posed before a restless crowd of soldiers, women, and children. In the background are the walls of Rome as they presumably once were. The lighting is as dramatically managed as it is in "The Oath of the Horatii," and

* These and many other pictures and designs are reproduced in *La France de la royauté à la nation*, originally published in Stuttgart and translated from the German of Friedrich Sirburg into French by François Ponthier in 1963. I take it that the French edition was published in Paris. There are many books containing such illustrations; for example, A.-J. Tudesq and J. Rudel, *1789–1848*, Paris (?), 1966, is full of fascinating illustrations, one of them (p. 127) the celebration of a marriage under the Republic, the bridal couple standing before a female figure that may or may not be Juno, holding an upright torch in her right hand and extending a wreath over the heads of the pair with her left hand. On the wall behind the happy couple are, again, two tablets bearing the text of The Rights of Man, crowned by a liberty cap; and the grouping of the figures is vaguely reminiscent of David's "Oath of the Horatii."

the picture presumably illustrates the philosophic dictum of Montesquieu that so long as the Romans were virtuous, republican, and warlike the state was safe. If the canvas suggests a scene from a Meyerbeer opera, it is nonetheless impressive and "heroic."

David was capable of tenderer scenes (an example is his "Cupid and Psyche," 1817, illustrative of Anacreontic classicism), and he anticipated the French vogue of Constable in his single landscape, "View of the Luxembourg Gardens," painted from his prison window when he was incarcerated after the fall of Robespierre. In addition to "The Oath of the Horatii," however, three canvases are more expressly related to the revolution: "Belisarius recognized by a Soldier" (1781), "The Death of Socrates" (1787), and, one of the masterpieces of all time, "The Death of Marat" (1793).* The Belisarius canvas, like the others slightly theatrical, reminded viewers of the fall of the mighty from high places, and "The Death of Socrates," theatrically lighted but excellently composed, is an example of classical virtue (somebody has suggested that in this picture Socrates replaces Christ). The magnificent "The Death of Marat," which has not in it a single antiquarian or classical motif, is possibly the greatest triumph of the classical revival in painting during the revolutionary decade. It is both realistic and antique in its emotional appeal, and at once justifies the revolution and reminds its leaders that assassination was a common crime in the ancient world. Marat is dead in his bathtub (how many Romans committed suicide in their baths?), his head bound up in a towel, the wound in his chest faithfully reproduced. His left hand holds a sheet of paper, his right arm falls over the side of the bath but still grasps the pen with which he had been writing; on a block of wood, oddly suggestive of a stele, is an inkwell, another pen, and a few more pieces of paper, and on this wooden oblong, as if engraven, is the legend: "À Marat. David." The simplicity is classical, the details naturalistic, the total effect one of the peace of death. It is proof of the depth and energy of revolutionary passion that in a later phase of this tumultuous period so magnificent a composition could be covered over with a coat of white paint. It is also possible that this canvas, so geometric in structure, so

---

* I pass over the unfinished "The Oath of the Tennis Court," a superb composition, and the equally unfinished "The Death of Barras," suggested by a falsified report to the Assembly by Robespierre the Incorruptible. The "Oath" is the better.

exact in detail, so vaguely religious in its general effect, helps to explicate the indifference with which death was contemplated by thousands in the revolutionary era.

Heroic classicism, mixed, as in David's later paintings, with romantic coloring, is found in other notable canvases of the period —Guérin's "The Return of Marcus Sextus" (1799), Ingres's "Vergil reading the Aeneid in the presence of Augustus, Livia, and Octavia" (1812), Gros's melodramatic "Sappho at Leucadia" (1801); and those who saw the great exhibition of the Council of Europe in London in 1972, "The Age of Neo-Classicism," need not be reminded of the way classicism or neoclassicism in one or another of its various phases permeated the art and life of the West during the revolutionary decade, the Consulate, and the Empire.

It affected the portraiture and the costuming of women; the female form seems pliably to alter its shape in accordance with the rapidity of alterations in fashion, which can be followed in the first volume of Oskar Fischel and Max von Boehn's *Modes & Manners of the Nineteenth Century* (4 vols., trans. M. Edwardes, London and New York, 1927). Corsets and wigs disappeared, the full skirt vanished, dresses grew narrower and waists higher until by 1793, say these historians, every woman looked as if she had a wen. By 1800 fashionable clothing (always *à la grecque*, or supposed to be), including shoes and ornaments, was not supposed to weigh more than eight ounces, the wife of a Swiss banker walked in the garden of the Tuileries clad only in a gauze veil, and in 1801 a lady trod the streets of Hanover clad in a chemise and a neckerchief. The bosom went up and hips disappeared. This female pliability can also be seen in the art of the period, in which many women seem to have no bones: examine from this point of view David's "Paris and Helen" (1789), and his portraits of Madame Vigée-Lebrun and Madame Récamier, Schick's "Frau Dannecker" (1802) (Schick worked mostly in Rome), Marie Benoist's totally different "Portrait of a Negress" (1800), Gérard's "Madame Récamier" (1805), Margarete Gérard's sentimental "Matrimonial Happiness' (1805?), and of course the female figures of Canova, from the absurd "Three Graces" through the elegant simplicity of "Pauline Borghese" to the austere domesticity of "Madame Mère" (Napoleon's mother seated in a curule chair!). When one turns to the line engravings of Fuseli and Blake, each of whom was in his own way interested in the revolution, entirely different sets of females meet the eye: in Fuseli women are more elongated than even Ingres's famous "Odalisque" of 1814, and in Blake women have no sexuality whatever. If I have wandered far from the French revolution proper, it will be noticed that none of these examples represents anything from the *ancien régime*. It is also evident that one moves from the antique stoicism of David's "Oath of the Horatii" to romantic Hellenism, but precisely where to draw a chronological line is an insoluble puzzle.*

iii

It would be possible at this point to see how the classical revival of the revolution affected many other elements in the life not only of France but of the Western world — furniture, silverware, the decoration of rooms, architecture, and much else, and how many of these tendencies developed into romantic Hellenism. But enough has been said, I think, to indicate that the French revolution found in its own version of the ancient world a vocabulary, a typology, an iconography that served as a new language for the republican hope in man. It is a commonplace that in 1789 and for a while thereafter forward-looking spirits in Europe and elsewhere looked upon the fall of the Bastille and the creation, however temporary, of a limited monarchy in France as a golden gateway into the radiant future of humanity. Tom Paine, Schiller, Condorcet, William Blake, young Wordsworth are representative names, and two famous lines in *The Prelude* beautifully express the momentary wonder of this expectation:

> Bliss was it in that dawn to be alive,
> But to be young was very Heaven.

But beginning in 1790 a counterrevolutionary literature, often as extreme in linguistic violence as that of the revolutionary super-

---

* Throughout this discussion I have been immensely aided by the magnificent catalogue issued for the great exhibition at the Royal Academy and the Victoria and Albert Museum, *The Age of Neo-Classicism*, London, The Arts Council of Great Britain, 1972. Perhaps this is an appropriate place to express a like indebtedness to *The Romantic Movement*, an equally magnificent catalogue of the fifth exhibition by this same Council of Europe at the Tate Gallery and the Arts Council Gallery, printed in London in 1959.

349

egoists, developed in Europe, and to some specimens of this state of mind I now turn. Saint-Just, speaking before the Convention November 13, 1790, had announced that Louis XVI should be judged as an alien enemy. A week later he declared that a vengeful and victorious tyranny will emerge from popular tumults in France, and that if the rights of men exist, they will then be written in the blood of the people on the tomb of liberty. From sentiments like these writers of the reaction took off.

Among the chief documents are Edmund Burke's famous *Reflections on the Revolution in France* (1790), which became an international influence upon its publication; Jacques Mallet du Pan's two pamphlets, *Considérations historiques sur la révolution française par un ami de l'ordre, de la liberté, des rois, et du bonheur des peuples* and *Considérations historiques sur la révolution française et sur les causes qui en prolongent la durée* (the first printed in London, the second in London and Brussels, in 1793); *Théorie de pouvoir politique et religieux dans la société civile, demontrée par le raisonnement et par l'histoire* by Louis-Gabriel-Ambroise, Vicomte de Bonald, published in Switzerland in 1796; Joseph de Maistre, *Considérations sur la France*, printed in 1796, with which, however, must be associated de Maistre's later writings, of which *Du Pape* (1817) is the most solid and the unfinished *Soirées de St. Petersbourg* the most interesting; Chateaubriand's *Essai historique, politique et moral sur les révolutions anciennes et modernes, considerées dans leurs rapports avec la révolution française*, also published in 1796; Friedrich von Gentz's many diatribes, among them "Der Ursprung und die Grundsache der amerikanischen Revolution verglichen mit den Ursprunge und den Grundsätzen der Französischen," from volume II of the *Historische Journal*, for May 1800, translated (or rather paraphrased) by John Quincy Adams as "The French and American Revolutions Compared" that same year; and Madame de Staël's vindication of her father, Necker, in *Considérations sur les principaux événements de la révolution française*, published in 1818 but written earlier. Because the British, particularly the British liberals, had been immensely pleased to see the French, as they thought, veering toward the British monarchical system, the reaction, most powerfully expressed by Burke, was diffuse among them. It includes Coleridge's "France: An Ode" (1798), occasioned by the French invasion of

Switzerland of that year, asking heaven's forgiveness because he had been deceived, and including such scathing passages as:

> O France, thou mockest Heaven, adulterous, blind,
>   And patriot only in pernicious toils!
> Are these thy boasts, champion of human kind?
>   To mix with Kings in the low lust of sway,
> Yell in the hunt, and share the murderous prey;
> To insult the shrine of Liberty with spoils
>   From freemen torn; to tempt and to betray?

Coleridge provided more rational discourse on the political theme in *The Statesman's Manual* (1816), which makes the Christian religion, especially the Bible, the best guide to the modern state. Wordsworth's counterrevolutionary sentiments are well known, and mention should be made of Robert Southey's *Letters from England by Don Manuel Espriella* (in three volumes, 1808?), a work which, though it deprecates revolution, mob rule, and bigotry and thinks every English schoolboy should have military training, by no means merits the neglect into which, like its author, it has fallen. A passage about Birmingham is as grim as anything in Dickens' *Hard Times*:

I am still giddy, dazzled with the hammering of presses, the clatter of engines, and the whirling of wheels; my head aches with the multiplicity of the infernal noises, and my eyes with the light of infernal fires, — I may add, my heart also, at the sight of so many human beings employed in infernal occupations, and looking as if they were never destined for any thing better. Our earth was designed to be a seminary of young angels, but the devil has certainly fixed upon this spot for his own nursery-garden and hot-house.

(2d ed., London, 1808, II, 56–57)

Southey is as much a humanitarian as Shelley, but as Crane Brinton puts it, "he soon discovered that revolutionary principles had not made men good; he characteristically jumped to the conclusion that they made men bad." The point in quoting Southey's paragraph is only to remind the reader that to be reactionary was not necessarily to be blind.

I turn to examine four of these writers — Burke, de Maistre, Chateaubriand, and Madame de Staël. To them, as to the others, the revolution was a primordial convulsion like the Flood. As Burke wrote in his later *Thoughts on French Affairs* (1791),

"This declaration of a *new species* of government, on new principles, (such it professes itself to be,) is a real crisis in the politics of Europe." Though he was himself a Protestant, Burke compared the divisive nature of the revolution in international politics to the Reformation, which had also split Europe in two. It is, he wrote in italics, "*a Revolution of doctrine and theoretic dogma,*" and, neatly turning classical antecedents against the revolutionaries, he went back to the states of Greece for an older example of "most cruel and bloody persecutions and proscriptions." If the French, announcing that a popular majority of taxable people in every country "is the perpetual, natural, unceasing, indefeasible sovereign," "master of the form as well as the administration of the state," and therefore cashiered their king, what monarch in Europe was safe? Burke, it is well known, had very little use for abstract doctrines of political science, and this particular piece of practical philosophy seemed to him utterly abhorrent.* But let us get back to the *Reflections.*

Burke's famous book, put together over a period of months, is irregular in structure and uneven in style. It purports to be a letter to a "gentleman in Paris" and is occasioned by a sermon delivered by Dr. Richard Price before a congregation of dissenters in London, "Discourse on the Love of our Country," printed and also sent abroad as representing the views of English "radicals," particularly of the Society for Constitutional Information and the Society for the Commemoration of the Glorious Revolution (Burke calls it the Revolution Society). It seems to Burke that Dr. Price both misunderstood and misrepresented the nature of English society and of the British government. For Burke, as for Wordsworth,

There is

One great society alone on earth,
The noble Living and the noble Dead.
(*The Prelude*, XI: 393–395)

---

* Burke's political conservatism is well known and has been much dwelt upon by liberal historians. Nevertheless there is considerable political prescience in *Thoughts on French Affairs.* For an account of radicalism in Great Britain, which Burke feared, see the book by Carl B. Cone already referred to, *The English Jacobins: Reformers in Late 18th Century England*, New York, 1968; and for an illuminating essay on the curious fusion of political radicalism with "illuminism," millenarianism, and dissent see the article by Clarke Garrett, "Joseph Priestley, the Millennium, and the French Revolution," *Journal of the History of Ideas*, 34 (January–March 1973), 51–66.

This society, divided, it is true, into nations, is linked together across the ages by custom, by property rights, by religion, by the realization that men, taken individually, are only a frail reed, as Pascal has said, and that wise and experienced statesmen

are afraid to put men to live and trade each on his own private stock of reason, because we suspect that this stock in each man is small, and that the individuals would do better to avail themselves of the general bank and capital of nations and of ages.

Man, Burke says flatly, is by his constitution a religious animal — a matter on which he quotes Cicero's *De legibus*; and connected with this truth is the truth that, though property, taken by itself, is "sluggish, inert, and timid."

the power of perpetuating our property in our families is one of the most valuable and interesting circumstances belonging to it, and that which tends the most to the perpetuation of society itself. It makes our weakness subservient to our virtue, it grafts benevolence even upon avarice.

The European world has for ages depended upon two principles: the spirit of a gentleman and the spirit of religion. "People," he says firmly, "will not look forward to posterity, who never look backward to their ancestors." There are indeed rights, but not as the French infer. Social rights (responsibilities?) include the right to do justice, the right to the fruits of one's industry, the right to the acquisitions of one's parents, the right to do what one can by himself, and the right to all that society can fairly do in his favor. But equal rights are not the same as equal things, and, writes Burke, "The rights of men are in a sort of *middle*, incapable of definition, but not impossible to be discerned."

As for the theory of a social contract, Burke is at his eloquent best in asserting his mystical belief in the historicity of society:

Society is indeed a contract . . . but the state ought not to be considered as nothing better than a partnership agreement in a trade of pepper and coffee, calico, or tobacco, or some other such low concern, to be taken up for a little temporary interest, and to be dissolved by the fancy of the partners. It is to be looked on with other reverence, because it is not a partnership in things subservient only to the gross animal existence of a temporary and perishable nature. It is a partnership in all science [knowledge]; a partnership in all art; a partnership in every virtue and in all perfection. As the end of such a partnership cannot be obtained in many generations, it becomes a partnership not only between those who are living, but between those who are dead and those who are to be born. Each contract of each particular state is but a clause in the great primeval contract of eternal society, linking the lower with the higher natures, connecting the visible and invisible world, according to a fixed compact sanctioned by the inviolable oath which holds all physical and all moral natures, each in their appointed place. . . . men move in the same direction, though in a different place. They . . . move with the order of the universe.

Matching the revolutionaries at their own game of seeking support from the classics, he again quotes Cicero (*De republica*) in support of his view of the eternal order of society: "That nothing, indeed, of the events which occur on earth is more pleasing to that supreme and prepotent God who rules the entire universe than these societies and associations of men, cemented by law, which are called states." *

Burke's central philosophy of the state is intellectually respectable. Aware, however, that "Many parts of Europe are in open disorder. In many others there is a hollow murmuring under ground; a confused movement is felt that threatens a general earthquake in the political world," conscious also that "at once to preserve and to reform" is a difficult political problem, in his anxiety to defame the revolution he uses any stick that will beat the French dog. He is blind to the manifest inequities in the Anglican church, to the stupidity and reactionary quality of the country gentlemen in his own country, and to the absurdities of the British system of parliamentary representation that had irritated the former American colonies. The beginning of the essay is a long and casuistical defense not merely of a society ordered in ranks and classes by divine providence but also of the theory that the principle of a hereditary monarchy had never been violated in England, neither by the Cromwellian regime nor by the transfer of the crown from the house of Stuart to the house of Hanover. He declares that the French nobility were for the most part "composed of men of high spirit and of a delicate sense of honor," and, blind to the deficiencies of Marie Antoinette, he writes one of

* Burke quotes Cicero in Latin. I borrow the translation from the admirable edition of the *Reflections* edited by Thomas H. D. Mahoney for The Library of Liberal Arts, Indianapolis, 1955. This edition is especially useful because it includes an analytical outline by Oskar Prest.

his most celebrated paragraphs in laudation of the injured queen:

It is now sixteen or seventeen years since I saw the queen of France, then the dauphiness, at Versailles, and surely never lighted on this orb, which she hardly seemed to touch, a more delightful vision. I saw her just above the horizon, decorating and cheering the elevated sphere she just began to move in — glittering like the morning star, full of life and splendor and joy. Oh! what a revolution! and what a heart must I have to contemplate without emotion that elevation and that fall! Little did I dream when she added titles of veneration to those of enthusiastic, distant, respectful love, that she should ever be obliged to carry the sharp antidote against disgrace concealed in that bosom, little did I dream that I should have lived to see such disasters fallen upon her in a nation of gallant men, in a nation of men of honor and of cavaliers. I thought ten thousand swords must have leaped from their scabbards to avenge even a look that threatened her with insult. But the age of chivalry is gone.

Revolutionary France "has not sacrificed her virtues to her interest, but she has abandoned her interest, that she might prostitute her virtue." The revolutionary leaders are "Roman confiscators," "atheistic libellers," "men who confound the right of a people with their power," impractical *philosophes* who think "it is a sufficient motive to destroy an old scheme of things because it is an old one." They have reduced the king to nullity, confiscated the church lands (Burke defends the French clergy), turned to paper money, set up arithmetical electoral units that "reduce men to loose counters," put together "a stock-jobbing constitution," and, in letting loose the reins of authority, "doubled the license of a ferocious dissoluteness in manners and of an insolent irreligion in opinions and practice, and . . . extended through all the ranks of life . . . all the unhappy corruptions that usually were the disease of wealth and power." Above all, they are mere theorists with no sense for political reality or the historical process that brings society into being, and no understanding of the truth that, since men are of necessity unequal in ability and temperament, only a fixed order among classes and some form of authority will preserve the state. He says with justice that the National Assembly is a body "without fundamental laws, without established maxims, without respected rules of proceeding, which nothing can keep firm to any system." And he prophesies that the next assembly will be worse.

But this is not his only prophecy. Two other passages reveal, amid all his prejudices, the prescience of Burke. They are to this effect:

The whole of the powers obtained by this revolution will settle in the towns among the burghers and monied directors who lead them [because] all things which conspire against the country gentleman combine in favor of the money manager and director,

an amazing prediction in 1790 of what Denis Woronoff in his book calls the bourgeois republic of 1794–1799; and

[Eventually] some popular general, who understands the art of conciliating the soldiers, and who possesses the true spirit of command, shall draw the eyes of all men upon himself —

and one remembers that Bonaparte was to become First Consul and military dictator of France at the very end of 1799. In the *Reflections* Burke's style frequently exhibits the elaborateness of syntax and figure one associates with romantic prose — for example, that of De Quincey — but, though his utterance is personal, he lacks the prepotent egotism of such political leaders as Marat and Robespierre.

The three French writers to whom we now come in the main follow the lines of Burke, but they all experienced the revolution at first hand as Burke did not, and it is true that each of them suffered in some degree under the Bonaparte regimes, a fact which, when they revised their essays, undoubtedly fed their prejudices. Burke was indignant and on occasion violent; de Maistre,* who studied him, was somber, pessimistic, and authoritarian, a predecessor of Nietzsche and perhaps of the "philosophy" of the Nazis. He was also a devout Catholic, who spent most of his life in poverty and exile.

For de Maistre man is a ferocious animal who must be controlled, his reasoning powers feeble and his instincts bloody. So long as he confines his reason to the sciences, though not always then, ra-

---

* My attention was first called to de Maistre by the brief but acute discussion in Georg Brandes' *Main Currents*. His power as a writer is slowly winning recognition. Two other discussions are: one by Isaiah Berlin in *The Hedgehog and the Fox*, London, 1957(?), where de Maistre's influence on Tolstoy's theory of history is maximized; and the preface to *The Works of Joseph de Maistre*, selected, translated, and introduced by Jack Lively, London, 1965. De Maistre's correspondence is also of great interest, and the *Soirées de St. Pétersbourg*, though lengthy, is a fascinating commentary on the affairs and philosophy of Europe from the point of view of an intelligent reactionary.

tionality will do him no harm and may do him good, but when he oversteps this boundary to dethrone God, not only deny the divine origin of authority but also substitute a theory of the state founded on the sands of flimsy philosophy and overlook his terrible tendency, ever since the fall of man, to commit crimes of the darkest dye, he is doomed in this world and presumably in the next. All authority emanates from God, who has created the papacy to indicate what rule must be in a criminal world. De Maistre does not so much advocate monarchy by divine right as argue that all political authority can be proper only as it has divine authority behind it. Murders, wars, and revolutions are part of the divine order following upon the fall of Adam; if the innocent perish, it is only that sacrificial offering (and here de Maistre anticipates Kierkegaard) which is symbolically represented by the command laid upon Abraham to sacrifice Isaac, by the blood offerings of the ancient Jews, by the sacrificial victims of the ancient world, and of course by the sublime instance of Jesus Christ. The world is wicked because man is given to wickedness, and this is true for de Maistre because, like Calvin, he accepts the antecedent will of God, who desires to save men and offers them salvation, and the consequent will of God, which, because men do not accept grace, declares that they cannot be saved. The French revolution is therefore as much an act of the will of God as the crucifixion; the death of the innocent on earth is no different from the death of the innocent Christ.

For de Maistre the revolution may have been the work of the devil but it was also a necessary episode in the history of the universe. The revolutionary governments have no possible chance to survive because their leaders hate Christianity and deny that the state must be sanctioned by the church, and because rationalism is a false power, once it passes beyond the limited sphere of "science," in which alone it can be more or less effective. It follows from premises like these that de Maistre abhors the revolution and that his abhorrence is divinely right, just as one's abhorrence of Satan is divinely right. Men must be governed, and in the long run there are only two principles of authority: the church and punishment. The church is incarnated in the papacy, which is immortal, though popes may die; punishment is exemplified in the executioner, a figure society supports and loathes. These two,

357

the priest and the headsman, are the only sure pillars of the state, a body which, when it is successful, makes war and, when successful, shelters abominable crimes. The theory of the state, including the impossibility of a democracy, is set forth in the work known in English as *Essay on the Generative Principle of Political Constitutions*; his doctrine of the infallibility of the papacy and the need for such a theorem is in *Du Pape* (1819); his defense of the headsman, one of the great rhetorical passages in nineteenth-century writing, is in the *Soirées de St. Pétersbourg,* in the first dialogue between a senator and a count. Nothing more powerful appears in any Gothic novel:

Je vous crois trop accoutumés à réfléchir . . . pour qu'il ne vous soit pas arrivé souvent de méditer sur le bourreau. Qu'est-ce donc cet être inexplicable qui a preféré à tous les métiers agréables . . . qui se présentent en foule à la force ou à la dextérité humaine, celui de tourmenter et de mettre à mort ses semblables? Cette tête, ce coeur sont-ils faits comme les nôtres? ne contiennent-ils rien de particulier et d'étranger à notre nature? Pour moi, je n'en sais pas douter . . . il naît comme nous; mais c'est un être extraordinaire, et pour qu'il existe dans la famille humaine il faut un décret particulier, un FIAT de la puissance créatrice. Il est créé comme un monde. Voyez ce qu'il est dans l'opinion des hommes, et comprenez, si vous pouvez, comment il peut ignorer cette opinion ou l'affronter! A peine l'autorité a-t-elle désigné sa demeure, à peine a-t-il pris possession, que les autres habitations reculent jusqu'à ce qu'elles se voient plus la sienne. C'est au milieu de cette solitude et de cette espèce de vide formé autour de lui qu'il vit seul avec sa femelle et ses petits, qui lui font connaître la voix de l'homme: sans eux il n'en connaîtrait que les gémissements . . . Un signal lugubre est donné; un ministre abject de la justice vient frapper à sa porte et l'avertir qu'on a besoin de lui: il part; il arrive sur une place publique couverte d'une foule pressée et palpitante. On lui jette un empoisonneur, un parricide, un sacrilège: il le saisit, il l'étend, il le lie sur une croix horizontale, il lève le bras; alors il se fait un silence horrible, et l'on n'entend plus que le cri des os qui éclatent sous la barre, et les hurlements de la victime. Il la détache; il la porte sur une roue: les membres fracassés s'enlacent dans les rayons; la tête pend; les cheveux se hérissent, et la bouche, ouverte comme une fournaise, n'envoie plus par intervalle qu'un petit nombre de paroles sanglantes qui appellent la mort. Il a fini: le coeur lui bat, mais c'est de joie; il s'applaudit, il dit dans son coeur: *Nul ne roue mieux que moi.* Il descend: il tend sa main souillée de sang, et la justice y jette de loin quelques pièces d'or qu'il emporte à travers une double haie d'hommes écartés par l'horreur. Il se met à table, et il mange; au lit ensuite, et il dort. Et le lendemain, en s'éveillant, il songe à tout autre chose qu'à ce qu'il a fait la veille. Est-ce un homme? Oui:

Dieu le reçoit dans ses temples et lui permet de prier. Il n'est pas criminel; cependant aucune langue ne consent à dire, par example, *qu'il est vertueux, qu'il est honnête homme, qu'il est estimable, etc.* Nul éloge moral ne peut lui convenir; car tous supposent des rapports avec les hommes, et il n'en a point.

Et cependant toute grandeur, toute puissance, toute subordination repose sur l'exécuteur: il est l'horreur et le lien de l'association humaine. Otez du monde cet agent incompréhensible; dans l'instant même l'ordre fait place au chaos, les thrônes s'abîment et la société disparait.*

Not even Schopenhauer takes a gloomier view of the inevitability of evil, the weakness and wickedness of man, and the futility of all doctrines of improvement.

Although de Maistre was a devout Catholic, there is something virtually Manichaean in his theories of the revolution and of man,

* I believe you too thoughtful . . . not to have meditated often on the executioner. What under heaven can be that incomprehensible kind of being who instead of any of the myriad pleasant occupations open to human strength and skill prefers the one of torturing and putting to death his own kind? Can such a head, such a heart, be of the same stuff as ours? Isn't something in them special and foreign to our nature? I can't doubt this myself . . . he is born as we are but he is an extraordinary being; it took a special decree of the creator, a FIAT, to get him into the human family. He was created — as a world is. Look at what he is in the opinion of other men and then understand, if you can, how he is able to face that opinion, or ignore it. Hardly do the authorities get him a place to live, hardly does he move in, when everyone else moves away where they won't have to look at it. In the midst of that isolation and in the sort of vacuum that forms around him he lives alone with his female and their young, who give him his only chance to hear a human voice; but for them he would hear only moans . . . He gets a funereal message; an abject agent of justice knocks at his door and tells him he is needed; he sets out; he comes into a public square thronged by an excited crowd. Someone hands over a poisoner, a parricide, or a blasphemer; he seizes him, he stretches him out and binds him on a horizontal cross, he raises his arm; then comes a horrible silence and nothing is heard but the crunching of bones as the bar comes down, and the screams of the victim. He takes the body off, puts it on a wheel; the shattered limbs laced around the spokes, the head hanging, hair on end, and the mouth, open like the door of a furnace, utters nothing except, from time to time, a few bloodsoaked words that beg for death. He has finished; his heart throbs, but with joy; he applauds himself, saying in his heart: No one works the wheel better than I. He comes down; he holds out a hand stained with blood, and, from a distance, justice tosses a few pieces of gold that he takes with him through a double line of men who shrink back in horror. He sits at his table and eats; he goes to bed and sleeps. And when he wakes the next day he thinks of everything but what he has done the day before. Is this a man? Yes, God admits him to his temples and allows him to pray, yet no tongue would be willing to call him *virtuous, decent, estimable, etc.* No kind of moral praise could ever befit him, for everything of the kind presupposes relationships with other men, and he has none.

And yet all greatness, all power, all discipline depend on the executioner; he is at once the horror of society and what holds it together. Take this incomprehensible element out of the world and at that instant order gives way to chaos, thrones go down, and society disappears.

a Satanic drive not shared by the austere and melancholy Chateaubriand, who considered that he was motivated by two great principles: the love of a charitable religion and a sincere attachment
to public liberty. A stately and stoic aloofness characterizes the
preface of his *Oeuvres complètes* of 1830, an expression of the
romantic *moi* at once elegant, impressive, and complacent:

J'ai entrepris les *Mémoires* de ma vie: cette vie a été fort agitée. J'ai
traversé plusieurs fois les mers; j'ai vécu dans la hutte des Sauvages et
dans le palais des rois, dans les camps et dans les cités. Voyageur aux
champs de la Grèce, pélerin à Jerusalem, je me suis assis sur toutes
sortes de ruines. J'ai vu passer le royaume de Louis XVI et l'empire
de Buonaparte; j'ai partagé l'exil des Bourbons, et j'ai annoncé leur
retour. Deux poids qui semblent attachés à ma fortune la font succes-
sivement monter et descendre dans une proportion égale: on me prend,
on me laisse; on me reprend dépouillé un jour, le lendemain on me jette
un manteau, pour m'en dépouiller encore. Accoutumé à ces bourrasques,
dans quelque port que j'arrive, je me regarde toujours comme un
navigateur qui va bientôt remonter sur son vaisseau, et je ne fais à terre
aucun établissement solide. Deux heures m'ont suffi pour quitter le
ministère, et pour remettre les clefs de l'hôtellerie à celui qui devoit
l'occuper.*

If de Maistre's mental processes may be said to resemble the dark,
Satanic mills of Blake, the aloof melancholy of Chateaubriand, so
sensitive to slight, so despairing of the present, so given to dreams
of the far away or the long ago, is that of an aristocratic Melmoth
or Wandering Jew, for whom the earth, especially in its political
aspect, can offer no permanent home. Like de Musset he at once
congratulates the younger generation and sorrows over it, that
"race innocente et libre," which knew neither the oppression nor
the military glories of the revolution, the Consulate, or the Empire:
"ils n'ont pris aucun engagement avec nos crimes ou avec nos

---

* I have undertaken the *Memoirs* of my life; that life has been a very agitated
one. Several times I have crossed the seas; I have lived in the huts of savages and
in the palaces of kings, in camps and in cities. As a traveler on the fields of Greece,
as a pilgrim to Jerusalem, I have seated myself on all kinds of ruins. I have seen
the passing of the realm of Louis XVI, and of the Empire of Bonaparte; I shared
the exile of the Bourbons, and I heralded their return. Two weights seem attached
to my destiny in a way such as to make it rise and fall equally. People have taken
me up, and dropped me again; then taken me up again, naked, and the next day
thrown a cloak over me, only to strip me of it once more. Accustomed to the
buffeting of these changing winds, wherever I go I see myself as a sailor who will
shortly embark again, and on land I set up no permanent dwelling. Two hours
have been enough for me to leave a ministry and hand the keys of the building
to the next occupant.

erreurs"; like de Maistre he laments "les temples détruits, la religion persecutée"; like Burke he finds a representative monarchy far preferable to a representative republic; like each of them he raises on high the standard of religion. On the other hand, by 1826, when he issued a revised version of the *Essai historique*, he inclined to think that manners and morals had improved, perhaps because in 1826 the "law of sacrilege," enacted under the reign of Charles X in France, imposed the death sentence for certain "sacrilegious" offenses. (In 1827 the Liberals won the election; in the Revolution of July 1830, Charles X was to be driven from the throne!)

The *Essai historique, politique et moral sur les révolutions anciennes et modernes, considerées dans leurs rapports avec la révolution française* purports to be a comparative historical study. A preliminary analysis sets forth six propositions to be examined, such as this one: among revolutions which of them can be compared to that in France in the light of the spirit, manners, and enlightenment of their eras? But Chateaubriand is neither comparative nor historical: all revolutions melt into anticipations of that in France. Thus chapters 13 and 14 deal with the revolution wrought by Lycurgus in Sparta, but Chateaubriand has only a superficial mastery of the history of Greece, and the real point is that the Jacobins took Lycurgus as their model; yet, even when they assassinated country gentlemen, confiscated private wealth, changed customs and usages, and abolished God, they did not achieve the egalitarianism of the Spartan state. Only a miracle could have accomplished this feat, and, once the Jacobins understood that they had failed, they resorted to criminality. The trumpet of the exterminating angel was heard in France. Everywhere the blood-stained guillotine, everywhere at night the sound of drums as young men, awakened at midnight, were hurried off by force to join the army, passing on their way the pale heads and hideous trunks of those who had tried to refuse. France in the Reign of Terror was sheer horror:

Tandis que les armées se composent, les prisons se remplissent de tous les propriétaires de la France. Ici, on les noie par milliers [Nantes]; là, on ouvre les portes des cachots pleins de victimes, où l'on y décharge du canon à mitraille [Lyon]. Le coutelas des guillotines tombe jour et nuit. Ces machines de destruction sont trop lentes au gré des bourreaux; des artistes de mort en inventent qui peuvent trancher plusieurs têtes d'un seul coup [Arras]. Les places publiques inondées de sang deviennent impracticables; il faut changer le lieu des exécutions: en vain d'immenses carrières ont été ouvertes pour recevoir les cadavres, on demande à en creuser de nouvelles. Vieillards de quatre-vingt ans, jeunes filles de seize, pères et mères, soeurs et frères, enfants, maris, épouses, meurent couverts du sang les uns des autres. Ainsi les Jacobins atteignent à la fois quatre fins principales, vers l'établissement de leur république: ils détruisent l'inégalité des rangs, nivellent les fortunes, relèvent les finances par la confiscation des biens des condamnés, et s'attachent l'armée en la berçant de l'espoir de posséder un jour ces propriétés.*

(*Oeuvres complètes*, Paris, 1830, I, 65–66)

An unfair account? Chateaubriand has no idea of being fair; all previous revolutions merely lead to the horror of this one. When you throw out God, you throw out all the Christian virtues. Is France any more virtuous because under the Directory they have changed a king for five masters?

In 1816 Madame de Staël wrote her *Considérations sur les principaux événements de la révolution française*, but left it incomplete; it was published in 1818 by her literary heirs and occupies volumes 12 and 13 of the *Oeuvres complètes*, brought out in Brussels in 1830. Its motivation is a justification of her father, M. Necker; and her belief is, naturally enough, that if the king, the notables, and the national assembly had followed his advice, France could have been peaceably transformed into a constitutional monarchy. She gives more weight to the example of the American revolution than do modern historians, makes out as good a case as she can for Lafayette (not a very good one), and severely reproaches Calonne for his insensate financial policy. The dismissal of her father occasioned the riots and the assassinations of July 14 (the fall of the Bastille), yet even that bloody affair had its grandeur:

le mouvement était national; aucune faction intérieure ni étrangère ne pouvait exciter un tel enthousiasme. La France entière le partageait, et

---

* While the armies assemble the prisons fill with all the landholders of France. In one place they are drowned by thousands [Nantes]; in another cannon loaded with grapeshot are fired into the open doors of cells crowded with victims [Lyons]. The blades of the guillotines fall day and night. These machines of destruction are too slow to please the hangmen; the artists of death invent some that can slice off several heads an once [Arras]. The public squares are so awash with blood that they can't be crossed; the scenes of execution have to be changed; great quarries are dug to take care of the bodies, but in vain, and the order goes out to dig new ones. Ancients of fourscore years, girls of sixteen, fathers and mothers, sisters and brothers, children, husbands, wives die, covered with each other's blood. Thus the Jacobins accomplish four aims at once on the road to setting up their republic: they destroy inequality of rank, level off fortunes, swell the treasury by confiscating the wealth of the condemned, and win over the army by encouraging the hope of getting these properties one day.

l'émotion de tout un peuple tient toujours à des sentiments vrais et naturels.*

Mirabeau was, naturally, not so great a man as her father, but the Constituent Assembly seems to her to have accomplished wonders. But, alas! the party of the left more and more prevailed, the wise advice of Necker was ignored (especially by Mirabeau), and royal authority was so sensibly diminished that an outraged king attempted to flee the country, after which the assembly fell more and more under the influence of abstract ideas, often expressed by Robespierre as he wormed his way into prominence: "Robespierre joignait de la métaphysique obscure à des déclamations communes, et c'était ainsi qu'il se faisait de l'éloquence," † a somewhat astonishing statement, inasmuch as she elsewhere compares unfavorably the orations read aloud from manuscript to the assembly with the informal speaking in the British House of Commons. Naturally enough, she favors the Girondins, who struggled daily to oppose "with intrepid eloquence" the denunciations, sharp as daggers, hurled against them.

It was characteristic of the Jacobins, she thought, to adopt and then suspend the constitution of 1793, and amid the despotism they created, the deaths of the king and queen and of reasonable men such as Malesherbes, Bailly, Condorcet, and Lavoisier destroyed the traditional glory of France. For the time allotted him Marat lived triumphant and alone: "sa figure était si basse, ses sentiments si forcenés, ses opinions si sanguinaires, qu'il était sûr que personne ne pouvait se plonger plus avant que lui dans l'abîme des forfaits. Robespierre ne put atteindre lui même à cette infernale sécurité.‡ Only the army, the spirit of which she greatly admires, kept a sort of peace in France by serving as its shield against foreign foes.

Robespierre attracts her special venom, partly because he had visited her father in 1789. He was not, she says, more able or more eloquent than others, but his political fanaticism had a quality of

---

* The movement was a national one; no faction, domestic or foreign, could have excited such enthusiasm. The whole of France shared it, and the stirring of a whole people always comes from true and natural emotions.

† Robespierre mixed obscure metaphysics with vulgar declamation, and the mixture made him eloquent.

‡ His face was so base, his sentiments so extreme, his views so sanguinary, that it was certain that no one could plunge deeper than he in that sink of crime. Even Robespierre himself could not get down to such infernal certitude.

calm and austerity that frightened his colleagues. She pictures him with something of the vividness of Carlyle, whose famous description may owe something to that of Madame de Staël:

Ses traits étaient ignobles, son teint pâle, ses veines d'une couleur verte; il soutenait les thèses les plus absurdes avec un sang-froid qui avait l'air de la conviction; et je croirais assez que, dans les commencements de la révolution, il a adopté de bonne foi, sur l'égalité des fortunes aussi-bien que sur celle des rangs, de certaines idées attrapées dans ses lectures, et dont son caractère envieux et méchant s'armait avec plaisir. . . . Danton était un factieux, Robespierre un hypocrite; Danton voulait du plaisir, Robespierre seulement du pouvoir; il envoyait à l'échafaud les uns comme contre-révolutionnaires, les autres comme ultra-révolutionnaires.*

But even Robespierre could not escape what he had been instrumental in creating. Madame de Staël describes the Terror as a descent, circle after circle, into the depths of Dante's Inferno:

Il semble qu'on descende, comme le Dante, de cercle en cercle, toujours plus bas dans les enfers. A l'acharnement contre les nobles et les prêtres on voit succéder l'irritation contre les propriétaires, puis contre les talens, puis contre la beauté même, enfin contre tout ce qui pouvait rester de grand et généreux à la nature humaine. Les faits se confondent à cette époque, et l'on craint de ne pouvoir entrer dans une telle histoire, sans que l'imagination en conserve d'ineffaçables traces de sang.†

Madame de Staël does not go back to antiquity for precedents, but no revolution in England has been thus terrible; as a result, "on dit aujourd'hui que les Français sont pervertis par la révolution."

But Robespierre finally fell, and shortly thereafter "l'irréligion la plus indécente," which had upset the social order and based crime on impiety, also collapsed. Robespierre's own colleagues turned against him.

* His features were ignoble, his skin pale, his veins of a green hue; he pushed the most absurd arguments with a self-controlled calm that looked like conviction; and I am quite persuaded that, at the beginning of the revolution, he was in good faith in adopting certain ideas about equality of fortune as well as of rank that he had picked up in his reading and that appealed especially to his envious, nasty character. Danton was seditious, Robespierre a hypocrite; Danton wanted pleasure, Robespierre only power; he sent some to the gallows as counterrevolutionaries and the rest as ultrarevolutionaries.

† One seems to go down circle by circle, like Dante, deeper and deeper into Hell. After his venom toward the nobles and the priests comes his bitterness toward property holders, then against talent, next against beauty itself, and in the end against anything great and generous in human nature that remained. Facts then become confused, and one fears to probe into such a story lest one's imagination be indelibly smeared with blood.

On vit donc cet homme qui avait signé pendant plus d'une année un nombre inouï d'arrêts de mort, couché tout sanglant sur la table même où il apposait son nom à ses sentences funestes. Sa mâchoire était brisée d'un coup de pistolet; il ne pouvait pas même parler pour se défendre, lui qui avait tant parlé pour proscrire.*

The details may not be strictly accurate, but the passage is sufficiently vivid.

Toward the end of her history Madame de Staël tries to be just to the good intentions of Bonaparte (who was to drive her into virtual exile), but though, when Bonaparte returned to Paris after the treaty of Campo Formio (1797) he had forced on the defeated Austrians, his qualities seemed to appeal to all those weary of turmoil, she was, says Madame de Staël, troubled by this popular adulation and felt a pronounced sentiment of fear. Even though in 1797 Bonaparte had no legal power, and though she saw him frequently, he intimidated her more and more. Small wonder that the last chapter of her history meditates on the fall of Napoleon as she had meditated on the fall of Robespierre:

Mais on ne peut se taire sur Bonaparte, lors même qu'il est malheureux, parce que sa doctrine politique règne encore dans l'esprit de ses ennemis comme de ses partisans. Car, de tout l'héritage de sa terrible puissance, il ne reste au genre humain que la connaissance funeste de quelques secrets de plus dans l'art de la tyrannie.†

In 1818, when her book was published, Madame de Staël had been dead about a year, foreign troops were evacuating the soil of France, the Ultras were slowly coming to control that kingdom, and events were shaping up to the revolution of 1830. By 1818 the romantic movement in French literature, which her book *De l'Allemangne* had done much to shape, was on its way to dominating the writing of a country that had once been dedicated to classicism.

* So this man, who for more than a year had signed an incredible number of sentences of death, lay there bleeding on the table where he had signed the doom of so many. His jaw was shattered by a pistol bullet; he could not even speak in his own defense, he who had spoken so often to condemn others.

† But one cannot be silent about Bonaparte, even when he is down on his luck, because his political doctrine still rules the minds of his enemies as it does those of his friends. For, out of all the heritage of his terrible power, humankind has retained only the dreadful knowledge of a few additional secrets about the art of tyranny.

XII

The Romantic Rebel

I have sketched the gradual disintegration of the high culture of the Western world in the eighteenth century under a variety of forces, including a rising tide of sensibility, a growing sense that the past was not as Voltaire and others had pictured it, and a feeling that a status society ordered in ranks and classes was not necessarily the eternal form of the state. We have seen that the romantics created a new theory of individualism, partly in consonance with and partly antagonistic to the "democratic" concept of the individual as citizen. They also developed a special theory of genius, some of the origins of which we have examined. And I have analyzed, however sketchily, some leading components in the two great revolutions of the eighteenth century, that in America and that in France, and simultaneously noted the emergence of two types of great personalities: the neoclassic hero as in the case of Washington, and examples of romantic egotism as in the instances of Rousseau and Robespierre. Movements of rebellion against an established order never wholly disappear; it was evident, for example, to Thomas De Quincey, a romantic recluse writing on Wordsworth in *Tait's Magazine* in September 1845, that the French revolution "has not even yet come into full action": "This mighty event was the explosion of a prodigious volcano, which scattered its lava over every kingdom of every continent, silently manuring them for social struggles; this lava is gradually fertilising all soils in all countries," and he named Milan, Rome, Naples, Vienna, and St. Petersburg as continuing centers of revolutionary activity.*

* The standard edition of De Quincey's *Writings*, edited by David Masson, that giant among Victorian literary scholars, came out in 1890 and was reprinted

Nevertheless, beginning in 1815, Europe sank into a kind of exhaustion after forty years of almost incessant war. There then came a minor eruption in 1820, a more formidable one in 1830, and a still more formidable disturbance in 1848, but these we must here pass over. One notes the paradox that the French revolution began by theoretically preaching the universalism of the rights of man and that, though this idea never disappeared (its Protean immortality included what came to be known as the religion of humanity), it also fed the divisive forces of emotionalized nationalism. That there is a frequent connection between the revolutionary spirit and the spirit of romanticism has, I hope, been evident. Unfortunately for historical simplicity, not all romantics were revolutionaries and some of them came to frown upon social upheaval, whereas both the American and the French revolutions made appeals more or less valid to antique precedents and adopted a vocabulary and an iconography that owed much to the classical world. There can be, it is clear, revolutions without romanticism and romanticism without revolution or at least without political revolution, although romanticism tends to imply some sort of radical break with some sort of current conventions, and often makes reference to an idealized world, compared to which the present condition of mankind is unsatisfactory. This does not imply that only the romantics dreamed of a fairer world, inasmuch as social reformers set up utopias of their own for an industrial society. Fourier is a case in point.

As the final chapter of this study hopes to show, "modern" man, more particularly nineteenth-century man, seems to work and live in what, following Spengler, one may call the Faustian tradition. In Germany even during the French revolution, and in the rest

by the AMS Press in 1964. The quotation in the text is from a long essay on Wordsworth, vol. XI, pp. 310–311. For De Quincey the Reign of Terror was a mere transitional phase. He notes in an essay first printed in *Blackwood's Magazine* in 1828 and collected into vol. X of the *Writings* that "the national convulsions by which modern France has been shaken produced orators," Mirabeau among them, but that authors such as Chateaubriand "have written the most florid prose that the modern taste can bear" (p. 121). In a set of essays on style, first published in *Blackwood's* in 1840–1841, he makes the interesting point that until the French revolution "no nation in Christendom except England had any practical experience of popular rhetoric; any deliberative eloquence, for instance; any forensic eloquence that was made public; any democratic eloquence of the hustings; or any form whatever of public rhetoric beyond that of the pulpit" (vol. X, p. 138).

of the Continent and in Great Britain after 1800, romanticism often remained rebellious without necessarily being revolutionary and perfectionist without necessarily being sociological. Therefore I propose in this and the following chapter to look at two types of the romantic egotist: the romantic rebel, whose protest is not so much directed against the state as against things in general; and the romantic dreamer, who, agreeing the present life is unsatisfactory, reverts to a past of his own creating, as Winckelmann did, or to a dream world of his own. This, too, may have some connection with revolutionary politics, yet it is difficult to think of E. T. A. Hoffmann, whose fantastic universe is *sui generis*, as a practical political revolutionary, just as it is difficult to imagine Wackenroder, who virtually invented a medieval era of his own, as a politician. Both types have their modern analogues, for their points of view anticipate what in our jargon one calls "alienation."

Despite the fact that there is no single body of romantic doctrine and despite the differentiations of the general movement by disparate nationalistic drives commonly involving the discovery, revaluation, or re-creation of a racial or national past,* there are some premises more or less common to romantic egotism. This body of general presuppositions lacks the neatness of the philosophy of the Enlightenment; nevertheless romantic art and philosophy were nourished by three interrelated, if occasionally incongruous, sources. These were Kantian and post-Kantian philosophy; a return after the revolutions to theology, Protestant or Catholic, that was

---

* The breaking up of romanticism as a cosmopolitan concept by the force of nationalism is especially evident in Germany after it became apparent to leading romanticists (principally of the so-called Second Romantic School) and to leading statesmen in Austria, Prussia, and lesser states that Napoleon was not to be a liberator but a dictator. The classic document is of course Fichte's *Reden an die deutsche Nation* (1808), skillfully phrased to avoid the censorship. Even before that date romantic poets were writing songs for the "War of Liberation," the Rhine became not a mere European river but a German stream, historic and symbolical, and a general return upon the Middle Ages as the age of faith and chivalry changed into a return upon a heroic German medievalism, powerful, unified, Christian — and Germanic. The climax of this mode of thought is presumably Hegel's assumption that if the rational was the real and the real was the rational, the German nation was to become real, rational, and "free," a model for the future of humanity. The topic is complex. There is an excellent brief discussion in Oskar Walzel, *German Romanticism* (translated by Alma Elise Lussky), New York, 1932, chapters vi and following; and see also the illuminating article, devoted, it is true, mainly to Adam Müller, by Goetz A. Briefs, "The Economic Philosophy of Romanticism," *Journal of the History of Ideas*, 2 (June 1941), 279–300.

virtually a revaluation of the relation between the soul and God; and inferences drawn from the rapid development of science in the decades under survey.

In the opinion of most historians the metaphysics of Kant (the *Kritik der reinen Vernunft* appeared in 1781 and was revised in 1787, the year the Notables assembled at Versailles) closes one chapter in the history of philosophy and opens another. The traditional eighteenth-century belief in universal rationalism had broken down. The world was neither as logical as Spinoza had thought nor as geometrically clear as it had seemed to Descartes. As one moves from these philosophers to Locke, from Locke to Berkeley, and from Berkeley to Hume, one notes the weakening and disappearance of faith in innate ideas. Locke had taught that all we know comes through the senses, and that our knowledge of an object in space — say, an apple — is individual in the sense that my sense of its redness is singular to me and cannot be communicated to anybody else. Yet the apple, to exist for me, must be presumed to exist in a universe having certain general characteristics, such as extension in space; and the mind, working on its sensory impressions, comes to recognize the existence of these general laws or principles of existence, among them, for example, the truth that causes have effects and effects have causes. Bishop Berkeley, however, inquired: if the particular redness of a particular apple is private to me, and if all my knowledge of the world "out there" comes to me only through my senses, why should the mind accept both the particularity in the apple *and* the general regularity of the outer world? It seemed to him that the only possible explanation is that God sustains both my subjectivity and the orderly world, each pattern paralleling the other. Each exists in God. But Hume inquired: if the only knowledge I have comes to me through my senses, how can I possibly arrive at a belief in the existence of God or in such a concept as the "law" of cause and effect? I can taste and smell and handle the apple and receive a distinct impression of it, and memories of my impression may often be revived in my mind, but I can neither handle nor touch nor smell nor see cause and effect. Is cause and effect anything more than a habit of congruency? I find certain things or events often follow upon certain other things or events, and it is convenient to call this relationship cause and effect, but this is merely a convenience not susceptible of proof. As for the existence of God, Hume examined all the arguments in favor of it and found all of them fallacious for much the same sorts of reasons. The individual psyche (in our terminology) was by him reduced to a casual bundle of sensory impressions and memories of impressions, and that was all.

The logic of Hume, it seems, confined my notion of what is real to my circumscribed experience as a finite being, to whose experience all tests of truth must be referred. Hume's skepticism was so profound that it left the usual doctrine of rationalism a shambles. Kant saw nothing wrong with Hume's logic as logic; what he discovered was that if you begin with the subjective experience of the individual, you can nevertheless construct an orderly world. True it is we can never know the world "out there"; that is, we can never know the objects that exist in it as in themselves they truly are. It is also perfectly true that I can have no sensory experience of an X I call cause-and-effect; yet objects cause me to have sensations, and though I can never know them as they really are, they exist in time and space as I do, since a timeless-spaceless world is an unthinkable condition if there are to be objects to be perceived and a mind to perceive them. It is true that time and space are not impinging upon my senses; what is true is that time and space are modes of thought without which all sensory experience is impossible. They are, in other words, conditions intellectually anterior to all sensory experience, pure categories without which neither we, nor our senses, nor the world is thinkable. Kant found certain other conditions-without-which regularity in sensory experience is impossible, and these he bound together into a single unitary principle, the "transcendental unity of apperception." "Transcendental" here means that the conditions which make sensory impressions possible must exist *before* experience (otherwise experience would not be); "apperception" means both the mind's perception of its own activities and the perceptions it has of things in themselves; and the "unity" of this famous phrase is, simply, individuation. In a parallel fashion Kant also restored a moral order, and to his own satisfaction asserted the existence of God as another condition-without-which what we think of as general sanity is impossible. Duty, for instance, is a categorical imperative; we cannot experience it as we experience an apple, but the world as experienced becomes nonsensical without our cognition (or our recognition) that there is an "oughtness" we accept, just as we accept time and space as preconditions to any experience of anything. There are two famous sentences in Kant's difficult prose that not only sum up his beliefs but also indicate how the Kantian transformation of philosophy referred "reality" to the world within rather than to the world "out there." The first is from the Conclusion of the *Kritik der praktischen Vernunft*:

Two things fill the mind with ever-growing wonder and awe, the more often and intensely the mind of thought is drawn to them: the starry heavens above me and the moral law within me.

The second is from his treatise on morals of 1797:

The only categorical imperative is this: act only on that principle through which you could at the same time will that your action should become a universal principle.

However carefully Kant might guard his logical proof for the a priori existence of time and space and insist upon the necessity of morality as action that can and should be capable of being universalized, it is clear that the weight of his analysis is thrown upon the subjective world rather than upon the world "out there." As we saw in discussing the romantic doctrines of individualism, post-Kantian philosophers such as Fichte seemed to twist the nature of individual existence into theories that could and did substitute, among romantic artists of all sorts, willfulness for will; or, if thinkers retained will as a central human characteristic, they seemed by a sort of logical jump either to argue that because the universe does not conform to my deepest wish I have a right to express my rebellion, or, more consistently, as in the case of Schopenhauer, to suppose that because pain and suffering are universal the will to live must forever batten on suffering. If the will were satisfied, it would by definition cease to exist. The romantics were interested in the wisdom of the East; and it is illuminating to remember that the Nirvana of Buddhism, the extinguishing of all desires in universal nihilism, parallels the pessimism of Schopenhauer. To will is to want, or to lack something desirable; if you school yourself to desire nothing, want vanishes and existence ends.

From the days of St. Paul the Christian faith has been analyzed and defended by rational arguments that make up the body of theology more or less common to all varieties of believers. The eighteenth century, however, though it had produced Bishop Butler's influential *The Analogy of Religion, Natural and Revealed, to the Constitution and Course of Nature* (1736), which concludes: "The whole, then, of [Christian] religion is throughout credible; nor is there . . . anything relating to the revealed dispensation of things, more different from the experienced constitution of things, than some parts of the constituents of nature are from other parts of it" — the eighteenth century, I say, turned the argument upside down and argued that if Christianity was not radically different "from the experienced constitution of things," and since the constitution of things predated the Christian era, why not, rationally speaking, insist that the constitution of things *was* older than Christianity? And if that be true, what was the logical evidence that proved Christianity to be truer than the constitution of things? Why not, as the deists argued, take the constitution of things as they obviously are as the proper basis for religion? Hence the vogue among intellectuals of deism; hence the famous Feast of the Supreme Being dear to the heart of Robespierre. But mere rationality in religious faith proved to be self-destroying, so that various movements, one of which was Pietism, returned to the religion of the heart. Some romantics rather favored Pietism because it represented an unspoiled state of the soul. More important, however, are two somewhat inconsistent positions. One was that institutionalized religion had not only failed to prevent the horrors of the French revolution but had also failed, because of its worldliness, to satisfy the thirst of the soul for spirituality. The other was that art was a more rewarding approach to faith than either the institutional church or its theology. Inconsistency arises from the fact that art neither corrected the excesses of the French revolution nor expressed anything more than the artist's own yearnings or opinions, scarcely a sound basis for systematic theology.

However this may be, the romantics tended to revolve endlessly around the relation of the finite human being to infinity. There were those who thought that a solitary search for faith rather than an institutionalized church was what they needed, and perhaps for this reason the hermit became a standard figure in romantic art. There were those who wanted the world to return to a simpler time, preferably the ages of faith, when Christian belief went hand in hand with chivalry, love was ennobling, all men were pure and all women were virtuous. Medieval art expressed this touching and noble simplicity of mind and humility of spirit. And there were those who, turning from theology because it was obsolete and from rationalism because it was shallow, saw the universe as dynamic, as a vast system of energy for good or evil, which they might admire or might attack. Hence it is that the romantics ran the gamut from saintliness to satanism, but it cannot be said that at either extreme theological rationalism had much to do with individual choices.

If it was possible to invoke illimitable energy as an evil thing, as many Gothic novels seemed to do, or if it was possible to return to the primal simplicity of goodness and adoration, one's choice, one's action or inaction commonly involved an element of ultrarational or mystical behavior. In either event it was assumed that the finite soul could as a matter of individual choice be opened to, or make contact with, the infinite. There is perhaps nothing new in this: in *Antony and Cleopatra* Cleopatra is made to exclaim, "I have immortal longings in me," but her craving is of a different order from Blake's belief that he saw the soul of his brother ascending from the dead body clapping his hands for joy, or the conviction of many German romanticists that art in general and poetry in particular were absolute modes of reaching infinite truth. In painting, the German Nazarenes by meekness, and in music Beethoven and Berlioz by violence, sought to lay hands on the kingdom of heaven.

Finally, romantic yearning found confirmation in curious beliefs suggested by or arising from science — too often from pseudoscience. Scientific historians are commonly not interested in scientific error but rather in the unfolding of scientific truth. But from 1763 onward, science seemed to promise wonderful short cuts to truth, new possibilities for the control of universal powers and for the expansion of the human mind. In the middle of the century Franklin had not merely demonstrated the kinship of lightning to electricity, he had suggested or seemed to suggest that electricity had many other marvelous properties. In the last quarter of the century Galvani had announced something he called "animal electricity," and even before that, Friedrich Anton Mesmer, who believed in astrology, had declared that "animal magnetism" was an occult force that permeated the universe and, properly directed, could cure diseases. In far-off America Dr. Elisha Perkins was to cure illness by stroking the patient's body with his metallic tractors, two rods that mysteriously conveyed a galvanic force to the body of the afflicted; his son, Benjamin Douglas Perkins, a graduate of Yale, was to go to London and there publish in 1798 *The Influence of Metallic Tractors on the Human Body*. In chemistry there was something equally mysterious called phlogiston, or "the principle of inflammability," which nobody could quite isolate but which, like magnetism, was part of the mysterious properties of the universe. Chemistry, moreover, depended upon chemical "affinities," an equally wonderful power that required certain elements to unite with other elements (or compounds) and form new compounds, all very mysterious.

Geology was equally romantic. Did the rocky strata of the earth originate in fire or in water? The Vulcanists argued for the one hypothesis, the Neptunists for the other, and both explanations found their way into the second part of Goethe's *Faust*. Mining, moreover, made steady advances, especially at the famous school of mines at Freiberg, where Abraham Gottlob Werner exerted a tremendous influence upon Europe for some forty years. Did mining, did the theories of the Neptunists and the Vulcanists confirm or deny the account of creation in Genesis?* Whether the theories were true or not, scientific mining revealed a new and fascinating world under the surface of the globe. Folklore told of kobolds and brownies; Swinburne's "obscure Venus of the hollow hill" held Tannhäuser in her power; somewhere in the buried vault of an ancient castle the great emperor Charles sat asleep, his long white beard flowing over a table, his knights sleeping around him, all waiting a horn-call that would waken them and send them forth to re-establish the universal empire of the Germans; the mysterious earth permitted dead lovers to rise out of their graves as in Bürger's "Lenore"; and there was the possibility of strange power emanating from underground for the benefit of those who knew the secret, as in Bulwer-Lytton's *Zanoni*.† Absurd? Anything was possible in a world in which it

---

* For a fascinating account of the extraordinary influence of geology on faith see Charles Coulston Gillispie's *Genesis and Geology*, Cambridge, 1951.

† For an account of occultism as a literary theme see Robert Lee Wolff,

was difficult to distinguish between the supposed powers of a Rosicrucian and the real discoveries of a Benjamin Franklin.

ii

The romantic rebel revolted against his lot not because, like Prometheus, he desired directly to promote the welfare of humanity but because, learning of colossal powers of this kind, or of the generations of men who had been previously happy, or because he yearned in his finitude to grasp the infinite, he desired to destroy or to exalt himself. He wanted to talk to God or the devil as an equal. Let me analyze three or four instances of romantic genius in rebellion.

I begin with Byron's *Manfred*, a dramatic poem of 1817, a work once thought so powerful that Robert Schumann, who created a beautiful musical setting for it,* burst into tears while he was reading the drama aloud to a circle of friends. The great Goethe declared that *Manfred* was an improvement on Hamlet's soliloquy about suicide.

The plot of *Manfred* is easily summarized. The period is vaguely in the past, presumably in the late feudal ages. The setting is in the high Alps and in the hall of Arimanes, somewhere in the underworld. The noble Manfred lives virtually alone in an Alpine castle, though there are servants. He is self-exiled from society and

---

Strange Stories and other Explorations of Victorian Fiction, Boston, 1971. This study, though in the matter of the occult chiefly concerned with Bulwer-Lytton, is equally applicable to uses of the pseudo-scientific in earlier fiction, such as Schiller's *Der Geisterseher*, Maturin's *Melmoth the Wanderer*, and Balzac's *Séraphita*. In *The Count of Monte Cristo* hashish dreams are directed to the salvation of the lovers; in Poe's "The Strange Case of M. Valdemar" hypnotism keeps a corpse alive and talking until, when the spell ends, it sinks into a mass of corruption; in the fourth act of Shelley's *Prometheus Unbound*, tyranny having been driven from its throne, all the sciences unite to create a new heaven and a new earth. But instances are innumerable.

* Schumann's overture to Manfred is still in the repertory of symphony orchestras, and there are recordings of it; the work as a whole is rarely produced. A recording of the entire melodrama (in the literal sense: Schumann's *Manfred* is a spoken play accompanied, or interrupted at intervals, by music) has been made by Sir Thomas Beecham, the Royal Philharmonic Orchestra, the B.B.C. Chorus, and a competent cast of speakers and singers, and, once the hearer accustoms himself to the declamatory style necessary for the projection of Byron's text (cut by Schumann), the effect is impressive. I derive Goethe's comment on the superiority of *Manfred* to Hamlet's soliloquy from Charles Burr's program notes for this recording, which is, I am told, out of print.

tortured by remorse for a mysterious crime: he has somehow
caused the death of Astarte, presumably his sister, since

> She was like me in lineaments — her eyes,
> Her hair — her features — all, to the very tone
> Even of her voice, they said were like to mine;
> But soften'd all, and temper'd into beauty.

Astarte shared his quest for "hidden knowledge" and possessed "a
mind / To comprehend the universe," together with all the "gentler
powers," including humility, and, cries Manfred:

> I loved her, and destroy'd her!
>
> .   .   .   .   .   .
>
> Not with my hand, but heart — which broke her heart;
> It gazed on mine and wither'd.

Tortured by remorse, he resolves to use his abnormal powers to
call before him "the spirits of earth and air," employing for that
purpose "a tyrant-spell"

> Which had its birthplace in a star condemn'd,
> The burning wreck of a demolish'd world,
> A wandering hell in the eternal Space.

The spirits appear and offer him sovereignty, power over the earth,
and control of the elements, but they are unable to offer him forgetfulness. At the end of this episode another spirit appears "in the
shape of a beautiful female figure" (Astarte, the sister who died
because of him), and Manfred collapses. We find him next on the
Jungfrau, where he soliloquizes upon the beauties of wild nature
and that "fatality to live" which tortures him, and, when he is
about to commit suicide by springing over a cliff, he is saved by a
chamois hunter, who takes him to his hut. Manfred is next seen
standing before a mountain cataract, from which he summons the
Witch of the Alps, who offers him great, if undefined, powers if
he will but obey her. Both because she cannot wake the dead and
because he fiercely insists upon his own will, he refuses —

> Obey! and whom? the Spirits
> Whose presence I command, and be the slave
> Of those who served me — Never!

Manfred then resolves to invoke the spirit of the dead Astarte, but for this purpose he must visit the dread hall of Arimanes, the "Prince of Earth and Air" — that is, Satan. Manfred will not bow down even to this dreadful monarch but with the aid of Nemesis he calls up the spirit of his beloved, who refuses to grant him either forgiveness or love but prophesies that tomorrow he will die. The last part of the poem takes place in Manfred's castle, where he is visited by an abbot, who labors in vain to reconcile Manfred to Christianity and to the society of other men. At a final meeting between Manfred and the abbot, a spirit appears (the tutelary genius of Manfred) to say that his last hour is at hand. The abbot again vainly intervenes; Manfred fiercely rejects the claim of the spirit to be his superior, exclaiming:

> I do not combat against Death, but thee
> And thy surrounding angels . . .
>   — I do defy — deny —
> Spurn back, and scorn ye!

and at the very end says to the Spirit (who, it appears, is accompanied by Demons):

> Back, ye baffled fiends!
> The hand of Death is on me — but not yours!*

His last words, addressed to the abbot, "Old man! 'tis not so difficult to die," are an affirmation of Byron's consistent belief that the quintessence of human individuality lies in the will — which Manfred in the first act identifies with

> The Mind — the Spirit — the Promethean spark,
> The lightning of my being.

* Echoes of the Faust story are suggested by Manfred's possession of supernatural powers, the appearance in the poem of various spirits, the fact that Manfred is filled with remorse for the death of Astarte, whose ghost he sees in the hall of Arimanes as Faust sees a double of Gretchen in the Walpurgisnacht scene in *Faust* I, the general contempt of Manfred for humanity, and the hidden powers of the earth, evident in the scene with the Witch of the Alps. Byron insisted that he had never read Marlowe's *Dr. Faustus*. He knew no German, though parts of *Faust* were once translated to him *viva voce* while he was living in the Villa Diodati on Lake Geneva. He composed the final act of *Manfred* in Venice, but this he rewrote upon the advice of William Gifford, John Murray's literary adviser. Byron himself protested that the poem was conceived and principally written in Switzerland, and that its "inspiration" was the Alps and "something else." That something else is glossed as his supposed incestuous relation with Augusta Leigh, his half-sister, so that when Lord Lovelace published documents concerning the Byron–Augusta Leigh relationship he entitled his volume *Astarte* (London, 1905, 1921).

His human will

> shall not yield to yours, though coop'd in clay!

Manfred's will power wins the admiration even of the demon world of Arimanes:

> Yet, see, he mastereth himself, and makes
> His torture tributary to his will.
> Had he been one of us, he would have made
> An awful Spirit.

This faint echo of Prometheus' resolve to endure torture rather than betray the human race to Zeus does not mean, however, that Manfred is in any sense either a philanthropist or a political revolutionary. On the contrary, his rebellion is against human finitude, as is evident from the following chain of passages:

> Sorrow is Knowledge; they who know the most
> Must mourn the deepest o'er the fatal truth,
> The Tree of Knowledge is not that of Life.

> There is a power upon me which withholds
> And makes it my fatality to live, —
> If it be life to wear within myself
> This barrenness of Spirit, and to be
> My own Soul's sepulchre . . .

> But we, who name ourselves its [the earth's] sovereigns, we
> Half dust, half deity, alike unfit
> To sink or soar, with our mix'd essence make
> A conflict of its elements and breathe
> The breath of degradation and of pride . . .

Manfred's joy was in the wilderness, and in "The difficult air of the iced mountain's top," and when he was compelled to return to the common life of humanity, "I felt myself degraded back to them, / And was all clay again." He dwells in despair, and recognizes that men

> are the fools of Time and Terror. Days
> Steal on us, and steal from us; yet we live,
> Loathing our life, and dreading still to die.

Recognizing the goodheartedness of the abbot, Manfred nevertheless announces that

> I disdain'd to mingle with
> A herd, though to be leader — and of wolves.
> The lion is alone, and so am I.

His final fierce assertion of scorn and independence is addressed to the spirit who has come to summon him to death:

> Thou hast no power upon me, *that* I feel;
> Thou never shalt possess me, *that* I know:
>
> .   .   .   .
>
> The mind which is immortal makes itself
> Requital for its good or evil thoughts, —
> Is its own origin of ill and end —
> And its own place and time: its innate sense,
> When stripp'd of this mortality, derives
> No colour from the fleeting things without,
> But is absorb'd in sufferance or in joy,
> Born from the knowledge of its own desert.
> *Thou* didst not tempt me, and thou couldst not tempt me;
> I have not been thy dupe, nor am thy prey —
> But was my own destroyer, and will be
> My own hereafter.

The force of rebellious solipsism cannot further go.

iii

Manfred belongs to no ascertainable nation and is not the chief of any group of persons exiled from society. In this he differs from Karl Moor, the hero of Schiller's *Die Räuber*, who heads a band of brigands in order to avenge himself upon the *mores* of society. So likewise does the hero of Heinse's *Ardinghello*, a novel in which a group of pirates vow to have all things in common and are necessarily the enemies of organized society. But Hugo's *Hernani* — though it includes the bandit motif and though Hernani is really a grandee of Spain who desires to avenge the death of his father, executed at the order of the former king — is of a different order of rebellion, even if it be argued that the Don Carlos of the play is a disguised satirical attack on Charles X, last of the Bourbon kings of France. Charles was overthrown about four months after the famous first night of *Hernani*, which occasioned the historic battle between the romanticists who applauded and the classicists who hissed, in Paris on February 25, 1830. (The revolution of

379

1830 took place during the first days of July.) It is true that in a preface dated March 9, 1830, Hugo says there is, or should be, a connection between liberty in literature and liberty in the state, but his liberty is not the antisocial anarchy of *Die Räuber* nor the communalism of *Ardinghello*: "Dans les lettres comme dans la société, point d'étiquette, point d'anarchie: des lois. Ni talons rouges, ni bonnets rouges." The modern reader, furthermore, finds it difficult to discover in Don Carlos many of the traits of Charles X, who, despite a dissipated youth, ruled as a relatively austere reactionary; Don Carlos, the future emperor Charles V, though for three acts he is engaged in the amorous pursuit of Doña Sol, in the last two acts is presented as a great and responsible ruler. Just before his election as emperor of the Holy Roman Empire, he utters a very long soliloquy before the tomb of Charlemagne, the ideational substance of which goes back to Hugo's early celebration of the sacrosanct qualities in throne and altar. The world was, it seems, happier when there was but one ruler — the emperor — and one head of a universal church — the pope. A note of humility creeps into Carlos' meditations:

> Etre empereur, mon Dieu! j'avais trop d'être roi!
>
> .   .   .   .
>
> Mais, moi! qui me fera grand? qui sera ma loi?
> Qui me conseillera?*

His first imperial act is to pardon the conspirators against his life, to restore Hernani to all his dignities, and to urge forward Hernani's marriage with Doña Sol. There may be occasional hits at the Bourbons in this lengthy drama, but they are not the conspicuous element of Hugo's famous play.

If it requires a special effort of the historical imagination, even with the aid of Schumann's music, to understand the powerful impact of *Manfred* on the younger generation of Europe in and after 1817–1818, the reading of *Hernani* is embarrassing. Perhaps its transformation into *Ernani*, an early Verdi opera, the libretto by Piave, is its proper fate. Piave, however, seized upon only the melodrama of *Hernani* and missed its deeper significance. Nevertheless it is difficult to resuscitate the faded glories of what was

---

* Be emperor, good Lord! Being king was too much for me! / . . . Me! Who will make me great? Who will guide me? / Who counsel me?

once a magnificent spectacle, a thrilling plot (three men fatally in love with one woman), a daring challenge to dramatic tradition, and a shocking innovation in the diction proper to French tragedy.

Everything is too pat, including the characters, who make sudden decisions on a *pundonor* basis, so that their reversals of attitude are rather *coups de théâtre* than true transformations of character. Doña Sol does little but suffer and make rash and mistaken promises, Don Ruy Gomez * is not so much a villain as an aging nobleman out of Gothic romance who has his revenge at the end, regrets it, and dies, and Hernani, though ostensibly motivated by a thirst to avenge his father, and elected by lot to assassinate the future Charles V, too quickly accepts the imperial pardon and forgets that he has pledged himself to die whenever Don Ruy Gomez demands it by blowing Hernani's horn — a horn like that blown in de Vigny's fine poem, "Le Cor" (1825), to announce the death of Roland:

> Dieu! que le son du Cor est triste au fond des bois!

The plot seems contrived and silly, the characters are too prone to make incredible speeches, and, despite all the costuming and the elaborate sets, Hugo does not revive the Spain of Charles V but gives us a sort of glorified magic-lantern show.

The story, though complex in the sense that it includes numerous disguises, theatrical changes of resolution, and sudden rescues, is simple and soon told. Hernani has withdrawn from all society to head a band of brigands, most of whom are also noblemen, partly to escape imprisonment or death and partly to discover ways of killing Don Carlos, king of Spain. Through some chance anterior to the play, Hernani has fallen desperately in love with Doña Sol, the young ward and niece of the aged Don Ruy Gomez, who plans to marry her himself. Don Carlos comes secretly to woo Doña Sol, who remains faithful to Hernani throughout, and who, when circumstances compel her to assent to a wedding with Don Ruy Gomez, conceals a dagger among her wedding jewels. Out of the highest possible motives the three men, discovering that they are rivals, each, to protect one rival against another, guards the life of his own "enemy."

---

* After the Spanish custom the don's full name is Don Ruy Gomez y Silva, and he is therefore sometimes referred to as Silva in the play.

For a time everybody saves the life of everybody else; but on one fatal occasion, Hernani, to show his gratitude to Don Ruy Gomez for shielding him in difficult circumstances from the anger of the king, gives Don Ruy Gomez his own horn, saying that when he, Hernani, hears the horn blow, he will render up his life. The sudden election of Carlos to be emperor requires Carlos to act magnanimously and in the crypt, before the tomb of Charlemagne, he forgives the conspirators. In the fifth act the happy marriage of Doña Sol and Hernani (Don John of Aragon) has just been celebrated when Don Ruy Gomez, disguised as a black masker, causes Hernani's horn to be blown and insists that our hero keep his oath; just before the final curtain Doña Sol and Hernani share a death by poison. Then Don Ruy Gomez, overwhelmed by the disaster he has precipitated, stabs himself, crying out in the last six syllables of the last hexameter in the text: "Morte! — Oh! je suis damné."

There is more to *Hernani* than naive melodrama, gorgeous language, and a succession of *coups de théâtre*, and that "more" is the conception of Hernani himself, who is not so much the *homme fatal* as a man doomed from the beginning by the conditions of the universe. He can, like Manfred, believe that "I loved her and destroyed her." But beyond that there is in Hernani something not so much primitive as primary. He honors, it is true, the code of the Spanish nobility with all its punctilio, but his rebellion against Spanish royalty is not so deep-seated that he cannot accept a royal pardon and resume his place at court. He rebels not so much against "tyranny" as against the conditions of life and is in fact like Manfred a primordial lover, whose true home is wild nature and whose love is destined to ensure the death of the beloved. Almost desperately he tries to persuade Doña Sol not to love him:

> Oh! ce serait un crime
> Que d'arracher la fleur en tombant dans l'abîme!
> Va, j'en ai respiré le parfum! c'est assez!
> Renoue à d'autres jours tes jours par moi froissés.
> Epouse ce vieillard! c'est moi qui te délie.
> Je rentre dans ma nuit. Toi, sois heureuse, oublie!*

* Ah! Would it be a crime / To pluck the flower as I fall into the depths! / Come, I have smelled its perfume, that's enough! / Join to some other life this life that I have damaged. / Marry this ancient [Don Ruy Gomez]. I free you to do it. / I go back into my dark. You be happy, forget! (Act II, scene iv.)

Not once but many times in his *tirades* he dwells upon his difference from other men:

> Parmi nos rudes compagnons,
> Proscrits, dont le bourreau sait d'avance les noms,
> Gens dont jamais le fer ni le coeur ne s'émousse,
> Ayant tous quelque sang à venger qui les pousse?
> Vous viendrez commander ma bande, comme on dit;
> Car, vous ne savez pas, moi, je suis un bandit!
> Quand tout me poursuivait dans toutes les Espagnes,
> Seule, dans ses forêts, dans ses hautes montagnes,
> Dans ses rocs, où l'on n'est que de l'aigle aperçu,
> La vieille Catalogne en mère m'a reçu.
> Parmi mes montagnards, libres, pauvres, et graves
> Je grandis . . .
> > Vous frissonez! réfléchissez encor.
> Me suivre dans les bois, dans les monts, sur les grèves,
> Chez des hommes pareils aux démons de vos rêves.
>
> .   .   .   .
>
> Me suivre où je suivrai mon père, — à l'échafaud.*

Not unnaturally Doña Sol exclaims:

> Etes-vous mon démon ou mon ange?
> Je ne sais. Mais je suis votre esclave . . .†

And in Act III, scene iv, one reads of Hernani's sense of doom:

> Tu me crois peut-être
> Un homme comme sont tous les autres, un être
> Intelligent, qui court droit au but qu'il rêva.
> Détrompe-toi. Je suis une force qui va!
> Agent aveugle et sourd de mystères funèbres!
> Une âme de malheur faite avec des ténèbres!
> Où vais-je? je ne sais. Mais je me sens poussé
> D'un souffle impétueux, d'un destin insensé.

---

* Among our rough companions? / Fugitives whose names the hangman knows already, / Men whose knives, like their hearts, are never unready, / Each driven by having a death to avenge? / You [Doña Sol] will come and command what they call a band? / Because — you don't know — I am a bandit! / When I was hunted everywhere, in every part of Spain, / Alone old Catalonia, in her woods, her peaks, / In her rocks where one is seen only by the eagle, / Took me in like a mother. / Among my mountain men, free, poor, austere, / I grew up . . . / You shudder! think once more. / To follow me in the woods, in the hills, on the strands, / Among men who are like the demons you dream about / . . . To follow me to where I shall follow my father — to the gallows. (Act I, scene iii.)

† Are you my demon or my angel? / I don't know, But I am your slave . . . (Act I, scene ii.)

Je descends, je descends, et jamais ne m'arrête.
Si parfois, haletant, j'ose tourner la tête,
Une voix me dit: "Marche!" et l'abîme est profond,
Et de flamme ou de sang, je le vois rouge au fond!
Cependant, à l'entour de ma course farouche,
Tout se brise, tout meurt. Malheur à qui me touche!*

In a still later scene with Doña Sol Hernani describes himself in a succession of wild natural figures:

Mon âme
Brûle . . . Eh! dis au volcan qu'il étouffe sa flamme,
Le volcan fermera ses gouffres entr' ouverts,
Et n'aura sur les flancs que fleurs et gazons verts.
Car le géant est pris, le Vésuve est esclave!†

including the fact that he once had the lightning for his sword; and when Don Ruy Gomez comes to demand that Hernani fulfill his fatal oath, Hernani compares the aged Don Ruy to a demon:

Si tu n'es pas un spectre échappé de la flamme,
Un mort damné, fantôme ou démon désormais,
Si Dieu n'a point encor mis sur ton front: "Jamais!"‡

This, and passages like it, are somewhat excessive even for a revolutionary; they are rather the words of a great cosmic rebel such as Milton's Satan, who, totally dissatisfied with the universal scheme of things, rebels for the sake of rebelling:

To bow and sue for grace
With suppliant knee, and deifie his power
Who from the terrour of this Arm so late
Doubted his Empire, that were low indeed,

---

* Perhaps you think me / A man like all the others, a being / Of intelligence, who drives straight at his dreamed-of goal. / See your mistake. I am an unleashed force! / A blind, deaf actor in dark mysteries! / A soul of misfortune made of shadow! / Where I go? I know not. But I feel myself pushed on / By a tempestuous wind, a mindless destiny. / I go down, I go down, and never do I stop. / If sometimes, panting, I dare turn my head, / A voice says: On! And the gulf is deep, / Whether from blood or flame I see red in its depths! / Meanwhile, along my wild path, / Everything is shattered, everything dies. Woe to whoever comes near me.

† My soul / Burns . . . Oh! Tell the volcano to put out its flame, / The volcano will close its half-opened gulfs, / And bear upon its slopes only flowers and green grass. / For the giant is trapped, Vesuvius is a slave! (Act V, scene iii.)

‡ If you are not a ghost escaped from Hell, / A dead man damned, phantom or ghost forever, / If God has not written on your brow: "Never!"

That were an ignominy and shame beneath
This downfall; since by Fate the strength of Gods
And this Empyreal substance cannot fail . . .
                    (*Paradise Lost*, I: 111–117)

This does not mean that Hernani is so grand a figure as Satan but only that Manfred, Hernani, and Satan are of the same category of minds. They believe that will is equal to theology.

Even more a cosmic rebel than Hernani is de Vigny's Moïse, depicted in a poem of 1822. The austerest of romantics — and there are those who would not classify him among the romantic poets — de Vigny, at least in his poetry, was attracted to the epic subject, the large theme, the great and philosophical person or event, as in *Eloa*, in which a "fallen" angel joins Lucifer, "Le Cor," which beautifully details the death of Roland as experienced at an epic distance, or "La Colère de Samson," obviously, like "Moïse," drawn from the Bible. His romanticism is shown in *Stello* (1831), which began to appear periodically in *La Revue des deux mondes* in 1831 as "Les Consultations du Docteur Noir, petit fragment d'un gros livre," a series of dialogues between Stello, a misunderstood poet, and Dr. Noir, who seems to represent rationality. In this work de Vigny thinks of poets who died in their prime — Chatterton and Chénier are examples — and finds poetic genius an extraordinary gift and a human misfortune. When Dr. Noir asks Stello: "Are you a poet?" the romantic Stello replies:

Je crois en moi, parce que je sens au fond de mon coeur une puissance secrète, invisible et indéfinissable, toute pareille à un pressentiment de l'avenir et à une révélation des causes mystérieuses du temps présent. Je crois en moi, parce qu'il n'est pas dans la nature aucune beauté, aucune grandeur, aucune harmonie qui ne me cause un frisson prophétique, qui ne porte l'émotion profonde dans mes entrailles, et ne gonfle mes paupières par des larmes toutes divines et inexplicables. Je crois fermement en une vocation ineffable qui m'est donnée, et je crois, à cause de la pitié sans bornes que m'inspirent les hommes, mes compagnons en misère, et aussi à cause du désir que je me sens de leur tendre la main et de les élever sans cesse par des paroles de commisération et d'amour. . . . de même je sens s'éteindre les éclairs de l'inspiration et les clartés de la pensée lorsque la force indéfinissable qui soutient ma vie, l'Amour, cesse de me remplir de sa chaleureuse puissance; et lorsqu'il circule en moi, toute mon âme en est illuminée; je crois comprendre tout à la fois l'Eternité, l'Espace, la Création, les créatures et la Destinée; c'est alors que l'illusion, phénix au plumage doré, vient se poser sur mes lèvres, et chante.*

These are, of course, the words of an imagined personage, but Stello is only thinly disguised, and de Vigny's quarrel with the universe is very much like Byron's and Hugo's in *Hernani*.

"Moïse," from the "Livre Mystique" section of the collected poems, goes back to the Pentateuch for its scene and its character. Soon after the poem opens, Moses is seen high on the mountain top of Nebo surveying both the host of Israel and the Promised Land he is never to enter. Most of the time in his monologue he speaks to the Lord in the cloud, through which alone, according to Deuteronomy, mortal man could come face to face with God. He utters a long apologia, each section of which concludes with the melancholy refrain:

> Laissez-moi m'endormir du sommeil de la terre.†

What has he not accomplished for the Eternal One? What secrets of the universe are not known to him? What miracles has he not wrought?

> Je commande à la nuit de déchirer ses voiles;
> Ma bouche par leur nom a compté les étoiles,
> Et dès qu'au firmament mon geste l'appela,
> Chacune s'est hâtée en disant: "Me voilà."
>
> .   .   .   .
>
> J'engloutis les cités sous les sables mouvants;
> Je renverse les monts sous les ailes des vents;
>
> .   .   .   .

---

* I believe in myself, because I feel in the depths of my heart a secret force, invisible and not to be defined, exactly like a foreshadowing of the future and a revelation of mysterious causes in the present. I believe in myself because in nature there is no beauty, no grandeur, no harmony that does not stir a prophetic shudder in me, that doesn't move me to the depths of my body, and doesn't swell my eyelids with wholly divine, inexplicable tears. I believe in an ineffable vocation that is vouchsafed me, and I believe, because of the endless pity that men, my companions in suffering, inspire in me, and also because of the need I feel to hold out a hand and lift them endlessly with words of sympathy and love . . . just so I feel flashes of inspiration, and the light of thought, darkened when the undefinable force that sustains my life, Love, stops filling me with its warming power; and when it circulates within me, my whole soul is lighted up; I believe I understand, all at the same time, Eternity, Space, Creation, created things, and Destiny; that is when Illusion, that Phoenix with golden wings, alights on my lips, and sings.

† Let me sleep the sleep of the earth.

Le fleuve aux grandes eaux se range quand je passe,
Et la voix de la mer se tait devant ma voix.

   .   .   .   .   .   .

Vos anges sont jaloux et m'admirent entre eux. —
Et cependant, Seigneur, je ne suis pas heureux.*

Why not? Moses rebels against the conditions of terrene existence:

Vous m'avez fait vieillir puissant et solitaire.†

The very conditions of leadership have separated him from humanity, left him glorious but melancholy:

J'ai marché devant tous, triste et seul dans ma gloire,
Et j'ai dit dans mon coeur: "Que vouloir à présent?"
Pour dormir sur un sein mon front est trop pesant,
Ma main laisse l'effroi sur la main qu'elle touche,
L'orage est dans ma voix, l'éclair est sur ma bouche.

   .   .   .   .   .   .

— O Seigneur! j'ai vécu puissant et solitaire,
Laissez-moi m'endormir du sommeil de la terre!‡

By an ironical twist the last section of the poem shows the mountain free of clouds but lacking Moses, as Joshua, pale and subdued, marches toward the Promised Land,

Car il était déjà l'élu du Tout-Puissant.§

De Vigny wrote in a letter in late December 1838: "The great name of Moses serves only as a *persona* (mask) for man in every century both modern and antique: the man of genius, weary of his eternal widowerhood, despairs on seeing his solitude vaster and more arid in proportion as he grows. Weary of his grandeur, he demands nothingness." This is identical with the thirst of Manfred

---

* I command the night to strip away her veils; / My mouth has counted, each by its name, the stars / And as soon as I beckoned to something in the firmament / Each thing hastened forth to answer: "Here am I." / . . . I bury cities under moving sands, / And overturn mountains with the wings of the wind; / . . . Great rivers draw aside to let me pass, / And the ocean's voice is silent when I speak. / . . . Your angels are jealous and admire me among themselves — / And even so, O Lord, I am not happy.

† You have made me grow old, powerful and alone.

‡ I walked ahead of all, sad and alone in my glory, / And I said in my heart: "What can I wish for now?" / My head is too heavy to sleep upon a breast, / My hand frightens the hand I touch, / The storm is in my voice, lightning is on my lips. / . . . — O Lord! I have lived powerful and alone, / Let me sleep the sleep of the earth.

§ For already he was the chosen one of the Almighty.

for extinction. Let us have done with this eternal tension between the conditions of mortality and infinitude.

Occasionally this total dissatisfaction with the finite universe was, as it were, checked and regularized, albeit the discipline had to come from within and not merely from without. An illuminating case is the last drama by the Prussian writer, Heinrich von Kleist (1777–1811), whose enigmatic personality was a puzzle to himself and has been a puzzle to interpreters ever since. His father died when Kleist was eleven; he once had a tutor named Martini, who said with considerable insight that Kleist's was a fiery soul not to be dampened; he served in the Prussian army from 1792 to 1797, when he resigned in disgust; he entered the university at Frankfurt an der Oder, where, it is said, his discovery of Kant's categorical imperative increased his despair, and he became engaged to the daughter of a general, an engagement he broke off in 1802. He wandered around Europe during the last years of his life, at one time resolved to enter the French army, at another time (after Jena) being made a prisoner by the French. He was usually poor and he was a haunted man. After failing to induce another woman to die with him, he arranged a double suicide on the banks of the Wannsee near Potsdam with a female friend, one Henriette Vogel, the two of them spending a cheerful evening together before the fateful morning. They also invited two guests for dinner the evening after their death, having arranged with the innkeeper to serve dinner for four! Kleist wrote poetry, essays, fiction, and plays. His tales are memorable because they have far more structural form than most German romantic fiction; a typical one is the tragic story of *Michael Kohlhaas* (1811), for which Housman's line: "Be still, my soul, and see injustice done," might serve as an ironic epigraph.

Kleist's plays were written in the last seven or eight years of his troubled life. They range from the melodrama of *Die Familie Schroffenstein* (1803), virtually a belated Storm-and-Stress play, through *Penthesilea* (1808), possibly his most characteristic tragedy, to *Prinz Friedrich von Homburg* (1810), which heads toward tragedy and ends as an example of self-discipline. Kleist's little essay on the puppet theater ("Ueber das Marionettentheater"), which appeared in the *Berliner Abendblätter* and purports to be a dialogue between Kleist and a male ballet dancer with an enthusiasm for puppetry, throws some light on Kleist's aesthetic beliefs. The amateur of puppet plays alleges that because puppets, though mechanically manipulated, follow beautiful lines mechanically and mathematically determined, they offer lessons to dancers; and the lesson is borne home by a singular contest between a bear and a skillful fencer, in which the bear always successfully parries the thrusts of the fencing-master's weapon. Perhaps Kleist is laughing at us, but the point of this enigmatic essay seems to be that the springs of action in the natural world are and must be different from, perhaps superior to, the actions dictated to us by skill, however excellent, or art, however ideal.

One commentator on Kleist (Marcel Brion in *L'Allemagne romantique*, Paris, 1962) seems to regard Kleist as virtually a somnambulist, and finds in his plays a dialogue between two states of being — what is possible and what is desirable. Art is a kind of somnambulism, in which the unconsciousness evokes and eventually discharges (as action) what the consciousness is directed to do. The only explanation for the queer state of being in which Prinz Friedrich finds himself when that play opens is a kind of self-hypnosis, which is later to dictate to him his rash action at the battle of Fehrbellin, June 18, 1675. The drama begins on the evening before the battle. The prince is a cavalry leader. The Electoral Prince of Brandenburg-Prussia has made a most careful and thoroughly Prussian plan of battle, which, indeed, brings victory over the Swedes. Instructions to the several divisions of his army are particular and minute, and it is specified that Prinz Friedrich and his cavalry are not to move from their posts without exact orders to do so. But when the play begins, the prince is discovered seated in a sort of trance under an oak tree in the palace garden weaving a laurel crown of victory. He can scarcely be aroused; and when he attends the general staff meeting he hears, but does not take in, the orders of battle. At what seems to him a crucial moment in the struggle, he suddenly gives the order to charge, an attack which routs the Swedes and in fact ensures victory. But he has disobeyed orders; the Electoral Prince declares that he must be court-martialed, and the sentence is death. Pleas to spare the prince are made to the Elector by various personages, including Natalie, who loves him, but the Elector will not yield unless Friedrich himself concedes the justice of the military sentence.

The conflict is therefore between the discipline of earth and the sudden insight of genius, a conflict within the soul of Friedrich himself. Friedrich tears up the petition for clemency signed by many, which the Electoral Prince has given him to read, and announces his decision:

> Ich will den Tod, der mir erkannt, erdulden.
>
> . . . .
>
> Ruhig! Es ist mein unbeugsamer Wille!
> Ich will das heilige Gesetz des Kriegs,
> Das ich verletzt, im Angesicht des Heers,
> Durch einen freien Tod verherrlichen!*

At the last moment he is pardoned. Before American readers dismiss this *coup de théâtre* as a thoroughly Prussian ending, let them remember that the dilemma of *Prinz Friedrich von Homburg* is like the dilemma of *Billy Budd*, the difference being that Melville sternly sends Billy Budd to execution whereas Kleist spares his erring prince. The philosophic point is that the transcendental rebel can be subdued, pardoned, or punished only by his own transcendental will.

iv

The transcendental rebel can be reconciled to things as they are in finitude only or mainly by a transcendental act of will, as in the example of Prinz Friedrich. The reconciliation comes about only as the romantic rebel accepts things as they are either because they afford glimpses into infinity or evidences of ideal beauty, a reconciliation that may be in a general sense religious, as in the Catholic revival and the Oxford movement; or because he reads them in a general sense as metaphysical, personal, or mystical symbols, as do many romantic dreamers, to whom we shall presently come. Perhaps the greatest example of reconciliation is the colossal instance of Beethoven, the towering genius who in the words of the subtitle of a popular biography "freed music." The phrase points to a factual half-truth and to a vaster mystery. The half-truth lies in the fact that all European music after Beethoven

---

* I shall suffer the death sentence which has been passed upon me. Be still! It is my determined will. I will honor the sacred law of war, which I violated, through a death freely elected on my part in the sight of the soldiers.

is richer, fuller, more various in tone color and harmony than it had been in the days of Haydn and Gluck; the unexpressed falsity in the phrase is twofold: first, Beethoven inherited, but did not invent, most of the musical forms that he superbly used — the sonata, the fugue, the rondo, the symphony, the variations on a single theme, the oratorio, the Singspiel, the Lied, the concerto, and so on, some of minor importance. These he twisted into personalized expressions. Second, Beethoven profited from the creation of the piano as a rich and self-sufficient solo instrument, from the movement of music out of private residences into the concert hall, from the increasing interest in, and exploitation of, musical personalities (the career of Paganini is a case in point), and from the gradual etiolation of the concept of the composer as an artist in his own right whom it was the duty of society, or an important part of society, to support. This change in the attitude toward art and artists Beethoven, a man who knew his own worth, did much to bring about. It is also a tragic truth that Beethoven's growing deafness, which, fortunately, came upon him only after he had reached maturity, altered the tonal and harmonic qualities of his composition: it is as difficult to think of the young Beethoven composing the last five string quartets (the opus numbers are 127, 130, 131, 132, and 135) as it is to think of Vivaldi composing the Fifth Symphony. Finally, although it is commonly, and rightly, said that Beethoven is in music what Shakespeare is in modern literature, the master of us all, Beethoven did not invent "romantic" music all by himself. The work of von Weber, Berlioz, Schubert, Schumann, Chopin, Liszt, and others, whether they were born in Beethoven's time or came after him, is as fully of the fabric of the romantic period as the Moonlight Sonata. It should also be remembered that Beethoven paid tribute to composers as apparently remote from him as Cherubini, whose *Médée* (1797), still performed, he heard in Vienna in 1802. Incidentally it should be said that Cherubini was far more involved in the French revolution and the fortunes of Napoleon than was Beethoven.

The innumerable and radical innovations that Beethoven made in harmony, key relationships, counterpoint, tempo, and orchestral coloring, and in giving an organic inner life not merely to sonatas, symphonies, choral works, and the like but also to parts within these compositions are matters for the musical theorist and the musicologist. Beethoven was not Tom Paine. That he radically altered the status of musical genius in the aristocratic society of Vienna is unquestionable. If, on the one hand, he composed the *Eroica*, he wrote the flaccid *Wellington's Victory; or, The Battle of Vittoria* in 1813 and published it in 1816, possibly the flattest piece of orchestral music he ever composed. He was equally capable of the mediocre *Consecration of the House*, an overture put together in 1822, and of "Adelaide" (1795), one of the masterpieces of song. He was, after all, a professional musician who, though he was singularly lacking in sound financial judgment, lived by selling his wares, so that he could accept a commission for twenty-five Scotch songs (1815–1816) because musical nationalism was commercially profitable, and for his own satisfaction in 1825–1826 write the Rabelaisian and outrageously funny *Rondo a capriccio* in G for the piano ("Rage over a Lost Groschen"), which is as much a product of Beethoven's genius as the String Quartet in B Flat (op. 133), written during the same years. They are all phases of the incomparable energy we call Beethoven. Mozart brought to a superb conclusion that superb elegance, not therefore lacking tragic depths, which is perhaps the greatest single legacy left us from the eighteenth-century world. Beethoven revolutionized music in the sense that he is the eternal dramatist of the soul, that quintessential problem of much, if not most, nineteenth-century art. Mozart lives with the muses and the graces, Beethoven on the cliff that received Prometheus.

When one thinks of Beethoven, one does not think of the run-of-the-mill music that he, like many another composer, turned out either to keep his hand in, or for pay; one thinks of the *Eroica*, the Fifth Symphony, the Seventh, the Ninth, the *Missa Solemnis*, the *Archduke Trio*, the overtures to *Egmont* and *Coriolanus* among others, the great piano and violin concerti, the "Waldstein," "Apassionata," and "Hammerklavier" piano sonatas, the sonatas for the violin or cello, and above all that incomparable expression of mystical peace, the "Arietta. Adagio molto semplice e cantabile" which concludes the last piano sonata (op. 111), and which follows at the right psychological distance the crashing chords of the introduction to the first part of the composition, eighteen bars in length, that promise the titanic struggle of the "Waldstein" but in fact end in transcendent reconciliation. No melody can be simpler than the

"Arietta," no set of variations (before Liszt) can be more professional and complex, yet no musical statement by Beethoven ever surpassed this incomparable expression of spiritual humility finding a peace that passes understanding.

Beethoven was not a political radical, albeit his struggle upward from being the grandson of a Flemish tailor and the son of an alcoholic musician to a position of virtual equality with the Austrian nobility, a genius who died, appropriately enough, in the midst of a hailstorm accompanied by thunder and lightning, is as good a proof of the rights of genius as the French Declaration is of the rights of man. His private life, as all the world knows, was plagued by family troubles, including the care of an irresponsible nephew (the fact that the nephew finally contracted a respectable marriage does not alter the fact that he was arrested by the police, attempted suicide, and was expelled from Vienna while he was under his uncle's care). Beethoven had no money sense and no sense of "belonging," he longed for affection and received instead admiration, his love affairs brought no peace to his restless soul, and, beginning about 1798, his growing deafness — that worst of catastrophes in the world of music — seemed a spiteful affliction of the gods. He grew more and more irascible, quarreled with staunch friends, and had perforce to live in the private world of his own art, a phrase that must not be construed in terms of any art-for-art's-sake movement. But if he was difficult as a personality, he was admired as a genius, and during the Congress of Vienna in 1814–1815 he was virtually the equal of the sovereigns of Europe. His will power was magnificent, his patience in working from source motives preserved in notebooks and on scraps of paper to the immense effectiveness of theme in his grander compositions was incomparable, and though like many another genius he was occasionally dull, he was never shoddy.

It is impossible to make words do the work of music, and I shall not try, but the unmistakable quality of Beethoven in his most characteristic masterpieces is dramatic intensity — not the dramatic intensity of the theater but the dramatic intensity of the soul. Despite the opinions of many musicologists to the contrary, I believe this dramatic intensity, in the works of his third period especially, was heightened by his deafness, which cut him off not merely from normal intercourse with mankind but also from the natural music of wood and field. It is true that the trained musician can read a score and comprehend it perfectly without necessarily hearing it played. But the gigantic inward struggle, the passionate alternation of protest and release in the subjective life of this composer had for him no echo in the outside world. Like William Blake, or Poe, or Hoffmann, he therefore built an inner universe of his own, though that universe of course lacks their fantasticality and is in the deepest sense both Biblical in its simplicity and Sophoclean in its movement from torture to release. One does not need to be a Christian to understand the "Et incarnatus est" of the *Missa Solemnis*, the "Benedictus," or the "Agnus Dei" of that masterpiece any more than one has to have been a prisoner to "understand" the "Prisoners' Song" ("O welche Lust!") of *Fidelio*. Berlioz was a romantic rebel. So, if in lesser degree, was Schumann. But the supreme example of titanic (though apolitical) rebellion passing into the infinity of peace among the romantics is the music of Ludwig van Beethoven. All Western music leads up to him, all Western music leads away from him, even our modern practitioners of *musique concrète*. Homer in the ancient world, Dante in the Middle Ages, Michelangelo in the ripeness of the Renaissance, Shakespeare in drama, and Beethoven in music — these are the five great pillars of such enduring culture as we still possess.

XIII

Romantic Dreamers
and Idealists

Probably all theory is a subjective correction of, or protest against, reality. Geometry, for example, is not in nature as we commonly gloss these two terms, nor is mathematics, at any level from the simplest arithmetic to Gödel's theorem that the higher branches of mathematics assert principles or propositions that are basically unprovable. Line, says Emerson, in Nature is not found. Chemistry is an exact science only in the laboratory under test conditions, themselves the result of elaborate artifice. However wonderful human achievement may be in physics or astronomy, there forever lurks in each science the possibility of the appearance of an X, which is, as it were, nature untamed or in the raw. In the main, natural action, it is true, is consonant with our presuppositions, but nature sometimes fails to perform according to formula. This geologists know, who analyze strata and rock and dust with wonderful acuity and who can define with accuracy areas of the earth where earthquakes are likely to occur — for example, the San Andreas fault — but who can never tell with certainty when a new tremor may shake some city in California. The history of medicine is a tale of finer and finer analysis, obliterating the errors of the past and exploring new areas of disease and pain, but any practicing physician feels that every new patient is an enigma, whose physiology or psychology may in the long run prove an insoluble riddle.

What is true of science, that most delicate and precise element of man's subjective theorizing, is necessarily also true of theology, of philosophy, of the social sciences, and of the arts. Thus in the world of fiction the naturalist claimed to record only what human material, forever chained to physical form, does or thinks it does, and this "objective" reporting, with only a little tinkering, was supposed to be a relatively exact record of human life. We have long since given up the naive naturalism of the nineteenth century; yet it is useful to note that fictional naturalism, when it succeeded, succeeded only by selectivity in the observer's mind, a selectivity among "natural" phenomena as naive as the assumptions of a fairy story. The naturalist writer inevitably left out three-fourths of life. What is true of naturalism is quite as true of classicism in the age of Louis XIV or of sentimentalism in the time of Marivaux and Richardson. Art, like thought, is a process of subjective selectivity. As Blake put it,

> The vision of Christ that thou dost see
> Is my vision's greatest enemy.

We speak, of course, of the "spirit of an age," a convenient verbal shorthand, a convention which helps us to organize what we call history. But the spirit of an age is nothing more than a loose set of pragmatical generalizations credible because in a given culture at a given time some group or groups of artists or philosophers tacitly agreed for a while to accept artifices in common so that they could "communicate" with each other and with their culture. French dramatists, for instance, set up elegant phrases for sexual attraction, among them "mes flammes," but they could not and did not therefore infer that the emotions of all men, real or imagined, have a mathematical identity. We recognize the common elements that make up classicality in music, or think we do;* yet within these strongly held conventions we do not mistake Corelli for Mozart, nor was there anything in the common postulates of Gluck and Piccinni to prevent their adherents from quarreling violently over the individual talents of the two composers.

When Winckelmann dreamed of the past, he dreamed of an Athens that never existed, and this idealization of Greece was a mode of protecting his dream from the coarse contact of fact. Neither the American nor the French republic succeeded in uni-

---

* On music see the remarkable analysis by Charles Rosen, *The Classical Style: Haydn, Mozart, Beethoven*, New York, 1971.

versalizing the "virtue" they attributed to the Rome of Brutus. We sometimes smile at the belief that there are eternal, absolute, and unalienable rights, although we take with great seriousness the doctrine of the libido, the id, the ego, and the super-ego, or did until experience and impatience began to modify these constructs. The romantic rebel appealed to a city in the skies that never existed, the political conservative assumed a past that was equally shadowy, the romantic nationalist conjured up a Gaul or an ancient Germany or a Celtic past or a heroic age in Scandinavia, each of which is, one fears, simplistic in its ideality.

If I now speak of the romantic dreamer, I unite him with, and differentiate him from, other thinkers or modes of thought. The union comes in his subjectivity, like the subjectivity of the scientist; the differentiation arises from the nature of his performance, expressed in a difficult essay, "On the Relation of the Plastic Arts to Nature" (1807), by Friedrich von Schelling, which argues that the artist is in nature but not of it. His materials are the elements of nature, yet his art must surpass nature; and art, the product of his soul, both acknowledges the existence of nature with all its imperfections and exults over nature because it raises expression to a superior level. The romantic dreamer tries to do precisely this.

The phrase "romantic dreamer" may be misleading. It seems to imply lack of will or of purpose, an idiosyncratic refusal to face "facts," a preference for escapism over reality. Some part of this implied reproach is true. But the great romantic is more than a daydreamer. Like the prophets of the Old Testament, the romantic dreamer possessed conviction that what he saw with his inner eye was reality and what he saw with his physical eyesight was mere semblance, a veil drawn for some inscrutable reason between him and eternity. Blake is again invaluable: you are led, he wrote,

> to believe a lie
> When you see with, not thro' the eye.

The romantic dreamer might desire change or reform as intensely as any other radical, but he might also come to the conviction, sometimes despairing, sometimes triumphant, as in the conclusion of Shelley's "Ode to the West Wind," that until the minds of all men are awakened to the glory of what is ideal, "tyranny," however glossed, remains unalterable. He therefore sets himself the task of communicating his vision of ineffable perfection to all mankind. Or the romantic dreamer may seek peace of soul as does the mystic, Christian or other, by concentrating on the world within him rather than by combatting the world without him.* To such personalities public activity seems on occasion to be so obviously self-defeating that they renounce it in favor of what are to them more attainable ends.

It is true that many leading romantic figures were simultaneously romantic dreamers and romantic rebels or romantic politicians. Carlos Baker, after quoting an amusing anecdote from E. M. Forster's *The Celestial Omnibus* about a man who boasted he had seven copies of Shelley in the house, dryly observes that there are, indeed, seven Shelleys — the radical reformer, the classical Hellenist, the romantic humanist, the lyricist, the philosophical poet, the tragedian of human corruption, and the unorthodox theist, a God-intoxicated man.

Coleridge was a poet, a philosopher, an editor, a propagandist, a critic, and a politician of sorts; he was also addicted to opium, like De Quincey, though it cannot be asserted with confidence that his most famous poems necessarily developed out of his opium dreams. The literary sources of these works have been patiently traced by John Livingston Lowes, and what Lowes calls the magic synthesis that worked in the deep well of Coleridge's unconscious yields us three of the most amazing dream poems in all English literature, "The Ancient Mariner," "Christabel," and "Kubla Khan." The first was completed, the other two were not. It is illuminating to know that when a minor poetess, Mrs. Anna Letitia Barbauld, complained that "The Ancient Mariner" had no moral, Coleridge replied that the great fault of the poem was the obtrusion of moral

---

* See in this connection the excellent introduction by A. Gillies to his edition of Wackenroder and Tieck, *Herzensergiessungen eines kunstliebenden Klosterbruders*, Blackwell's German Texts, Oxford, 1966. Among other valuable observations, the editor says that when art and religion were at a low ebb in Germany this book gave a new impetus, launched a notable revival, in both fields. The *Herzensergiessungen* seems to have been the first formidable challenge to Winckelmann's contention that Greek art, as he understood it, was absolute and supreme. The book is, among other things, a prose poem in praise of Dürer and Raphael, and also something of a catch-all (like *Wilhelm Meister*). Note in "Das merkwürdige musikalische Leben des Tonkünstlers Joseph Berglinger" that Berglinger, refusing to become a physician, leaves home in pursuit of music, returns to his father's deathbed, expresses his feelings of guilt and alienation in an "Oratorium," and dies, destroyed by his imagination and his love of music, the art to which all romanticism aspired.

sentiment into a work that should have been pure imagination. As for the unfinished "Christabel," the best guess is that the point of the tale was to have been the salvation of the wicked by the virtuous, a sufficiently practical aim for both a Christian and a conservative.

"Kubla Khan" is "a vision in a dream" and persistently remains a fragment because, if we are to believe Coleridge, "a person on business from Porlock" interrupted him as he was writing down his vision, which "passed away like the images on the surface of a stream into which a stone has been cast, but, alas! without the after restoration of the latter." One can perhaps be grateful to the person from Porlock, thus unconsciously responsible for a fine example of the fragmentary dream poem, some fifty lines which have no logical meaning but which educe a universe of wonder.

> In Xanadu did Kubla Khan
> A stately pleasure-dome decree:
> Where Alph, the sacred river, ran
> Through caverns measureless to man
>   Down to a sunless sea.
> So twice five miles of fertile ground
> With walls and towers were girdled round:
> And there were gardens bright with sinuous rills,
> Where blossomed many an incense-bearing tree;
> And here were forests ancient as the hills,
> Enfolding sunny spots of greenery.

Suddenly we learn of a deep chasm

>   which slanted
>   Down the green hill athwart a cedarn cover,

that this chasm "with ceaseless turmoil seething" sends forth the water of a fountain, intermittently and terribly tossing up dancing rocks, and that here is the source of the mysterious river, which, after

> Five miles meandering with a mazy motion
>
>   .   .   .   .   .   .
> . . . reached the caverns measureless to man,
> And sank in tumult to a lifeless ocean:
> And 'mid this tumult Kubla heard from far
> Ancestral voices prophesying war!

Precisely what this war is to be we never learn, for, after a magical description of the shadow of the dome of pleasure, we suddenly turn to a totally unrelated theme:

> A damsel with a dulcimer
> In a vision once I saw:
> It was an Abyssinian maid,
> And on her dulcimer she played,
> Singing of Mount Abora.

Scholarship can locate the literary origins of the Abyssinian maid and of Mount Abora, which, however, appears on no terrestrial map — nor does this matter, for again the dream changes, when we learn that the power of poetry and music is absolute, that music alone can build the pleasure dome, and that the poet is a personage to be feared:

> Beware! Beware!
> His flashing eyes, his floating hair!
> Weave a circle round him thrice,
> And close your eyes with holy dread,
> For he on honey-dew hath fed,
> And drunk the milk of Paradise.

Why the milk of Paradise and why its danger? Why the Abyssinian maid? Why the dangerous chasm, and the ancestral voices, and the mysterious pleasure dome, that

> miracle of rare device,
> A sunny pleasure-dome with caves of ice!

No reason can be asked or given, except perhaps that of Poe at the end of "Israfel":

> If I could dwell
> Where Israfel
>   Hath dwelt, and he where I,
> He might not sing so wildly well
>   A mortal melody,
> While a bolder note than this might swell
>   From my lyre within the sky.

Rational explanation of the dream is as impossible as explanation of its philosophical or public meaning. This is no escape from "reality," but a reality more compelling than what we think of as ordinary and actual.

The evocation of a world of vision is notably characteristic of many German romantic poets, with whom the word *Traum* recurs a countless number of times. Any handy anthology of German verse will illustrate this fact. Here is a celebrated quatrain by Ludwig Tieck:

> Mondbeglänzte Zaubernacht,
> Die den Sinn gefangen hält,
> Wundervolle Märchenwelt,
> Steig auf in der alten Pracht.

Poetry among the Germans, said Madame de Staël, was perpetually trying to approach the condition of music. Here is Clemens Brentano's "Abendständchen":

> Hör, es klagt die Flöte wieder,
> Und die kühlen Brunnen rauschen.
> Golden wehn die Töne nieder,
> Stille, stille lass' uns lauschen!
>
> Holdes Bitten, mild Verlangen,
> Wie es süss zum Herzen spricht!
> Durch die Nacht, die mich umfangen,
> Blickt zu mir der Töne Lichte.*

Brentano seems to be the first to have discovered the Lore Lay above Bacharach on the Rhine, but Brentano's admirable poem on this story has been eclipsed by Heinrich Heine's "Die Lorelei," which not even the Nazis could suppress: they had to pretend it was a ballad, the authorship unknown. It appeared in the "Die Heimkehr" section (1823–1824) of his *Buch der Lieder*:

> Ich weiss nicht, was soll es bedeuten,
> Dass ich so traurig bin;
> Ein Märchen aus alten Zeiten,
> Das kommt mir nicht aus dem Sinn.
>
> Die Luft ist kühl und es dunkelt,
> Und ruhig fliesst der Rhein;
> Der Gipfel des Berges funkelt
> Im Abendsonnenschein.

* The German quotations run: (from Tieck) Moonlit night of magic, that catches the mind in its spell, O wonderful fairytale world, rise up in ancient splendor; (from Brentano) Listen, the flute is sorrowing again, and the cool springs are rippling; the golden notes drift down, let us listen quietly, quietly. A lovely demand, a faint desire — how sweetly it speaks to the heart! Through the night which surrounds me the illumination of these notes gleams on me.

Die schönste Jungfrau sitzet
Dort oben wunderbar,
Ihr goldnes Geschmeide blitzet,
Sie kämmt ihr goldenes Haar.

Sie kämmt es mit goldenem Kamme,
Und singt ein Lied dabey;
Das hat eine wundersame,
Gewaltige Melodei.

Den Schiffer im kleinen Schiffe
Ergreift es mit wildem Weh;
Er schaut nicht die Felsenriffe,
Er schaut nur hinauf in die Höh.

Ich glaube, die Wellen verschlingen
Am Ende Schiffer und Kahn;
Und das hat mit ihrem Singen
Die Lore-Lei getan.*

Another version of the *femme fatale* theme? A parable? A vision of evil? A striking instance of the ballad revival? None of these matters: we have turned from the world-as-it-is to the world as perhaps it might have been. And, again illustrating the complexity of romantic temperament, let us not forget that the creator of this world-famous fairy tale is also the author of the satirical *Deutschland*, perhaps the only long poem in European literature to satirize a nation in its entirety, of cynical parodies of the Christian heaven, and of stinging prose essays that are part of the literature of the Young Germany movement which preluded the revolutions of 1848.

There is no clear connection between "Die Lorelei" and Heine's political liberalism, just as there seems to be no connection between

---

* I do not know what it can mean that I am so sorrowful; but a legend from ancient times will not go out of my head. The air is cool, it darkens, the Rhine quietly flows; the top of the mountain glitters in the evening sunshine. The lovely maiden sits up there, beautiful; her golden jewelry flashes, and she combs her golden hair. She combs it with a golden comb and sings a song meanwhile that has a miraculous and powerful melody. With its wild sorrow it grips the sailor in his little boat; he does not see the rocky ledge, for he looks only upward. I believe that in the end the waves drowned the sailor and his boat; and this the Lorelei did with her singing.
There have been a hundred attempts to turn "Die Lorelei" into English verse, but none of them is ever quite successful, such is the magic of its simplicity. Some of the words in the original are archaic in form.

Tieck's romantic moonlit forest and Brentano's murmuring sounds on the one hand and politics or religion on the other. One might find the general conditions of human existence unsatisfactory and so dream of a world in which, for example, all honest work was done by honest craftsmen and all great work was art, as Tieck does in *Franz Sternbalds Wanderungen* (1798), an "old German tale," which Wackenroder helped to create, or in Wackenroder's *Herzensergiessungen eines kunstliebenden Klosterbruders* (1797), to which Tieck contributed such items as the sections "Sehnsucht nach Italien" and "Brief eines deutschen Malers in Rom." The book is an extraordinary mixture of mystical outpourings concerning religion and art. In such ahistorical retreats into history the writer turns away from the classical dream of Winckelmann to another dream universe in which artists such as Dürer and Raphael satisfy man's unending thirst for beauty and holiness. So, too, the fictions of Jean Paul Richter have for their central characters no persons with continuing responsibilities of the common sort. Life is spent amid a sort of Disneyland of unexpected events, comic catastrophes, and whimsical characters contrived after the admired model of Laurence Sterne.*

To the dreaming writer (who, to be sure, may work hard enough at his craft) the universe he summons up seems at once richer and more unpredictable than man's ordinary humdrum existence. The dreamer may produce a fairy tale for adults, such as Brentano's *Geschichte vom braven Kasperl und schönen Annerl* (1817) or Tieck's *Der blonde Eckbert* (1796),† but neither these nor Tieck's

---

* This seems to be generally true. Thus the hero of *Hesperus* (1792–1794) has a protean capacity for changing not only his mind but his personality, and, says one commentator, the author gives him three souls, a sentimental one, a philosophical one, and a humorous one. The hero of *Siebenkäs* (1795–1796) has a split personality, which he tries to bind together by humor. Richter at one point addresses Siebenkäs: "Dear hero, please remain one!" The great exception to the general observation is Richter's influential *Titan* (1800–1803), the hero of which "would like to storm through heaven like a cascade" and demands of nature perpetual energy. But the more famous character in this novel is Roquairol, whom physical strength and sensuality force into an evil whimsicality that ends in suicide. Roquairol is described as a child of the century who unfortunately finds nothing in which he can believe. In general the nearest English equivalent to what is most characteristic in Richter is Carlyle's *Sartor Resartus*, published in book form in 1836. Carlyle had previously brought out four volumes of German "romances" (1827).

† These days of Freudian analysis of literary productions are perhaps prepared to take "dream" literature somewhat more seriously than did the nineteenth century. Thus in her essay, "Ludwig Tieck's 'Der blonde Eckbert': A Psychological

strange drama *Der gestiefelte Kater* (1797), the hero of which is a
cat and the audience for which is sometimes on the stage and sometimes in the auditorium, can compare, say, with *Candide* as a reading of life, though *Der gestiefelte Kater* has its satirical touches.

In truth a good many romantics, whether they were politically
minded or no, found the same pleasure in constructing a world of
beautiful impossibilities as the Gothic novelists found in putting
together their tales of terror. For example, there is no evident
"public" meaning to Keats's *Endymion*, or to "The Eve of St.
Agnes," unless one chooses to think that Madeline in "The Eve"
is somehow the victim of oppression. If she be, it is sheer folly to
waste time putting platters of sweets, including

> jellies smoother than the creamy curd,
> And lucent syrops, tinct with cinnamon,

at the side of her bed before Porphyro wakes her by playing "her
hollow lute" and singing "La belle dame sans merci." Shelley's
wan poet in *Alastor; or, the Spirit of Solitude* (1816), his first major
work, flees from the world of men, including

> His cold fireside and alienated home,

pursues "Nature's most secret steps," goes to the vale of Cashmire,
where a veiled maid speaks to him in "low solemn tones" about

> lofty hopes of divine liberty,
> Thoughts the most dear to him, and poesy;

then, after a trancelike sleep, is taken on a remarkable journey in
a boat

> long abandoned, for its sides
> Gaped wide with many a rift, and its frail joints
> Swayed with the undulations of the tide.

Reading," *PMLA* 85 (May 1970), 473–486, Victoria L. Rippere argues that this
fairy story has a latent no less than a manifest meaning. Bertha steals jewels and
causes the death of two animals in Tieck's narrative. This commentator argues
that on a latent level the story is that of the failure of a narcissistic child to attain
the norm of social adaptation prescribed for her in a workaday world; for this
critic the story has an inner psychological coherence not previously apparent.
Whether Tieck knew that he was indulging in fancies about incestuous marriage
and sexual development (or lack of development) is a nice point in the historical
interpretation of literary works. One cannot, however, wholly shrug off this
approach.

The boat, however, proves unsinkable and at long last carries the poet to

> a tranquil spot, that seemed to smile
> Even in the lap of horror,

where nobody else has ever been, and there he dies, his last sight being one of the great moon. We learn incidentally in a coda to the tale that

> Heartless things
> Are done and said i' the world,

but the dream landscapes, a mixture of beauty and terror, do nothing for politics as Shelley's *The Mask of Anarchy*, written in 1819, four years later, does something for politics by excoriating the stupidity of the so-called Peterloo massacre:

> Let the fixèd bayonet
> Gleam with sharp desire to wet
> Its bright point in English blood,
> Looking keen as one for food.
>
> .   .   .   .   .
>
> And that slaughter to the Nation
> Shall steam up like inspiration,
> Eloquent, oracular;
> A volcano heard afar.

The landscape of dream is also found in the work of a figure more familiar to Americans, Edgar Allan Poe. Whatever one may think of "The Raven" as a poem, the house, the bird, the episode, and the somnambulistic dreamer are creations out of space, out of time, for in "The Raven" time by and by is frozen into immobility. Where Poe's "Al Aaraaf" takes place nobody really knows; the universe of discourse in which it exists has nothing to do with common life. A living woman and a particular Richmond house suggested Poe's famous short lyric, "To Helen," but the poem is, like "Kubla Khan," a dream vision:

> Helen, thy beauty is to me
>   Like those Nicéan barks of yore,
> That gently, o'er a perfumed sea,
>   The weary, way-worn wanderer bore
> To his own native shore.

On desperate seas long wont to roam,
  Thy hyacinth hair, thy classic face,
Thy Naiad airs have brought me home
  To the glory that was Greece
And the grandeur that was Rome.

Lo! in yon brilliant window-niche
  How statue-like I see thee stand,
  The agate lamp within thy hand!
Ah, Psyche, from the regions which
  Are Holy Land!

There is no use protesting the confusion of Helen and Psyche, of seas that are both desperate and perfumed, just as it is useless to ask who the weary, way-worn wanderer may be and to what native shore he is returning. Common sense does not matter in a visionary universe which includes "The Haunted Palace," "The Conqueror Worm," and "The City in the Sea":

Lo! Death has reared himself a throne
In a strange city lying alone
Far down within the dim West.

.   .   .   .   .

There shrines and palaces and towers
(Time-eaten towers that tremble not)
Resemble nothing that is ours.
Around, by lifting winds forgot,
Resignedly beneath the sky
The melancholy waters lie.

Eventually

Down, down that town shall settle hence,
Hell, rising from a thousand thrones,
Shall do it reverence.

The same world, half vision, half nightmare, in Poe's tales creates the whirlpool that drowns the ship in "Ms. Found in a Bottle," and "some large, old decaying city near the Rhine" where Legeia was born, she whose beauty of face had "the radiance of an opium-dream," whose eyes were large and strange, whose mind was encyclopedic, and whose will power momentarily conquered death. It also contains the strange, decaying house of Usher, the mere sight of which creates "an utter depression of soul" and the inhabitants of which have baffled criticism and scholarship ever since the story was written.* Here, too, are the catacombs where Montresor chained and walled up Fortunato in "The Cask of Amontillado"; the strange gardens of "The Domain of Arnheim" and "Landor's Cottage"; and the "alley Titanic" "hard by the dim lake of Auber" "in the misty mid region of Weir," where the poet on a moonlit October night "pacified Psyche and kissed her," but could not bring Ulalume back to life because "the pitiful, the merciful ghouls" had sent a spectral moon to prevent the resurrection of the dead. Poe was not without satirical force and logical acumen, and that he had political views, conservative in tone, is proved by a queer story of his entitled "Mellonta Tauta." It is also true that he was a professional journalist and often a hack writer, not to speak of being a critic of worldwide influence. But when one thinks of Poe, one thinks first of all of these weird landscapes, these zombies, the uncanny minds and extraterrestrial powers of the masks he created in his poems and stories.

ii

If one compares the passages of poetry and the tales I have just cited to such standard eighteenth-century productions as *Candide*, or Addison's "Ode," or *Nathan der Weise*, it is evident that a radical change has occurred in the sensibility of the Western world. It seems a fair guess that one important cause for these dream poems, these odd pictures of the universe, this evocation of a half-world of fairyland or purgatory is cultural and political frustration of the artist's desire to express himself. After 1789 and especially after 1799 both the political and the cultural climate changed. Repressive measures in Great Britain and Ireland, the Alien and Sedition laws in the United States, waves of terrorism in France and in some of its satellite states, censorship, which grew increasingly heavy-handed in the Napoleonic world, and the obstinate resolve of the Congress of Vienna after 1815 that Europe should see no more revolutionary convulsions † damped or diverted for a

* For a sampling of the wide variety of interpretations occasioned by "The Fall of the House of Usher," see *Poe Studies* 5 (1), June 1972. These range from incest to a theory of *Doppelgängerei*.

† The best possible study of the tension between repression and progress, as well as that between forward-looking minds and conservative, but by no means unin-

time the minds of ardent youth, weary of war. Some went to live in voluntary exile, Shelley and Byron among them. Others stayed at home and changed their system of values, as did Coleridge and Wordsworth. In Germany, after the tumultuousness of the Storm and Stress period, many writers turned to a mystical view of Catholicism or of the Middle Ages or, just before and during the War of Liberation, to a feverish nationalism that produced valuable propaganda but that also paved the way for reactionary censorship. It was impossible to build Jerusalem in England's green and pleasant land, and some who tried to do so, such as Joseph Priestley, fled to America. Other radicals were deported and occasionally hanged. Madame de Staël was forced into exile by Napoleon. A younger generation in France, once it got over the burden of warfare and the gloom of defeat, was temporarily divided between a mystical adherence to throne and altar and a desire to return, if possible, to the better parts of the tenets of revolution. Concerning the ministry of Pitt and the following years, the Reverend Sydney Smith remarked that it was an awful time to be alive for those who entertained liberal opinions. Smith was speaking of Britain; his remark was applicable to much of Europe. In South America, it is true, patriotic armies destroyed the Spanish colonial empire and threatened that of Portugal, but they so often quarreled among themselves that dictatorship resulted from these contests quite as often as a genuine republic. It must be remembered that some extreme revolutionaries thought society must be totally destroyed before it could be rebuilt.

In such an environment idealism and personality, if they were to be expressed, had to disguise themselves as fairy tales, as history, as theories of education, as landscape, as dream, even as narratives of man's inhumanity to man, since inhumanity at least implied that humanity was somehow thinkable. The dream, of course, might be turned almost against the will of the dreamer (or with his consent) into a nightmare, but nightmares of such a kind were preferable to some sorts of actuality. The landscape in "Kubla Khan" might

telligent, statesmen in Great Britain during the period is the first volume of Elie Halévy's incomparable *A History of the English People in the Nineteenth Century*, vol. I, most easily available as *England in 1815*, a paperback edition published in London and New York, 1961. Despite the title, the book is an admirable survey of tendencies in English politics, economics, and thought virtually from the accession of George III, and does not confine itself to 1815.

be populated by either seraphs or demons; at least it was not populated by bankers, bureaucrats, or a Biedermeier bourgeoisie. Whatever crimes a Roderick Usher committed, he was neither Ferdinand VII of Spain nor Nicholas I of Russia. The Lorelei cruelly caused the death of an innocent sailor; she was not responsible for the massacre of Greeks by the Turks or of Turks by the Greeks. If at the end of "The Eve of St. Agnes" Madeline and Porphyro flee into the storm, they are certainly not being sent to Botany Bay by a reactionary British judge. The poet in *Alastor* freely decides to leave mankind, but not because he is being victimized by Ferdinand I, the despotic king of Naples. The restlessness of the romantic dreamer is therefore understandable, and so is the quality of his visionary protests, because his protests were so far historically justified that the Congress of Vienna could no more restrain revolt than Wordsworth's sonnet against the projected Kendal and Windermere Railway could stop railroad building in the industrial revolution.

There is, however, a more fundamental element than frustrated romantic egotism in the poems and stories I have cited. The world in "Kubla Khan" is a curiously restless world, a world in which enormous rivers do incredible things. Tieck's moonlight and Brentano's murmuring springs have some sort of secret property. The Lorelei is doubtless folklore, but that mysterious witch also incarnates some special power beyond the control of humanity. I need not expatiate on the inexplicable performances of natural forces in Shelley's *Alastor*, or in Poe's poems, or in "The Fall of the House of Usher" and in others of his tales. The great fact is that the comfortable universe of Locke and Newton, the *Encyclopédie* and the Royal Society — and I call it comfortable because its operations were supposed to be both comprehensible and predictable — was turning into a universe of energy, and this energy was enigmatic (as in *Faust*), possibly even demoniac. Either the human personality would so expand itself that it could confront and perhaps control a dynamic universe or it must retreat before the demons of electricity, of steam, of earthquake, of tidal wave, or some other vast manifestation of cosmic power.

The romantic dreamer was also the cosmic visionary at times, at once accepting and protesting against vast forces beyond the explanation of religious creeds. This note of energy, of gigantism, even of ferocity begins more and more to appear in all the arts. The story of Medea comes from classical mythology, but when even so relatively "quiet" a composer as Cherubini in his *Médée* of 1797 gets through with his heroine, she is no classical woman of the Winckelmann sort but the incarnation of superhuman vengeance. *Der Freischütz* (1821) of Karl Maria von Weber is supposed to be the first German opera, which is perhaps true, but the composer said that the most important line in his composition is the statement by Max, the hero: "Doch mich umgarnen finstre Mächte!" ("But the dark powers enmesh me.") The "dark powers" are incarnate in the demoniac Samiel, differentiated from all the other characters by not being given a line to sing. Samiel's earthly home is a wolf-glen like a bottomless pit of hell, so deep the moon cannot penetrate the ghastly cloud forms floating in it; and Max, like Faust, catches horrid glimpses of one he knew in normal life: he sees the spirit of his mother lying in her grave and warning him to go back before he falls into the power of Samiel. In the end a mysterious hermit appears from nowhere and saves Max and his sweetheart from destruction, and the villainous Kaspar dies. A folk story? Yes. But, says von Weber, I deliberately gave a dark orchestral coloring to the whole to emphasize the sinister and nameless terrors of the wild. Protest and nightmare also shape Berlioz' first great concert success, the *Symphonie fantastique* of 1830. A sequel, the far inferior *Lélio; ou la retour à la vie* of 1831, at least makes explicit that the symphony is supposed to be an opium nightmare in the soul of a lover struggling against the forces of destiny. In the same period the virtuosity of Paganini (1782–1840), whose skill as a performer is supposed never to have been equaled, was explained by the assumption that he had sold himself to the devil — a legend Paganini did nothing to disclaim. Call the devil Mephistopheles, put him into Goethe's poem, and he becomes an agent of energy, one half of a Manichaean division of the universe between destruction and creation.

The same transformation of tranquillity into dynamism, and at that a dynamism felt to be superhuman, appears in painting. To pass from the agrarian peace of Constable's "The Cornfield" to the wild thrust of viaduct and rushing train out of a stormy sky in Turner's "Rain, Steam, and Speed" is to pass from a world in which man controls nature to a world in which energy is beginning to control man. "Nature" in Watteau or Sir Joshua Reynolds or Benjamin West is tapestry or stage set, a mere backdrop for the activities of humanity. General Wolfe died in battle on the Plains of Abraham outside the walls of Quebec, a setting sufficiently picturesque, one would think, to attract the attention of a painter. But when one looks at West's painting of 1770, now in the National Gallery of Canada, the setting might be anywhere, since the background is principally composed of sunlight and cloud, and the entire emphasis of the painter is on a human action, translated, it is true, into heroic proportions. So Mrs. Siddons as the Tragic Muse in Sir Joshua's portrait of her sits in a curule chair with two shadowy figures behind her, heroic, indeed, but shrouding her chair from "nature." If, however, one turns to the masterpiece of young Théodore Géricault, "The Raft of the 'Medusa,'" which dates from 1818–1819, one finds, indeed, the theme of human action, more particularly of social protest, since the wreck of the ship was supposed to have been a political scandal, but on the canvas the pitiful remnants of humanity are unequally pitted against the ocean and the gale. Some of them are dead, some of them are dying, some of them are in despair, and a heroic few — those with strength enough to do so — are attempting to signal a distant ship. The composition is in a sense as classically patterned as is "The Death of General Wolfe," but the theme is not that of dying for a glorious victory, the theme is one of the cruelty of inhuman nature and the alternation of selfishness and self-sacrifice in man. So likewise in Delacroix's "The Massacre of Chios" (1822; repainted 1824) in the Louvre, the helplessness of the victims and the inhumanity of the conquering Turks are emphasized by a vast landscape that stretches beyond the helpless prisoners into infinity.* Géricault's explorations of the madhouse, Goya's studies of war, assassination, torture, and stupidity, Delacroix's fascination for battles, animals playing or in combat, African *convulsionnaires*,

---

* In the art histories this sometimes comes out as "The Massacre at Scios" or at Scio.

If one looks in chronological order at such notable canvases as Copley's "Watson and the Shark" (1778), Fuseli's "The Nightmare" (1785; and again in 1790), Washington Allston's "The Deluge" (1804), John Martin's gigantic illustration for Gray's poem "The Bard" (1817), and J. M. W. Turner's "The Slave Ship" (1830), one must be impressed, I think, by the decreasing importance of human power in the universe, at least as these painters and others like them interpret nature and man.

Dante and Vergil in hell, and the death of Sardanapalus seem to me attempts to reach the utmost bounds of human life, to examine the human potential, and to judge it against the energy, incessant and inexplicable, of the universe. For Delacroix the spirit of man is presumably invincible, as in what may be his best-known work, the revolutionary "Liberty Guiding the People at the Barricades" (1831), to which I shall come in the next chapter.* The revolutionary impulse did not die.

iii

How strengthen personality against tyranny? How lead man to feel at home in a universe of vast, elemental force? How simultaneously enrich the lonely individual and renew the social forwardness which was the best part of the political revolutions? Perhaps "romantic dreamer" is inappropriate. Let us replace it either by "writers having a vision" or by "writers exhibiting Coleridge's esemplastic imagination."

I suspect most specialists would find it difficult to think of Goethe as a visionary; yet the imagination that produced *Faust*, to which we shall come, was not of the order of imagination that produced *Robinson Crusoe* or *Tom Jones*. *Faust*, says Stuart Atkins, is principally a succession of dream visions, especially *Faust II*, in which Goethe tries to encompass world history. The puzzle of Goethe's mind and temperament is nowhere greater than in the interpretation of the *Wilhelm Meister* books, the most influential *Bildungsroman* ("education into culture") ever written. Yet the two *Wilhelm Meister* novels are essentially invertebrate, the second more so than the first. The work began in 1777 as *Wilhelm Meisters theatralische Sendung*, which was expanded into *Wilhelm Meisters Lehrjahre* in 1795–1796. After a long interval,

---

* Yet Delacroix was capable of writing, on May 1, 1850: "La nature ne se soucie ni de l'homme ni de ses travaux, ni en aucune manière de son passage sur la terre. Qu'il invente et construise des merveilles ou qu'il vive comme une brute, pour la nature c'est tout un. Le vrai homme est le sauvage; il s'accorde avec la nature comme elle est. Sitôt que l'homme aiguise son intelligence, agrandit le cercle de ses idées, en perfectionne l'expression, acquiert des besoins et l'intelligence nécessaire pour les satisfaire, il s'aperçoit que la nature le contrarie en tout. Il faut qu'il s'applique à lui faire continuellement violence; elle, de son côté, ne demeure pas en reste." *Eugène Delacroix: Sa Vie et ses oeuvres*, Paris, 1865, pp. 465-466.

this was followed by *Wilhelm Meisters Wanderjahre** in 1821, revised and enlarged in 1829. Nowadays one finds the story rather incredible, its central personage being a character lacking any clear-cut individuality, even though *Wilhelm Meisters Lehrjahre* is supposed to chronicle his growth into maturity. The Wilhelm Meister of the *Wanderjahre* has little connection with the Wilhelm Meister of the first book except identity of name. Long after the *Lehrjahre* had been published, Goethe referred to his hero as a sad dog. The central difficulty is that Goethe could not make up his mind whether he was writing a philosophic romance, a *Märchen*, a picaresque novel, a polemic, or a moral tale. "Realistic" events are found cheek by jowl with such visionary concepts as the Society of the Tower, like the Free Masons or the Rosicrucians, who for some mysterious reason watch over young Wilhelm Meister in part I and send him under equally mysterious authority to wander around Europe in part II. But let us first summarize the story.

Wilhelm Meister is the son of a prosperous middle-class German commercial man. The son has been indulged at home. In his youth and adolescence he develops a passion for the theatrical world and gets involved with an actress of somewhat doubtful virtue named Mariana, by whom, though he does not know it for a long time, he has a son called Felix. Recovering from the shock of her apparent faithlessness, he is sent by his father to collect debts in various parts of the world. In the course of collecting these he rescues an unhappy pair of lovers from the law and from the anger of the girl's parents. The parents consent to the marriage of the daughter to her lover, a rather feckless strolling player named Melina. By and by a group of actors gathers around Melina, one of whom, a light-hearted girl named Philina, has an escort (gentleman friend?) named Laertes. Wilhelm also meets with some strolling acrobats, who seem to him to mistreat an androgynous child named Mignon. Wilhelm rescues Mignon, who becomes his faithful follower. With Wilhelm's money (his father's?) the

* *Wanderjahre* offers some difficulty to translation. Inasmuch as the Society of the Tower determines to "educate" Meister by requiring him to see life by wandering about Europe, a means by which he traverses various strata of post-Napoleonic society, "travels" will not quite do, since traveling implies some fixed goal, "wandering" implies a willfulness Meister is supposed to avoid, and "journeyings," though not good, is about as close as one can come in English to the purport of the title.

Melinas form a theatrical troupe, Wilhelm joining it as a sort of gentleman critic, and the company is invited by a count to perform in his castle. Wilhelm falls in love with the countess, but after a somewhat improbable contretemps in which the count mistakes Wilhelm for his own double, Wilhelm's advances are repulsed, the company takes to the road and is attacked by robbers, and Wilhelm is knocked unconscious. He comes to with his head in Philina's lap and learns that they have been rescued by a beautiful Amazon, of whom he has caught some glimpses. An old harper materializes for no good reason and seems to be especially interested in Mignon and Felix, who, thinks Wilhelm, is the son of Aurelia, sister of the actor-manager of the troupe. Wilhelm proposes to produce *Hamlet*, his father dies and leaves him all his property, a fire breaks out, and while Wilhelm is helping to extinguish it Mignon runs in to tell him that the harper is bent on murdering Felix in the basement of the castle in which the company is lodged. Wilhelm decides that the harper is insane and places him in the custody of a clergyman, he himself taking on the care of the two children. He has meanwhile been attracted to Aurelia, who dies, though not before telling Wilhelm (and the reader) the sad story of her unhappy love affair with one Lothario. After various other episodes Wilhelm finds he has all the while been under the secret guidance of members of the Society of the Tower, who have exposed him to these various incidents (and others) in order to educate him into maturity. By and by he meets Natalia, the beautiful Amazon who had rescued the actors from attack. Her he eventually marries. It also appears not only that Felix is his son by Mariana, whom he had not married, but also that Mignon, who dies, is the daughter of the crazed harper by an incestuous union. We are to believe, once Wilhelm is admitted to the Society of the Tower, that this apprenticeship to life has freed him from confusion and that he is now, or will shortly become, an unbiased personality to whom the world of practical affairs and the world of art and philosophy are equally familiar.

Apparently, however, Wilhelm's education is not complete, since in *Wilhelm Meisters Wanderjahre* he goes on a somewhat aimless set of travels, accompanied by Felix, with the remarkable provision laid down by the Society that he shall not stay more than three days in one place. During the course of his journeyings he meets a modern incarnation of the Holy Family, complete to a carpenter shop and an ass. Felix acquires from a cave a mysterious golden box nobody can open, a geologist instructs him, and he and the boy enter a sort of fairy garden, the iron gates of which mysteriously shut behind them. They are, however, well treated. Another set of adventures follows. As Natalia represented feminine wisdom in the *Lehrjahre*, so a woman named Makaria (Makarie) now represents sagacity. The golden box is left through the instigation of Makaria and an astronomer (astrologer?) for an antiquarian to examine. There follows another set of confusing interpolations — for example, a tale about a Nutbrown Maid. Wilhelm puts his son in a school run by some wise pedagogues, and father and son eventually resume their travels. (Any probable time element in the *Wilhelm Meister* books is nonexistent.) Felix is attracted to a girl named Hersilia, who has acquired a magnetic key intended to open the mysterious box. But the key breaks in two, Felix tries to embrace Hersilia, she repulses him, and he dashes away and falls unconscious beside a stream, where his father, now a surgeon (how did he become one?) restores him to consciousness. There is finally a vague general agreement that everybody should go to America. The contemporary reader may be pardoned if he wonders why this literary farrago made so much noise in the world of the French revolution, the Napoleonic empire, and the Congress of Vienna.

Though he could not wholly escape from the spirit of his age, Goethe denied many tenets of the romantic school, including, one supposes, the extreme statement of Wackenroder in the *Herzensergiessungen* that "it is man's holiest business to bow the knee before art and to bring adoration and eternal, boundless love to art." "Art," Wackenroder says a little later, "is a fearful and forbidden fruit: whoever has once tasted its sweet and innermost juice is forever after lost to the appeal of the busy world." This was not, to put it mildly, the view of the mature Goethe; yet he also felt he was in the tradition of the romantic genius, of the "God-like creator" theory of the poet, whose origins, as we have seen, go back at least to Young and Shaftesbury. Inchoate the world may appear, and especially did it so appear after the French revolution, the Napoleonic adventure, and the dominance of the Holy Alliance. In some sense Goethe in the *Wilhelm Meister* books sets up an antiworld that is more satisfactory and intelligible because it is run by comprehensive powers (the Society of the Tower). As for art, we have the futility of Wilhelm Meister's theatrical obsession and, conceivably, the odd story of the harper, who takes what he conceives to be proper vengeance into his hands in trying to kill Felix and who, judged by any sensible standard, is insane. Meister, who begins with adolescent yearnings after the make-believe of the stage, which he mistakenly thinks will interpret "reality" for him, and who as a result merely tumbles from one scrape into another, ends soberly as a physician who has had wide experiences.

Goethe also seems to share the views of Madame de Staël and others about the superiority of female sagacity and insight. The various women who cross Wilhelm's path lack the vividness of Margarete in *Faust*, although George Witkowski in his fine interpretation of Goethe says that, as compared with the male characters, they are more full-blooded. Yet Goethe's attempt at a universal social analysis of the Western world, besides getting hopelessly involved in side issues (like the chapter on a beautiful soul or the account of the Nutbrown Maid), seems to be typological rather than idiosyncratic; that is, if a woman like Philina has a certain vividness, the Natalia whom Wilhelm marries and the Makaria in the *Wanderjahre*, who is supposed to be a sort of sybil, are little more than philosophical symbols or metaphors. If *Faust* is a vision of the world which succeeds, *Wilhelm Meister* is a vision of the world which does not quite come off: the events are too often either melodramatic or drearily symbolical and the structure, especially of the second novel, too invertebrate.

Yet Goethe had a vision of social import. Wilhelm Meister's experiences are in a sense an anticipation of Tennyson's famous remark: "We cannot live in art alone." Goethe, however, is wise enough to see also that we cannot live without art — that is, without some sort of value system that involves something higher than a cash bond as the sole nexus between man and man. The Society of the Tower is also called "those who renounce": what they renounce (amid a good deal of hocus-pocus) is the self-seeking quality of romantic individualism, something that Wilhelm Meister is required to learn through trial and error and something that, once he has matured, he leads his son to learn, first through the school to which Felix is sent, and second through some passionate errors on Felix's part, from which he barely escapes with his life.

If one compares the *Wilhelm Meister* novels with, say, *Tom Jones*, one finds in Fielding's masterpiece no nonsense about a secret society living in a castle, or golden boxes opened with a magic key, or mystical injunctions (as in the *Wanderjahre*) to practice three reverences — for that above, for that below, and for that within. Yet Fielding, who was not in the least the Olympian Goethe was, also has his preachments, not metaphorical but direct. His *Bildungsroman*, which tells how a young scapegrace stumbles into maturity, is divided into books, and most of the books begin with what used to be called a moral essay, sometimes on the nature of art (literature) and sometimes on the wisdom of living in the world. Fielding also has his interpolated tales that lead away from his central theme, and, like Wilhelm Meister, Tom Jones is guided toward personal fruition: "Thus . . . we have at length brought our history to a conclusion, in which, to our great pleasure, though contrary, perhaps, to thy expectations, Mr. Jones appears to be the happiest of all mankind." Guidance exists; Jones finds his proper place in society, and so, we are supposed to believe, does Wilhelm Meister. *Tom Jones* is a better novel but lacks a total vision of life; *Wilhelm Meister* is badly constructed, but it yields a vision of mankind. I think this is what Henry Hatfield has in mind when he says of the *Wanderjahre* that it is the most Christian of Goethe's major works, but that the Christianity is tempered with humanism. The philosophic outlook is better than the art, but the philosophic outlook, which affirms social individuality rather than romantic self-pity, anticipates much in the nineteenth century, for example, Carlyle's *Sartor Resartus*.*

iv

If to think of Goethe as a visionary seems at first difficult, to think of Sir Walter Scott as a visionary is at first glance totally

* Even though Goethe was dubious about romanticism, the totality of *Wilhelm Meister* seems to me to fulfill a good many of the conditions pro or anti laid down in the illuminating article by Eugene N. Anderson, "German Romanticism as an Ideology of a Cultural Crisis," *Journal of the History of Ideas* 2 (June 1941), 301–317, including the assumption that the highest criterion of value to the romantics consisted in an individuality's containing its own justification and its own purpose.

absurd. Yet Scott is by no means the simple-minded costume romancer whose *Ivanhoe*, conscientiously taught in American high schools, gave all literary classics a bad name. If there were seven Shelleys, there were also seven Scotts: the antiquarian, the poet, the lawyer, the country gentleman, the learned editor, the biographer, the novelist; and despite the excellence in its time of *The Minstrelsy of the Scottish Border* and the appeal, now faded, of *Marmion* and *The Lady of the Lake*, the novelist is the central or supreme Walter Scott. (It should be said that Scott was enough of an experimental romantic poet to take over the novel meter of Coleridge's *Christabel* after hearing it read out loud.) The twenty-six Waverley novels laid the foundation for nineteenth-century fiction and, what is more important, altered the mode of conceiving and writing history. Gibbon, it is true, comes before Scott and is sufficiently colorful for those who will read him, but Scott radically affected men's conception of the vital relation to the present and to the past.

It is, I think, significant that only one of his novels, and that an inferior one, *St. Ronan's Well*, is set in present time. It must also be allowed that after the financial collapse he suffered Scott wrote some of his dullest books for money; an example is his twenty-fifth novel, *Count Robert of Paris*, in which the Great Unknown virtually parodies himself. But one judges Shakespeare's excellence and influence not by *Titus Andronicus* but by *Hamlet*; and, given that Scott's fictions are unequal in merit and that, as in *Wilhelm Meister*, there is much in even the more masterly books that one could spare, Scott had a vision of mankind partially comparable to that of Burke and partially comparable to that of Goethe. A basic difference is, however, a distinction in the sense of time. Historical time with Scott is of the essence. His great vision is therefore two-fold: he looks back upon various epochs in Western history and, like Macaulay, whom he anticipates, finds them lacking in solidity and citizenship, however colorful or however valuable their modes of life may have been. He thought of the web of history as a great seamless whole; in his more distinguished fiction he tried both to revivify time past with all its imperfections on its head and also to trace the living filaments that bind past time to the present time. Novels such as *Waverley, Quentin Durward, Woodstock, Rob Roy, The Fortunes of Nigel, The Bride of Lammermoor,* and *The*

Heart of Midlothian are not merely products of a sweeping historical vision but also depictions of what is gone and what is. On the whole, Scott thinks his native country and, for that matter, most of Europe, now Napoleon is out of the way, better off with what is.

I suggest that an important passage from *Wilhelm Meister* is a proper epigraph for the better novels of Scott:

Nicht von Irrtum zu bewahren ist die Pflicht des Menschenerziehers, sondern den Irrenden zu leiten, ja ihn seinem Irrtum aus vollen Bechern ausschlürfen zu lassen, das ist die Weisheit der Lehrer. Wer seinen Irrtum nur kostet, hält lange damit Haus, er freuet sich dessen als eines seltenen Glücks; aber wer ihn ganz erschöpft, der muss ihn kennen lernen, wenn er nicht wahnsinnig ist.*

Scott allows his young heroes, none of whom, perhaps, passes beyond typicality, to drain the cup of error to its dregs, but he also allows them to return to the normal course of human life. And this return is more than convention; it is an acceptance by Scott of the facts of actual life as the world must learn to accept them. The first of the novels represents his general outlook.

A tale of youthful follies cured, *Waverley* (1814) is the story of its hero's involvement and disinvolvement with the amateurish Stuart rebellion of 1745, and, equally, of his involvement and disinvolvement with romantic sentimentality and his adjustment to the troubled world of George II of England and, by analogy, to Europe of the post-Napoleonic era. He is the son of a family of which one branch (his uncle's) inclines to the Stuart cause, the other branch (his not altogether admirable father's) to the Hanoverian line. He is brought up by his uncle at Waverly-Honour,† where his education is self-willed and romantic: he spends more time dreaming over romances and romantic tales of chivalry by Spenser, Ariosto, and the like, either in "a large Gothic room" or a solitary tower, than he does learning anything so commonsensical as the management of a country estate. Having been commissioned a captain in a royal regiment stationed in Scotland, he then obtains

---

* It is not the duty of one who educates men to protect them from making mistakes, but to guide the erring one, even to the point of allowing him to drain the cup of wrongdoing to its dregs. That is the wisdom of the teacher. He who does no more than taste of error has it with him for a long time, and, indeed, rejoices in it as at a special happiness, but he who drinks it wholly must come to comprehend it unless he is insane. (*Wilhelm Meister's Lehrjahre*, VII, ix.)

† "Honour" is a legal (and real-estate) term referring to a seignory of several manors held by one baron or other lord.

a leave of absence, during which he visits Tully-Veolan, an estate near the Highlands, owned by the pedantic and whimsical Baron Bradwardine, who has a pretty daughter, Rose, and a crazed follower, David Gellatley. The reader is made aware of the emptiness of "chivalry" when, after a drinking bout, the baron goes off to fight a comic duel in defense of his honor — a scene that might have been written by Jean Paul Richter.

A cattle raid precipitates Edward into the Highlands, where he is exposed to romantic adventures, romantic scenery, and the persuasive charm of Fergus MacIvor, head of a Highland clan, at once older, shrewder, more impetuous, and more impractical than Edward. Fergus has a sister (out of an opera by Donizetti) named Flora, who sings to her harp by a waterfall and expresses undying devotion to the cause of the Stuarts. She is, however, more mature than Edward Waverley and refuses his hand, telling him his proper future is with Rose Bradwardine and the management of a settled estate. A series of "adventures" follows, half veiled from the reader, the beginnings of a rising on the part of the Young Pretender against the Hanoverian king. Meanwhile Waverley, long overdue at his post, fails to receive letters, cleverly intercepted by the Highlanders, summoning him back to his regiment, and is finally relieved of his command. Stung by this imputation of treachery, he decides to follow Fergus into the ranks of the Young Pretender's undisciplined forces, but on his way to join the Jacobites he is involved in a quarrel with a blacksmith and had up before a local magistrate of the Hanoverian party. He is then recaptured by the Highlanders through a stratagem, meets the Pretender, participates in the Jacobite victory at Preston, takes captive an English officer named Talbot, whose life he saves from the wild Highlanders, and by and by finds himself involved in a senseless quarrel about a point of honor with the harebrained Fergus MacIvor. They are reconciled. But the Stuarts are beaten at Clifton, Edward is cut off from that army, and Fergus is sent as a prisoner to Carlisle to be sentenced to death. Waverley gets to London in disguise, is befriended by Colonel Talbot, and finally marries Rose Bradwardine, the baron's estate having been somewhat improbably restored to Bradwardine through the efforts of Colonel Talbot and Bradwardine's faithful servitor, Bailie MacWheeble. Flora seeks refuge in a convent in France.

Thus summarized, *Waverley* seems to be little more than a cloak-and-sword romance. But neither *Waverley* nor the better books in the Waverley romances can be thus dismissed; and I concentrate on *Waverley* not merely because it is the first of a series of novels that set all reading Europe ablaze but also because it is cleverly plotted as a *Bildungsroman* and is not a mere adventure novel. In the opening chapter, in the concluding chapter (which, after the manner of Richter or of Laurence Sterne is whimsically entitled "A Postscript, Which Should Have Been a Preface"), and in a preface to the third edition (printing), Scott pours scorn on sentimental romance, the mere Gothic novel, and affected imitations of Cervantes. He is scornful also of Waverley's education and of his callow youth spent in an ideal world of dream, "which became daily more delectable." Scott is amused by the estate of the Baron of Bradwardine, but he is not unaware of the fact that Edward's introduction to it is by means of the crazed, if faithful, David Gellatley, virtually a parody of romantic minstrelsy, and is equally aware that the comic duel fought by the Baron has originated in an insensate drinking bout at the baron's table. Scott pities the baron when, toward the conclusion of the work, Bradwardine has to go into hiding, served only by the faithful David. To Waverley the Highlands are, indeed, "romantic" and the violent deeds he is made aware of are like a dream. But though the hero is momentarily seduced into the Jacobite army, he abhors civil war, and finds that the relations of officers and men to the Young Pretender are highly personal rather than military. Scott once or twice brings Edward into contact with harsh reality, as when in chapter xxx Edward finds himself surrounded by an irrational rabble at Cairnvreckan, has his life threatened by a red-hot bar of iron, and shoots in self-defense only to be arrested. After experiencing the indiscipline of the Pretender's retreating army, defeated at Clifton, Waverley discovers that ordinary Cumberland farmers are far more trustworthy than Donald Bane Lane (Bean Lean) the Highlander or, from one point of view, even Fergus MacIvor. If the ending is a hurried fairy-tale close — the Bradwardine estate is miraculously restored — if Edward marries Rose with unexpected suddenness, and if he is forgiven his desertion of the English army with totally unhistorical rapidity, these things do not matter — novels used to conclude in this summary fashion. The important element in

Waverley lies neither in these things, nor in the heroic death of Fergus MacIvor, nor in the fusion of fanatical devotion and clear-eyed common sense of Flora MacIvor when she sends Waverley back to Rose Bradwardine and a quiet domestic life:

. . . high and perilous enterprise [she tells Rose] is not Waverley's forte . . . I will tell you where he will be at home, my dear, and in his place — in that quiet circle of domestic happiness, lettered indolence, and elegant enjoyment, of Waverley-Honour . . . he will repeat verses to his beautiful wife, who will hang upon his arm; and he will be a happy man.

The important element in *Waverley* is Scott's vision of history, and of the relation of history to the present. He had lived through the American revolution, the French revolution, and the Napoleonic wars, and he had decided (like Burke) that the essential elements in society were family, property, and order.

For it will be noted that our hero recoils at last from being involved in a merely romantic enterprise and returns to the solid pattern of life which he scorned in his adolescent years. His ultimate mentor is not Fergus MacIvor but the sobersided Colonel Talbot, who, however improbably, manages to rescue Tully-Veolan from ruin so that Waverley can marry Rose Bradwardine. Waverley has had his adventures. He is matured and saddened by them, and Scott, though his heart was emotionally attracted to the Jacobite cause, did not allow his head to follow his heart. As in *Rob Roy*, so in *Waverley*, the hero and the author are reconciled to a Burkian view of society and a Macaulayan belief in progress. We read in the last chapter:

There is no European nation which, within the course of half a century, or little more, has undergone so complete a change as this kingdom of Scotland. The effects of the insurrection of 1745 — the destruction of the patriarchal power of the Highland chiefs . . . the total eradication of the Jacobite party . . . commenced this innovation. The gradual influx of wealth and extension of commerce, have since united to render the present people of Scotland a class of beings as different from their grandfathers as the existing English are from those of Queen Elizabeth's time . . . the change, though steadily and rapidly progressing, has, nevertheless, been gradual; and like those who drift down the stream of a deep and smooth river, we are not aware of the progress we have made, until we fix our eye on the now distant point from which we have been drifted.

But even Scott's acceptance of modernity is not the whole point. He has a *vision* of history, a panorama of what the Western world had been at various eras from 1097–1099, the date of *Count Robert of Paris*, to *St. Ronan's Well*, which is supposed to take place in 1812. This vision undoubtedly dates back to his boyish reading, his "raids" after border ballads, his antiquarian sense, and his Scotch nationalism, and is part of the general set of his mind. Except for his shrewd practical sense Scott could have said, like Teufelsdröckh in *Sartor Resartus*:

We sit as in a boundless Phantasmagoria and Dream-grotto; boundless, for the faint star, the remotest century, lies not even nearer the verge thereof; sounds and many-coloured visions flit round our sense . . . What are all your national Wars, with their Moscow retreats, and sanguinary hate-filled Revolutions, but the Somnambulism of uneasy Sleepers? This Dreaming, this Somnambulism is what we on Earth call life . . .

Scott simultaneously feared revolution and loved history, respected the solid mercantile virtues (this is especially evident in the dénouement of *Rob Roy*) and admired the great eras of the past, which were to him — and in this respect Scott, the conservative, is, oddly enough, like Condorcet the radical — stages in the inevitable progress of mankind. Edgar Johnson, in his great, definitive biography of Scott, quotes two scholars who have specialized in interpreting for modern times the meaning of the work of the Wizard of the North. Says one of them, Karl Kroeber: Scott was the first artist to conceive of history as the evolution of competing styles of life. Francis Hart, the second specialist, remarks upon Scott's avid interest in the fateful impact of the past — of any great period of the past — upon the present time. Neither remark is a mere truism. Sir Walter Scott, who had lived through so many wars and revolutions, by the intensity with which he summoned up, imperfectly perhaps, his visions of the past, altered the writing of history in all the Western world. What is even more wonderful, he altered man's sense of the meaning of the past. To theorists of the American revolution the English seventeenth century, for example, was a convenient cupboard of documents to plunder; to the great figures of the French revolution Greece and Rome were, so to speak, lighthouses by which to steer the storm-tossed vessel of the French republic one and indivisible; to Walter

Scott, however, stoic though he might be, history was the living visible garment of God, or, in Carlyle's version of the speech of the Earth-Spirit in *Faust*:

> In Being's floods, in Action's storm,
> I walk and work, above, beneath,
> Work and weave in endless motion!
>> Birth and Death,
>> An infinite ocean!
>> A seizing and giving
>> The fire of Living:
>
> 'Tis thus at the roaring Loom of Time I ply,
> And weave for God the Garment thou seest Him by.

The nineteenth-century sense of the past as development owes more to the author of *Waverley* than even literary historians realize. The private vision of "Kubla Khan" turns into a general dream that, age by age, mankind steadily improves. The dreamer grows less metaphysical but, in coming back to reality, he does not return to the Scottish Common Sense interpretation of the world.

XIV

Faustian Man

In 1914 a youngish Oberlehrer named Oswald Spengler, born in a town in the Harz Mountains, a region that had been the last stronghold of German paganism, completed the manuscript of a monumental work he called *Der Untergang des Abendlandes.* He could not publish his book until July 1918, when its pessimistic conclusion both fitted the mood of the time and antagonized liberal hope in postwar Europe. Spengler was accused of having furnished the Nazis their philosophical basis, but as the Nazis adopted or adapted almost anybody they liked as philosophical precursors including Hegel and Wagner, the accusation was but partly true. The book aroused furious controversy. When the first volume was translated into English (Alfred A. Knopf brought out an American edition in 1926) this controversy spread to the New World. The points at issue were partly scholarly, partly philosophic, partly political, and partly sheer emotionalism. Who was this unknown that he should seize boldly upon universal history — politics, the arts, the sciences, philosophy — weave them into a continuous pattern, and come out with the conclusion that the West, particularly Europe, was facing inevitable decay?

Even in German the book was difficult reading; and the English translator, faithful to the original, did little to simplify the task of understanding it. Here, for example, is a passage from the Atkinson translation (page 390), which is based on Spengler's revised edition of 1922 and faithfully reflects the original:

When the intellect looks back from *its* sphere, the Become, the aspect of life is reversed, the idea of Destiny which carries aim and future in it having turned into the mechanical principle of cause-and-effect of

425

which the centre of gravity lies in the past. The spatially-experienced is promoted to rank above the temporal living, and time is replaced by a length in a spatial world-system. And, since in the creative experience extension follows from direction, the spatial from life, the human understanding imports life *as a process* into the inorganic space of its imagination. While life looks on space as something functionally belonging to itself, intellect looks upon life as something *in* space. Destiny asks: "Whither?" Causality asks, "Whence?"

Most readers found this hard going. Spengler created a good many German compounds, neologisms, and the like; and, moreover, some common German words offer difficulties to any translator. One such is *Geist*, which Atkinson renders as "soul." "Soul," however, has Christian connotations Spengler did not intend, and in such compounds as *Zeitgeist* it means only the spirit of the times.

There is, wrote Spengler, no natural science without a precedent religion; that is, the assumptions of science in any culture are, on the whole, predetermined by the religious traditions of that culture. He discusses three great general cultures, the Apollinian,* a term he owes to Nietzsche, the Faustian, a term he owes to Goethe, and the Magian, a term he seems to owe to the interpretation of the Far East, Saracenic and Arabian history, Sanskrit literature, and the like by a good many romantics and by authors whose interest in the wisdom of the ancient East was awakened by eighteenth-century inquiry or romantic philology. Perhaps for that reason the epigraph for the whole book is a short poem by Goethe from the *Zahme Xenien*, or "good-natured" epigrams, that parallel the satirical *Xenien*, often harsh in tone, in his collected poetry. Here is the epigraph:

> Wenn im Unendlichen dasselbe
> Sich wiederholend ewig fliesst,
> Der tausendfältige Gewölbe
> Sich kräftig ineinander schliesst;
> Strömt Lebenslust aus allen Dingen,
> Dem kleinsten wie dem grössten Stern,
> Und alles Drängen, alles Ringen
> Ist ewige Ruh in Gott dem Herrn.†

* I give the term as Atkinson rendered it, rather than "Apollonian," the more usual form in English.
† Paraphrased (one can scarcely say translated) by John S. Dwight in 1838 (Dwight was an American admirer of Goethe): "And while throughout the self-same motion / Repeated on forever flows, / The thousandfold o'erarching ocean [!] / Its strong embrace around all throws; / Streams through all things

This is essentially the idea of nature in Goethe's *Faust* and suggests the great hymn by the archangels in the "Prologue in Heaven" of that masterpiece. Goethe had a lively interest in the wisdom of the ancient East, so that a good many poems, notably in his fine collection of 1819, the *West-östlicher Divan*, are "Oriental":

> Gottes ist der Orient!
> Gottes ist der Occident!
> Nord- und südliches Gelände
> Ruht im Frieden seiner Hände.*

Magian culture — embodied in such religions as the Persian, the Jewish, the Hindu, the Mohammedan, the Christian, and the Manichaean — produces, according to Spengler, algebra, a mode of reasoning about unknown, guessed-at, or fluctuating quantities; astrology, which illumines the interdependence of humanity and the universe; and alchemy, the mother of modern chemistry, which seemed to him in 1922 still to depend upon mysterious affinities, or if not that, then to have had as its original postulates mystical assumptions of this sort. It will be remembered that one of Goethe's major novels is *Die Wahlverwandtschaften* (*Elective Affinities*) of 1809, in which four persons are, by a mysterious force akin to chemical affinities, drawn irresistibly into new and unlooked-for relationships against their moral judgments.

Of more moment for our purposes are Apollinian culture ("soul," says the translator) and Faustian culture. Apollinian culture includes that of ancient Egypt no less than that of antiquity in the usual sense. Its characteristic product is Euclidean geometry, which assumes that space is "out there" and can be objectively measured and divided. The vast temples of the Egyptians, like the monuments of the pharaohs and the statues of their gods, all erected under the unchanging heaven of the Nile, do not so much defy time as stand outside of it. Such a culture produces not merely geometry but mechanics and can think of atoms only in terms of physically discrete particles of matter, not, as the moderns do, as

---

the joy of living, / The least star thrilleth fond accord; / And all their crowding, all their striving / Is endless rest in God the Lord." This is a fine example of the truth of the Italian apothegm, *traduttore, traditore*.
* "God is of the East possess'd, / God is ruler of the West; / North and South alike, each land / Rests within his gentle hand." This translation is by Edgar A. Bowring. Needless to remark, there is very little about God in Spengler, but a great deal about men's notions of a living universe.

centers of energy. History in Apollinian culture may be narrative but is scarcely development, for the world in Apollinian culture is a perpetual repetition of pattern or else the slowly revolving cycle of the Great Year. When Heraclitus remarked it is impossible to step into the same river twice, he assumed as a matter of course that the stream is "there," that its flow is fixed, and that his senses report the stream as it really is. Following Winckelmann, though at a great distance, Spengler postulates that the nude statue is Apollinian, and so is the sensuous cult of the Olympian gods; and that a primary difference between a fresco by Polygnotus and an oil painting by Rembrandt is that in the one the body is defined by contours, in the other by light and shade. If one puts aside Christianity, the roots of which, according to Spengler, are in Magian culture, it is a fair inference that the classicism of the seventeenth century and the neoclassicism of the eighteenth, or much of it, still included many leading elements of Apollinian culture; for example, the geometrical spirit of Descartes and the mechanics of Newton. In a sense the success of the Americans in reconstituting a republic and the attempts of the French to do the same thing are functions of a continuing Apollinian theory of the state.

It is a convenient transition to Spengler's discussion of the Faustian "soul" to quote at this juncture a sentence by him, at once fatuous and penetrating: "What we call Statics, Chemistry, and Dynamics — words that as used in modern science are merely traditional distinctions without deeper meaning — are really the respective physical systems of the Apollinian, Magian and Faustian souls." For Spengler the Faustian world view was evident in world history long before either the Faust legend or Goethe's poem. Faustian culture seemed to him to have blossomed with the birth of the Romanesque style in the tenth century; and as with Hegel, so with Spengler, the Faustian "soul" is primarily, though not solely, exemplified in Germanic culture. The symbol of the Faustian "soul" is the assumption that there is pure and unlimited space. Among its chief developments are Galilean dynamics; the Madonna ideal in Dante's Beatrice and in the last line of *Faust*; deep self-consciousness and introspection; a personal (personalized?) culture evident in memoirs, autobiographies, retrospects, and prospects; and, above all, the great assumptions and discoveries of modern

428

science, such as polarized light-rays, errant ions, flying and colliding gas particles (Spengler was writing when the Wilson cloud-chamber effect was new), magnetic fields, electric currents and waves, and so on, including n-dimensional geometry, or a geometry that cannot be reported directly to the senses but is an extension of the ego into thought. The upthrust of Gothic architecture, not content like that of the Greeks or the Egyptians to enclose a space and so deny space generalized, the mental or physical adventurousness of persons like Columbus and Copernicus, the idea that motion is process, not a mere spatial change of bodies — all these Spengler cites as exemplars of the Faustian world view.

There is, he stipulates, an inner relation between atomistic theory in modern terms and the Faustian "soul" in music and the other arts. The assumption of science is that inner vision is intellectually dependable; yet inner vision implies, or springs from, loneliness, and this loneliness, this longing for infinity, this need for solitude, distance, and abstraction, is Faustian. To Faustian man the idea of nature is that of a dynamic of unlimited span, a physics of the distant (compare our moon-landings and the report of some of the astronauts that they experienced religious peace). Spengler quotes from Goethe the statement: "Nature has no system. It has Life, it is Life and succession from an unknown centre to an unknowable bourne." Modern science tries to meet the implied difficulty by dealing only with what has become, not with what is becoming; that is, even when a contemporary physical theorist replaces cause by statistical probability, he is saying nothing intellectual about the future, he is merely cumulating a series of similar episodes scattered along the time-line of past events. Modern man has not, however, obtained either happiness or satisfaction from contemplating or using the result of what, in Spengler's thinking, is little more than a summation of introspective formulae. The space I individually know as a person is not the space of physical theorizing; time past is for me no longer "time" but the memory or record of an event I can in no wise re-experience; and against this intellectual nihilism I perpetually strive, though I know I strive in vain.

What the two great revolutions, American and French, left to modern man was therefore not stability but striving. The Lord says to Mephistopheles in the "Prologue in Heaven" of *Faust I*:

Ein guter Mensch in seinem dunklen Drange
Ist sich des rechten Weges wohl bewusst.

That is, a human being in whom there is usually some degree of the good, or of knowing that there is a good, is of necessity conscious and, in his struggles to live, knowingly or half-knowingly aware that there is rectitude or righteousness somewhere. This emphasis upon striving is what separates the nineteenth century from the eighteenth century with its status society, and is the principal legacy of the revolutionary years to the world of the West. It is also a central element in mature romanticism.

ii

I speak of course of Europe and the West after 1815. Striving was not in 1815 evident among peoples or persons. When Western man emerged from more than half a century of conflict — from the Seven Years War to Waterloo — he was weary of contentiousness, whether in the military, the economic, the religious, the political, or the aesthetic field. The great and hopeful revolutionary movements had, indeed, basically altered the outlook of man, but they had then been hidden by the vast shadow of Napoleon. The greatest despot of the age, after gigantic struggles that raged from Moscow to Brussels, lay imprisoned and dying on a distant island. The Western world, except for the confused wars and dislocations of the nascent Latin American republics (the royal house of Portugal had emigrated to Brazil), acquiesced in the peace settlements of Metternich, by no means everywhere bad. G. K. Chesterton once noted the appositeness of a line in Mrs. Browning:

And kings crept out again to feel the sun.

But the kings, the dukes, and the rest were not all tyrants, though they were, of course, aristocrats, among whom three sovereigns — the czar of Russia, the emperor of Austria, and the king of Prussia — solemnly promised to govern their subjects in the spirit of Jesus Christ.

A vast silence fell on the world during the years when the artillery ceased to roar and the drums to beat. In the magnificent preface to his *Confession d'un enfant du siècle* (1836) Alfred de Musset, born in 1810, described his generation, conceived between

430

two battles and born to the sound of cannon, as suffering from lassitude of spirit, the *mal du siècle*. Benjamin Constant, who sometimes seems to have been on every side in politics and to have been intimate with every sort of woman, in 1816 published *Adolphe*, a strange and penetrating narrative, the hero of which is not, like Werther, moved by passion to suicide but instead deserts his mistress from sheer boredom and, standing at her deathbed, feels virtually nothing: "the air I breathed seemed harsher, the faces of men I met more indifferent to me; all nature seemed to tell me I would now cease to be loved forever." This is romantic egotism in reverse. Shelley, along with Blake the most consistently radical of the English romantic poets, in 1819 wrote his "Ode to the West Wind," a poem that, though it expresses a general hope that his thoughts, driven over the world like dead leaves, may quicken a new birth, pictures the author as helpless:

> I fall upon the thorns of life! I bleed!
>
> A heavy weight of hours has chained and bowed
> One too like thee: tameless, and swift, and proud.

Even Byron, who became for Europe the great type of romantic rebel, though in *Childe Harold* IV:xcviii he wrote that Freedom's

> banner, torn but flying,
> Streams like the thunder-storm *against* the wind,

in the same poem spoke of mankind and the Congress of Vienna in these hopeless terms:

> The yoke that is upon us doubly bowed,
> And the intent of Tyranny avowed,
> The edict of Earth's rulers, who are grown
> The apes of him who humbled once the proud,
> And shook them from their slumbers on the throne,

though once

> nursing Nature smiled
> On Infant Washington. Has Earth no more
> Such seeds within her breast, or Europe no such shore?

In Germany, despite the promise of Prussian nationalism, Schleiermacher, Adam Müller, and Heinrich von Kleist were haunted by the allure of death. Schleiermacher was concerned with

431

the theological implications of the idea of death; Müller wrote in 1809 that no one understands love, that every sacrifice, every surrender is a kind of death; and Kleist committed suicide in 1811, leaving behind him correspondence known as his "Death Letters." In Dresden meanwhile Arthur Schopenhauer, who had once taken a mild interest in the movement for Prussian nationalism (he went so far as to buy military equipment) meditated on the hopelessness of life and published in 1819 *Die Welt als Wille und Vorstellung*, which celebrates suffering as the eternal condition of humanity. Only through art, especially the art of music, can the human being reach the blessedness of nihilism, the peace of eternal repose:

. . . what remains after the entire annulling of the will, is, for all those who are yet full of the will, indeed nothing. But, on the other hand, for those in whom the will has turned again, and has denied itself, this our own so very real world, with all her suns and Milky Ways, is — Nothing.*

But the sense of striving was merely stunned, not stupefied. The Declaration of the Rights of Man and of the Citizen and the American Declaration of Independence had not lost their power. After 1789, over most of the Western world, men had become citizens, not subjects. The concept of absolute monarchy, though it seemed to survive in Russia, in the kingdom of Naples, perhaps in the Papal states, and in the Austrian empire, was now obsolescent if not obsolete. The truths of the revolutions were perhaps for historians to analyze; the myth of the revolution was alive and powerful. The myth of the revolution was Janus-faced, or at least painted in two colors, blood-red and sunrise-gold. Men were horrified by the blood-lust of 1793 and the slaughter of the Napoleonic wars; but men were also cheered to believe there was a mystic entity called sometimes the people, sometimes humanity.

The idea of the people was unfortunately confused by notions of race and nationalism, and the idea of humanity was criss-crossed by various religious revivals, most of them reactionary. Among these were the celebrations of the sacrosanct qualities of the throne and the altar by Lamartine and Hugo in their younger years, and the revival of Catholicism when the pope returned to political

---

* This is the famous concluding sentence of Schopenhauer's first volume. It will be noted that for Schopenhauer the will is *striving*, though the blindness of an irrational struggle to live creates the endless suffering of existence.

power.* The Jesuits were resuscitated, the Papal states were re-instituted, the Oxford movement shaped itself in England (Keble's sermon, "National Apostasy," preached in 1833 against the right of the state to interfere with the structure of the church, is a significant document), Wordsworth celebrated the historical validity of the Anglican church in his *Ecclesiastical Sonnets* (1822), and in distant America deism, formerly thought to be the religion of the frontier, was overwhelmed by evangelical revivalism. Mysticism, once crudely represented by Madame de Krüdener, the religious "friend" of Alexander I of Russia, proved to be a growing force in Russian culture during and after the Napoleonic wars. In Rome, just before the end of the Napoleonic regime, a group of German painters known as the Nazarenes, Overbeck and Cornelius among them, turned painting into a religious exercise; and the French and Belgian Liberal Catholic movement, which sought to unite "God and Liberty," was condemned by Rome in 1832 and again in 1834. The best-known figure in Liberal Catholicism was Lamennais, whose paper *L'Avenir* had been launched in 1830 and whose best-remembered book is *Paroles d'un croyant* (1834). But Lamennais's book, written against both church and state, seemed to Gregory XVI "false, calumnious, rash, leading to anarchy, contrary to the Word of God, impious, scandalous, and erroneous." When in 1830–1832 political revolution broke out in the papal states, Austrian troops restored order, and the papal secretary of state, Luigi Cardinal Lambruschini, yielded as little as possible to "progress" and did as much as possible in Rome and elsewhere to restore "authority."

But a new credo, heir in some respects of Robespierre's cult of the Supreme Being and shaped by Saint-Simon, Comte, and Fourier, disputed the empire of religious faith. The sans-culottes, the plebs, the mob, the populace, had become "the people," whose voice was supposed to be the voice of God. The new secular theology was to produce its epistles to the gentiles in the novels of George Sand, in Lamartine's *History of the Girondins*, in Victor Hugo's *Les Misérables*, in the verse of Heinrich Heine, and in the poetry of Walt Whitman, but its original apostles, not counting the revolu-

---

* Rightly or wrongly the two papal decretals condemning liberal Catholicism are supposed to have been the result of pressure from Czar Nicholas I and Prince Metternich, who once proudly informed his wife: "I, too, am a Power."

tionaries, were Saint-Simon (1760–1825), Auguste Comte (1798–1857), and François Marie Charles Fourier (1772–1837), whose phalansteries, of which Brook Farm was an imperfect example, were to be miniature industrial societies perfectly ordered. The biography of Claude Henri de Rouvroy, Comte de Saint-Simon, is incredible. A descendant of the author of the famous *Mémoires* of the age of Louis XIV, he was imprisoned by an outraged father; broke out of jail; was bitten by a mad dog; became a colonel in the French army in America; knocked senseless by a cannon ball, was about to be thrown overboard from a French ship when he was discovered to be still alive; anticipated the building of the Panama Canal; was imprisoned for almost a year by Robespierre; lost all his estates and all his income; became the director of a municipal pawnshop and after that a librarian; twice tried to commit suicide; fascinated people by his conversation and repelled them by his eccentricities. He once distributed sixty handwritten copies of his *Mémoire sur la science de l'homme* (1813) among persons he thought eminent, but for present purposes two titles by him, *De la Réorganisation de la société européenne* (1814) and *Le Nouveau Christianisme* (1825) are important. Saint-Simon proposed, among other things, the reorganization of the world under the direction of twenty-one men of genius, who were, among other delightful tasks, to force the rich to enlighten the poor. He thought the Catholics were even greater heretics than the Protestants, he had little use for the Bible, but he considered (like other romantics) that the universal leadership of the medieval church was a proper model for a new religion, the creed of which would enforce progress for all mankind, more particularly among the poor. Some of his followers, despairing of the timidity of the male sex, hoped to discover a female messiah for a Saint-Simonian church, which, however, was dissolved by the courts.

Comte was a more reasonable man, who began as secretary to Saint-Simon and went on to deliver a series of lectures from 1826 to 1829, published as his influential *Cours de philosophie positive*. Because of the strain they involved, he once attempted to commit suicide. The lectures appeared in six volumes from 1830 to 1842, and were eventually followed by the *Système de politique positive* (1852–1854), which was dedicated to the memory of his dead mistress. The name of Comte is now indelibly associated with the science of sociology, but here one has to notice mainly his positivistic religion, which was to replace Christianity. After the fashion of the French revolutionaries, there was to be a new calendar, in which each month was to be devoted to honoring one of the chief occupations of society, not excluding the industrialists. In this cult womanhood is to be exalted somewhat after the manner of Corinne, Lucinde, and Shelley's *Epipsychidion*, and there is to be a "positive" committee composed of Frenchmen, Englishmen, Germans, Italians, and Spaniards, plus four women, which is, apparently, to direct the affairs of the world, for it is to be joined eventually by representatives of the black and yellow races. There is also to be a Church of Positivism, into which any "child of humanity" is to be initiated at the age of fourteen, unless he proves "radically" incompetent. Among other duties the Positive Church will constantly execrate the memory of such tyrants as Napoleon and continuously honor such figures as Joan of Arc, King Alfred, and Mohammed. If this seems a touch fantastic, what of Fourier, who dreamed of "anti-lions" that would be docile, who believed in "lifemanship," and who thought the human race, organized into phalansteries, might philosophically practice free love?

Doubtless all this is to a rational mind silly enough, but consider this passage from Book V of Victor Hugo's *Les Contemplations*, an untitled poem dated 1846:

> Pourquoi le fiel, l'envie,
> La haine? Et j'ai vidé les poches de la vie.
> Je n'ai trouvé dedans que deuil, misère, ennui.
> J'ai vu le loup mangeant l'agneau, dire: Il m'a nui!
>
> . . . .
>
> Hélas! j'ai vu la nuit reine, et, de fers chargés,
> Christ, Socrate, Jean Huss, Colomb; les préjugés
> Sont pareils aux buissons que dans la solitude
> On brise pour passer; toute la multitude
> Se redresse et vous mord pendant qu'on en courbe un.
> Ah! malheur à l'apôtre et malheur au tribun!
> On avait eu bien soin de me cacher l'histoire;
> J'ai lu; j'ai comparé l'aube avec la nuit noire,
> Et les quatre-vingt-treize aux Saint-Barthélemy;
> Car ce quatre-vingt-treize où vous avez frémi,
> Qui dut être, et que rien ne peut plus faire éclore,
> C'est la lueur de sang qui se mêle à l'aurore.

Les Révolutions, qui viennent tout venger,
Font un bien éternel dans leur mal passager,*

and much more, including:

Quand le sang de Jésus tombe en vain, goutte à goutte,
Depuis dix-huit cents ans, dans l'ombre qui l'écoute;

. . . .

Quand la guerre est partout, quand la haine est partout,
Alors, subitement, un jour, debout, debout! †

Perhaps this is all merely literary. But beginning in 1820 popular
revolts, rebellions, and revolutions stirred the Western world until
1848. Indeed, one can go on to 1871 (the Paris Commune) and
the break-up of empires during and after World War I. Always
these struggles, whether they were staged in the Low Countries,
Germany, France, the Austrian empire, the German states, Russia,
Poland, Italy, the Iberian peninsula, or elsewhere involved a four-
fold conflict, the forces including the government in power,
frequently monarchical; the aristocracy and the rich bourgeoisie;
labor in the cities plus young student rebels and artists; and peasants
on the land. Always the intent was for a more nearly perfect
realization of the rights of man. Nothing, of course, was simple:
the "people," or large segments of them, were sometimes archcon-
servatives, and the forces of control, commonly labeled reactionary
by those of a revolutionary philosophy, were themselves divided,
since there were liberal rulers and reactionary rulers; a few forward-
looking employers (an example is Robert Owen, the Welshman)
and a great many conservative ones, who felt that God had created
the poor so that Christians might feel benevolent; liberal theologians

* Why the gall, the envy, / The hatred? I've emptied out life's pockets / And
found nothing but sorrow, wretchedness, boredom. / I've watched the wolf eat
the lamb and say, He did me harm! / . . . Alas, I have seen benightedness
triumph, and in chains / Christ, Socrates, John Huss, Columbus; closed minds /
Are like the briars in the woods / You break so you can pass; the rest / Straighten
and tear you while you are bending one. / Ah, plague on the apostle, and on the
magistrate! / They took good care to hide history from me; / I've read; I've
compared the dawn with the dark night, / And the Ninety-Three's with the
Saint Bartholomew's days; / For that Ninety-Three that set you aquiver, / Which
had to be, and which nothing can bring about again, / Is the glare of blood that
mixes with the dawn. / Revolutions, which come to avenge everything, / Create
an eternal Good amid a transient Evil.
† When Jesus' blood has fallen drop by drop in vain / For eighteen hundred
years into the listening shadows; / . . . When war is everywhere and so is hate,
/ Then suddenly, one day, Arise, Arise!

436

and passionate supporters of the status quo; political leaders who trusted the people, and other leaders who manipulated them. The voice of the people was perhaps the voice of God, but labor unions were forbidden in France by the law passed in 1791 by Le Chapelier, an ardent revolutionary who profoundly believed that freedom would be curtailed by collective bargaining. There were similar restrictions in other countries, for example, Great Britain.

Perhaps the best way to understand these intermittent revolutions, sometimes aborted, sometimes led astray, sometimes successful, is to study Delacroix's social masterpiece of 1831, "Liberty Leading the People," especially if one remembers that Delacroix had said a few years earlier, "J'étais enchanté de moi-même." All the social forces of the Europe of 1830 save science meet in this picture, and even science is represented by the musket with bayonet affixed that Liberty carries in her left hand. The scene is somewhere in Paris during the Revolution of July 1830. A barrier has been surmounted, and the symbolical figure of Liberty, a vigorous "classical" woman with bare breasts and bare feet, a gun in one hand and a flag held aloft in the other, is leading the people in a victorious charge. Before her on the ground are the dead bodies of two or three fallen patriots, and a dying revolutionary raises himself to gaze upon her valiant figure. On her left is a youth flourishing two pistols, on her right a solid citizen grasping a musket and wearing a top hat. Behind these is an agitated crowd armed with whatever weapons they have been able to seize. A section of pre-Haussmann Paris lies behind her, but the background is mainly filled with swirling clouds of the smoke of battle as the citizens and she charge irresistibly on. The coloring, the activity, and the composition are all romantic — here is no stately commemorative battle-picture. Liberty herself is Hellenic and suggests Rude's "La Marseillaise" in her vigor. The details are as realistic as those in Géricault's "The Raft of the 'Medusa,'" and the subject is contemporary. Above all, one is moved by the irresistible *surge* of the picture, even in the quiet galleries of the Louvre. The spectator feels that he should get out of the way before the revolutionaries trample him down. Classicism in the figure of Liberty, romanticism in the restlessness, realism in the details, and sociological vitality unite to make this one of Delacroix's masterpieces.

iii

This sense of striving, this surge after something just out of reach, this yearning to pass beyond experience is characteristic of the new men of the nineteenth century, though it was prophesied here and there by men of the previous age. It appears in the replacement of the neat universe of Buffon by an activist universe of becoming, as evolution shaped scientific thought. It appears in romantic paintings by Delacroix, Géricault, J. M. W. Turner, William Blake, and Caspar Friedrich, the wild canvases of John Martin, and the grandiloquence of Thomas Cole, pictures which can scarcely be contained by the frames which bound them. The first two piano sonatas of Beethoven are still within the confines of the sonata form as Haydn shaped it, though Haydn would probably have disapproved of the Largo Appassionato of the second sonata on the ground that it was excessively personal. But with Beethoven we pass through the emotional tensions of the "Pathétique" and the fury of the Presto Agitato of opus 27, no. 2 (the "Moonlight") to the titanism of the "Hammerklavier" and, eventually, to the attainment of divine peace in the last movement of opus 111 (Sonata 32). A similar striving after unutterable things distinguishes the late string quartets from the early ones, just as the *Missa Solemnis* is no ordinary piece of liturgical music but an agonized dialogue between Beethoven and his God. A like passionate determination to pass beyond the bounds of humanity into the infinite is evident in Berlioz, whose *Requiem* ("Grande Messe des morts," opus 5) of 1837, is, again, no mere musical formulary for the Roman Catholic service but an immense expression of the religion of humanity — music, said De Vigny, that is wild, convulsed, and sorrowful, dedicated to those who had died in the revolution of 1830. One has to await Verdi's requiem for Manzoni, whose five sons participated in the revolution of 1848, to parallel this titanic striving after eternity. The struggle to overcome limits and express infinity is also evident in the eternal tension between theories of science and theories, or rather actions, of a political sort in the period. Thus Haeckel thought he had solved the riddle of existence in his *Natürliche Schöpfungsgeschichte* of 1867, a theme to which he returned in his pretentious *Die Welträtsel* in 1889, books of the genre to which Spengler belongs. But there is also the melancholy personalism of Heinrich Heine's "Enfant perdu," which begins:

Verlorner Posten in dem Freiheitskriege,

says that the poet has battled thirty years in vain for liberty, announces his coming death, declares some other warrior will take his place, and concludes that his sword is still unbroken — the only thing that's broken is his heart.

Two great poetical masterpieces of the first part of the nineteenth century drew together, each in its own way, most of the great forces of revolution and romanticism that this book has dealt with, and through an analysis of each of them we may see how these two movements, the one political, the other aesthetic and philosophical, were transmitted to the later nineteenth century. The first is an English poem, a critical inspection and history of the growth of a creative mind; the second, a dramatic poem, is shaped by the life history of the greatest German poet of his age but is also a panorama of the world. The first is Wordsworth's *The Prelude*, issued in its final form in 1850; the second is Goethe's *Faust*, completed in 1831 and brought out in 1832. The publication of the English poem followed the revolutions of 1848 by two years; the German drama that of the revolution of 1830 by the same lapse of time.

Analysis of *The Prelude*,* like the study of *Faust*, has become

* There is a rich literature about Wordsworth, and readers dissatisfied with the superficiality of my discussion of *The Prelude* may profitably turn to the various editions of William Wordsworth's letters and Dorothy Wordsworth's letters and journals, listed in any competent bibliography of Wordsworth or of English romanticism. The standard biography is now Mary Moorman, *William Wordsworth*, 2 vols., Oxford, 1966–1967, but one should also consult Edith C. Batho, *The Later Wordsworth*, New York, 1933, and Helen Darbishire, *Wordsworth*, London, 1953. Willard L. Sperry, *Wordsworth's Anti-Climax*, Cambridge, Mass., 1935, is still invaluable. The text of the 1805 version of *The Prelude* was edited and published by Ernest De Selincourt; a convenient edition is that of 1933, London, easier to handle than the original Clarendon edition of 1928; De Selincourt here gives us "the text of the Poem as it was completed in May 1805 and read to Coleridge in the following winter," and an abridged version of his original notes. A second edition of De Selincourt's work, revised by Helen Darbishire, was issued in 1959. Of many studies concerned with Wordsworth's personal development and with *The Prelude* as a document revelatory of that development the following seem outstanding: Arthur Beatty, *William Wordsworth: His Doctrine and Art in Their Historical Relations*, 3rd ed., Madison, Wisconsin, 1960; William Warner Douglas, *Wordsworth: The Construction of a Personality*, Kent, Ohio, 1968; Geoffrey Durant, *Wordsworth and the Great System: A Study of Wordsworth's Poetic Universe*, London, 1970; Geoffrey H. Hartman, *The Unmediated Vision: An Interpretation of Wordsworth*, New York, 1966; the

virtually a major branch of learning. The text of 1850 is not the original text of the fourteen books now comprising the poem, parts of which were composed before 1800, and most of which was written in 1804–1805. Other fragments apparently intended for the poem are scattered here and there in Wordsworth's works, and *The Prelude*, furthermore, has the curious distinction of being a great work intended to find out whether its author could write a great work, to be called *The Recluse*, the concluding sections of the completed portion of which tell us of Wordsworth's intention to fuse into a single whole his interpretation of Man, Nature, and Human Life. He blandly requests the aid of a greater muse than Urania, since he proposes to attack a greater theme than that of Milton, namely,

> How exquisitely the individual Mind
> (And the progressive powers perhaps no less
> Of the whole species) to the external World
> Is fitted: — and how exquisitely, too —
> . . . .
> The external World is fitted to the Mind.

Nor is that all. He implores the "prophetic Spirit" which inspires

> The human Soul of universal earth
> Dreaming on things to come

to aid him because this mysterious spirit possesses

> A metropolitan* temple in the hearts
> Of mighty Poets,

and will, Wordsworth hopes, bestow on him the gift of "genuine insight" and "star-like virtue," because he wants to discuss a theme so great as to

---

second volume of Raymond Dexter Havens, *The Mind of a Poet*, 2 vols., Baltimore, 1941; Henry J. F. Jones, *The Egotistical Sublime: A History of Wordsworth's Imagination*, London, 1954; David Perkins, *Wordsworth and the Poetry of Sincerity*, Cambridge, Mass., 1964; Newton P. Stallknecht, *Strange Seas of Thought: Studies in William Wordsworth's Philosophy of Man and Nature*, 2nd ed., Bloomington, Indiana, 1958; and, standing a little apart from these, Abbie Findlay Potts, *Wordsworth's Prelude: A Study of Its Literary Form*, Ithaca, New York, 1953. No two specialists quite agree on the interpretation of *The Prelude*; the discussion in the text may be a poor thing but it is at least mine own.

* "Metropolitan" is here used in the sense of all-inclusive; as, for example, in the days before Algeria became independent it was said to be part of "metropolitan" France.

The quoted matter is from "The Recluse," ll. 816–821, 837–840, 852–859; it can also be found in Wordsworth's Preface to *The Excursion* (1814).

> sort with highest objects, then — dread Power!
> Whose gracious favour is the primal source
> Of all illumination, — may my Life
> Express the image of a better time,
> More wise desires, and simpler manners; — nurse
> My Heart in genuine freedom: — all pure thoughts
> Be with me.

Once more one has the yearning for something beyond, for some "illumination" to spring from a mysterious "primal source." It has been made a matter of reproach to Wordsworth that he revised *The Prelude* before publishing it and that these revisions gloss over, omit, or conceal important crises in his own life (for example, the love affair with Annette Vallon). But inasmuch as the rule in literary comment is to accept as final the last text of a work to come under the eye of its author, we may fairly take the 1850 text as saying what Wordsworth meant to say.

The poem runs to fourteen books and to nearly 8,000 lines. In general, Books I–IV tell the story of Wordsworth's infancy, boyhood, and youth; Book V has to do with the development of his imagination; Books VI–VII graduate him from Cambridge, send him to London, and indicate his approach to maturity; Book VIII continues this story, but also looks back on the narrative and seeks its meaning; Books IX–XI are principally concerned with his residence in France and the effects upon him of the hope and disillusion of the French revolution; and Books XII–XIV state his theory of the development of his own imagination as well as his theory of the relation among mystical vision, Nature as a transcendent power, Reason as defined by ideal philosophy, intuition, and the various phases of love, which rise from mere animal affection to the highest degree of spiritual love, the "intellectual Love" also found in Aquinas and Dante. The poem concludes with tributes to Dorothy Wordsworth, to the poet's wife, and to Samuel Taylor Coleridge, who had insisted that this "history" be brought

> To its appointed close: the discipline
> And consummation of a Poet's mind.
> (XIV: 303–304)

The Prelude belongs among the great confessional books that explain the interplay of God, the cosmos, and the human psyche.

Of these the *Confessions of St. Augustine*, Dante's *Divine Comedy*, and Tennyson's *In Memoriam* are memorable examples. So, like-wise, in its queer way is Rousseau's *Confessions*, and in another fashion Byron's *Don Juan*. But our present concern is with Words-worth.

Nobody has ever pretended *The Prelude* is easy reading. It is impossible to sustain a blank verse poem of this inordinate length at a high level. Wordsworth's style varies from the extreme flat-ness of:

> And at the *Hoop* alighted, famous inn,

through passages so syntactically confused, one has to read them twice, to such haunting pronouncements as the famous outburst of self-consciousness in Book IV:

> Magnificent
> The morning rose, in memorable pomp,
> Glorious as e'er I had beheld — in front,
> The sea lay laughing at a distance; near,
> The solid mountains shone, bright as the clouds,
> Grain-tinctured, drenched in empyrean light;
> And in the meadows and the lower grounds
> Was all the sweetness of a common dawn —
> Dews, vapours, and the melody of birds,
> And labourers going forth to till the fields.
> Ah! need I say, dear Friend! that to the brim
> My heart was full; I made no vows, but vows
> Were then made for me; bond unknown to me
> Was given, that I should be, else sinning greatly,
> A dedicated Spirit.
>
> (323–337)

This easy transition from accurate description of landscape to a feeling of supranormal meaning in the scene is characteristic of Wordsworth at his best; it is also in a sense what the poem is all about; that is, the transmogrification of the world as we know it into the world as it ought to be known (an emanation of infinity), and the concomitant discovery than man, if only certain obstacles are cleared away, may by intelligence and desire be promoted to that higher state of being which is Genius. Is Wordsworth's case, in his opinion, mere chance? The double problem of the poem is this: Wordsworth dimly feels that he is working out his spiritual destiny, but he also profoundly feels that his destiny is being worked out for him by some sort of higher power vaguely known in child-hood that has to be consciously sought after in maturity.

I have said that *The Prelude* is not easy reading. Like most auto-biographies it is frequently false to fact. In later years the Words-worth who once thought there might be something in William Godwin's philosophical anarchy wrote *Ecclesiastical Sonnets*, a rhymed history of the Church of England, "that stream" which had borne England unharmed through the ages because of her Christian belief,

> THAT STREAM upon whose bosom we have passed
> Floating at ease while nations have effaced
> Nations, and Death has gathered to his fold
> Long lines of mighty Kings — look forth, my Soul!

We may pass over this view of history to note that the writer who was made poet laureate in 1843 was more anxious to depict the consistency of his life than to chronicle the varying stages of re-bellion he had passed through. *The Prelude* of 1850 is the way Wordsworth wanted to picture himself to posterity. He had the same right to do so as Benvenuto Cellini or Mark Twain had to alter the past by omission, evasion, and invention. This general truth does not, however, alter the value of the poem as an example of development through striving. Wordsworth came to possess what he believed to be the right view of God, of the cosmos, and of Man, especially Man exemplified in himself — sublime egotism, as somebody calls it, but nonetheless valuable.

Wordsworth faced but only partially solved a greater difficulty than a mere rearrangement of the past. In a work rightly subtitled: "Growth of a Poet's Mind — An Autobiographical Poem" (such was his intention and that intention he carried out), he was juggling more themes than even his thousands of lines could carry. *The Prelude* includes a number of landscapes, persons, remembered events — a poor French peasant girl leading a cow; the bust of Newton at Cambridge; stealing a boat as a little boy and rowing it with a mountain seemingly coming after him; the hour he heard somebody cry, "Robespierre is dead!"; a country fair with its lame man, its blind man, its peepshow, a pretty girl trying to sell farm produce, and the morning light on the silent rocks around; a small boy hooting at the owls; the poet's own life as an alien in revolutionary Paris, cut off from the tumult and as

> careless as a flower
> Glass'd in a green-house, or a parlour shrub
> That spreads its leaves in unmolested peace.
>   (IX: 87–89)

Such units he frequently describes as vividly as does Marcel Proust in *Remembrance of Things Past*.

But Wordsworth was a solitary by temperament. Orphaned at an early age, separated from his brothers and sisters, deprived for long years of a debt due him and his brothers and sisters, put under the legal guardianship of uncles who wanted to make a respectable man out of a ne'er-do-well and a potential college dropout, obstinately refusing to take up any profession that would bring in a regular income and not infrequently lying about his plans, then miraculously dowered by a dying consumptive with a legacy, Wordsworth, looking back on these episodes and inventing others, wants the reader to feel that they were all somehow divinely ordered, that his obstinacies were part of an overall scheme, that both consciously and unconsciously he clung to the pattern of what the education of a genius ought to be. The reader sometimes finds it puzzling to know how much to believe. There are time-gaps in the narrative, discrepancies, a precocity that may or may not have been true at these earlier stages, and, more unpleasantly, a flavor of patronage that springs from egotism, not from the sublime egotism of romantic theory.

The poem is also the history of Wordsworth's political experience, a matter of still greater consequence, since the Wordsworthian paradox is that one of the most subjective of romantic writers was throughout his life deeply concerned with public issues. His first experience with egalitarian life was during his boyhood and youth; he found among the "dalesmen" where he grew up a simple democracy he more or less took for granted. For a time he thought to find democracy repeated on a larger scale in France during the earlier months of the revolution. His bitter experience with the Lowther family (Lord Londsdale finally paid up only in 1802, when Wordsworth was thirty-two) convinced him of the insensibility of the upper classes to the poor; and though at Cambridge he momentarily yielded to the dissipations of careless undergraduates, he led there an essentially nonsocial existence. His walking tour with Robert Jones in France and Switzerland was the kind of vagabond trip that many contemporary undergraduates, hard put to it for ready cash, now embark on; and Wordsworth's residence in France in 1791 and 1792, mainly at Orléans and Blois, and his liaison with Annette Vallon, his refusal to engage in any sort of professional training, and his vague notions of "writing," are all the sort of thing one finds common nowadays among young men who are rather self-consciously "alienated" from society. As all the world knows, Wordsworth was outraged by the smugness of the Bishop of Llandaff, who, like Burke, spoke up for things as they were in Britain; he was deeply hurt when Britain went to war with revolutionary France, and shocked by reports of the bloody events in France. *The Prelude* records this personal political history, and records also the poet's growing acquiescence in Burke's philosophy of tradition and development,* to the acceptance of which Wordsworth was helped by Coleridge. Indeed, Wordsworth's sense of being at home amid the old customs of Windermere and the Lake District generally, set forth in *The Prelude*, seems to show that his youthful radicalism, his bitterness against society as he found it — for example, during his residence in London — was really something against the grain, though at the time perfectly sincere:

> Not in my single self alone I found,
> But in the minds of all ingenuous youth,
> Change and subversion from that hour. No shock
> Given to my moral nature had I known
> Down to that very moment.
>
> (X: 266–270)

This shock was not merely because Britain was at war with France, but also because

---

* In addition to the direct praise of Burke in Book VII (512–543), in which the aging Burke is pictured as one who

> launches forth,
> Against all systems built on abstract rights,
> Keen ridicule; the majesty proclaims
> Of Institutes and Laws, hallowed by time;
> Declares the vital power of social ties
> Endeared by Custom; and with high disdain,
> Exploding upstart Theory, insists
> Upon the allegiance to which men are born,

see also the Burkian flavor of Wordsworth's commentaries on his own youthful misreading of history (VIII: 617–664, IX: 465–501, X: 331–355, and XII: 52–74).

> Frenchmen had changed a war of self-defence
> For one of conquest, losing sight of all
> Which they had struggled for.
>
> (XI:207–209)

Obstinate by nature, Wordsworth claims he still clung to a revolutionary philosophy, and the struggle to pass beyond Godwin became painful:

> In such strange passion, if I may once more
> Review the past, I warred against myself —
> A bigot to a new idolatry —
> Like a cowled monk who hath forsworn the world,
> Zealously laboured to cut off my heart
> From all the sources of her former strength;
> And as, by simple waving of a wand,
> The wizard instantaneously dissolves
> Palace or grove, even so could I unsoul
> As readily by syllogistic words
> Those mysteries of being which have made,
> And shall continue evermore to make,
> Of the whole human race one brotherhood.
>
> (XII:75–87)

To distinguish between the artifice of liberty, equality, and fraternity, on the one hand, and the natural (or supernatural) mystical brotherhood he knew in the countryside or in any natural or pastoral solitude, on the other hand, takes a great deal of writing. This task in one sense is the main theme of *The Prelude* and in another sense is related, but not central to, the purport of the subtitle: the growth of a poet's mind.

An equally important element is a succession of dreams and visions either remembered or expanded by the memory or, in the extreme case, invented. Since Wordsworth is under no obligation to give chapter and verse for these strange mental phenomena, it is impossible to know which of these episodes or what part of any one of them is remembered, even in a loose sense, and what part is the product of later wishful thinking. Their importance to the poem and to its theme of struggling upward toward "truth" makes them significant elements in this autobiography of genius. The episodes vary in importance and in emotional immediacy. In considering them, two matters must be kept in mind: first, the poem was written for Coleridge, to whom frequent reference is made in

446

The Prelude and to whom such supernatural solicitings were, so to speak, expected proofs of genius in a man he held to be among the greater English artists; and, second, the whole purport of the poem is to demonstrate

> a faith
> That fails not, in all sorrow, my support,
> The blessing of my life,
>
> (II:443–445)

as he says early in the work; and, as he writes in the concluding book:

> Imagination having been our theme,
> So also hath that intellectual Love,
> For they are each in each, and cannot stand
> Dividually. — Here must thou be, O Man!
> Power to thyself; no Helper hast thou here;
> Here keepest thou in singleness thy state:
> No other can divide with thee this work;
> No secondary hand can intervene
> To fashion this ability; 'tis thine
> The prime and vital principle is thine,
> In the recesses of thy nature, far
> From any reach of outward fellowship,
> Else is not thine at all. But joy to him,
> Oh, joy to him who here hath sown, hath laid
> Here, the foundations of his future years!
>
> (XIV:206–220)

In other words, these moments of vision were either valid or they were not; because Wordsworth believed they were valid, they become important episodes in the history of his imagination. He is completely honest in his understanding of the slippery quality of a writer's psychology:

> Humility and modest awe, themselves
> Betray me, serving often for a cloak
> To a more subtle selfishness; that now
> Locks every function up in blank reserve,
> Now dupes me, trusting to an anxious eye
> That with intrusive restlessness beats off
> Simplicity and self-presented truth,
>
> (I:243–249)

a passage that does infinite credit to Wordsworth's integrity, though it may not be sublime as verse.

447

The passages in question include vaguely remembered child-hood impressions that the universe was more than the sensory universe. Among the simpler are, for example, the mingled sense of delight and guilt engendered by stealing the boat (I:357-414); the sense of possessing two consciousnesses (II:31-33); the feeling that his education at Cambridge was not academic but "natural":

> there's not a man
> That lives who hath not known his god-like hours,
> And feels not what an empire we inherit
> As natural beings in the strength of Nature;
>   (III:190-193)

the meeting with a "meagre man," all "a desolation, a simplicity," whom Wordsworth steered to a cottage of refuge (he seems to have taken no responsibility on himself).

A curious visionary experience on Mount Snowdon, when the moon "hung naked in the firmament" over a mist that hid all but the tops of the adjoining hills and through a rent in the mist

> Mounted the roar of waters, torrents, streams
> Innumerable, roaring with one voice,
>   (XIV:59-60)

gave the poet the feeling of a universal

>   mind sustained
> By recognitions of transcendent power,
> In sense conducting to ideal form
> In soul of more than mortal privilege.
>   (XIV:74-77)

More mysterious is a dream about an Arab in V:50-139, the Arab being both Euclid and Don Quixote, a dream that has something to do with Wordsworth's aspiration to become a poet of the rank of Shakespeare and Milton. Like it is a moment on Salisbury Plain near Stonehenge, where he had a sudden fearful vision of the past (XIII:312-349), which Coleridge seems to have glossed as hints that Wordsworth's mind

>   had exercised
> Upon the vulgar forms of present things,
> The actual world of our familiar days,
> Yet higher power.
>   (XIII:355-358)

But more important was the sudden glory of the moon shining upon the ocean of mist around Mount Snowdon, since by this experience, with all the twistings of the rest of the poem behind him, Wordsworth concludes that he is really in touch with "a mind / That feeds upon infinity," that Nature is the counterpart of that "glorious faculty / That higher minds bear with them as their own," that such minds "are truly from the Deity," that the "endless occupation for the Soul" in contemplating a universe thus morally free, whatever the world's physical limitations, is alone "genuine liberty," and that, finally, custom and natural philosophy (the science of Wordsworth's time) merely

> substitute a universe of death
> For that which moves with light and life informed,
> Actual, divine, and true.
>
> (XIV: 160–162)

In sum, Wordsworth has traced "the history of a Poet's mind," knows that he has been called upon to do the work of genius, and has a duty to other men to

> Instruct them how the mind of man becomes
> A thousand times more beautiful than the earth
> On which he dwells, above this frame of things
>
> . . . . . .
>
> In beauty exalted, as it is itself
> Of quality and fabric more divine.
>
> (XIV: 448–454)

In his dark striving Wordsworth, always conscious of the right way, has in fact drawn near the abode where the eternal are. There are hundreds of unsolved riddles in *The Prelude*, but one point is clear: men may rise on stepping stones of their dead selves to higher things. It is also illuminating to discover that seldom or never in this huge autobiography does Wordsworth record any speech or conversation of his own.

iv

The Prelude is one of the great introspective triumphs of romanticism, a large part of it turning on the poet's varying attitudes toward the French revolution. I have said it belongs to that class of confessions which deals with God, the cosmos, and humanity. On reflection one must admit that God plays so minor a role in the poem, He may be said not to appear at all, His role being taken by the wisdom and spirit of the universe. Wordsworth's universe, however, has but small scientific structure; it is rather the poet-philosopher's projection of what he thinks the universe ought to be. When, however, one turns to Goethe's *Faust* one finds not only God and His emissaries but also, disguised as late medieval or early Renaissance cosmology, a universe of becoming as well as a universe of being. Faust himself begins as a late medieval conjuror, but the poem was so long in the making and Goethe was so many-sided a man that the hero fuses into one being late medieval man, Renaissance man, neoclassical man (in his search for Helena), and modern man, or at least the modern man of Goethe's time and perhaps even of ours, since we, too, have been humbled by the terrible energies of the universe released in atomic destruction. Goethe manages to make all this conformable to his system of values because, among other reasons, he takes over the machinery of Christianity without Christian belief. God, the archangels, Mephistopheles, heavenly choirs, and, on earth, the Catholic church are all parts of the poem, but there is in it no Christ the Redeemer, no thought of an immortal soul in the theological sense, no "conversion," and no penitence, but only human remorse. His universe is Copernican, not Ptolemaic, its central principle is energy, an energy so great that it frightens Faust; yet it is also a universe in which the sun comes up like thunder, moonlight has special powers, meadows and fields are, literally, curative agencies, and — a necessary part of the Faust legend — one can go backward and forward in time: backward to a vague Homeric world and forward, as in Act V of *Faust II*, to a universe of commerce, irrigation, and mercantile wealth.

The thrust of the poem, which runs to 12,111 lines of verse, not to speak of a few lines of prose, is upward and onward. It is a poem of becoming. Faust, we are told, is to experience everything, and the playhouse is to represent all creation, the hero to move from earth downward to hell and upward to heaven. If he does not literally go to hell, he experiences two witches' nights, the Walpurgisnacht of *Faust I* and its classical equivalent in *Faust II*. Faust moves from the loneliness of an academic life shut off from the rest of mankind through the little world (that is, the world of private, individual desire) into the great world of statesmanship, aesthetics, war, and commerce. Mephistopheles transforms him (he is apparently in his later middle age when the drama begins) into a fiery younger man, though not a callow youth, and Faust lives to be a hundred, when he is stricken blind, Care takes over, and he dies, after which, unburdened by his manifold sins, his immortal part is borne aloft in spite of all Mephistopheles can do to retain it. Just before his death Faust utters an epitome of the liberal ideas of the nineteenth century, compounded of revolutionary and romantic idealism:

> Nur der verdient sich Freiheit wie das Leben,
> Der täglich sie erobern muss.

The nearest Faust comes to the personal satisfaction he yearns for is just before his death when, a blind old man, he thinks the Lemures, who are really digging his grave, are workmen cutting canals to drain his land, redeem it from the sea, and so create the possibility of a happy life for future millions:

> Solch ein Gewimmel möcht' ich sehn,
> Auf freiem Grund mit freiem Volke stehn.
> Zum Augenblicke dürft' ich sagen:
> Verweile doch, du bist so schön.

One notes that even this is in the subjunctive mood: "*If* I could see the work going on, then I *might* say to the passing moment, remain with me." Mephistopheles has a cynical word about Faust's unaccountable pleasure in accepting civic responsibility:

> Ihn sättigt keine Lust, ihm g'nügt kein Glück,
> So buhlt er fort nach wechselnden Gestalten;
> Den letzten, schlechten, leeren Augenblick
> Der Arme wünscht ihn fest zu halten.
> Der mir so kräftig widerstand,
> Die Zeit wird Herr, der Greis hier liegt im Sand.
> Die Uhr steht still —
>
> Er fällt, es ist vollbracht.*

* Bayard Taylor has at least the right nineteenth-century flavor, and his versions of these passages run: "He only earns his freedom and existence, / Who daily conquers them anew." "And such a throng I fain would see, / Stand on free soil among a people free! / Then dared I hail the Moment fleeting: / 'Ah, still delay —thou art so fair!'" (The last line is pretty bad.) "No joy could sate him, and suffice no bliss! / To catch but shifting shapes was his endeavor! / The latest, poorest, emptiest Moment — this, — / He wished to hold it fast forever. / Me

451

But time never stands still, and no earthly life is ever "complete," so that the mystical scenes show us the spiritual being of Faust drawn upward amid choirs of music into that other world where love, intellect, sexual desire, and the incompleteness of the earth are rounded into a supreme unity:

> Alles Vergängliche
> Ist nur ein Gleichniss;
> Das Unzulängliche
> Hier wird's Ereigniss;
> Das Unbeschreibliche
> Hier ist's gethan;
> Das Ewig-Weibliche
> Zieht uns hinan.*

The Faust legend haunted Goethe from about his twentieth year (possibly from his childhood) until his death. Part I, which has the form (or formlessness) of a late medieval morality play, was more or less complete in 1808; Part II, arranged in five acts but really, like Part I, a succession of episodes, was not formally completed until the whole vast poem was published in 1832. The third act of *Faust II* was once separately printed as *Helena* in 1827. Before his death Wordsworth had reorganized *The Prelude* into relative order and had given it a style harmonious with itself. But the forty-five scenes of *Faust* are written in various styles, some scenes reaching back to Goethe's *Sturm und Drang* days, others starting out in the relatively obsolescent style of Hans Sachs and easing into more normal, "modern" rhythms, and still other parts being influenced by the German love for Calderón or by Goethe's interest in Euripidean tragedy. The vocabulary is equally varied in this vast "tragedy," something that most English translators are unable to cope with, and Goethe specialists point out the affinities between the varying metrical effects of the verse and the varying purposes of the several episodes.

---

he resisted in such vigorous wise, / But Time is lord, on earth the old man lies. / The clock stands still — / He falls; and it is finished, here!" Though I find occasional fault with Bayard Taylor, he seems to me to have given us the "classical" English version of *Faust*.

* These lines are virtually untranslatable, and in their mingling of intellect and mystery are among the greatest passages in Goethe. The sense is something like this: "All things that have been done are but as an allegory or metaphor. What was impossible on earth is here brought to fruition. What man cannot comprehend (the indescribable) is here completed; and the eternality of womanhood [creativity] still urges us onward."

The Faust legend seems to have originated in the first half of the sixteenth century, and Goethe's Faust begins as a late medieval or early Renaissance scholar of high repute who, having exhausted all the normal branches of knowledge, turns to magic, once thought to be an extension of science; while in *Faust II* his former assistant, Wagner, now grown mature, is seen manufacturing a miniature human being (Homunculus) by alchemical and magical formulas. Goethe in his lordly way does not feel any duty to write a consistently historical drama, but uses only so much history as suits his purpose. A good many "historical" episodes, such as the emperor and his court in *Faust II*, more than hint at the decay of the monarchical state in Goethe's own time and include materials from the French revolution, such as the issuing of paper money and a battle that, though fairylike, brings to mind the cannonading at the Battle of Valmy. Victory in the battle is won by the appearance in the emperor's army of three giants conjured up by the magic of Mephistopheles:* like other characters and elements in *Faust II* these are allegorical figures, to which Goethe resorted in his effort to picture time, the world, and history, or at least so much classical and medieval history as went into the making of Act III of *Faust II*, where Faust, like the Frankish barons of the thirteenth century, is supposed to occupy a medieval castle near Sparta (the ruins of the medieval fortress of Mistra, three miles from the site of ancient Sparta, still attract the tourist).

Specialists in *Faust* are able to fit most things in it into some sort of coherent world view, but the modern reader has, one fears, only a mild interest, if any, in the Walpurgisnacht and the attached

* Goethe refers to II Samuel 23:8, though he really means verses 8–11. Therein one reads that in his battles against the Philistines King David enlisted Adino, Dodo, and Shammah, three "mighty men" who wrought havoc on the enemy, Adino, for example, slaying eight hundred of the Philistines when he lifted up his spear. Goethe replaces the Hebrew names with Raufebold (Fight-hard, Bully), Habebald (Seize-quick), and Haltefest (Hold-fast). Once the camp of the anti-emperor is entered by the imperial forces, a fourth allegorical figure appears, this time female, by name Eilebeute (Quick-loot), who tries to seize the treasure chest of the rebel army. If one takes these allegorical figures for what they are worth, adds that the command of the imperial forces is eventually given to Mephistopheles, and that Mephistopheles wins the battle by, among other magical means, seeming to drown his opponents with a phantom flood, one concludes that Goethe had few illusions about warfare, including the Napoleonic campaigns. Mephistopheles' magic flood recalls Napoleon's breaking the ice with artillery fire at Austerlitz, thereby drowning hundreds of the enemy in the ice-cold waters of Lake Satschan.

"Walpurgisnachtstraum, oder Oberons und Titanias goldne Hochzeit" of Part I, in the overelaborate Renaissance carnival that takes up altogether too much of *Faust II*, Act I, the scholarly and even pedantic "Classische Walpurgisnacht" of Act II, and a good deal of Act III, partly because Goethe in his enthusiasm for the ancient world let these passages get out of hand and partly because the modern reader lacks the mythological, literary, and historical knowledge to tell him what is going on. There is, for instance, a good deal of obsolete geology in a lengthy discussion among Thales, Anaxagoras, and others in the concluding scenes of Act II, and though the decision of Homunculus to throw himself into the sea, whence life arose, at the end of the act is proof that Goethe was alert to contemporary scientific theory, his crowding the stage with Sirens, Nereids, Tritons, Dorides, Psylli, Marsi, not to speak of Nereus, Proteus, and Galatea, whatever it may do for pageantry, obscures rather than clarifies meaning.* Yet if one takes *Faust* as a whole, as Dryden said of Chaucer, here is God's plenty.

Doubtless to most Americans *Faust* is Gounod's opera, a theatrical, though not a dramatic, masterpiece; or if not that, Berlioz's choral symphony, *The Damnation of Faust* or, perhaps, Boito's *Mefistofele*, the only one of the three best-known musical compositions on the theme that does justice to Goethe's "Prologue in Heaven." With the exception of Busoni, musicians tend to concentrate on the seduction, insanity, and death of Margarete as the point of the tragedy. Yet out of the more than 12,000 lines in the total poem, something less than 1500 suffices for Margarete, a tribute to Goethe's genius, since in this brief space he creates a three-dimensional character that has impressed itself upon the imagination of the world. The story of Gretchen is usually interpreted as a tale of female innocence betrayed. Goethe, however, is more subtle, for the girl who laments the loss of her first box of jewels and, on finding the second, takes to wearing them secretly in the house of a neighbor of somewhat questionable morality may be said to know something of the worldly ways of mankind.

---

* Moreover, in preceding parts of the Classical Walpurgisnight we have had Sphinxes, Nymphs, Dactyls, Griffins, gigantic Ants, Pygmies, Lamiae, and Cranes, not to speak of Erichtho (a witch), Chiron, Manto, and other names which send one to a classical dictionary. The Carnival Masquerade of Act I, modeled on a Renaissance *trionfo*, has more characters in it than are necessary for the point of the show, which is that reckless prodigality gets nowhere as a form of public finance.

Margarete is flattered by the amorous attention of a social superior, and, of course, her fate represents a kind of self-immolation on behalf of love, rewarded by sending her beyond the reach of Mephistopheles. This ending parallels that in an inferior, though theatrically brilliant, success by Dumas, known in English as *Camille*, the concluding line of which is: "God will forgive her, for she loved much." Goethe was not a Christian, but he was most emphatically no Calvinist and did not believe in eternal damnation.

Margarete is an appealing figure, but the four personages who more importantly concern us are the Lord and the cosmos He has created; Mephistopheles, who is, rather against his will, a dynamic, if negative, part of that cosmos; Faust, who may be taken to represent, if not all humanity, then the intelligent part of mankind; and Helena, that dream of perfect beauty which has haunted Western man since the days of Homer. In a sense Helena may be thought of as Margarete idealized; as Stuart Atkins rightly points out in one of the finest analyses of *Faust* in English,* a large part of *Faust II* is best thought of as a succession of dreams, and these visions reach a climax when Faust meets Helena precisely in the middle of *Faust II*, in Act III, the classical place for dramatic climax. Their dream child, Euphorion, dies, and Helena, after one last embrace of Faust, fades into a cloud, as do, ultimately, her veil and her garment:

> Ein altes Wort bewährt sich leider auch an mir:
> Dass Glück und Schönheit dauerhaft sich nicht vereint.
> Zerrissen ist des Lebens wie der Liebe Band,
> Bejammernd beide, sag' ich schmerzlich Lebewohl!
> Und werfe mich noch einmal in die Arme dir.
> Persephonia, nimm den Knaben auf und mich.†
>
> (ll. 9939–9944)

The Lord speaks only thirty-three lines in the poem, but the songs of the archangels in the "Prologue in Heaven," a voice at the

* Stuart Atkins, *Goethe's Faust: A Literary Analysis*, Cambridge, Mass., 1958. The book is rich and full, its only fault being that Atkins tries to justify almost everything in the poem.

† In me an ancient word unfortunately proves true; namely, that happiness and beauty do not unite in any lasting form. The bond of love and the bond of life alike are broken and I, sorrowing for both, sadly say farewell, and throw myself into your arms once more. Persephone, receive my boy (Euphorion) and me.

Persephone is of course the goddess of the underworld, who, according to Swinburne, "Waits for each and other, / She waits for all men born."

end of *Faust 1* which announces that Margarete is saved, and the numerous choirs and solo voices which make glorious the ending of the whole drama may be thought of as surrogates for the Almighty, not to speak of the "symbol" of the Macrocosm, which Faust does not see, and the Earth Spirit whom he does see and who terrifies him. The common note of these supernal voices is that the universe is orderly activity:

> Der Anblick gibt den Engeln Stärke
> Da keiner dich ergründen mag,
> Und alle deine hohen Werke
> Sind herrlich wie am ersten Tag.*
>
> (ll. 267–270)

But the changeless splendor of creation does not negate creativity, striving upward, the continuing struggle of finite mind to grasp infinite things, so that when Mephistopheles, aware of the despair of Faust, tells the Lord that nothing seems to subdue his discontent, the Lord answers that the very restlessness of this learned man is part of the scheme of things. In sum the contrast is between Mephistopheles' interpretation of human egotism as not much greater than animal selfishness, and the Lord's "scheme," in which earthly egotism is a stage of development toward egotism of the sublime — the rich development of personalities evident in the concluding choirs of *Faust* and the ultimate goal of Goethe's ideal of *Humanität*. For, in truth, Goethe and the social reformers of the first half of the nineteenth century were not, in the ideals they dreamed of, very far apart.

In the Lord's dynamic scheme of things there must be some force that will operate to keep man from mere contentment, since contentment is tantamount to apathy, spiritual sloth, and that ending of development which is death. This force is incarnated in Mephistopheles, who is a far more intricate character than the red-cloaked devil of the opera. When he first reveals himself to Faust, Mephistopheles frankly confesses that he is the power that always denies (and destroys) and nevertheless, in spite of his lust for negation, a power that wills evil and ends by creating good. Darkness in Goethe's universe is the primordial base of being, just

---

* Its aspect gives (continues to give) strength to the angels although none can fathom it (the cosmos); and all your great works are as wonderful as they were on the day of their creation.

as light and the action of light (Goethe had a special theory that light both cleaves to and flows from bodies, that is, is corpuscular) are evidence of creativity. For this reason, when Faust is stricken blind, he dies. Mephistopheles is a Proteus-like character in this masterpiece, taking on all sorts of shapes, assuming all sorts of tasks, and defeated, somewhat unfairly, one must think, when the roses scattered on him by angels bearing away the immortal part of Faust turn into flames and stick like pitch and sulphur to his neck, head, heart, and liver — a rather incongruous mode of shaming the devil. Mephistopheles has wit, coarseness, cynicism, supernal power, and a crafty worldly wisdom, but he is also oddly short-sighted, since he is told from the beginning that Faust's aspirations will always outrun whatever pleasures Mephistopheles may find or invent. Mephistopheles begins to tempt Faust at the lowest possible level, that of the sensuality and animalism of the scene in Auerbach's Cellar and that in the Witch's Kitchen; he passes on to the less sensual allure of earthly love (Margarete's devotedness awakens in Faust a sense of shame), then offers his victim the kingdom of this world in Acts I, II, and IV of *Faust II*, all laid in an empire tottering to its fall. At Faust's request in Act III a somewhat bewildered Mephistopheles, strangely disguised, proves or discovers that a dream of mortal perfection (the Helena episode) remains a dream, and in Act V, turning Faust into a protocapitalist and incidentally causing the deaths of innocent persons, Mephistopheles loses his victim forever.

Goethe felt under obligation to retain a great deal of the hocus-pocus of the Faust legend, and added mystifications, sometimes humorous, sometimes serious, of his own. But whatever one can say against Mephistopheles and all he symbolizes, it cannot be said that he is ever dull, even though his own pleasures are occasionally subhuman.

Faust himself is more, however, than a protocapitalist who, late in life, discovers the pleasures of philanthropy and planning. Committed of necessity to retaining the main elements of the Faust legend, an important ingredient in German nationalistic feeling, Goethe begins with a Faust who has studied everything, tries by magic to penetrate to the powers of the universe, is frightened by what he conjures up (as modern man is frightened by atomic energy), is ready to commit suicide, is rescued by an Easter chorus in a nearby church singing about a Christ who is "growing into rapture" ("Ist er in Werdelust / Schaffender Freude nah"), then mingles with the common people, and eventually succeeds half unwittingly in conjuring up the devil (Mephistopheles). But if Goethe retains many aspects of the legend, his Faust is more nearly a *uomo universale* of the Renaissance than he is a late medieval scholar; and though nobody can rightly call the drama a revolutionary document, Faust revolts against organized learning, against his father's practice of medicine, against animality, against the imperfections of a run-of-the-mill love affair, and against the stupidity with which the state is governed. His ideal is that dream of classical beauty which Winckelmann imposed upon the German intellect, together with a dream nation exemplified by the castle near Sparta, where an imaginary Germany and an imaginary Hellas are momentarily made one. His thirst for the unattainable disturbs both his private life and the public world; but in the act of dying he sketches the outlines of such a modern state as the revolutionaries dreamed of:

> Eröffn' ich Räume vielen Millionen,
> Nicht sicher zwar, doch thätig-frei zu wohnen.
> Grün das Gefilde, fruchtbar; Mensch und Heerde
> Sogleich behaglich auf der neuesten Erde,
> Gleich angesiedelt an des Hügels Kraft,
> Den aufgewälzt kühn-emsige Völkerschaft.
> Im Innern hier ein paradiesisch Land,
> Da rase draussen Fluth bis auf zum Rand,
> Und wie sie nascht gewaltsam einzuschiessen,
> Gemeindrang eilt die Lücke zu verschliessen.*

Faust's vision has nothing to do with the industrial order or with the proletariat who played such ambiguous roles in the city revolutions of 1848. The revolutionary movements of 1848 were on the whole both futile and badly managed (think of the quick replacement of Lamartine by Napoleon III or of the restoration

---

* Perhaps because he was an American, Bayard Taylor, it seems to me, has rendered this passage (ll. 11,563–11,572) rather effectively: "To many millions let me furnish soil, / Though not secure, yet free from active toil; / Green, fertile fields, where men and herds go forth / At once, with comfort on the newest Earth, / And swiftly [!] settled on the hill's firm base, / Created by the bold, industrious race. / A land like Paradise here, round about: / Up to the brink the tide may roar without, / And though it gnaw, to burst with force the limit, / By common impulse all unite to hem it." Taylor's search for rhymes has mildly falsified the passage, but he is not responsible for the unexpected appearance of a hill ("Hügel") on Faust's "made" land.

of Prussian and Austrian "authority").* But Faust has left the whole imperial order behind him (Act IV) and pictures a society not incomparable with American dreams of a perfect agricultural nation in the 1780's and the 1790's, or the physiocratic notion of prosperity in eighteenth-century France, or the communalism of Saint-Simon, Comte, and Fourier in the first half of the nineteenth century. Goethe may have been a statesman but he was no economist, however manifold his genius; yet at the conclusion of his great drama Faustian man is onward-going man, a creature who denies Mephistophelean cynicism, a spiritualized entity who firmly believes that time and the tendency of the universe are on the side of progress toward individual and social perfection. In the long career of Faust, mainly composed of follies and failures, Goethe embodied the hopes, the dreams, and the progress of the human race. The modern ecologist or environmentalist creates, in fact, the ideal that Goethe sketched in the final scenes of *Faust* and that is, from the point of view of old-line laissez-faire economics, quite as revolutionary as Tom Paine or Fourier.

v

I have tried in this book to follow with sympathy, if not with profundity, some of the principal elements in the two great convulsions which shook Western civilization between the end of the Seven Years War in 1763 and the American Civil War of 1861. The shock waves of revolution did not subside with the final overthrow of Napoleon in 1815. On the contrary they reappear in 1820, in 1830, in 1848, and in the American Civil War, which was a revolution in that it sought to impose upon the American nation by violence an interpretation of the Constitution which seemed to leaders of the Confederacy a proper union of the states as against the increasing concentration of power in Washington, which was defended by the Federal armies. (I am aware that the Federal troops attacked first.) For that matter the Parisian Commune of 1871, after the fall of Napoleon III and the victory of the armies of the fire-new German Empire, was a recurrence to principles emotionally advocated in the France of the 1790's. I have said

* For an excellent overview see Priscilla Robertson, *Revolutions of 1848: A Social History*, Princeton, 1952.

earlier that change of government by revolutionary violence seems to me more characteristic of modern states than Americans like to think. They prefer the peaceful process of voting in a representative republic. But because the American revolution and the French revolution, each in its way, are paradigms of almost all revolutions since their time, including that outlined in the Communist Manifesto of Marx and Engels, there is no need to continue this book through the Balkan revolutions, the Russian revolutions, and the Chinese revolutions.

A fundamental question is whether revolutionary changes have increased the happiness of men. With all his dry logic Jeremy Bentham did not succeed in shaping a felicific calculus (his phrase) by which to measure contentment, and I know no way of weighing the average happiness of human beings in the 1770's and the 1790's as against their average happiness in the 1970's. One fact, however, seems indisputable. The two great revolutions succeeded in ridding North America and western Europe of an obsolescent feudal system. Yet it is a nice question whether in the course of time the feudal system might not have quietly withered away more or less peacefully by reason of its own inadequacy, as, in fact, it has dwindled into mere pageantry in the British Isles. On the other hand the weakening and eventual disappearance of the feudal system in the nineteenth century did nothing to abolish American Negro slavery, or the oppression of Indians and mestizos in most of Latin America by a small, elitist governing class, though again it seems to me probable that slavery would have disappeared because on most plantations it was a wasteful form of wholesale agriculture, founded in inefficiency and exhausting the soil.

If one looks at actual rather than at conjectural history, the revolutionary convulsions, despite slavery, seem chiefly to have benefited the United States of America, since the history of France after 1799 is a strange alternation of tyranny and libertarianism. Throughout the nineteenth century and into the earlier decades of the twentieth Lincoln's declaration that this country was the last, best hope of man made considerable sense for a variety of reasons, including the easy access in North America of human beings to space. During this stretch of time, moreover, and especially after the Civil War, the United States was annually enriched by the in-coming of thousands upon thousands of immigrants who, finding no hope of lasting contentment in their own countries, trooped to the New World. They might have been better received, they ought not to have been exploited, but in the long run and until recent years the melting-pot theory, that latest form of the religion of humanity, really seemed to work. I think Condorcet would have approved. It was not until after World War I, the Great Depression, World War II, and its tumultuous aftermath that the golden dream of Columbia, the gem of the ocean, the home of the brave and the free, became a little tarnished.

Nowadays book after book takes for its theme the folly of the American dream, the loss of American innocence, or, in general, the ending of the rainbow vision of the United States. If one were to take these studies literally, we are to end not with a bang but with a whimper. The dreariness of this literature is evident to any thoughtful reader, but a condition, not a theory, confronts us in the tumultuous and often irrational pressure of "ethnic" groups, disgruntled youth, criminal gangs, and so on. Is this a passing phase of adjustment, or has the great inheritance of the American revolution really failed the United States? An eighteenth-century constitution which really worked through most of the nineteenth century may not necessarily be the proper frame of government for the problems of the twenty-first century, which is almost upon us.

Putting aside the fading away of the feudal system and the passing of monarchy as the only rational form of the state, one may still ask whether Western man is happier because there were revolutions in 1775 and 1789. It seems at least doubtful. In France, for example, the scandal of the Dreyfus case of 1894–1906 differs in kind but not in malodorousness from the Diamond Necklace scandal of 1784–1785; the cynicism of Balzac's critique of society in *La Comédie humaine*, which pictures society in the post-Napoleonic world, is echoed by the cynicism of Zola's Rougon-Macquart series, which pictures the society of the Second Empire; and the brutality, callousness, and terror of Vichy France are awkwardly reminiscent of France under the Terror. If one takes a more general view, one would be hard put to prove that the rule of the bourgeoisie in the Western world during the nineteenth century was an improvement on the rule of monarchy in the century that preceded it. People starved in France under Louis

XIV; people starved in Ireland in the 1840's. Life, argued Josiah Royce at the conclusion of his *The Spirit of Modern Philosophy* (1892), is sufficiently significant to be at any rate tragic, a profound observation that springs from the latter decades of the Victorian world, a time when philosophy and literature seem to have been more and more addicted to a melancholy blacker than that of the romantics. Lincoln and Bismarck were contemporaries, and Bismarck ran a state far more efficiently than did Lincoln. Most of us, however, prefer Lincoln. Was the German Empire of William II a genuine improvement for human life over the Holy Roman Empire of the German People snuffed out by the Napoleonic wars? Happy, runs the proverb, is that people whose annals are short. Having given up its dream of empire, Sweden now contents itself with playing well the role of a secondary power and is said to have one of the best programs for the care of the individual and of the family in modern times. Are the Swedes happier than they were when they took Marshal Bernadotte for their king? The suicide figures do not seem to say so. The Greeks, the Italians, the Spanish, the Irish — are they more, or less, comfortable in this postrevolutionary century than they were when Byron died at Missolonghi, Tom Moore was producing his *Irish Melodies*, and Manzoni published *I Promessi Sposi*? To ask the question is to answer it. One is reminded of Mark Twain, who, when he was asked whether he had any racial prejudice, replied that yes, he had one: if a man belonged to the human race, that was bad enough for him.

This, however, is not the whole story. It will have been observed that my discussion of romanticism is inconclusive. True, I have tried to see in Wordsworth's *The Prelude* and Goethe's *Faust* the shaping of modern man, or at least man of the nineteenth century, and I trust my analysis justifies the supposition. Both poems are great exercises in the romantic *moi*, which, throughout this study, I have taken as a central theme. The romantic notion of the individual seems to me to illuminate the profound difference between individuality as it is conceived in contemporary times and individuality as it was conceived by somebody like Pope. Romanticism does not end with *Faust* or *The Prelude*. It goes marching on. It produces Wagner's *Ring*, the sardonic drama of Ibsen, less a realistic than a rebellious poet, *War and Peace*, a novel in which social causation is nothing and character is everything, and in our own time the work of Ezra Pound and Robert Frost. Despite all his social-service agencies, his labor unions, his fantastic belief that psychiatry or anthropology or sociology or a structureless religion will somehow make him happy, modern man is solipsistic, a frail but independent being surrounded by mysterious enemies known as "They." The great, the unique contribution of romanticism to modernity is the insistence that every human being is a distinct and autonomous entity, whatever theories of education or of sociology or of political science or of evolution may say to the contrary. This, rather than economic determinism or Marxian theory or the ideal of the democratic state ("one man, one vote"), is the startling gift of romanticism to modern society. It is, I suggest, a more lasting contribution than those made by the American and French revolutions.

At this point it is important not to fall into the easy trap of liberal weekly journals with their incessant complaint of the badness of government. It is equally important not to fall into the somewhat more complex but equally fallacious assumption of somebody like Max Nordau in *Degeneration*, a book which takes refuge in the simplistic doctrine that all modern art and therefore all modern society is sick. That way madness lies — the madness of "sick" humor, the underground press, the so-called subculture of youth (was there ever a time when youth did not have a sub-culture?), and the assumption that to live in a commune is fully to discharge all one's civic responsibilities. That way also lies the insanity which confuses human love with the sexual act in even its unpleasing variations.

Man is more than the sum of his blunders. The state has been with us longer than the youth commune, and is likely to be with us for a long time to come. The grave central problem of our day is not the destruction of the state or of institutions or of ordinary forms of decorum by casual violence; the great central problem of the Western world is how to adjust the civic processes descending from the American and the French revolutions to the romantic theory that every human being is an inviolable end in himself. I do not find this answer on the shores of Walden Pond. The answer is to be found, if it ever is to be found, in the nature of man, that rare and curious species who is at home neither in the animal world nor in the spiritual universe of our ancestors. I think the answer, if there be one, is hinted at in William Faulkner's Nobel Prize speech of 1950, the conclusion of which is substantially as follows:

I decline to accept the end of man. It is easy enough to say that man is immortal simply because he will endure: that when the last ding-dong of doom has clanged and faded from the last worthless rock hanging tideless in the last red and dying evening, that even then there will still be one more sound: that of his puny inexhaustible voice, still talking. I refuse to accept this. I believe that man will not merely endure; he will prevail. He is immortal, not because he alone among creatures has an inexhaustible voice, but because he has a soul, a spirit capable of compassion and sacrifice and endurance. The poet's, the writer's duty is to write about these things. It is his privilege to help man endure by lifting his heart, by reminding him of the courage and honor and pride and compassion and pity and sacrifice which have been the glory of his past.

This sense of an indestructible center of all human individuality is the enduring gift of romanticism to modern times, and in saying so I do not overlook either religion, or general history, or the political idealism that produced the Declaration of the Rights of Man and of the Citizen. There cannot be citizenship unless there is man, and the rights of man is a phrase essentially without meaning unless one believes, as the romantics did, that each human being is more than the totality of his own history.

Appendix

Index

THE DECLARATION OF THE RIGHTS OF MAN AND OF THE CITIZEN

The representatives of the French people, organized in National Assembly, considering that ignorance, forgetfulness, or contempt of the rights of man are the sole causes of the public miseries and of the corruption of government, have resolved to set forth in a solemn declaration the natural, inalienable, and sacred rights of man, in order that this declaration, being ever present to all the members of the social body, may unceasingly remind them of their rights and their duties; in order that the acts of the legislative power and those of the executive power may be at each moment compared with the aim of every political institution and thereby may be more respected; and in order that the demands of the citizen, grounded henceforward upon simple, incontestable principles, may always take the direction of maintaining the constitution and the welfare of all.

In consequence the National Assembly acknowledges and declares in the presence and under the auspices of the Supreme Being, the following rights of man and of the citizen.

1. Men are born and remain free and equal in rights. Social distinctions can be based only upon public usefulness.

2. The aim of every political association is the preservation of the natural and imprescriptible rights of man. These rights are liberty, property, security, and resistance to oppression.

3. The origin of all sovereignty is essentially in the nation; no body and no individual can exercise authority that does not plainly proceed from it.

4. Liberty consists in the power to do anything that does not injure others; accordingly, the exercise of the natural rights of each man has for its limits only those that secure to other members of society the enjoyment of these same rights. These limits can be determined by law.

5. The law has the right to forbid such actions as are injurious to

society. Nothing can be forbidden that is not interdicted by law and no one can be constrained to do what it does not order.

6. Law is the expression of the general will. All citizens have the right to take part in person or by their representatives in its formulation. It must be the same for all, whether it protects or punishes. All citizens being equal in its eyes are equally eligible to all public dignities, places, and employments according to their capacities, and without other distinction than that of their virtues and their talents.

7. No man can be accused, arrested, or detained except in cases determined by law and according to the form it has prescribed. Those who procure, expedite, execute, or cause to be executed arbitrary orders ought to be punished. But every citizen summoned or seized in virtue of the law ought to render instant obedience; by resisting he makes himself guilty.

8. The law ought to establish only penalties that are strict and clearly necessary, and no one can be punished except by virtue of a law established and made public prior to the offense, and legally applied.

9. Every man being presumed to be innocent until he has been found guilty, if it is thought necessary to arrest him, all severity that may not be needed to secure his person should be strictly suppressed by law.

10. No one ought to be disturbed because of his opinions, even religious, provided that their manifestation does not disturb the public order as established by law.

11. The free communication of ideas and opinions is one of the most precious of the rights of man. Every citizen can therefore speak freely, write, and print, subject to his responsibility for the abuse of this freedom in cases determined by the law.

12. The guarantee (protection) of the rights of man and of the citizen requires a public force. This force is instituted for the benefit of all and not for the personal benefit of those to whom it is entrusted.

13. For maintaining the public force and for the expense of administration a general tax is indispensable. It ought to be equably apportioned among all citizens according to their means.

14. All citizens have the right to ascertain by themselves or by their representatives the necessity of any public tax, to consent

freely to it, to follow the uses of it, and to determine the amount, the assessment, the collection, and the duration of the tax.

15. Society has a right to call for an accounting from every public agent in its administration.

16. Any society in which the guarantee of rights is not secured or the separation of powers not determined has no constitution whatever.

17. Property is a sacred and inviolable right. No one can be deprived of it unless public necessity, legally established, demands it under the condition of a just and prior indemnity.*

---

* This is based on what seems to be the standard translation by F. M. Anderson, but I have slightly modified his version.

Index

The index has been prepared by Glenn T. Odell with the assistance of Richard M. Ludwig.

Index

Storm and Stress movement, 129n, 274, 284, 388
Stuart, James, 147
Sturm und Drang, see Storm and Stress movement
Style Directoire, 323
"Suffolk Resolves," 153, 183
Sugar Act of 1764, 179
Sweden, 462; social structure in 18th century, 35
Swift, Jonathan, 57, 120, 269
Swinburne, Algernon Charles, 374
Switzerland, tension in, 309

Taine, Hippolyte, 298
Talleyrand-Périgord, Charles Maurice de, 34, 327
Tallien, Jeanne Marie Ignace Thérésa, 323
Tandy, Napper, 224
Taxation, British-colonial problems, 189
Taylor, Bayard, 451n, 452n, 458n
Taylor, Jeremy, 89
Tea Act, 183, 195
Tennent, Rev. Gilbert, 172
Tennis Court Oath, 290, 315
Tennyson, Alfred, Lord, 416
Terror, the, 322, 361, 364
Thermidorean reaction, 292, 320
Third Estate, 314, 315
Thirty Years War, 8–9
Thomas à Kempis, 89
Thompson, Benjamin, *see* Rumford, Count
Thompson, J. M., 290, 301
Thompson, Sir William, 22
Thomson, George, 103
Thomson, James, *The Seasons*, 107–109
Tieck, Ludwig, 101, 104n, 247, 258, 275, 287n, 398n, 401, 403
Tilly, Charles, 299
Tocqueville, Alexis de, *The Old Regime and the French Revolution*, 297–298
Tooke, Horne, 276
Townshend, Charles, 36
Townshend acts, 163, 176, 195
Transcendental rebel, 390
Transcendental unity of apperception, 242, 370
Transcendentalism, German, 242
Translations, 18th century, of the classics, 124–126
Trevelyan, George Otto, 218
Trumbull, John, *M'Fingal*, 176
Tudesq, A. J., 325, 346n

Tudor, William, 212
Turgot, Robert Jacques, 58, 70
Turner, J. M. W., 2, 233, 410, 411n, 438
Twain, Mark, 462
Tyler, Moses Coit, 153, 209

Uhland, Johann Ludwig, 101
Unitarianism, 170
Unity and harmony, 18th century, 116–117
Universe, 18th century interpretation of, 63–65
Universe of energy, and the romantics, 409
Urban proletariat, France, 328
Utilitarian theory, 151

Vallon, Annette, 441, 445
Van Dyck, Anthony, 118
Van Tieghem, Paul, 93
Vauvenargues, Luc de Clapiers, Marquis de, 59, 81
Veit, Dorothea Mendelssohn, *see* Schlegel, Dorothea
Verdi, Giuseppe, 12, 325, 380, 438
Vergil, 118, 132, 137
Vergniaud, Pierre Victurnien, 127, 336
Vermont, particularism in, 165
Versailles, 19
Vico, Giovanni Batista, 59
Viëtor, Karl, 133
Vigée-Lebrun, Marie Anne Elizabeth, 260
Vigny, Alfred de, 438; "Le Cor," 381, 385; "Moïse," 385, 386–388; *Stello*, 385–386
Vinal, Rev. William, 164
Violence, 18th century, 27–28, 33
Virginia: particularism in, 166; Anglican clergy in, 174
Visconti, Ennio Quirino, 122–123
Volney, Constantin François de Chasseboeuf, Comte de, 341
Voltaire (François Marie Arouet), 13, 14, 21, 25, 26, 34, 58, 60, 62, 70, 78, 117, 119, 121, 333, 343, 344; *Candide*, 64; *Dictionnaire philosophique*, 61; *Siècle de Louis XIV*, 14
Voss, Johann Heinrich, 124
Vovelle, Michel, 301
Vulcanists, 374
Vulpius, Christiana (Frau von Goethe), 41
Vyverberg, Henry, 80

Wackenroder, Wilhelm Heinrich, 247,

486